VALUATION AND RISK MANAGEMENT
IN ENERGY MARKETS

Valuation and Risk Management in Energy Markets surveys the mechanics of energy markets and the valuation of structures commonly arising in practice. The presentation balances quantitative issues and practicalities facing portfolio managers, with substantial attention paid to the ways in which common methods fail in practice and to alternative methods when they exist. The material spans basic fundamentals of markets, statistical analysis of price dynamics, and a sequence of increasingly challenging structures, concluding with issues arising at the enterprise level. In totality, the material has been selected to provide readers with the analytical foundation required to function in modern energy-trading and risk-management groups.

Glen Swindle is the managing partner and co-founder of Scoville Risk Partners, a global professional services and analytics firm focused on the energy and commodities sectors. He has held senior positions at Constellation Energy, where he ran the Strategies Group for the merchant energy business, and at Credit Suisse, where, as managing director, he was responsible for significant aspects of the North American energy business, running structured trading teams, and more broadly as co-head of power and natural gas trading. Previously he held tenured positions at the University California–Santa Barbara and Cornell University. He currently holds an adjunct faculty position at New York University, where he lectures on energy valuation and portfolio management. He is also on the Energy Oversight Committee for the Global Association for Risk Professionals' Energy Risk Professional Program and is a frequent speaker at panel discussions and webinars. He holds a Ph.D. in applied mathematics from Cornell University, an MSE in mechanical aerospace engineering from Princeton, and a B.S. in mechanical engineering from Caltech.

VALUATION AND RISK MANAGEMENT IN ENERGY MARKETS

GLEN SWINDLE

Founder Scoville Risk Partners LLC

CAMBRIDGE
UNIVERSITY PRESS

CAMBRIDGE
UNIVERSITY PRESS

32 Avenue of the Americas, New York, NY 10013-2473, USA

Cambridge University Press is part of the University of Cambridge.

It furthers the University's mission by disseminating knowledge in the pursuit of
education, learning and research at the highest international levels of excellence.

www.cambridge.org
Information on this title: www.cambridge.org/9781107539884

First published 2014
First paperback edition 2015

A catalogue record for this publication is available from the British Library

Library of Congress Cataloguing in Publication data
Swindle, Glen.
Valuation and risk management in energy markets / Glen Swindle.
pages   cm
Includes bibliographical references and index.
ISBN 978-1-107-03684-0 (hardback)
1. Energy industries–Finance.   2. Commodity futures.   3. Investments–Mathematical
models.   4. Financial risk.   I. Title.
HD9502.A2S95   2014
332.64′4–dc23   2013027353

ISBN 978-1-107-03684-0 Hardback
ISBN 978-1-107-53988-4 Paperback

Contents

VI   Additional Topics

Preface

In the summer of 1998, I was working at a hedge fund in Bermuda and contemplating returning to the United States, the plan being to continue working in a fixed-income quantitative role of some sort. Fortunately, I suppose, a former student of mine at Cornell, Dana Thorpe, strongly encouraged me to look into the energy markets, particularly electricity. Dana had worked in this area for a few years and described the modeling and risk-management state of affairs as being in a nascent stage and largely virgin territory.

As it turned out, several shops had already been systematically building very solid analytics, architected by some of the now best-known minds in the business, and academics were becoming increasingly interested in energy. However, despite the considerable efforts of regiments and brigades of researchers, including groups that I have had the opportunity to run over the years, Dana's assessment made fifteen years ago feels disturbingly close to the truth even now.

My first significant tour of duty in energy was at Constellation Power Source (CPS), at the time the name of the merchant arm of Constellation Energy. Initially, CPS was a joint venture between Goldman Sachs and Baltimore Gas & Electric (BG&E). Perceptions of hubris aside, Goldman management was shrewd enough to know that when entering a business as peculiar and complex as electricity, it might not be a bad idea to partner with people who have been working within the context of the physical system for decades. In many respects this collaboration was successful, with first-rate trading systems and risk-management experience afforded by Goldman coupled with the seasoned skepticism and engineering knowledge of BG&E.

While personalities and value systems converged over the years, a striking feature of the operation was the yawning gap between the valuation system (which is, in fact, quite impressive) and the realities facing the teams running the assets. The risk system could accommodate the litany of conventions of physical and financial settlement of any commodity, notably the hourly or subhourly calculations that are required. Forward valuation was also extremely flexible, provided that transactions were represented as derivative constructs with all the implicit assumptions underpinning complete markets and risk-neutral valuation. This is true of most risk systems, both commercial and in-house. Transactions must be boiled down to a representation that requires forward curves, implied volatilities, implied correlations, and all the other usual inputs, each of which is presumed to be tradable in some fashion.

The problem that confronted portfolio managers, and does to this day, is that many commonly traded structures in energy involve risks that trade so rarely and in such small size that market activity is at best an indication of how others are assessing the risk. At worst, such can be outright disinformation to confuse market participants in advance of large transactions or auctions. In such situations, any notion of market completeness is moot. Extrinsic value as ascertained in idealized settings simply cannot be captured. Structures that look like quantos cannot be hedged when one leg does not trade at all.

Other ways of thinking about valuation and risk are required.

In the course of what follows, much of the standard liturgy on valuation of energy structures will be described in full detail. However, substantial attention also will be paid to the ways in which common methods fail and to alternative methods when they exist. In some situations, the conclusion will be that researchers and practitioners simply do not yet know how to properly handle some transactions. Rather than being bad news, this is what makes the field of energy trading and structuring particularly vibrant: even after several decades of thought, open problems abound.

This book is descendant from a sequence of lectures that I started giving each spring at New York University in 2008. I was working at Credit Suisse at the time, and the bank accommodated and supported the effort over the following years to have practitioners interacting directly with financial engineering students, no small number of which I have seen on the desks at the bank in subsequent years. Ultimately, these lectures evolved into a collection of material that will hopefully prove useful for "quantitative types" with a commercial orientation entering the business and joining a trading desk.

This book is structured in six parts. Part I is an overview of some of the distinguishing features of energy markets and a survey of important fundamental and econometric attributes of the core markets discussed – crude oil and refined products, natural gas, and electricity. Part II covers basic "zeroth-order" valuation before moving into a more detailed analysis of the empirical features of price dynamics and the implications for managing swaps books. While the content of the first two parts is clearly oriented toward "stylized facts" about markets, modeling in the absence of such information is not a good idea.

Bona fide valuation activities begin in Part III, which is a survey of standard methods for dealing with the simplest "nonvanilla" structures that arise in practice. Part IV discusses modeling approaches from a more general perspective, exploring the dialectic between the tractability of various modeling paradigms and their consistency with empirical facts and utility in practice. In Part V we explore the application of these methodologies and their limitations in three settings that have challenged practitioners for years – natural gas storage, tolling transactions (generation hedges), and variable-quantity swaps. Finally, in Part VI we turn to broader considerations at the level of enterprise risk management and control, concluding with a discussion of the future of energy markets.

It sounds (and sounded to me) like a routine affair to convert a reasonably seasoned sequence of lectures into a book, but the experience was anything but straightforward. While all remaining errors are mine, this work would be a pale shadow of itself were it not for the remarkable efforts of many of my colleagues and friends. Michael Coulon, formerly at Princeton and now at the University of Sussex, and Radu Haiduc at Credit Suisse proofed the entirety of the manuscript at a level of detail and "no holds barred" critique that simply defies description. Their input not only reduced the error count by an order of magnitude but also improved the manuscript at a fundamental level. Richard Lassander was a close collaborator on large parts of the book, particularly those focused on fundamental aspects of the markets and trading, not to mention his help on the dauntingly high-dimensional task of index creation. Eric Grannan and Peter Jenson made numerous suggestions and helpful comments. Sheela Kolluri, a statistician in the pharmaceuticals business and lecturer at Columbia, provided the refreshing perspective of someone completely outside the business. Stefan Revielle and Soumya Kalra provided a great deal of assistance on data and many helpful comments and insights along the way. I would also like to express my appreciation to Rene Carmona for numerous invitations to conferences and workshops, in addition to a continuing sequence of fascinating discussions when we manage to find time to meet in Princeton.

I was introduced to the Cambridge team by Robert Dreesen, who assisted in many ways in guiding the process and for whose assistance I am grateful. In addition, this work benefited substantially from the efforts of Scott Parris and Kristin Purdy, and more recently Karen Maloney, as well as the Cambridge team broadly. Thanks also to two anonymous referees whose input and critique were very helpful.

Last, and certainly most, my wife, Adviti Muni, not only carefully and repeatedly proofed the manuscript, but more important, she also provided the critical ingredient of encouragement at those moments when I was inclined to back-burner the effort in favor of the incessant barrage of other seemingly, but fleetingly, more pressing matters.

This book is graphically and data intensive. While specific sources are mentioned for "one-offs" throughout the text, in general, most data were either sourced from Bloomberg LLC, notably weather, spot, and forward price data, as well as implied volatilities, or were drawn from my lectures written when I was at Credit Suisse.

Part I

Introduction to Energy Commodities

Energy has been traded in one form or another for centuries, with modern energy markets emerging at the launch of the NYMEX[1] West Texas Intermediate (WTI) crude oil contract in 1983. Subsequent growth has been significant, with an expanding array of physical and financial instruments traded across almost all energy commodities. This evolution has been driven by a trend toward deregulation in markets such as natural gas and power that, until relatively recently, were essentially fully regulated. The past decade has also witnessed growing interest among institutional investors in energy, and commodities more broadly, as a new component of investment portfolios.

While the level of complexity of energy markets has increased rapidly, practitioners have often found themselves depending on analytical methods that were inherited directly from those used in other asset classes, often with only cosmetic modifications. Energy commodities, however, exhibit important differences from other markets, which at times imperil the validity of conventional approaches to valuation and hedging.

There are two basic features of energy that together result in price behavior that can be dramatically different from that of other asset classes. The first is that for a variety of reasons, including weather events and infrastructure failure, fluctuations in supply and demand for many energy commodities can change rapidly on daily or even hourly time scales. The second is that it costs real money to move a commodity through time or between locations. One cannot electronically transfer ownership and delivery of natural gas from Louisiana to Boston on a cold winter day as one could, for example, title to a bond.

---

[1] NYMEX, short for the New York Mercantile Exchange, is one of the primary exchanges for energy futures trading and clearing. Although NYMEX was acquired by the Chicago Mercantile Exchange (CME) in 2008, we will refer to legacy energy futures contracts as NYMEX contracts.

The facilities required to store or transport energy vary in cost, with coal and crude oil relatively easy to store and transport, natural gas much more challenging and costly, and electricity expensive to move and effectively unstorable in meaningful quantities at any cost. In each of these markets, however, storage capacity by region and transport capacity between regions is finite. When limits to infrastructure are tested, through mechanical failure, unusually high supply or demand, or extreme levels of inventory, price behavior is affected.

The first consequence of these fundamental aspects of energy markets is that energy prices are significantly more volatile than benchmarks in equities, rates, and currencies. Higher volatility affects an array of commercial considerations, including stability of pricing during the negotiation of potential transactions, investment decisions relating to asset development or acquisition, and the capital required to support trading operations and collateral requirements.

A second consequence is that energy markets exhibit a much higher degree of "specialness," that is to say, negative forward yields or rapid changes in relative pricing between closely related commodities. Liquidity in energy markets, as in most asset classes, is usually concentrated in a few benchmark commodities. The practical consequence of chronic specialness is that energy portfolios often have risk profiles that are very high dimensional – not in the sense of a large number of closely related tradables such as a few hundred Treasury bonds outstanding on any given day but in the sense of distinct locational and temporal delivery that can dislocate rapidly and unpredictably from the benchmarks most commonly used to hedge. Specialness, and the resulting high-dimensional attributes of typical portfolios, is the fundamental challenge in energy risk management.

In the next few chapters we will survey basic stylized facts about energy commodities prices, the typical framework in which commodities prices are analyzed, and essential fundamental facts underpinning the workings of energy markets.

1

Context

What makes energy commodities different from other asset classes?

Many seasoned risk managers in other asset classes consider energy trading as simply more of a "white knuckle" experience than other businesses. This view is often based in part on the empirical observation, easily gleaned from any screen with West Texas Intermediate (WTI) or Brent oil futures prices, that energy commodities can exhibit exceptionally high volatility. The relatively frequent blowups of energy trading desks reinforce the image. Noteworthy instances of abuse of market mechanics, such as in the case of Enron and other power marketers in California in the early 2000s, accompanied by index manipulation in natural gas, and culminating more recently with the Amaranth spectacle and FERC[1] actions against several power marketers, add credence to the notion that energy markets can be challenging environments in which to operate.

Much of this perception, however, is based on very high-level views of the more newsworthy mishaps, with only cursory knowledge of the commercial realities of energy markets and the risk-management practices that are required to run an energy trading operation. Energy markets serve much more of a purpose than simply providing a few well-capitalized hedge funds an arena in which to speculate on the direction of global energy prices. Most trading activity involves balancing variations in supply and demand across time and between locations. This occurs both on short time scales, so-called cash desks that move commodities from supply centers to demand centers on a daily basis, and on the long time scales involved in the construction of a new refinery, pipeline, or generator, activities which often require significant hedging programs to support the sizable financing required.

---

[1] The Federal Energy Regulatory Commission (FERC) is the U.S. regulator responsible for energy infrastructure and power markets.

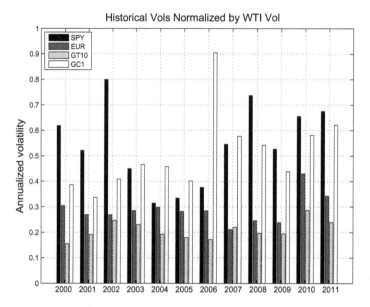

Figure 1.1. Ratio of realized volatilities by calendar year for various assets to WTI.

The distinguishing features of energy price dynamics affect market participants in different ways, an understanding of which is central to the development of useful risk-management and valuation frameworks.

Volatility

There are several reasons to view energy commodities as fundamentally different from other traded assets. First among them is that energy prices consistently exhibit higher levels of volatility compared with other asset classes. Figure 1.1 shows the realized volatility for a set of historical prices representing a cross section of commonly traded assets normalized by the realized WTI volatility by calendar year. Given a price series $p(n)$, the realized volatility (often referred to as *historical volatility*), is defined as

$$\left[250\sum_n R^2(n)\right]^{1/2} \tag{1.1}$$

where $R(n) = \log[p(n)/p(n-1)]$ denotes the price returns. The factor 250 is approximately the number of trading days in a year. We have chosen the Standard & Poor's (S&P 500) Exchange-Traded Fund (ETF) Index (SPY) for equities, the euro (EUR) denominated in U.S. dollars (USD) for currencies, the first traded futures contract for gold (GC1), the generic 10-year U.S. Treasury bond (GT10) for rates,[2] and the first futures contract for WTI

---

[2] GT10 volatility was proxied by the product of duration (assumed to be 7.5 years) and change in yield.

Table 1.1. *Returns statistics (2000–2011)*

Statistic	WTI 1st Month	WTI 1 Year	NG 1st Month	NG 1 Year
σ (1 day)	0.024	0.020	0.034	0.022
$p_{1,99}$ (1 day)	0.067	0.055	0.091	0.059
σ (10 day)	0.072	0.058	0.104	0.068
$p_{1,99}$ (10 day)	0.225	0.170	0.269	0.177

crude oil. WTI is an abbreviation for West Texas Intermediate, which is a particular specification of crude oil deliverable at Cushing, Oklahoma; the futures contract serves as one of the world benchmarks for energy prices.[3]

The realized volatility of WTI has been consistently and meaningfully higher than that of the other series, with the exception of the gold contract, which reached volatilities of roughly 90 percent of WTI in 2006. The average annual volatility ratios were much lower across all the references assets, with a low of 21 percent for GT10 to a high of 55 percent for SPY.

While the realized volatility in energy commodities is systematically higher than that of other comparables, options markets exist on numerous energy benchmarks, often with considerable depth. Given that options can be used to mitigate volatility risk, one might be tempted to dismiss high energy volatility as merely a curiosity. On the contrary, higher volatility affects the commercial operations of a business in many ways, some of which simply cannot be easily managed using options.

Consider Table 1.1, which shows returns statistics for the WTI and Henry Hub natural gas (NYMEX NG) futures contracts. These results are for the first contract and the first calendar strip prices[4] over one- and ten-trading-day intervals. The statistics shown are the standard deviation σ as well as the greater of the absolute value of the first and 99th percentiles, denoted by $p_{1,99}$. One can expect prices to move routinely 6 to 7 percent over a ten-business day (two-week) period, with changes of over 15 percent not unexpected.

These statistics, while just another way of restating the high-volatility premise, do help to add perspective to transaction mechanics. Most sizable transactions involve exposure to multiple years of commodity prices, so the calendar strip statistics are the more pertinent. Suppose that you are negotiating the purchase or sale of an energy asset, for example, a collection of

---

[3] Most global crude oil trading references the other benchmark, namely, the Brent futures contract. We will use both WTI and Brent throughout as context requires.

[4] A calendar strip price is the average of the futures or forward prices for a given calendar year and should be thought of as the price for delivery of the commodity over the course of the next twelve months. In this case we are using the arithmetic average without discounting and the volumetric considerations discussed in Chapter 2.

oil or natural gas production fields, or a large natural gas power-generation asset. The value of each of these examples is approximately linear in the underlying fuel price. For an acquirer paying significant sums, often in excess of $1 billion, as well as for the lenders supporting such an activity, a 15 percent change in value over two weeks can be highly problematic. Simply converging on an acquisition price in the course of negotiations can be challenging. Hedging the exposure of a large transaction, once completed, must also occur on relatively short time scales in order to avoid the potentially large changes in value.

High volatility also affects collateral postings and increases credit exposure, resulting in higher capital requirements for energy trading operations. Whether exchange-traded or over the counter (OTC),[5] hedging activities are almost always accompanied by collateral posting requirements. The larger the potential swings in the mark-to-market of trading operations, the more cash or functional equivalents such as letters of credit (LCs) are required for daily operations.

A more subtle but severe consequence of high energy price volatility arises when the underlying business premise involves an inherent asymmetry in collateral posting requirements. A relatively recent example is the case of retail energy providers (REPs), which are companies that contract and serve the energy requirements of end users; these could be residential consumers, commercial customers (e.g., stores, restaurants, and the like), and some industrial customers. The REP is short energy to each of its customers. To hedge its aggregate short position, the REP typically makes forward purchases of the energy commodities via exchange-traded or OTC markets.

A collateral posting asymmetry arises from the fact that the customers to whom the REP is short are not margined (imagine if your utility or REP was calling you for margin against your expected future annual energy usage!), whereas the energy purchases are margined. Everything works fine, provided that macro energy price levels don't change too much or, better yet, if they increase. However, if prices decrease, the REP must post collateral against its long energy hedges. If the price decrease is severe enough, the collateral calls can be lethal.[6]

Figure 1.2 shows the time series of rolling calendar strips for WTI, NYMEX natural gas and PJM[7] power prices. PJM is a power market in the eastern United States and the largest such market in North America.

---

[5] Over-the-counter trades are bilateral trades between two counterparties that are not exchange trades.

[6] The history of commodities trading is replete with examples of cash-flow crises sustained by market participants due to collateral posting asymmetries, the most notorious though somewhat dated example being that of Metallgesellschaft.

[7] PJM stands for the original states involved in the market, namely, Pennsylvanin, New Jersey, and Maryland. The PJM Interconnection now spans a large swath of the Midatlantic states.

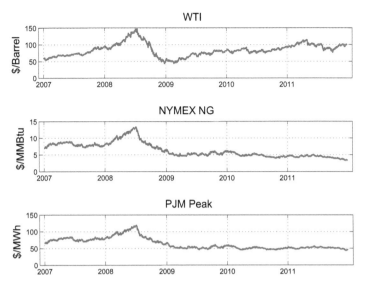

Figure 1.2. History of rolling calendar strips for U.S. energy benchmarks.

Imagine that, as manager of an REP, you purchased significant hedges in mid-2008. This would be a routine aspect of your portfolio-management practices, arguably even more sensible at the time given that many commodities research teams were forecasting ever-increasing energy prices. Fast forward a few months after energy prices had collapsed by a factor of roughly three; cash-flow distress among many natural shorts such as the REPs with long hedges was unprecedented and resulted in many companies exiting the business.

Figure 1.2 also illustrates the common macro structure in the price dynamics in the run-up to and the aftermath of the credit crisis. Although the price dynamics of each distinct energy commodity is affected by idiosyncratic drivers, prices at times can be broadly coupled by global events.

Specialness

Another feature of energy commodities that distinguishes them from other asset classes is the concept of "specialness." This term is borrowed from bond markets, in which demand for a particular bond is high, often due to the fact that it is "cheapest to deliver" (CTD) into a bond futures contract; see [BBLP05] for a more detailed discussion. Such bonds can trade at a significant premium to roughly comparable bonds and are said to be *trading special*. Figure 1.3 shows a snapshot of yields for U.S. Treasuries as a function of duration. Several bonds stand out as having anomalously low yields; these are the CTDs into their respective bond futures contracts.

The supply of a CTD bond available for delivery into a futures contract is limited. Finite issuance at inception is an a priori limit to supply. In addition,

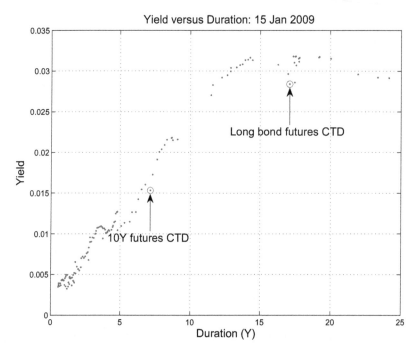

Figure 1.3. U.S. Treasury yields versus duration. (*Credit Suisse–Global Market Analytics Group.*)

passive investors often hold much of the original issuance, reducing the amount of the bond available for trading. The result can be a higher price for the CTD and a commensurately lower yield. The way this works in practice is that traders who have a short position in bond futures contracts need to procure the CTD for delivery. Once delivery is made, the supply stress on the CTD is alleviated, and yields will (probably) return to normal. The CTD is obtained via a reverse repo, where the bond is borrowed from someone who has it, and cash is lent in return at the repo rate. If the supply stress on the CTD is significant, the repo rate can be very low – to obtain the CTD you are lending at rates far below market rates.

This phenomenon is well understood by bond traders, although now and again surprises occur when market participants fail to predict a low supply of a CTD. If you are hedging your risk using liquid on-the-run (most recently issued) bonds and some part of your portfolio unexpectedly goes special, portfolio management becomes challenging. The term *special* is also used more broadly in financial markets in reference to any particular asset that is trading at an unusual premium to comparables. Major economic disturbances can result in extreme levels of specialness with severe consequences for some. The Russian financial crisis of in 1998 resulted in a global drop in commodities prices that had its origins in the Asian financial crisis roughly a year earlier. During the ensuing turbulence, U.S. swap spreads (the spread between dollar interest-rate swaps and U.S. Treasuries) widened to historic levels. Treasuries "went special" relative to swaps as a result of a flight to safety, causing some well-known hedge funds to fail. The credit crisis of 2008 also witnessed the breakdown of many ostensibly stable relationships between financial and cash instruments.

Although financial markets have certainly experienced dramatic and painful periods of widespread specialness, these are sporadic and certainly not the norm. Financial markets are stabilized by various institutions, such as the Federal Reserve and the European Central Bank (ECB), that have historically been successful at controlling the supply of credit as needed and that act in a generally predictable manner. In addition, electronic transfer of ownership of assets has reduced transaction costs and time lags, increasing the efficiency of the marketplace.

In contrast, energy commodities are often going special and frequently very special. One might even go so far as to say that specialness is the norm.

Supply and demand variations are more extreme in energy markets, and one cannot electronically wire a shipment of crude oil or natural gas to a location in which demand is high. Physical storage and transportation constraints can arise suddenly and result in significant locational and temporal price variations. Energy markets are also lacking the stability induced by large stabilizing bodies. The Organization of Petroleum Exporting Countries (OPEC), and Saudi Arabia in particular, attempt to stabilize energy prices, again with much less success than central banks have had in financial markets. National petroleum reserves also factor into the governing mechanisms of energy markets, but with much less predicability regarding both deployment and ultimate effect. In addition, the characteristic time scales for equilibration of structural supply-demand imbalances can be significant because of the substantial time and capital required to build the necessary infrastructure.

The upshot is that a single commodity delivered at two different times or locations can behave functionally as two entirely different assets.

Figure 1.4 shows the NYMEX natural gas (NG) futures price curve on a particular date. The points in the plot represent the prices for natural gas to be delivered in each of the contract months as of the end of the trading day January 25, 2010. The quasi-periodicity (and lack of monotonicity) of prices is due to seasonal variations in demand. Heating demand in the winter in North America results in far higher consumption than during the rest of the year; this results in the seasonal premia. The winter months are special relative to the summer; a chronic state of affairs. In the language of repos, if you wanted to borrow the commodity during the high-priced winter months and return it during the lower-priced summer months, you would be lending cash at negative (in some cases very negative) interest rates.

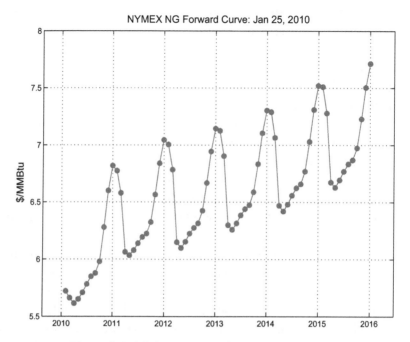

Figure 1.4. NYMEX natural gas forward curve.

Spot prices show even more dramatic and less predictable behavior. The term *spot price* refers to the price for delivery of a commodity *now*, that is, for nearly immediate delivery. The operational definition of *immediate delivery* always involves a lag that is a function of the time required for a supplier to arrange the logistics of shipping and delivery. For example, the spot price for natural gas is usually established the day before delivery.

Figure 1.5 shows daily spot prices and returns for Henry Hub, the delivery location underpinning the NYMEX natural gas contract (we will talk more about this in Chapter ?). By *spot returns*, we mean $\log(p_{d+1}/p_d)$, where p_d denotes the spot price on day d. We are taking liberties here, because returns are only well defined for a series of prices of the *same* underlying asset or deliverable. Commodity prices at two different delivery times are related only insofar as the commodity can be readily stored in the sense that an increase or decrease in inventory at known cost can be readily effected. An extreme case that illustrates this point is power, which is effectively unstorable, rendering this definition of returns highly questionable. Caveats aside, the results serve the purpose of illustrating the rapid variation in the value of a commodity at almost identical delivery times; daily returns are frequently in excess of 500 percent in magnitude.

Locational specialness also distinguishes energy commodities from other asset classes which are largely devoid of geographic disparities. Changes in demand and constraints in transportation can result in the appearance of rapid locational value disparities. Figure 1.6 shows results for a natural

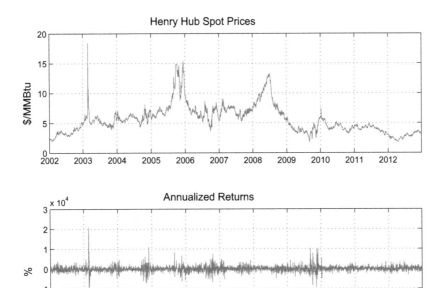

Figure 1.5. Henry Hub spot prices and returns.

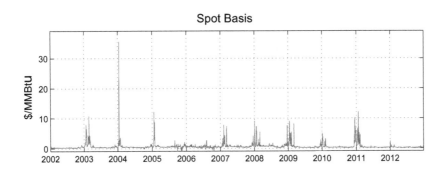

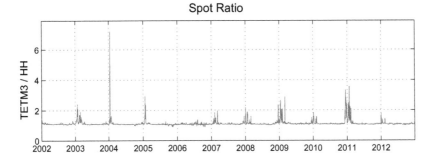

Figure 1.6. TETM3 spot and basis.

gas delivery location in the northeastern United States – TETM3 versus Henry Hub. The difference between TETM3 and Henry Hub, referred to as the *basis between the locations*, is shown in the top plot, and the ratio, which normalizes for price level, is shown in the bottom plot. TETM3 is typically premium to Henry Hub because of transportation costs and generally higher demand.[8] This premium is also reflected in the forward markets, with TETM3 trading consistently above NYMEX futures prices. The substantial premia in TETM3 prices occurs because of fluctuations in temperature-driven demand in the winter. The extreme events are typically due to low temperatures, which result in demand that exceeds available pipeline capacity.

Locational specialness across commodities occurs when infrastructure cannot keep up with spatial disparities in supply and demand. This can occur as a result of sudden changes in supply or demand, time lags such as shipping times for crude oil, or sudden failure of infrastructure such as a pipeline or power-transmission outage. Demand fluctuations are often weather-dependent and can be anticipated a few days in advance. In contrast, infrastructure failure is hard to predict and, because of the "Poisson process[9] nature" of such failures, is challenging to hedge.

Benchmark Hedging and High Dimensionality

In most asset classes, the number of distinct tradable instruments is very large, and each market has its idiosyncratic conventions regarding which instruments will be used to concentrate liquidity – the so-called benchmarks. In Treasuries, for example, while outstanding bonds number in the hundreds, the most recent issuances (the on-the-runs) are the benchmarks. For equities, the broader indices are the benchmarks, not only in the sense of performance metrics for investors but also from the risk-management perspective of being the fastest avenue to reduce risk in an equities portfolio.

The situation is the same in energy. The NYMEX WTI and ICE Brent futures contracts,[10] which we will discuss shortly, are the global crude oil benchmarks. For North American natural gas and power markets, the NYMEX natural gas (NG) contract is at the apex of liquidity concentration. It is through the use of benchmark tradables that large risk positions can be rapidly, though not totally, hedged.

---

[8] In 2013, however, TETM3 spot prices realized at a discount to Henry Hub at a frequency that had not been witnessed historically due to the geographic distribution of shale gas production, with forward markets also exhibiting a discount in the summer months.

[9] *Poisson processes* are defined by a sequence of arrival times, with the time between arrivals independent and exponentially distributed so that knowledge of the previous arrival times provides no conditional information about the time of future arrivals.

[10] ICE stands for Intercontinental Exchange which is a major exchange and electronic trading platform for energy, as well as other commodities and asset classes.

Energy is produced and consumed at many different locations and often with highly seasonal attributes; this is the origin of the large number of traded products that span locational and temporal hedging requirements. Energy markets typically trade risk in a hierarchical fashion, with the benchmark at the apex. Slightly less liquid products, sometimes referred to as *hubs*, often trade as a spread to the benchmark. Less liquid locations trade as spreads to the hubs. Beyond this, most risk positions are typically inventoried, being hedgable only if unusual circumstances arise.

On inception of a transaction, the usual sequence of events is that the benchmark instruments are used to reduce the risk position to a spread or basis between the transaction and the benchmark. Subsequent hedges, generally requiring substantially longer periods of time, are then effected to transfer the hedge to positions that are "closer" to the transaction, both locationally and temporally. In cases where the transaction involves delivery at particularly illiquid locations or tenors, a residual spread exposure may be inventoried for the life of the transaction.

This process of telescoping hedges from the benchmark to the actual risk is common. In energy markets, high volatility and chronic specialness make the risk of any outstanding spread position considerably greater than is typical in other asset classes.

Conclusion

Two fundamental aspects of commodities that are distinguishing features of energy commodities are consistently high levels of realized returns volatility and chronic specialness in prices. High volatility affects commercial activities in numerous ways, including

- Impeding convergence on transaction price of complex structures
- Affecting capital requirements and collateral demands on market participants
- Dramatically shortening time scales at which hedging programs must be effected

Specialness in energy is both common and significant in magnitude. A commodity for delivery at a particular time and location can exhibit dramatically different price dynamics from the same commodity deliverable at a different time and location, even when the times and locations are seemingly "close." The instruments available for a portfolio manager to efficiently hedge the risks in a typical energy portfolio are often confined to a few liquid or quasi-liquid benchmarks. The set of such tradables is therefore typically far smaller than the number of ways that a commodities portfolio can go special. The result is that energy portfolio managers have to deal with high-dimensional risk positions with significant gaps between the risks and the instruments available to hedge. Much of what follows expands on the challenges and partial solutions that commodities traders and strategists have crafted to close these gaps.

2

Forwards and Carry

Commodities trading is based on forward contracts and delivery. Forwards, swaps, and futures constitute the basic underlying tradables primarily because most market participants do not have access to storage facilities in which to carry the commodity forward in time. A bond or an equity can be purchased at any time to cover a short position sometime in the future. This involves paying funding costs but does not require elaborate infrastructure, in contrast to most commodities. As a consequence, most trading and hedging in commodities occur in the forward markets. A closely related fact is that one cannot readily infer forward prices from spot prices in energy. For equities, bonds, or even gold, market participants are able to make reliable estimates of the funding costs and other components of carry, such as dividends and warehouse storage, in order to calculate the cost of getting the commodity from now (spot) to a later (forward) delivery time. For energy, and consumption commodities more broadly, carry costs can be inferred only through forward prices. This renders forward prices as the natural underlying price variables.

Forwards, Futures, and Swaps

We have already encountered forward pricing in Figure 1.4, which showed the natural gas forward curve on a particular date. Figure 2.1 shows the forward curve for West Texas Intermediate (WTI). Each point on the plot represents the price for WTI crude oil delivered in subsequent months as of January 15, 2009.

To formalize this concept, we will denote the forward price observed at time t for delivery at time T by $F(t, T)$.[1] In the case of a delivery interval, this will be replaced by $F(t, T, T+S)$, where $[T, T+S]$ defines the delivery

---

[1] For expository reasons, we will usually work in continuous time. In practice, everything is in discrete time, be it natural gas delivery on a daily basis or power prices traded at the hourly level. Modifications for discrete time valuation are straightforward.

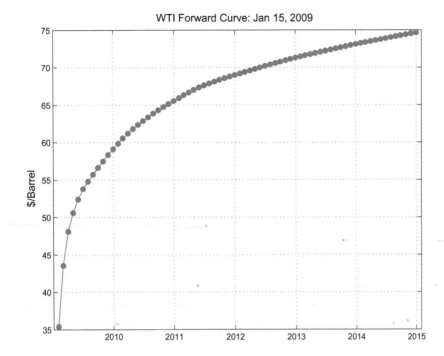

Figure 2.1. NYMEX WTI forward curve.

interval over which ratable (uniform) delivery of the commodity is assumed. Commodities forwards reference calendar months as the delivery window at all but the shortest tenors, where in some cases daily, weekly, or "balance-of-month" contracts trade.[2] For a given contract month m, we may abbreviate notation along the lines of $F_m(t)$ or $F(t, T_m)$. Finally, the first live contract is often referred to as the *prompt* contract or the first *nearby* contract. The nearby convention extends to other contracts; for example, the second nearby is the second contract actively traded.

At the inception ($t = 0$) of a forward contract for delivery at time T, the contract is struck at $K = F(0, T)$, ignoring bid-offer spreads and assuming that the transaction occurred at prevailing market prices. At a later time $t > 0$, when the prevailing market price for the same delivery time is $F(t, T)$, the value of the trade to the holder of the long position (the buyer) is

$$V[t, F(t, T)] = d(t, \tau) N[F(t, T) - K] \tag{2.1}$$

where τ denotes the settlement time, N the notional, and $d(t, \tau)$ the discount factor to time τ prevailing at time t. Discounting is required because

---

[2] Futures contracts in commodities, as well as some financial instruments, use arcane abbreviations for calendar months: F, G, H, J, K, M, N, Q, U, V, X, and Z correspond to January through December. For example, the December 2010 contract would be referred to as Z10.

settlement occurs in the future (the story is a little different for futures contracts, which we will discuss later). As a consequence of (2.1), the delta[3] for a forward is the discounted notional:

$$\Delta \equiv \frac{\partial V}{\partial F(t,T)} = d(t,\tau) N \tag{2.2}$$

The value of the forward in (2.1) is a linear function of the forward price $F(t,T)$. Linear instruments, as well as more complex structures, are usually categorized according to the following:

- Does the trade require physical delivery of the commodity, or is it financially settling on a prescribed commodities price index?
- Is the trade through an exchange, or is the trade bilateral (also referred to as *over the counter* or *OTC*) with specific credit-support agreements in place between the two counterparties?

A *swap* is a financially settling OTC trade. If it is exchange traded, then it is called a *listed swap*. A *forward contract* is an OTC trade requiring physical delivery. If it is exchange traded, then it is a *futures contract*. The term *futures contract* is also used by practitioners in reference to some financially settled instruments, or those with a delivery option to settle physically or financially.

Each of these trade types requires specification of the following attributes:

- *The underlying commodity.* While this may seem like a trivial point, it is actually more complex than meets the eye. In other asset classes there is rarely ambiguity – one USD or one share of an equity is unambiguous. Physical commodities, in contrast, are identical only in the case of electricity. The multitude of crude oils produced (referred to as crude oil *streams*) globally have a wide variety of characteristics, most notably sulfur content and density, that affect their ultimate value. For natural gas, the presence of other liquids and gases, as well as moisture content, affects value. Commodities contracts specify quite precisely the attributes that constitute acceptable delivery into a contract, with codified adjustments in settlement value as a function of the characteristics of the product actually delivered.[4]
- *Delivery.* When and where the commodity will be delivered for physical contracts or which price index will be used in financial trades.
- *Price.* The price per unit commodity to be paid.
- *Notional.* The quantity of the commodity to be delivered or defining financial settlement. Most energy commodities have a standard notional referred to as a *lot*. For example, one lot of crude oil is 1,000 barrels.
- *Settlement.* The terms defining how and when the commodity will be delivered and payment made between the two counterparties.

---

[3] Common notation for all derivatives is $\Delta \equiv \partial V/\partial X$, where X is an underlying price. Here the underlying is the forward price F.

[4] The closest analogue in financial markets is the use of conversion factors in bond futures.

Appendix D surveys the common tradables in energy markets. The following few illustrative examples will appear frequently in what follows.

Example 1: *WTI and Brent Futures*

The NYMEX WTI futures contract is one of the world energy benchmarks. The notional quantity for one contract is 1,000 barrels, which, as mentioned earlier, is one lot. As with all futures, trading for a given contract month ceases at a defined futures expiration date prior to the contract month. In the case of the WTI contract, this is roughly two-thirds of the way through the previous contract month. For example, the October 2012 contract expired on September 20, 2012.[5] On expiration of a given contract traders holding long positions in the contract are matched with those holding short positions; by definition, there are equivalent volumes of each. The shorts must deliver 1,000 barrels per contract of specific grades of crude oil at Cushing, Oklahoma, sometime during the delivery month, and the longs must take delivery and pay the final settlement price.

In recent years idiosyncrasies related to the delivery location of the WTI contract resulted in substantial and prolonged decoupling from global crude oil prices. As a result, despite complications of its own, the Brent futures contract which trades on ICE,[6] is now viewed as the dominant crude oil benchmark. The namesake of this futures contract is the Brent field in the North Sea. Depletion of the Brent field and the resulting drop in delivered volumes resulted in expansion of the set of deliverable crude oil streams used to define the final futures settlement price – the so-called BFOE basket.[7] The settlement and delivery mechanics of Brent contracts are more complex than for WTI futures. The Brent contract is described by the exchange as physically settling with an option to settle financially on the ICE Brent Index. This index is based on the arithmetic average of what are essentially physical forward trades for the first two delivery months (with the second nearby price linearly adjusted to a first nearby equivalent using the average price at which spreads between the two contracts traded). Physical settlement is through negotiated transactions referred to as *exchange-for-physical* or *EFP transactions*, in which specific grades and

---

[5] Contract expiration dates are defined by an exchange holiday calendar and a date rule, usually articulated verbally in exchange rules. Functionally risk systems often apply the rule in a scripted form. In the case of WTI, the date rule is "s-m+24d-0b-3b," which can be read from left to right as "move to the start of the month in question, go back one month, move forward twenty-four calendar days, move to the nearest business on or before this date, and then back three business days."

[6] ICE is the Intercontinental Exchange and one of the largest trading and clearing companies in commodities and more broadly. ICE screens are ubiquitous on energy trading desks.

[7] BFOE stands for Brent, Forties, Oseberg, and Ekofisk, all North Sea crude oil streams with distinct delivery points.

delivery locations are priced as a spread to the futures settlement price.[8] The circular nature of this settlement mechanism makes it difficult to categorize the contract as physically or financially settling. See [Car12] for a more detailed discussion of the Brent market. Nonetheless, the majority of physical crude oil trading references the Brent futures contracts.

Example 2: *WTI Swaps*

Swaps are typically closely related to the analogous futures contract (if such exists). The standard WTI swaps fix on the average first nearby contract price during the contract month. Cash settlement for a contract month is $N[p_{\text{float}}(m) - K]$, where N is the notional quantity, K is the swap strike, and the floating price $p_{\text{float}}(m)$ is

$$p_{\text{float}}(m) = \frac{1}{K_m} \sum_{d \in m} F_1(d) \tag{2.3}$$

where K_m is the number of trading days in month m, and $F_1(d)$ denotes the settle price of the first traded contract on day d. Recalling the contract expiry for WTI futures described in the preceding example, the floating price is comprised of roughly a two-thirds weighting of one contract price and a one-third weighting of the following contract.[9]

Example 3: *Natural Gas Futures*

The NYMEX NG natural gas futures contract is another noteworthy benchmark. The contract size is 10,000 MMBtus. Delivery occurs ratably (uniformly) over the delivery month at Henry Hub, Louisiana. Futures expiration is three business days prior to the delivery month.

Example 4: *Natural Gas Penultimate Swaps*

There are many variations of natural gas swaps, but the most common is the penultimate swap, which settles on the futures price for the same contract month four business days prior to the delivery month, that is, on the next-to-last trading day of the analogous futures contract. Its popularity as an instrument is due to the fact that options on natural gas futures expire on the same day, rendering this swap particularly useful for hedging options. Settlement occurring one business day before the futures contract is referred to as *penultimate settlement*. The settlement amount is based on the difference between the futures penultimate settlement and the strike at which the

---

[8] EFPs are common in commodities markets and allow counterparties with long and short futures contracts to exchange their respective offsetting futures positions for physical delivery of a desired specification and location at a negotiated spread to the futures price at the time the EFP is executed.

[9] While simple enough in concept, this causes a bit of headache in the design of risk systems in that a WTI swap for a single contract month will have nonzero delta exposure to two distinct futures prices.

trade was done. For example, suppose that an October 2011 swap for one lot per day (referred to as *one-a-day*) was entered into on July 1, 2011, at a price of \$4.372/MMBtu. The penultimate price was settled at \$3.827 on September 27, 2011. Because there are thirty-one days in October, the total notional is 310,000 MMBtus, resulting in a cash settlement (from the long perspective) of $310,000(\$3.827 - \$4.372) = -\$168.950$.

Example 5: *Gas Daily Swaps*

An example of swaps for which settlement is not directly related to a futures contract are the Gas Daily (GD) swaps. Financial settlement is based on the initial strike of the swap and the average Gas Daily Index published by Platts[10] for the relevant delivery locations. This index is constructed from a survey of market participants and is intended to be a representative spot price for natural gas transactions on a given day at a specific location. For example, in a Gas Daily Henry Hub swap for December 2015 struck at \$5.20, the buyer will receive

$$N \sum_{d \in \text{Dec15}} (p_d - \$5.20) \tag{2.4}$$

from the seller at settlement, where p_d denotes the GD price on day d, and N is the daily notional. If the preceding sum is negative, the buyer is paying the seller.

In contrast to the preceding futures and swaps examples, forwards contracts are physical purchases or sales that are not executed or cleared on an exchange. In a physical transaction, no reference to an underlying settlement price is required. The commodity is delivered as per the specifications of the trade confirmed by the short to the long. What the holder of the long position does with the commodity on delivery is not part of the contract, but presumably any use of the commodity amounts to the economic equivalent of buying or selling the commodity at the prevailing market price.

The floating price p_d in Example 5 is referred to as a *spot price* which, as discussed earlier, is the price for immediate delivery. Formally, we will represent a spot price by $F(t,t)$, where t indexes current time. In practice, the price is usually established slightly before the delivery time, rendering the distinction between spot and forward somewhat arbitrary. In the case of natural gas, for example, trading for delivery on day d occurs on day $d-1$, which is when the index print is established. For power, the spot price can be set a day before, hours before, or immediately at delivery. For coal, in which logistics and shipment are more daunting issues, *spot* can refer to a time lag between trade date and delivery measured in weeks or months. Spot prices

---

[10] Platts, Argus, and other index providers publish daily and monthly price indices for a vast array of energy products, many of which are used for transaction settlement.

are therefore forward prices with near-term delivery as determined by the physical logistics of the market.

Liquidity and Strips

Participants in markets with a large number of closely related tradables usually converge to conventions which enhance liquidity. In the case of U.S. Treasuries, for example, the set of bonds that can be traded on any given day numbers in the hundreds, but liquidity is concentrated in the most recently issued bonds of a given tenor (the *on-the-runs*) as well as in the Treasury futures markets. This concentration of trading activity in a smaller set of instruments reduces transaction costs, increasing the efficiency of the marketplace overall.

For energy commodities, the benchmarks such as WTI, Brent, and NG are proxies for less liquid locations. Even for these benchmarks, the dimensionality remains high simply because of the large number of contract months if we consider hedging at tenors of five to ten years. Within each energy market, conventions have evolved to avoid diluting liquidity.

Figure 2.2 shows the *open interest*, namely, the number outstanding contracts, in the WTI futures contracts on a specific date. The open interest, as well as the daily volume (not shown), is highest in the closest and most volatile months. However, at intermediate tenors, the liquidity is concentrated in the June and December contracts, and at the longest tenors, almost

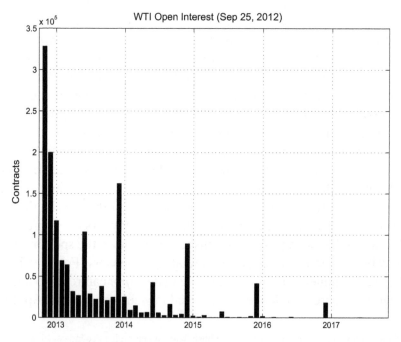

Figure 2.2. NYMEX WTI open interest by contract.

entirely in December contracts. For crude oil futures, in which there is no seasonality in price, this convention concentrates liquidity without any deterioration in the utility of the contract from a risk-management perspective. There is no hedging program that would require a position in November five years out as opposed to December. December WTI contracts are the analogue of the on-the-run Treasuries at various maturities.

Another way that the markets concentrate liquidity is through the trading of strips. The term *strip* refers to a set of adjacent months. A calendar strip (*cal strip*) is comprised of the twelve months of a calendar year. *Cal14*, for example, refers to the delivery period consisting of the twelve months comprising the year 2014. Swaps and forwards often trade as strips, especially at longer tenors. A strip is simply the union of a set of individual contract months; settlement, and in the case of physical contracts delivery, occurs on a monthly basis. For commodities with seasonality, such as natural gas, seasonal strips concentrate liquidity. In natural gas, the commonly traded strips are seasonal: the winter strips, which consist of November through the following March, and the summer strips, which consist of April through October. Seasonality matters, and these strips concentrate liquidity while acknowledging the specialness of the winter months. At longer tenors, calendar strips are the norm.[11]

Broker- and exchange-traded strips trade at a single fixed price, which means that each contract in the strip is struck at a price that is different from the price were it traded stand-alone. Given a set of monthly contract prices, the fair-value of the strip $m \in \{K, \ldots, L\}$, which we will denote by $F_{K:L}$, must satisfy

$$\sum_{m=K}^{L} N_m [F_m - F_{K:L}] d(t, \tau_m) = 0 \qquad (2.5)$$

where τ_m denotes the settlement times and N_m the monthly notionals. Strips can trade either as constant volume in each contract month (e.g., 1,000 barrels per month) or as a fixed rate (e.g. one lot per day or, in the parlance, *one-a-day* for the calendar year). In the latter case, the notionals N_m will vary by month because of differing day counts. From (2.5) we conclude that the fair value for the strip must satisfy

$$F_{K:L} = \frac{\sum_{m=K}^{L} N_m F_m d(t, \tau_m)}{\sum_{m=K}^{L} N_m d(t, \tau_m)} \qquad (2.6)$$

This equation relates strip prices to the forward curve.[12]

---

[11] Another reason that strips are commonly traded is ergonomic. The logistics of tracking and quoting individual contract prices for tenors of many years can be burdensome and prone to error.

[12] In practice, (2.6) is frequently used to infer changes in monthly prices from liquid quoted strip prices, which entails some form of interpolation.

Options as Related to Swaps

Options markets exist in tandem with the preceding linear instruments, and expiration can result in either financial or physical settlement. Mechanics and liquidity vary by commodity and tend to mirror conventions for futures and swaps.

WTI Options

The standard exchange-traded WTI options expire three business days before the futures contract expires and offer American exercise into a futures contract. Such listed options are associated with the WTI futures contract. The second commonly traded option is related to WTI swaps and settles similarly on Asian average of the first nearby. For example, an Asian call option struck at K in contract month m will have a settlement value of $\max[p_{\text{float}}(m) - K, 0]$, where the floating price was defined in (2.3).

Natural Gas Options

Listed natural gas options are American and exercise into the related futures contract one business day before (*penultimate*) expiry of the futures contract. OTC options that settle financially on the futures penultimate price are also traded. In each case, penultimate swaps are clearly convenient hedging instruments because they expire at the same time.

Annual *swaptions* are also commonly traded in natural gas. These exercise near the end of one calendar year into a swap for the next calendar year struck at the option strike K. The value of a call at expiry τ is therefore $\max\{\frac{1}{12}\sum_m d(\tau, T_m)[F(\tau, T_m) - K], 0\}$ per unit notional.

Daily options are on the opposite end of the spectrum of delivery time scales. For example, Gas Daily fixed strike options are related to Gas Daily swaps in Example 5. A call for a given contract month m is actually a strip of calls with settlement given by[13]

$$N\sum_{d\in m}\max(p_d - K, 0) \tag{2.7}$$

More common in the natural gas markets are forward starters in which the strike K is replaced by the forward price for the delivery month just before the beginning of the month.

Two features stand out in the preceding examples. First, vanilla energy options markets involve optionality across widely varying time scales. At the

---

[13] Here the payout is implicitly autoexercise or lookback–positive if the realized spot price index exceeds the strike in the case of a call. In practice, most daily options in natural gas and power are exercised manually the day before. We will discuss this in greater detail in Chapter 8.

long end of the spectrum are the annual swaptions, exercising into calendar swaps; on intermediate time scales are the options exercising into monthly delivery. Exposure to short-time-scale volatility is provided by daily options, which provide the holder with a strip of daily exercising/settling options.

The second attribute is in fact a significant structural limitation of the energy options markets. Expiration is usually "close" to the delivery interval for vanilla energy options. Unlike interest-rate swaptions, markets that offer an "MxN" palette (*M* years of expiry into an *N*-year swap) or midcurve options in Eurodollars, all vanilla energy options expire just before delivery. It is not clear why this added dimension of varying expiry has not appeared in commodities markets. However, this limitation will turn out to make the valuation and hedging of even mildly exotic options structures much more challenging than when options span both expiry and delivery/settlement dimensions.

Forward Yields and the Carry Formalism

We have discussed forward curves from the perspective of the price for a commodity at a particular forward delivery date and location. Alternatively, forward curves can be viewed from a yield-curve perspective. We saw in Figures 1.4 and 2.1 that forward curves can both increase and decrease dramatically. When forward prices are decreasing with tenor, the curve is said to be *backwardated* or *in backwardation*. When forward prices are increasing with tenor, the curve is said to be *in contango*. Usually backwardation is associated with supply stress: people need the commodity now and are willing to pay a premium for it. Conversely, contango is associated with supply excess; contango provides an incentive to store the commodity for future use, thereby alleviating the current glut. The significant contango in Figure 2.1, at the height of the credit crisis, was a result of market anticipation of excess supply due to reduced global economic activity.

Figures 2.3 and 2.4 show the WTI and NG forward curves at a variety of dates. These figures are interesting in that they illustrate both the fact that forward curves can vary between backwardation and contango, in some cases exhibiting mixed states, and showing the large range of prices spanned by these commodities over the past few years.

To begin to quantify how contango incentivizes an inventory build and, conversely, backwardation a reduction in inventory, it is necessary to view commodities forward curves from a yield perspective. The forward yield at time $y(t, T, T + S)$ is the annualized forward rate at time t implied by borrowing to buy the commodity forward at time T and sell it later at time $T + S$:

$$y(t, T, T + S) = \frac{1}{S} \log \left[\frac{F(t, T + S)}{F(t, T)} \right] \tag{2.8}$$

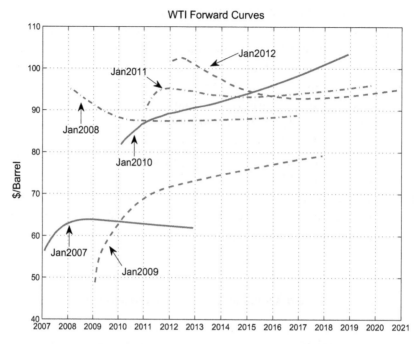

Figure 2.3.   WTI historical forward curves.

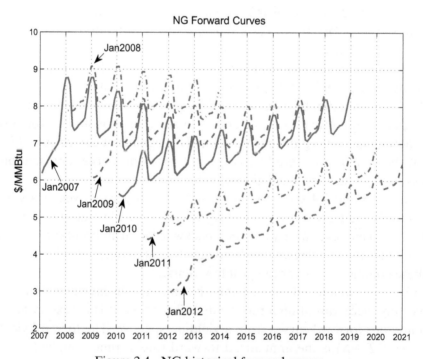

Figure 2.4.   NG historical forward curves.

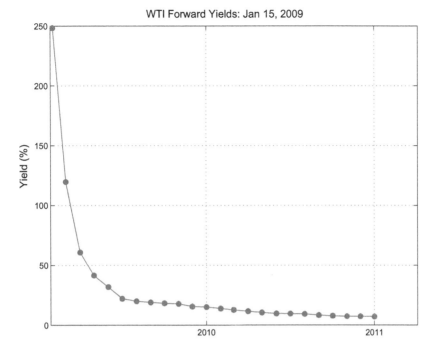

Figure 2.5. WTI monthly forward yields.

Negative forward yields imply that market participants are willing to pay a premium for earlier delivery; buyers for near-term delivery are effectively lending at negative interest rates.

Forward yields can exhibit extreme values. Figure 2.5 shows the WTI monthly forward yields (that is $S = 1/12$) for the same date, January 15, 2009, as Figure 2.1. A belief that a supply glut would result from the credit crisis, which was in full swing at the time, resulted in astonishingly high forward yields, exceeding 200 percent annualized. This was clearly the result of a remarkable global economic meltdown.

For seasonal commodities, in contrast, forward yields of mixed sign and of significant magnitude are more the norm than the exception. Figure 2.6 shows the forward yield corresponding to Figure 1.4. Note that the yields exceed 50 percent and fall below −100 percent on the boundaries between the summer and winter seasons.

The yield-curve paradigm is the starting point for a significant body of research in part because of the analogy with financial assets. The utility of this train of thought remains debatable, but at a minimum, the carry formalism discussed later provides some intuition and insight into commodities price dynamics.

For purely financial assets, the presence of decreasing forward curves presents an apparent arbitrage opportunity: Why not short the commodity at the high prices and repurchase at the low prices? This question is frequently

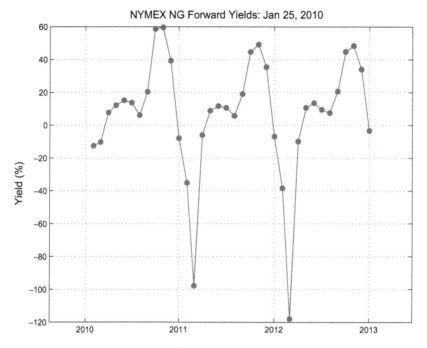

Figure 2.6. NG monthly forward yields.

the first response of bond traders unacquainted with energy markets. The answer is that you probably could affect this reverse repo[14] if you really wanted to. However, the lender of the commodity, being fully aware of the forward curve, will charge accordingly. If you borrow the commodity now (at time t) at a time of high prices, posting the purchase price as cash collateral (this is the embedded loan), agreeing to return the commodity at a later time $t + S$ corresponding to lower forward prices, at which time the cash is returned to you, the yield you will earn on your cash will be the forward yield $y(t, t, t + S)$. When the curve is backwardated, this yield is negative. There is no arbitrage opportunity. In practice this deal structure, referred to in the business as a *park-and-loan*, usually involves repo in the natural direction, namely, buying in the cheaper months and storing to the expensive months when demand is higher.

Carry arguments are most straightforward for investment assets with no dividends or storage costs, in which case the forward price is given by

$$F(t, T) = F(t, t)e^{r(t,T)(T-t)} \qquad (2.9)$$

where $r(t, T)$ denotes the funding rate from t to T, which is usually assumed to be the London Interbank Offered Rate (LIBOR). More generally, the

---

[14] A reverse-repo entails acquiring the desired asset or commodity and lending the cash value at inception and reversing the transaction at a later time by returning the asset or commodity and receiving the cash and accrued interest.

result is

$$F(t,T) = F(t,S)e^{r(t,S,T)(T-S)} \tag{2.10}$$

where $r(t,S,T)$ is the forward funding rate on the interval $[T,T+S]$. This is a direct result of absence of arbitrage. If $F(t,T) > F(t,t)e^{r(t,T)(T-t)}$, then borrowing to purchase the asset at the spot price $F(t,t)$ while simultaneously selling the asset forward results in a riskless gain. The converse applies for the reversed inequality, provided that you can short the asset.

This train of thought is easily extended to commodities held primarily as an investment asset, such as gold, by including the cost of storage. Using a somewhat idealized representation of storage costs as an instantaneous forward cost $q(t,T)$, the generalization of (2.9) is

$$F(t,T) = F(t,t)e^{[r(t,T)+q(t,T)](T-t)} \tag{2.11}$$

The implication of these results is that forward curves for investment assets without dividends are always in contango.

We know, however, that for energy commodities (and consumption commodities in general), backwardation is frequently observed. For a consumption commodity, basic arbitrage arguments can only support the following inequality:

$$F(t,T) \leq F(t,t)e^{[r(t,T)+q(t,T)](T-t)} \tag{2.12}$$

This fact is a direct application of the preceding argument: by definition, you can always buy the commodity at the spot price and sell the commodity forward. However, if strict inequality in (2.12) holds, an attempt to do the reverse, namely, shorting the commodity in the spot market, requires being able to borrow the commodity from someone in possession of it. If the commodity is special in the sense of high immediate demand, as discussed earlier, the rate of interest at which you are effectively lending in a reverse repo is negative. This is exactly the same situation as when bonds go special and is the origin of the inequality. The decoupling of the repo rate from typical funding rates results in the forward curve being backwardated.

Reconciliation of these facts with a yield-curve formalism requires an equality in (2.12). This is accomplished by defining the convenience yield $\eta(t,T)$ that yields the desired equality:

$$F(t,T) = F(t,t)e^{[r(t,T)+q(t,T)-\eta(t,T)](T-t)} \tag{2.13}$$

Exactly what this accomplishes is debatable. At a minimum, it is a way of thinking about specialness from a yield perspective. However, all that can be observed from the traded markets is $r(t,T)$ and $F(t,T)$, which allow one to discern $q - \eta$, not the two components separately. Participants in the natural gas markets know that if the spread between winter and summer months rises, increasing the profit a storage owner can make by injecting in the summer and selling in the winter, the cost to lease storage rises in tandem. Storage owners will charge what the market will bear. The cost to lease storage is in reality a function of forwards and volatilities as opposed to an input, rendering (2.13) recursive in nature.

For energy commodities, there is a finite amount of available storage, whether it be crude oil storage tanks or salt caverns in which to store natural gas. One would expect the marginal cost of storage to increase as storage levels increase; as less is available, it costs more to lease. Forward curves do in fact exhibit an inventory response that is consistent with $q - \eta$ increasing as inventory decreases. This relationship has been known by practitioners and academics for many years and has been a subject of great deal of research, starting with Kaldor in 1939 [Kal39] and including notably French and Fama [FF87], Ng and Pirrong [NP94], and Geman and Ohana [GO09]. Deaton and Laroque [DL91], followed by Routledge, Seppi, and Spatt [RSS00], have constructed risk-neutral-based inventory models to study the effects of inventory on price volatility. Recently, Gorton, Hayashi, and Rouwenhorst [GHR07] built and tested equilibrium inventory models to examine the effects of inventory on risk premia.[15] This body of research, which we will return to later in Chapter 10, is referred to as the *theory of storage*.

It is very difficult to reliably estimate global crude oil stocks primarily because of the challenge of obtaining timely and reliable estimates from many countries. A commonly used proxy is the oil inventory in Organisation for Economic Co-operation and Development (OECD) countries, which is compiled and released on a monthly basis and shown in Figure 2.7. Figure 2.8 shows a scatterplot of the forward yield between the first two cal strips of the WTI forward curve yields versus OECD crude oil stocks from January 2003 to December 2011. Note the obvious pattern, with low inventory levels being associated with low forward yields. At any given inventory level, the conditional standard deviation of yields is at least several percentage points wide, making this result of questionable utility from a statistical arbitrage perspective. The theme, however, is clear – low inventory is associated with negative forward yields and conversely.

Figure 2.8 implies that $q - \eta$ is low when inventories are low and spare storage capacity abounds. It remains unclear whether the forward curve is the tail or the dog: do inventory levels respond to the forward curve or vice versa? In reality, the two are recursively related, but there is compelling evidence that both inventory levels and, moreover, available storage capacity are a function of the forward curve. The period of time right after the inception of the credit crisis provided a very good example of the dynamic nature of storage.

---

[15] Recent surveys include the previous reference as well as [Cul04].

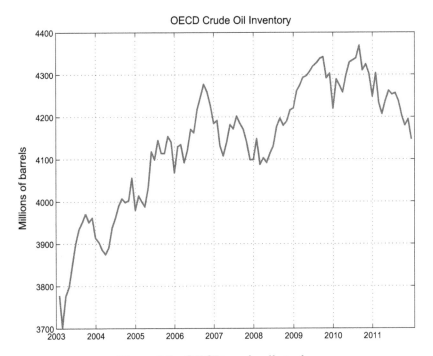

Figure 2.7. OECD crude oil stocks.

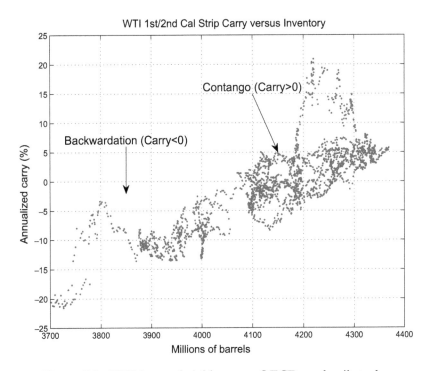

Figure 2.8. WTI forward yields versus OECD crude oil stocks.

Crude oil stocks rose significantly, as seen in Figure 2.7. Recall Figures 2.1 and 2.5, which showed the WTI forward curve in significant contango, with forward yields nearing 200 percent annually. Owners of storage can earn the forward yields net of funding costs, which were nearly zero at the time, courtesy of central bank intervention. There was a great deal of money to be made by buying crude oil in the spot markets and selling forward a few months – provided that one had the ability to store the commodity. According to Argus Media [Ltd11], approximately fifty very large crude carriers (VLCCs) stored over 100 million barrels of crude oil during this time frame. This was true globally; if you could find something to hold it, you stored it.

The moral of the story is that both the quantity of available storage capacity increased due to short-term innovations, namely, the use of tankers, and the marginal cost of storage was ultimately set by tanker leasing rates. This situation would have been challenging to predict only a few months earlier and was clearly a function of the forward prices for crude oil. The interactive nature of inventory, forward yields, and as we will see later, the covariance structure of returns are the genesis of some of the most challenging valuation problems in energy markets.

Conclusion

Energy commodities trade for forward delivery/settlement, and there are a variety of linear and nonlinear instruments available for risk transfer.

- Linear instruments (forwards, futures, and swaps) involve either physical delivery or financial settlement.
- Forward pricing references contract months, except at very short tenors.
- Liquidity at long tenors is typically concentrated at benchmark contract months or strips.
- Options tend to parallel forward and futures conventions, with an important structural limitation arising from the fact that standard options in energy markets expire near the delivery period. This feature limits the information about volatility structure that can be gleaned from traded products.

Forward curves for consumable commodities, and energy in particular, exhibit structure that is dramatically different from that of financial assets.

- Energy forward curves can exhibit varying monotonicity and forward yields of high magnitude of both positive and negative sign.
- When yields are positive, forward prices are increasing with tenor (contango), and when negative, prices decrease with tenor (backwardation).
- The carry formalism decomposes yields into borrowing costs, storage costs, and convenience yield, although market data provide visibility into only the sum of the storage and convenience-yield components.
- The cost of storage is endogenous, being a function of traded markets, rendering the carry formalism primarily a stylized description of forward markets.

In light of the preceding yield formulation, it should come as no surprise that much of the mathematics developed for valuation and hedging has drawn from other fields in financial engineering, notably, interest-rate derivatives. One of the distinguishing features in energy, however, is the feedback mechanism between the forward-curve dynamics and inventory response: high forward yields incentivize an increase in inventory and conversely. The dynamics of forward curves depends on inventory levels and the behavior of storage operators, and inventory decisions depend on the state of the forward curve and the covariance structure of returns. Effective modeling of this interaction is one of the major unresolved issues in energy markets.

3

Macro Perspective

High volatility and specialness in energy markets result in more challenging trade execution, larger capital requirements and diminished effectiveness of benchmark hedging in contrast to other asset classes. Given these challenges, it is reasonable to ask why energy is traded as extensively as it is. Part of the answer is an inclination of some market participants to prop trade, with the higher volatility and peculiarities of the markets providing an interesting arena to do just that. The real driver, however, is risk transfer between producers and consumers.

The life cycle of energy commodities begins with the production or extraction of the raw commodity, which is then converted and transported as required and ultimately consumed. Energy commodities must be created, moved through space and time, and transformed into a usable form. This has been true from the inception of human control of energy sources, initially involving very simple processes such as harvesting wood, drying it, and hauling it to the fireplace. Over time, the level of sophistication has created a "virtuous" cycle in which greater energy availability has resulted in more efficient extraction and transport methods and ultimately greater demand. There are two immediate consequences of these technological advances.

The first is that major sources of energy are often found at considerable distances from the locations of ultimate consumption, resulting in large regional imbalances with consequences ranging from international capital flows to geopolitical risks to the reliability of energy supply. The decades-long trade imbalances between the United States and the Middle East, only recently being alleviated with increased extraction of natural gas and oil from shale, and European concerns about the reliability of natural gas supply from Russia are just two examples.

The second is that increasing amounts of capital and time are required to complete the development and construction of new infrastructure. Deep-sea drilling rigs, natural gas and oil pipelines, and combined-cycle generators require large amounts of capital. When such projects are funded in part by debt, as is often the case, lenders must be concerned about the exposure of a project to commodity price volatility and regulatory changes.

Geographic imbalances and capital requirements for infrastructure are the primary reasons for the existence and sophistication of modern energy markets. Our dominant focus will be on three commodities classes: crude oil and refined products, natural gas, and electricity. We will digress into related markets such as coal, emissions, and weather, but most of our attention will be directed to these three markets.

Units and Orders of Magnitude

Most trading activity in crude oil and refined products references barrels, gallons, or metric tons to define notional quantities. These are volumetric and weight units and not energy units per se, such as MMBtus (an MMBtu is one million British thermal units) or gigajoules. One barrel of crude oil is equivalent to

- 42 gallons
- Approximately 5.4 MMBtu[1]
- 0.1364 metric tons

Natural gas markets use both volumetric units – cubic feet or cubic meters – and energy units – most commonly MMBtus or gigajoules. One MMBtu is equivalent to

- Approximately 1,000 cubic feet (cf) of natural gas
- 1.05 GJ
- 0.025 metric tons of crude oil

Power is measured in units of megawatt-hours (MWh) or kilowatt-hours (kWh). Roughly 7 MMBtus of natural gas is required by an efficient combined cycle generator to produce one MWh of electricity. One MWh of electricity powers approximately 1,000 U.S. households for one hour. While consumption varies dramatically by region and time of year, with usage in climates requiring air conditioning being higher, this is a useful rule of thumb. Another way to put this electricity demand into context is to consider what would be required to store the electricity used by a typical household in one day. The answer, assuming 100 percent conversion efficiency, is the potential energy stored by lifting a 1,000 kg (a rather small car) to a height of over 8.8 km. Electricity is very hard to store in useful quantities.

World Energy Trends

World energy consumption has increased consistently and rapidly over the past century. Figure 3.1 shows energy consumption by fuel type in common

---

[1] This figure is based on conversion factors used in [BP12]. Estimates vary. For example, the U.S. Internal Revenue Service actually ascribes 5.8 MMBtu to a barrel of crude.

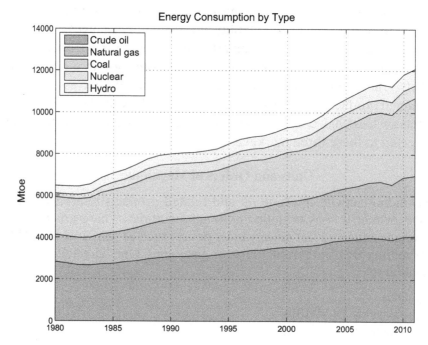

Figure 3.1. Global energy consumption by type. (*Source: BP Statistical Review of World Energy 2012.*)

units of metric ton oil (toe) or million metric ton oil equivalent (Mtoe) [BP12]. This growth in energy consumption has been highly predictable, aside from a small drop in 2009 resulting from the credit crisis. Annual global consumption in 2011 stood at a little over 12,000 Mtoe, which equates to the energy content of approximately 85 billion barrels of crude oil. Using a reference price of $100/barrel of crude oil, this equates to a notional value of 8.5 trillion USD; for comparison, global gross domestic product (GDP) in 2011 was approximately 70 trillion USD according to the World Bank. This comparison is only approximate because the cost per unit of energy varies dramatically across the different energy sources, some such as coal being much cheaper than crude oil.

Crude oil is the dominant energy source, although natural gas and coal are experiencing higher growth rates. Driven by Asian economic development, the increase in coal consumption has been spectacular in the last few years, a fact that certainly stands in contrast to the growing chorus of concern about global carbon emissions. Nuclear, hydro, and renewable energy sources in general satisfy a relatively small fraction of global energy requirements.

Energy consumption has important regional structure, as seen in Figure 3.2 (see [BP12]). Most of the past fifty years were characterized by the dominance of North America and Europe in consumption, but by 2003, the Asia Pacific region took the lead. This growing dominance of Asia Pacific

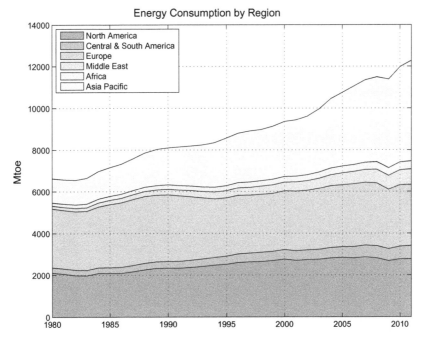

Figure 3.2. Global energy consumption by region. (*Source: BP Statistical Review of World Energy 2012.*)

energy requirements is coincident with the significant increase in global coal consumption, both being driven in large part by the export of industrial and manufacturing activities from Western countries.

Crude Oil and Refined Products

Crude oil production and consumption patterns mirror these regional imbalances. Figure 3.3 shows annual consumption of crude oil, including all refined products, at a regional level. Most crude oil is consumed in North America, Europe, and Asia.

In contrast, the production of crude oil, shown in Figure 3.4, is more localized and in different parts of the globe, with the Middle East the largest regional producer. This imbalance is illustrated for three of the regions in Figure 3.5. The reversal in the trend in the North American deficit starting in the late 2000s has accelerated as a result of increasing oil production from unconventional methods, particularly shale extraction in the United States. In contrast, consumption in the Asia Pacific region has increased at almost the same offsetting rate, with the upshot being that a great deal of crude oil needs to make its way from one part of the world to another.

The demand for crude oil exhibits finer structure when viewed on shorter time scales. This is illustrated in Figure 3.6, which shows monthly crude oil consumption globally in the top plot, as well as a linear regression of

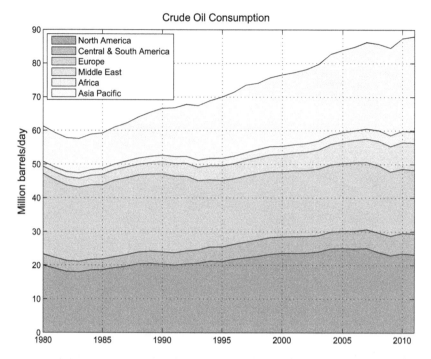

Figure 3.3. Global crude oil consumption by region. (*Source: BP Statistical Review of World Energy 2012.*)

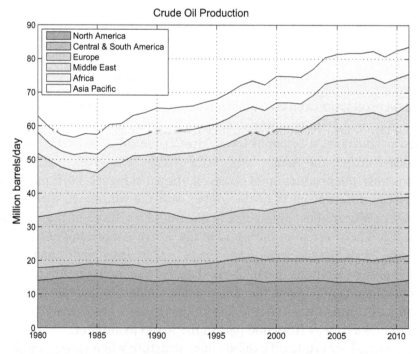

Figure 3.4. Global crude oil production by region. (*Source: BP Statistical Review of World Energy 2012.*)

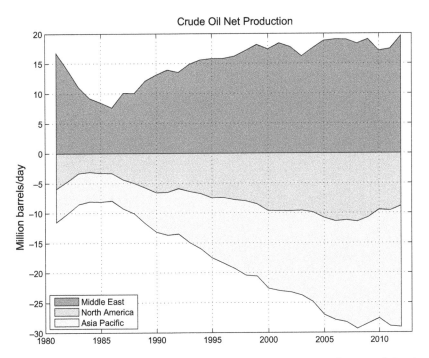

Figure 3.5. Net crude oil production by region. (*Source: BP Statistical Review of World Energy 2012.*)

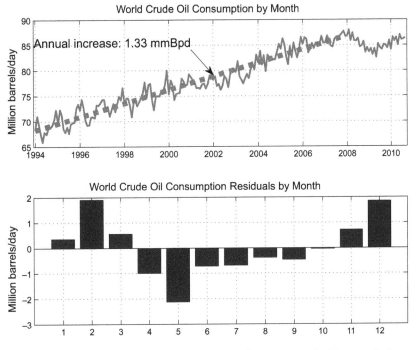

Figure 3.6. Monthly world oil consumption. (*Source: U.S. Energy Information Administration.*)

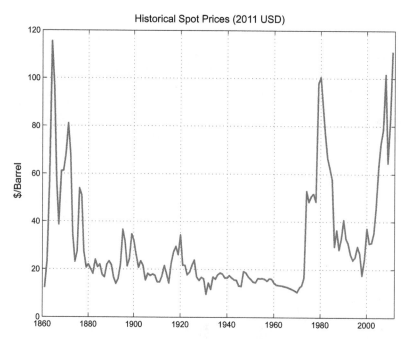

Figure 3.7. Historical crude oil spot prices in 2011 USD equivalent. (*Source: BP Statistical Review of World Energy 2012.*)

monthly consumption using data through the end of 2007 – that is, before the inception of the subsequent credit crisis. Over this period, the average annual increase in consumption was 1.33 million barrels per day (bpd), with daily global usage peaking at approximately 88 million bpd. This was followed by a drop of roughly 4 million bpd during 2009, before consumption resumed at roughly the same precrisis growth rate. The lower plot shows the average residual from the regression by month,[2] where one can see that heating requirements in the northern hemisphere result in above-average consumption during the winter months.

As one of the global energy benchmarks, the NYMEX West Texas Intermediate (WTI) crude oil futures contract provides some of the best historical oil price data, although it only started trading in 1983, well after the oil crisis in the 1970s. Figure 3.7 shows a concatenation of historical energy prices including U.S., Arabian, and Brent spot prices denominated in 2009 USD (see [BP12]). The high prices near the end of the 1800s have to be taken in context because crude oil did not have the relevance that it gained with the development of modern transportation methods. Note that the prices in mid-2008, adjusted for inflation, exceeded the previous peak in the late 1970s

---

[2] The linear regression is of the form $C_m = \alpha + \beta T_m + \epsilon_m$, where C_m denotes monthly consumption, and T_m is the time associated with the month (referenced to an arbitrary starting date). The residuals ϵ_m are grouped by calendar month and averaged.

in real terms. This was remarkable given that these recent high prices were not associated with any events as explicit and coordinated as the drivers of the oil crisis in the 1970s.

Crude oil is often discussed as if it refers to a single commodity, while in fact it is a general term for a commonly appearing type of hydrocarbon mixture, the attributes of which vary significantly by the reservoir and field from which it is extracted. Crude oil is also rarely ultimately consumed by end users, who instead require products such as gasoline and heating oil. Crude oil must be refined, in addition to being shipped, trucked, or transported by pipeline. Refining typically occurs after long-haul transport because this avoids requiring either multiple fleets for transporting different refined products or the time-consuming and costly requirement to clean tankers. Crude oil is usually shipped or piped to local refinery clusters (e.g., Louisiana or Houston in the United States), refined, and then transported by truck or pipeline to local destinations.[3]

To leading order, any given "stream" of crude oil is characterized by two dominant attributes: sulfur content and density or gravity. Higher sulfur content makes a crude oil stream harder to refine because of the corrosive by-products and requires efforts to reduce sulfur content in the resulting products for the purpose of emissions reduction. Crude oils with high sulfur content are referred to as *sour*, while those with relatively low sulfur content are called *sweet*. The products resulting from refining, appropriately referred to as *refined products*, are characterized in large part by their volatility, with highly volatile products such as gasoline being more valuable than heavier products such as fuel oil. Light (low-density) crudes have a higher percentage of volatile hydrocarbons, which results in a higher yield of more valuable refined products, in contrast to heavy crudes, which yield a higher fraction of less valuable heavy products.

An array of technologies has been developed to maximize the value of the resulting product mix (see [Dow09]), but the fact remains that a better crude going into a refinery results in a more valuable product stream at a lower cost. Figure 3.8, constructed by [Res], shows a set of crude oil streams scattered by attribute. The American Petroleum Institute (API) density on the *x* axis is a standard industry metric that is inversely related to actual density; it is therefore an increasing indication of value. Note the negative correlation between sulfur content and API density – less valuable crudes tend to suffer from both ailments of high sulfur and low density. Each of the various streams shown and many others are traded, transported, and refined, although only a few have the status of benchmark price references.

---

[3] There is a trend toward refinery development near the well head, which is resulting in an increase in shipment of refined products, but the norm remains long-haul transport followed by refining.

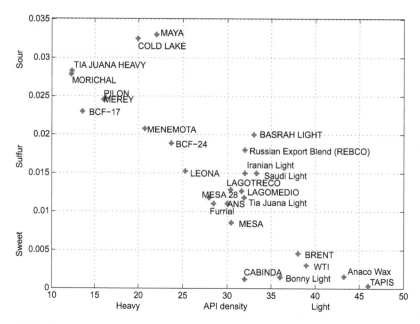

Figure 3.8. Crude oil streams by sulfur content and density. (*Source: Credit Suisse Research.*)

Figure 3.9 shows the historical spot prices for four benchmark crudes. Whereas prices clearly follow macro energy trends, the relatively low prices of Maya stands out visibly and is due to its sour and heavy attributes relative to, say, WTI or Brent crudes (see in Figure 3.8).

Using WTI as the benchmark, the price differentials or basis prices defined as $p(d) - p_{WTI}(d)$ are more interesting. The basis prices shown in Figure 3.10 are driven largely by differences in sulfur content and density, shipping rates for crude cargos, and inventory levels. Brent and WTI have relatively similar attributes, while Dubai (not shown in Figure 3.8 but in the cluster located at roughly 30 API and 0.015 sulfur) is less valuable; Maya, in the upper left corner is at the "bottom of the barrel" so to speak. A visual inspection of the Dubai and Maya basis prices would seem to suggest a relationship to price level, and this is in fact the case, as shown in Figure 3.11. In general, higher oil prices are associated with higher global economic activity and an increasing premium for the more desirable products such as gasoline.

The choice of a benchmark price to define basis is more than an arbitrary statistical decision. Given the multitude of crude oils that trade, it is clearly not viable to have visible liquid spot and forward markets for all of them. The need to establish credible market-based pricing for transactions across a wide variety of commodity types is handled via benchmark pricing in which contracts fix or settle as a basis to a defined benchmark. For example, the pricing of a nonbenchmark crude oil transaction will often be defined as a constant spread to a linear combination of WTI and Brent, all components of

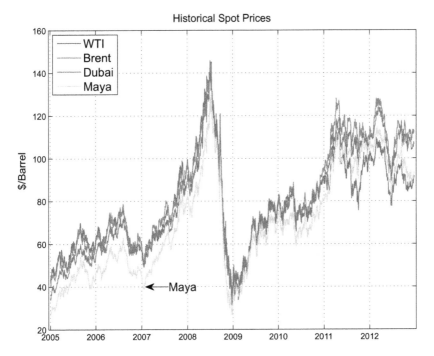

Figure 3.9. Crude oil spot prices by stream.

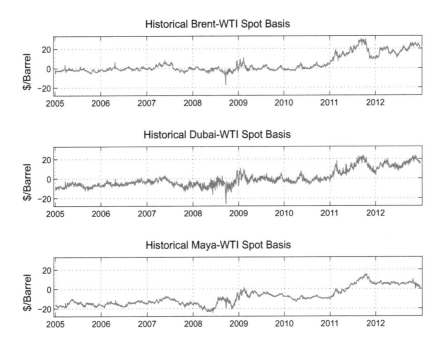

Figure 3.10. Crude oil spot basis versus WTI by stream.

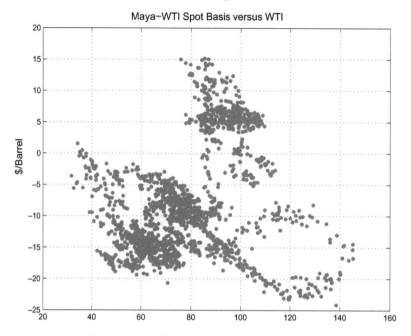

Figure 3.11. Maya spot basis versus WTI.

which are negotiated. Historically, WTI has served as a benchmark for most North American oil transactions, and Brent has served the same purpose for European, Middle Eastern, and Asian markets.

Brent futures are a slightly different breed because they can be settled financially or physically, as mentioned in Chapter 2. Most global oil shipments reference Brent prices. All other crude futures and swaps markets are much smaller in outstanding notional and daily volume. Recently, however, issues have arisen with both WTI and Brent contracts that have given way to increasing concern about their viability as global benchmarks.

In the case of Brent, the deliverable has had to be redefined repeatedly to accommodate the depletion of the original Brent fields. In a sense, what a Brent futures contract actually means has been and continues to be a moving target.

The WTI contract has been experiencing a far more dramatic fall from grace owing to the land-locked nature of the delivery location. Recall the basis prices shown in Figure 3.10. Note that all the crude oil spreads with respect to WTI rose meaningfully starting at the end of 2010. This would suggest something idiosyncratic about WTI during this period, given that the phenomenon is observed across crude oils of widely varying attributes. This apparent anomaly provides us with another example of the effects of inventory on commodities prices.

The United States is divided into five Petroleum Administration for Defense Districts (PADDs) for which statistics including inventory are

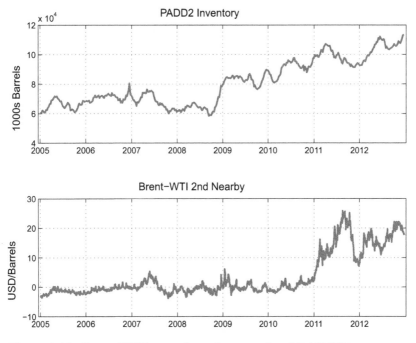

Figure 3.12. Brent-WTI second nearby spread and PADD2 inventory.

compiled. As discussed earlier, WTI futures contracts require delivery at Cushing, Oklahoma, which is in PADD2 in the Midwest. Inventory levels in PADD2 started rising dramatically in 2010 as a result of increasing imports from Canada and a lack of local demand in PADD2, coupled with limitations on export pipeline capacity. The resulting surplus of inventory during this time period drove the price of WTI down relative to other crude oils, diminishing the viability of WTI as a global benchmark and causing a migration to the Brent futures contract traded on the Intercontinental Exchange (ICE).[4]

The upper plot in Figure 3.12 shows the time series of weekly inventory at PADD2. The lower plot shows weekly averages of the spread between Brent and WTI second nearby contract prices. The relationship between the Brent-WTI spread versus inventory is clear in the scatter shown in Figure 3.13. The moral of the story is that analysis of commodity price spreads in the absence of information about key drivers such as inventory levels is done at your peril. A physical driver, in this case a high level of imports into a region with limited native demand and export capacity, is affecting the traded markets exactly as one would expect it to. Even with inventory as a regression variable, the response appears to be nonlinear, and the standard deviation of

[4] To punctuate the point, the U.S. Energy Information Administration used Brent oil futures in price forecasting energy prices in its *Annual Energy Outlook 2013*, a substantial departure from the traditional use of the WTI benchmark in previous AEOs.

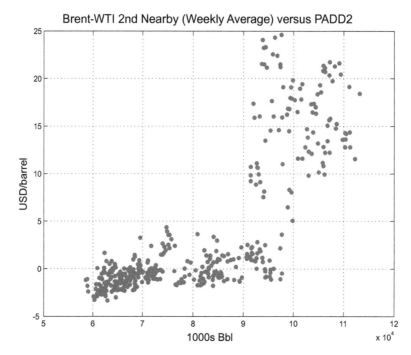

Figure 3.13. Brent-WTI second nearby spread versus PADD2 inventory.

the spread conditioned on inventory level is of the order of several dollars; speculative trading based on this analysis would be a high risk affair.

The purpose of crude oil production and trading is to provide inputs to refineries that produce the energy-wielding products on which so much of society depends.[5] Refinery yields vary by technology and desired output. In the United States, roughly 50 percent of the yield is comprised of gasoline and light distillates, predominantly gasoline.[6] The middle distillates, consisting of diesel, heating oil, and kerosenes (including jet fuel), constitute about 35 percent of the output. Finally, the heavy distillates such as residual fuel oil and asphalt account for roughly 15 percent of output[7] [Dow09] [EIAa].

Each of the three main categories subsumes a number of distinct refined products. The most commonly traded and liquid markets are gasoline (light), heating oil or gas oil (middle) and, residual fuel oil or *resid* (heavy). These have liquid spot markets and, in the case of the gasoline and heating oil,

---

[5] See [Kam12] for more detailed discussion of crude oil and refined products.

[6] Often gasoline is viewed as a distinct product, and light distillates refers to other products such as naphtha.

[7] While these figures conveniently sum to 100 percent, this is not the whole story because a number of other products result from the refining process in smaller volumes. This would seem to violate a conservation law because the refining process creates more than 100 percent of input. These are, however, volumetric figures, and because products such as gasoline have a lower specific gravity than the input crude oil, volumetric yields should sum to a number in excess of 100 percent. This is referred to as *refinery gain*.

Figure 3.14. Gasoline, heating oil, and residual fuel oil New York harbor (1st nearby prices).

futures markets with significant depth. Figure 3.14 shows the spot prices for these three products delivered at New York harbor.[8] Gasoline and heating oil trade in units of gallons, and their prices have been converted to USD per barrel for comparison with crude oil prices.

The prices of each product follow, as expected, global trends, with an obvious discount for resid.

The price series in Figure 3.14 alone shed little light on the economics of refiners, for whom revenue is driven by the spreads between the prices of the refined products and the costs of the input crude oil. Such spreads, referred to as *crack spreads*, can be written in the form[9]

$$\vec{w}^{\dagger}(t)\vec{p}(t) - p_{\text{Crude}}(t) - V(t) \tag{3.1}$$

where $\vec{p}$ denotes the vector of spot prices for the products, p_{Crude} is the spot price for the input crude, $\vec{w}$ denotes the palette of products the refiner is choosing to produce at time t, and V is the variable cost of refining in the production configuration $\vec{w}(t)$. Modern refineries have flexibility to adjust the mix of products, which is why $\vec{w}$ is, in practice, a function of time.

---

[8] The Chicago Mercantile Exchange (CME) changed the specifications of the classic heating oil futures starting with the May 2013 contract month to delivery of Ultra-Low Sulfur Diesel, although the contract symbol HO continues to be used.

[9] The superscript † denotes the transpose of the vector.

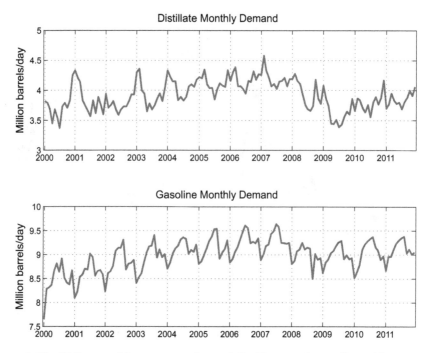

Figure 3.15. U.S. monthly consumption of distillate and gasoline. (*Source: U.S. Energy Information Administration.*)

Figure 3.15 shows U.S. monthly demand of distillate (which includes heating oil) and gasoline. The apparent seasonality of each of these demand series is more obvious when monthly averages are taken as shown in Figure 3.16. Distillate usage clearly peaks in the winter because of the heating season. Gasoline consumption, on the other hand, peaks in the summer in what is commonly referred to as the "driving season," with demand dropping precipitously at the start of the typical school year in September. This seasonality in demand is also manifest in forward curves, just as in the case of natural gas.

Demand seasonality is what makes refinery flexibility and storage useful. Refineries tune their output to produce more gasoline prior to the driving season and likewise for heating oil as winter approaches. Figure 3.17 shows the monthly averages of inventory statistics published by the U.S. Energy Information Administration for distillate and motor gasoline. Each series shows an inventory buildup before the peak consumption months. The ability to seasonally tune the relative amounts of gasoline and heating oil produced, storing the products in advance of peak consumption, ultimately results in lower cost for end users.

Although the term *crack spread* applies to the generic form $\vec{w}^\dagger \vec{p}(t) - p_{\text{Crude}}(t)$, the crack spreads most commonly discussed and traded are the simple spreads between single products and crude oil, for example,

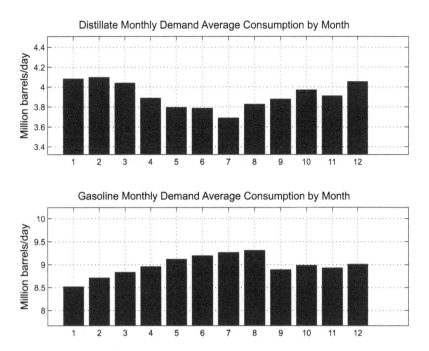

Figure 3.16. Average U.S. monthly consumption of gasoline and heating oil by month.

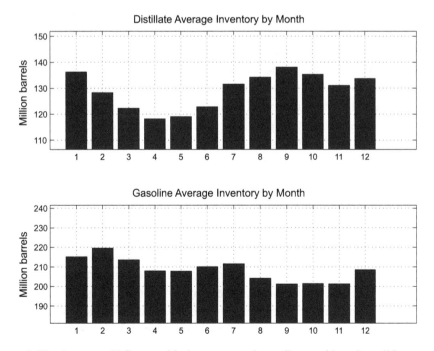

Figure 3.17. Average U.S. monthly inventory of gasoline and heating oil by month.

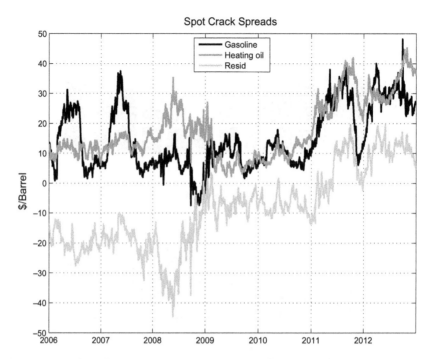

Figure 3.18. Gasoline, heating oil, and spot crack spreads (1st nearby prices).

$p_{\text{Gasoline}} - p_{\text{Crude}}$, or a few industry standards such as the commonly referenced 3:2:1 spread: $2p_{\text{Gasoline}} + p_{\text{HeatingOil}} - 3p_{\text{Crude}}$. Each of these corresponds to a specific choice of $\vec{w}$ in (3.1).

Figure 3.18 shows the crack spreads of the products in Figure 3.14 versus WTI. The discount of the residual crack to that of gasoline and heating oil is pronounced. The production of resid is an apparent money-loser for large intervals of time, at least when viewed as an individual product. However, although the goal of refiners is to minimize the relative fraction of heavy products, even under the best conditions these are an inevitable result of refining and do in fact sell for positive prices.

Natural Gas

Over the past decade, crude oil consumption has risen at a slower rate than that of coal and natural gas. The increase in coal consumption has been driven by Asian energy demand. The story with natural gas is more complex because rapid improvements in technology have yielded much greater recoverable reserves than even remotely contemplated twenty years ago. In addition, significant strides in shipping as liquified natural gas (LNG), increasingly efficient conversion to electricity via combined-cycle generation, and a relatively low carbon footprint have resulted in an increase in "market share" that seems likely to continue for the foreseeable future.

The fundamental complexity in crude oil markets is the spectrum of attributes, with refining costs and product yield varying widely by stream. Crude oil is relatively easy to transport via pipeline or tanker. For natural gas, the situation is the opposite. While delivery specifications define limits on water content and the presence of various gases and liquids, to a good approximation, natural gas is one and only one thing – methane. The challenge is getting it from where (and when) it is produced to where (and when) it is required.

Initially this challenge was addressed by either state-owned energy companies or privately owned vertically integrated utilities supervised by government regulators primarily because of the large capital costs and long investment horizon involved in building the required pipelines and storage facilities. After decades of regulated investment, the notion that competition could result in more efficient capital allocation began to get traction; of course, this was occurring as part of a broader paradigm that included other industries such as telecommunications. Ultimately, the past two decades have witnessed significant deregulation in natural gas markets, especially in the United States and parts of Europe.

Deregulation in natural gas markets has involved issues that pertain to any natural monopoly in possession of infrastructure essential to the overall commercial endeavor. The activities required to provide end users with natural gas can be divided into four categories: (1) production and short-term transport to pipeline networks, (2) transport by pipeline, (3) storage, and (4) sale and distribution to end users. Of these four activities, production and distribution are clearly amenable to competitive merchant activities; pipeline systems and, arguably, storage constitute the critical infrastructure to which producers and distributors would need fair access in order to function competitively.

The mechanisms by which these four components of the natural gas supply chain have been unbundled vary,[10] but the premise is that competitive natural gas markets are predicated on the ability of market participants to procure access to transportation and storage in a fair and transparent fashion. This has increased merchant investment with associated financing and hedging requirements, ultimately yielding the array of swaps and options markets currently traded.

Statistics for natural gas usage are typically quoted in billion cubic feet (bcf) per day, with total global consumption in 2011 of just over 300 bcf/day. Figures 3.19 and 3.20 show natural gas production and consumption, respectively, by global region. Europe/Eurasia and North America are both the largest producers and consumers of natural gas, in contrast to crude oil, in which the Middle East dominates production.

---

[10] For a survey of deregulation in the United States, see [Har06]; for European markets, see [Tre08].

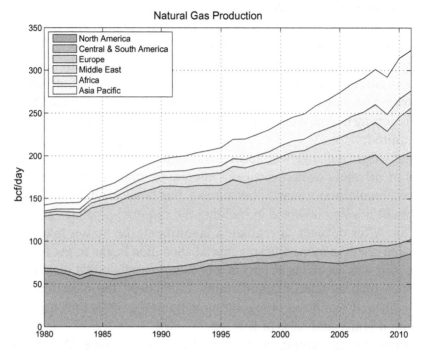

Figure 3.19. Global natural gas production by region. (*Source: BP Statistical Review of World Energy 2012.*)

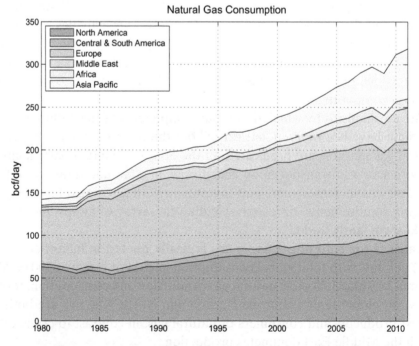

Figure 3.20. Global natural gas consumption by region. (*Source: BP Statistical Review of World Energy 2012.*)

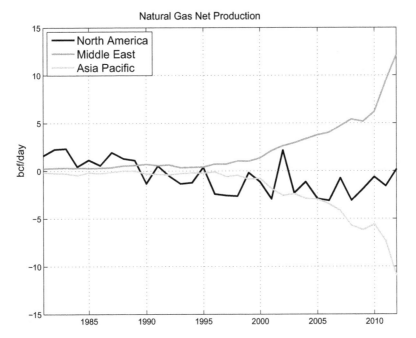

Figure 3.21. Net regional natural gas production. (*Source: BP Statistical Review of World Energy 2012.*)

Net production rates are shown in Figure 3.21 for the same regions as shown earlier for crude oil. Here we see the growing footprint of the Middle East more clearly as increasing LNG liquefaction and transport capacity have yielded commercial value for natural gas that was a by-product of oil production and that historically would have been simply flared. The Asia Pacific region is experiencing accelerating rates of both production and consumption, but with a rapidly expanding deficit. The most dramatic change, however, is that North American production has been rising steadily since 2005 owing to increasing rates of shale gas production and assessments of recoverable natural gas reserves in the United States that have been offsetting decline in Gulf production. Figure 3.22 shows U.S. natural gas production, consumption rates, and net production. Prior to the late 2000s, the concept of the United States transitioning to a potentially significant natural gas exporter was unthinkable. It is now likely, with sites and facilities originally intended for large-scale LNG imports being constructed or reengineered for export.[11]

Until recently, natural gas has been a commodity that is largely segmented by geography. Figure 3.23 shows the amount of traded natural gas flows by

---

[11] Because such facilities require approval by both the Department of Energy (DOE) and the Federal Energy Regulatory Commission (FERC), regulatory uncertainty is one of the dominant factors preventing reliable estimates of future exports.

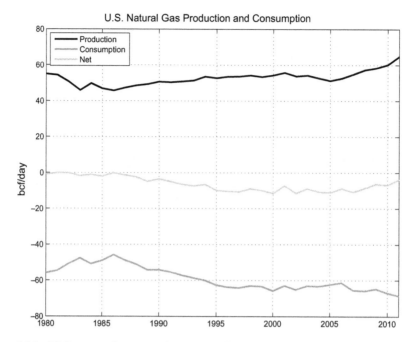

Figure 3.22. U.S. natural gas production and consumption. (Source: BP Statistical Review of World Energy 2012)

Flow by Pipeline	Imports	Exports	Net	Consumption	Ratio (%)
North America	12.45	12.45	0.00	83.57	0.00%
South & Central America	1.51	1.51	0.00	14.95	0.00%
Europe and Eurasia	45.43	43.55	1.88	106.53	1.76%
Middle East and Africa	3.60	6.86	-3.26	49.63	-6.56%
Asia Pacific	4.18	2.80	1.38	57.14	2.41%
Flow by LNG	Imports	Exports	Net	Consumption	Ratio (%)
North America	1.68	0.20	1.48	83.57	1.77%
South & Central America	1.06	2.32	-1.26	14.95	-8.45%
Europe and Eurasia	8.77	1.91	6.86	106.53	6.44%
Middle East and Africa	0.45	18.12	-17.67	49.63	-35.61%
Asia Pacific	20.04	9.45	10.59	57.14	18.54%

Figure 3.23. 2011 Global natural gas flows (bcf/day). (*Source: BP Statistical Review of World Energy 2012.*)

pipeline and by LNG shipping, along with net import volumes as a percentage of local consumption. While increasing global LNG transport capacity has started to couple regional markets, net imports as a fraction of consumption are still quite small for two of the largest consuming regions, North America and Europe/Eurasia, both of which remain relatively isolated markets. In contrast, the Asia Pacific region is more closely linked to external markets, with deficit-driven LNG imports comprising over 18 percent of consumption.

The United States is the dominant consumer in North America, burning natural gas at the rate of roughly 67 bcf/day or approximately 24 tcf (trillion

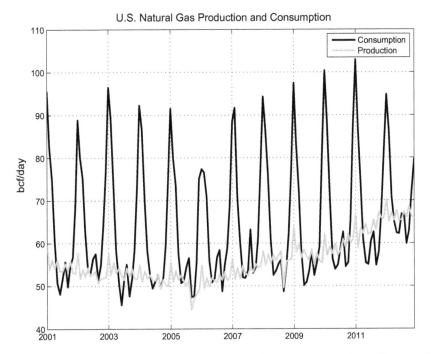

Figure 3.24. Monthly U.S. natural gas consumption and production. (*Source: U.S. Energy Information Administration.*)

cubic feet) per year in 2011. As with heating oil, North American demand is highly seasonal. Figure 3.24 shows U.S. monthly consumption and gross production. Note the high winter peaks and the relatively mild summer peaks in consumption, the latter due to air-conditioning power demand resulting in increased dispatch of natural gas – powered generation.

Gas storage facilities are used to bridge the gap between the high seasonality in demand and the slowly varying nonseasonal production rate. Figure 3.25 shows the working natural gas inventory,[12] as published by the U.S. Energy Information Administration on a weekly basis. This figure shows the seasonal response of inventory, with injection during the summer months and withdrawal during the winter, largely resolving the mismatch between supply and demand profiles in Figure 3.24.

Understanding this inventory process and the implications for price dynamics is harder than it sounds. First, if we expect inventory levels to affect forward yields, as we saw for oil in Figure 2.8, then seasonality must first be removed by subtracting an estimate of what the markets view as

---

[12] *Working storage* is the storage capacity that can used to inject and withdraw natural gas repeatedly. *Total storage capacity*, in contrast, includes pad gas which cannot be cycled. Gas storage typically occurs in natural formations such as salt caverns or aquifers, on which technology is built that controls the flow of gas. These structures require a minimum fill level, in industry parlance *pad gas*, before cycling can occur. Any natural gas volumes above the pad gas volume constitute working storage, which is the only natural gas constituting usable inventory.

"normal" inventory levels as a function of time of year. Further complicating matters is the fact that inventory levels must be gauged against total working storage capacity, which changes as new storage facilities are added – data on this are limited. Finally, the fact is that nobody really knows exactly how much natural gas could be removed from existing storage facilities if required. Most estimates put the figure at slightly over 4.2 tcf as of 2012, according to the U.S. Energy Information Administration, or roughly one-sixth annual consumption. Whether it is, in fact, possible to remove all natural gas designated as working inventory or whether one can remove even more by extracting pad gas is not known with certainty.

Despite these challenges, it is possible to construct reasonable analytical approaches that shed some light on the price response to inventory levels. Most market research defines normal inventory levels using somewhat arbitrary historical averages of inventory by time of year; often the five-year average is used. While simple and easy to validate, such approaches have weaknesses, not the least of which are small sample size and potential non-stationarity in capacity. The results of a more sophisticated approach are shown in the second series appearing in Figure 3.25. This is an estimate of normal storage levels as a function of time which was constructed as follows. First, U.S. Energy Information Administration estimates for total storage capacity by year were used to estimate a linear capacity growth of about 20

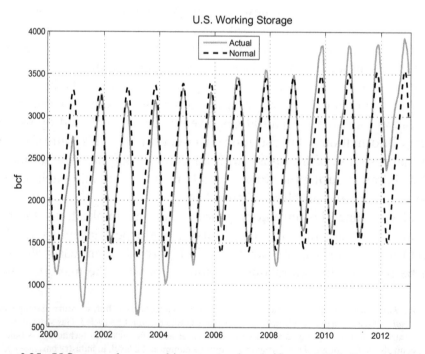

Figure 3.25. U.S. natural gas working storage level. (*Source: U.S. Energy Information Administration.*)

Figure 3.26. U.S. natural gas working storage level residual.

bcf/year over this period. This drift in capacity was used to detrend the inventory series, the result of which was a fit with a Fourier series with the number of modes selected using an out-of-sample forecasting criterion. The resulting expected storage $\bar{S}(t)$ is of the functional form

$$\bar{S}(t) = \alpha + \beta t + \sum_{k=1}^{K} [\gamma_k \sin(2\pi kt) + \delta_k \cos(2\pi kt)] \tag{3.2}$$

with t measured in units of years, and where the parameters $\left[\alpha, \beta, \vec{\gamma}, \vec{\delta}\right]$ are estimated using linear regression. Out-of-sample selection methods yield $K = 2$ as the optimal number of modes, and the result is shown as the second series in the Figure 3.24.

Equipped with this estimate for normal inventory levels $\bar{S}(t)$, we can now calculate the departure of inventory from normal levels, which we will refer to as the *storage residual*: $R(t) \equiv S(t) - \bar{S}(t)$, where $S(t)$ is the storage level at time t. Figure 3.26 shows historical values of the storage residual, which, as we will see, is an important explanatory variable for price dynamics.

Spot price behavior is affected by inventory level. We saw in Figure 1.5 that two regimes where large and sudden spot price increases occurred were in the winter seasons of 2000–2001 and 2002–2003. Both were periods of significant storage deficit. There were other instances of substantial price

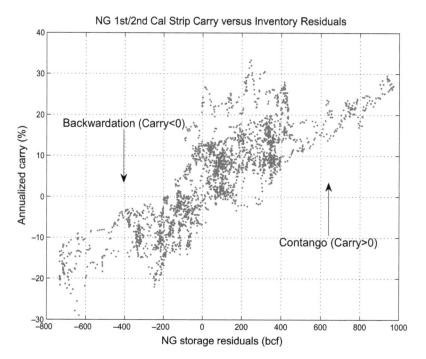

Figure 3.27. NG forward yield versus storage residual.

increases, such as late 2005, which was a response to the uncertainty surrounding the effects of hurricanes Katrina and Rita. The price increases
from 2007 to mid-2008, subsequently followed by the infamous sell-off, were
driven by global macroeconomic events. These examples were the result
of specific identifiable causes, leaving us with a stylized fact about natural
gas markets: low inventory levels tend to be associated with high spot price
volatility.

Turning next to forward yields, recall Figure 2.8, which showed forward
yields for WTI versus Organisation for Economic Co-operation and Development (OECD) inventory. The lack of meaningful seasonality in oil prices
and inventories rendered this a simpler exercise than for seasonal commodities. For natural gas, the storage residual is the deseasonalized inventory
metric. Figure 3.27 shows the annualized forward yield for the first two calendar strips versus the storage residual from 2003 through 2012. As with
the crude oil example, the structure is unambiguous: departure of inventory
levels from normal result in predictable backwardation and contango.

The seasonality in the natural gas forward curve adds a dimension to the
inventory effect in natural gas that is absent from the nonseasonal forward
dynamics of oil. It is reasonable to expect that the spread between winter
and summer months would increase, from a yield perspective, as inventory decreases. Historically, one of the most commonly discussed and traded
spreads in natural gas has been the March–April spread. Referring again to

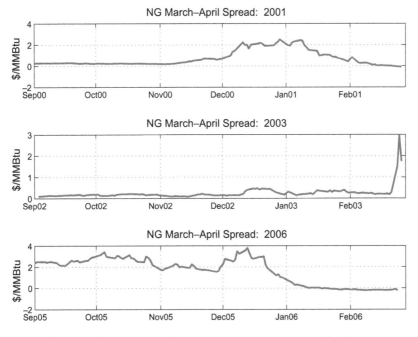

Figure 3.28. Sample NG March–April spread realizations.

Figure 1.4, it is clear that the forward curve can exhibit a meaningful drop between these two contract months across all tenors. This spread, which is of interest to traders because it serves to define the premium between the end of winter and the beginning of the injection season, has at times traded at very significant premia. It is, however, interesting that the March–April spread has settled at or near parity with only one exception, namely, in 2003, when inventory levels were low. Figure 3.28 shows sample realizations of the active March–April contract spread. The first two plots show the years 2001 and 2003, both years of inventory deficit. The third plot is for 2006, when inventory was roughly normal. The 2003 example illustrates how tight inventory can result in nontrivial spreads at settlement. In all other cases it was a concern about potential deficits that pushed this spread to high levels, only to see it settle near parity.

Another illustration of the effect of inventory levels on price spreads is afforded by the extreme storage residuals in January 2001 and January 2002, the former of significant deficit, the latter of surplus. Figure 3.29 shows the respective forward curves for these two dates. Note the obviously lower price for the surplus case, as well as the difference in backwardation versus contango for the deficit and surplus situations already discussed. Figure 3.30 shows the monthly forward yields. Seasonal forward yields are far more significant in the low-inventory situation. Also of note is that the effect clearly diminishes with tenor, as one would expect given that the distribution of $R(T)$ should converge to a stationary distribution as T increases. Even if the

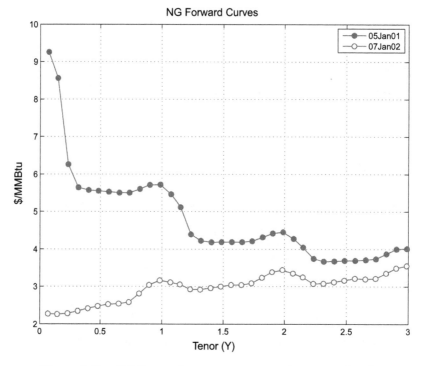

Figure 3.29. NG forward curves at extreme inventory levels.

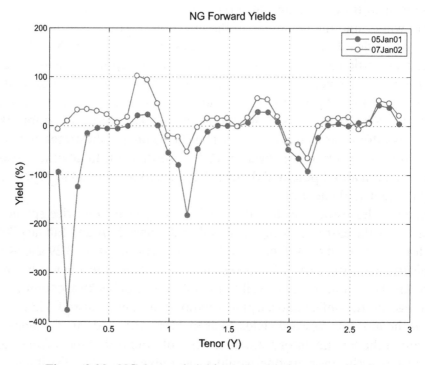

Figure 3.30. NG forward yields at extreme inventory levels.

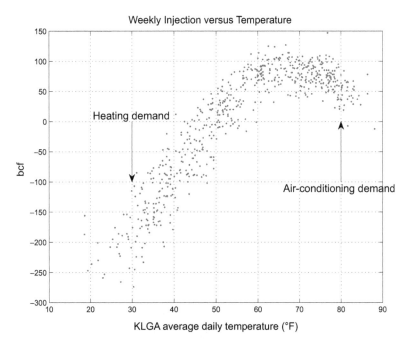

Figure 3.31. Weekly change in U.S. natural gas inventory versus New York temperature.

departure from normal levels is significant, the effect on spreads and forward yields will diminish with tenor – current information is less relevant for longer tenor forward prices.

These three examples support a second stylized fact: specialness, both on long tenors and seasonally, is highest at low inventory levels.

Participants in the natural gas markets spend a great deal of time and money trying to understand the dynamics of natural gas inventory. As with so many phenomena in traded markets, natural gas inventory is affected by short-term drivers that are often amenable to statistical analysis and long-term influences that are typically much harder to model.

Of the short-term drivers, weather is the most obvious. Figure 3.31 shows the weekly change in inventory scattered against average temperature at LaGuardia Airport in New York City from January 2000 to December 2011. Cold temperatures drive withdrawal. The drop in injection rates at high temperatures is due to air-conditioning demand. Adding judiciously selected weather stations around the country increases the predictive power of temperature regressions. Many trading desks use an array of temperature inputs and other variables to attempt to predict the weekly change in inventory in an effort to get a short-term trading advantage.[13]

---

[13] The relatively recent availability of large and timely data sets on pipe flows at a granular level means that they are now frequently used for the same purpose and can yield short-term predictions

The impact of macro drivers, such as the credit crisis or the increasing shale gas production in North America, is harder to discern in the inventory series given short-term weather-driven demand fluctuations. The effect of the credit crisis is the easier to see, with the rapid inventory buildup from a deficit of roughly 200 bcf in early 2008 to a surplus of over 400 bcf by the end of 2009 in lock step with the OECD oil inventory increase shown in Figure 2.7 during this period. The impact of increasing shale gas production is, of course, superimposed on this.

Shale gas is produced by the hydraulic fracturing or *fracking* of rock formations to facilitate the recovery of trapped natural gas. Technological improvements in such methods of extraction have resulted in a dramatic change in estimates of natural gas reserves in North America. The production profile has been remarkable. In 2000, shale gas production was nonexistent. By 2006, production was approximately 2 bcf/day; by 2010, it stood at roughly 11 bcf/day, or approximately 20 percent of total U.S. production. In 2012, shale gas production had roughly doubled to over 22 bdf/day. This increase in production is forecasted by some to continue at a rate that will result in over 30 bcf/day in 2020 [EIA]. As we saw in Figure 3.21, surplus was almost achieved in 2011, and it is highly likely that this trend will continue, with the United States transitioning from a net importer to an exporter of natural gas.

The effect of this likely surplus on U.S. natural gas prices in comparison with global energy prices has been pronounced. It was common only a few years ago for market participants to discuss the ratio of WTI or Brent to NG, the rationale being that refined products, such as heating oil and residual fuel, have a degree of substitutability with natural gas. In addition, the fact that many LNG contracts in Europe and Asia have been priced in reference to crude oil benchmark for many years (arguably) helps to couple the markets to some degree. Figure 3.32 plots the ratio of the Brent[14] and Henry Hub (NG) rolling calendar strips, which exhibits a near-total decoupling of domestic U.S. natural gas markets from global energy benchmarks.

The relationships of U.S. natural gas prices and those of the rest of the world also have changed. Figure 3.33 shows several spot price series for notable world benchmarks. The trading hub for natural gas in the United Kingdom is the National Balancing Point (NBP). The NBP is a virtual hub about which forward markets are traded, notably the ICE U.K natural gas futures contracts, which settle and deliver at the NBP.[15] On the European

---

of changes in inventory that are much more accurate than weather-based approaches. One advantage of weather-driven models, however, is that simulation of weather realizations can yield useful longer term predictions for inventory that are hard, if not impossible, to achieve with pipeline flow data.

[14] We chose to use Brent in this figure because of the impact of the Cushing inventory on WTI prices.

[15] Natural gas trades in pence/therm in the United Kingdom; the price series in Figure 3.33 has been converted to USD using prevailing GBP exchange rates.

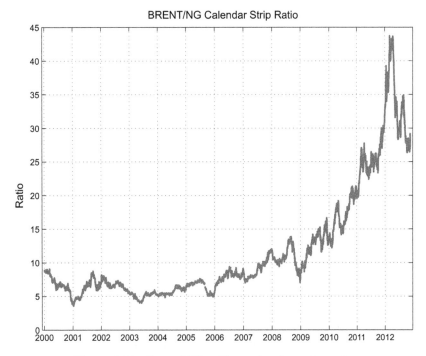

Figure 3.32. Brent/NG rolling calendar strip ratio.

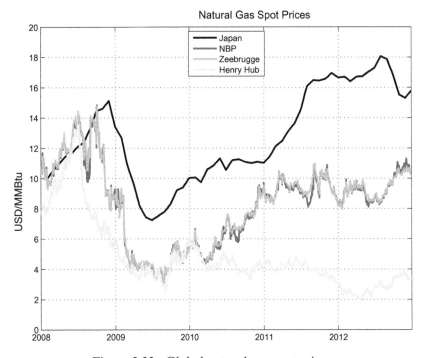

Figure 3.33. Global natural gas spot prices.

Continent, two major hubs are the Title Transfer Facility (TTF), which is a virtual hub in the Netherlands, and the Zeebrugge Hub in Belgium. Zeebrugge is connected to the NBP via the Interconnector, which allows balancing between the locations and ultimately results in the closely coupled prices. In contrast, Asian natural gas supply deficits are met by LNG imports from the Middle East and Russia, with the price differentials exhibited by the Japanese LNG import price series. Note that U.S. natural gas prices did not experience the 2010 post – credit crisis increase that international spot prices exhibited, again evidencing the decoupling of the U.S. market from global markets.

The mechanics of European and Asian natural gas markets, with traditional oil benchmark pricing conventions and long-term legacy contracts, limit adaptability to a global natural gas merchant environment afforded by LNG. European markets, given the presence of spot trading hubs, are closer in spirit to the North American markets. However, Japanese natural gas import prices and Asian prices broadly remain meaningfully decoupled from global spot pricing, even including the LNG transport basis, and the general belief is that this dichotomy will persist for the foreseeable future.

Price spreads of the magnitude of Japanese versus U.S. prices are a significant enticement to market participants. It is likely that the next few years will witness an increase in the export capacity from the United States, but the impact on European and Asian markets is likely to be muted owing to regulatory limits on export volumes as well as the limited spot market pricing mechanisms afforded by Asian markets. For now, North American markets are left to their own devices to reach an equilibrium, with power markets being a significant mechanism for demand enhancement.

Electricity

Electricity, otherwise referred to as *power*, is at the apex of energy commodities. All other energy commodities can be converted into power through one form of generation or another. Although commonly traded and modeled as any other energy commodity, it is debatable whether or not power is actually a commodity at all. It is essentially unstorable, rendering its price an instantaneous manifestation of a multitude of other energy prices. Electricity is a real-time clearing market between a palette of input fuels. Adding to this peculiar nature of electricity as a traded deliverable, the rich set of structured power transactions that commonly occur and the rapidly changing technological and regulatory landscape make electricity arguably the most interesting and challenging of the energy markets.[16]

---

[16] For a more extensive discussion of parts of this section see [KS04]

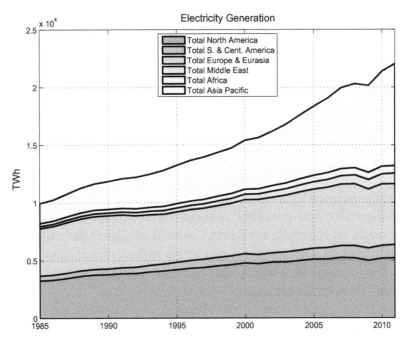

Figure 3.34. Historical global power generation. (*Source: BP Statistical Review of World Energy 2012.*)

Total world electricity generation in 2011 was approximately 22,000 tera-watt hours. Assuming 100 percent efficiency in conversion of primary energy sources to power, and making the appropriate conversions, this is approximately 15 percent of the total global primary energy consumption. In 2010, approximately 60 percent of world electricity was generated using fossil fuels, the rest being predominantly supplied by hydro and nuclear in nearly equal amounts [IEA10][OECD10]. An efficient combined-cycle generator requires roughly 7 MMBtu of natural gas to yield one megawatt-hour of power, which is equivalent to 3.4 MMBtu in energy content – a conversion efficiency of roughly 50 percent. The implication is that accounting for conversion efficiency would at least double the 15 percent figure, illustrating the importance of power generation in global energy markets.

Figure 3.34 shows total historical annual generation by region. North America, Europe/Eurasia, and the Asia Pacific are the three dominant electricity producers, with Asia Pacific as the largest producer since roughly 2003 [BP12]. Total global electricity generation actually dropped in 2009 as a result the impact of the credit crisis. Although we have already observed the same demand destruction in oil and natural gas, electricity consumption had increased without pause from the early part of the twentieth century, rendering this drop in demand a remarkable and largely unforeseen event.

For most societies, electricity is central to the viability of lifestyle and commercial processes. The fact that electricity cannot be stored in any meaningful quantity results in a need for infrastructure and systems to ensure continuous reliability. Electricity is costly to transport; transmission lines are expensive to build, and often substantial legal and regulatory hurdles must be overcome prior to construction. Once built, transmission over appreciable distances incurs losses. The result is that electricity systems and markets are usually organized locally or regionally.

As with natural gas, the initial stages of electricity markets were invariably an undertaking of state-run entities or vertically integrated private utilities under the auspices of state regulators because of the significant capital requirements and daunting investment horizons. Initially, most electricity was generated by large hydro, coal, or nuclear facilities that, because of both their size and potential environmental impact or simply because of constraints on location, were often located at significant distances from population centers. Generation construction therefore was not the only significant cost; transmission from plants to demand centers added substantially to required investment capital.

By the 1990s, circumstances had changed, and deregulated power markets appeared in something of a patchwork in parts of the United States and Europe, as well as in a few other countries, such as Australia and New Zealand. In addition to the growing acceptance that competitive markets allocate capital more efficiently, technological advancements also helped to catalyze deregulation [Tre08]. The introduction of combined-cycle natural gas generation changed the landscape because it afforded the prospect of smaller and very efficient generators with lower environmental impact, which meant that generation could be located closer to population centers. The truly breathtaking costs of large plant builds with associated transmission were no longer a requirement, which meant that merchant financing of infrastructure became a more tenable prospect.

The delivery of power to end users has four components: generation, transmission, supply, and distribution. *Generation* is the process by which electricity is created using a variety of technologies and energy sources. *Transmission* refers to long-distance high-voltage transmission, which serves to link sources (generation) to sinks (demand centers). *Supply* is the activity of procurement and sale of power directly to retail customers. *Distribution* refers to local transmission from high-voltage lines directly to end users. Because owners of transmission and distribution systems have a natural monopoly, deregulation has focused on creating competitive markets in the generation and supply activities, leaving the natural monopoly of transmission and distribution as separate public or private enterprises under regulated cost structures.

Deregulated power markets are administered by independent organizations that ensure orderly market clearing and system reliability. Electricity markets vary in the details of implementation but can be grouped broadly

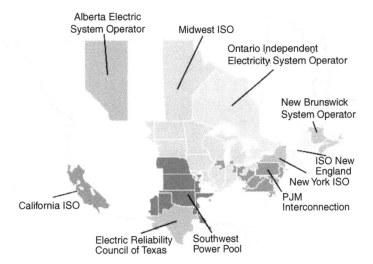

Figure 3.35. North American deregulated power markets. (*Source: ISO/RTO Council.*)

into three categories: pool markets, markets with bilateral trades, and electricity exchanges. In *pool markets*, all electricity generation and demand must be bid into a single clearing market, which sets the spot prices for all market participants. *Bilateral markets* are similar, with the primary distinction being that spot prices are set via market clearing of positions *net* of bilateral trades. *Electricity* (or *power*) *exchanges*, as the name suggests, are voluntary markets in which generators and suppliers can offer and bid respectively.

Ultimately, regardless of market design, an independent entity, either private or state-sponsored, is responsible for administering market clearing, balancing, and system reliability. Such administrators are referred to as *independent system operators* (ISOs) or *regional transmission organizations* (RTOs) in U.S. markets and as *transmission systems operators* (TSOs). Figure 3.35 shows the layout of the deregulated markets in the United States and Canada [Cou].

The PJM RTO in the Midatlantic region is the largest market in United States, both by quantity of power consumed and by the liquidity and depth of the related derivative markets. It is also the most mature U.S. market, having evolved gradually and without major regulatory perturbation since the late 1990s. Other mature markets in the United States include the New York ISO, the New England RTO, and the Texas marketplace run by the Electricity Reliability Council of Texas (ERCOT). California has been involved in electricity deregulation since the 1990s, but significant regulatory and market mechanics changes arising from the western power crisis of 2000–2001 resulted in a number of years of regulatory change and as of 2012 is still generally viewed as a relatively unpredictable marketplace.

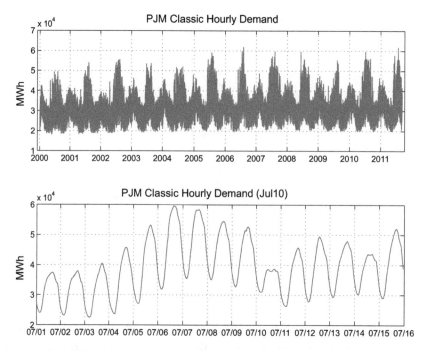

Figure 3.36. Hourly PJM demand.

Power demand, otherwise known as *load*, varies rapidly with time in a manner than can be difficult to predict, even with sophisticated weather-based regressions. The upper plot in Figure 3.36 shows hourly load for a subset of the PJM market referred to as PJM Classic.[17] Demand is dual peaking (two peaks per annum) with maxima in the summer and winter and minima during the so-called shoulder months of late spring and early fall. The lower plot shows a few days of the same demand series, from which it is clear that there are also periodicities on the daily time scale. Weekend demand is visibly distinct from that of weekdays.

Temperature is the primary driver of power demand. Figure 3.37 shows a scatter plot of PJM Classic load at 4 p.m. versus the average daily temperature in Philadelphia from 2004 through 2010.[18] High-quality load forecasting would use more than the daily average temperature at a single weather station, but a lot can be gleaned from this figure. First, the nature of dual peaking demand is manifest as heating drives a demand increase at low

---

[17] As with many ISOs, PJM has grown geographically as specific control areas joined the ISO over the years. Total PJM load would show obvious discontinuities when each control area was added. PJM Classic is a fixed subset of the total system that provides an element of stationarity of data for statistical analysis and for exotic swaps settlement, as discussed in Chapter 15.

[18] *Average temperature* here is defined as the arithmetic mean of the daily high and low hourly temperatures; this is the same definition that is used in most weather derivatives. KPHL is the weather station name.

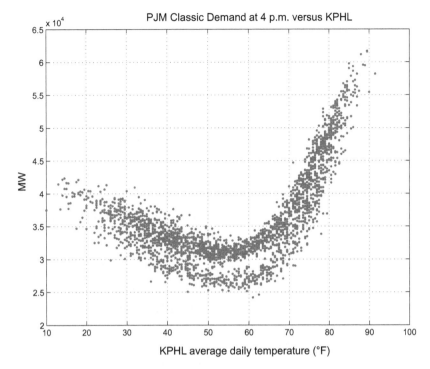

Figure 3.37. PJM classic load at 4 p.m. versus average daily temperature at KPHL.

temperatures, but one which pales in comparison with the air-conditioning-driven demand at high temperatures. Note that this is similar to the natural gas injection scatter shown in Figure 3.31, although natural gas demand peaked at low temperatures. A second and more subtle observation relates to the visible gap at loads between roughly 50 and 65°F, which is another manifestation of the difference in demand on business versus nonbusiness days.

One consequence of the fact that electricity demand and price vary on short time scales is that forwards and swaps, which assume ratable delivery over a day, do not always provide enough granularity for portfolio managers. On the other hand, trading hourly forwards clearly would be prohibitively cumbersome. Forward markets in power have evolved to partially accommodate the conflicting requirements of a need for simplicity in market mechanics and intraday variations in demand by trading standard groups of hours, or *buckets*. Power forwards reference ratable delivery over standard time buckets, which roughly demarcate high-demand versus low-demand periods as follows:

- Peak:
  - Eastern markets: 7 a.m. to 11 p.m. EST Monday through Friday excluding holidays

- ○ Western markets: 7 a.m. to 11 p.m. PST Monday through Saturday excluding holidays
- ○ Texas (ERCOT): 6 a.m. to 10 p.m. CST Monday through Friday excluding holidays
- Offpeak: The complement of peak

The Eastern and ERCOT peak buckets are often referred to as "5x16"; in the Western markets, it is "6x16". Offpeak is often split into nights ("7x8") and the weekend peak, "2x16" ("1x16" in the West), although swaps on these separate buckets are much less liquid.

The basic problem confronting electricity markets is the design of market-clearing mechanics that can meet highly variable demand, such as that just shown, at as low a cost as possible while maintaining a high degree of reliability. There are several reasons why this is a particularly challenging affair. First, the cheapest generation available is usually the least flexible in output, which implies that any market-clearing algorithms must couple different delivery periods – optimization is fundamentally control theoretic in nature. Second, an electricity system receives power from generators (sources) and delivers power to end users (sinks) at thousands of *nodes* or *busbars* that are connected by transmission lines of finite capacity. This renders the optimization problem extremely high dimensional in nature. Third, infrastructure, notably generating units and transmission lines, can fail unpredictably. Finally, the differential equations governing alternating-current (ac) power systems are nonlinear and challenging to solve in reasonable time.

A detailed discussion of how system administrators deal with these issues is not our intention here, but many references exist; see, for example, [Har06] or rules manuals of the various ISO/RTOs, which are the ultimate authorities on the mechanics of their respective markets. Here we will only discuss the essential facts about generation and market clearing.

Generation is best grouped into two classes: fossil fuel and non-fossil-fuel generation. Generation powered by coal, natural gas, or refined products fall into the first category and differ from the other sources in that these generators convert a *traded* energy commodity into electricity. Non-fossil-fuel generation includes hydro, wind, solar, and nuclear. Nuclear generation stands out in the category because it certainly converts a (nonfossil) fuel into into electricity; of note, though, is that the prevailing cost of uranium at any moment is difficult to assess, and the fuel itself does not trade in the sense of natural gas or crude oil. It is generally accepted that nuclear generation provides power at low, slowly varying marginal cost.

A fossil-fuel generator is essentially a physical manifestation of a spread option between input fuels and power prices. If the price of power is higher than the cost of generation, as implied by the prevailing fuel price, then it makes sense to generate; otherwise, it does not. Non-fossil-fuel generation can be thought of as fixed-price options, with the strike defined by the cost of nontraded inputs and normalized maintenance costs.

Whereas the engineering characteristics of physical generation are very complex, the primary consideration is to define two key variables. First, how much will a generator produce at any time t, which we will denote by Q_t. Second, how much of the input fuel is required to produce each megawatt-hour of power at time t, which we will denote by H^*. The conversion ratio H^* is referred to as the generating unit's *heat rate*. The unit heat rate is an attribute of the generator and does not depend on market prices.

If we denote the spot price of power using our forward price convention by $F(t,t)$ and the spot price of the fuel by $G(t,t)$, then optionality embedded in generation can be viewed as having the payoff

$$\max[F(t,t) - H^* G(t,t), 0] = G(t,t) \max\left[\frac{F(t,t)}{G(t,t)} - H^*, 0\right] \quad (3.3)$$

Spreads of the form $F(t,t) - H^* G(t,t)$ are referred to as a *spark spreads*; spark spreads depend on the reference heat rate H^*. The ratio of the market price of power to the market price of the fuel $F(t,t)/G(t,t)$ is called the *market heat rate*, or, in this case, the *spot market heat rate*. This optionality is easily summarized – generate if the market heat rate exceeds the unit heat rate.

While simple in the preceding context, actual generators are encumbered by additional complexities that can affect the operation of power markets and the hedging requirements of asset owners. A fuel-driven generator has the following relevant characteristics or close analogues:

1. *Operating limits.* If running ($Q_t > 0$) the generator has a low operating limit, (LOL) and a high operating limit (HOL): $Q_{min} \leq Q_t \leq Q_{max}$.
2. *Start costs.* Transitioning from $Q_t = 0$ to $Q_t > 0$ incurs costs which can depend on the current fuel price.
3. *Thermal effects.* The operating limits Q_{min} and Q_{max} can depend on ambient temperature and are therefore effectively seasonal. The maximum output level of a generator is referred to as its *capacity*.
4. *Varying heat rate.* The unit heat rate depends on the quantity being generated: $H^* = H^*(Q_t)$.
5. *Ramp rates.* The rate at which the quantity being generated Q_t can change is limited by *ramp rates*: $q_{min} \leq dQ/dt \leq q_{max}$.
6. *Minimum downtimes.* When a unit transitions from $Q_t > 0$ to $Q_t = 0$, it must remain at $Q_{t+s} = 0$ for a minimum downtime $s \leq s_{min}$.
7. *Operating costs.* The more a unit runs, the more costly it is to maintain, which is often approximated by a fixed cost per megawatt-hour generated known as the *variable operation and maintenance* (VOM).

There are many implications of these attributes, but an important one is that generators can run at lower levels (i.e., near Q_{min}) even when sustaining losses (i.e. when the market heat rate is below the unit heat rate) in order to avoid start costs and constraints on minimum downtimes. As a result, the dispatch of units involves nontrivial intertemporal optimization, and market-clearing algorithms must optimize subject to generator constraints.

A typical market such as PJM will have many hundreds of generators. Simply listing the attributes for each generator does little in the way of providing a qualitative understanding of the collection of available generation. A standard remedy to this problem is to portray supply in the order of marginal cost from cheapest to most expensive, assuming maximum output of each generator at prevailing fuel costs and ignoring constraints. Such an ordering of available generation in a given region is usually referred to as the *generation stack* or simply *the stack*.

The lowest-price generation is usually comprised of wind, solar, and other renewable sources. In some cases, particularly for wind generation, tax incentives exist in the form of production tax credits that subsidize generation on a per-megawatt-hour generated basis. The result is that the marginal cost of such units can be negative; as long as the sum of the spot price and the tax incentive is positive, it makes sense to generate.

Next in the stack is hydro; once a dam with generating turbines is built, the marginal cost to generate is very low. Nuclear generation follows; as with hydro, nuclear generation involves very large initial capital expenditures but relatively low marginal cost once operating. Nukes are highly efficient but ramp slowly and once offline usually take days to return to maximum output.

Coal generation is generally next in the stack, with marginal costs varying widely based on coal price, often including transport costs as well as costs or constraints on emissions. Coal generation is also slow to start and slow to ramp. As we will discuss later, the drop in natural gas prices caused by the proliferation of shale gas production has rendered the obvious hierarchy with natural gas generation dubious.

Following coal, depending on relative prices of natural gas and coal, are combined-cycle natural gas generators and fuel oil generation, which start and ramp more quickly. The most expensive fossil-fuel generation consists of natural gas – or distillate-fired jet turbines called *peakers*, which can start very rapidly to meet unanticipated fluctuations in supply or demand.

Finally, demand-side management contracts, also referred to as *demand-response contracts*, are a relatively recent development and one of growing importance. Such contracts usually occur between large retail customers and their suppliers or local utilities and give the supplier the option to require the customer to reduce consumption. Typically, there are a defined number of hours per year that such an option can be exercised; the supplier typically will exercise the option at times when demand and spot prices are high. The effect of reduced consumption is equivalent to additional generation.

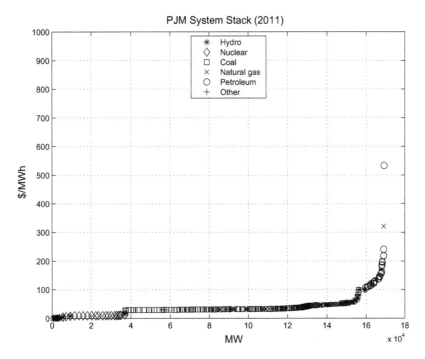

Figure 3.38. PJM supply stack circa 2011.

Consequently, such contracts are sometimes considered part of the stack and are usually more expensive than even peaking units.

A stack is formally constructed from a set of generator capacities $[C_1,\ldots,C_N]$ sorted so that the associated marginal costs in \$/MWh $[p_1,\ldots,p_N]$ are increasing. The stack is a graph of p_n versus $\bar{C}_n \equiv \sum_{1 \le k \le n} C_k$, for $1 \le n \le N$. Figure 3.38 shows an approximate rendition of the supply stack for PJM as of 2011. This typical portrayal of a stack exhibits the broad structure; however, the composition of the stack by generation type is hard to discern. Figure 3.39 shows the stack from the perspective of the composition of the generation capacity by fuel, effectively plotting $\bar{C}_n$ as a function of p_n. Here the general hierarchy of cost by fuel type is more easily discerned. With the relatively low natural gas prices in 2011, some natural gas units are in fact comparable, on a marginal-cost basis, with the more expensive coal units. At lower natural gas prices, additional coal generation would be displaced by natural gas. Less coal will be burned, and power price dynamics could be affected, with offpeak power prices likely to be increasingly coupled with natural gas prices. This phenomenon, known as *coal switching*, is a simple illustration of the nonlinearities that can arise as fuel prices change

The relative placement of each type of generation in the stack is visible another way. Figure 3.40 shows the installed capacity of generation in the United States by type using data compiled by the U.S. Energy Information Administration. Compare the relatively modest 10 percent of capacity that

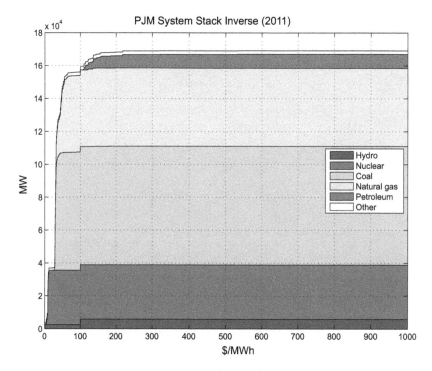

Figure 3.39.   PJM supply stack circa 2011.

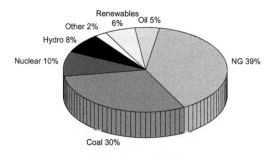

Figure 3.40.   U.S. power generation capacity by source (2011). (*Source: U.S. Energy Information Administration.*)

nuclear generation comprised with the 20 percent of actual megawatt-hours generated, as shown in Figure 3.41. This is due to the low position on the stack that nuclear occupies. The same phenomenon was manifest for coal generation, with 30 percent capacity versus 45 percent of megawatt-hours generated. The opposite was true for natural gas, which, because of its position further up the stack, is dispatched less frequently.

Many trading desks make price forecasts and trading decisions using methods that effectively superimpose expected demand onto the supply stack. Because demand is generally inelastic, the point of intersection of

U.S. Generation by Source (2011)

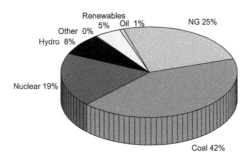

Figure 3.41. U.S. power generation by source (2011). (*Source: U.S. Energy Information Administration.*)

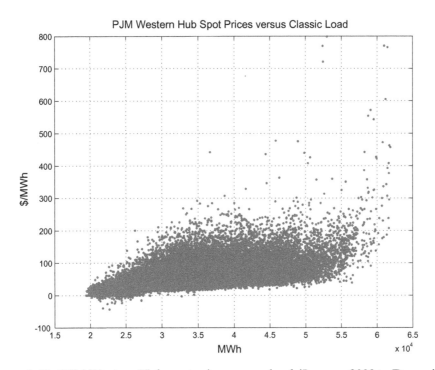

Figure 3.42. PJM Western Hub spot prices versus load (January 2003 to December 2011).

a load forecast with the stack could be viewed as an estimated spot price. Such a train of thought can yield useful qualitative attributes. For one thing, the actual relationship between realized spot prices and loads immediately exhibits the stacklike structure shown in Figure 3.42, which plots historical PJM Western Hub spot prices versus load. In addition to the general increase in price with load, note also the occasional negative clearing price that results from optimal generation dispatch – it is better for a nuke to keep

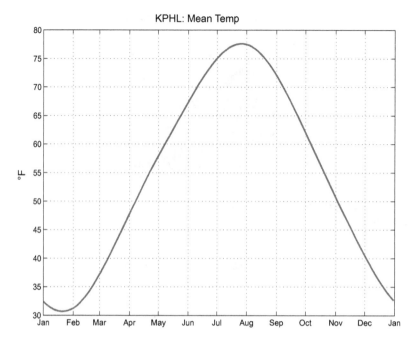

Figure 3.43. Mean temperature at KPHL.

generating during low-demand hours, even at a negative price, rather than shut down.

Proceeding a bit further with the stack paradigm, consider Figure 3.43, which shows the expected temperature[19] in Philadelphia, which is located in PJM.

The results of Figures 3.36 and 3.37 imply that demand peaks in the summer, with a smaller peak in the winter. If we superimposed such an expected demand on the stack in Figure 3.38, a reasonable hypothesis is that expected spot power prices should peak in the summer with a smaller peak in the winter. The forward curves exhibit precisely this dual peaking structure, as shown in Figure 3.44.

This was a heuristic and somewhat obvious result. More can be obtained. For example, it is reasonable to expect that the variance of spot prices would peak in the summer given that demand is closest to the end of the stack. However, pushing such stylized analysis to a level where actionable price forecasting is attained is very challenging for several reasons.

First, the stack is not static. Not only do generators sustain forced (unplanned) outages owing to mechanical failures, but planned maintenance is usually derived as a function of the forward curve. Figure 3.45 shows the time series of available nuclear generation. The typical nuke requires roughly a month for refueling and maintenance once every eighteen months,

---

[19] This is the result of methods discussed in Chapter 10.

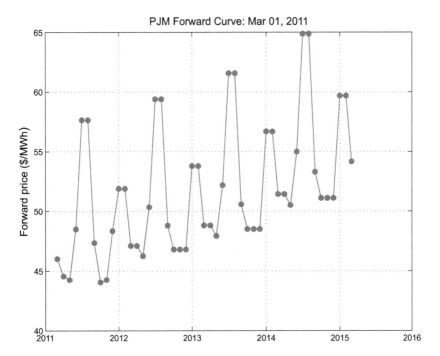

Figure 3.44. PJM peak forward curve.

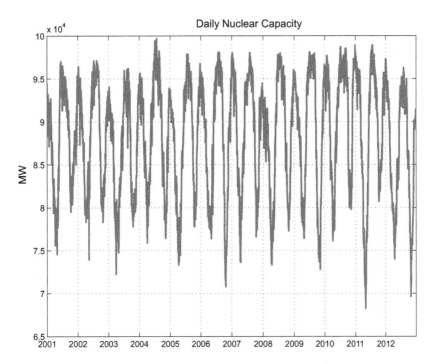

Figure 3.45. U.S. available nuclear capacity.

and this figure shows that such maintenance is usually scheduled in the shoulder months, where the economic loss is minimized. The stack therefore varies in composition seasonally and is subject to random perturbations as a result of outages.

Second, in competitive markets, generators often bid their capacity above their marginal costs. How individual units are bid is a tactical decision made independently by owners of generation, and such bidding strategies can change over time. Quantifying future bidding behavior of hundreds of generators is a serious obstacle to construction of stack-based pricing forecasts.

Third, and most important, the stack is only a stylized rendition of how power markets work (see [Kam12] and [KS04]) Most competitive markets are nodal markets, typically referred to as *locational marginal pricing* (*LMP*) *markets*. In LMP markets, the spot price at each node at which generation can deliver power or load can receive it is established via an optimization methodology referred to as *security-constrained optimal dispatch*. Generators and loads submit offers and bids, respectively, at an hourly time scale, usually the day before delivery (the *day-ahead market*) and then in a second auction the day of delivery (the *real-time market*). Market-clearing computations are performed subject to reliability constraints, hence the phrase *security constrained*, that ensure that the resulting configuration of generation dispatch, transmission, and load are stable to certain perturbations in the physical system deemed by the system operator as warranting concern. Spot prices are the shadow prices at each node resulting from this optimization; that is, the spot price for power at any node is the cost of incremental additional demand at the node.[20]

In general, transmission constraints and losses result in nodal prices that are not uniform over the system, rendering a "stack view" little more than a caricature of the physical system. However, the typical behavior of power markets is that transmission and stability constraints result in subsets of the system (groups of nodes) that have very similar market-clearing prices; these subsets are referred to as *congestion zones* or simply *zones*. Liquid swaps markets almost always reference zonal or hub prices which are averages of a set of nodal prices in a particular congestion zone.

There is a purity to the LMP market design. Every participant is paid or charged a well-defined and justifiable economic value of the commodity at every instant of time and at every location, with costs due to losses and congestion fairly allocated. The argument in favor of such a design goes further

---

[20] In addition to the price of the commodity, stability of the power system requires that some generation be held in reserve for reliability purposes. The need for such reserve supply, which must be compensated for not being dispatched, results in several additional traded products referred to as *ancillary services* that consumers must procure, in addition to the power itself. The details vary significantly by market, but forward markets for such products are only liquid at short tenors.

– such a market design clearly incentivizes the building of new generation or transmission where such will receive higher prices or revenues, ultimately reducing the cost of power for the end user.

Viewed from the perspective of an asset purchaser or a trader attempting to hedge a portfolio of generation, nodal pricing can pose significant challenges. Swaps liquidity is concentrated at hubs, but economic exposures are at the nodes. The future decisions of other market participants or regulators can affect the economics of an asset in ways that are challenging to hedge and nearly impossible to predict. On the face of it, this is no different from the problem confronting any investor in any commercial enterprise. However, the behavior of electricity systems is notoriously difficult to model, and in an LMP market, investors have to bear the risks of the node-to-hub spreads, which in simpler market designs would be socialized across market participants. The quest for idealized equilibrium, with thousands of locational prices, has had the effect of complicating valuation and hedging. There is a compelling argument that competitive markets at the zonal or regional levels constitute a more effective balance between efficient allocation of costs and the transparency required for rational long-term investment decisions.

Conclusion

Each of the markets that we surveyed in this chapter is a mechanism by which supply and demand are matched. The important drivers of price dynamics are global energy trends coupled with technological features that are unique to each market. The central themes were

- Global energy consumption has risen consistently, interrupted by a few periods of relatively minor drops owing to geopolitical or global economic turmoil.
- Crude oil remains the dominant source of energy, with coal and natural gas rapidly gaining ground. Of particular note are unconventional sources of natural gas production, which are affecting the energy landscape significantly.
- Energy markets and infrastructure, including shipping, pipelines, and storage, exist to accommodate local imbalances between producing and consuming regions and locations, as well as variations in demand.

The details of how supply and demand are balanced vary significantly by commodity. The challenge with crude oil and refined products is the lack of uniformity of the underlying commodity – each crude stream is unique in its characteristics. With natural gas, the product is uniform – transportation and storage are the primary challenges. For power, which is an instantaneous manifestation of a variety of input commodities, the near-total absence of storage spawns technological and modeling challenges that are distinct from those of other commodities.

The presence of inventory smooths price dynamics, dampening short-term variations in supply and demand and lowering costs to end user. In the absence of storage, as in the case of power, markets are designed and operated in a manner that ensures stability of supply exogenously. The features of each of these commodities markets motivate the hedging activities and resulting structures that we will discuss in what follows. Next, however, we turn to the mechanics of the instruments most commonly used by traders to effect risk transfer.

Part II

Basic Valuation and Hedging

All markets have limitations in the instruments that can be efficiently traded. The broader the set of liquid tradable instruments in a market, the more effectively risks embedded in exotic structured trades can be hedged. As the collection of available price data expands, calibration of valuation models becomes less dependent on statistical estimation of unhedgeable parameters, reducing modeling risk. In most markets, concerns about market depth and liquidity revolve primarily around the options available for model calibration. In energy markets challenges arise at the much more basic level of swaps and forwards.

We saw in Part I that energy is produced and consumed at many physical locations. However, swaps liquidity is typically limited to a few benchmarks such as West Texas Intermediate (WTI) and Brent for crude oil, Henry Hub or National Balancing Point (NBP) for natural gas, and PJM Western Hub for U.S. power. The result is that many energy portfolios have risks of very high dimensionality, while portfolio managers have relatively few hedging instruments at their disposal. Successfully navigating the challenges of such portfolios depends greatly on analysis of forward dynamics and sensible application of the results.

The situation is even more severe in the energy options markets, where liquidity is typically concentrated at even fewer benchmarks and at shorter tenors. To compound matters, the types of options that are traded shed relatively little light on the term structure of volatility for any given forward price, which results in exposure to modeling risk in situations that would, in most other markets, be viewed as quite routine.

Construction of hedging strategies for complex swaps books and design of realistic commodities pricing models begin with an understanding of the dynamics of forward prices. We start Part II with a review of the basic tenants of risk-neutral valuation, establishing some very general results and describing the original risk-neutral framework for derivatives on futures –

a modification of standard Black-Scholes to accommodate futures prices as the underlying tradable known as Black-76. We will then turn to analysis of the empirical attributes of forward price dynamics and conclude with practical applications of these results to the management of swaps books.

4

Risk-Neutral Valuation

Valuation of options structures in energy often follows the same paradigm as in other asset classes. A model for price dynamics is posited, ideally motivated by empirical features of the underlying price dynamics, calibrated to market prices that are available, and then used to price nonstandard structures. The integrity of this approach is predicated on many assumptions, widely discussed in the general mathematical finance literature, that collectively imply the ability of market participants to replicate derivative payoffs by trading the underlying asset [Hul12], [Wil07]. In this chapter we will survey basic derivatives valuation methodology as it pertains to commodities, emphasizing some important facts about commonly traded instruments. All the results here will involve standard arbitrage arguments and apply to any forward or futures contract [Shr04].

The key results that we will establish are

1. Forward prices are martingales[1] under the risk-neutral measures used to value derivatives on forwards. This is to be expected because there is zero cost of entry for forward contracts, and drifts in risk-neutral price processes result from the cost to fund positions.
2. Forwards and futures prices are functionally identical. While technically different, the corrections are very small.
3. American options on forwards should never be exercised early.
4. American options on futures in which the premium is paid at trade inception, commonly referred to as *equity-style options*, can be optimal to exercise early. The alternative *futures-style options*, in which the premium is paid at expiration, are never optimal to exercise early. Both types of options are traded on various exchanges.

---

[1] A stochastic process X_t is a martingale under measure $E[\cdot]$ if $E[X_t | \mathcal{F}_s] = X_s$, where $\mathcal{F}_s$ is the filtration, or information, at time s. Martingales are drift-free.

Black-76

Of the preceding four facts, the first is the most important because it immediately constrains the processes that can drive forwards, simplifying matters
considerably in comparison with cash instruments such as stocks with their
associated funding rates and dividend payments. The original derivatives
valuation framework for forwards and futures is Black-76 [Bla76]. As the
name would suggest, this approach is simply Black-Scholes without the funding costs, with returns of the forward price $F(t, T)$ normally distributed and
the price process governed by geometric Brownian motion (GBM) with
constant volatility σ:

$$\frac{dF(t, T)}{F(t, T)} = \sigma \, dB_t \tag{4.1}$$

This is the process for a specific forward or futures contract under the risk-
neutral measure, and no explicit relationship is specified between contracts
of different tenor. Equation (4.1) is easily integrated:

$$F(t, T) = F(0, T) \, e^{-\frac{1}{2\sigma^2} t + \sigma B_t} \tag{4.2}$$

and closed-form valuation is identical to Black-Scholes if one sets the dividend rate equal to the risk-free interest rate, thereby zeroing the cost of
carry. Details are provided in Appendix A.

The simplicity of the Black-76 approach is its virtue. If the activities of a
desk are confined to trading standard "vanilla" options with no off-market or
exotic risks, this valuation framework can accomplish most, if not all, of what
is required for reliable valuation and functional greeks. Once commercial
activities extend beyond vanilla products, however, more is required.

The martingale property of forwards is seen by some as suspect given the
folklore that commodities prices mean revert, the argument being that if
prices get too high, demand will fall, production will increase, and substitution of alternatives will collectively pull prices back down, and conversely.
We will see later that mean reversion in spot prices is a concept that is distinct from that of forward prices and that mean reversion in forward prices
is not nearly as obvious as many are tempted to think. The martingale property, however, applies under the risk-neutral measure. Suppose, however,
that the dynamics of forwards under the *physical* measure is specified by

$$dF(t, T) = \mu [t, F(t, T)] \, dt + \sigma F_t dB_t \tag{4.3}$$

with μ of a form implying mean reversion to a stationary expected value L;
for example, $\mu(t, F) = -\beta(F - L)$, where β is the mean-reversion rate. The
key point is that even if prices mean revert in reality, under the risk-neutral
measure, the martingale property holds. Derivatives valuation would still

proceed using (4.1) because the drift in (4.3) is rendered moot due to delta hedging, as shown in Appendix A.[2]

The key results just listed are very general and predicated only on the standard arbitrage pricing conditions required for a complete market [Shr04]. Model specification of the form used in Black-76, however, is very specific – returns are normal and volatility constant. In the next chapter we discuss the statistical properties of commodities forward curves, in part to understand the limitations of Black-76.

The remainder of this chapter is a somewhat technical exposition of the preceding four basic results, and the reader can proceed to the next chapter without liability.

Equivalent Martingale Measures

Risk-neutral valuation is predicated on the selection of a reference asset, or *numeraire*, the price of which is used to discount other asset prices. Subject to conditions guaranteeing the existence of a unique equivalent measure under which all discounted prices are martingales, the price of any derivative payoff is obtained by calculating the expected discounted payoff with respect to this equivalent martingale measure.

Denoting the reference asset price by D_t and the prices of all assets being driven by stochastic processes $\vec{X}_t$, the value of a derivative at time t with payoff $U(\vec{X}_T)$ is

$$\frac{V(t,\vec{X}_t)}{D_t} = E_D\left[\frac{U(\vec{X}_T)}{D_T}|\mathcal{F}_t\right] \tag{4.4}$$

Here E_D is the risk-neutral measure using the reference asset price D_t, and $\mathcal{F}_t$ denotes the information (filtration) available at time t [Hul12], [Wil07]. The choice of reference asset is usually a matter of convenience; a good choice can make seemingly challenging problems routine.

The most commonly arising reference assets in finance are the money-market and the zero-coupon bond:

- *Money-market measure.* The reference asset is the money-market account M_t, which appreciates at the spot interest rate r_t: $dM_t = r_t M_t dt$. The associated martingale measure will be denoted by $\tilde{E}[\cdot]$.
- *T-forward measure.* The reference asset is the unit-notional zero-coupon bond at time t maturing at T, the value of which is simply the discount factor: $d(t,T) = \tilde{E}\left[e^{-\int_t^T r_s ds}|\mathcal{F}_t\right]$. The associated martingale measure is referred to as the *T-forward measure*, which we will denote by $\tilde{E}^{(T)}[\cdot]$.

---

[2] One could construct drifts that are singular enough so that F would be confined to a finite interval, in which case this result would not hold, but that is not considered a particularly relevant concern in practice.

The money market and zero-coupon bonds relate naturally to the mechanics of funding a transaction. We will see later that in commodities, a third reference asset arises naturally in situations where payoffs depend on spreads between prices; in this case, using one of the commodities as a reference asset simplifies calculations considerably.

Martingale Property of Forward Prices

Our first key fact can now be stated more precisely. Forward prices are martingales under the T-forward measure $\tilde{E}^{(T)}$, and futures prices are martingales under money-market measure $\tilde{E}$. The distinction arises from funding considerations associated with the futures margin accounts.

Starting with forwards, let V_s denote the value of a forward contract established at time t with delivery at time T for $t \leq s \leq T$. We know the following:

- $V_t = 0$; the cost of entry for a forward contract is zero.
- $V_t/B(t,T)$ is a martingale under the T-forward measure.
- At expiration, $d(T,T) = 1$, and the forward payoff is $V_T = F(T,T) - F(t,T)$.

The first two facts yield

$$0 = \frac{V_t}{d(t,T)} = \tilde{E}^{(T)}\left[\frac{V_T}{d(T,T)} \mid \mathcal{F}_t\right] \tag{4.5}$$

Coupled with the last fact, this result implies the martingale property.

Futures contracts, in contrast, are effectively exchange-margined forward contracts. A futures contract is marked-to-market on a daily basis, with the futures exchange publishing settlement prices at the close of each trading day based on trades executed in the final minutes of trading. The change in the value of a customer's trades, as calculated using the settlement prices, is reflected in the balance of a customer's margin account. Margin requirements vary among exchanges and are typically quite complex owing to provisions that attempt to net offsetting positions in closely related contracts. For our purposes, however, margining means that the value of the futures contract is zero at the end of each trading day. This contrasts with forwards, where the value is known to be zero only at inception.

The fact that a position in a futures contract generates daily cash flows, which accrue at a spot interest rate,[3] results in a distinction between futures prices and forward prices. We will denote a futures price by $\tilde{F}(t,T)$ to distinguish it from the analogous forward price $F(t,T)$.

Proceeding in discrete time, note that the mark-to-market due to margining implies that the value of the position is reset to zero at the next margining

---

[3] The fact that the interest rate earned on margin accounts is not identical to other more commonly used short rates is being ignored here.

time $t+\delta$:

$$0 = \tilde{E}\left[M(t,t+\delta^-)V_{t+\delta^-}|\mathcal{F}_t\right]$$
$$= \tilde{E}\left\{M(t,t+\delta^-)\left[\tilde{F}(t+\delta^-,T) - \tilde{F}(t,T)\right]|\mathcal{F}_t\right\}$$

where $V_{t+\delta^-}$ is the value of the position just before $t+\delta$. Here we are working under the money-market measure. The short rate r_t is known at time t, so $M(t,t+\delta) = e^{-r_t\delta}$ is $\mathcal{F}_t$-measurable, yielding

$$\tilde{F}(t,T) = \tilde{E}\left[\tilde{F}(t+\delta,T)|\mathcal{F}_t\right] \tag{4.6}$$

This establishes the martingale property of futures prices under the money-market measure. Moreover, the delta of the futures contract is the notional due to the margining protocol, in contrast to a forward contract, in which the delta is the discounted notional.

It is worth noting that the result in (4.6) applies to any cash-margined derivative. The fact that this was a linear payoff was never used in the preceding argument – an observation that we will use shortly in the context of options.

Forwards versus Futures

Forwards and futures are distinguished only by the margin cash flows that futures positions sustain. A simple argument establishes equivalence of forward and futures prices in the case that interest rates are deterministic. A long forward position initiated at time t will have a terminal payoff of $F(T,T) - F(t,T)$. A futures trading strategy that holds a position of $\alpha(s)$ futures contracts for $s \in [t,T]$ will yield a payoff of

$$\int_t^T \alpha(s)\, e^{\int_s^T r_u du}\, d\tilde{F}_s \tag{4.7}$$

because each differential cash flow $\alpha(s)d\tilde{F}_s$ accrues at the spot rate to the terminal time T. As for forwards, this futures trading strategy involves zero initial investment. By choosing $\alpha(s) = e^{-\int_s^T r_u du}$, the futures strategy results in a terminal value of $\tilde{F}(T,T) - \tilde{F}(t,T)$. By assumption, the forward and futures contracts require delivery of the same commodity at the same time, so the two prices at expiry must be identical: $F(T,T) = \tilde{F}(T,T)$. It follows that $F(t,T) = \tilde{F}(t,T)$; otherwise, there would be an obvious arbitrage opportunity.

To obtain a more general relationship between forwards and futures for the case when interest rates are dynamic, we need to be viewing both prices through the same measure. Choosing the money-market measure, the zero price of entry of a forward contract can be written as

$$0 = \tilde{E}\left\{[F(T,T) - F(t,T)]e^{-\int_t^T r_s ds}|\mathcal{F}_t\right\}$$

which yields

$$F(t,T) = \frac{\tilde{E}\left[e^{-\int_t^T r_s ds} F(T,T) | \mathcal{F}_t\right]}{B(t,T)} \tag{4.8}$$

For futures, recall that (4.6) implies $\tilde{F}(0,T) = \tilde{E}[F(T,T)]$.

Taking the difference of the two results yields the price difference:

$$F(0,T) - \tilde{F}(0,T) = \frac{1}{B(0,T)} \left\{ \tilde{E}\left[e^{-\int_0^T r_s ds} F(T,T)\right] - \tilde{E}\left[e^{-\int_0^T r_s ds}\right] \tilde{E}[F(T,T)] \right\}$$

This result can be written in a slightly more intuitive form:

$$F(0,T) - \tilde{F}(0,T) = \frac{1}{B(0,T)} \text{cov}\left[e^{-\int_0^T r_s ds}, F(T,T)\right] \tag{4.9}$$

A first consequence of this result is a generalization of the deterministic interest-rate result: if the price process is uncorrelated with interest rates, then the preceding covariance is zero, and the two prices are identical. More generally, if the covariance between interest rates and prices is positive, then the covariance between the discount factor and prices in (4.9) is negative, and the futures price exceeds the analogous forward price. This is reasonable – in this scenario the margin account for a long futures position tends to be credited when rates are high and debited when rates are low, which enhances the value of the futures contract relative to the forward, resulting in a higher futures price.

Does this covariance effect really matter? Historical data suggest not. Equation (4.9) can be written as

$$\frac{\tilde{F}(0,T)}{F(0,T)} - 1 = -\text{cov}\left[\frac{e^{-\int_0^T r_s ds}}{B(0,T)}, \frac{F(T,T)}{F(0,T)}\right] \tag{4.10}$$

Figure 4.1 shows a scatter of the forward ratio $F(T,T)/F(T-1,T)$ versus the following proxy for the first term in the covariance in (4.10):

$$\left[1 + r_1^{(12)}\right] \prod_{m=1}^{12} \left[1 + \frac{r_m^{(1)}}{12}\right]^{-1}$$

where $r_m^{(n)}$ is the n-month USD LIBOR rate at the beginning of month m for each contract month spanning January 1992 to December 2010. While the correlation is nontrivial (increasing rates tending to be associated with increasing WTI prices), the covariance, which is what affects the price ratio, is very small.

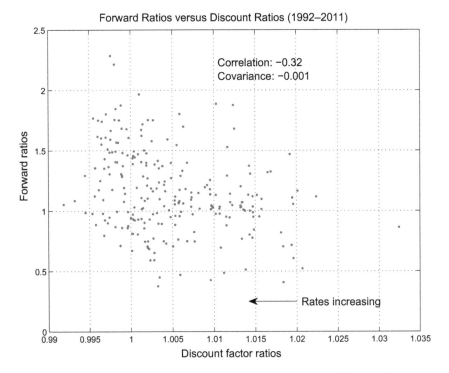

Figure 4.1. Effect of correlation on futures/forwards spread.

American Optionality

We turn now to the third key fact – the American feature of an option on a forward contract is trivial. The argument is simple and informative for the case of a standard call or put.

Consider an American call option with strike K expiring at time $T_e \leq T$. At any time $t \leq T_e$, the option holder can exercise immediately into a long forward contract with forward (undiscounted) value $F(t, T) - K$. Alternatively, the holder could short an at-the-money (ATM) forward and hold the option to expiration yielding the payoff

$$V(T) = \begin{cases} F(t, T) - F(T_e, T) & \text{if } F(T_e, T) < K \\ F(t, T) - K & \text{otherwise} \end{cases}$$

This dominates the former payoff. The sale of the forward contract served to lock in the intrinsic value, swapping the call into an out-of-the-money put, as shown in Figure 4.2 in the situation where $K = 8$ and the current forward price is $F(t, T) = 10$.

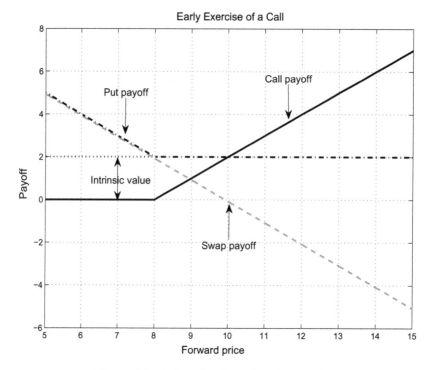

Figure 4.2. Suboptimality of early exercise.

While harder to portray visually, this result is true for any convex payoff $f(\cdot)$ of the forward price. By Jensen's inequality,[4] we have:

$$f[F(t,T)] = f\left\{\tilde{E}^{(T)}[F(T_e,T) \mid \mathcal{F}_t\}\right) \leq \tilde{E}^{(T)}\left\{f[F(T_e,T)] \mid \mathcal{F}_t\right\} \qquad (4.11)$$

where we have used the fact that the forward price is an $\tilde{E}^{(T)}$ martingale. The first term is the undiscounted value of the immediate exercise at time t, while the last term is the undiscounted value of the option. It follows that such options are never optimal to exercise early.

Our final key fact pertains to exchange-traded American options on futures. The mechanics of these options vary by exchange and fall into one of two categories:

- *Equity style.* Options with up-front premium payments.
- *Futures style.* Those without up-front premia.

Equity-style options are standard on the CME/NYMEX, while options on ICE exist in both forms. See [Wha86] and [Ovi06] for related discussions.

Starting with equity-style options, a call option gives the holder the right to acquire, on exercise,

---

[4] Jensen's inequality states that for any convex function f and random variable X, $f(E[X]) \leq E[f(X)]$ provided that these expected values exist.

- A futures contract
- A cash balance of the difference between the futures price and option strike

Given the up-front premia, equity-style options sustain a cost of carry that can make early exercise optimal. To see this, note that, on exercise of, say, a call at time t, the immediate value to the holder is $\tilde{F}(t, T) - K$. If the option is in-the-money, as interest rates increase with everything else held constant, including the futures price, the immediate payoff and the *forward* value of the option do not change. However, the latter needs to be discounted from settlement time T to current time t. Therefore, there is a level of interest rates where the value of immediate exercise exceeds the value of continuing to hold the option, implying that the value of the American option is strictly higher than that of its European analogue.

Futures-style options are simply another form of a futures contract. At trade inception, there is no cost of entry. Denoting the price of the option at time t by P_t, the margin account is credited or debited according to changes in P_t. Recalling that (4.6) holds for any cash-margined derivative, we know that

$$P_t = \tilde{E}[P_T \mid \mathcal{F}_t]$$

Considering the case of a call, on exercise at any time t, the holder of the option receives a position in the futures contract and sustains a cash flow equal to the difference between the futures price and the strike less the *current* market price of the option: $\tilde{F}(t, T) - K - P_t$. Because the option payoff is convex, it follows from Jensen's inequality that

$$\left\{ \tilde{E}\left[\tilde{F}(T_e, T) \mid \mathcal{F}_t \right] - K \right\}^+ \leq \tilde{E}\left\{ [\tilde{F}(T_e, T) - K]^+ \mid \mathcal{F}_t \right\} = \tilde{E}[P_{T_e} \mid \mathcal{F}_t] = P_t$$

which means that the value of immediate exercise is nonpositive. This argument only required convexity of the payoff, so the implication is that American options of this type are never optimal to exercise early.

The fact that some markets such as CME/NYMEX WTI crude options are equity style with a nontrivial American feature means that obtaining implied volatilities from options prices is model-dependent. Even using a simple model such as (4.1), this requires either lattice-based valuation methods or approximation methods (see, for example, [Shr04]). For short-tenor options in what has been a generally low-interest-rate environment in the past decade, this can be ignored, but care must be taken for options with longer maturity.

Conclusion

The four basic facts underpinning the discussions in this chapter were all direct implications of arbitrage pricing methods and were independent of modeling paradigm.

- Forwards and futures are martingales under the appropriate risk-neutral measure – for forwards, it is the T-forward measure; for futures, it is the money-market measure. This distinction is not usually significant in practice, and the two prices are typically nearly identical.
- The Black-76 model for forwards/futures is Black-Scholes without the drift, thereby yielding the required martingale property. Option valuation formulas and techniques are simple modifications of the cash-based approach.
- American optionality is never relevant for options on forwards and only affects options on futures in the case where the option premium is paid up-front, so-called equity-style options. Low-interest-rate environments diminish the effect.

These results are predicated on the assumption that the underlying market satisfies the usual no-arbitrage conditions. In many situations, these assumptions are reasonable. However, as we will see in the subsequent chapters, circumstances often arise where these assumptions are seriously flawed, and market incompleteness cannot be dismissed as merely a higher-order correction.

5

Dynamics of Forwards

Empirical analysis of price returns is an essential component of the development of valuation methods in any asset class. The design of hedging strategies, construction of investor index products, and model selection for derivatives valuation each rely heavily on statistical estimates of moments and models of returns processes. Energy commodities present some unique challenges: the effects of seasonality and inventory on covariance structure are significant; forward price volatility decays rapidly with tenor; returns are highly nonnormal. These features are juxtaposed on markets in which options liquidity is concentrated at short tenors and near the money, and trading activity in correlation products is minimal, constraining the availability of market-implied information about returns distributions.

A casual examination of forward prices shows that correlations in returns between different contracts of the same commodity can be quite high. Figure 5.1 shows several nearby price series for West Texas Intermediate (WTI); recall that the nth nearby contract is the nth contract currently trading. A nearby price series is the concatenation of a set of nearby prices across trading dates. Variations between the different prices are discernible, but the dominant feature is that these price series are tightly coupled, suggesting high correlations between price returns of the series of forward contracts. This is the case, as we will see shortly.

Reconciliation of high returns correlations with the empirical fact that forward curves can show periods of significant backwardation and contango requires that the volatility of forward prices decrease with tenor, a feature that we will refer to as *volatility backwardation*. Forward prices at short tenors are significantly more volatile than at long tenors, which is why large variations in forward yields can arise in tandem with high returns correlations.

Nontrivial term structure of volatility and correlation is of central importance to hedging programs. For example, we saw in Chapter 2 that liquidity

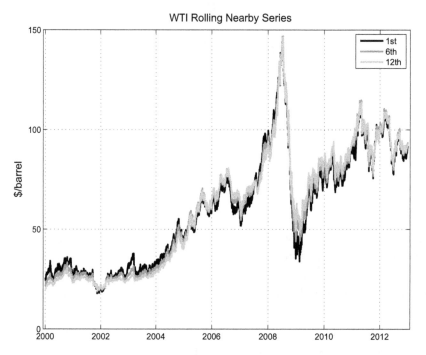

Figure 5.1. WTI nearby price series.

in commodities futures contracts is highly concentrated at short tenors. This incentivizes traders to use near-dated contracts to hedge longer-term risks – so-called stack-and-roll hedging, which we will examine closely in Chapter 6. Constructing hedges in which short-tenor positions hedge long-tenor risks requires a framework for estimating and modeling the term structure of volatility and correlation.

Option pricing is also affected. The constant-volatility assumption implicit in Black-76 must be reconsidered when valuing option structures with non-standard features. Even simple departures from "vanilla" options are cause for concern. Consider, for example, pricing and hedging a WTI option that expires three *months* before the underlying futures contract (recall that the listed WTI option expires three business days before futures expiry). If volatility is heavily backwardating, that is, if instantaneous returns volatility is decreasing rapidly with the tenor of the contract, prices calculated using an assumption of constant volatility could be seriously flawed.

In what follows, we will examine

- *The empirical distribution of forward yields.* Is there a bias toward backwardation or contango? Is there a relationship between forward yields and commodity index performance?
- *The term structure of volatility.* How rapidly does volatility backwardate, and are there effective parameterizations of the effect?

- *The term structure of correlations*. How does the correlation between the returns of $F(t, T)$ and $F(t, T + S)$ depend on the tenors of the two contracts?
- *The distribution of returns*. How flawed is the assumption of normal returns?

Our analysis will use the WTI and natural gas (NG) futures contracts as primary working examples. Despite the flaws of the WTI contract, WTI remains a deep futures market with a long data series, and the empirical results apply broadly across energy commodities.

Dealing with Contract Rolls

Empirical analysis of commodities returns is encumbered by a technical annoyance: contracts expire. Unlike interest-rate swaps, for example, where each trading day yields a set of effectively identical data comprised of swap rates at approximately identical tenors, for commodities, the underlying contracts march relentlessly toward expiry. The market data available for analysis is therefore of the form $F(t_n, \vec{T}_n)$, where $\vec{T}_n$ denotes the set of contract months active on date t. The tenor of all contracts $\vec{T}_n - t$ changes with t. Volatility and correlation analysis requires stationary (or nearly stationary) data, and the data of the form $F(t_n, \vec{T}_n)$ are not stationary. Not only are tenors changing with time, but discontinuities arise when the first active contract expires.

There are two common approaches to dealing with this problem. The first is to construct returns series from nearby price series. This approach does not mean calculating returns from a nearby price series; this would result in anomalies at contract roll dates where returns would be between two distinct contract prices.[1] This "return" between the price of the second nearby versus the first nearby on the previous date can be anomalously large in magnitude. The correct approach is to generate returns for each individual forward contract and then concatenate these returns into nearby returns series, thereby avoiding spurious returns at roll dates.

A second approach is to build constant-maturity forwards from which returns are calculated. On each day, the prevailing forward prices are interpolated onto a fixed-tenor grid. This yields forward data of the form $F(t, t + \vec{\Delta})$, where Δ denotes a fixed set of tenors. Such data are analogous to the interest-rate swaps data and are ostensibly a stationary rendition of forward prices on which returns analysis can be performed.

Each of these approaches is technically flawed in some way. The nearby approach ignores the fact that the tenor associated with each return series is varying by roughly one-twelfth of a year in a periodic fashion. The constant-maturity approach, on the face of it, avoids this issue. However, problems

---

[1] If we let t_k denote the last trading day for the first active contract $T_k(1)$, then the return generated using the simple (and flawed) approach would be $\log\{F[t_{k+1}, T_k(2)]/F[t_k, T_k(1)]\}$.

can arise at roll dates as a result of the effect of the change of data on the spline, which can cause spurious jumps at the short end of the forward curve. Despite the technical differences, the statistical results obtained from either approach are usually consistent.

Forward Yields: Backwardation versus Contango

Two closely related issues have garnered the attention of several generations of researchers:

- What drives forward yields, and is there a bias toward backwardation or contango?
- Is there a systematic drift (risk premium) in commodities forward prices, and if so, what are the drivers?

These issues revolve around two distinct phenomena that, because of their similar nature and common vernacular, are easy to confuse.

Recalling the carry formalism as per (2.13), empirical analysis of forward yields is equivalent to analysis of modified convenience yields: $\tilde{\eta} \equiv q - \eta$. Traders and energy research teams use the terms *backwardation* and *contango* to refer to negative and positive values of the forward yield (2.8), respectively, fully inclusive of funding costs. Forward yields are directly observable from market forward or futures prices, and hence their statistical attributes and the impact of fundamental drivers can be estimated.

The second issue pertains to a bias in the forward price relative to expected future spot prices, expectation in this case referring to the *physical measure*. We know that under the risk-neutral measure $F(t, T) = \tilde{E}[F(T, T)]$, where $F(T, T)$ is the final settlement price or the spot price. This need not hold under the physical measure $E[\cdot]$, and the spread

$$\mu(t, T) \equiv E[F(T, T)] - F(t, T) \qquad (5.1)$$

is the expected increase (drift) in the forward price $F(t, T)$ over the time interval $[t, T]$. This drift, or risk premium, is of considerable interest to index investors who are making "physical-measure decisions." The challenge is that $E[F(T, T)]$ is not observable.

Theories and empirical analysis pertaining to $\mu(t, T)$ abound. A longstanding thesis is that forward curves of consumable commodities exhibit a bias toward $\mu(t, T) > 0$; that is, forward prices are statistically below expected future spot prices. This postulated phenomenon is referred to as *normal backwardation*, and results in the confusing vernacular. The theory of normal backwardation dates back to Keynes [Key50] and Hicks [Hic46]. The essence of the argument is that producers of a commodity tend to hedge more than consumers, being less diversified in economic activity – often producing only a single commodity. Consumers, in contrast, typically rely on a variety of input resources and have comparatively diverse exposure to multiple risks. This asymmetry, it is posited, results in selling pressure in futures markets, pushing futures prices below expected spot prices and effectively providing compensation in the form of the premium $\mu(t, T) > 0$ to speculators willing to fill the void.

It is true that for many commodities, producers are larger and more organized entities than consumers, which are often simply individual customers purchasing food or gasoline and, as such, are neither inclined nor able to hedge. In a modern economy, however, there are certainly many counterexamples. Airlines are naturally short energy and are active hedgers in the oil and products markets. Utilities and other retail energy providers can be short power to customers and are also active hedgers. Moreover, there are empirical studies that cast doubt on the hedging asymmetry explanation. For example, analysis by Gorton, Hayashi, and Rouwenhorst [GHR07] rejects the hypothesis that there is a significant correlation between hedging pressure, defined as the aggregate position of commercial exchange positions (as reported by the CFTC[2] in its *Commitment of Traders Report*), and *future* drift in forward prices.

A set of alternative approaches to forward yields and risk premia, grouped under the rubric of the *theory of storage* alluded to in Chapter 2, formalizes the relationship between forward yields and inventory. We have already encountered several instances of a relationship between inventory levels and forward yields. Examples included crude oil forward yields versus OECD inventory in Figure 2.8 and a similar relationship with natural gas calendar strip yields versus inventory relative to seasonal norm in Figure 3.27. We will discuss this theoretical framework more in Chapter 12, but one consequence of particular relevance is that backwardation (in the yield sense) is related to normal backwardation in the sense of positive drift $\mu(t, T)$.

The heuristic argument, appearing more formally in equilibrium models,[3] is that an increase in net demand results in a decrease in available inventory. This should result in two effects. First, spot or short-tenor forward prices should increase more than long-tenor forward prices because market expectations typically posit an equilibration to normal inventory levels. Second, the actions of those in possession of inventory tend to mitigate price fluctuations. By selling inventory when spot prices are high relative to forward prices and increasing inventory when spot prices are low, owners of storage capacity reduce the variance of returns at all tenors. However, at low inventory levels, the degree to which this can occur is reduced. Hence one

---

[2] The Commodities Futures Trading Commission (CFTC) regulates futures trading and increasingly over-the-counter (OTC) trading in commodities in the United States as a result of the Dodd-Frank bill.

[3] See, for example, a model developed by Gorton, Hayashi, and Rouwenhorst [GHR07] that incorporates risk-averse hedgers in the presence of inventory optimization

would expect higher volatility in the short run, which would clearly affect
the risk premia of forward prices; hedgers should expect to pay more in
the way of nonzero $\mu(t, T)$. The upshot is that the two forms of backwardation, namely, negative forward yields and positive risk premium, should be
related.

The preceding issues arise naturally in the context of commodity
exchange-trade funds (ETFs) or index products designed to allow investors
to participate in the commodities markets. The mechanics of such investment vehicles is to purchase a notional equivalent of the first nearby contract
(or contracts in the case of indices with exposure across multiple commodities) and to "roll" the position to the next traded contract, in a codified
manner, as the first nearby approaches expiry. There is no choice but to roll
the position. Failure to do so would result in taking physical delivery, which
index and fund managers are not equipped to do.

Each roll is done dollar for dollar, because the current notional value must
be pushed to the next contract. Typical protocols involve rolling the position
over a number of days, but assuming, for ease of exposition, that the roll
occurs at one moment in time, conservation of value implies

$$N_1 F(t_{\text{roll}}, T_1) = N_2 F(t_{\text{roll}}, T_2) \tag{5.2}$$

where N_1 is the notional in the first nearby just prior to the roll, and N_2 is the
resulting notional in the second (and soon to be come first) nearby contract.

As a consequence of (5.2), index returns are typically closely approximated by the returns of the first nearby contract. The initial value of the
index (per unit notional) is $V_0 = F(0, T_1)$. Assuming, for simplicity, that
rolls occur exactly at maturity of each futures contract T_n and applying (5.2)
recursively give us the value of the index at any future time t:

$$V_t = \left[\prod_{n=1}^{N(t)} \frac{F(T_n, T_n)}{F(T_n, T_{n+1})} \right] F(t, T_{N(t)+1}) \tag{5.3}$$

for $T_n < t \leq T_{n+1}$, where $N(t) = \max\{n : T_n < t\}$ is the number of rolls that
have occurred by time t. The term in brackets is simply the number of
contracts that the index is holding at time t. For example, at the time of
the first roll T_1, the value of the index $V_{T_1} = F(T_1, T_1)$ is converted into
$F(T_1, T_1)/F(T_1, T_2) \, T_2$ contracts.

The important point is that the value of the index evolves according to
the changes in the current first nearby price $F(t, T_{N+1})$. This means that the
index returns are identical to the first nearby *returns* series, and this is where
contango and backwardation come into play. Figure 5.2 shows the price trajectory for the first nearby contract for WTI over the course of 2009, as well
as the index price that an investor would have experienced by summing the

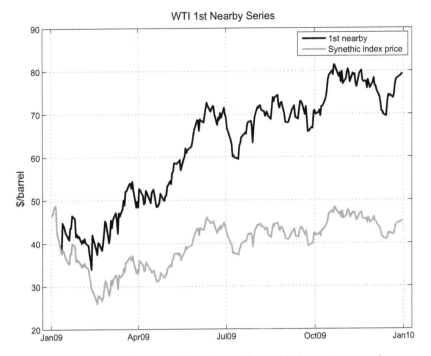

Figure 5.2. WTI first nearby price and cumulative returns series.

first nearby returns. This was a period of high contango. It is the index-price series that is relevant to financial investors. Investors who opted to go long oil by purchasing a position in an index or ETF during this period realized an annual return of -3 percent, while optically the first nearby price series gained over 50 percent.

There is often a notion among investors that the index is "malfunctioning" when the nearby price looks so lucrative in comparison with the index price. This is not the case; in fact, this misconception is identical to making the mistake of calculating returns from the first nearby price series rather than first calculating individual contract returns and then concatenating them. Recall from Chapter 4 that under the risk-neutral measure, forwards are martingales; under this measure, holding a forward contract from t to $t + \delta$ will have zero expected profit and loss (P&L).[4]

Taking this a step further, the forward price for the index V for settlement at time T is independent of T – the forward curve for the index is flat. To see this, the forward price is given by $\tilde{E}[V_T]$, which can be calculated recursively. Using (5.3), for $t \in (T_N, T_{N+1}]$, conditioning on $\mathcal{F}_{T_{N(t)}}$, and applying

---

[4] While this is not true in general under the physical measure, because risk premia can result a drift in the forward price, additional analysis is required beyond simply looking at the next nearby price for an estimate of where the current nearby price will be at expiry.

the martingale properly for $F(t, T_{N(t)+1})$ yield

$$\tilde{E}\left[V_t | \mathcal{F}_{T_{N(t)}}\right] = \left[\prod_{n=1}^{N(t)} \frac{F(T_n, T_n)}{F(T_n, T_{n+1})}\right] F\left(T_{N(t)}, T_{N(t)+1}\right)$$

which becomes:

$$\tilde{E}\left[V_t | \mathcal{F}_{T_{N(t)}}\right] = \left[\prod_{n=1}^{N(t)-1} \frac{F(T_n, T_n)}{F(T_n, T_{n+1})}\right] F\left(T_{N(t)-1}, T_{N(t)}\right)$$

Recursively conditioning on each $\mathcal{F}_{T_n}$ yields $\tilde{E}[V_t] = F(0, T_1) = V_0$. This applies for any t, so the forward curve for V is flat.

The risk-neutral measure is in general not the same as the physical measure. The point, however, is that the forward value of the index is the current spot value, and only owners of storage capacity can earn the forward yield. Index investors looking at a steeply rising forward curve should not be expecting to see such gains. In fact, the opposite is the case. Risk premia matter.

If, for example, a forward price is sustaining a positive drift in the physical measure, the case of $\mu(t, T) > 0$ in (5.1), then investors with long positions are enjoying positive expected returns. In a contango environment, it is natural to expect negative returns because a given contract price $F(t, T)$ "rolls down the curve." Periods of contango are associated with excess inventory. Being long during such periods incurs a tax of sorts as the value of the index will tend to drift as $dF(t, T_N)/dt$, which is negative if the curve is in contango. When the index rolls, physical market participants are essentially agreeing to take delivery of the product. In a period of surplus inventory, storage is scarce, and contango is effectively compensating the owners of storage for use of their facilities.[5]

A complete econometric analysis across commodities is beyond the scope of this work. However, as an example of such analysis, recent WTI forward dynamics suggests that positive risk premia are associated with backwardation, and conversely. Using WTI data from Jan2000 to Dec2012,[6] the returns of the second nearby can be regressed against forward yields:

$$r_2(d) = \alpha + \beta y_{1,2}(d) \tag{5.4}$$

---

[5] Bouchouev [Bou11] explores this issue in detail and posits that the increasing role played by financial investors in index products, who are generally inclined toward long positions, is resulting in a new paradigm of "normal contango" owing to positive hedging pressure on forward prices. In this case it is storage operators, as opposed to hedgers, who are reaping the benefits of the negative risk premia [$\mu(t, T) < 0$].

[6] WTI is particularly useful in this analysis because of the high levels of contango experienced as a result of inventory builds in the latter part of this data set as discussed in Chapter 3.

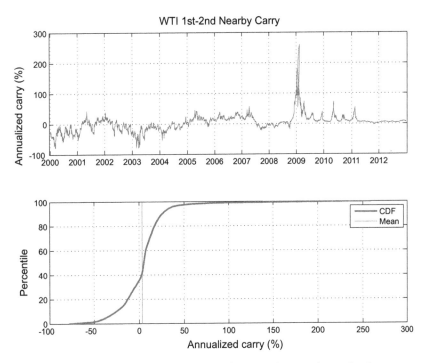

Figure 5.3. WTI forward yield (first and second nearbys).

Here $r_2(d)$ is the daily return of the second nearby, and

$$y_{1,2}(d) \equiv 12 \log \left[\frac{F(t_d, T_2)}{F(t_d, T_1)} \right] \qquad (5.5)$$

is the forward yield of the first two nearby contracts. The result is $\beta = -0.0030y_{1,2}$.[7] Annualized, this amounts to a drift corresponding to 74.75 percent of that implied by the forward yield, which is significant and gives credence to the notion that long positions in commodities indices tend to perform better in backwardated environments. Statistically forward prices tend to roll up or down the curve in backwardated and contango environments, respectively.

Given the relationship in (5.4), the presence or absence of a systematic bias toward backwardation is relevant to investors contemplating index investments. In what follows, we will examine WTI as an example of a non-seasonal commodity and NYMEX natural gas as a seasonal commodity. See [GHR07] for a more complete treatment of the empirical relationship between drift and forward yields across a broad set of commodities.

Figure 5.3 shows the yield between the first and second nearby contracts for WTI: $12\log[F(t, T_2)/F(t, T_1)]$ from January 2000 through December

---

[7] The standard deviation of β is 0.0016, or, equivalently, a Z-score of 1.872.

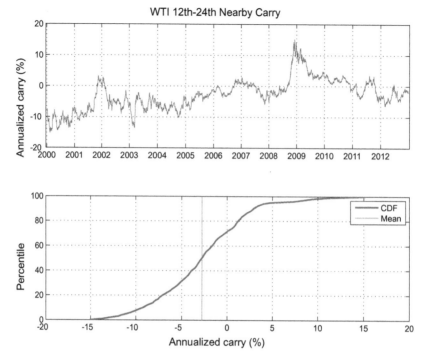

Figure 5.4. WTI forward yield (twelfth and twenty-fourth nearbys)

2012. The large contango in aftermath of the credit crisis is clearly visible. The lower plot shows the distribution function of the yield. Over this time period, the probability of being in contango was nearly 60 percent. The story is different at longer tenors. Figure 5.4 shows the same statistics for the twelfth and twenty-fourth nearby contracts. In this case, the curve at longer tenors was backwardated roughly 70 percent of the time. The different forward yield statistics between the two cases is due to the inventory effects at Cushing, forcing near-term yields into contango as a result of the inventory glut. In contrast, during this same time period, the Brent forward curve was in backwardation and contango with almost equal probability at short tenors.

Turning to natural gas, forward yields for seasonal commodities will generally oscillate between contango and backwardation as nearby contracts move up and down the forward curve. A simple way to strip out seasonality is to consider the first two rolling calendar strips, the results of which are shown in Figure 5.5. The forward curve was in contango approximately 60 percent of the time, skewed in recent years by the shale gas glut.

This analysis of forward yields included all components of carry: storage costs, convenience yield, and funding. Funding costs induce a bias toward contango, as seen in (2.13). If an investor takes cash and starts a program of buying the first nearby and rolling to the next nearby as in (5.2), the

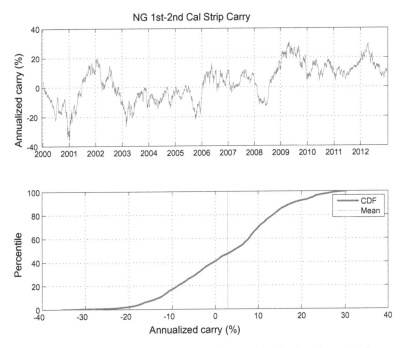

Figure 5.5. NG Forward Yields (1st and 2nd calendar strips)

collateral posting for futures contracts is a fraction of the notional value; the rest of the cash will simply earn the short rate. Furthermore, the collateral in the margin account also accrues interest. Moreover, some (although not all) index investment vehicles pay total returns, which passes this accrued interest through to the investor. It is therefore more appropriate to consider forward yields net of funding costs.

Defining modified forwards as $\tilde{F}(t,T) = F(t,t)e^{-r(t,T)(T-t)}$ leaves purely storage and convenience yield effects. Figure 5.6 shows the distribution functions for the resulting modified forward yields for WTI. The bias toward backwardation is meaningfully greater for the longer-tenor forward yields than for the unadjusted forward yields, with the backwardation occurring over 80 percent of the time once adjusted for financial carry.

Term Structure of Volatility and Correlation

We turn next to the term structure of realized volatility and correlation. This topic affects many aspects of portfolio management, from the design of hedging strategies to the valuation of nonstandard options structures, and its importance is due in large part to the limited types of options that are most commonly traded in energy markets.

We saw in Figure 2.2 the rapid decay in volume and open interest for the WTI futures contract. Concentration of liquidity at short tenors is a universal feature of energy commodities which results in traders using stack-and-roll

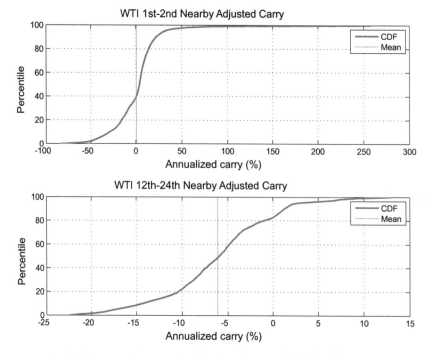

Figure 5.6. WTI forward yields net of funding costs.

hedging methods (using near-dated futures contracts to hedge longer-dated positions), especially on the execution of sizable long-tenor transactions. The issue at hand is how to determine optimal hedge ratios. Given a position Δ_T on contract T, the goal is to find a Δ_S on another, more liquid contract S so that

$$\Delta_T dF(t,T) \approx \Delta_S dF(t,S) \tag{5.6}$$

Phrased more formally, this can be stated as a minimum-variance problem commonly discussed in financial engineering and reviewed in Appendix B (see [Hul12]):

$$\min_w \mathrm{var}\left[dF(t,T) - wdF(t,S)\right] \tag{5.7}$$

The solution to this problem is given in (B.9):

$$w(t,S,T) = \frac{F(t,T)}{F(t,S)} \frac{\sigma(t,T)}{\sigma(t,S)} \rho(t,S,T) \tag{5.8}$$

where $\sigma(t,T)$ is the local (time t) returns volatility for contract T, and $\rho(t,S,T)$ is the returns correlation between contracts S and T. Any practical implementation of this result requires estimation of the joint returns covariance. This is the simplest among many applications of empirical volatility and correlation estimates.

The result (5.8) is general, applicable to both seasonal and nonseasonal commodities. The nonseasonal case is much simpler, however, because the

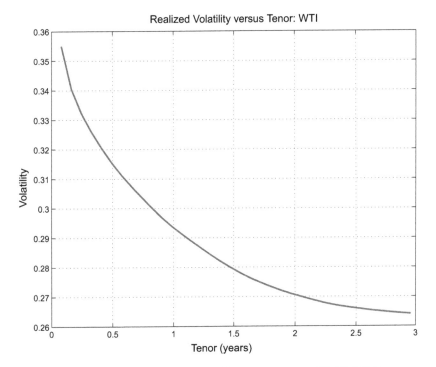

Figure 5.7. WTI returns volatility versus tenor (2005–2008).

local volatility can be parameterized as $\sigma(T - t)$ and the returns correlation as $\rho(S - t, T - t)$, thereby reducing the dimensionality of the estimation problem. Figure 5.7 shows the standard deviation of returns versus tenor for WTI using data from 2005 to 2008.[8] Here we are using the constant-maturity interpolation method, with the grid of relative tenors $\vec{\Delta}$ corresponding to thirty-day increments in delivery times. The return for grid point Δ_i is

$$r_i(t) \equiv \log \left[\frac{F(t+\delta, t+\delta+\Delta_i)}{F(t, t+\Delta_i)} \right] \qquad (5.9)$$

The time lag δ, over which returns were calculated, was set to ten trading days, and the returns standard deviation was annualized by multiplying by a factor of $\sqrt{250/\delta}$.

The systematic decrease in returns volatility with tenor is commonly referred to as the *Samuelson effect*. This backwardation of volatility arises across most markets with an underlying concept of a forward, but the magnitude of the decrease is particularly high for energy commodities. This empirical behavior is also manifest in implied volatilities. Figure 5.8 shows the implied volatilities for WTI on November 25, 2009, where backwardation occurs at all but the shortest tenors. The volatility contango observed

[8] We have chosen this estimation window for consistentcy with a working example in Chapter 7.

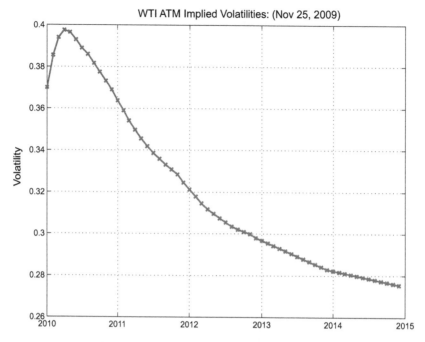

Figure 5.8. WTI ATM implied volatilities.

in the first few contracts is not typical but does occur at times and poses nontrivial modeling questions that we will discuss later.

It will be useful to parameterize the decay of volatility shown in Figure 5.7. Maximum-likelihood estimation (MLE) of stochastic models that are multifactor extensions of Black is commonly attempted in the literature, but these are laden with challenges involving nonnormality and nonstationarity of volatility. We will discuss this topic later, but for the moment we will opt now for simple curve fitting of the standard-deviation estimate by tenor.

Exponential forms will prove to be particularly tractable, but a semilog version of the results, shown in Figure 5.9, clearly demonstrates that the decay of volatility with tenor is not readily handled with a single exponential. Two exponentials, however, fit the data effectively. Using the form

$$\sigma^2(T-t) = \sum_{j=1}^{2} \sigma_j^2 e^{-2\beta_j(T-t)}$$

$$= \sigma_1^2 \left(e^{-2\beta_1(T-t)} + \lambda e^{-2\beta_2(T-t)} \right) \tag{5.10}$$

and minimizing the L^2 error of the empirical variance over the free parameters σ_1, β_1, β_2, and λ yield the results shown in Figure 5.10. We chose to use the second form because a single volatility parameter appears in front of the term that defines backwardation; this will be useful in calibrating one-factor models to implied volatilities.

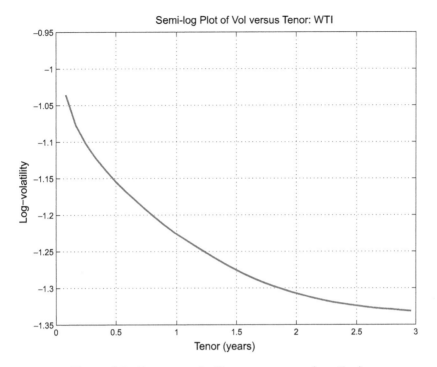

Figure 5.9. Returns volatility versus tenor (semilog).

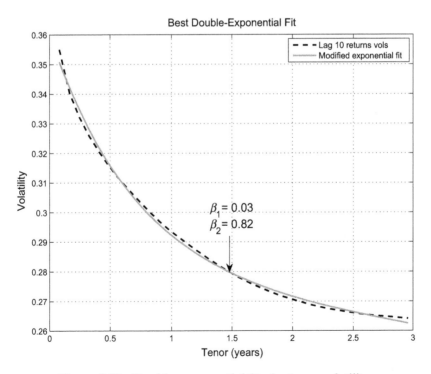

Figure 5.10. Double-exponential fit of returns volatility.

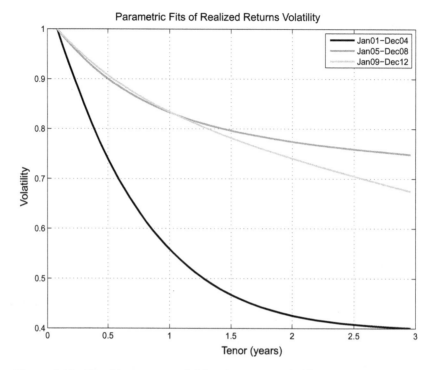

Figure 5.11. Double-exponential fit of returns volatility: multiple epochs.

Before applying such parameterizations of volatility as in Figure 5.10, it is worthwhile to assess the stability of such estimates. The results for the minimum L^2 error using ten-day returns fit are shown in Figure 5.11 using data starting at three different nonoverlapping four-year intervals with starting dates January 2001, January 2005, and January 2009. The results have been normalized to unity at the first nearby. Clearly, the rate of volatility backwardation can change meaningfully over different epochs.

Another way to look at this is to consider how the realized volatility of a price at long tenor relates to that of a shorter tenor. Figure 5.12 shows the rolling four-year estimate of the volatility at tenor $T = 1$ to that at tenor $T = 60$ days; the higher the ratio, the flatter the volatility term structure. The estimates are indexed to the end of the estimation interval. Realized returns volatility started to flatten substantially in the mid-2000s, interestingly coincident with the trend toward inclusion of commodities as an asset class in investment portfolios.

Just as volatility exhibits a nontrivial term structure, returns correlations also do so. Correlation has a two-dimensional structure $\rho(T,S)$ between returns at tenor T and S:

$$\rho(T,S) \equiv \langle r_T, r_S \rangle \tag{5.11}$$

where r_T is the forward return at tenor T as defined in (5.9). There are at least two qualitative features that we should expect:

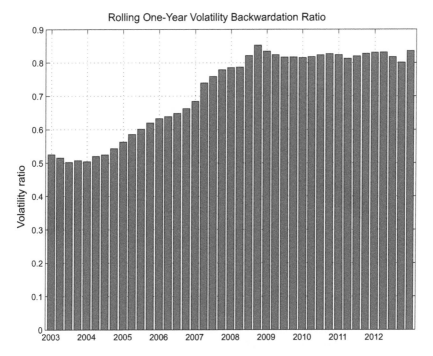

Figure 5.12. Four-year rolling estimate of volatility ratios: one year versus 2M.

- $\rho(T, T+S) \uparrow$ as $S \downarrow$. Correlations increase as contracts become closer in delivery period.
- $\rho(T, T+S) \uparrow 1$ as $T \uparrow$. At long tenors, the correlation between returns of two contracts of fixed tenors approaches unity; far enough out the curve, all prices behave similarly.

These features are manifest in Figure 5.13, which shows the correlation surface between the daily nearby returns of WTI between 2005 and 2008. A one-dimensional cross section that is pertinent to the hedge ratio (5.8) is shown in Figure 5.14, which plots the returns correlation between the first nearby and other nearby series versus tenor. As the tenors between the two delivery times increases, the correlation decreases, as expected.

An alternative view of the correlation structure of forward returns is via principal-components analysis (PCA). PCA reduces the dimensionality of the joint returns processes and is a basic tool in the design of risk metrics. The PCA decomposition is of the form

$$\vec{r}(t) = \sum_j \lambda_j^{\frac{1}{2}} \Phi_j\left(\vec{\Delta}\right) Z_j(t) \tag{5.12}$$

where, as before, $\vec{\Delta}$ is indexing either the tenor grid or the nearby contract, and the returns are for a time step t to $t + \delta$. Here $\{\lambda_j, \Phi_j\}$ are the eigenvalues/eigenvectors of the covariance matrix of the returns series, and $\vec{Z}$ are

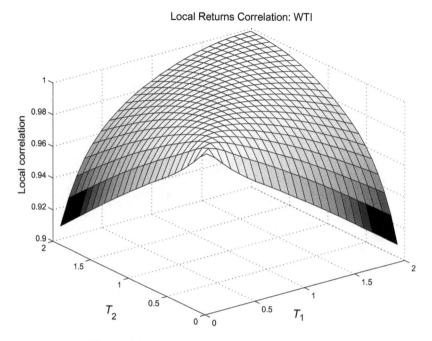

Figure 5.13. WTI returns correlation surface.

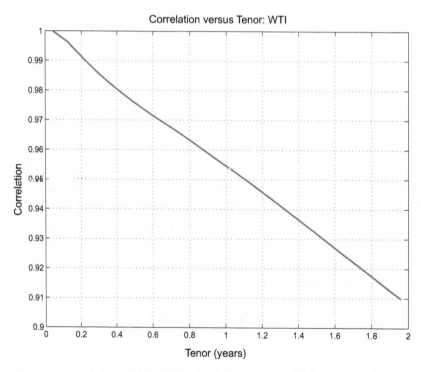

Figure 5.14. Correlation of WTI returns as a function of tenor using nearby returns series.

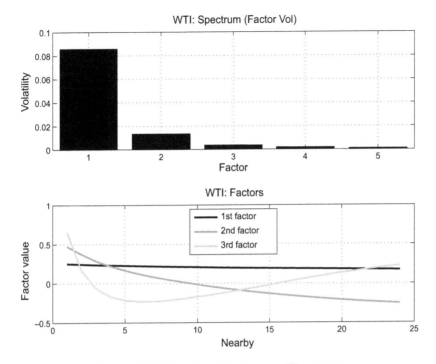

Figure 5.15. Results of PCA on WTI returns.

uncorrelated unit variance random variables. The interpretation is that each of the uncorrelated random variables $Z_j(t)$ perturbs the forward curve via returns of the shape $\lambda_j^{\frac{1}{2}} \Phi_j(\vec{T} - t)$.

Figure 5.15 shows the results for WTI using data on the first twenty-four nearby contracts from 2002 through 2012. The top plot shows the factor standard deviations $\sqrt{\lambda_j}$. The first two factors comprise over 97 percent of the variance. The bottom plot shows the first three factors. As expected, the first factor decays with tenor, and the second factor exhibits the usual structure of having one sign change, in this case at a tenor of approximately one year.

Analysis of volatility and correlation structure for commodities with seasonal structure is a much more challenging affair, and most methods currently used are somewhat ad hoc in nature. Using NYMEX NG futures as our working example, complexities are already manifest in standard PCA. As a seasonal commodity, the rote application of PCA is questionable because volatility should no longer be parameterized as $\sigma(T - t)$ but more generally as $\sigma(t, T)$; the absolute time of the delivery is relevant for commodities that are systematically special in high-demand months.

Ignoring this concern for the moment, Figure 5.16 shows the results for standard PCA using the same dates and contracts as for WTI earlier. The slower decay in the spectrum in comparison with WTI suggests that seasonality increases the dimensionality of forward dynamics. In addition, the third

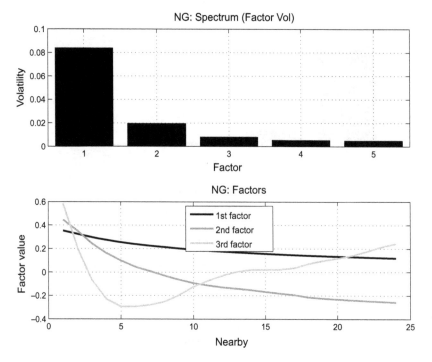

Figure 5.16. Results of PCA on NG returns.

factor already shows the vestiges of seasonality, revealing the limitations of our liberal use of standard PCA in a nonstationary setting.

Various extensions of PCA to handle seasonality have been proposed, usually involving nontrivial assumptions regarding the structure of $\sigma(t, T)$. For example, [CC13] assumes that returns are of the form

$$\vec{r}(t, T) = s(t) \sum_j \lambda_j^{\frac{1}{2}} \Phi_j\left(\vec{\Delta}\right) Z_j(t) \tag{5.13}$$

with $s(t)$ of annual periodicity. The seasonal adjustment $s(t)$ is estimated initially using, for example, the first nearby contract or a strip of contracts and applying standard averaging or Fourier methods. PCA is then applied to the normalized returns $r(t, T)/s(t)$. This is a compelling heuristic, supported by the seasonality in $s(t)$ shown in Figure 5.17, which used the three-year calendar strip (twenty-four nearby contracts) and normalized results over a calendar year. However, the resulting PCA analysis is largely unchanged. Figure 5.18 shows the change in spectrum and eigenvalues from the original results, as well as the factors resulting from the analysis. The differences are small – the change in the spectrum is under 1 percent for each of the first five factors. Moreover, the factors themselves are optically identical to the results in (5.16). The correlation structure is more complex than the representation embodied in (5.13).

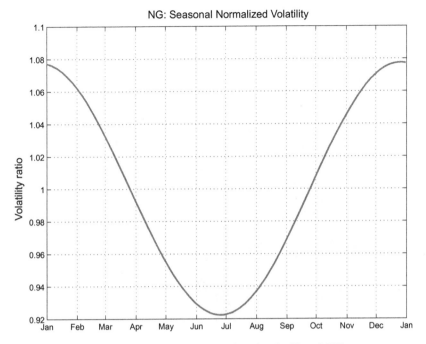

Figure 5.17. Seasonality in local volatility (NG).

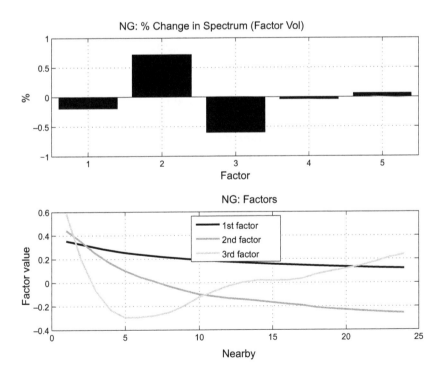

Figure 5.18. Results of modified PCA on NG returns.

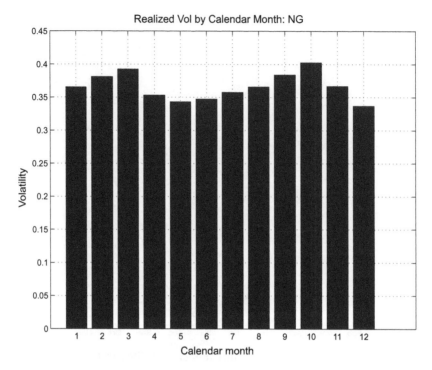

Figure 5.19. Natural gas returns volatility by calendar month (2002–2012).

Natural gas exhibits volatility periodicities in T that are consistent with fundamental facts about the commodity. Figure 5.19 shows the realized volatility (annualized) by calendar month using contract months spanning 2002 through 2012. For each contract month, the volatility was calculated over the interval from thirteen months to one month before expiration. All results were grouped by calendar month, so all January contracts were averaged. Note in particular the higher volatility for contracts near the end of winter and at the peak of the hurricane season, both periods of significant potential supply stress.

Natural gas volatility also exhibits seasonality in local time t; some times of the year are systematically more volatile (for the entire forward curve) than others. Figure 5.20 shows the realized returns variance with accompanying error bars for a rolling calendar strip binned by time of year. Seasonality in local time is higher in the winter months and perhaps affected by the superposition of the hurricane season.

Correlation structure is even more complex. Market participants tend to believe that returns between contracts in the same season, injection (summer) or withdrawal (winter), are more correlated with each other than those between seasons; for example, January 11 and 12 are more correlated than January 11 and October 11. Some evidence of this folklore is shown in Figure 5.21, which shows returns correlations between the first nearby and

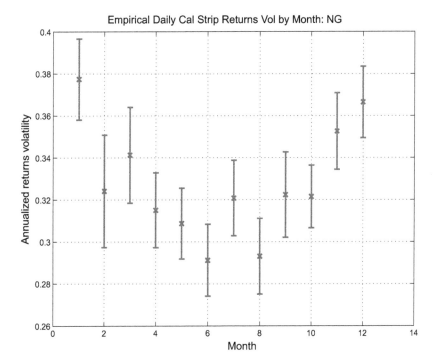

Figure 5.20. Natural gas rolling calendar strip volatility by time of year.

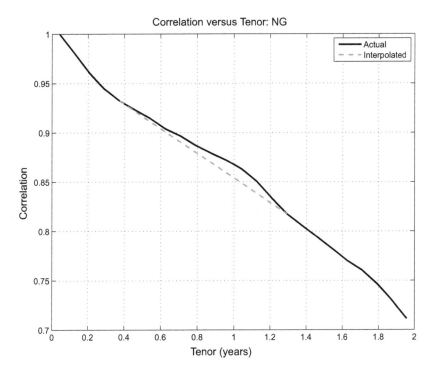

Figure 5.21. Correlation of NG returns versus tenor.

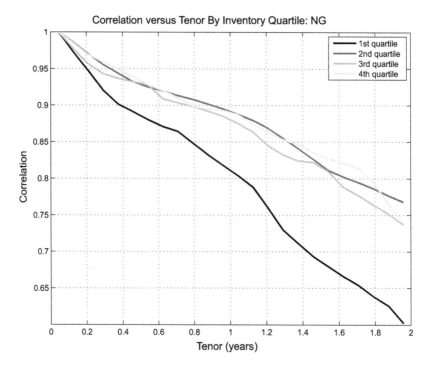

Figure 5.22. Correlation of NG versus tenor conditioned on inventory levels.

other nearby contracts. Unlike WTI, there appears to be a higher correlation at roughly a year from the current nearby than one would expect by interpolating between the short- and long-tenor correlations.

More daunting, however, is the impact of inventory on correlation structure. We saw earlier that inventory affects forward yields in a reasonable way; high inventory is associated with contango which incentivizes the injection of surplus commodity. This theory of storage also has consequences for correlation structure. Inventory serves to "smooth" forward curve dynamics. If a forward curve is too "rough," then storage owners will buy forward, where prices are low, and sell when they are high, smoothing the forward curve.[9] At low levels of inventory, short-tenor contract returns can decouple from those of longer tenors. Figure 5.22 shows the same results as in the preceding figure by quartile of departure of inventory from normal shown in Figure 3.26, the first quartile corresponding to low levels of inventory and the fourth to the highest. Note the much more rapid decrease in correlation as tenor increases at low inventory levels.

The implications of this last result are significant: volatility and correlation structure depends on inventory level. Valuation and hedging methodologies

---

[9] This can be formalized in some idealized settings in which rigorous bounds on forward dynamics are given by storage value [ADS02].

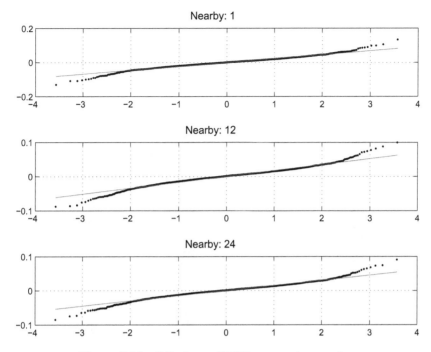

Figure 5.23. QQ plots of WTI returns by nearby.

should incorporate inventory, either directly or proxied by some function of forward yields, into the dynamics of the forward curve. The upshot is that seasonality and inventory effects result in meaningfully increased structure and complexity in volatility, with commensurately more complex modeling and risk-management issues.

Returns Distributions

We will conclude this chapter with some empirical results on the nature of the returns distribution. Figure 5.23 shows QQ plots of daily returns for the first, twelfth and twenty-fourth nearby contracts for WTI from 2002 through 2012. The associated Kolmorogov-Smirnoff statistics unambiguously reject the hypothesis of normality.

Figure 5.24 shows the kurtosis[10] as a function of lag; for example, lag 15 means that returns are being calculated over fifteen-day increments. Returns kurtosis does not appear to decrease with lag.

This nonnormality could arise as a mixture of distributions with a wide range of volatilities. Figure 5.25 shows the time series of kurtosis of fifteen-day returns for the twelfth nearby calculated over rolling one-year intervals

---

[10] The kurtosis of a random variable X is $E\left[(X-\mu)^4\right]/\sigma^4$, where μ and σ are the expected value and standard deviation of X, respectively. Normal distributions have a kurtosis of 3.

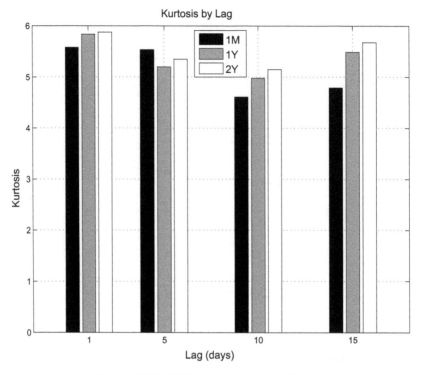

Figure 5.24. WTI returns kurtosis by lag.

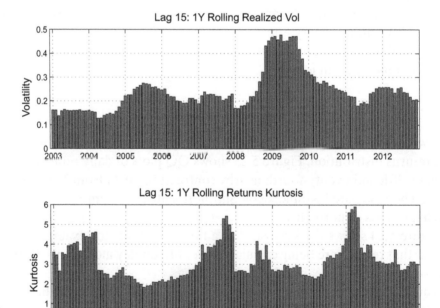

Figure 5.25. WTI moving fifteen-day returns kurtosis (twelfth nearby).

(the dates are the starting month of the averaging window). Realized annualized returns volatility is also shown. Note the varying kurtosis as well as the obvious mixture of distributions. This figure suggests that at least some of the apparent nonnormality is due to the returns being a mixture of realized volatilities, pointing to a stochastic volatility component of the dynamics.

Conclusion

The empirical behavior of forward dynamics has the following key features:

- Empirical returns exhibit a systematic decrease in volatility with tenor – volatility backwardates.
- Correlation between contract returns decays with difference between tenors, with the rate of decay fastest at short tenors.
- Volatility and correlation structure exhibit nonstationary features; in particular,
  o Historical volatility backwardation has decreased systematically, with much greater rates of decrease with tenor in the 2001 to 2004 time frame than in recent times.
  o Correlation structure is clearly correlated with inventory level.
- Seasonality results in significantly greater structure (complexity) in volatility and correlation surfaces.
- Returns, viewed over long time scales, are nonnormal largely due to mixtures of very different volatility levels.

These phenomena affect the decisions that portfolio managers make in practice – from construction of hedging strategies of large illiquid positions to the selection of valuation models for more complex options structures. It also motivates the decisions that risk and control groups make in the design of risk metrics and limits. We will see in what follows that most of the modeling that is applied in practice does not attempt to accommodate all these features at once. Efforts to do so usually result in unwieldy models and unstable calibrations. The pragmatic objective is the design of valuation methods that come close to capturing the features relevant to any particular setting and understanding where breakdowns in the methodologies can occur.

6

Swaps Books

Energy is produced and consumed at myriad locations and across tenor, and supply and demand must balance locationally and temporally. The risks of such portfolios therefore, are, often high-dimensional. Risk management of such portfolios is effected primarily with linear instruments: swaps, forwards, and futures. There is a tendency in the field of financial engineering to focus on complex structures, relegating the topic of the management of swaps positions to a lesser status, perhaps owing to the fact that the mathematics of the former appears more interesting. Whereas options structures in energy trading do play a significant role because of the embedded optionality in many physical assets, linear instruments are the risk-transfer workhorses.

Our focus so far has been on contracts with commonly acknowledged liquidity – the benchmarks. Benchmark trades typically constitute the dominant component of hedging programs; however, many energy portfolios span much broader locational and temporal risks. Swaps portfolios can have a very high-dimensional risk profile, and their level of complexity can become far greater than one might expect, confounding efforts to display risk in usable forms, making sensible profit and loss (P&L) attribution elusive, and rendering the design of effective controls challenging.

In this chapter we will first survey the chain of risk transfer that occurs through linear instruments. We will then build on some of the results from the Chapter 5 to describe methods of organizing risk and ascribing P&L to risk drivers.

The number of variations of swaps and forwards is quite large, and often the distinctions are technical. In Appendix D we survey some commonly traded instruments by commodity, only a few of which we will use in the examples that follow. However, extension to other commodities and settings should be clear. Furthermore, the examples that follow will be in the context of swaps in which settlement is financial. Each of these examples has a physical delivery analogue. If a swap is used to mitigate physical risk, it is usually replaced by the associated physical contract at some point prior to delivery, if required. Physical portfolios are operationally more challenging, requiring personnel and systems to effect scheduling and delivery of the commodity, but from the perspective of commodity price risk, there is little distinction.

Linear instruments can be categorized according to which of the four basic risks are transferred.[1]

- Macro price-level risk for which benchmark contracts are typically used at trade inception
- Time-spread risk originating from changes in forward yields or, equivalently, backwardation and contango
- Basis-price risk arising from locational price variations, usually between less liquid delivery points and benchmark delivery points
- Cross-commodity risk involving price differentials between one commodity, often a benchmark, and other commodities into which it is converted [Examples of this risk category, which one could describe as *conversion risk*, include crack spreads between refined products and crude oil prices, as well as spreads between power and input fuels such as natural gas (spark spreads) or coal (dark spreads).]

We will discuss these risks and how they are handled through a sequence of sample trades.

Managing Price-Level and Time-Spread Risk

Here we will explore the first two risks in the preceding list using the following trade example:

Trade 1

On May 31, 2011, you enter into a transaction in which you buy 2/day (2 lots per calendar day) of Henry Hub natural gas for financial settlement over the term January 12 to December 18.

In a transaction such as this, in which a large volume of a benchmark commodity is bought or sold over a long tenor, the first step in the hedging process is usually to enter into an offsetting trade at shorter tenor where liquidity is greater and execution more efficient. Assuming that we use the Cal12 strip to hedge, the resulting delta profile is shown in Figure 6.1. This is an example of *stack-and-roll hedging*; the term *stack* refers to stacking short-tenor hedges against long-tenor risk; *roll* refers to the subsequent process of moving (rolling) the hedge to longer tenors by buying/selling the short-tenor position and selling/buying the long-tenor equivalent as liquidity permits. The ultimate goal is to completely (or nearly completely) neutralize the risk.

---

[1] Other swaps transfer "market mechanics" risks. For example, *pen-last swaps* convert a penultimate settlement swap to a standard futures settlement. These are used to manage risks in portfolios with both types of contracts as expiration approaches. We will not go into such swaps in much detail, but numerous references exist that describe them. A good natural gas reference is [Stu97].

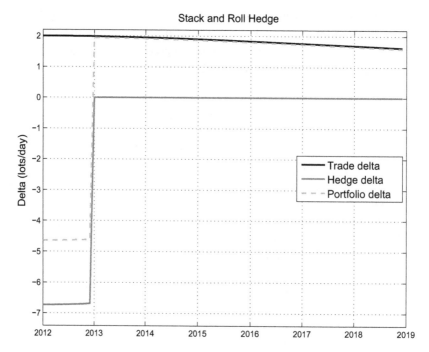

Figure 6.1. Stack-and-roll delta profile.

Note that there are variations in delta by contract month due both to discounting and to day count because the swaps were defined as volumetric rates per day.

How did we arrive at the choice of selling -6.75/day of the Cal12 strip, as shown in Figure 6.1? In Appendix B we discuss the construction of minimum-variance hedges using one contract to hedge another, with the hedge ratio given in (B.6). Here we are using a set of contracts for both the original risk position and the potential hedge, in this case a calendar strip. The Cal12 strip is represented by weights $\vec{w}$ corresponding to the exact volumes per month of the calendar strip (1/day), with the original 2/day purchase corresponding to $\vec{W}$ over the seven-year strip. Letting $\vec{w}_*$ and $\vec{W}_*$ denote these respective weights multiplied componentwise by the discount factors to the contract settlement dates, the minimum-variance problem becomes:

$$\min_{\alpha} \mathrm{var}\left[\alpha\left(\vec{w}_*^{\dagger} d\vec{F}\right) + \vec{W}_*^{\dagger} d\vec{F}\right] \qquad (6.1)$$

The unknown α is the quantity of the Cal12 strip to be used as a hedge. Defining the vectors obtained from componentwise multiplication, $\vec{\eta} \equiv \vec{w}_* \vec{F}$ and $\vec{\zeta} \equiv \vec{W}_* \vec{F}$, the solution is

$$\alpha = -\frac{\vec{\eta}^{\dagger} A \vec{\zeta}}{\vec{\eta}^{\dagger} A \vec{\eta}} \qquad (6.2)$$

where A is the matrix of the returns covariance between the set of contract months spanning the problem at hand. The numerator is the covariance between the risk that we want to hedge $\vec{W}_*^\dagger d\vec{F}$ and the risk of the strip that we will use to effect the hedge $\vec{w}_*^\dagger d\vec{F}$; the denominator is the variance of the hedge value. The ratio of the two gives the optimal hedge quantity, as shown in Appendix B.

Another way to look at (6.2) is to consider the situation in which the first PCA factor is the only driver; that is, all other factors have zero variance. In this situation, (6.2) reduces to

$$\alpha = -\frac{\vec{\zeta}^\dagger \vec{\Phi}_1}{\vec{\eta}^\dagger \vec{\Phi}_1} \tag{6.3}$$

or, more intuitively, to

$$0 = \left[\alpha\vec{\eta} + \vec{\zeta}\right]^\dagger \vec{\Phi}_1$$

where $\vec{\Phi}_1$ is the first PCA factor. The optimal hedge does what we would expect: create a portfolio that is orthogonal (delta-neutral) to the first factor. This is the approach that we used to calculate the hedge shown in Figure 6.1.

We opted for this factor-oriented method of hedge construction for several reasons. First, the returns for the original trade and the hedge are dominated by the first factor. Second, because the original trade and the hedge instruments span calendar years, seasonality is less of an issue than if we were trying to hedge, say, the winter strip Nov12-Mar13 with the summer strip Apr12-Oct12. Finally, implementation is simple, although a technical point warrants mention that we discuss in the next paragraph.

The results shown in Figure 5.16 used interpolated forward data with a tenor of two years. As the hedging problem here involves a much longer tenor, extrapolation is required. We could have performed a PCA decomposition on a longer time frame, but limited liquidity at longer tenors makes returns data, and ultimately PCA results, of no greater validity than extrapolation. As with the volatility fitting done in Chapter 5, we used a two-factor exponential fit with the results shown in Figure 6.2. The extrapolated values were then used for Φ_1 in (6.3), with the strip weights $\vec{w}$ corresponding to the unit volume Cal12 hedge and $\vec{W}$ to the original seven-year swap. Note that the effective discount factor must be removed in converting the solution $\vec{w}_*$ to $\vec{w}$.

At this point the first step of using benchmark hedges to control price level risk has been completed. This was the *stack*. The next step is the *roll*, in which the short-tenor hedges are replaced with longer-term hedges. This amounts to buying back some of the hedges in Cal12 and selling further-dated calendar strips. The commonality of this situation is evidenced by the fact that calendar spreads (or *rolls*, as they are referred to on trading desks) are quoted and quite liquid. In crude oil these usually take the form of a

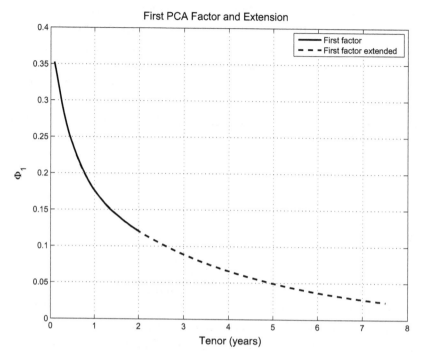

Figure 6.2. First-factor extrapolation for natural gas (NG).

swap or futures contract on the spread between two contract months; at long tenors, the Dec-Dec spreads are the points of liquidity. Calendar spreads are quoted with the convention that backwardation is premium. For example, if a Dec14-Dec15 spread is trading at −$3.30, this means that the December 14 contract is priced $3.30 below the December 15 contract. For natural gas, monthly spreads are quoted at short tenors; at longer tenors, liquidity is concentrated in calendar-strip spreads. As with oil, calendar spreads are quoted with the same convention of backwardation premium.

In practice, implementation of stack-and-roll hedging is not as clean as the situation portrayed earlier, in which calendar strips are executed and then neatly rolled from one year to the next. Idiosyncrasies in the various markets often result in client trades that do not coincide with calendar strips. In natural gas, the seasonal spreads (winter and summer) are highly liquid and therefore, are, useful in hedging programs. They do not, however, coincide with calendar strips. In power markets, ISOs[2] and utilities often design hedging programs around *planning years* that span June to the following May. The energy exposures of such trades are often hedged using calendar strips, which results in stub exposures at either end of the transaction. Regardless of the origin, the reality is that flow books in energy develop a roughness

---

[2] Recall from Chapter 3 that ISOs, or Independent System Operators, administer the operations of some electricity markets.

to their delta profiles – entropy increases. One of the tasks of the portfolio manager is to keep this under control and continuously "mop up" delta debris at the monthly contract level as exposures roll into more liquid tenors.

Managing Locational Spread Risk

The stack-and-roll method of handling limited liquidity at long tenors is used for nonbenchmark exposures as well. The principle remains the same. The mechanics of transferring risk from benchmark hedges to nonbenchmark exposures is the challenge to which we now turn. This is the basis category of risk transfer and is third in our list of risk types.

Trade 2

On May 31, 2011, you enter into a transaction in which you buy 4/day of Cal12 TETM3 natural gas, financially settling on the Gas Daily index.

TETM3, short for TETCO M3, is a delivery location for natural gas from the Tennessee pipeline in the northeastern United States. We saw in Figure 1.6 that the basis between TETM3 and Henry Hub spot prices can be exceptionally volatile. Trade 2 is an example of a Gas Daily swap in which settlement is based on a locational price index derived from surveys of trading activity as published by Platts.

The liquidity in Gas Daily swaps, while high relative to many delivery locations, is significantly lower than in NYMEX natural gas futures. Therefore, at trade inception, the first order of business is to neutralize the macro price risk using the benchmark futures or swaps. Once accomplished, a sequence of trades will then be executed to hedge the locational price risk. The first question is therefore how much of the benchmark contract should we sell?

Figure 6.3 shows the two forward curves on the trade date in question. The significant differences in price levels and seasonal structure suggest that a one-to-one hedge, that is, using the same volumes, is probably naive.

One train of thought is to follow the preceding approach of calculating hedge ratios using estimated returns covariances. The delivery period is a calendar strip, and as with Trade 1, this allows us to avoid seasonality issues. Using rolling calendar strips to compute the hedge ratio (B.9) yields a hedge ratio of $w \approx 1.04$; that is, we should sell 1.04 MMBtu of Henry Hub natural gas for every MMBtu of TETM3 exposure, which amounts to a sale of 4.17/day. In practice, swaps trade in units as small as $\frac{1}{4}$/day, so the hedge would end up being a sale of 4.25 contracts per day.

Another approach is to study the price relationships directly. Figure 6.4 shows rolling calendar strips of TETM3 versus Henry Hub from January 2007 through May 2011. The origin of this coupling, as with most locational basis settings in commodities, is the existence of tangible infrastructure costs.

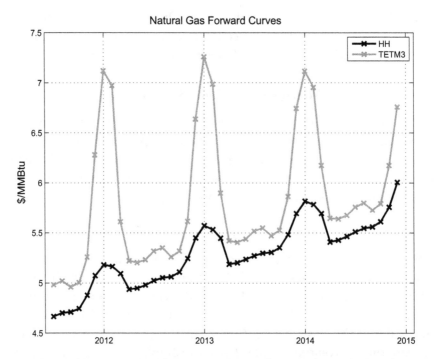

Figure 6.3. TETM3 and NYMEX forward curves (May 31, 2011).

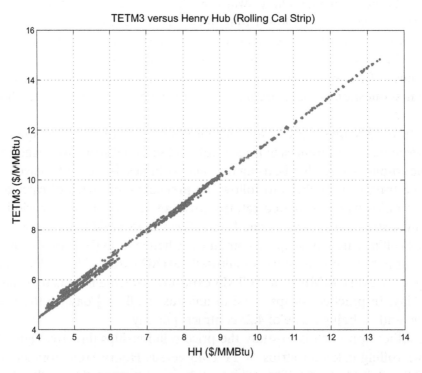

Figure 6.4. TETM3 versus Henry Hub (rolling calendar strips).

In the case of natural gas, pipelines run from Louisiana to the northeastern United States, and flow is almost[3] always from the Gulf Coast to the cold regions. Furthermore, pipeline tariffs typically involve three components:

- A fixed capacity charge that the owner of transportation rights pays the pipeline company
- A variable charge paid on volume transported, usually articulated in cents per MMBtu
- A fuel charge in terms of percent of fuel transported, which economically amounts to the shipper paying a percentage of the spot price of the commodity at the time of transport

The capacity charge is paid every month regardless of usage and consequently is a sunk cost that does not affect the daily decision to transport; a decision that is driven by the second and third components. Viewed as an option, transport should occur when the spot price differentials make it economical:

$$p_D - (1+b)p_H - a > 0 \tag{6.4}$$

where the subscript D denotes the delivery (or basis) location, and the subscript H denotes hub. In this relationship, a is the variable charge and b is the volumetric charge. Furthermore, statistical analysis of spot price data using models based on the form shown in (6.4) yields estimates for a and b that are close to the tariff costs.

Before proceeding with regressions motivated by (6.4), it is useful to look a little closer at the relatively large width of the scatter at low price levels in Figure 6.4. Figure 6.5 shows the price-ratio F_D/F_H versus F_H using rolling calendar strips. The structure shown in what we have labeled as "Regime 1," consisting of data prior to July 2009, is at least optically consistent with a relationship of the form $F_D = \alpha + \beta F_H + \epsilon$. Alarmingly, however, two subsequent regimes appear to have occurred since, and as of our trade date, Regime 2 is in play. These regime changes, which probably resulted from market response to infrastructure and supply or demand changes occurring during this period, clearly point to risks that we would not have discerned had we relied purely on the returns analysis.

The results of the linear regression for Regime 2 are shown in Figure 6.6. The fit clearly captures the most salient features, and the estimated parameter values are for Regime 2 are $\alpha \approx 0.34$ and $\beta \approx 1.07$.

The hedge ratios implied by estimation of price relationships are close to those obtained from the covariance method. Differences can be understood by writing the linear price relationship in returns form:

$$\frac{dF_D}{F_D} = \frac{dF_H}{\alpha + \beta F_H} \tag{6.5}$$

---

[3] For a more detailed discussion see [Kam12].

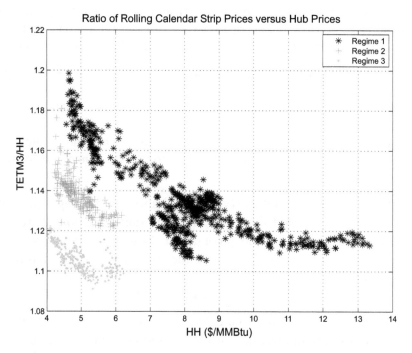

Figure 6.5. Price ratio versus price level (rolling calendar strips).

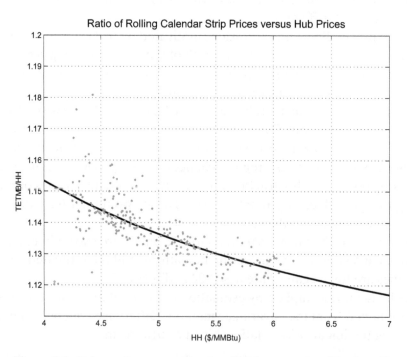

Figure 6.6. Price ratio versus price level with regression (Regime 2).

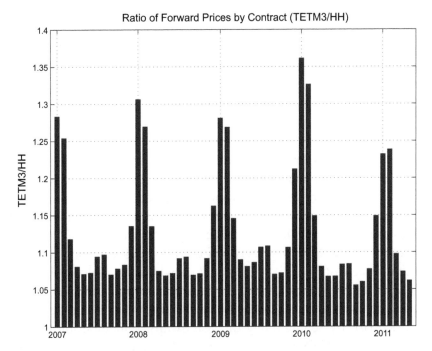

Figure 6.7. TETM3/NYMEX ratio estimate by contract month.

The volatility of F_D is now clearly price-level-dependent: $\sigma_D = \sigma_H/(\alpha + \beta F_H)$, a feature not accounted for by the basic covariance calculation.[4] This nonlinearity in returns volatility is real, and the price regressions imply a hedge volume (once rounded) of 4.25/day. Although this result happens to coincide with the minimum-variance returns-based approach once rounded to the nearest tradable contract size, the approaches are fundamentally different, and the results can differ meaningfully. We prefer the priced-based regression methods and will see why in our next example on cross-commodity risk.

Before concluding our analysis and hedging program for Trade 2, it is worth pointing out that had we been dealing with a hedging problem that required seasonal analysis, the problems confronting us would be significantly more complex. Figure 6.7 shows estimates of the form $p_D/p_{Hub} = \beta + \epsilon$ by contract month using the trailing one year of historical data for each contract. Note the seasonality in the ratio, which is also apparent in the forward curves – winter months exhibit much higher spot price volatility, and the risk premia are commensurately higher.[5]

---

[4] We could, of course, attempt to modify the returns regressions to account for price dependence, but the differentiation of price series implicit in returns will simply make estimation harder.

[5] We used this regression form because monthly estimates of a linear model $p_{Delivery} = \alpha + (1 + \beta)p_{Hub} + \epsilon$ show spurious results for α and β for some months. A more refined analysis

Returning to our hedging program for Trade 2, after we have sold the 4.25/day of Henry Hub swaps, we are still left with significant basis risk, as evidenced by the regime changes seen in Figure 6.5. In addition, the swap that we have entered into fixes on daily spot prices, whereas the benchmark hedge expires before each delivery month. Were we to stop here, not only would we have basis risk, but at each futures contract expiry we would be left with a full exposure to natural gas prices during each cash month. Two common tradables exist to solve this problem.

The first are basis swaps, which settle on the difference between a monthly locational price survey and the expiration price of the associated futures contract. Several data services publish monthly price surveys for a variety of delivery locations; these are based on transactions done during the five business days preceding each delivery month, a period known as *bid week*. Basis swaps settle on the difference between the bid-week price and the futures settlement price $F_D(T_{\mathrm{BW}}, T_m) - F_H(T_e, T_m)$, where T_m denotes the delivery month, T_e is the expiration date of the futures contract, and T_{BW} is the time corresponding to bid week.[6] As liquidity permits, we would hedge the locational price risk by selling 4/day of basis swaps, remembering to buy the additional $\frac{1}{4}$/day of NYMEX gas that resulted from the higher volume of the initial hub sale.

This leaves us with the final remaining risk, namely, that the basis hedge will expire just before each delivery month, whereas our Gas Daily swap length has not expired. The instrument that is traded to mitigate this risk is known as an *index swap*, which settles on the difference between the basis price and the Gas Daily index: $\sum_{d \in M}[p_{\mathrm{GD}}(d) - F_D(T_{\mathrm{BW}}, T_m)]$, where $p_{\mathrm{GD}}(d)$ denotes the Gas Daily spot price on day d. Once we have sold 4/day of index swaps, we are now fully hedged.

The mechanics of these two instruments, which effectively telescope from the futures price to the Gas Daily fixing, may seem arcane. However, these trade types constitute a logical decomposition of the risks embedded in our original swap. Every market, whether it be crude oil and refined products or power, has trade mechanics that are idiosyncratic but usually logical when viewed in context. Nonetheless, the thought process behind our hedge construction in the two trades just discussed is common:

- Estimate the hedge ratio for a viable benchmark hedge, and execute the hedge.
- Roll the hedge from the benchmark to the inventoried risk either through calendar rolls or basis hedges, unwinding the benchmark hedge pro rata.

This train of thought also applies to our fourth risk category, conversion risk, to which we turn to now in the context of power.

---

incorporating seasonality into a single regression problem across all contract months is required here.

[6] We have taken a little license with notation because $F_D(T_{\mathrm{BW}}, T_m)$ is really a five-day average of prices for physical delivery over the contract month.

Managing Cross-Commodity Risk

Trade 3

On May 31, 2011, you enter into a transaction in which you buy 400 MW of Cal15 PJM 5x16 power, financially settling on the real-time spot price as published by the PJM ISO.

PJM on-peak power swaps are among the most liquid in the North American power markets. If this purchase had been for Cal12 settlement, life would be simple. You would simply sell 400 MW of Cal12 swaps, which would take all of about an hour, thereby locking in whatever margin was associated with the original transaction less whatever transaction costs you sustained in the sale.

Calendar-strip PJM peak swaps are much less liquid at tenors of more than a few years, and a staged hedging strategy similar to those discussed in the preceding trades often would be required. One option would be to stack and roll using Cal12 PJM, much as we did in Trade 1 for natural gas. Another option, and one used more commonly, is to sell Cal15 Henry Hub natural gas swaps and then opportunistically convert the natural gas short into a power short in Cal15.

This is a common problem in conversion structures – the best available benchmark hedge can involve a different commodity. For end users of refined products such as airlines, as another example, hedging individual refined-product price exposure usually first involves a crude oil hedge and then crack-spread transactions as they become achievable at a reasonable cost. As with the locational hedging example in Trade 2, analysis is required to ascertain optimal hedge ratios.

Analysis of conversion is often very similar to that of locational price differentials that we just discussed. Figure 6.8 shows the PJM and HH forward curves, as well as the market heat-rate curve. Recall that the market heat rate is the ratio of the forwards $H(t, T) = F(t, T)/G(t, T)$, where F and G denote power and natural gas forward prices, respectively. We saw in Chapter 3 that power forward prices are highest in the summer, which is when natural gas forward prices are lowest. Electricity demand for air conditioning pushes expected loads further up the generation stack during summer months, resulting in comparatively higher market heat rates.

Practitioners frequently do the simple calculation of converting the power delta to an equivalent natural gas delta using the market heat rate:

$$\tilde{\Delta}(T) \equiv \Delta(T)\frac{F(t, T)}{G(t, T)} \qquad (6.6)$$

where Δ denotes the power delta, and $\tilde{\Delta}$ is the natural gas equivalent. The units are clearly correct because the right-hand side reduces to MMBtus as

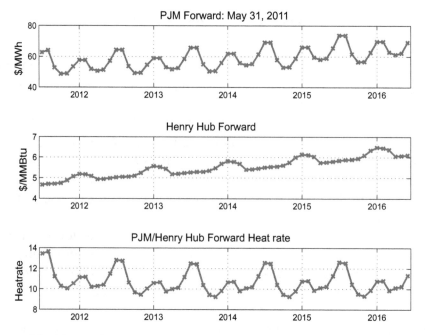

Figure 6.8. PJM and Henry Hub forwards and market heat rates (May 31, 2011).

it should:

$$[\text{MWh}] \left[\frac{\$}{\text{MWh}} \right] \left[\frac{\text{MMBtu}}{\$} \right] = \text{MMBtu} \tag{6.7}$$

In the case of Trade 3, the Cal15 market heat rate is 11.14. Using (6.6), for every MWh of power that we had purchased in the sample trade, we would sell 11.14 MMBtus of natural gas. The total notional for the swap is the product of the number of on-peak days in 2015 (256) and the notional (400) multiplied by the 16 hours in the peak bucket. This yields a total notional of 1,638,400 MWh. Converting to a natural gas hedge (which is delivered over all 365 days), the result is a sale of 5.00 lots per day of natural gas rounded to the nearest $\frac{1}{4}$/day. This is how many desks would craft their hedges.[7]

Paralleling our analysis of natural gas basis, Figure 6.9 shows rolling calendar strips for power versus Henry Hub natural gas using data from January 2007 through May 2011.[8] The dominant linear relationship between power and natural gas prices is indeed reminiscent of the gas-basis result in Figure 6.4, but with a visibly higher variance.

---

[7] A similar forward price-ratio approach could have been taken with natural gas basis in Trade 2, but often basis traders let the form of the tariff guide hedging decisions, which yields results quite close to those that we presented in that case.

[8] Note that by this we mean the ratio of the calendar-strip prices, not an average of the calendar-strip heat rates. As in the basis setting, there is significant seasonality in monthly heat-rate contracts, which renders the ratio of the averages distinct from the average of the ratios, but for now we will work on the calendar-strip level.

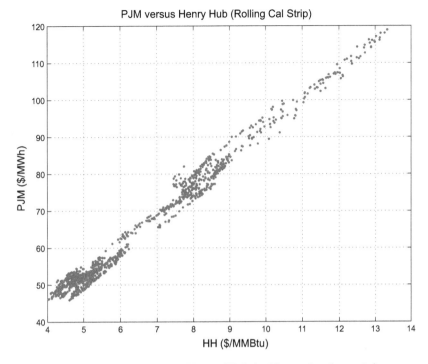

Figure 6.9. PJM versus Henry Hub (rolling calendar strip).

The market heat rate clearly depends on natural gas price level, as shown in Figure 6.10. Using the simple linear model $F(t,T) = \alpha + \beta G(t,T)$ yields the fit shown and an implied hedge ratio of $\beta = 8.02$ MMBtu/MWh. For comparison, a returns-based approach results in a substantially different effective heat rate of 7.63.

This result is *very* different from the basic heat-rate conversion, with hedge ratios differing by 30 percent. Instead of selling 5.00 contracts per day of natural gas implied by the price-ratio approach, this approach results in selling only 3.50 per day. The nonlinear form of the heat rate implied by the fit in (6.10) has lowered the required delta considerably. The fact that the heat rate increases as the gas price decreases effectively dampens the response of the power price. Because $F(t,T) = G(t,T)H(t,T)$, we have

$$\frac{dF}{dG} = H + G\frac{dH}{dG} \tag{6.8}$$

The second term is negative, at least as implied by our regression, yielding a lower gas-equivalent delta than obtained from the simple assumption that $dF/dG = H$.

The natural gas hedge, in this case selling 3.50 per day, can be put in place very quickly given liquidity in natural gas futures. The next step is to swap the natural gas short into the desired power short. In many cases this is done in the obvious way – sell the power as liquidity permits, buying back a

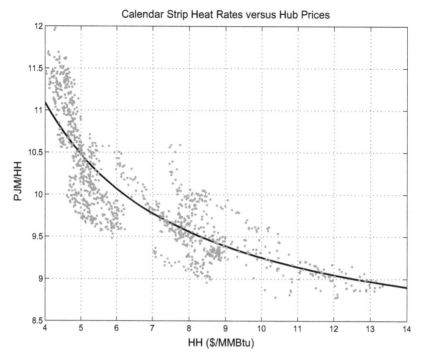

Figure 6.10. PJM/Henry Hub heat rate versus Henry Hub (rolling calendar strip).

pro-rata amount of the natural gas short. In some markets, for example, in ERCOT,[9] power is often priced and traded as a heat-rate transaction. When quoted in terms of a heat rate, the reference natural gas price is usually NYMEX NG futures. For example, a quote of 9.0 heat rate for a single contract month is at inception a floating price for power. Once the natural gas futures contract fixes at the usual expiration date, the price for power is fixed as the product of the heat rate and the futures settlement. If in our working example, the natural gas futures contract expired at $5.00/MMBtu, the price for power in the trade would then be fixed at $45/MMBtu. This method of trading power is quite natural; by bundling the two components into a single transaction, the natural gas hedge has (at least to a good approximation) already occurred.

Managing High-Dimensional Swaps Books

All the trades that we have just discussed, as well as the hedges used, were linear in form. Viewed individually, these trades are quite simple – valuation and risk are matters of basic arithmetic. The preceding examples, however, serve to show that hedging activities can immediately increase the set of deltas to which a portfolio is exposed because of liquidity concentration

---

[9] The Electric Reliability Council of Texas (ERCOT) adminsters the Texas power market.

at benchmarks and idiosyncrasies of market mechanics. As a result, many energy swaps books are of very high dimension from a risk perspective.

To illustrate this point, suppose that you are monitoring a swaps port-folio with both Henry Hub and PJM, the benchmarks for natural gas and power, as well as, say, ten gas-basis locations and fifteen PJM locational (zonal) forwards spanning a tenor of five years. All production-risk systems in commodities work on the basis of contract months; in our example here, we have 1,620 contract months of exposure, all rather closely related. Furthermore, if properly hedged, large exposures may exist at individual delivery locations offset by positions at the benchmark or other more liquid locations. This is by no means an unusual state of affairs for a power book.

In a setting such as this, what happens when you see a daily P&L that is not what you expect? Most risks systems will generate P&L explanation reports that will show the change in value by delivery location and contract month, or by trade. However, given the sheer number of exposures, such displays are bewildering, with very large and offsetting positions by location. Explaining daily P&L and the salient risk composition of such portfolios in a cogent form requires more thought.

The preceding hedge-construction examples suggest an organization of risk that is more effective than simply a rote display of results by tenor and location. The order in which we hedged transactions earlier – benchmark hedging at trade inception, followed by subsequent transactions that tele-scoped the hedge to the desired location – motivates a hierarchical approach to risk management that is pertinent to almost all situations in commodities. In the sample setting of North American natural gas and power, the top of the hierarchy is the NYMEX natural gas contract. Regional natural gas – basis hubs (we use the word *hub* to denote the most liquid basis locations) are usually the next in the hierarchy. Below these are less liquid natural gas – basis locations and regional power hubs, followed by zonal and nodal power locations.

The result is a branching tree, a caricature of which is shown in Figure 6.11, which we will discuss in more detail in Chapter 16. Every contract month is organized in such a fashion. Each node on the tree is identified by an index $\mathcal{I}$ indicating its location in the hierarchy; the forward price associated with each location in the tree is $F_{\mathcal{I}}$. This forward price will be related to the price of its parent one level up $F_{\pi[\mathcal{I}]}$, where $\pi[\mathcal{I}]$ denotes the parent. For example, assuming the Northeast NG hub (e.g., TETM3) corresponds to $\mathcal{I} = (2,1)$, its parent, the NYMEX NG contract, is $(1,1) = \pi[(2,1)]$. Once such a branching tree is constructed, connected pairs of nodes require a functional relationship between prices:

$$F_{\mathcal{I}} = \Phi_{\mathcal{I}}\left(F_{\pi[\mathcal{I}]}\right) + \epsilon_{\mathcal{I}} \tag{6.9}$$

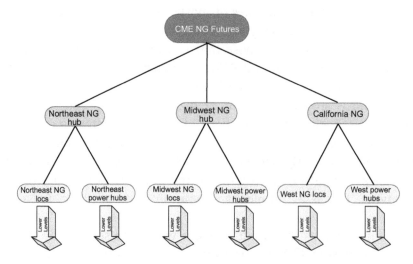

Figure 6.11. A sample North American natural gas/power risk hierarchy.

We have written this in the form of a regression result where ϵ denotes a residual by analogy to the regressions that we used earlier. These regressions are good candidates first because of their simplicity of form but also because risk and P&L attribution should be consistent with the methods used for hedge construction.

Once the price relationships are specified, risk and P&L analysis are transparent and consistent with hedging methods. The portfolio delta at node $\mathcal{I}$ is the sum of the native exposure at this node and that of all its child nodes; we denote this by $\tilde{\Delta}_{\pi[\mathcal{I}]}$. Computing the portfolio delta at the benchmark location (Henry Hub in our example) for each contract month is just an application of the chain rule at each level of the tree:

$$\tilde{\Delta}_{\pi[\mathcal{I}]} = \Delta_{\mathcal{I}} \frac{d\Phi\left(F_{\pi[\mathcal{I}]}\right)}{dF_{\pi[\mathcal{I}]}} \qquad (6.10)$$

This computation is performed iteratively up the tree, summing exposures along the way, resulting in a total portfolio delta $\tilde{\Delta}_{(1,1)}(m)$ for contract month m.

The utility of such a hierarchical risk organization for energy portfolios cannot be overstated. A head trader trying to monitor the risks across a number of traders or desks has little hope of gleaning much of anything staring at a spreadsheet of several thousand deltas. Having total risk exposures at each level of the tree allows fast analysis of portfolio risk.

The same applies to P&L attribution, working down the tree. On any given trading day, all the prices in the hierarchy can change. How much can be related to the change in the benchmark price $F_{(1,1)}$ from day $d-1$ to day d? This is a reasonable question, the answer to which is simple to calculate using the total exposure to this risk factor:

$$\tilde{\Delta}_0 \left[F_{(1,1)}(d) - F_{(1,1)}(d-1) \right] \tag{6.11}$$

Proceeding down the tree, the impact on portfolio value resulting from the risk factor corresponding to any price node in the tree is the product of the total equivalent delta at the node and the associated unexplained price change:

$$\tilde{\Delta}_\mathcal{I} \left[\epsilon_\mathcal{I}(d) - \epsilon_\mathcal{I}(d-1) \right] \tag{6.12}$$

The result is an allocation of P&L across risk factors that is logical and intuitive.

The hierarchical approach also adds clarity to the construction of basic risk metrics such as value-at-risk (VaR), which we will discuss at length in Chapter 16. A properly constructed hierarchy parallels the liquidity in the markets, with the benchmark at the top node being most liquid. In many situations, only the first few levels exhibit meaningful trading activity on a daily basis. This means that whatever marking apparatus each trader is using – intuition, spreadsheets of varying degrees of complexity, or more advanced statistical models – the fact is that the daily changes in the prices at nodes further down the tree are not merely dominated by their parent nodes but often are *entirely* driven by such except for sporadic remarking.

The implications for VaR and other statistical risk metrics are significant. Price- and credit-risk exposure can be very large in lower levels in the hierarchy without affecting standard metrics. Historical data do little to safeguard against such situations, rendering VaR-like approaches inherently limited. Position limits are the logical recourse, but closely related risk can be scattered across many locations, thereby not triggering any flags. Once again, deployment of a hierarchical risk structure resolves many of the issues; as risk is summed up the tree, the effective risk at any node represents the total risk at closely related locations and on which limits can sensibly be applied.

Conclusion

The unifying theme of the topics in this chapter is that the mechanisms for hedge construction are typically sequential, proceeding from the use of liquid benchmark hedges through a set of telescoping trades in which the hedge is either rolled out in tenor or propagated to the desired delivery location and commodity. The way in which this is done in any given market is idiosyncratic, but the concept pertains to all markets:

- Relationships between the target risk and the instrument used to hedge can be nonlinear and can exhibit regime shifts.
- Nonlinearities can affect the calculation of the appropriate hedge ratios.

- The risk profile of many energy swaps books can be high dimensional because of the long time scales required to hedge spread risk between illiquid delivery points and benchmark hedges.
- Hierarchical organization of risk, in which less liquid risks are aggregated to more liquid benchmarks, facilitates more efficient risk analysis and P&L attribution.

The analysis required to relate the price at one tenor/location/commodity to another serves to define a sequence of hierarchical risk calculations. The integrity of the portfolio management and risk analysis depends on sensible construction of the risk hierarchies and valid estimation methods for posited price relationships.

Part III
Primary Valuation Issues

The valuation framework of Black-76 provides a zeroth-order model in which forwards are martingales, volatility is constant, and returns are normal. The martingale attribute is robust, being a direct consequence of the assumptions underpinning all risk-neutral valuation. The assumptions of constant volatility and normal returns, however, are definitely at variance with the empirical behavior of forward prices. When does this matter?

In Part III we will explore three central features of commodities price dynamics and related structures: backwardation of volatility, skew, and correlation. Each of these features require enhancements of some form to Black-76 to even begin to sensibly price commonly occurring structures. We will not posit a holistic pricing framework that solves all problems and is consistent with all empirical results. Our goal here is to adapt Black-76 as required to (arguably) handle these three core risks while pointing out limitations and deficiencies as appropriate.

The problems that we will discuss here are those in which risk-neutral valuation is generally believed to be a defensible approach. In reality, no market is complete; certainly no one who has ever managed structured options portfolios would think otherwise. The applicability of risk-neutral pricing methods depends on just how incomplete the market is. In many practical settings, a model of price dynamics involves parameters that cannot be inferred from the market prices of instruments that actually trade liquidly. Changes in such parameters are hard to hedge, which means that the validity of pricing and risk results depends on the stability of these parameters. In what follows we will be paying particular attention to what is estimated and the risks associated with such estimates.

Part III.

Positions Valuation ...

7

Term Structure of Volatility

The purpose of any derivatives pricing framework is to use an underlying model of price dynamics to make valuation inferences from observable market prices. The pricing engine effectively serves as either an interpolation or extrapolation device from prices of liquid "vanilla" forwards and options to prices for nonstandard or exotic structures. Exactly what constitutes an *exotic option* can be debated, but a good working definition is any option structure for which valuation depends on modeling assumptions regarding the structure of local volatility and correlation that cannot be implied from liquid tradables. It follows, therefore, that the more limited the set of vanilla options in a market, the less complex a structure has to be to warrant designation as exotic.

Nonstandard Expiry

In the case of energy markets, vanilla options have a universal and limiting feature: expiry is always very near the delivery date. Recall, for example, listed options on crude oil, in which options expiration is three days before the related futures contract expiry; options on natural gas futures expire one business day before futures expiration. Unlike interest-rate swaptions markets, which span an MxN grid (*M* years expiration into an *N*-year swaption), energy options markets can be thought of as spanning a one-dimensional grid. All that is available in the way of volatility information for a contract month with tenor T is the volatility implied by the vanilla options over the time interval to expiry $[0, T^{(e)}]$, where $T^{(e)} \lessapprox T$. The implications of this limitation are significant, rendering seemingly innocent variations of option structures challenging to value and hedge.

Consider, as an example, options on exchange-traded funds (ETFs) or indices, which by construction usually reference the current nearby. As discussed in Chapter 5, the value of the index is obtained iteratively through contract rolls:

$$V_t = \left[\prod_{n=1}^{N(t)} \frac{F(T_n, T_n)}{F(T_n, T_{n+1})} \right] F(t, T_{N(t)+1}) \tag{7.1}$$

for $T_n < t \le T_{n+1}$, where $N(t)$ is the number of rolls that have occurred by time t. The returns for V_t therefore are, identical to the returns for contract n over the time interval $t \in (T_{n-1}, T_n]$. Consequently, the value of an option on the index expiring at time τ must depend on the implied volatilities of all contracts that will have first nearby status during the time interval $[0, \tau]$. Because the time interval in which the nth contract has first nearby status $[T_{n-1} < t \le T_n]$ is not the same as the vanilla option term $[0, T_n^{(e)}]$ (except perhaps for the first time interval), valuation requires assumptions regarding local volatility.

Another commonly occurring example is provided by *price-hold structures*. In many circumstances, a structured trade is part of a larger underlying deal, for example, financing the purchase of an asset such as a generation unit. It is common for a transaction to be contingent on a variety of uncertain factors, some of which are simply not market-driven, such as regulatory approval. In situations such as this, a trading desk can be asked to put a price on the structured hedge that is to remain on offer for a prescribed period of time, usually coincident with when the contingencies are expected to be resolved.

A price-hold put, for example, has a payoff of the form

$$\max\left\{ K - V\left[F(\tau, \vec{T}) \right], 0 \right\} \tag{7.2}$$

where V is the value of the contemplated hedge. Such a structure can be used to floor a transaction price at the level K. If the structure V is comprised solely of swaps or forwards, unless the expiry τ and the underlying swaps happen to coincide exactly with traded options, valuation of the price hold involves assumptions about local volatility. In fact, it is common for V to have embedded optionality, in which case (7.2) is a compound option with additional complexities.

There are countless variations of options structures that have risk to model design and calibration based on the limited vanilla options that trade. So-called TARN[1] structures, in which a strip of standard listed options is packaged with a defined maximum total payout of the options strip, trade sporadically in energy markets. Many commodities index desks offer a dizzying array of exotic structures with nonstandard energy components.

---

[1] TARN is an acronym for Targeted Redemption Notes.

Structured notes, in which coupons vary according to the dynamics of baskets of commodities, are another source of exotic optionality. The list of structures in which valuation requires local volatility and correlation assumptions is constantly evolving, and attempting to catalog it would be a fruitless endeavor. The point of the example that we will work through subsequently is that even relatively simple options structures provide modeling challenges that are nontrivial.

Consider the following situation:

Working Problem

On February 18, 2009, you are asked by the sales desk to price WTI December 11 at-the-money (ATM) European straddles with expiration on December 17, 2009.

The vanilla listed option expiration date for the December 11 contract is November 15, 2011, so the requested expiration is almost two years earlier and is, consequently, a straddle with the same nonstandard exercise feature of the price-hold payoff (7.2). Although a very simple structure, the exercise is illuminating.

The market data pertinent to this problem are shown in Figure 7.1. The implied volatilities correspond to ATM European options with standard listed expiration dates.[2]

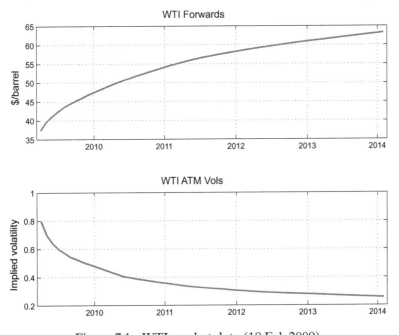

Figure 7.1. WTI market data (18 Feb 2009).

[2] Recall from Appendix D that listed WTI options are American. In many risk systems, European volatilities are marked in some fashion, and American option-valuation methods are used to ensure

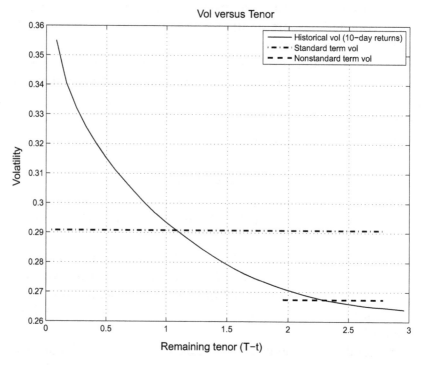

Figure 7.2. Local and term volatilities for the working problem.

The relevant times for the working problem are

- December 11 contract expiry: $T = 2.784$.
- December 11 standard option expiry: $T^{(e)} = 2.740$.
- Nonstandard option expiry: $T^* = 0.827$.

In addition, on the trade date, we have

- The forward price: $F(0, T) = 57.970$.
- The implied volatility for the standard option: $\bar{\sigma}_{T^{(e)}} = 0.308$.

Given that realized volatility backwardates, the naive approach of applying Black valuation using $\bar{\sigma}$ over the interval $[0, T^*]$ would appear to have
the potential of overvaluing the option due to the backwardation of volatility. Figure 7.2 shows historical returns volatility by tenor from January 2005
to December 2008 in the solid curve. In this figure, the local volatility is a
function of the tenor of the December 11 contract, so the origin is the local
volatility as the contract expires on November 15, 2011. The local volatility
at the pricing date February 18, 2009, is the volatility at $T^{(e)} = 2.740$. Local

consistency with the listed options prices. Standard approaches to American valuation are discussed
in many sources, for example, [Hul12] and [Shr04], and we have nothing new to add to the subject.
All working examples will be confined to European exercise.

volatility starts low at long tenors and increases as remaining tenor $T - t$ decreases to zero.

The "Standard term vol" line shows the term volatility[3] for December 11 implied by the empirical result. Note that this is not calibrated to the implied volatility in the working problem but simply integrates the historical profile to illustrate the effect of backwardation. The "Nonstandard term vol" line corresponds to the term volatility using the historical returns profile over the life of the nonstandard option $[0, T^*]$.

The point being made is intuitively reasonable: if volatility of a contract starts low and increases systematically over the life of the contract, then an option on the December 11 forward contract for the period $[0, T*]$ should have a lower implied volatility than that for the vanilla option over $[0, T^{(e)}]$. When asked about this, most options traders would agree with this train of thought. However, the simplicity of the argument (and ultimately its flaw) is that we are only using the market data for the December 11 contract. Nonetheless, we will see this approach through to completion and then work to improve it.

Time-Varying Volatility

The most straightforward way to accommodate volatility backwardation is to allow the volatility in the Black framework to be time-varying:

$$\frac{dF_t}{F_t} = \sigma(T - t)dB_t \tag{7.3}$$

where F_t denotes the December 11 forward price. Exactly the same arguments as those shown in Appendix A yield the following generalization of the Black partial differential equation (PDE) for the forward (undiscounted) value of our option:

$$\frac{\partial V}{\partial t} + \frac{1}{2}\sigma(T - t)^2 F^2 \frac{\partial^2 V}{\partial F^2} = 0 \tag{7.4}$$

We are using the forward value to eliminate discounting for ease, discounting being applied trivially to the forward value in the case of constant interest rates.

A simple change of time-variable argument (see Appendix A) results in the value of an option expiring at time τ being the solution to the standard Black PDE:

$$\frac{\partial V}{\partial s} + \frac{1}{2}\bar{\sigma}_\tau^2 F^2 \frac{\partial^2 V}{\partial F^2} = 0 \tag{7.5}$$

---

[3] The adjective *term* in this case means over the time period from the present to the relevant expiry or settlement date. This *term volatility* means the volatility over the interval in question. Likewise for phrases such as *term correlation*.

using a variance equal to the average variance of the time-varying volatility over the valuation interval $[0, \tau]$:

$$\bar{\sigma}_\tau^2 = \frac{1}{\tau} \int_0^\tau \sigma^2(T-t) dt \qquad (7.6)$$

This well-known and intuitively reasonable result is a consequence of the fact that volatility is deterministic.[4] All that is required now to complete this first cut at valuing the nonstandard option is to construct a sensible estimate of $\sigma(T-t)$ that is consistent with the implied volatility of the vanilla option.

Recall the parametric form (5.10):

$$\sigma^2(T-t) = \sigma_1^2 \left[e^{-2\beta_1(T-t)} + \lambda e^{-2\beta_2(T-t)} \right] \qquad (7.7)$$

The parameters $\vec{\eta} \equiv [\beta_1, \beta_2, \lambda]$ collectively define the backwardation rate of local volatility. In what follows, we will use the results of the estimation done in Chapter 5 and shown in Figure 5.10: $\bar{\beta} = [0.025, 0.817]$ and $\lambda = 0.631$.

Using (7.7) in (7.6) yields

$$\begin{aligned}
\bar{\sigma}_\tau^2 &= \frac{1}{\tau} \int_0^\tau \sigma^2(T-u) \, du \\
&= \frac{\sigma_1^2}{\tau} \int_0^\tau \left(e^{-2\beta_1(T-t)} + \lambda e^{-2\beta_2(T-t)} \right) dt \\
&= \frac{\sigma_1^2}{\tau} \left[\Psi(T, \tau|\beta_1) + \lambda \Psi(T, \tau|\beta_2) \right]
\end{aligned} \qquad (7.8)$$

where we have simplified appearances by defining the results of the integrations:

$$\Psi(T, S|\beta_j) \equiv \frac{e^{-2\beta_j(T-S)} - e^{-2\beta_j T}}{2\beta_j} \qquad (7.9)$$

Calibration consists of setting σ_1 so that the implied volatility obtained from (7.8) with $\tau = T^{(e)} = 2.740$ is equal to the market implied volatility $\bar{\sigma}_{T(e)} = 0.308$, which yields

$$\sigma_1^2 = \frac{\bar{\sigma}_{T(e)}^2 T^{(e)}}{\left[\Psi\left(T, T^{(e)}|\beta_1\right) + \lambda \Psi\left(T, T^{(e)}|\beta_2\right) \right]} \qquad (7.10)$$

Using (7.7) with this value of σ_1 exactly reprices the vanilla option; our simple model is now calibrated.

The final step is to use (7.8) with $\tau = T^*$ to obtain the term volatility for our nonstandard option, the result of which can be expressed as a ratio of

---

[4] This result also holds if volatility is stochastic and independent of the underlying price process [Hull2].

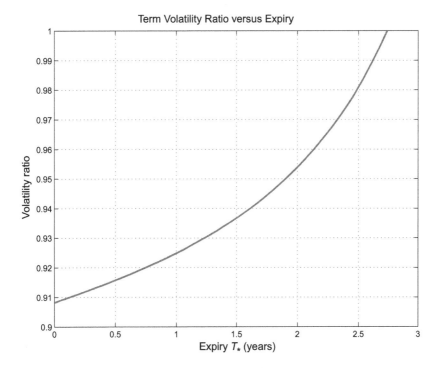

Figure 7.3. Volatility ratio ζ versus tenor.

the nonstandard variance to the vanilla variance:

$$\zeta^2(T^*) \equiv \frac{\bar{\sigma}_{T^*}^2}{\bar{\sigma}_{T^{(e)}}^2} = \frac{T^{(e)}}{T^*}\left[\frac{\Psi\left(T,T^*|\beta_1\right)+\lambda\Psi\left(T,T^*|\beta_2\right)}{\Psi\left(T,T^{(e)}|\beta_1\right)+\lambda\Psi\left(T,T^{(e)}|\beta_2\right)}\right] \tag{7.11}$$

While visually unpleasant, the volatility ratio $\zeta(T^*)$ is simple to calculate, and the basic features are intuitive.

Figure 7.3 shows ζ as a function of T^*. The ratio is unity when $T^* = T^{(e)}$ and decreases the farther T^* is from the vanilla expiry $T^{(e)}$.

The effect of volatility backwardation is also as expected: the greater the level of backwardation (in this case parameterized by higher values of λ, holding the values of β fixed), the larger is the effect on implied volatilities. Figure 7.4 shows the volatility ratio for three values of λ as a function of T^*.

Ultimately, the value of options is what matters. Figure 7.5 shows the difference in the dollar price for the ATM straddle obtained using the back-wardated volatility versus that using naive Black for different values of λ. Note that the impact diminishes as time to expiry T^* approaches zero; the volatility correction might be larger, but the pricing correction is driven by the difference in total variance $\left(\bar{\sigma}_{T^*}^2 - \bar{\sigma}_T^2\right)T^*$, which vanishes as $T^* \to 0$. The largest price difference is at intermediate values of T^*, where the difference in returns variance is largest.

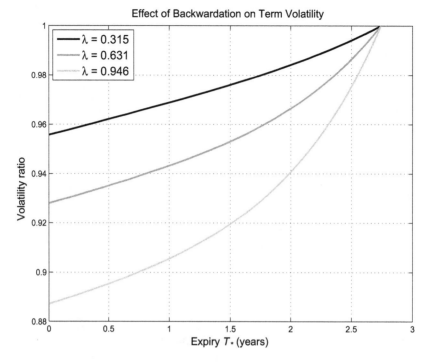

Figure 7.4. Volatility ratio ζ versus tenor for varying backwardation rates.

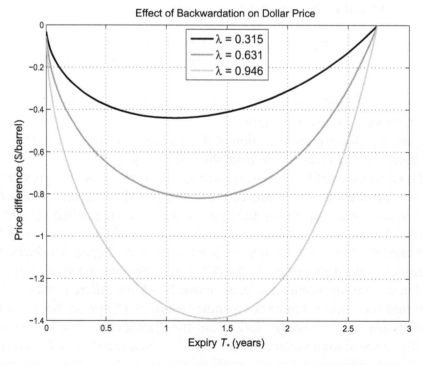

Figure 7.5. ATM option value versus tenor by backwardation rate.

Working Problem Solution (Single-Contract Approach)

Using the preceding results with the market data as specified in the working problem yields an implied volatility for the option of $\bar{\sigma}_{T*} = 0.284$ and a value of \$11.908. The ostensibly more sophisticated approach of backwardating the implied volatility yields a lower option value than that obtained from the naive application of Black, which is \$12.916.

We turn now to the hedging strategies implied by this single-contract method. The implied volatility $\bar{\sigma}_{T*}$ earlier was calculated with the double-exponential parameterization of local volatility, with the prefactor σ_1 set to yield the market implied volatility of the vanilla option $\bar{\sigma}_{T^{(e)}}$. The parameters $\vec{\eta} \equiv [\beta_1, \beta_2, \lambda]$ are statistical estimates and are therefore risk parameters. Here we will assume that $\vec{\eta}$ is constant and focus on hedging the standard Greeks.

Beginning with vega hedging, assume that we are long the nonstandard option with a value function V. At any particular time t, the goal is to hold a quantity $q(t)$ of a vanilla option with standard expiry $T^{(e)}$ and value function U so as to neutralize exposure to changes in the implied volatility $\bar{\sigma}_{T^{(e)}}$:

$$\frac{\partial(V+qU)}{\partial \bar{\sigma}_{T^{(e)}}} = \frac{\partial V}{\partial \bar{\sigma}_{T*}} \frac{\partial \bar{\sigma}_{T*}}{\partial \bar{\sigma}_{T^{(e)}}}\bigg|_{\vec{\eta}} + q\frac{\partial U}{\partial \bar{\sigma}_{T^{(e)}}}\bigg|_{\vec{\eta}} \qquad (7.12)$$

The first term arises by application of the chain rule, yielding the product of the conventional vega for the nonstandard option and the sensitivity of the term volatility $\bar{\sigma}_{T*}$ to the market implied volatility $\bar{\sigma}_{T^{(e)}}$ assuming that $\vec{\eta}$ is constant.

Constructing a vega hedge is now merely arithmetic. Figure 7.6 shows the evolution of vega of both the target option V and the vanilla option U in the top figure, assuming that the underlying price $F(t,T)$ is constant. The lower figure shows the evolution of $q(t)$. This vega hedge will require repeated rebalancings of the short vanilla option hedge, which can result in large cumulative transaction costs in practice. In some markets, notably power, the significant bid-offer spreads in the options market would seriously impede effecting anything but the coarsest approximation to this hedging strategy.

A second issue also emerges in this working problem. Vanilla options markets consist exclusively of options that expire near the delivery month. Using this modeling paradigm, it is not possible to simultaneously eliminate vega and gamma risks. Figure 7.7 shows the evolution of gamma for the two options as well as the resulting gamma path for the vega-hedged portfolio under the same assumption of unchanged forward price. Note the severe divergence of the total gamma $t \uparrow T^*$, which clearly could be problematic near expiry.

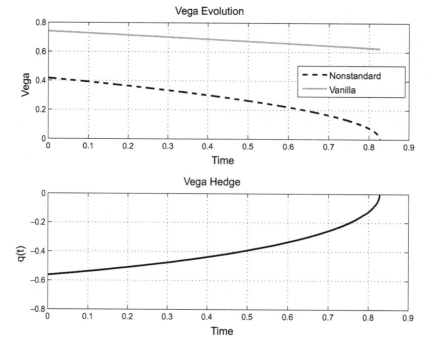

Figure 7.6. Vega hedging using single-contract market data.

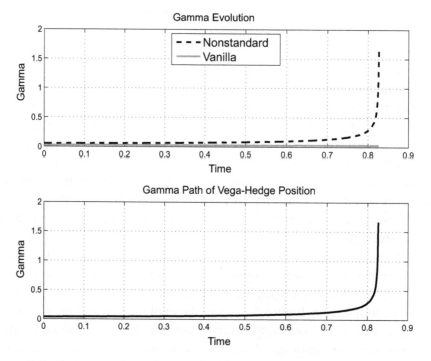

Figure 7.7. Gamma paths under vega hedging using single-contract market data.

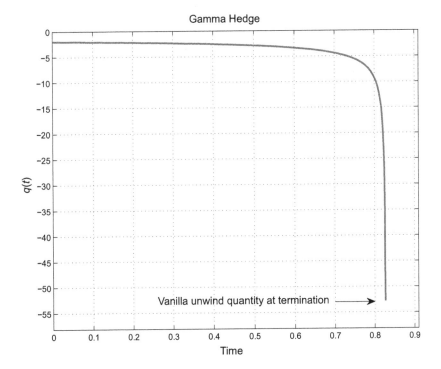

Figure 7.8. Gamma hedge quantity using single-contract market data.

Suppose instead that we focus on hedging gamma by instantaneously selling the required quantity of vanilla options to zero the portfolio gamma.
Figure 7.8 shows the evolution of the required hedge quantity to maintain gamma neutrality under the assumption of constant forward paths. The
gamma of the nonstandard option is diverging as $t \uparrow T^*$ because we have held
the forward price constant and the option is ATM. In contrast, the vanilla
option gamma remains finite because expiry is in the future. The result is that
we would need to hold increasing quantities of the vanilla option as expiry
approaches; a position that would have to be unwound at expiry. This illustrates the "dual" problem, where large vega exposures can arise by hedging
gamma.

One way to understand this is to explicitly address delta-hedging slippage
if realized volatility is different from that modeled. Assume that we have
sold an option payoff $u(F_T)$ at price $V(0, F_0)$, where V is the solution to
basic Black-76 (see Appendix A):

$$\frac{\partial V}{\partial t} + \frac{1}{2}\sigma^2(T-t)F^2 \frac{\partial^2 V}{\partial F^2} = 0$$

where we are using our calibrated local volatility $\sigma(T-t)$. Suppose that the
actual evolution of forwards turns out to be consistent with a different local

volatility surface:

$$\frac{dF_t}{F_t} = \tilde{\sigma}(T-t)dB_t$$

What is the hedging error sustained by working with the wrong model?

Ito's formula provides the evolution of our value function under the actual dynamics:

$$V\left(T^*, F_{T^*}\right) = V(0, F_0) + \int_0^{T^*} V_F(t, F_t)\, dF_t$$

$$+ \int_0^{T^*} \left[V_t + \frac{1}{2}\tilde{\sigma}^2(T-t)F_t^2 V_{FF} \right] dt$$

where V_{FF} is the gamma of the option. The actual economics of the dynamic hedging of the option using $\Delta = V_F$ yields a random payoff $\hat{V}$ given by

$$\hat{V}\left(T^*, F_{T^*}\right) = V(0, F_0) + \int_0^{T^*} V_F(t, F_t)\, dF_t$$

$$= V(0, F_0) + \int_0^{T^*} V_F(t, F_t)\, dF_t$$

$$+ \frac{1}{2}\int_0^{T^*} \left[V_t + \frac{1}{2}\sigma^2(T-t)F_t^2 V_{FF} \right] V_{FF}\, dt$$

where the second equality uses the fact that V satisfies (7.4), so the last integral is identically zero.

The result of delta hedging is therefore $\mathcal{E} \equiv \hat{V}(T^*, F_{T^*}) - V(T^*, F_{T^*})$:

$$\mathcal{E} \equiv \frac{1}{2}\int_0^{T^*} \left[\sigma^2(T-t) - \tilde{\sigma}^2(T-t) \right] F_t^2 V_{FF}\, dt \qquad (7.13)$$

This result is consistent with intuition – if we are short a convex pay-off ($V_{FF} > 0$) priced with a volatility that was lower than what is realized ($\sigma < \tilde{\sigma}$), then we will lose money by simply delta hedging according to our specified model.

The expression for $\mathcal{E}$ relates vega to expected path integrals of gamma. Because we do not have options on the same forward contract with various expiration dates, we can either neutralize vega (the entire integral), the instantaneous gamma, or some weighted combination but not both gamma and vega.

Modeling Extensions: "Big-T" versus "Little-t"

The approach of using a deterministic volatility calibrated to the implied volatility of the relevant contract is not unreasonable; after all, it involves a relatively minor modification of standard Black-76 and yields results that are, on the face of it, consistent with the stylized fact that volatility back-wardates. Our construction of hedging strategies, however, was constrained by the fact that the entire modeling paradigm was restricted to the use of options on a single underlying contract, all of which have the attribute of expiring near the start of the contract month.

We saw in Chapter 6 that the first factor in PCA was by far the dominant source of volatility – to leading order, the forward curve is moving in tandem. It would stand to reason that we could gain a lot by approaching the problem using all contracts and traded options. This is the tack that we will take now.

The single-contract dynamics in (7.3) can be extended in a one-factor setting by explicitly identifying the contract dependence in the following way:

$$\frac{dF(t,\vec{T})}{F(t,\vec{T})} = \sigma(t,\vec{T})dB_t \tag{7.14}$$

where $\vec{T}$ denotes the array of contracts currently in play at time t. Our first approach to the working problem was equivalent to calibrating each contract independently of the other contracts using a local volatility of the form

$$\frac{dF(t,\vec{T})}{F(t,\vec{T})} = \sigma(\vec{T})\Phi_{\vec{\eta}}(\vec{T}-t)dB_t \tag{7.15}$$

where

$$\Phi_{\vec{\eta}}(T-t) \equiv \left(e^{-2\beta_1(T-t)} + \lambda e^{-2\beta_2(T-t)}\right)^{1/2}$$

Here $\sigma(\vec{T})$ is equivalent to σ_1 in (7.7) and obtained for each contract exactly as done in (7.10). Under this modeling paradigm, the implied volatility of a contract $\bar{\sigma}_{T_j}$ affects only $\sigma(T_j)$ and no other $\sigma(T_k)$, $k \neq j$. Because we are modifying the basic volatility profile $\Phi_{\vec{\eta}}(T-t)$ by a function of T, we will call this *big-T calibration* going forward. In assuming that $\sigma(t,\vec{T}) = \sigma(\vec{T})\Phi(\vec{T}-t)$, all that we have accomplished is to formally couple the dynamics of all contracts. Implied volatilities of each contract are calibrated separately, and no information content is shared between contracts.

An alternative is to consider the form $\sigma(t,\vec{T}) = s(t)\Phi(\vec{T}-t)$ and to assume a piecewise constant form for $s(t)$

$$s(t) = s_j \mathbf{1}_{\{T_{j-1}^{(e)} < t \leq T_j^{(e)}\}}$$

so that the local volatility is s_j when the jth contract is the next to expire (the first nearby). Calibration involves setting the values of $\{s_j\}_{j=1}^{J}$ to be consistent with the implied volatilities of contracts $[1,\ldots,J]$, where J is the last contract relevant to the valuation problem. We will refer to this as *little-t calibration*.

The little-*t* form for the local volatility has significantly different implications than the big-*T* form. The little-*t* formulation assumes that stochastic perturbations affect the entire set of forward-contract returns. If circumstances transpire to affect the implied volatility for near-dated contracts, longer tenors will follow suit. It is typical for unanticipated events to result in periods of higher volatility for the entire forward curve (hence the dominance of the first PCA factor). Information embodied in local volatilities of near-dated contracts should be relevant to the local volatilities of longer-dated contracts. If an event, for example, the formation of a tropical disturbance that could be a threat to production in the Gulf of Mexico, is viewed by the markets as likely to yield a short-term period of high volatility for the next few weeks, little-t calibration can handle this. An increase in s_1 results in higher local volatility for the *entire* forward curve during the life of the first nearby only. Big-T calibration, on the other hand, requires that each $\sigma(T_j)$ increase, resulting in higher local volatility for each forward contract over its entire life.

Figure 7.9 depicts the two calibration approaches in such a situation for a single contract with maturity at $T = 1$. The plots show the model-estimated instantaneous volatility as a function of spot time t through the evolution of a single contract. Note that big-T calibration "interprets" information with a shift of this estimated volatility through the life of the contract, in contrast to little-t, which perturbs the volatility near $t = 0$.

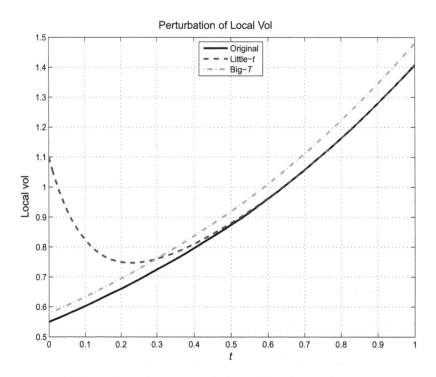

Figure 7.9. Big-T versus little-t calibration response.

The response of the local volatility to events resulting from the little-t approach is clearly more reasonable than that obtained from the big-T formulation, but the actual situation is almost certainly ambiguous. Recall Figure 5.19, which illustrated a meaningful seasonality of volatility by contract calendar month; this is clear evidence for seasonality in T that would not be captured in the little-t formulation. Within the confines of deterministic volatility, parameterizations of a hybrid form $\sigma(t, T) = s(t)\Phi(T-t)\sigma(T)$ are probably more appropriate, although such an approach requires estimation of a larger parameter set. We will return to this issue at the end of this chapter, proceeding now with the working problem using the little-t approach.

The Little-t Approach

In the little-t approach, the implied volatility $\bar{\sigma}_{T_j}$ is a function of $[s_1, \ldots, s_j]$; conversely, the value of an implied volatility $\bar{\sigma}_{T_j}$ affects the local volatilities s_k for $k > j$ via a bootstrap calibration. Using the same double-exponential parameterization of volatility backwardation, calibration requires

$$\bar{\sigma}_J^2 T_J^{(e)} = \sum_{j=1}^{J} s_j^2 \int_{T_{j-1}^{(e)}}^{T_j^{(e)}} \left(e^{-2\beta_1(T_J-t)} + \lambda e^{-2\beta_2(T_J-t)} \right) dt$$

The intuition behind this is that during each time interval $\left[T_{j-1}^{(e)}, T_j^{(e)}\right]$, the local volatility s_j is affecting all contracts in play. Local volatility is still a decreasing function of tenor, consistent with our empirical observations.

The result is a bootstrap solution for calibration:

$$s_J^2 = \frac{\bar{\sigma}_J^2 T_J^{(e)} - \sum_{j=1}^{J-1} s_j^2 \mathcal{I}\left[T_{j-1}^{(e)}, T_j^{(e)}, T_J\right]}{\mathcal{I}\left[T_{J-1}^{(e)}, T_J^{(e)}, T_J\right]}$$

where we have defined

$$\mathcal{I}[t_1, t_2, T] \equiv \int_{t_1}^{t_2} (e^{-2\beta_1(T-t)} + \lambda e^{-2\beta_2(T-t)}) \, dt$$

Each s_J depends only on values of s_k for $k < J$ and the implied volatility at $\bar{\sigma}_J$; hence this is a bootstrap calibration starting with s_1 and proceeding out through the valuation horizon.

The result of this calibration for our working problem is shown in Figure 7.10. Note that $s(t)$ is rapidly decreasing in t. The trade date for this problem was in the immediate aftermath of the credit crisis, a period

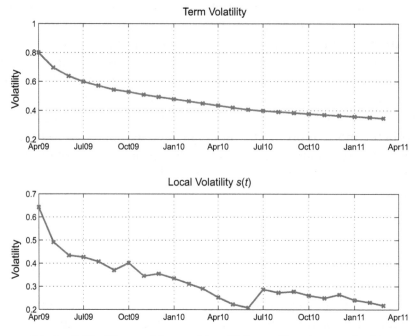

Figure 7.10. The working problem little-*t* calibration result $s(t)$.

of extreme volatility accompanied by a high rate of volatility backwardation. Traders were anticipating high volatility in the near future, and this is reflected in high values of $s(t)$ at short tenors as well as a rapid decay.[5]

With our calibrated values of $\vec{s}$ in hand, the next step is to construct the implied volatility for the December 11 contract over the interval $[0, T^*]$ by summing the contributions of each of the intervening intervals. The interval $[0, T^*]$ is decomposed into

$$0 < T_1^{(e)} < T_2^{(e)} \cdots < T_{J(T^*)}^{(e)} < T^* \tag{7.16}$$

where J^* denotes the last contract with expiration before T^*. When the local time t is in the interval $(T_{j-1}^{(e)}, T_j^{(e)}]$, the local volatility for contract T is $s_j \Phi(T - t)$, and the total contribution of this interval to the term variance of contract T is $s_j^2 \mathcal{I}\left[T_{j-1}^{(e)}, T_j^{(e)}, T\right]$. The total term variance is obtained by summing the contributions of each interval, with the last interval truncated at time T^*:

$$\bar{\sigma}_{T^*}^2 T^* = s_1^2 \mathcal{I}\left[0, T_1^{(e)}, T\right] + \cdots + s_{J^*}^2 \mathcal{I}\left[T_{J^*-1}^{(e)}, T_{J^*}^{(e)}, T\right] + s_{J^*+1}^2 \mathcal{I}\left[T_{J^*}^{(e)}, T^*, T\right] \tag{7.17}$$

---

[5] The roughness of $s(t)$ is due to kinks in the marked implied volatility, often barely visible. This roughness is an artifact of simple interpolation methods by traders or exchanges between liquid contracts months.

The result is a term volatility of $\bar{\sigma}_{T*} = 0.404$ and an option value of 16.892. This result is in stark contrast to the naive Black value of 12.916, as well as to the big-T result 11.908. The high values of $s(t)$ near $t = 0$ imply a high volatility for *all* contracts, which yields a result that is very different from the lower "intuitively reasonable" results of the big-T approach.

The differences in hedging strategies are also significant. In constructing a vega hedge, we now have exposure to s_j for every contract j: $1 \le j \le J^*$. An exact vega hedge amounts to constructing a portfolio so that exposure to s_j for all $j \le J^*$ is zero. In what follows, we will assume that we are using vanilla ATM straddles for contracts $\vec{T} \equiv [T_1, \dots, T_{J(T*)}]$ with value functions $\vec{U}$. The hedge quantity $\vec{q}$ must solve the linear system

$$A\vec{q} = -\vec{v}, \qquad \text{where} \quad A_{i,j} = \frac{\partial U_j}{\partial s_i} \quad \text{and} \quad v_i = \frac{\partial V}{\partial s_i}$$

Note that A is lower triangular because the exposure of the jth option does not have exposure to an s_i for $i > j$. Figure 7.11 shows the options positions required. While the dominant contribution to the hedge is in the January 2010 contract, the last active contract J^* actually corresponds to the February 2010 contract, since the January 2010 contract expired one day before December 17, 2009. This results in the small residual vega in the February contract.

The dominance of the January option in the hedge is understandable. Under this modeling paradigm, selecting the option with the expiry closest

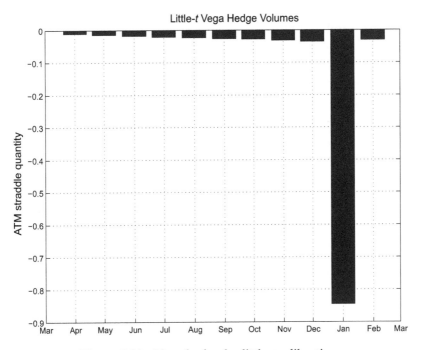

Figure 7.11. Vega hedge for little-t calibration.

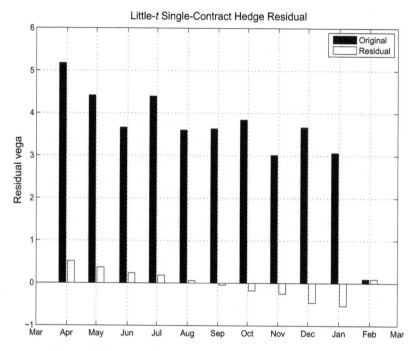

Figure 7.12. Residual vega using dominant vanilla hedge.

to that of our nonstandard option is the obvious choice – the vegas of the two options depend on the same s_j values. In practice, no sensible portfolio manager would actually bother with the relatively small quantities over the shorter-tenor vanilla options and would choose to use the dominant vanilla option. This results in the vega profile shown in Figure 7.12, which is a very small residual risk.

The merit of the little-t approach is further validated by the gamma profile assuming constant forwards. Two contracts are now in play with this hedge, namely, the nonstandard option on contract T and the vanilla option $T_{J(T^*)}$, so technically gamma is a two-dimensional matrix. To map things to a single T-gamma in this one-factor framework, note that

$$dF(t, T_j) = \left[\frac{\sigma(T_j - t)F(t, T_j)}{\sigma(T - t)F(t, T)} \right] dF(t, T)$$

The second-order Ito term in the evolution of U_j can be written as

$$\frac{1}{2} \frac{\partial^2 U_j}{\partial F_{T_j}^2} d\langle F_{T_j}, F_{T_j} \rangle = \frac{1}{2} \frac{\partial^2 U_j}{\partial F_{T_j}^2} \left[\frac{\sigma(T_J - t)F(t, T_J)}{\sigma(T - t)F(t, T)} \right]^2 d\langle F_T, F_T \rangle \qquad (7.18)$$

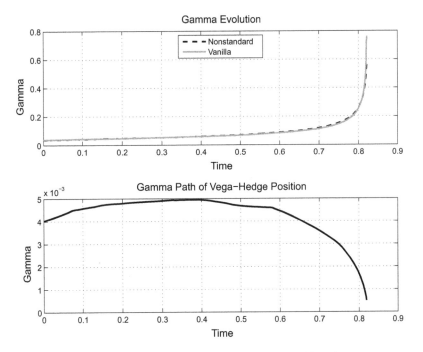

Figure 7.13. Gamma paths using little-*t* calibration.

where $d\langle F_T, F_T \rangle = \sigma^2(T-t)F_T^2 dt$ is the quadratic variation of F_T. The T-gamma equivalent of U_j is therefore

$$\frac{\partial^2 U}{\partial F_{T_j}^2} \left[\frac{\sigma(T_J - t)F(t, T_J)}{\sigma(T-t)F(t, T)} \right]^2$$

Figure 7.13 shows the constant-forward gamma trajectories of each option as well as the gamma trajectory for the vega-hedged position. Note the very small residual gammas in contrast to the big-*T* results.

A Comparison of the Two Approaches

Among deterministic volatility approaches, the big-*T* and little-*t* approaches are at modeling extremes. For a given parametric form of $\Phi(T-t)$, calibration in the big-*T* formulation is done contract by contract. Its advantage is simplicity: calibration is unambiguous, and Greeks pertain only to any given underlying contract. The price for this simplicity is that no information is gleaned from options on other contracts. This restricts potential hedging strategies and, given the dominance of the first PCA factor, is a significant sacrifice for simplicity.

By contrast, the little-*t* approach involves a bootstrap to generate local volatilities $\vec{s}$, and calibration uses information from all contracts. This is reasonable given the empirical results and facilitates using options across

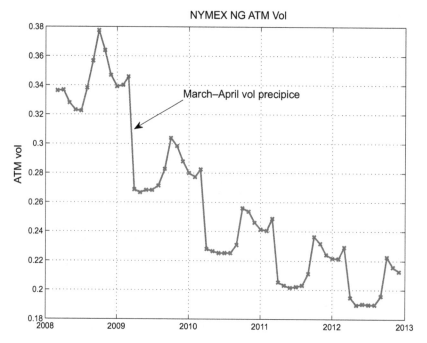

Figure 7.14. NG ATM implied volatilities (January 31, 2008).

contracts for hedge construction, mitigating the divergences that plagued the big-T hedging strategies. The disadvantage, however, is that for a prescribed form of $\Phi(T-t)$, calibration can fail.

The origin of calibration failure, at, say, contract k, is that high levels of term volatility $\bar{\sigma}_j$ for $j < k$ can result in a value of integrated variance for contract k that exceeds that implied by the term variance $\bar{\sigma}_k^2 T_k^{(e)}$.

$$\sum_{j=1}^{k-1} s_1^2 \mathcal{I}\left[T_{j-1}^{(e)}, T_j^{(e)}, T\right] > \bar{\sigma}_k^2 T_k^{(e)}$$

The local volatility in time interval k would have to contribute a negative variance, something that is obviously not possible. This situation can arise using estimated forms of Φ in seasonal commodities such as natural gas. Figure 7.14 shows the ATM volatilities for the NYMEX natural gas (NG) contract on January 31, 2008. As with the forward curve, implied volatilities for NG typically change markedly between seasonal boundaries, particularly between the March and April contracts, although much less so since the inception of the shale gas revolution. At such seasonal boundaries, care must be taken to avoid little-t calibration failure.

To illustrate how this can occur, suppose for the moment that we choose the simpler form for local volatility backwardation $\Phi^2(T-t) = e^{-2\beta(T-t)}$.

Letting $\mu(T) = \bar{\sigma}_T^2 T$ and $\zeta(t) = s^2(t)$, calibration amounts to solving

$$\mu(T) = \int_0^T \zeta(t) e^{-2\beta(T-t)} dt$$

Differentiating this with respect to T yields

$$\frac{\partial \mu(T)}{\partial T} = \zeta(T) - 2\beta \int_0^T \zeta(t) e^{-2\beta(T-t)} dt$$

If the implied volatility $\bar{\sigma}(T)$ decreases at a sufficient rate, $\partial \mu(T)/\partial T < 0$. If, moreover, we reduce β to a sufficiently low level, lowering the rate of backwardation of Φ, the second term on the right-hand-side will be small enough in magnitude that we must have $\zeta(T) < 0$, clearly an impossibility because ζ is a variance. This is calibration failure, the origin of which is implied volatilities backwardating too slowly for the form of Φ to "keep up." The solution is to backwardate Φ faster or to use a hybrid approach employing nonconstant values of $\sigma(\vec{T})$.

Conclusion

Limitations in the nature of vanilla options markets induce model risk for even relatively simple structures. Assumptions must be made regarding local volatility. We considered two particular modeling paradigms, as well as the potential for hybrid approaches, in dealing with structures with nonstandard expiry. In all cases, some estimate for the functional form of backwardation rate $\Phi(T - t)$ is required. Given Φ, the choice of the local volatility model $\sigma(t, T) = s(t)\Phi(T - t)\sigma(T)$ was ours to make. The two models that we examined:

- *Big-T*: Calibration based on single-contract implied volatilities where $s(t) \equiv 1$ with $\sigma(T)$ calibrated to options on $F(t, T)$
- *Little-t*: Calibration using the entire term structure with $\sigma(T) \equiv 1$ with $s(t)$ calibrated via bootstrap to options of all tenors

The point of this analysis is that two reasonable approaches to valuation of mildly off-market options structures can yield very different results and that reliable market data do not resolve the selection of model. Additional thought and assumptions are inherent to the enterprise.

The dominance of the first PCA factor is what leads us to ultimately favor the little-t paradigm between the two extremes. The key assumption underpinning this approach is that forward curve dynamics are to leading order one-dimensional. This allowed us to use information from options on all contracts to complete a construction of the local volatility trajectory. We will see later in our discussion of multifactor models, however, that higher factors can be relevant, especially at extreme values of inventory levels.

8

Skew

Among the many assumptions underpinning the Black framework, one of the most noteworthy is that returns are taken to be normally distributed – an assumption at variance with empirical observations. While most traded asset classes exhibit nonnormal returns, the effect is particularly pronounced in energy markets, a fact that is reflected in the implied volatility surfaces that often exhibit extreme skew. Many common structures cannot be valued properly without accounting for skew in some fashion. Moreover, assumptions about skew dynamics can have meaningful effects on the delta-hedging regimen of all options portfolios, even those comprised solely of "vanilla" options.

The goal in this chapter is to introduce some common skew-dependent structures, working through basic valuation and hedging. We will also discuss empirical results on the dynamics of energy volatility surfaces with implications for both hedging programs and the design of models that can be calibrated to implied volatility surfaces.

Common Structures

The simplest and by far the most commonly transacted energy structures with skew dependence are *collars*, sometimes referred to as *fences*. A collar consists of a long/short combination of a high-strike call and a low-strike put of equal notional size. The payoff is therefore of the form

$$N \max[F(T_e, T) - K_{\text{call}}, 0] - N \max\left[K_{\text{put}} - F(T_e, T), 0\right]$$

where N is the notional and $K_{\text{put}} < K_{\text{call}}$. These are almost always transacted with strikes that bound the prevailing forward price: $K_{\text{put}} < F(0, T) < K_{\text{call}}$. Note that if the two strikes are equal, this payoff is that of a simple swap. The component options are usually vanilla – exchange-traded or OTC look-alike. In most circumstances, the transaction is free of premium, in which case

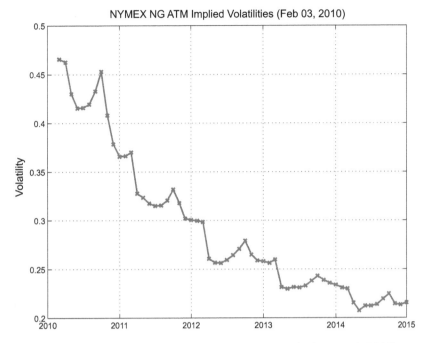

Figure 8.1. NG ATM volatility term structure (February 3, 2010).

these are called *costless collars*.[1] The demand for collars arises from naturals, producers, or consumers who want to bound their price exposure at some threshold. While the simplest (and some might argue the best) hedges available to producers and consumers are swaps or forwards, options structures such as these are frequently transacted. Consider the following.

Working Problem

On February 3, 2010, a producer indicates interest in hedging Cal11 natural gas (NG) price exposure for two-a-day by selling calls at $1 premium to the current forward strip and buying Cal11 puts struck at K; both calls and puts are NYMEX-listed options. What K should you quote?

As with forward prices, the implied volatilities for natural gas exhibit marked seasonality both in term structure and in skew. Figure 8.1 shows the term structure of at-the-money (ATM) volatilities on the pricing date. Volatilities are clearly highest in the withdrawal season and lowest during the injection season. Within the withdrawal season, the highest volatilities are often in the earlier months due to a combination of effects: in the returns numerator, this is at the tail end of hurricane season as well as the beginning

---

[1] The term *costless* is a bit of a euphemism because the profit to the dealer is embedded in the location of the strikes. Costless collars should be viewed as "costless" only insofar as no up-front premium changes hands.

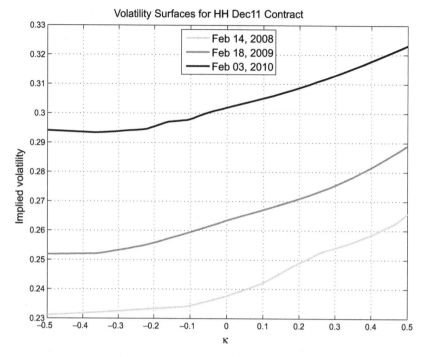

Figure 8.2. Implied volatility surfaces for December 2011 NG at multiple dates.

of exposure to cold weather; in the denominator, prices are typically lower in October and November relative to, say, January. This results in higher expected returns volatility.

The volatility surface for a given contract month evolves as the underlying contract approaches expiry. Figure 8.2 shows volatility surfaces for the December 2011 contract on a sequence of trade dates. The x axis is log of the price ratio: $\kappa \equiv \log(\pi)$, where the price ratio π is defined as the ratio of strike to underlying price: $\pi = K/F$. Note that the levels of implied volatility are increasing as time to expiry decreases, as one would expect given volatility backwardation. Call skew[2] until recently has been the norm for natural gas, particularly in the winter months when potential demand stress due to cold weather results in higher forward prices, higher implied volatilities, and greater call skew. Figure 8.3 shows the same sequence of volatility surfaces normalized by the ATM volatility. As expiry is approached, the relative level of skew is actually decreasing with time, likely a manifestation of the a systemic drop in call skew resulting from shale gas production.

---

[2] *Call skew* is the situation in which implied volatility is increasing with strike level above the forward price; *put skew* is the situation when implied volatilities are decreasing with strike level below the forward price. *Mixed skew* or *smile* is when both occur.

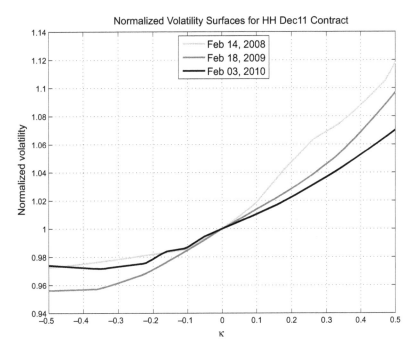

Figure 8.3. Normalized volatility surfaces for December 2011 NG at multiple dates.

Figure 8.4 shows skew for NG on February 3, 2010, for a summer and winter contract that affords a comparison between volatility surfaces in the injection and withdrawal seasons. Note both the lower volatility in the summer months and the markedly reduced skew in comparison with the winter contract. In Chapter 3 we discussed the secular drop in North American NG prices, even with global energy prices rising in 2010 and 2011, as increased shale gas production and estimated reserves decoupled North American natural gas from world energy markets. This has coincided with the appearance of put skew, especially in summer months, which prior to 2010 was essentially unheard of.

Returning to the working problem, the Call1 strip price is $6.335, and the call strike, by client request, is $1 higher at $K_{\text{call}} = \$7.335$. For perspective on the size of the transaction, the notional volume is approximately $46.245 million in undiscounted value. Any transaction such as this involves an assessment of hedging costs by the trader taking the position. In most circumstances, trader judgment and rules of thumb pertain (whether or not this is the right way to do things is debatable). Here, in the spirit of codifying matters for well-defined calculations, we will assume that initial swap hedging costs (and margin) are $0.05/MMBtu, and we will parameterize volatility hedging costs by $\alpha + \beta |\pi - 1|$, where

- $\alpha = 0.01$ (one volatility point)
- $\beta = 0.05 = 0.005/0.1$ (one-half a volatility point per 10 percent move in price ratio)

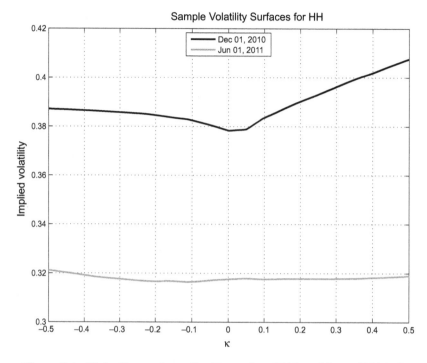

Figure 8.4. Volatility surfaces for December 2010 and June 2011 NG.

The point here is that the bid-offer spread for options increases as one moves further away from the money. These parameters are selected to be reasonable and are not calibrated or based on historical analysis, although such could be done.

The first thing to notice in valuing this structure is that while the call strike is fixed, the natural gas forward curve is highly seasonal, resulting in varying levels of skew across the individual contracts. Figure 8.5 shows both the forward prices and the variation of κ for the call side of the structure by contract month; note that the winter months are near-the-money, whereas the summer months are distinctly out-of-the-money.

Given the vanilla nature of the component options, the first step is to value the twelve calls using the volatility look-up heuristic: specifically the implied volatility used for a given strike K is $\bar{\sigma}(\kappa_m)$, where $\kappa_m = \log[K/F_m]$ for each contract month m. There are two approaches to marking a volatility surface. The first is to specify a set of implied volatilities for a grid of strikes for each contract month; the grid can be defined in various ways, but the concept is simple. In this case, volatility look-up implicitly relies on an interpolation mechanism to define $\bar{\sigma}(\kappa)$ from the marked volatility grid – think of linear or cubic splines. Alternatively one can specify a parametric form for volatility surfaces that depends on a set of parameters $\vec{\eta}$: $\bar{\sigma}(\kappa) = \phi_{\vec{\eta}}(\kappa)$, where the parameters are calibrated to fit marked volatilities, minimizing a metric of

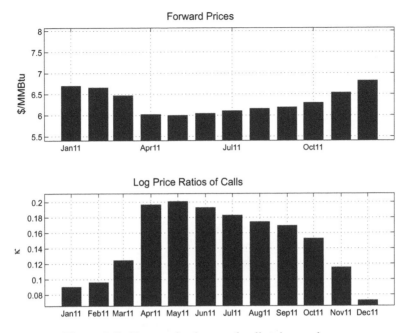

Figure 8.5. Forward prices and call strip κ values.

some type. One has to take care that the parametric form is arbitrage-free for the space of allowed parameters $\vec{\eta}$.[3]

The second step in the working problem is to scan over put strikes K_{put}, once again using volatility look-up. Figure 8.6 shows the value of the structure in units of $/MMBtu as a function of K_{put}. The breakeven strikes are shown for midvalue, excluding transaction costs ("No TC"), as well as including transaction costs as prescribed earlier ("Including TC"). Note that the inclusion of transaction costs pushes K_{put} lower, as it should – you as the dealer are giving the client something of less value, namely, a lower strike put, to compensate you for your hedge costs and margin. Another observation is that the breakeven put strike $5.686 is substantially closer to the forward strip price than the call strike due to skew. As the dealer, you are getting the calls that, due to the prevailing call skew at the time, are providing you with more value per unit distance of strike from ATM than you are giving up in puts.

Aside from vanilla swaps or forwards, the collar structure is the simplest hedge for producers and consumers. Often, however, hedgers have a predisposition for more complex structures. A common example, especially popular in the 2007–2008 time frame, are *knockout swaps*. These are standard swaps with embedded European binary options, which results in

---

[3] An arbitrage problem arises if a volatility surface increases with strike at a rate that would imply that higher strike calls were worth more than those at lower strikes; equivalently, call spreads of negative value and similarly on the put side.

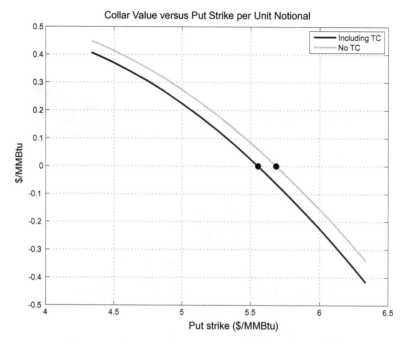

Figure 8.6. Collar value as a function of put strike.

a payout that looks like a swap but vanishes above or below the knockout strike.[4] Figure 8.7 shows an example of the terminal payout of such a structure. This payoff is shown from the dealer's perspective and is a situation in which the client is selling natural gas.

The purpose of this structure for the hedger is that it gives the appearance of a sale of natural gas at a price above the prevailing market price. This "above market" sale, of course, comes at a cost – namely, the possibility that the hedge could evaporate exactly when it would be needed most, namely, in low-price environments. This structure amounts to the seller of the commodity embedding an inherently speculative element in the hedging program, reflecting the belief that prices may fall a little, but not a lot. At least one well-established natural gas producer in the United States transacted large volumes of knockout swaps before the commodity price sell-off in 2008, resulting in extremely poor performance of its hedging program and a white-knuckle experience for both shareholders and management.

From the perspective of the dealer, managing a portfolio of knockout swaps is anything but trivial. Valuation and booking are often accomplished using tight call or put spreads to approximate the binary, as shown in Figure 8.8, as well as to allow a buffer in the hedging program – something

---

[4] The use of the term *knockout* is poetic license commonly taken on energy desks, at times confusing financial engineers who appropriately interpret the phrase as relating to barrier options. In this case, the term *knockout* is intended to describe the vanishing of the swap hedge below a certain strike.

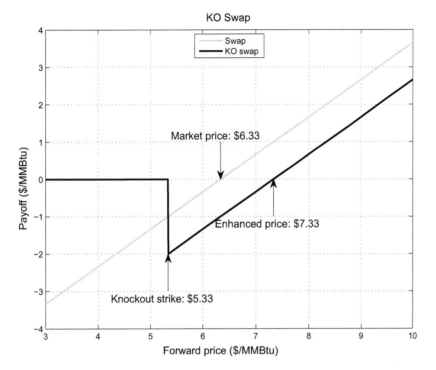

Figure 8.7. Knockout swap payoff.

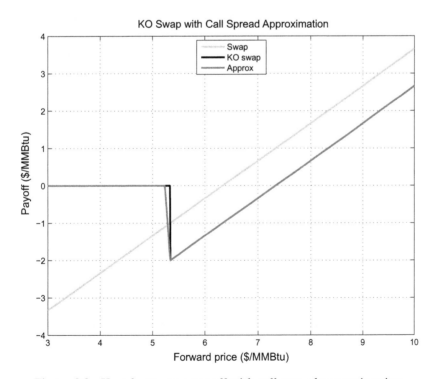

Figure 8.8. Knockout swap payoff with call spread approximation.

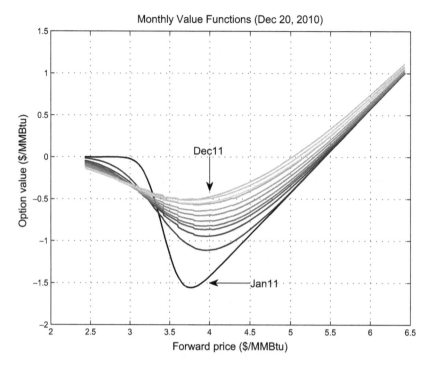

Figure 8.9. Knockout cal11 knockout swap value functions.

akin to an inexplicit reserve. Moreover, tight call spreads with strikes separated by say $0.10 are in fact quoted and traded in the broker markets,
allowing for hedging these structures, at least if the volumes are not too
large.

Valuation of the binary, which is the limiting case of call spreads with
converging strikes and diverging volumes, is highly sensitive to the slope of
the volatility curve:

$$\frac{N}{\Delta}\left\{V[F,K,\bar{\sigma}(K)] - V[F,K-\Delta,\bar{\sigma}(K-\Delta)]\right\} \approx N\left(\frac{\partial V}{\partial K} + \frac{\partial V}{\partial \bar{\sigma}}\frac{\partial \bar{\sigma}}{\partial K}\right)$$

Figure 8.9 shows the value as a function of the underlying forward prices for
each monthly structure in a Cal11 payoff with strikes ATM $\pm$ $1 as seen from
December 20, 2010. The appearance of these value functions at longer tenor
is deceptively benign. Unless the binaries have been hedged with tight call
spreads, near-expiration hedging activities devolve into a game of Russian
roulette if the underlying forward price is near the binary strike; the January
2011 value function is already showing signs of this in the figure.

More complex structures requiring proper skew modeling, not merely
volatility look-up, do arise from client hedging programs, although they
are much less common than the structures discussed so far. One type of
modification is to apply a maximum total payout constraint on a strip of

collars, so-called TARN features.[5] These structures require modeling the joint dynamics of all underlying forward contract prices, ideally accommodating term structure of volatility, correlation between contracts, and skew. This requires multifactor models, which we will discuss in a later chapter.

Another structure that also trades on occasion is a proper knockout swap, in which the option payoff is zero if any settlement price of the underlying contract during the life of the option crosses a specified knockout barrier. The mathematics behind this is well developed in a variety of settings, whether skew is modeled by local volatility surfaces, stochastic volatility models, or jump diffusions. We will not discuss valuation mechanics of exotic structures that commonly appear across asset classes because this territory is well grazed in the literature both broadly (e.g., [Gla04], [Hul12], [Wil07]) and in the energy space (see [CS00], [EW03]). Rather, we will turn to some empirical results as they relate to the design of hedging strategies and the relevance of commonly used models.

Skew Dynamics: Sticky versus Floating

While the collar and knockout structures can be handled by volatility look-up, skew dynamics affects the design of hedging programs for options portfolios. Ideally, on entering a transaction, the trader will flatten the position shortly thereafter, capturing the margin embedded in the pricing. In practice, options liquidity can be problematic for a number of reasons: far out-of-the money strikes, large binary positions, or even mismatches between strikes at which liquidity is present at the time of transaction versus those in the structure. The result is that even vanilla flow options portfolios are rarely flat. In many cases, nontrivial convexities are maintained in the portfolio for some period of time.

Most portfolio managers who have had the experience of taking over distressed energy options books found portfolios comprised of a large number of options of varying strikes and tenors, often not particularly balanced. The high volatility of the underlying commodity price can rapidly move options liquidity, which is concentrated near-the-money, away from the strikes where client transactions have occurred. Traders, faced with the choice of paying increased transaction costs now or waiting to flatten the position opportunistically, often will choose the latter. It may very well be that some use of the second option is beneficial, but experience shows that too much of the "wait for a better price to hedge" philosophy can result in bad outcomes.

---

[5] TARN is an acronym for *target accrual redemption note*, in which target or capped payout features are appended to an underlying structure.

This leads to the following question: How does the volatility surface behave as a function of the forward price? This question has implications for the effective delta of any options portfolio, even those comprised solely of vanilla options.

This basic question can be refined as follows: Given a prescribed change in the underlying forward price, what inference can be made about the change in the implied volatility surface? In the context of energy commodities, which often show pronounced skew, assumptions about the dynamics of volatility surfaces as a function of changes in forward prices can affect the value of delta meaningfully.

The volatility look-up protocol implicitly assumes that the ATM volatility does not change because of forward price movements. This is commonly referred to as the *floating-skew convention* because the default estimate for the new volatility surface given the new forward price is that the volatility surface shifted in tandem with the forward price with shape unchanged. As prices move, the volatility surface appears fixed when viewed in reference to the forward price but changes for any fixed strike option. By using the form $\bar{\sigma}(\kappa)$ earlier, we have implicitly been using a floating-skew convention.

The other hypothesis most frequently discussed is *sticky skew*, in which the volatility surface is parameterized by absolute strike $\bar{\sigma}(K)$. Here the volatility surface is fixed with respect to option strike and moves when viewed from the reference of the prevailing forward price $F(t,T)$.

The value functions for an option at strike K takes the following forms for the two hypotheses:

$$
V[t,F,K,\bar{\sigma}(\cdot)] = \begin{cases} V[t,F,K,\bar{\sigma}(K)] & \text{Sticky skew} \\ V\{t,F,K,\bar{\sigma}\,[\log(K/F)]\} & \text{Floating skew} \end{cases} \tag{8.1}
$$

where we have eliminated extraneous arguments (such as tenor and rates) from the value function. As a consequence, delta under the floating-skew hypothesis is not the standard delta obtained from Black but is rather the total derivative:

$$
\frac{dV}{dF} = \frac{\partial V}{\partial F} + \frac{\partial V}{\partial \bar{\sigma}} \cdot \frac{d\bar{\sigma}\,[\log(K/F)]}{dF} \tag{8.2}
$$

To illustrate the effect, consider the volatility surface for the December 2008 NG Dec08 contract on February 14, 2008 shown in Figure 8.10. For a call with strike corresponding to a price ratio $\pi = 1.20$, we have

$$
\frac{d\bar{\sigma}\,[\log(K/F)]}{dF} < 0
$$

This is so because as the forward price F increases, the price ratio K/F decreases, so $\bar{\sigma}(\kappa)$ decreases due to the call skew. Therefore, the skew-adjusted *floating* delta will be lower than the *sticky* (Black) delta. The

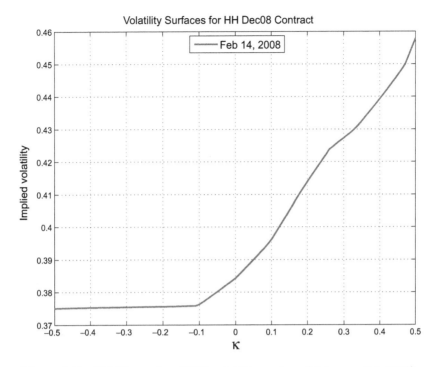

Figure 8.10. NG December 2008 volatility surface (February 14, 2008).

magnitude of the second term in (8.2) can be significant. In this example, the forward price is $F = 50.40$, and the strike corresponding to $\pi = 1.20$ is $K = 11.62$, with the comparative results

- Sticky skew: $\Delta = 0.365$
- Floating skew[6]: $\Delta = 0.304$

From the perspective of the trader hedging the position, this is a significant difference.

So which of these paradigms is more consistent with empirical behavior? The results are not particularly compelling in part because any difference between the two approaches appears to be small relative to daily changes in implied volatility levels. For example, an analysis of Henry Hub monthly volatilities in which contracts in the range January 2008 to December 2010 were used between twelve months and one month to contract expiry yields ambiguous results.[7] For each trading day t, forecasts for the volatility surface on the next trading day $t + dt$ were made for price ratios π in the interval $[0.8, 1.2]$. The sticky forecast is that the volatilities for options at strikes

---

[6] The skew-adjusted delta is obtained perturbatively by moving F to $F + 0.10$, interpolating the volatility skew array and evaluating the option.

[7] The last month of life of the option was excluded because of the potential distortions arising from small values of the term variance $\bar{\sigma}^2 T$.

$\vec{K} = \vec{\pi} F(t, T)$ are unchanged:

$$\hat{\sigma}_S(\vec{K}) = \bar{\sigma} \left[t, \frac{\vec{K}}{F(t, T)} \right]$$

The floating forecast is that the new volatility will be

$$\hat{\sigma}_F(\vec{K}) = \bar{\sigma} \left[t, \frac{\vec{K}}{F(t + dt, T)} \right]$$

The error used is the L^2 norm of estimate versus actual: $\|\hat{\sigma}(\vec{K}) - \bar{\sigma}(t + dt, \vec{K})\|_2$. The two paradigms yielded nearly equivalent performance, with a floating error of 0.0132 and a sticky error of 0.0136. In each case, the prediction error is of the order of a volatility point, which is substantial; clearly, there are other drivers of the volatility surface beyond merely the dynamics of the underlying forward curve.[8] This is far from a complete study, but it serves to illustrate the fact that the nature of the dynamics is not obvious. The opinions of natural gas options traders vary widely on this point, and the truth is probably somewhere between the floating- and sticky-skew hypotheses.

Parameterizing Skew

The search for more sophisticated models that handle skew using a single stochastic process starts with an understanding of the empirical behavior of the volatility surface, not merely the sticky versus floating issue earlier, but also on the effects of tenor and fundamental variables on skew dynamics. We will focus again on West Texas Intermediate (WTI), which eliminates the seasonality issues that continue to challenge modeling efforts.

Figure 8.11 shows skew for the WTI December 2011 contract on three dates. Crude oil volatility surfaces have historically exhibited both call and put skew regimes as well as both. As seen for natural gas, as the tenor of the contract decreases, the implied volatility typically increases. It is interesting to note, however, that the minimum volatility in the surface is often achieved at strikes that are greater than the forward price (i.e., $\kappa > 0$). To examine relative levels of skew, as before, we put these on an equal footing by normalizing the volatility surfaces by the prevailing ATM volatility at each date; this is shown in Figure 8.12. Skew (in this case, put skew) is more extreme at shorter tenors.

Two questions arise naturally from these figures. First, was the use of price ratio κ as the metric for strike versus forward price the right thing to do?

---

[8] The topic of whether the volatility surface is driven solely by forward dynamics has, to the surprise of anyone trading options books, garnered a fair amount of attention within the academic community. This work goes under the term *unspanned stochastic volatility*. See, for example, [TS09].

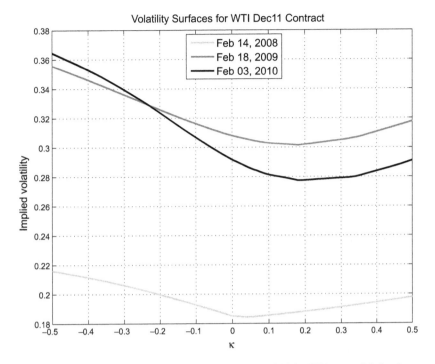

Figure 8.11. Volatility surfaces for December 2011 WTI at multiple dates.

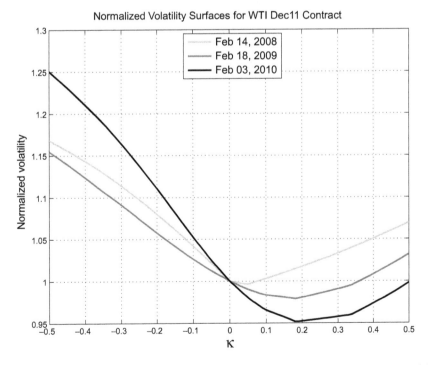

Figure 8.12. Normalized volatility surfaces for December 2011 WTI at multiple dates.

Second, why did we choose to normalize skew by ratios to ATM volatility as opposed to, say, differences?

On the first question, much of the literature on the subject of volatility dynamics parameterizes skew as a function of $\kappa \equiv \log(K/F)$, thereby preserving a natural returns orientation. However, if we think of skew as a perturbation around a GBM price process, the returns distribution has a standard deviation that scales as $\bar{\sigma}\sqrt{T}$. A more natural parameterization of strike distance is therefore $\lambda \equiv \kappa/\bar{\sigma}\sqrt{T}$. This term appears, of course, in the Black-Scholes option pricing formulas, and it is conventional to take one additional step and parameterize skew in terms of the Δ of standard options.[9]

Using call option implied volatilities, as the Δ of a call decreases with strike, it is conventional to preserve the natural monotonicity by using $\bar{\sigma}(1-\Delta)$ or, equivalently, the negative of the delta of the put at the same strike. Thus, in what follows, $\bar{\sigma}(0.9)$, for example, refers to a strike that is above the underlying price, corresponding to a call with $\Delta = 0.1$ or put with $\Delta = -0.9$. Finally, because the Δ of an option depends on the implied volatility, this reasoning is a bit circular; however, the natural "engineering" solution and market convention is to obtain strikes from Δ values calculated using the ATM volatility.

Recalling that the (undiscounted) delta of a call struck at K is $\Delta_K = \Phi(d_1)$, where $\Phi(\cdot)$ denotes the standard normal distribution function, and

$$d_1 = \frac{\ln(F/K) + \frac{1}{2}\bar{\sigma}_{\mathrm{ATM}}^2 T}{\bar{\sigma}_{\mathrm{ATM}}\sqrt{T}}$$

a given Δ corresponds to a strike K given by

$$K = Fe^{\left[-\bar{\sigma}_{\mathrm{ATM}}\sqrt{T}\Phi^{-1}(1-\Delta) + \frac{1}{2}\bar{\sigma}_{\mathrm{ATM}}^2\right]}$$

This provides the mapping between strike and Δ used in parameterizing volatilty surfaces by delta.

The second question pertains to the appropriate way to think of the magnitude of skew. Does skew scale with volatility level? Analysis is complicated by the fact that skew can be put call, or mixed in direction and varying with tenor. In the following analysis, the tenor is fixed, and a one-year constant-maturity volatility surface is created using linear interpolation of the volatility grid from January 2007 to December 2010.[10] Figure 8.13 shows a scatter plot of the standard deviation of the implied volatilities on the Δ grid: $\vec{\Delta} \equiv [0.4, 0.5, 0.6]$ (effectively the L^2 norm) versus the implied volatility at $\Delta = 0.5$, which we have termed the *ATM volatility*. Notice the

---

[9] Options traders use volatility for fixed strikes when discussing specific trades or quotes but use volatility as a function of Δ in more qualitative discussions.

[10] The tenor was $T = 0.9863$ purely due to grid construction.

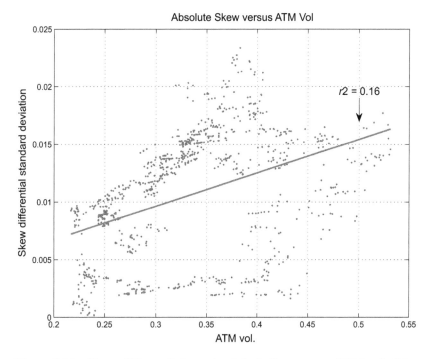

Figure 8.13. Skew differential standard deviation versus ATM volatility.

increase in this skew metric as a function of volatility level, as evidenced by the linear regression. Alternatively, if we replace the standard deviation of the implied volatilities with the standard deviation of the ratios, specifically $\mathrm{std}\left[\bar{\sigma}(\vec{\Delta})/\bar{\sigma}(0.5)\right]$, the results are as shown in Figure 8.14. This has no discernible dependence on volatility level and hence points to the fact that the ratio of the implied volatilities to the ATM volatilities is the more natural representation of skew.

Effect of Inventory

What drives skew?

Daily variations in flow can have meaningful short-term effects. Large transactions of the type described in the working problem can result in temporary demand for option hedges that can distort the volatility surface; this is true in all markets, not just energy. In addition, as we will see in the next section, skew changes systematically with tenor. On longer time scales, however, fundamental drivers are relevant, most notably inventory levels.

Figure 8.15 shows normalized skew versus OECD crude oil inventory levels using the same one-year-tenor interpolated data over the same time

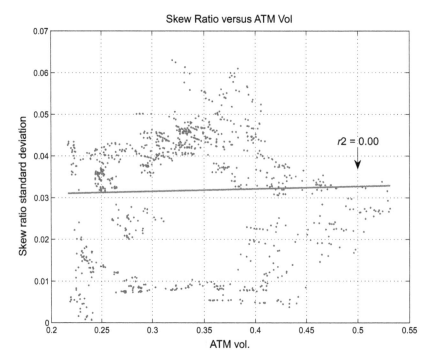

Figure 8.14. Skew ratio standard deviation versus ATM volatility.

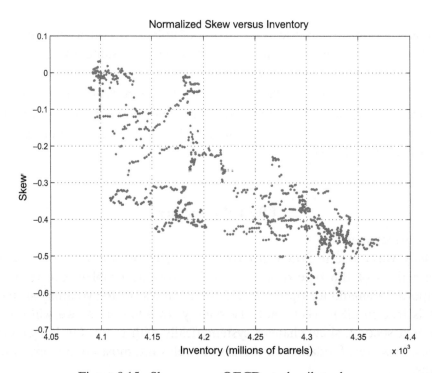

Figure 8.15. Skew versus OECD crude oil stocks.

period.[11] With a skew metric defined as the slope of a linear interpolation of $\bar{\sigma}(\vec{\Delta})$ versus the same grid $\vec{\Delta} \equiv [0.4, 0.5, 0.6]$, normalized skew is calculated the same way with the modification that the regression is on the normalized volatilities $\left[\bar{\sigma}(\vec{\Delta})/\bar{\sigma}(0.5)\right]$. Put skew (corresponding to a negative slope) increases systematically as inventory levels increase. Heuristically, at high inventory levels, negative fluctuations in demand (increases in net supply) are harder to absorb into inventory than positive fluctuations are to alleviate. This results in skew to the downside. Inventory levels have a significant effect on the dynamics of implied volatility surfaces.

Skew Dynamics: Effect of Tenor

There is an important remaining question: How does skew behave as a function of tenor? Our snapshots of NG and WTI volatility surfaces earlier suggest an increase in prevailing skew as option expiry is approached.

Focusing on crude oil, WTI skew can exhibit put or call skew, as well as mixed skew, as seen in Figure 8.12. To characterize "how much skew" is present, we first interpolate implied volatility series by tenor for a grid $\mathcal{I}$ of κs or Δs (e.g., $\mathcal{I} \equiv \vec{\Delta} = \{0.4, 0.5, 0.6\}$ would use the skew at these values of Δ), thereby creating a constant-maturity representation. For each trading day t, we compute the maximum departure of the ratio of the implied volatilities to the reference (ATM) volatility, which we will refer to as the *normalized skew*:

$$S(t, t+\tau) \equiv \max_{K \in \mathcal{I}} \left| \frac{\bar{\sigma}_K(t, t+\tau)}{\bar{\sigma}_{K^*}(t, t+\tau)} - 1 \right|$$

Here K denotes the strikes in the grid $\mathcal{I}$, and K^* denotes the reference strike corresponding to $\kappa = 0$ or $\Delta = 1/2$. We have suppressed some notational rigor here because the strikes $K \in \mathcal{I}$ depend on both t and τ, but the concept should be clear: $S(t, t+\tau)$ represents how much variation in volatilities is present across a range of strikes relative to the reference (ATM) volatility at tenor τ. Finally, we calculate the average value

$$\bar{S}(\vec{\tau}) \equiv \frac{1}{N} \sum_{n=1}^{N} S(t_n, t_n + \vec{\tau})$$

over the data set for a grid of tenors $\vec{\tau}$, thereby yielding a profile of the typical skew level as a function of tenor.

Figure 8.16 shows the results using data from 2007 through 2010 and choosing the interval based on price ratio π: $\mathcal{I} = \{\pi \in [0.8, 1.2]\}$. Viewed from this perspective, skew is clearly diverging as $\tau \to 0$. If we look at the

---

[11] The period January 2007 to December 2010 is before the large decoupling of WTI from global markets for the idiosyncratic reasons discussed in Chapter 3.

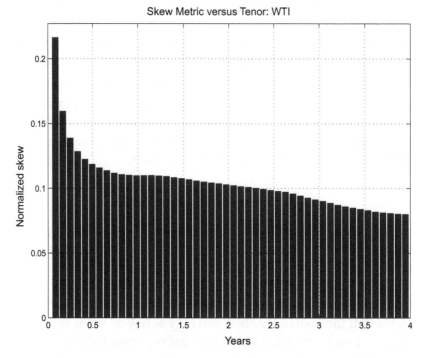

Figure 8.16. WTI skew versus tenor (price-ratio metric).

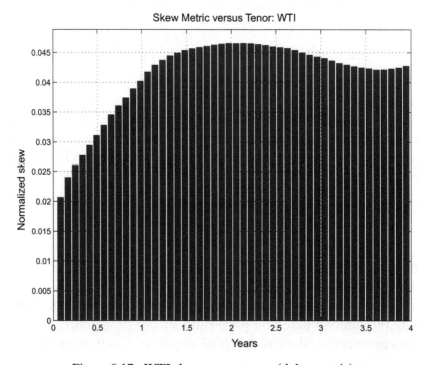

Figure 8.17. WTI skew versus tenor (delta metric).

same phenomenon from a delta perspective, the picture is more interesting. Figure 8.17 shows the results using $\mathcal{I} = \{\Delta \in [0.4, 0.6]\}$. This is qualitatively different and shows that skew viewed on a length scale consistent with the width of the returns distribution is initially an increasing function of tenor, out to a range of approximately two years, and then decreasing at longer tenors.[12]

A Digression on Power Options

Our previous analysis was focused exclusively on WTI and NG. Power options and their volatility surfaces can exhibit much higher implied volatilities and skew, at least for some option types, than we have seen so far. Liquidity away from the ATM options is severely limited, however, so our discussions of volatility structure will remain more heuristic than those for WTI and NG earlier. The close relationship between natural gas and power would suggest that for similar option types, specifically for options with monthly exercise, many of the features would be similar between the two commodities.

For power options, the underlying is one of the standard swaps or forwards, with delivery in the peak or off-peak buckets as described in Chapter 3. Most options liquidity is in the peak products, with limited trading volume in off-peak options. As with the swaps markets, the standard notional is 50 MW in eastern markets and 25 MW for the west. There are three commonly traded option types.

- *Swaptions.* These are options in which exercise results in a swap position in a strip of contracts at a fixed strike K. The most commonly traded swaptions are *calendar swaptions*, in which the underlying is a calendar strip. Exercise is usually a week or two before the first delivery month and is specified by trade. The terminal value of the swap at option expiry τ is $V_\tau = 1/12 \sum_m d(\tau, T_m)[F(\tau, T_m) - K]$. For example, a call swaption has a value at expiry of $\max(V_\tau, 0)$. As options on a basket of forward contracts, valuation of swaptions involves modeling the joint dynamics of multiple forward prices.
- *Monthly options.* These are options that exercise into swaps, or in some cases physical power, for settlement or delivery in a single contract month. Exercise is usually two business days ("$-2b$") before the delivery month in the eastern U.S. markets and five business days ("$-5b$") for the west. The value at expiration is based on the difference between $F_m(T_e) - K$ for contract month m, where K is the strike and T_e denotes option expiry. For example, the value of a call at expiration is $N_m \max[F_m(T_e) - K, 0]$, where N_m denotes the number of MWh in the delivery

---

[12] The slight increase visible near four years is an artifact resulting from what is effectively a smaller data set for the longest tenors.

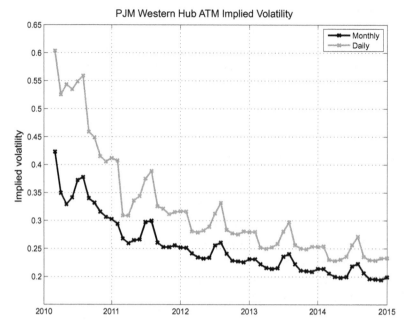

Figure 8.18. PJM ATM volatility term structure (February 3, 2010).

bucket for the month.[13] These options are the closest analogue to monthly listed
options in natural gas.

- *Daily options.* Daily options also trade by contract month. A daily option for
  a particular month for peak power consists of a set of distinct options, one for
  each peak delivery day in the month (typically twenty to twenty-two options in
  a month depending on day count and holidays). The typical form is for manual
  (phone) exercise by 10 a.m. one business day before the delivery day, and the settlement amount is $\sum_{d \in m} \mathbf{1}_{E_d}[F(d,d) - K]$, where $d \in m$ denotes the active delivery
  days in the option during month m, and E_d denotes the event that the option was
  exercised for day d.[14,15] Less commonly traded are autoexercise, which settle on
  $\sum_{d \in m} \max[F(d,d) - K, 0]$; this is lookback exercise.

Implied volatilities for power exhibit seasonality that is consistent with
the power forward curve. Figure 8.18 shows the ATM implied volatilities for monthly and daily options in PJM. Daily volatility is dramatically
higher than monthly volatility at short tenors – a manifestation of the

---

[13] We have ignored discounting here; settlement on the swap is almost always in the following month,
and risk systems will, of course, apply the discounting to the settlement date.

[14] The notation $\mathbf{1}_A$ is referred to as the *indicator function* for event A and takes the value 1 if A
occurs; zero otherwise.

[15] Note that $\mathbf{1}_{E_d}[F(d,d) - K]$ can be negative. This arises when, at the time of exercise the price for
next-day power, $F(d-1,d)$ is in the money, and the option is exercised. However, the final index
$F(d,d)$ as computed by the ISO can be out-of-the-money, hence resulting in a negative value.
This does not mean that the trader erred. On exercise on $d-1$, the power is presumably sold
immediately (in the case of a call option) at the price $F(d-1,d)$, thereby locking in the intrinsic
value.

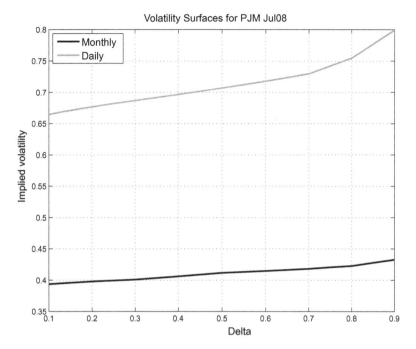

Figure 8.19. PJM volatility surface for July 2008 and October 2009 contract (March 3, 2008).

high spot volatility observed in power prices. In addition, as with forward prices, summer implied volatilities are systematically higher than other contract months, once again reflecting that market participants are aware of Figure 3.42, where high variance in spot prices occurs at the highest levels of demand, which typically occur in the summer months. Note also that the difference between monthly and daily ATM volatilities decreases with tenor, as it should. As tenor increases, the returns variance increases, and the forward price at expiry is increasingly likely to be far from the current forward price, in which case the two options types are economically equivalent.[16]

There can be a significant difference in skew between monthly and daily power options. Figure 8.19 shows monthly and daily volatilities for the July 2008 contract as of roughly three months prior to delivery. Note the high levels of implied volatility and skew for the daily options, which are more pronounced than for monthly options.

It is commonly stated that power is the most volatile energy commodity, for that matter, the most volatile of all commodities. This statement is usually made with daily implied volatilities in mind. However, a more appropriate comparison is between natural gas implied volatilities for listed

---

[16] They are, however, not ergonomically equivalent because the trader still must manually exercise each daily option, even when the options are flagrantly in the money.

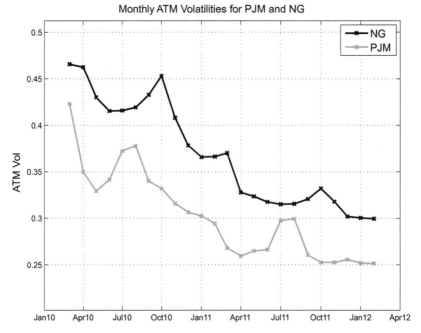

Figure 8.20. NG and PJM monthly ATM volatilities (February 3, 2010).

(monthly) options and those for monthly power options.[17] In this case, the results are not what many would expect. Figure 8.20 shows the term structure for the ATM NG and PJM monthly options. The reason that monthly power volatilities are lower than for the natural gas analogues is due to the nonlinear relationship between power and natural gas prices discussed in Chapter 6. Recall Figure 6.10, which showed that the forward heat rate: $H(t,T) = F(t,T)/G(t,T)$, where F and G denote power and natural gas forward prices, increases systematically as natural gas prices decrease. The model used in Chapter 6 was the linear form $F(t,T) = \alpha + \beta G(t,T) + \epsilon(t)$, which fits the observed heat-rate behavior tolerably well. If we assume that the residuals $\epsilon(t)$ are stationary with relatively small variance in comparison with cumulative natural gas returns, then power returns can be written as

$$\frac{dF(t,T)}{F(t,T)} = \frac{\beta dG(t,T)}{\alpha + \beta G(t,T)} < \frac{dG(t,T)}{G(t,T)}$$

where the inequality is holds because $\alpha > 0$. The behavior of the heat rate as a result of changing natural gas prices serves to dampen the power price fluctuations and explains why monthly power volatilities are almost always meaningfully lower than their analogous natural gas implied volatilities.

---

[17] Daily options of a forward-starting form, namely, the IFERC/Gas Daily options described in Appendix D, are traded in natural gas, although they are much less liquid than daily options in power.

Skew Dynamics: Implications for Model Selection

The empirical characteristics of skew dynamics provide some guidance as to potentially viable modeling approaches. Valuation of many skew-dependent structures requires stochastic processes that are at least roughly consistent with the empirical dynamics of volatility surfaces and that can be calibrated to observed market data. In what follows we will briefly survey the features of common approaches to modeling volatility surfaces, in addition to discussing the challenges in applying these in the context of energy markets.

The development of approaches to handle skew across a broad array of asset classes has typically focused on three general modeling paradigms, some of which have been used in tandem:

- Local volatility
- Stochastic volatility
- Jump diffusions

The following summary draws heavily on Gatheral's rendition of the subject [Gat06].

The local volatility approach developed by both Dupire [Dup94] and Derman and Kani [DK94] modifies the Black-Scholes framework by allowing local volatility to depend on the underlying state variable. In the context of Black, this modification is of the form

$$\frac{dF_t}{F_t} = \sigma(t, F_t)dB_t \tag{8.3}$$

Under such dynamics, the function $\sigma(t, F_t)$ can be inferred from the option value surface

$$\sigma^2(t, K; F_0) = \frac{\partial C/\partial T}{\frac{1}{2}K^2(\partial^2 C/\partial K^2)} \tag{8.4}$$

where $C(T, K)$ is the value of the call with strike K expiring at time T. It is assumed that the options markets have enough liquidity to generate smooth interpolates of the value surface $C(T, K)$.

There are two major problems with this approach. The first is common across the asset classes to which this has been applied, in particular, equities, in which the skew dynamics implied by (8.3) is simply at variance with what is observed. Local volatility models imply that volatility surfaces move in the opposite direction of the change in the underlying (one might call this *antifloating*) [HKLW91]. The second commodities-specific problem is that unlike in equities, where you have a fighting chance of constructing a continuous surface of call option prices on the *same* underlying, in energy, the only available option prices for the specific underlying $F(t, T_m)$ expire at $T_m^{(e)} \lesssim T_m$. The difficulties in constructing a useful continuous surface $C(T, K)$ in equities are well known; in commodities it is impossible, at least within the framework of modeling a single underlying forward contract. This limitation is the reason that skew modeling in energy is inherently a multi-factor endeavor, which complicates matters greatly.

The stochastic volatility approach has more traction. The general framework is given by the following joint diffusions:

$$dF_t = \Phi(T-t)v_t F_t dB_t^{(1)}$$
$$dv_t = \alpha(t, F_t, v_t)dt + \eta\beta(t, F_t, v_t)dB_t^{(2)}$$

where η denotes the "volatility of volatility," and the correlation between the driving Brownian motions is $\langle dB_t^{(1)}, dB_t^{(2)} \rangle = \rho dt$. This is the form specified in [Gat06] modified by $\Phi(T-t)$ to accommodate volatility backwardation. This form is too general for tractable solutions, and the search for quasi-tractable subsets of this class of diffusions has yielded some viable candidates that rely on transform methods to obtain European option pricing formulas.[18]

One such is the Heston model, which in our setting takes the form

$$dF_t = \Phi(T-t)v_t F_t dB_t^{(1)}$$
$$dv_t = \lambda(v_t - v^*)dt + \eta\sqrt{v_t}dB_t^{(2)} \tag{8.5}$$

It is unclear whether the transform methods can accommodate the backwardation modification $\Phi(T-t)$, but the basic attributes that have been established for the $\Phi \equiv 1$ case shed light on what we can expect from this slightly modified form.

The asymptotic behavior of skew as a function of tenor for (8.5) with $\Phi \equiv 1$ is well understood (see [Gat06]). Parameterizing skew using price ratio or κ, specifically not reducing the length scale by $\bar{\sigma}T^{1/2}$, the typical skew profile for stochastic volatility models shows an initial increase with tenor, transitioning ultimately to decreasing skew at long tenors. Comparing this with the visual portrayal in Figure 8.16, one can immediately see problems. The asymptotic decrease at long tenors is consistent with empirical behavior. However, the observed decrease in skew at short tenors suggests that unless we use a tortured set of time-varying parameters, a pure stochastic volatility framework will fail to match the behavior at both short and long tenors.

The third general approach to skew modeling is via jump diffusions, in which jumps driven by a Poisson process are superimposed on the standard Brownian-motion returns [Gat06]. The basic framework is

$$\frac{dF_t}{F_t} = \mu_t dt + \Phi(T-t)[\sigma dB_t + (J-1)dq_t] \tag{8.6}$$

---

[18] The criterion for fast computation of vanilla options is to facilitate calibration; exotics usually require simulation-based approaches, which are much more time-consuming but viable if not included in calibrations.

where dq_t is a Poisson process with jump rate $\lambda(t)$[19] independent of B_t, and the jump size J is a random variable, independent of B_t and q_t, with density f_J having support on $[0,\infty)$. At each Poisson event, F_t jumps to JF_t. To preserve the martingale property for F, the drift needs to compensate for the expected jump size occurring at rate $\lambda(t)$:

$$\mu_t = -\lambda(t)E(J-1) \tag{8.7}$$

This expression is referred to as the *compensator* for the jump process.

Jump diffusions are a much less subtle way of forcing skew than stochastic volatility. However, the somewhat "spiky" behavior of energy spot prices has engendered interest in applying this class of models to energy options, particularly in power. Positive jumps have a negative compensator μ_J that results in behavior that is consistent with intuition – positive jumps yield positive (call) skew.

It is known that jump diffusions exhibit rapid decay of skew beyond a characteristic time scale, which is at variance with the slow decay shown in Figure 8.16. Jump diffusions alone do not appear to be up to the task of explaining the empirical behavior of skew dynamics. However, the asymptotic behavior at long tenors is what stochastic volatility models (arguably) get right. Together, each could potentially handle behavior at different tenors, leading naturally to hybrid models combining the two approaches, so-called stochastic volatility/jump diffusion models.

The hybrid of stochastic volatility and jumps is appealing because the approach is effectively fusing the rapid initial decay of jump diffusions with a slower T^{-1} decay at longer time scales. However, calibration is problematic in the commodities setting once again because of the limited set of traded options. In equities, calibration is more tractable by separation of time scales – short-tenor options can be used to calibrate jump parameters; long-tenor options can be used to calibrate stochastic volatility parameters. Modification of the little-t approach from Chapter 7 along the lines of

$$\frac{dF_t}{F_t} = \mu_t dt + \Phi(T-t)\left[v_t dB_t^{(1)} + (J-1)dq_t\right] \tag{8.8}$$

$$dv_t = \lambda(v_t - v^*)dt + \eta\sqrt{v_t}dB_t^{(2)} \tag{8.9}$$

could potentially facilitate calibration using separation of time scales as in equities.

---

[19] $dq_t = 1$ with probability $\lambda(t)dt$ and 0 otherwise.

Conclusion

The issues that we have surveyed relating to skew dynamics and its impact on valuation and hedging have yet to be definitively resolved – no real consensus has been reached, and research continues. A few themes stand out, however:

- The significant levels of skew observed in energy markets makes even basic issues, such as the appropriate computation of Greeks, ambiguous and model-dependent.
- Among the common approaches to skew modeling, the dynamics of skew exhibits qualitative features that suggest elements of both stochastic volatility and jumps.
- Calibration of hybrid price processes governing a single forward price combining stochastic volatility and jumps is challenging because of the limited set of traded options.
- Multifactor models extending the little-t approach from Chapter 7 could potentially render calibration of hybrid models tractable.

The fact that skew dynamics is so clearly related to inventory and hence, by extension, forward yields suggests that more sophisticated (and arguably yet to be developed) models will ultimately be required to unify the relationship between forward yields, returns correlations, and skew.

9

Correlation

Up to this point, our focus has been on single-commodity options structures. These are commonly used by producers and consumers to hedge their natural positions, as well as by speculators or investors desiring levered exposure in some form. As a general rule across asset classes, however, options markets of meaningful depth usually result from "natural" sources of optionality. Mortgages provide the best and certainly the largest example. Typical home mortgages have embedded prepayment options that are a major reason for the existence of closely related interest-rate swaptions markets. For energy markets, it is infrastructure, essential to the basic balancing of supply and demand, that is the natural source of "steel in the ground" optionality.

A power generator is, to a first approximation, an option to convert a fuel to electricity – a call option on the spread between the input and output commodity prices. A natural gas pipeline connecting one delivery point to another is an option on the spread between two locational prices. A natural gas storage facility, as we will see later, is a complex structure that can loosely be thought of as a combination of options on the spread between forward prices with different delivery times.

Spread options are by far the dominant natural source of optionality in energy markets. It is in the valuation and hedging of spread options that correlation risk first arises. The methods commonly used to value spread options are discussed in standard references [Hul12, Shr04], although the very high correlations that usually arise in energy spread options raise issues that are not typically encountered in other contexts, such as equities basket options.

Common Correlation Structures

Single-commodity spread options come in two basic flavors: time spread and locational spread. The former have a natural source of optionality in storage facilities; the latter in shipping, transportation (pipelines), and transmission (power lines).

The most common time-spread structures are calendar spread options (CSOs), which are options on underlying spreads of the form $F(\tau, T_2) - F(\tau, T_1)$, where τ denotes expiry.[1] A CSO straddle, for example, has a payoff of the form $|F(\tau, T_2) - F(\tau, T_1)|$. In general, there is also a strike K to accommodate forward yields: $F(\tau, T_2) - F(\tau, T_1) - K$. Markets in CSOs are not particularly deep, and liquidity is concentrated in the benchmark futures contracts such as West Texas Intermediate (WTI) and natural gas (NG).

Calendar swaptions in natural gas and power provide another example. The terminal value of a swaption is based on the present value of the swap at exercise:

$$S_\tau \equiv \sum_m d(\tau, T_m) w_m [F(\tau, T_m) - K]$$

where w_m is the notional quantity of the swap in contract month m, which can vary due to day count.[2] A call swaption, for example, has a terminal payoff of the form $\max(S_\tau, 0)$. While not often considered spread options, swaptions are, in fact, options on a linear combination of contract prices $\vec{w}^\dagger F(\tau, \vec{T})$ and therefore warrant this classification.

Turning to locational optionality, basis options settle on spreads of the form $S_\tau \equiv F_2(\tau, T) - F_1(\tau, T)$, where subscripts index different delivery locations. This is an idealization of the actual mechanics since in most instances each leg fixes at slightly different times and with different averaging conventions. These are technical points in the greater scheme of things.

The various option types just listed can be combined. For example, locational time-spread options, while much less common than CSOs, can arise naturally as hedges for time-spread risk between say Brent and WTI, where delivery times also can be distinct due to the time required to ship crude oil between Europe and the United States.

Multiple-commodity spread options arise naturally from conversion infrastructure such as power generation and refineries. The primary purpose of these structures is to hedge the value of an asset in order to facilitate financing the purchase of an existing asset or to fund the construction of a new asset. A lender is generally not inclined to assume the commodity-linked default risk and requires that the value of an asset against which financing is sought be hedged for some period of time.

---

[1] The term *calendar* can be misinterpreted as referring to options on spreads between calendar strips. Most CSOs are, in fact, on monthly spreads.

[2] Note that here and in what follows, for ease of notation, we will assume that settlement is either at delivery or option exercise as convenient. In practice, settlement often occurs at other dates defined by the trade confirm, and the modification of discounting is straigthforward.

Tolling deals are structures designed to hedge a power generator that converts a fuel or, in some cases, multiple fuels into electricity. The term *tolling* is often rigorously interpreted as meaning a transaction in which the buyer of the option has operational control of the generator and is responsible for physical procurement of the fuel and sale of the electricity. Financially settling transactions of the same mathematical form are more common; these are often referred to as *heat-rate options* or *spark-spread options*. Here we will simply use the term *tolling* for both cases.

The typical tolling deal involves daily optionality: exercise for day d results in a spark-spread swap of the form $F_B(d,d) - H_*G(d,d)$, where F_B denotes the power price for a particular delivery bucket B (e.g., "5x16"), and G denotes the fuel price, usually natural gas. The heat rate H_* defines the spark spread underlying the transaction and is typically close to that of a generator being hedged.

The exercise convention is almost always manual (by phone) exercise on the day preceding delivery, usually before 10 a.m. The manual exercise payoff is $[F_B(d,d) - H_*G(d,d) - V]\mathbf{1}_{E_d}$, where E_d denotes the event that the option was exercised on day $d - 1$. Much less commonly traded "autoexercise" tolls have a lookback payoff for day d of $[F_B(d,d) - H_* G(d,d) - V]^+$. In either case, the valuation problem is of the form

$$V = \tilde{E}\left\{\sum_m d(0, T_m)C \sum_{d \in B(m)} [F_B(\tau_d,d) - H_*G(\tau_d,d) - V]^+\right\} \quad (9.1)$$

where m indexes calendar months, d is days, and τ_d denotes the exercise date for day d. Also, $B(m)$ denotes the days in the month m corresponding to the delivery bucket, C denotes the capacity (hourly quantity), and V is a strike in units of \$/MWh. Usually C is between 50 MW (for small OTC broker trades) to over 1,000 MW for large asset hedges. Typical combined-cycle generators or groups thereof will have capacities between 400 and 2000 MW.

OTC tolls transacted over the broker markets, which are always financial, involve up-front premium payment. Larger tolls arising from asset hedging programs are usually structured with monthly capacity payments over the life of the transaction. This serves to mitigate credit risk because the owner of the asset (and the seller of the toll) is often unrated and is using the asset as collateral for the transaction. Tolls are usually quoted in one of the following two forms (in what follows, V is the present value of the toll and C is the capacity in megawatts)[3]:

- *Up-front premium (USD/MWh).* This is the broker market convention obtained by:

$$\frac{V}{\sum_m Q_m} \quad (9.2)$$

---

[3] In power, our examples are taken from U.S. markets, hence the USD currency convention.

where $Q_m = C\sum_{d\in B(m)} N_h(d)$ is the monthly notional calculated from the number of hours N_h in the bucket B on day d.

- *Monthly capacity payment (USD/kW-mo)*. Monthly payments are typically quoted in USD/kilowatt-month, calculated as

$$\frac{V}{1,000C\sum_m d(0,T_m)} \tag{9.3}$$

Note that $V/[\sum_m d(0,T_m)]$ is the monthly annuity that has present value equal to V. The factor of 1,000 simply converts the result to the result kilowatts from megawatts.

Crack spread options are another example of conversion optionality. These are options on the spread between the prices of a refined product, or a basket of refined products, and a reference crude oil price:

$$\max[F_{\text{Product}}(\tau,T) - F_{\text{Crude}}(\tau,T),0] \tag{9.4}$$

The product is usually heating oil or gasoline, although other commonly traded crack spread options reference multiple products, in which case the underlying spread is of the form $\vec{w}^\dagger \vec{F}_{\text{Products}}(\tau,T) - F_{\text{crude}}(\tau,T)$, where $\vec{w}$ defines the weights defining the refined products basket. The options are usually either monthly exercise or Asian lookback. Crack spreads options are typically traded in "vanilla" form and, unlike tolling deals, are usually less tailored to specific assets.

Each of the preceding structures has a common mathematical form, and all require as valuation inputs the relevant forwards and implied volatilities surfaces, as well as the new ingredient – pairwise returns correlations.

Basic Spread Option Valuation: Margrabe

There is a substantial body of work on a variety of methods to "properly" value spread options and related physical assets. Some are risk-neutral-based and predicated on dynamic hedging; others depart from the assumption of market completeness and are predicated on models, usually simulation-based, of the physical measure. The unambiguous starting point for spread option valuation, however, is the framework developed by Margrabe [Mar78], which effectively extended Black-Scholes to options on spreads when underlying prices are driven by GBMs. While more sophisticated approaches can yield different results, the qualitative results for valuation and hedging obtained via Margrabe are shared by most enhanced models.

The Margrabe pricing framework, derived in Appendix A, values options on spreads between two assets, for example, a call option with expiry τ and terminal payoff $\max[F(\tau,T_1) - H_*G(\tau,T_2),0]$. In our context, F and G are the forward prices of two possibly distinct commodities with potentially different delivery locations and times. H_* is a multiplier, which in the case of distinct commodities is a conversion factor such as a heat rate of a generator.

The starting premise in Margrabe is two underlying GBM drivers:

$$dF(t, T_1) = \sigma_F F(t, T_1) dB_t^{(F)}$$
$$dG(t, T_2) = \sigma_G G(t, T_2) dB_t^{(G)}$$

The correlation between the two Brownian motions is ρ. As shown in Appendix A, the value of this call spread option is given by

$$V[0, F(0, T_1), G(0, T_2)] = d(\tau)[F(0, T_1)N(d_1) - H_* G(0, T_2)N(d_2)] \quad (9.5)$$

with

$$d_{1,2} = \frac{\log\left[\frac{F(0,T_1)}{H_* G(0,T_2)}\right] \pm \frac{1}{2}\hat{\sigma}^2}{\hat{\sigma}} \quad (9.6)$$

where

$$\hat{\sigma}^2 = \tau\left(\sigma_F^2 + \sigma_G^2 - 2\rho\sigma_F\sigma_G\right) \quad (9.7)$$

Extensions to deterministic volatility where $\sigma_{F,G} \equiv \sigma_{F,G}(T-t)$ to accommodate volatility backwardation are straightforward, as we will see in our first example.

Application to CSOs

The following shows a sample of broker chat pertaining to WTI CSOs on April 15, 2011:

> 9:11:13—CSO K/M -0.50 call 2/12 (ref-0.58)
> 09:56:18—CSO N/Q -0.30 straddle..49/65
> 09:58:41—CSO N/Q -0.30 straddle..50/60
> **10:00:01—CSO N/Q 0.00 call 12/20 (ref-0.31)**
> 10:00:21—CSO N/Q -0.30 straddle..52/60
> 10:03:18—CSO K/M -0.50 call 2/10 (ref-0.58)
> 10:36:07—CSO N/Q -0.30 straddle..52/59
> 11:10:27—CSO M/N -1.00 put 8/15 (ref-0.48)
> 11:36:08—CSO N/Q-1.00 put 6/16 (ref-0.30)

Consider the 10:00:01 post. This is a two-way market for a call CSO on the July 2011–August 2011 contracts. The strike is $K = 0.00$. Note that in the CSO pricing convention, the strike defines the payoff spread via

$$S(t) \equiv F_1(t) - F_2(t) - K \quad (9.8)$$

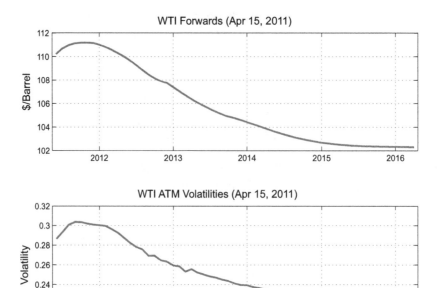

Figure 9.1. WTI market data (April 15, 2011).

where the subscripts denote the order of months listed in the spread. For this particular CSO, we have $S_t = F_{N11}(t) - F_{Q11}(t)$. The payoff of the call is $\max\left[S(T_1^{(e)}), 0\right]$, where $T_1^{(e)}$ denotes the standard option expiry for the WTI N11 contract, and the bid-offer shown is \$0.120 at \$0.200. The last component of the quote "(ref-0.31)" means that the reference spread at the time of quote is $S(0) = -0.310$.

We will now proceed to apply Margrabe to this CSO, accounting for volatility backwardation, to obtain a market implied correlation ρ. Figure 9.1 shows the WTI forward and at-the-money (ATM) volatility at the close of April 15, 2011. The relevant market data for our problem are

- Forward prices: $F(0, T_1) = 110.680$ and $F(0, T_2) = 110.960$.
- ATM volatilities: $\bar{\sigma}_1 = 0.293$ and $\bar{\sigma}_2 = 0.301$.

Three issues confront us:

- *Current spread.* The spread at close is different from the spread at quote: $110.680 - 110.960 = -0.280 \neq -0.310$.
- *Term structure of volatility.* The second contract expires after the CSO expiry $T_2^{(e)} > T_1^{(e)}$.
- *Skew.* The required strike $K = 0$ differs from the market spread -0.310.[4]

The first is benign given the relative stability of spreads. In lieu of a contemporaneous set of forwards, which would be available in practice on the

---

[4] In addition, nonnormal returns implied by skew affect spread option valuation. We will discuss this later in this chapter.

desk in real time, we will adjust the second forward: $F(0,T_2) = F(0,T_1) + (-0.310) = 110.990$.

For the second matter, because the working problem involves two different contracts, with local volatility exposure on the longer-tenor contract, we will use the little-t parameterization

$$\frac{dF(t,T)}{F(t,T)} = s(t)\Phi(T-t)dB_t \tag{9.9}$$

where, as in Chapter 7, we will assume

$$\Phi^2(T-t) = e^{-2\beta_1(T-t)} + \lambda e^{-2\beta_2(T-t)} \tag{9.10}$$

with $\bar{\beta} = [0.065, 1.049]$ and $\lambda = 0.469$.[5] Once we have decided how to handle skew, we will apply this calibration to obtain the term volatility $\bar{\sigma}_2(T_1^{(e)})$ for contract 2 over $[0, T_1^{(e)}]$.

The issue of skew is more subtle. There is ambiguity as to what volatility to use because the skew for each underlying is defined in terms of fixed strike options. In the spread option setting we have what are effectively floating strikes, in that each leg is acting as a strike for the other. A common approach (and one that makes purists cringe) is to use the forward price of the opposing leg to define moneyness, which we will refer to as the *volatility look-up* approximation. This look-up heuristic for an option on the spread $F_1 - F_2 - K$ involves using price ratios (or equivalently Δs) from each respective volatility surface in terms of the strike implied by the opposing leg; specifically,

- The implied volatility used for F_1 references moneyness using $F_2 + K$:

$$\pi_1 = \frac{F(0,T_2) + K}{F(0,T_1)}$$

- The implied volatility used for F_2 references $F_1 - K$:

$$\pi_2 = \frac{F(0,T_1) - K}{F(0,T_2)}$$

This is an "engineering" solution, and there are indeed errors sustained in this approach. Numerical tests suggest that the errors can be relevant, in excess of the change in value implied by the bid-offer spreads on the underlying volatilties in some situations. The ease of implementation and computational efficiency of the volatility look-up heuristic are compelling; however, when used, the effect of approximation should be estimated. We will return to this topic later in this chapter.

As we started to see in Chapter 8, addressing volatility backwardation and skew in single-commodity structures is already fraught with challenges.

---

[5] These parameters were estimated with the same method used previously with data from 2007 to 2010.

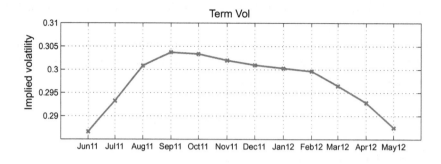

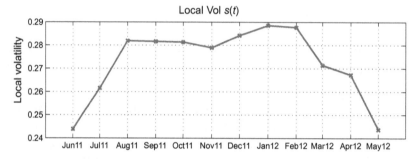

Figure 9.2. WTI local volatility (April 15, 2011).

Adding to this the requirement for multifactor models that will arise shortly, as well as coupling two commodity price processes to address spread options, is quite a tall order and one that arguably remains unresolved.

The strike K is zero in our current problem, so $\pi_1 = 1.003$ and $\pi_2 = 0.997$. These near-unit values of the price ratios mean that we will simply be using the ATM volatilities (this will not be the case in our second example involving tolls).

On calibration, we have the required set of local volatilities $[s_1, s_2, \ldots]$ shown in Figure 9.2. Proceeding as we did in (7.17) yields the term volatility $\bar{\sigma}_2(T_1^{(e)}) - 0.286$; note that the implied volatility for the first leg is the same as for the vanilla option $\bar{\sigma}_1$.

Now that we have obtained the term volatilities of the two legs, we can apply Margrabe across a range of correlations. The inputs to Margrabe, aside from the correlation ρ, are

- Forwards prices: $F(0, T_1)$ and $F(0, T_2)$
- Term volatilities: $\bar{\sigma}_1$ and $\bar{\sigma}_2(T_1^{(e)})$
- The time to expiry: $T_1^{(e)}$
- The discount factor $d(0, T_1^{(e)}) = 0.9996$[6]

---

[6] In this case, as well as in some subsequent examples, the discount factor is of almost no relevance given the near-zero interest rates prevailing during recent years courtesy of our central banks. Nonetheless, we include this for completeness.

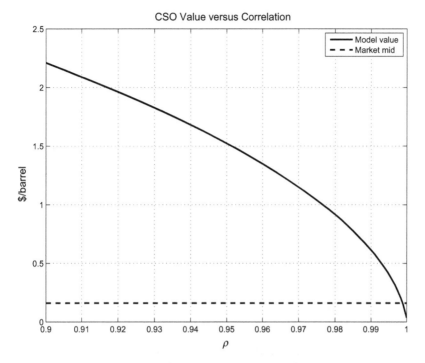

Figure 9.3. CSO value versus correlation.

Figure 9.3 shows the results using the basic Margrabe formula for a call as a function of correlation ρ. Note that the midvalue of 0.16 corresponds to an implied correlation of $\rho = 0.9988$, which is effectively implying unit correlation between the two legs. A lower rate of backwardation in our parameterization of local volatilty would lower the implied correlation. However, the near-unit implied correlation suggests that the market view at the time was that this CSO was rather boring. Nonetheless, several important themes stand out in this analysis.

First, spread options on the difference between two commodities prices increase in value as the correlation decreases. In addition, the sensitivity to the correlation ρ can be significant as $\rho \to 1$ when the forwards and volatilities are nearly equal, which was the case in this example.

Second, the extrinsic value of the spread option need not be zero even at unit correlation because, in general, $\bar{\sigma}_1 \neq \bar{\sigma}_2(T_1^{(e)})$. At unit correlation, the volatility $\hat{\sigma}$ that enters the Margrabe formula given in (9.7) is

$$\hat{\sigma}^2 = T_1^{(e)} \left[\bar{\sigma}_1 - \bar{\sigma}_2(T_1^{(e)}) \right]^2$$

When the two relevant volatilities are not equal, $\hat{\sigma} > 0$, resulting in positive extrinsic value.

Finally, very high correlations can occur for commodities spread options. In fact, as we will see later, situations arise where implied correlations in the range of mid-90s occur even when empirically estimated correlations are much lower – a topic that we will discuss at various points going forward.

Application to Tolls

Although tolls are usually daily exercise, here we will consider a toll with monthly exercise, dealing with the more challenging daily variety once we have multifactor models at our disposal. Monthly tolls do not trade over the broker market, and when they arise, they are almost always part of structured transactions. Many of the issues that we encounter here, however, will be pertinent to the more common daily exercise structures.

Consider a monthly exercise tolling deal with the following terms:

- Pricing date: January 11, 2010
- Commodities: PJM Western Hub 5x16 and Henry Hub natural gas
- Heat rate $H_* = 11.0$
- Delivery monthly July 2010
- Exercise is standard penultimate settlement (-4b) of NYMEX NG
- Notional: 400 MW

Recall that standard exercise for monthly power options is "−2b"; for simplicity, we will assume that PJM monthly options also expire "−4b" in the calculations that follow. We will also assume financial settlement at expiration.

Comment

A heat rate of $H_* = 11.0$ is high compared with the most efficient combined-cycle generators, which are just below 7. Natural gas generators with a heat rate above 10 are considered *peakers*, which are dispatched infrequently to capitalize on (and to alleviate) short-time-scale price spikes. Monthly tolls would rarely be used as hedges for high-heat-rate generation. We have used this heat rate to push the option close enough to the market heat rate to make things interesting.

As for most power options, the notional just quoted is in units of megawatts – a megawatt is a rate, in this case 400 MWh per hour. The number of NERC[7] business days in July 2010 is 21, so the total notional of this toll is

$$Q \equiv 400 \times 21 \times 16 \times 400 = 134,400 \text{ MWh} \tag{9.11}$$

The relevant forward prices on these pricing date are

- $F(0, T) = \$69.650/\text{MWh}$
- $G(0, T) = \$5.603/\text{MMBtu}$

---

[7] NERC is the North American Electric Reliability Corportation, self-described as "a not-for-profit entity whose mission is to ensure the reliability of the Bulk-Power System in North America."

If we convert the natural gas leg by the toll heat rate to units of $/MWh (recall that the units of H_* are MMBtu/MWh and the units of G are $/MMBtu), the second fuel leg of the option has a forward price (in $/MWh) of $11.0 \times 5.603 = \$61.633$. Note that the market heat rate is $H = 69.650/5.603 = 12.431$, which is higher than the tolling heat rate $H_* = 11.0$, so this option is in-the-money. Finally, the discount factor is 0.999.

On the face of it, we do not have a volatility backwardation issue as we did in the CSO setting because the respective legs are expiring (by assumption) at their vanilla expiry. In our initial cut, we will simply use term volatilities and discuss implied term correlations; this will be a straightforward application of Margrabe.

As with the CSOs, we will use the volatility look-up heuristic:

- $\pi_F \equiv \dfrac{H_* F_G(0,T)}{F_P(0,T)} = 0.885$
- $\pi_G \equiv \dfrac{F_P(0,T)}{H_* F_G(0,T)} = 1.130$

The results of the volatility look-up, depicted in Figure 9.4, are $\sigma_F = 0.393$ and $\sigma_G = 0.445$.

We now have to grapple with what correlation should be used. There is no broker market for monthly tolls from which to calibrate correlation. In this

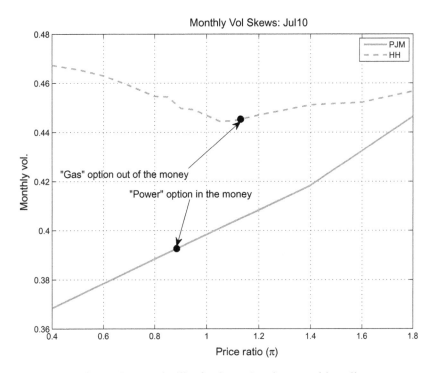

Figure 9.4. Volatility look-up for the monthly toll.

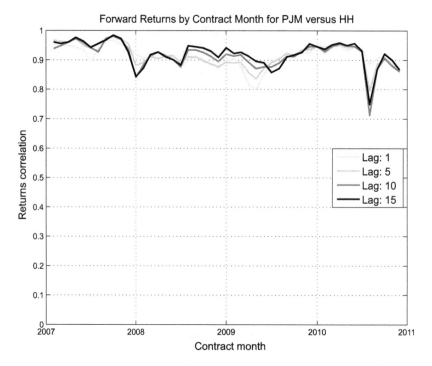

Figure 9.5. Empirical returns correlation by contract: PJM versus NYMEX NG.

situation, we have little choice but to rely, at least in part, on empirical analysis. Figure 9.5 shows the returns correlation by contract month estimated over a one-year trailing window using several time scales (lags) for returns. Returns at lag L are defined as $\log[F(d,T)/F(d-L,T)]$. There are two reasons for considering returns for $L > 1$. First, hedging activity will turn out to occur on the time scale of days. Second, longer lags are less sensitive to anomalies in historical marks.[8]

Looking at the results in Figure 9.5, it might be tempting to conclude that there were price-data errors driving the low correlations that are visible in the August 2010 contract. This turns out not to be the case. Figure 9.6 shows the heat-rate history for this contract. A hot and high-priced July in PJM drove market expectations for the August contract, resulting in a rather meaningful breakdown in correlation between power and natural gas forwards for this delivery month.

This is admittedly a simplistic analysis of correlation that does not account for possible seasonal effects, volatility backwardation, or a term structure of correlation – one would expect that correlations would decrease as the contract month approaches delivery and short-term drivers of power prices

---

[8] Imagine a day in which the power trader is on vacation and the natural gas trader marks the power curves keeping heat rates constant when in fact they have changed; this is not supposed to happen, but in practice it does.

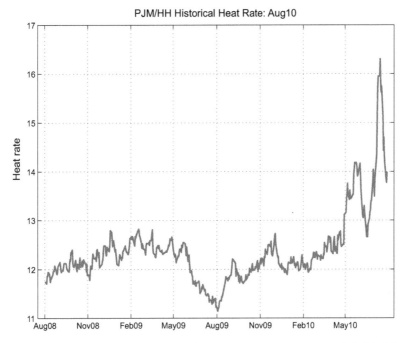

Figure 9.6. August 2010 heat-rate history for PJM versus NYMEX NG.

such as local temperature forecasts and generation outages begin to manifest in the power forwards. We will examine correlation more closely in Part IV when we transition to the multifactor setting. For now, it is reasonable to work under the assumption that term correlations are in the low to middle 90s (in percent).

The results for our working problem are shown in Figure 9.7 for a range of correlations. In what follows, we will take $\rho = 0.90$ as our working implied correlation, which yields a value of

- Up-front: $ 8.809/MWh
- PV: $1,183,881
- $/kW-mo: $2.964

The fraction of intrinsic value to total value is 0.909.

The Value Surface

A natural representation of the value of a spread option with zero strike is given in (A.21), which in the present setting takes the form

$$V[0, F(0, T_1), G(0, T_2)] = d(\tau)G(0, T)[H(0, T)N(d_1) - H_*N(d_2)] \quad (9.12)$$

with

$$d_{1,2} = \frac{\log\left[\frac{H(0,T)}{H_*}\right] \pm \frac{1}{2}\hat{\sigma}^2}{\hat{\sigma}} \quad (9.13)$$

Primary Valuation Issues

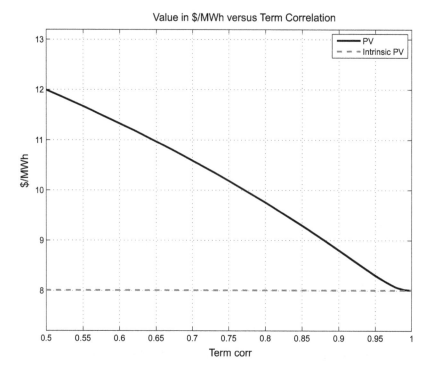

Figure 9.7. Monthly tolling value versus term correlation.

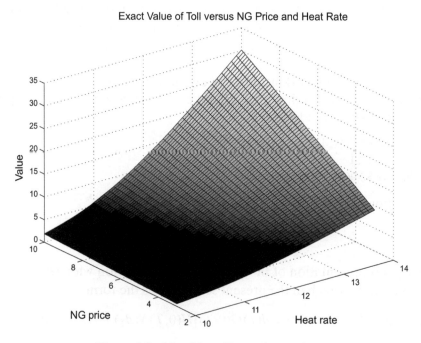

Figure 9.8. Monthly tolling value surface.

The implication is that if the forward heat rate $H(0,T)$ is held constant, the value of the option is linear in $G(0,T)$. Figure 9.8 shows the value surface for the toll, where it is clear that the highest values are achieved at high natural gas prices and high heat rates.

Delta and Gamma

Turning our attention to hedging, the deltas for the spread option are as shown in (A.23) and (A.25). When modified by discounting and the conversion factor H_* as in (A.33), as well as multiplied by the notional (9.11), we get

$$\frac{\partial V}{\partial F} = d(\tau)QN(d_1) \qquad \frac{\partial V}{\partial G} = -d(\tau)QH_*N(d_2) \tag{9.14}$$

In our working example, the power delta is 112,978 MWh, which is 337 MW or roughly seven 50-MW blocks; this is what would be sold to hedge this toll. The natural gas delta is -119.312 lots or 3.85/day, which rounds to $3\frac{3}{4}$ per day.

The gamma for a spread option is a matrix (or Hessian):

$$\Gamma = d(\tau)Q\frac{N'(d_1)}{\hat{\sigma}}\begin{bmatrix} \dfrac{1}{F(0,T)} & -\dfrac{1}{G(0,T)} \\ -\dfrac{1}{G(0,T)} & \dfrac{F(0,T)}{G^2(0,T)} \end{bmatrix} \tag{9.15}$$

The diagonal terms are both positive, as expected, given the similarity of the valuation results to single-commodity options. The cross-gamma term is negative: increasing the value of the second leg $G(0,T)$ lowers the moneyness of the option, thereby reducing $\partial V/\partial F$.

Collectively, Γ as a matrix is positive-definite; for any vector $\vec{\alpha}$,

$$\vec{\alpha}^\dagger\Gamma\vec{\alpha} = d(\tau)Q\frac{1}{F}\frac{N'(d_1)}{\hat{\sigma}}\left(\alpha_1 - \frac{F}{G}\alpha_2\right)^2 \geq 0 \tag{9.16}$$

This is to be expected: a spread option is an option – when delta-hedged, all directions point up.

In our example, the Γ takes the value

$$\Gamma = \begin{pmatrix} 3564 & -44,307 \\ -44,307 & 550,771 \end{pmatrix} \tag{9.17}$$

Units are important here: $\Gamma(1,1)$ is in units of Q/F or MWh^2/\$, which is more appropriately thought of as MWh/(\$/MWh) – the change in the power delta $\partial V/\partial F$ per change in the notional price of power. Similarly $\Gamma(2,2)$ has units MMBtu/(\$/MMBtu) and $\Gamma(1,2)$ has units of MWh/(\$/MMBtu) or MMBtu/(\$/MWh), however you choose to view it.

Because Γ is positive semidefinite and symmetric, it is interesting to diagonalize the matrix to see where the convexity is – or rather is not. Note that the determinant of Γ is zero, and the matrix is singular. The eigenvalues are

$$\lambda_1 = 0$$
$$\lambda_2 = d(\tau)Q\frac{N'(d_1)}{\hat{\sigma}}\left[\frac{1}{F(0,T)} + \frac{F(0,T)}{G(0,T)^2}\right]$$

The eigenvector corresponding to $\lambda_1 = 0$ is[9]

$$\vec{v}_1 = \begin{bmatrix} \dfrac{F(0,T)}{G(0,T)} \\ 1 \end{bmatrix} \qquad (9.18)$$

This is saying that there is no convexity when $\Delta F = H\Delta G$, that is, when the market heat rate $H(t,T)$ is constant. This is easily seen from (9.12), where the value surface, viewed as a function of gas price and heat rate, is linear in $G(0,T)$ when $H(0,T)$ is held fixed.

The second eigenvector is

$$\vec{v}_2 = \begin{bmatrix} 1 \\ -\dfrac{F(0,T)}{G(0,T)} \end{bmatrix} \qquad (9.19)$$

Convexity is maximal for price changes in which $\Delta G = -H\Delta F$. This is in a direction that is not particularly relevant to empirical natural gas and power dynamics: in this direction, a \$1 increase in forward power prices is associated with a roughly \$12 drop in natural gas prices, hardly an expected event.

Impact of Contract Size on Hedging

The high empirical correlations that we saw earlier imply movements that are predominantly in the $\vec{v}_2$ zero-convexity direction. This begs the question: How much would prices have to move to yield a change in Δ that could actually be hedged? Recall that you can only trade 50-MW blocks of power in eastern U.S. power markets.

Figure 9.9 shows the change in power delta (converted to MW) as a function of a change in heat rate holding natural gas prices constant: To see a change in delta of 50 MW requires a drop in heat rate of nearly 0.50 point.

To put this in context, Figure 9.10 shows a history of the forward heat rate for the July 2010 contract as well as the distribution of five-day heat-rate changes. Heat-rate changes of the magnitude required to result in a 50-MW change in power delta for our toll are not particularly frequent occurrences on the time scale of a week, suggesting that attempting to monetize extrinsic value by delta hedging is not going to be a particularly fruitful affair. A

---

[9] Here $\vec{v}$ is not of unit norm, but it is more intuitively useful, as shown here.

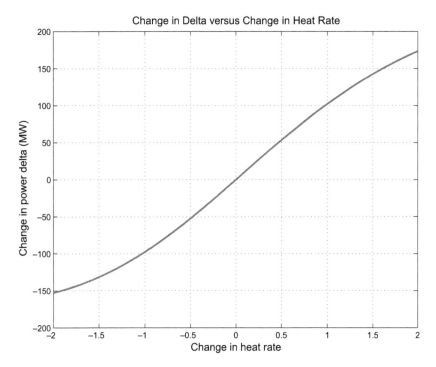

Figure 9.9. Change in power delta (MW) versus change in heat rate.

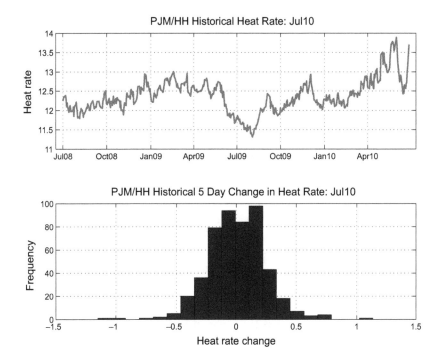

Figure 9.10. July 2010 heat-rate history and histogram of five-day changes.

400-MW toll is considered to be of noteworthy size. While the toll we analyzed here involved monthly exercise, the 50-MW contract size is also a very
significant market friction for daily structures.

This point is often either unknown or unspoken. Contract size in commodities hedging, particularly in power, severely impacts one's ability to
capture modeled extrinsic value and results in a level of incompleteness
that certainly must give one pause before applying the basic tenants of
risk-neutral valuation.

Vega

The Margrabe valuation formula in (9.5) is identical to a call option with
underlying price F struck at $H_*G(0,T)$, with the modification that the term
volatility is given by (9.7):

$$\hat{\sigma}^2 = \tau\left[\sigma_F^2 + \sigma_G^2 - 2\rho\sigma_F\sigma_G\right] \equiv \tau\tilde{\sigma}^2 \tag{9.20}$$

The standard vega calculation yields

$$\frac{\partial V}{\partial\hat{\sigma}} = d(\tau)F(0,T)N'(d_1) \tag{9.21}$$

As for a single underlying option, the vega with respect to the term volatility
is positive. Applying the chain rule yields the vegas with respect to the two
underlying volatilities:

$$\frac{\partial V}{\partial\sigma_F} = \frac{\partial V}{\partial\hat{\sigma}}\frac{\partial\hat{\sigma}}{\partial\sigma_F} = d(\tau)F(0,T)N'(d_1)\frac{\tau^{\frac{1}{2}}(\sigma_F - \rho\sigma_G)}{\tilde{\sigma}} \tag{9.22}$$

where the second equality is obtained by implicit differentiation of $\partial\hat{\sigma}^2/\partial\sigma_F$.
By symmetry, we also have

$$\frac{\partial V}{\partial\sigma_G} = d(\iota)F(0,T)N'(d_1)\frac{\tau^{\frac{1}{2}}(\sigma_G - \rho\sigma_F)}{\tilde{\sigma}} \tag{9.23}$$

The implication is that

$$\text{sign}\left(\frac{\partial V}{\partial\sigma_F}\right) = \text{sign}(\sigma_F - \rho\sigma_G)$$

$$\text{sign}\left(\frac{\partial V}{\partial\sigma_G}\right) = \text{sign}(\sigma_G - \rho\sigma_F)$$

because $\tilde{\sigma}$ is positive.

An important consequence is that one of the vegas will be negative if

$$\min\left(\frac{\sigma_F}{\sigma_G}, \frac{\sigma_G}{\sigma_F}\right) < \rho$$

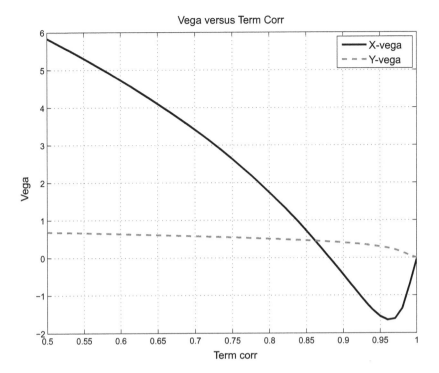

Figure 9.11. Tolling vegas versus correlation.

Moreover, we know from our working examples that correlations, both estimated and implied, often are very close to unity.

It is often assumed that a long option position has positive vega, or in this case vegas. Commodities spread options often violate this notion, but the intuition is simple: if the correlation of the two assets is high, and if $\sigma_F > \sigma_G$, then any increase in σ_G reduces the volatility of the spread $\hat{\sigma}$. Increasing the lower volatility allows the associated underlying price to "keep up with" the changes in the price of the higher-volatility leg, thereby lowering the option value.

Returning to our monthly tolling example, natural gas volatility exceeded that of power, and the correlation threshold for negative vega is $\sigma_F/\sigma_G = 0.882$. We expect, therefore, to see $\partial V/\partial \sigma_F$ be negative. This is in fact the case, as seen in Figure 9.11, which shows both vegas as a function of correlation.

Nonzero Strikes: Numerical Methods

In practice, one typically encounters nonzero strikes:

$$V[0, F(0,T), G(0,T)] = d(\tau)\tilde{E}\left\{[F(\tau,T) - H_*G(\tau,T) - K]^+\right\} \qquad (9.24)$$

The presence of a nonzero strike precludes the closed-form solutions obtained in Appendix A. In the tolling setting, values of the peak power forward prices historically have been of the order of $50 to $100 depending on natural gas prices and delivery location; the value of the strike K represents variable operation and maintenance (VOM) costs, which are typically between $3 and $6 per MWh. The strike K is therefore often a nontrivial percentage of the underlying commodities prices.

There are two ways to proceed: numerical integration or approximation methods. In most settings, the number of underlyings is small – typically just two. This renders numerical integration tractable and preferred, especially given modern computational capabilities. We will, however, discuss approximation methods, many of which were developed to deal with higher-dimensional baskets such as those that arise in equities and for which quadrature is not a viable approach. These continue to be used by some practicitioners and commercial risk systems.

The key observation for the direct approach of numerical integration is that conditional on $G(\tau, T)$, the distribution of $F(\tau, T)$ remains log-normal:

$$G(\tau, T) = G(0, T)e^{\sigma_G B_G(\tau) - \frac{1}{2}\tau\sigma_G^2}$$

$$F(\tau, T) = F(0, T)e^{\sigma_F\left[\rho B_G(\tau) + \sqrt{1-\rho^2}W\right] - \frac{1}{2}\tau\sigma_F^2}$$

Conditioning on $G(\tau, T)$ or, equivalently, setting $B_G(\tau) = \tau^{1/2}z$, yields

$$F(\tau, T) = F(0, T)e^{\left(\rho\sigma_F\tau^{1/2}z - \frac{1}{2}\tau\rho^2\sigma_F^2\right)}e^{\left[\sigma_F\sqrt{1-\rho^2}W - \frac{1}{2}\tau\left(1-\rho^2\right)\sigma_F^2\right]} \tag{9.25}$$

Denoting the "modified" forward and strike by

$$\tilde{F}(0, T)(z) \equiv F(0, T)e^{\rho\sigma_F\tau^{1/2}z - \frac{1}{2}\rho^2\tau\sigma_F^2}$$

$$\tilde{K}(z) \equiv K + G(0, T)e^{\sigma_G\tau^{1/2}z - \frac{1}{2}\tau\sigma_G^2}$$

we have:

$$V[0, F(0, T), G(0, T)] = \int_{-\infty}^{\infty} \mathcal{B}\left[\tilde{F}(0, T), \tilde{K}, T, \sigma_F\sqrt{1-\rho^2}\right]\phi(z)\,dz \tag{9.26}$$

where $\mathcal{B}$ denotes basic Black valuation of a call option, and $\phi(z)$ is the standard normal probability distribution function (pdf). The benefit of this calculation is that $\mathcal{B}$ can be evaluated analytically, thereby avoiding the need for a two-dimensional quadrature. Various methods can be used. A fast and simple approach, especially for prototyping, is to create a uniform probability grid by letting $\mathcal{I} \equiv \{\frac{1}{N}, \ldots, (N-1)/N\}$ and then letting $\mathcal{Z} \equiv N^{-1}(\mathcal{I})$. The integral is then approximated as

$$V[0, F(0, T), G(0, T)] \approx \sum_{z \in \mathcal{Z}} \mathcal{B}\left[\tilde{F}(0, T), \tilde{K}, T, \sigma_F\sqrt{1-\rho^2}\right] \tag{9.27}$$

More sophisticated quadrature methods typically would be used in production settings.

Nonzero Strikes: Moment Methods

Numerical integration is fast enough to render approximate solutions necessary. Nonetheless, a number of approximation methods are standard in many production risk systems, and it is useful to have an assessment of the accuracy of the methods.

One class of approaches is based on the approximation that the dynamics of $\tilde{G}(t,T) = G(t,T) + \tilde{K}$, with $\tilde{K} \equiv K/H_*$, is close to that of a GBM when $\tilde{K}$ is small. Note that K is normalized by H_* so that $F(t,T) - H_*\tilde{G}(t,T)$ is the required spread. The approximation methods distinguish themselves with respect to how the volatility $\sigma_{\tilde{G}}$ is obtained from σ_G. Once calculated, valuation is rote application of Margrabe.

Two well-known approaches are

- *The Kirk approximation* [Kir95]. The simple heuristic underpinning this approach is that the size of the returns is altered by the constant K based on the *initial* value of second leg[10]:

$$\sigma_{\tilde{G}} = \sigma_G \frac{G(0,T)}{G(0,T) + \tilde{K}} \tag{9.28}$$

- *The Levy approximation.* This is a moment-matching method based on the observation that a log-normal random variable L has the following moments:

$$E(L) = e^{\mu + \frac{1}{2}\sigma^2}$$
$$E(L^2) = e^{2(\mu + \sigma^2)}$$

from which we have:

$$\sigma^2 = \log\left[\frac{E(L^2)}{E(L)^2}\right]$$

For a spread option with nonzero strike, if we assume that $G(t,T) + \tilde{K}$ is log-normal, the following must hold:

$$\tau\sigma_{\tilde{G}}^2 = \log\left\{\frac{E\left[(G(\tau,T) + \tilde{K})^2\right]}{E\left[G(\tau,T) + \tilde{K}\right]^2}\right\} \tag{9.29}$$

$$= \log\left\{\frac{G^2(0,T)e^{\sigma_{\tilde{G}}^2 T} + 2\tilde{K}G(0,T) + \tilde{K}^2}{\left[G(0,T) + \tilde{K}\right]^2}\right\}$$

where the second equality follows from

$$E\left[G^2(\tau,T)\right] = G^2(0,T)E\left(e^{2\sigma_{\tilde{G}}B_\tau - \frac{1}{2}\sigma_{\tilde{G}}^2\tau}\right) = G^2(0,T)e^{\sigma_{\tilde{G}}^2\tau} \tag{9.30}$$

by the properties of moment-generating functions of normal random variables.

---

[10] See [AV11] for a more refined exposition and minor modification of this method.

These two approximation methods are practically the same in the relevant parameter regimes. Expanding (9.29), we have

$$\tau\sigma_{\tilde{G}}^2 = \log\left[1 + \frac{G^2(0,\tau)\left(e^{\sigma_G^2\tau} - 1\right)}{G^2(0,\tau) + 2\tilde{K}G(0,\tau) + \tilde{K}^2}\right]$$

$$\approx \frac{G^2(0,\tau)}{G^2(0,\tau) + 2\tilde{K}G(0,\tau) + \tilde{K}^2}\left(e^{\sigma_G^2\tau} - 1\right)$$

$$\approx \tau\sigma_G^2(0,\tau)\frac{G^2(0,\tau)}{\left[G(0,\tau) + \tilde{K}\right]^2}$$

which is exactly the Kirk approximation. The approximate equivalence holds when both $\sigma_G^2\tau$ and $\tilde{K}$ are small.

Figure 9.12 compares the results of these approximations with those of the quadrature (numerical integration) for our tolling example as a function of strike K. As expected, the Kirk and Levy approximations are practically identical, and the accuracy is quite good. Recall, however, that we are dealing with a situation in which expiry $\tau = 0.452$ is reasonably small. If, for simplicity, we keep all market data the same but increase the expiration time to $\tau = 4$, the errors start to become relevant, nearly 1 percent at typical strikes, as seen in Figure 9.13.

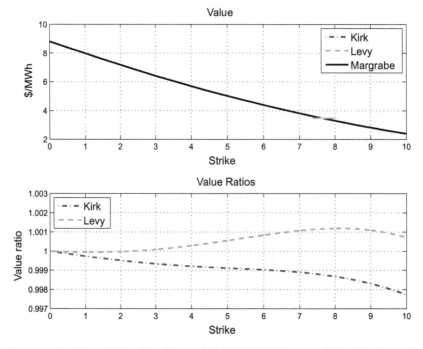

Figure 9.12. Comparison of approximation methods: short-tenor case.

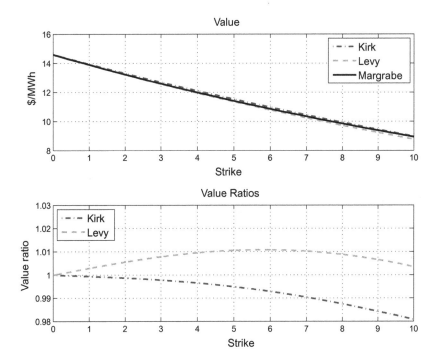

Figure 9.13. Comparison of approximation methods: long-tenor case.

The speed with which quadrature can be applied leaves little need for deployment of these methods in production risk systems.

Nonzero Strikes: Modeling the Spread

The underlying premise of Margrabe is that both underlying prices are modeled and calibrated separately to market data and that correlation assumptions are what tie them together. Another train of thought in the effort to arrive at closed-form valuation formulas for nonzero strikes involves positing that the relevent spread itself is governed by a diffusion – a reduction to a single factor. This method is described in a survey by Carmona and Durrleman [CD03] that compares methodologies for valuing spread options and that we will follow closely here. As we will see, there are significant problems with modeling the spread directly, although this approach is also commonly used.

Unlike an asset price, which is of positive value, a spread can take either sign. The simplest spread model is arithmetic Brownian motion with drift, sometimes referred to as the *Bachelier model*:

$$dS_t = \mu_S S_t dt + \sigma_S dB_t \tag{9.31}$$

where S_t is a spot (cash) price spread. The drift μ must account for costs of carry, dividends, and storage.

Because we are focusing on forward spreads of the form $S_t \equiv F(t,T) - H_* G(t,T)$, the martingale property of the two underlying legs is inherited by S_t so that

$$dS_t = \sigma_S dB_t \tag{9.32}$$

This simple diffusion yields straightforward pricing formulas, and some practicioners favor this approach for perceived simplicity.[11]

There are different ways to implement calibration and valuation using (9.32). The simplest is to calibrate S to the current forwards, which is trivially accomplished by setting $S(0) = F(0,T) - H_* G(0,T)$. One then sets σ_S to match a traded spread option, assuming that a liquid market exists for the spread option in question. Working under this assumption, we have

$$m_\tau \equiv E(S_\tau) = F(0,T) - H_* G(0,T)$$
$$s_\tau^2 \equiv \mathrm{var}(S_\tau) = \sigma_S^2 T$$

Option valuation is then a simple direct integration; for example, the value of the call $\max(S_\tau - K, 0)$ is

$$
\begin{aligned}
V(0, S_0) &= e^{-r\tau} E\left[(m_\tau + s_\tau Z - K)^+\right] \\
&= e^{-r\tau} E\left[(m_\tau - s_\tau Z - K)^+\right] \\
&= e^{-r\tau} \int_{-\infty}^{\frac{m_\tau - K}{s_\tau}} (m_\tau - K - s_\tau z)\,\phi(z)\,dz \\
&= e^{-r\tau}\left[(m_\tau - K)\,N\left(\frac{m_\tau - K}{s_\tau}\right) + s_\tau \phi\left(\frac{m_\tau - K}{s_\tau}\right)\right]
\end{aligned}
\tag{9.33}
$$

where, as usual, N and ϕ are the standard normal cumulative distribution function (cdf) and pdf, respectively. The second equality results from the symmetry of the distribution of Z and yields a simpler formula at the end.

The most important consequence of this result is that, by construction, the deltas of the two legs always have the ratio H_* because

$$\frac{\partial V}{\partial G} = \frac{\partial V}{\partial S}\frac{\partial S}{\partial G} = -H_* \frac{\partial V}{\partial S}\frac{\partial S}{\partial F} = -H_* \frac{\partial V}{\partial F}$$

regardless of the prevailing forward prices of the two underlying commodities. This result is an immediate consequence of the calibration assumptions and is questionable, as we will show shortly.

Another obvious weakness to this approach is that the vegas that a trader has to deal with expand with each new spread – each new spread volatility $\sigma_S(H_*)$ is an additional risk parameter for every new H_* traded. Each $\sigma_S(H_*)$

---

[11] We could add backwardation of volatility by allowing σ to be a function of time, but the purpose here is to discuss the distinctions between the arithmetic versus Margrabe approaches.

vega is unrelated not only to other spread vegas but also to vegas of the underlying volatilities σ_F and σ_G. Furthermore, we know that there must be a relationship because setting $H_* = 0$ is in fact a single-commodity option with $F(t, T)$ as the underlying.

A more sophisticated approach to modeling the spread directly is to calibrate s_τ^2 to the implied volatilities and correlations of the two underlying legs. The reason for proceeding this way is that consistency with single-commodity options markets is maintained, and the point of modeling the spread is that closed-form solutions for nonzero strikes are maintained via (9.33). Standard moment-generating function calculations (see [CD03]) yield

$$s_\tau^2 = F(0,T)^2 \left(e^{\sigma_F^2 \tau} - 1\right) - 2F(0,T)G(0,T)\left(e^{\rho \sigma_F \sigma_G \tau} - 1\right) + G(0,T)^2 \left(e^{\sigma_G^2 \tau} - 1\right) \tag{9.34}$$

It is worth contrasting the results with those obtained using Margrabe quadrature.

We will begin by examining the differences as a function of $H(0,T) \equiv F(0,T)/G(0,T)$ in the case of zero strike ($K = 0$) using our working example. While the spread modeling is intended to facilitate closed-form solutions for nonzero strike, robustness of results to underlying market data is important, and starting with $K = 0$ has its advantages. Rewriting (9.34) as

$$s_\tau^2 = G(0,T)^2 \left[H(0,T)^2 \left(e^{\sigma_F^2 \tau} - 1\right) - 2H(0,T)\left(e^{\rho \sigma_F \sigma_G \tau} - 1\right) + \left(e^{\sigma_G^2 \tau} - 1\right) \right] \tag{9.35}$$

we see that when $K = 0$, the value of (9.33) takes the simpler form

$$V(0, S_0) = e^{-r\tau} G(0,T) \Psi[\tau, H(0,T)] \tag{9.36}$$

where

$$\Psi[\tau, H(0,T)] = [H(0,T) - H_*] N\left[\frac{H(0,T) - H_*}{\eta_\tau}\right] + \eta_\tau \phi\left[\frac{H(0,T) - H_*}{\eta_\tau}\right]$$

and

$$\eta_\tau \equiv \left[H(0,T)^2 \left(e^{\sigma_F^2 \tau} - 1\right) - 2H(0,T)\left(e^{\rho \sigma_F \sigma_G \tau} - 1\right) + \left(e^{\sigma_G^2 \tau} - 1\right) \right]^{1/2}$$

The point of (9.36) is that as with the Margrabe result (9.12), the value also scales linearly with $G(0,T)$ if we hold $H(0,T)$ constant. This means that we only need to focus on the heat rate in contrasting the approaches.

Figure 9.14 shows valuation comparisons between Margrabe and the spread model for the monthly toll. Note the degrading performance as the market heat rate decreases relative to the tolling heat rate $H_* = 11.0$ when viewed as a ratio. Greeks also exhibit inaccuracies. Figure 9.15 shows the

Primary Valuation Issues

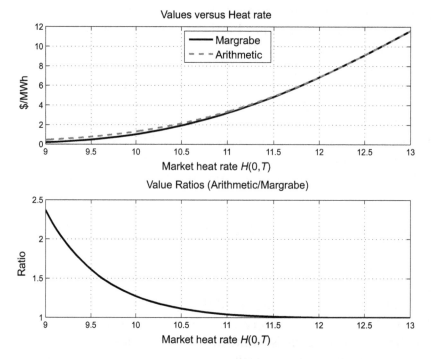

Figure 9.14. Value comparison of spread model to Margrabe.

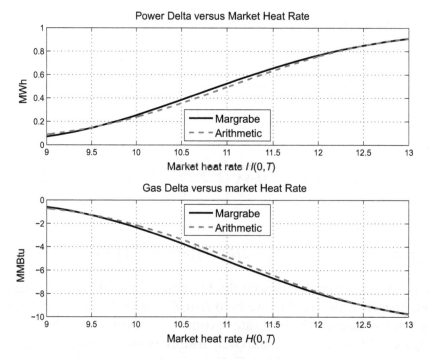

Figure 9.15. Delta comparison of spread model to Margrabe.

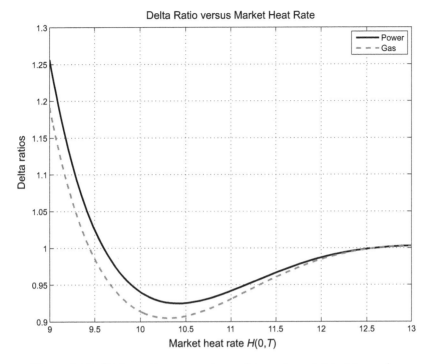

Figure 9.16. Delta ratio comparison of spread model to Margrabe.

power and natural gas deltas (per unit notional), which might appear acceptable. However, viewed as ratios, the situation becomes more questionable,
as shown in Figure 9.16, where the deltas can differ by as much as 25 percent
over the heat-rate range shown.

Finally, Figure 9.17 shows the hedge ratios, that is, the ratio between
power and gas deltas. The first observation is that as with the other preceding metrics, the departure between the two methods increases as $H(0, T)$
decreases. More interesting, however, is to note that in both cases the
hedge ratios required are altogether different from $H_* = 11.0$ implied by
the simple-minded application of spread valuation first discussed.

This analysis shows that one must view spread models with caution. However, the purpose of the spread approximation is to handle nonzero strikes.
Figure 9.18 shows results similar to the preceding analysis but by strike K.
A nonzero strike in effect lowers the market heat rate, hence the similarities with earlier results. Likewise for Greeks and for hedge ratios, which we
show in Figure 9.19.

Ultimately, the computational challenges of numerical integration are
minimal, rendering approximations typically unnecessary – that is, unless
there is a reason to believe that modeling the spread is somehow justified
empirically. This, however, does not seem to be the case. We have seen
before that ratios between commodities prices exhibit nonlinear structure

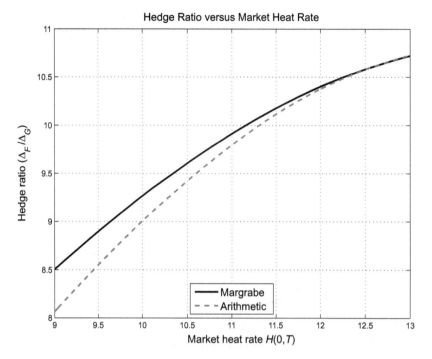

Figure 9.17. Hedge ratio comparison of spread model to exact.

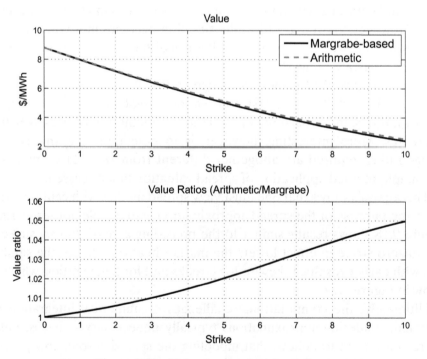

Figure 9.18. Value comparison by strike.

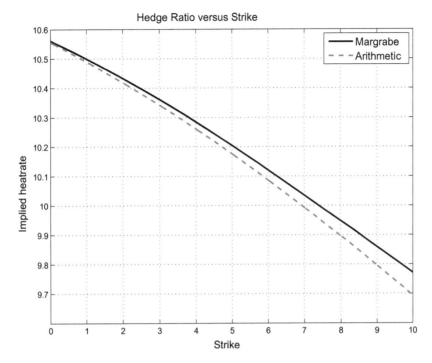

Figure 9.19. Hedge ratio comparison by strike.

versus one of the single-component prices. For example, in Figure 6.10 we saw that heat rates expand as the natural gas price in the denominator decreases. The following figures show similar results in the settings of spark spreads and heat rates.

Figure 9.20 shows the behavior of the heat rate versus the natural gas price in the top figure and, more pertinently, the $H_* = 11$ spark spread $F(t, T) - H_* G(t, T)$ versus the gas price in the lower figure. Treating each idiosyncratic spark spread as a separate underlying stochastic process omits the systematic response to natural gas prices shown here, which is ultimately the origin of the nontrivial power and natural gas deltas discussed earlier.

Turning to crack spreads, Figure 9.21 shows the results for the unit crack spread ($H_* = 1$) between heating oil and WTI. While the unit crack spread $F_{HO}(t, T) - F_{WTI}(t, T)$ is arguably nearly independent of WTI prices, ratios other than $H_* = 1$ would exhibit more structure, and refiners are not always asking for hedges at exactly the ratios implied by the commonly traded crack spreads.

The point is that even in a primitive way, Margrabe dynamics with properly set volatilities and correlations exhibit structure qualitatively similar to that shown in these figures. Later we will discuss more sophisticated methods than correlated GBMs for generating realistic distributions of multiple commodity prices. However, one-factor diffusion models of commodity spreads

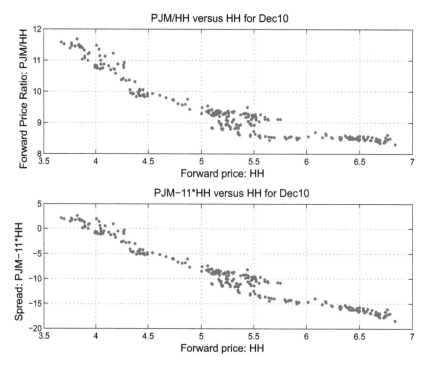

Figure 9.20. PJM versus Henry Hub December 2010: heat rates and spark spread.

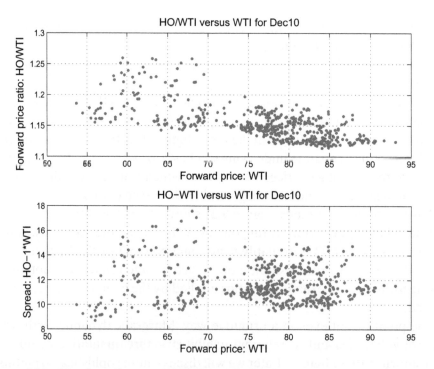

Figure 9.21. Heating oil versus WTI December 2010: conversion ratios and crack spread.

simply cannot generate these empirical features, making the case for separate stochastic processes driving each commodity leg compelling, even if a computational cost is involved.

The Volatility Lookup Heuristic and Correlation Skew

The treatment of skew via the volatility look-up approach based on price ratio was purely heuristic. Some researchers have examined this subject; see, for example, work by Alexander and Venkatramanan [AV11], although rigorous bounds on errors sustained by this method have yet to be established.

Numerical tests are the fastest way to shed some light on this issue. As an example, consider the following jump-diffusion setup:

- A spread option with tenor of $\tau = 1/2$ year
- Power and gas forwards of $F(0, T) = \$100$ and $G(0, T) = \$10$
- Heat rates spanning the interval $8 \leq H_* \leq 12$

The simulation results that follow are based on 10^6 independent standard normal deviates $\vec{Z}_n$, where each $\vec{Z}_n \in \mathbb{R}^2$. Poisson jumps with an arrival rate of four per year and a size of two were added to $Z_{n,1}$. The $\{\vec{Z}_n\}_{n=1}^N$ were normalized to unit standard deviation and linearly transformed to yield $\vec{X}_n$ with correlation $\rho = 0.90$; this results in skew for both commodities. The resulting returns (to time τ) distributions were normalized to have a standard deviation of 0.50 and 0.60 for the two legs, respectively. Figure 9.22 shows the skew for the two legs.

Given these nonnormal joint returns distributions with volatility levels and skew that are qualitatively similar to those seen in market data, we can now compare Monte Carlo valuation, which we will label "exact," versus the value obtained using the volatility look-up heuristic. Figure 9.23 shows the results comparing exact valuation with the volatility look-up methods as a function of heat rate. The top plot shows the value of the toll using the two approaches. The coincidence of the results is deceptive. The middle plot shows the percentage premium of the approximation over the exact value. Most transacted tolls correspond to heat rates below 10, where the errors in this experiment are under 2 percent. That said, 2 percent is a big number when applied to the fully loaded value of the toll – including intrinsic value. The bottom plot shows the ratios of extrinsic values, which are more ominous, with low heat rates seeing ratios above 1.5. Another way to characterize this error is shown in Figure 9.24, in which the difference in extrinsic value is converted into an equivalent change in σ_G by dividing the difference by the σ_G-vega. Here we see that the error in extrinsic value can be several volatility points, which is at least a factor of two larger than the typical bid-offer spread of, say, natural gas volatility at such tenors and strikes.

The moral of the story is that while this is an appealing heuristic and one that is easy to implement, valuation errors cannot be ignored, and valuation

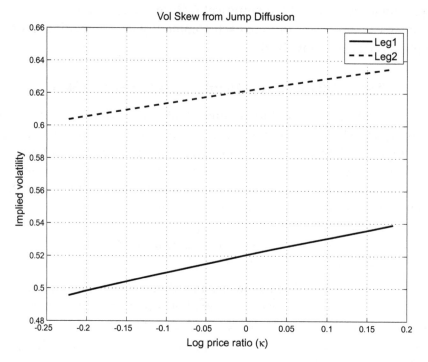

Figure 9.22. Volatility skew from joint jump-diffusion process.

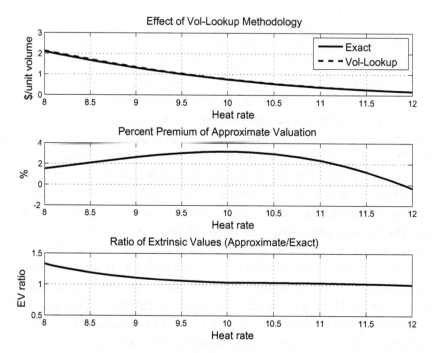

Figure 9.23. Toll valuation comparison: exact versus volatility look-up.

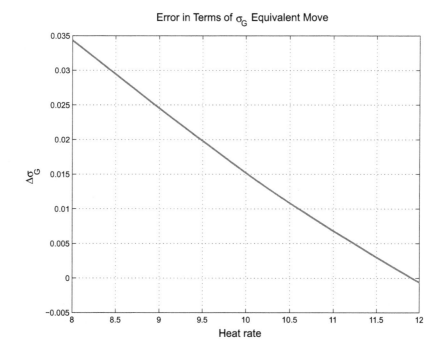

Figure 9.24. Extrinsic value error converted to $\Delta\sigma_G$.

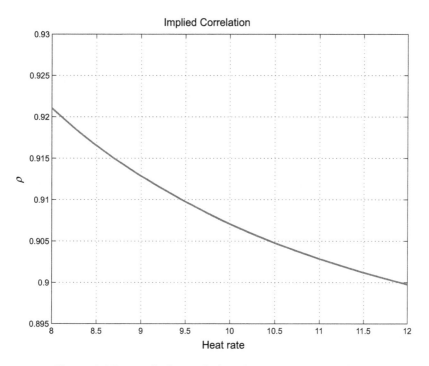

Figure 9.25. Implied correlation skew from exact values.

adjustments based on more sophisticated off-line[12] simulation methods are used by some practitioners to calculate valuation adjustments.

The numerical experiment also can be used to illustrate how the appearance of a correlation skew can arise purely out of volatility skew. If we calculate a Margrabe implied correlation based on the exact values and relevant market data (forwards and volatilities obtained by look-up and therefore including skew effects), the implied correlation varies with heat-rate as seen in Figure 9.25. Note that this is purely an artifact of the interaction of skew with the Margrabe formulation. The underlying correlation structure of returns was the same for each heat rate H_*. This exhibits another basic weakness of applying skew heuristics to spread options – namely, that skew risk can manifest as spurious correlation risk simply due to the look-up heuristic (see [AV11]).

Conclusion

Spread options constitute the major source of natural optionality arising from energy infrastructure and the related hedging requirements for financing, acquisition, and earnings management. Analysis of spread options requires the additional complexity of correlation.

The key results are

- The Margrabe formula is based on the assumption that the underlying price processes are correlated geometric Brownian motions and yield an exact solution for spread options with zero strikes.
- Convexity in a spread option is zero in the direction implied by the conversion factor (H_*): $\Delta F = H_* \Delta G$. Gamma is greatest in the orthogonal direction.
- The implied correlations of spread options in energy markets can often be quite high, resulting in vegas of mixed sign.
- High implied correlation also means that the dominant forward price changes are in the zero-gamma direction, which can result in a severe impact on the ability of the hedger to monetize the extrinsic value due to standard traded contract size.
- For spread options on two commodities with nonzero strikes, numerical quadrature is preferable to approximation methods, whether based on moment matching or on modeling the underlying spread directly.
- Heuristic methods to deal with skew in the Margrabe setting induce errors that can be relevant at conversion factors H_* well away from the money and also induce the appearance of correlation skew.

---

[12] The term *off-line* means not in production risk systems that run batch valuation on a daily basis.

Part IV
Multifactor Models

In Part III we addressed a series of problems that focused almost exclusively on structures with payoffs depending on the price process of a single underlying contract. Single-factor models were sufficient to establish reasonable valuation and to craft hedging programs provided that sensible decisions were made regarding model form and calibration.

Many franchise and merchant energy desks confront far more complex situations, including structures that depend in a nontrivial way on multiple forward prices and options structures with exercise mechanics on a range of time scales. A simplistic approach is to push the use of single-factor models to more complex situations, approximating multiple contract payoffs as arising from the dynamics of a single diffusion and using entirely separate models for different settings even if these are obviously closely related.

Multifactor models can provide (somewhat) holistic frameworks for valuation of large classes of related structures. The resulting benefit is that comparable risk metrics and hedging programs can be used for portfolios consisting of a broad set of trade types.

We will start by discussing the motivations for the deployment of multifactor models in the context of energy structures. This will be followed by the introduction of a standard Gaussian multifactor forward model that maintains a high degree of tractability while dramatically increasing the types of structures that can be handled collectively. We will conclude with a survey of various multifactor modeling paradigms, the relationships between them, and their relative strengths and weaknesses.

10

Covariance, Spot Prices, and Factor Models

The term *multifactor model* is very broad, encompassing any modeling framework in which multiple stochastic processes, often correlated Brownian motions, drive a set of asset prices. We know from the factor analysis in Chapter 5 that the volatility of the second PCA factor is certainly present, with a volatility of roughly 20 percent of that of the first factor for crude oil and natural gas. This would suggest that structures with non-linear dependence on multiple forward prices will require something more than a single Brownian motion. Moreover, single-factor models do not provide the flexibility required to unify and synthesize closely related market data.

Consider the following questions:

- How should we value more complex structures in which the payoff depends explicitly on the joint dynamics of many forward prices? These can arise in relatively simple settings such as strips of "vanilla" options structures with a total capped payout (TARN structures) or more complex situations such as natural gas storage, which requires a control theoretic framework applied to the entire forward curve.

- How do we accommodate the broad separation of time scales in price dynamics from "long-wavelength" features in which the entire forward curve moves in tandem (think of the first factor) to spot price dynamics? For example, in power, price dynamics is driven by factors with characteristic time scales of the order of a few days.

- How do we construct models that can be calibrated efficiently to multiple option types? This is closely related to the preceding point. In the context of crude oil, European, American, and Asian options all commonly trade. Monthly and daily options, in addition to annual swaptions, trade in power and natural gas markets.

- Liquidity in correlation structures is concentrated at short tenors (if any liquidity exists at all) in any given market. How can we extrapolate to correlation structures at longer, less-liquid tenors? This pertains not only to the intracommodity setting but also to cross-commodity structures such as tolls, which depend on the nontrivial behavior of returns correlations between the two underlying prices.

223

Most important, how do we handle all of this in a tractable setting? Quests for extremely realistic models usually result in valuation behemoths that can be prohibitively slow and too unstable for deployment in production risk systems. Although the relentless improvements in computational speed have helped matters, the search for viable models that are consistent with relevant empirical observations and market data continues.

Factor Models

Our first valuation efforts started with nonstandard option expiration in Chapter 7. There we saw that even for option structures depending on only one underlying forward price, using the information embedded in the implied volatilities of *all* contracts yielded more sensible results. We approached this problem in a single-factor setting defined in (7.14):

$$\frac{dF(t,\vec{T})}{F(t,\vec{T})} = \sigma(t,\vec{T})dB_t \tag{10.1}$$

where one Brownian motion drove the dynamics of the entire forward curve. At the time our focus was on the construction of reasonable forms of $\sigma(t,T)$, and because we were not dealing with spreads, we argued that the dominance of the first factor provided some justification for this approach.

An obvious and quite general extension of (10.1) ascribes a distinct Brownian driver to each contract:

$$\frac{dF(t,T_j)}{F(t,T_j)} = \sigma_j(t,T_j)dB_t^{(j)} \tag{10.2}$$

with the Brownian motions in general correlated: $\langle dB_t^{(i)}, dB_t^{(j)} \rangle = \rho_{ij}(t)$. This specification alone does not accomplish very much. The real challenge is crafting parameterizations of the volatility functions and the correlation structure that facilitate efficient calibration and valuation while maintaining consistency with empirical facts so that extrapolation from sparse market data is plausible.

Broadly speaking, there are two approaches to reducing general multifactor specifications such as (10.2) to more tractable forms. One approach starts by using diffusions to jointly describe the dynamics of the spot price and the instantaneous convenience yield, from which forward prices and implied volatilities are calculated. The other proceeds in the HJM tradition (see [HJM92]), with specification of forward returns factors and calculation of the drifts required in a risk-neutral setting. These two modeling paradigms are analogous to the distinction between short rate and factor models in interest rates [BR96]. We will compare these approaches in a later chapter;

for now, however, we will focus on Gaussian HJM-style models of the form

$$\frac{dF(t,T)}{F(t,T)} = \sum_{j=1}^{J} \left[\sigma_j(\cdot)\Phi_j(T-t)dB_t^{(j)} \right] \tag{10.3}$$

The volatilities $\sigma_j(\cdot)$ are usually functions of either spot time t or delivery time T, precisely the little-t and big-T dichotomy from Chapter 7. In addition, the factors Φ are almost always chosen to be exponentials for reasons of tractability, in which case the dynamics take the form

$$\frac{dF(t,T)}{F(t,T)} = \sum_{j=1}^{J} \left[\sigma_j(\cdot)e^{-\beta_j(T-t)}dB_t^{(j)} \right] \tag{10.4}$$

The factor decay rates β_j will turn out to be mean-reversion rates of underlying diffusion processes, but for now, the intuition is that the factor $e^{-\beta(T-t)}$ affects the forward curve at delivery time scales of $1/\beta$. A low β factor drives the forward curve "globally," while a factor with a high value of β primarily affects nearby forward prices.

The Gaussian exponential modeling (GEM) framework was introduced in the energy setting by Clewlow Strickland [CS99] and is a straightforward extension of the original HJM modeling in the rates setting [HJM92]. Other researchers introduced precursors to this framework, notably [Gab91]. Although this modeling approach is commonly used, it is by no means the only way to describe the multifactor dynamics of commodities forward curves. We will discuss other approaches, many of which are, broadly speaking, quite similar to (10.4), in Chapter 12.

How useful are factor models of this form at addressing our preceding set of questions?

Aside from its obvious limitations, that is,

- Returns are normal, and skew requires ad hoc approaches, and
- Covariance surfaces are stationary and deterministic,

the form of (10.4) is robust enough to make compelling representations of covariance structure, spot dynamics, and cross-commodity correlations.

Multifactor models are effective at unifying the valuation of many different option types on the same underlying commodity forward curve. However, multifactor models do not eliminate and, in fact, can increase the need for parameter estimation. There are rarely enough liquid options to calibrate all parameters of a model, and inference is almost always required to fill in the gaps.

The nature of the given commodity market and the structures that are typically traded play an important role in guiding model selection. A useful dichotomy categorizes markets according to the time scales involved in typical structures:

- *Long-time-scale markets.* These are commodities markets in which most traded structures involve time scales at or beyond monthly delivery. Crude oil and closely-related refined products, as well as coal, are examples of such commodities because typical swaps and options refer to monthly delivery or averages of the first nearby contract prices. In such markets, there is a limited notion of the price of the commodity for immediate delivery. Price-reporting agencies such as Platts and Argus publish "spot" prices for crude oil, but these are based on trades with delivery extending into the delivery period of the first benchmark contract [Fat11]. This effectively puts a lower bound on pricing time scales.

  The primary modeling goal in such markets is the valuation and hedging of multiple contract structures. The factor decay rates are either obtained through estimation using historical returns or set by calibration to multiple traded options types. These are usually in the ranges of $\beta_1 \in [0, 0.5]$ and $\beta_2 \in [1, 10]$, corresponding to factors that affect the forward curve on time scales of many years and fractions of a year, respectively.

- *Short-time-scale markets.* In these markets, which include natural gas and power, there are well-defined spot prices that play a central role in contract mechanics and risk management. Swaps and options structures referencing daily (or even hourly) spot prices commonly trade.

  The primary modeling goals in these markets is the valuation and hedging of both single-commodity and cross-commodity correlation structures, usually with daily spot price exposure. As we will see shortly, in these markets it is imperative to have a high-β factor to accommodate the spot price dynamics. While one can bolt a third factor onto the long-time-scale paradigm, it is more common to use two factors, with $\beta_1 \in [0, 0.5]$ and $\beta_2 >> 10$, thereby avoiding the complexity of calibration associated with three or more factors.

As we proceed, it is important to bear in mind that risk-neutral valuation constructs are devices for interpolation and extrapolation, using market data to make inferences about the value of illiquid, nonstandard products. Significant modeling risk arises when one is extrapolating to valuation at tenors beyond which markets typically trade or to options structures that are meaningfully different from vanilla products. A good example is afforded by the CSOs discussed in Chapter 9. As could be seen from the broker chat shown, liquidity in CSOs is typically at short tenor and for specific contract months. Valuation of any structure involving correlations at long tenors is an enterprise in extrapolating from limited correlation information at short tenors. With this thought in mind, we turn to covariance structure.

Long-Time-Scale Covariance Structure

For a modeling framework to deal with more complex structures with limited market data, it must be flexible enough to generate covariance structures that are reasonably close to those observed empirically. Recall the correlation surface for WTI shown in Figure 5.14, which exhibited the expected asymptotic behavior of the instantaneous correlation $\rho(T,S)$ in T and S. How effective are models such as (10.4) at replicating such correlation surfaces?

The correlation between the two Brownian motions in the two-factor setting could be time-varying, but in what follows we will assume that it is a constant $\rho_{1,2}$. In this case, the local volatility at time t takes the form

$$\sigma^2(T-t) = \sigma_1^2 e^{-2\beta_1(T-t)} + \sigma_2^2 e^{-2\beta_2(T-t)} + 2\rho_{1,2}\sigma_1\sigma_2 e^{-(\beta_1+\beta_2)(T-t)} \quad (10.5)$$

which subsumes the form (5.10) that we found to be a useful parameterization of the empirical volatility term structure.

Setting $t = 0$ without loss of generality, the instantaneous correlation between contracts T and S is

$$\rho(T,S) = \frac{\sigma_1^2 e^{-\beta_1(T+S)} + \sigma_1\sigma_2\rho_{1,2}\left(e^{-(\beta_1 T+\beta_2 S)} + e^{-(\beta_2 T+\beta_1 S)}\right) + \sigma_2^2 e^{-\beta_2(T+S)}}{\sigma(T)\sigma(S)}$$

$$(10.6)$$

The free parameters in (10.6) are

- The difference in the decay rates $\beta_2 - \beta_1$
- The volatility ratio $\lambda = \sigma_2/\sigma_1$
- The cross-factor correlation $\rho_{1,2}$

The fact that the volatility ratio and the difference in βs values are the relevant free parameters can be seen by noting that the returns of the T contract can be written as $\sigma_1 e^{-\beta_1 T}\left(dB_t^{(1)} + \frac{\sigma_2}{\sigma_1}e^{(\beta_1-\beta_2)T}dB_t^{(2)}\right)$; the prefactor $\sigma_1 e^{-\beta_1 T}$ does not affect the correlation matrix.

These three free parameters provide a considerable degree of flexibility, and sample correlation surfaces are shown in Figure 10.1 for two volatility ratios with $\vec{\beta} = [0.2,3]$ and $\rho_{1,2} = 0$.

The high-β factor serves to decouple the short-tenor returns from longer tenors – the higher the volatility ratio, the lower is the correlation. The factor correlation $\rho_{1,2}$ serves a similar qualitative purpose, with local correlation increasing as $\rho_{1,2}$ increases. A visual comparison of the lower plot in the figure with the empirical surface looks promising.

We can proceed more rigorously by optimizing over our parameter set to see how close we can get the model covariance to fit the empirical covariance – we are using the covariance so as to obtain estimates for β_1 and σ_1 and not merely for $\beta_2 - \beta_1$ and λ. Figure 10.2 shows the results of minimizing the Frobenius norm[1] of the difference of the empirical and exponential covariance matrices using WTI returns from January 2007 to December 2010.

---

[1] The Frobenius norm of a matrix A is $\sqrt{\sum_i \sum_j A_{i,j}^2}$

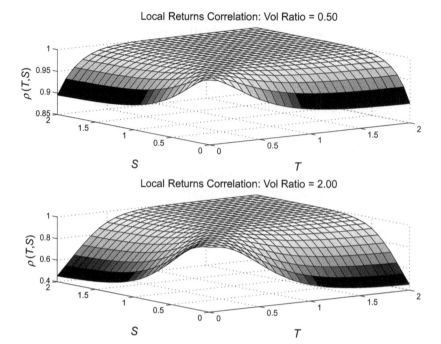

Figure 10.1. Sample two-factor local correlation surfaces.

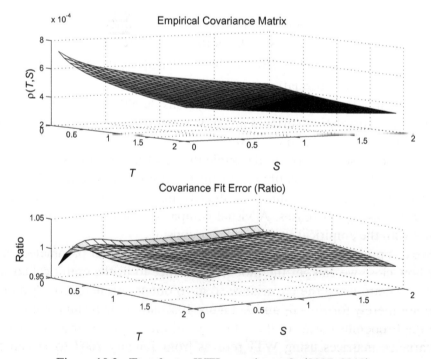

Figure 10.2. Two-factor WTI covariance fit (2007–2010).

The top figure is the empirical covariance matrix; the lower figure is the ratio of the empirical to the estimated. The optimal decay rates are $\vec{\beta} = [0.106, 1.528]$; the first factor decays at a tenor of nearly ten years; the second, at about eight months. The estimated correlation between the factors is $\rho_{1,2} = 0.119$, and the respective factor volatilities (on the time scale of one trading day) were $\vec{\sigma} = [0.022, 0.013]$.

This parametric fit of the empirical covariance matrix is arguably acceptable. The short-tenor fitting errors are of the order of a few percent, which would affect valuation of near-term CSOs, although fitting methods are easily designed to weight shorter-tenor results more heavily. Some modelers espouse using three (or more!) factors, which expands the number of free parameters meaningfully and results in even "better" fits. The consequence of course, is a more challenging calibration, with more dependence on parameter estimation and potentially a lack of stability of results due to over-fitting and the related problem of local minima in calibration. The main point, however, is that flexibility in covariance structure, coupled with, as we will see shortly, a high degree of analytical tractability, has made factor models of the form (10.4) quite popular in practice.

The estimated time scales on which the first two factors act are typically quite consistent across commodities – the first factor having a characteristic time scale of many years and the second of the order of a year. If we proceeded with natural gas or power in a similar vein, perhaps making adjustments for seasonality, we would obtain similar results. Of equal interest, however, is the fact that cross-commodity correlations also exhibit a nontrivial structure that becomes much more understandable in the multifactor setting. Figure 10.3 shows the average daily returns correlation between PJM and Henry Hub using contracts between January 2007 and December 2010 as a function of tenor.

No adjustments were made for seasonality. Note the systematic drop in correlation at short tenors. This behavior is real, and commodities prices that are highly correlated at long tenors typically exhibit a drop in correlation as short-term information (e.g., weather forecasts or announcements of generator or transmission outages) decouple the two markets.

As with intracommodity correlations, this phenomenon could be handled by time-varying correlation $\rho(T - t)$ between the two commodities' price returns in a Margrabe setting. However, such behavior arises much more naturally using (10.4) for each commodity. The first long-wavelength factors in both power and natural gas can be highly correlated, while the second high-β factors can have a lower correlation. At long tenors, the high-β factor has been "washed out," and correlations are high; as tenor decreases, the influence of the second factor becomes manifest, lowering the local correlation. Behavior such as that shown in Figure 10.3 falls naturally out of a simple relationship between the respective two-factor models.

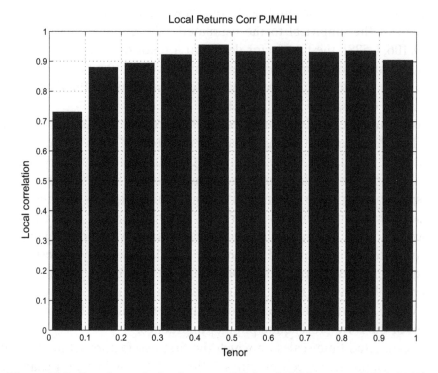

Figure 10.3. Local correlation between PJM and NG by tenor (2007–2010).

The drop in intercommodity correlation at short tenors is due to short-time-scale information, idiosyncratic to either market. Such short-time-scale information leads naturally to power and natural gas spot price dynamics and the related issue of short-time-scale optionality.

Multiple Time Scales in Options

Options in natural gas and power span the broadest time scale of deliverables among energy commodities. One approach to dealing with multiple option types is to simply treat each of these separately with its own one-factor model. For less complex trading operations, such as hedge funds with proprietary trading activities confined to the basic vanilla options types, this approach may be sufficient. It is simple, unambiguous, and extremely reliable from an operational perspective. Only a few volatility matrices need to be marked, and extrapolation to nonstandard structures is not required.

For more complex operations, this approach is wanting. If you are trading many options products, such as Asian options, quarterly swaptions, forward starters, and autoexercise daily options, in addition to the vanilla options, the absence of a unifying model means that vegas of each option type are unrelated to the others; hedging a less-liquid options structure with more liquid options is outside the framework. The number of volatility surfaces can be very large, and maintaining a handle on the total macro vega risk of a portfolio is challenging, if not impossible.

The breadth of time scales in natural gas and power markets is a good example of how multifactor models help to order one's thoughts. Before delving into this, it is useful to review the basic options structures in these markets, which are discussed in more detail in Appendix D:

- *Annual swaptions.* These are fixed-strike options exercisable just before the start of a calendar year into a calendar swap.
- *Monthly options.* These are fixed-striked options that exercise just before the beginning of the delivery month into either a swap or a forward. Monthly options can trade as single-contract months or as seasonal or annual strips.
- *Daily options.* These are a set of fixed-strike daily "optionlets" usually exercising one business day before delivery/pricing date. As with monthly options, these trade as single-contract months or as seasonal or annual strips. For peak ("5x16") power options, the number of optionlets is equal to the number of business of days in the particular month (typically twenty to twenty-two).
- *Daily options – forward starters.* As with the fixed-strike daily options, these structures constitute a sequence of daily options. The difference is that the strike is set based on the final settlement price for monthly delivery, hence the term *forward starter* becaue the strike is floating up until the delivery month. These are most common in natural gas markets, in which the settlement price is typically the bid-week price (recall that the bid-week price is a volumetric average transaction price for delivery in the upcoming month over the week prior to the delivery month).

Commonly traded options in natural gas and power involve characteristic delivery time scales that span years to days. Judicious choice of decay rates $\vec{\beta}$ can facilitate unified valuation of these disparate option types.

Spot Price Dynamics

Daily swaps and option structures exist because spot price dynamics exposes market participants to risks that cannot be hedged using annual or monthly structures. We saw in Chapter 8 that the difference in implied volatilities for monthly and daily options can be significant (see Figure 8.18). These differences at short tenors suggest a rapidly decaying high-β behavior in the heuristic of exponential factor models.

It is not entirely clear how one should define spot returns for energy commodities, particularly a nonstorable commodity such as power. Returns measure the percentage changes in the price of a *single* thing. In the absence of storage, power delivered at one time is a different commodity from power delivered at another time. Even for storable commodities such as natural gas, limits on inventory, as well as injection and withdrawal rates, can be binding constraints during periods of extreme supply-demand imbalance, decoupling pricing relationships between adjacent delivery periods.

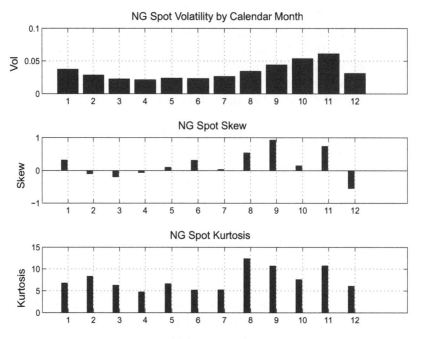

Figure 10.4. Statistics for Henry Hub classical spot returns.

Setting these concerns aside for the moment, it is useful to have a look at the behavior of spot returns defined in the typical fashion $\log\left(p_{d+1}/p_d\right)$. Figure 10.4 shows the realized returns volatility, skew, and kurtosis by calendar month for Henry Hub natural gas from January 2004 to December 2011. Over the total data set, the realized spot volatility was 0.036. This is a volatility on the time scale of one trading day; annualized, the value is roughly a factor of 2 greater than typical monthly implied volatilities for natural gas but certainly of the same order of magnitude. Binned by calendar month, seasonality is visible, with realized volatility (annualized) approaching 100 percent in early winter. There also appears to be seasonality in volatility as well as in skew (arguably) and kurtosis. Of note is that the kurtosis, calculated over the entire data set, is 14.579.

Turning to power, which is effectively not storable, Figure 10.5 shows the same results for PJM Western Hub peak daily spot prices. Here we see returns volatility that is almost an order of magnitude higher than for natural gas. The average spot volatility was 0.287; annualized, this is close to 450 percent. Also, surprisingly, kurtosis is much lower than for the natural gas case, with an average of 4.971.

The problem with using the classical definition of returns for spot prices in power, and perhaps for natural gas as well, is that the presence of large short-term variations and rapid mean reversion can cause drift in spot prices of a magnitude that affects the estimation of volatility and correlation. In the language of (10.4), this corresponds to a "spot" factor with high β and σ.

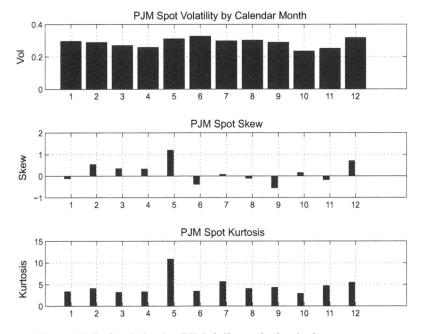

Figure 10.5. Statistics for PJM daily peak classical spot returns.

In Appendix C, it is shown in (C.25) that spot returns drift at the slope of $\log F(t,T)$ at $T=t$:

$$\frac{dF(t,t)}{F(t,t)} = \frac{\partial \log F(t,T)}{\partial T}\Big|_{T=t} + \sum_j \sigma_j dB_t^{(j)} \tag{10.7}$$

In the high-volatility – high-mean-reversion setting, this term can be large – a manifestation of the limited ability to store a commodity.

A more useful definition of spot returns is

$$\xi_t \equiv \log\left[\frac{F(t,t)}{F(0,t)}\right] \tag{10.8}$$

which relates the return of the spot price in reference to the initial forward price for the same delivery time. The issue of carry from one time period to the next is rendered moot; returns as defined by ρ_t reference the same commodity delivered at the same time and same location. For the purposes of estimation, one needs to take $t \ll 1$, in which case we have, courtesy of (C.27),

$$\xi_t \sim \sigma_2 \left(\frac{1-e^{-2\beta_2 t}}{2\beta_2}\right)^{1/2} Z \tag{10.9}$$

where Z is a standard normal random variable. This expression is devoid of the confounding effect of large drift in spot prices and a preferable definition of spot returns.

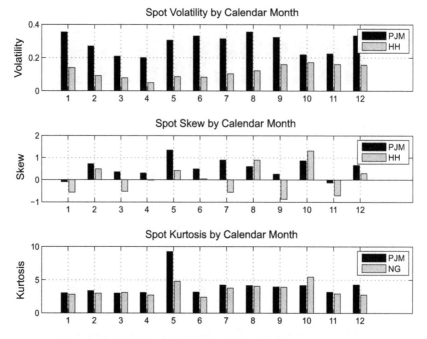

Figure 10.6. PJM and Henry Hub spot returns statistics.

To this end, using a beginning-of-month contract settlement as the reference price, and referencing time t to the settlement date of the contract T_e, the modified spot returns takes the form

$$\tilde{\xi}_d \equiv \log\left[\frac{p_d}{F_m(T_e)}\right] \tag{10.10}$$

where $F_m(T_e)$ is the settlement price for the last trading day of the standard futures or forward contract for delivery in month m, and p_d denotes the daily spot price a given day d in this month.[2] Because this settlement price is the cost for uniform delivery of power or natural gas over the delivery days in the month, this serves as the reference price $F(0,t)$ in (10.8).[3]

Figure 10.6 shows historical spot returns statistics for PJM and Henry Hub as defined in (10.10) by calendar month in the sense that all returns in January during the interval January 2004 to December 2011 were viewed as a single data set. The top plot shows the seasonality in spot returns volatility. Power spot volatility is dual peaking in summer and winter, whereas natural gas peaks solely in the winter. The skew statistics in the middle plot seem largely devoid of structure. Kurtosis is slightly greater in power, in part

---

[2] For power, a daily spot price is the average hourly spot prices over the delivery bucket. So a "5x16" daily spot price is the average of the sixteen peak hourly spot prices over the day.

[3] This definition will, of course, fail for negative daily spot prices, and the analysis here does not apply to markets with negative daily average spot prices.

because of a price spike contributing to the high kurtosis in May. However, the existence of fat tails in the summer months is evident.[4]

The spot returns (10.10) also provide a mechanism for estimating mean-reversion rate: β_2 in a two-factor world. In Appendix C [see Eq. (C.30)] it is shown that over short time scales, the correlation of spot returns decays as

$$\langle \xi_t, \xi_{t+s} \rangle = e^{-\beta_2 s} \tag{10.11}$$

The point is that the rate of decay of the spot return autocorrelation function (ACF) is determined at short time scales ($t << 1$) by the fast "spot" factor, as one would expect.

We will apply this result directly to power price data momentarily, but first it is interesting and informative to analyze the effects of the dominant fundamental driver of spot prices – weather. Reliable weather data at a large number of meteorologic stations spans fifty years or more, as opposed to, at best, a little over a decade of power price data of questionable stationarity. Analysis of weather correlation provides a guide as to what time scales are pertinent to both power and natural gas spot price dynamics.

Figure 3.42 showed the relationship between PJM Western Hub spot prices and PJM Classic Load. The conditional variance of price given load var$(p_h|L_h)$ is quite large; knowing only L_h, it would still be hard to prop trade based on the conditional mean. This is due in part to other relevant variables, notably fuel prices and seasonal maintenance cycles. More sophisticated regression-based models, which remove the effects of seasonality and fuel prices, reduce price forecasting error significantly. Load is, however, a primary determinant of the distribution of spot prices. We also saw the effect of temperature on realized load in Figure 3.37. Together these two observations imply what all power traders know – temperature is a primary driver of spot power prices.

Figure 10.7 shows historical daily average temperature at KPHL, a NOAA[5] weather station in Philadelphia in the heart of the PJM power market. Daily average temperature refers to the arithmetic average of the daily high and low temperatures measured on the respective day rounded to the nearest $1/2°$F; it is not an hourly (or continuous) average of realized

---

[4] For skew, the estimator is

$$\frac{\sqrt{N(N-1)}}{N-2} \frac{\frac{1}{N}\sum_n [x_n - \hat{\mu}]^3}{\hat{\sigma}^3}$$

where N is the sample size, and $\hat{\sigma}$ is the unbiased estimator of the standard deviation. Similarly for kurtosis, the estimator is

$$\frac{(N+1)N^2}{(N-1)(N-2)(N-3)} \frac{\frac{1}{N}\sum_n [x_n - \hat{\mu}]^4}{\hat{\sigma}^4} + 3\left[1 - \frac{(N-1)^2}{(N-2)(N-3)}\right]$$

[5] The National Oceanic and Atmospheric Administration.

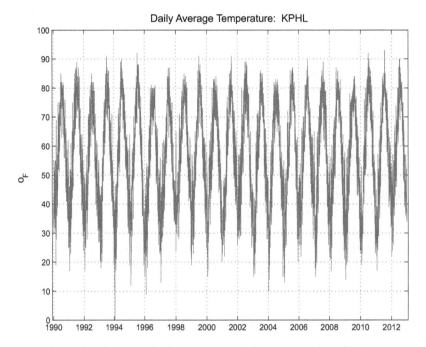

Figure 10.7. Historical average daily temperature at KPHL.

temperatures. This definition of daily average temperature is the primary underlying index in weather derivatives markets and is used for simplicity of calculation and verification. It also suffices as a regression variable in most price risk analysis, with relatively little to be gained by inclusion of finer structure.

The seasonality in daily average temperature should come as no surprise to anyone paying attention to his or her surroundings. However, in order to extract correlation structure, we need to deal with seasonality in the mean and variance of daily temperature distributions. A common and effective modeling approach starts with the premise that daily temperature τ has dynamics of the form

$$\tau_d = \mu(d) + \sigma(d)X_d \tag{10.12}$$

where d denotes day and X_d is a stationary time series, of a simple ARMA model.[6] The subtleties occur in the parameterization and estimation of $\mu(\cdot)$ and $\sigma(\cdot)$, as well as the form of X.

We will proceed here using the following parameterization:

$$\mu(d) = \alpha_0 + \alpha_1(d - d_*) + \sum_{k=1}^{K} \left\{ c_k \cos\left[2\pi k \Phi(d)\right] + d_k \sin\left[2\pi k \Phi(d)\right] \right\} \tag{10.13}$$

---

[6] Auto-Regressive Moving Average models; see [BD02].

which includes a drift α_1 and a Fourier representation for seasonality. Here d_* is an arbitrary reference date, and $\Phi(d)$ is the fraction of the year corresponding to d: $\Phi(d) = [d - BOY(d)]/365$, where $BOY(\cdot)$ is a mapping of a day to the beginning of its calendar year. A similar form is used for $\sigma(\cdot)$, which also shows seasonal behavior.

Estimation involves model selection – choosing the number of modes K, as well as accepting or rejecting the presence of a systematic drift ($\alpha_1 \neq 0$). This requires using out-of-sample selection criteria to avoid overfitting.[7] The method that we used here is brute force – selecting a sample fraction of, say, 1 percent, sequentially removing intervals of this fraction of the data, estimating using the remaining data, and calculating the out-of-sample estimation error on the removed data. Model selection involves selecting parameters that minimize the average out-of-sample forecast error over the entire data set. Using this approach yields

- $\alpha_1 \approx 1.25 \times 10^{-4}$, which is approximately $0.045°\text{F/year}$.
- $K = 3$ for both μ and σ.

These results vary by weather station. Cities with high population growth in warm climates such as Phoenix, Arizona, can exhibit much higher drifts. The goal in each case, however, is to produce a stationary set of residuals.

The preceding regressions yield the profiles for the mean $\mu(d)$ and standard deviation $\sigma(d)$ of daily average temperature for 2011 shown in Figure 10.8. The lower variance in summer months is common in North America.

The residuals from the regressions are

$$\hat{X}_d \equiv \frac{\tau_d - \mu(d)}{\sigma(d)} \tag{10.14}$$

which can be used to estimate parametric forms for X. Here our goal is to get some clarity on spot price dynamics through the ACF:

$$\rho(j) = E\left[X_d \cdot X_{d-j}\right] \tag{10.15}$$

Figure 10.9 shows ρ and the implied β obtained via

$$e^{-\beta(j)(j/365)} = \rho(j) \tag{10.16}$$

Were the residuals amenable to an AR(1) model of the form

$$X(d) = \alpha X(d-1) + Z_d \tag{10.17}$$

with Z_d independent random variables, then the implied $\beta(\cdot)$ would be a constant. Here we see a decay corresponding to just under three days

---

[7] Selecting a value of K that is too high yields what to the naked eye is obviously an overfit, with periodicities that we know from experience are not present in weather.

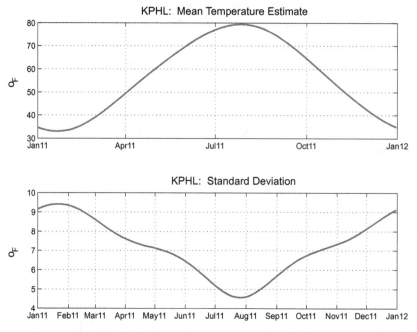

Figure 10.8. KPHL: mean and standard deviation temperature profiles.

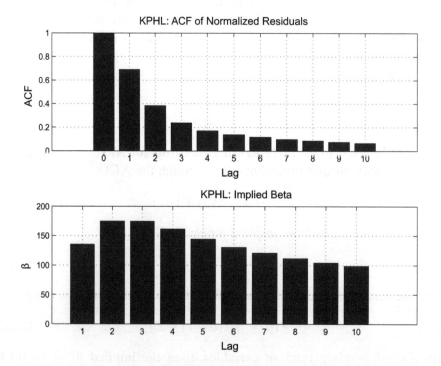

Figure 10.9. ACF and implied β for KPHL regression residuals.

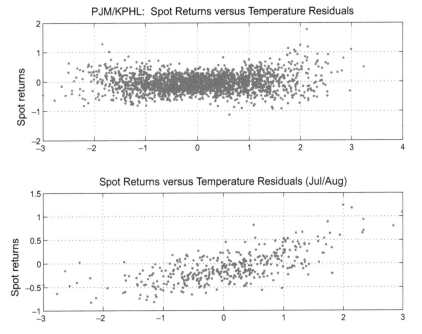

Figure 10.10. PJM spot returns versus Philadelphia temperature residuals (2007–2010).

($\approx 365/130$) at lag 1, followed by a faster decay at intermediate lags, ultimately settling down to a decay rate of between three and four days at longer lags. This would suggest that the modeling of spot price dynamics would require values of β in the second (or higher) factor of order 100.

Before turning directly to power price data, the relationship between temperature $X(d)$ and spot power prices is more than a heuristic. Figure 10.10 shows power spot returns as defined in (10.10) versus the temperature residual that we have just analyzed. The top plot shows a scatter of spot price returns versus the temperature residual series $X(d)$ over the period 2007–2010. The distribution of spot returns is affected by the temperature residual at both low and high departures from normal. The effect, however, is obscured by seasonality. The lower plot shows the results including only data for July and August, the months comprising the summer seasonal strip in power. Here the dependence of $\tilde{\rho}_d$ on $X(d)$ is much more discernible.

Turning to the direct analysis of spot price data, Figure 10.11 shows both the ACF and the implied β by lag for PJM Western Hub "5x16" daily spot returns. Note that by concatenating monthly returns series, we are making the assumption that the boundary effects at each change of monthly fixing is not a significant issue. In addition, we are ignoring the weekday/weekend distinction in the time intervals, a data issue that is not present in temperature analysis. Nonetheless, the results are of comparable magnitude with

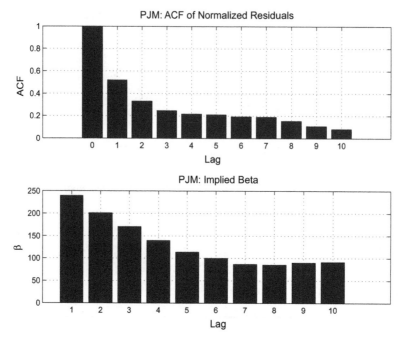

Figure 10.11. ACF and implied β for PJM spot returns (2007–2010).

those obtained in the analysis of temperature, which helps to validate that spot price dynamics imply mean reversion time scales on the order of a few days.

The preceding analysis was for power – the commodity that exhibits the most dramatic spot price dynamics. The effect of storage reduces volatility and increases correlation times. The results of the same spot returns analysis for Henry Hub natural gas are shown in Figure 10.12. Note the marked reduction in implied values of β, which implies mean reversion times of the order of a week or two, which is several times greater than for power.[8]

A Caricature of Spot Volatility

The rapid decay in correlations between both temperature and spot returns in the case of power, and even for natural gas, motivates a simple caricature of spot price dynamics. Inverting our working definition of spot returns in (10.10), and assuming that daily spot returns are uncorrelated, spot price dynamics would take the form

$$F(t,t) = F_m(T_e)e^{\zeta Z_d - \frac{1}{2}\zeta^2} \tag{10.18}$$

where the Z_d are independent (of both F_m and other Z values) standard normal random variables, and ζ is the spot volatility. The interpretation is

[8] The origin of the difference in monotonicity of $\beta(j)$ between power and natural gas is not clear.

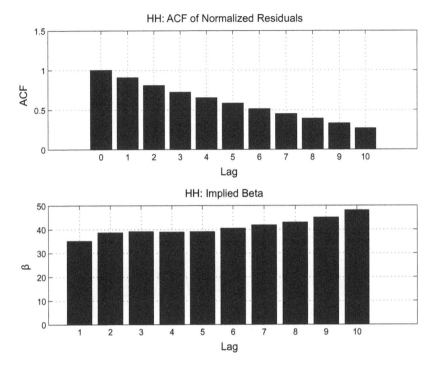

Figure 10.12. ACF and implied β for Henry Hub spot returns (2007–2010).

that the spot price on each day d is the monthly contract settle $F_m(T_e)$ price perturbed by a random and independent spot return Z_d. The presence of the $\frac{1}{2}\zeta^2$ term in the exponential ensures the required martingale property.

If we also assume that $F_m(t)$ is driven by a GBM in the traditional Black-76 setting, then this "model" can be thought of as a formal limit of a two-factor form of (10.4) with $\beta_1 = 0$ and $\beta \to \infty$. This caricature of short-time-scale dynamics couples spot prices to monthly contract prices. As such, it provides us with a method for relating monthly and daily options prices, but in a much simpler way than the more rigorous form in Chapter 11.

We will denote monthly implied volatilities by $\bar{\sigma}_M$ and daily by $\bar{\sigma}_D$; if there is any skew pertinent to the discussion, these will be functions of strike. Before proceeding, the meaning of $\bar{\sigma}_D$ warrants explanation because it pertains to the strip of daily options in the contract month. Market price is the only unambiguous attribute of anything that trades, and implied volatilities can depend on convention. Technically, the implied volatility for daily options satisfies the following equation for the observed market value V_t of the option:

$$V_t = d(t, T_S)\tilde{E}_t\left\{\sum_{d \in m} \max\left[F(\tau_d, t_d) - K, 0\right]\right\} \qquad (10.19)$$

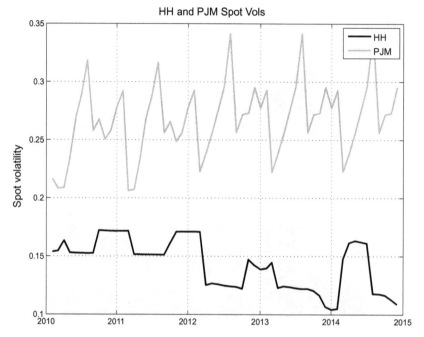

Figure 10.13. PJM and Henry Hub spot ATM spot volatility by contract month (January 11, 2010).

for a strip of daily calls where T_S is the settlement date. Here τ_d denotes expiry of option d, and each expectation depends via Black on $\bar{\sigma}_D$. In practice, because the vega for the options varies slowly with t_d at all but the shortest tenors, this is typically replaced by

$$V_t = d(t, T_S) N_m \tilde{E}_t \left(\max\left\{ F(\tau^*, t^*) - K, 0 \right] \right\} \tag{10.20}$$

where t^* corresponds to the midpoint of the month, and N_m are the number of exercise days in the month.[9] Calculating $\bar{\sigma}_D$ using either (10.19) or (10.20) is a routine numerical inversion.

Equation (10.18) and the approximation (10.20) yield the following basic relationship between σ_D and σ_M:

$$\sigma_D^2 T_D = \sigma_M^2 T_e + \zeta^2 \tag{10.21}$$

where $T_D \approx T_m + (1/24)$; that is, halfway through the delivery month. The monthly and spot variances are additive because of the assumption of independence of Z_d and $F_m(t)$. Figure 10.13 shows the at-the-money (ATM) spot volatility ζ by contract month for PJM Western Hub and Henry Hub using monthly and daily volatilities on January 11, 2010. By solving (10.20) for ζ,

---

[9] While seemingly a very casual convention, errors induced by this approximation are well within the bid-offer spread.

we have in a sense calibrated our first single-commodity multifactor model formally corresponding to (10.4) with $\vec{\beta} = [0, \infty]$.

Although this model is only a caricature of a proper multifactor model, many traders and analysts use the spot volatility ζ to assess potential trading opportunities involving spreads between daily and monthly options. Moreover, the conceptual content is almost exactly what will transpire as we work through similar calibration and valuation issues using exponential Gaussian factor models in Chapter 11.

Conclusion

A number of features of energy markets lead us inevitably toward the development of multifactor models:

- Historical forward dynamics exhibits covariance structure that a one-factor model will have difficulty replicating. Valuation of structures such as CSOs, as well more complex structures such as natural gas storage, requires empirically reasonable returns covariances.
- Empirical attributes of the term structure of cross-commodity correlation, which would require awkward correlation parameterizations using single-factor models, arise naturally from correlated multifactor models.
- The broad separation in time scales of price dynamics from global factors that act on time scales of many years to spot price dynamics in power and natural gas with correlation time scales of only a few days can be accommodated easily using multifactor models.
- Statistical analysis of fundamental drivers, notably weather, yields results that are consistent with spot returns behavior and that can be used to estimate factor decay rates.

As we transition to applying (10.4) in Chapter 11, the computations become more complex. However, the underlying approach is conceptually identical to the simple caricature of spot price dynamics introduced earlier. Equipped with a set of market implied volatilities for options spanning multiple time scales, calibration of factor volatilities follows naturally.

11

Gaussian Exponential Factor Models

Financial modeling is a tradeoff between reality and tractability. The use of Brownian motions to model returns, when precious few asset classes are consistent with normal returns, is the prototypical example. There is, however, a lot to be said about the utility of Black-Scholes. Exponential factor models for yield curves and commodity forwards are another example of a balance between tractability and reality. These models can capture several, though certainly not all, important empirical features of price dynamics. In this chapter we will discuss in detail the Gaussian exponential factor models of the form (10.4) covering calibration to market data as well as application to specific valuation problems.

We saw in Chapter 10 that the covariance structures and separation of time scales achievable through the Gaussian exponential model (GEM) framework are broad. In addition, the exponential structure and assumptions of normality yield exact solutions in many situations and efficient numerical approaches in others. Some of the underlying calculations in what follows have been relegated to Appendix C in an effort to highlight the essential concepts.

Exponential Factors and Ornstein-Uhlenbeck (OU) Processes

Gaussian exponential models (GEMs) are of the general form

$$\frac{dF(t,T)}{F(t,T)} = \sum_{j=1}^{J} \sigma_j(\cdot)e^{-\beta_j(T-t)}dB_t^{(j)} \tag{11.1}$$

where the local volatilities $\sigma_j(\cdot)$ are deterministic functions of either spot time t, delivery time T, or both. The Brownian motions can be correlated. The fact that the factors and volatilities are deterministic implies that the distribution of the forward curves $F(t,\cdot)$ is jointly log-normal. Multifactor models of this form are effectively souped-up versions of Black, expanding achievable covariance structure and breadth of time scales in dynamics but skirting the issue of skew. In our applications we will be working in the two-factor setting ($J = 2$); in practice, three factors are the most that one will see deployed in production settings, and even this is rare.

The utility of exponential factors has been appreciated in financial engineering for some time. The key feature, as shown in Appendix C, is that if the volatility functions are separable in the sense that $\sigma_j(t, T) = v_j(t)\sigma_j(T)$, then $F(t, T)$ can be represented as

$$F(t, T) = F(0, T)e^{\sum_{j=1}^{J}\left[\sigma_j(T)e^{-\beta_j(T-t)}Y_j(t)\right] - \frac{1}{2}V(t,T)}$$ (11.2)

where the Y_j processes satisfy

$$dY = -\beta Y_j dt + v(t)dB_t^{(j)}$$ (11.3)

and $V(t, T)$ is the variance of the sum of stochastic integrals given in (C.4). Diffusions of the form

$$dY = -\beta Y dt + \sigma dB_t$$ (11.4)

for constant σ are called *Ornstein-Uhlenbeck (OU) processes*. The form (11.3) is a generalization with time-varying volatility.

It is important to realize that (11.2) is simply saying that

$$F(t, T) = F(0, T)e^{X - \frac{1}{2}\sigma_X^2}$$ (11.5)

where X is the normal random variable:

$$X = \sum_{j=1}^{J}\left[\sigma_j(T)e^{-\beta_j(T-t)}Y_j(t)\right]$$ (11.6)

The implications are:

- The forward prices distributions are analytically tractable and described by a *finite* set of OU (or closely related) processes. The initial forward curve $F(0, T)$ and the values of $\vec{Y}(t)$ define the entire forward curve $F(t, T)$ for all tenors T. This is extremely useful for path-dependent structures, including natural gas storage, which we will encounter later, and avails to us a set of numerical methods that would otherwise not be applicable.
- The exponential factors are consistent with the basic heuristics of volatility decay and have the flexibility to closely approximate empirical returns covariances.

We will illustrate the use of multifactor models in a single-commodity setting using two working problems. First, however, we have to address the issue of calibration of these models to market data.

Calibration

A common misconception is that production risk systems at sophisticated shops feed all observable market prices to a calibration engine, which adjusts all free parameters of the "house" model to fit the market data. In practice, this is rarely done. Such optimizations are nonlinear and laden with local minima that render the calibration process extremely time-consuming and the results unpredictable.

Typically calibration tools are provided to trading desks to facilitate the efficient marking of a few parameters that change daily in tandem with the most commonly traded options in the particular market. Other free parameters are adjusted in a more ad hoc fashion, if and when less commonly traded structures are seen quoted or if econometric estimates suggest that changes are warranted.

In crude oil markets, it would be typical to calibrate a two-factor model to match the prices of listed monthly options and Asian options, which commonly trade. When CSOs or American/European spreads trade, adjustments to the mean reversions rates $\vec{\beta}$ or the correlation parameters can be made. For natural gas, the instruments to which one would naturally gear daily calibration are swaptions, listed options or OTC look-alikes,[1] and daily options (typically forward starters). Less liquid structures such as CSOs are accommodated with other free parameters. In power, monthly and daily options are the most commonly traded options, with swaptions a close third.

Ideally, an efficient computational method maps market data to the fast-changing parameters; for example, if the fast parameters are the local volatilities $\vec{\sigma}$ and the prices of the liquid tradables $\vec{\pi}$, then a mapping

$$\vec{\sigma}(\cdot) = \Psi_{\vec{\beta},\rho}[\vec{\pi}] \tag{11.7}$$

yields the term structure of the volatilities based on the observed prices $\vec{\pi}$. Constructing Ψ for any given market is a nontrivial enterprise, and there is little value here in working through the forms of Ψ for the variety of situations that can arise, many of which involve nonlinear relations that are not amenable to closed-form solution.

In what follows, we will consider two working problems that involve optionality at the daily time scale. Structures with daily optionality are, in many respects, the most challenging to value and hedge. We will approach these problems using (11.1) in the two-factor setting; monthly and daily options will be used for calibration.

We have two factors and, for each contract month, two implied volatilities, namely, monthly and daily. The goal is to set σ_1 and σ_2 to be consistent with

---

[1] *Look-alike* means an OTC derivative that has features that are identical to a listed futures or options contract

the market prices for these two option types. To do this, we need to have tractable pricing formulas. We will assume that the mean reversion rates $\vec{\beta}$ are specified. Moreover, for ease of exposition, we will also assume that the Brownian motions are uncorrelated ($\rho = 0$), in addition to working in the big-T setting; the little-t setting involves a bootstrap modification akin to that used in Chapter 7.

Starting with daily volatility, a single daily option with delivery T expiring u time units before the delivery date has an implied volatility of

$$
\sigma_{T,u}^2 = \frac{1}{T-u} \sum_{j=1}^{2} \int_0^{T-u} \sigma_j^2(T) e^{-2\beta_j(T-s)} \, ds
$$

$$
= \frac{1}{T-u} \sum_{j=1}^{2} \sigma_j^2(T) \left(\frac{e^{-2\beta_j u} - e^{-2\beta_j T}}{2\beta_j} \right) \tag{11.8}
$$

The time interval between exercise and delivery u is different due to the presence of nonbusiness days, notably weekends. This matters in a very high-β_2 market as such as power.

Daily options are traded by contract month, and calibration involves solving for the sum of the individual daily option prices. Alternatively, a useful approximation is to average implied volatilities under the assumption that the market quote is referring to a single option at the midpoint of the month.

$$
\bar{\sigma}_D^2(m) T_{\text{mid}}^{(m)} = \frac{1}{N} \sum_{d \in m} \sigma_{T_d, u_d}^2 \tag{11.9}
$$

where m indexes contract month, $T_{\text{mid}}^{(m)}$ is the midpoint of month m, and $\bar{\sigma}_D$ is the daily volatility.

Together (11.8) and (11.9) result in a linear equation that must be satisfied by the two unknowns σ_1 and σ_2:

$$
D_1 \sigma_1^2 + D_2 \sigma_2^2 = \bar{\sigma}_D^2(m) \tag{11.10}
$$

The coefficients D_1 and D_2, while not pleasant to compute by hand, are simple to evaluate numerically.

We turn next to monthly options, for which some notation is useful:

- T_1 and T_2 will denote the beginning and end of the delivery month.
- T_e will be the expiration of the monthly option.
- $\sigma_M(m)$ will denote the implied volatility for the monthly option.
- F_m will be the initial monthly forward price.

It will be understood by context that T_1, T_2, and T_e are indexed by month m.

The exact expression for the monthly forward price at expiration is obtained from (11.2):

$$F_m \frac{1}{N_d} \sum_{d \in m} e^{\sigma_j \sum_j e^{-\beta_j(T_d - T_e)} Y_j(T_e) - \frac{1}{2} V(T_e, T_d)} \tag{11.11}$$

where N_d is the number of days in the month.

A comment is in order regarding the use of a single value for $F(0, T) = F_m$ for all days in month m ($T \in [T_1, T_2]$), at the same time that we are modeling daily structure at expiration. Viewed at the daily level, the initial forward curve being used here is a step function in tenor T, with constant values over each delivery month. One can use interpolation methods to create daily forward curves that are consistent with monthly forward prices. The distinction has meaningful effects in natural gas storage, where we will explore this more. For now we will proceed using the constant forward price at the daily level over a contract month.

Sums of log-normals as in (11.11) are not log-normal, which is an annoyance. One way around this problem is exact numerical quadrature or simulation coupled with nonlinear solvers. Alternatively, one can resort to moment matching. It can be shown that using the Levy approximation and assuming that $\sigma_M^2 T_e << 1$ result in

$$T_e \bar{\sigma}_M^2 \approx \text{var} \left\{ \frac{1}{T_2 - T_1} \int_{T_1}^{T_2} \left[\sum_j \sigma_j e^{-\beta_j(T - T_e)} Y_j(T_e) \right] dT \right\} \tag{11.12}$$

where we have returned to continuous time for ease. Using the fact [see (C.15) in Appendix C] that

$$\text{var} \left[Y_j(T_c) \right] = \left(\frac{1 - e^{-2\beta_j T_e}}{2\beta_j} \right) \tag{11.13}$$

this can be reduced to:

$$T_e \bar{\sigma}_M^2 = \sum_j \sigma_j^2 e^{-2\beta_j(T_1 - T_e)} M_j^2(T_1, T_2) \left(\frac{1 - e^{-2\beta_j T_e}}{2\beta_j} \right) \tag{11.14}$$

where

$$M_j(T_1, T_2) \equiv \left[\frac{1 - e^{-\beta_j(T_2 - T_1)}}{\beta_j(T_2 - T_1)} \right] \tag{11.15}$$

As with daily options, the requirement for monthly options is of the form

$$M_1 \sigma_1^2 + M_2 \sigma_2^2 = \bar{\sigma}_M^2(m) \tag{11.16}$$

The approximations that we used to reduce this to a linear form are useful in practice. Provided that we evaluate monthly options using the same approximations, this is self-consistent. Moreover, there is also nothing preventing the use of nonlinear solvers to reduce or eliminate the need for such approximations. The relevant point is that we are using the two liquid options types to solve for the two unknown factor volatilities, and the approach that we have followed is computationally efficient.

In the big-T paradigm calibration for a single contract month involves nothing more than calculating the coefficients ($\vec{D}$ and $\vec{M}$) and solving the linear system

$$\begin{pmatrix} D_1 & D_2 \\ M_1 & M_2 \end{pmatrix} \begin{pmatrix} \sigma_1^2 \\ \sigma_2^2 \end{pmatrix} = \begin{pmatrix} \sigma_D^2 \\ \sigma_M^2 \end{pmatrix}$$

Under the little-t paradigm, a bootstrap is required, in addition to solution of a similar linear system.

To summarize the procedure:

- Obtain σ_M and σ_D from market data, adjusting for skew via the volatility look-up heuristic.
- Compute $D_1, D_2, M_1,$ and M_2.
- Solve the preceding linear system.
- Use the resulting σ_1 and σ_2 for structure valuation.

The results, of course, depend on the mean reversion rates $\vec{\beta}$. Before proceeding to working examples, it is interesting to examine these calibration results as a function of the mean reversion rates. Figure 11.1 shows σ_1 and

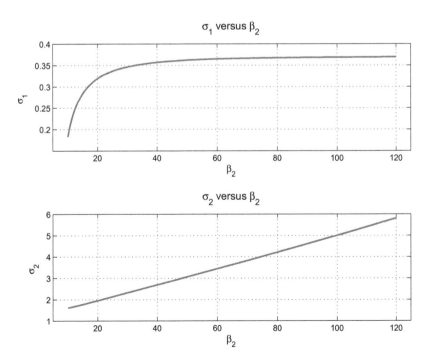

Figure 11.1. Calibrated σ values as a function of β_2.

σ_2 for October 2010 as of pricing date Febuary 3, 2010, for varying β_2 with $\beta_1 = .3$, which will be our default assumption. Note the increase in both σ_1 and σ_2 with increasing β_2; as mean reversion rates increase, more factor volatility is required to be consistent with the implied volatilities. This is merely a manifestation of the nature of the underlying OU processes. The limiting stationary variance of an OU process with parameter β_j is $1/2\beta_j$, as shown in (C.16). In (11.2) this corresponds to a factor variance of $\sigma_j^2/(2\beta_j)$. To yield the same normal returns variance, the factor variance must increase because $\sigma_j \sim \sqrt{\beta_j}$.

Valuation Examples

Our first example involves a relatively straightforward extrapolation using the commonly traded daily and monthly options in power to price and hedge a forward-starting option. Forward starters are much more common in natural gas markets than in power markets, but the problem serves as a good example of the use of multifactor models to accommodate nonstandard options types. In fact, the inverse problem of extracting daily fixed-strike volatilities from forward starter quotes would be required to calibrate these models to quoted natural gas options.

Working Problem

Price an October 2010 forward-starting daily straddle on PJM Western Hub "5x16" power as of pricing date Febuary 3, 2010, with the following terms:

- The notional is the standard lot size of 50 MW.
- Monthly index: ICE PJM Western Hub "5x16" with settlement one business day prior to the delivery month.
- Daily index: PJM RT "5x16" daily average price as published by the PJM ISO.

The pricing date is the same as in our previous calibration example. On this date, the initial forward price for the October 2010 contract is 50.40. We need to evaluate

$$\tilde{E}\left[\sum_d |F(T_d, T_d) - F_m(T_f)|\right] \tag{11.17}$$

where T_f refers to the date of fixing ("-1b," the previous business day), and F_m denotes the monthly contract price. The approach that we will follow is commonly used for forward starters [Hul12]. Focusing on one particular day d, the first step is to condition on $\mathcal{F}_{T_f}$ and calculate

$$\tilde{E}\left[|F(T_d, T_d) - F_m(T_f)| \big| \mathcal{F}_{T_f}\right] \tag{11.18}$$

Because our processes are log-normal, this is rote application of Black for an at-the-money (ATM) option – for example, the value of a call is

$$C(T_f, F) = e^{-r(T_d - T_f)} F_m(T_f) [\Phi(d_1) - \Phi(d_2)] \tag{11.19}$$

where $d_{1,2} = \pm \frac{1}{2} \sigma_{T_f, T_d} \sqrt{T_d - T_f}$ (the simplified form results from the fact that the strike is the forward in this calculation). Here σ_{T_f, T_d} denotes the volatility over the time interval $[T_f, T_d]$.[2]

All that remains is for us to calculate σ_{T_f, T_d} in the multifactor setting. Note that in our simple caricature model, the result is the spot volatility: $\sigma_{T_f, T_d} = \zeta$.

The evolution of F from T_f to T_d is

$$F(T_f, T_d) = F_m(T_f) e^{\sum_{j=1}^2 \left[\int_{T_f}^{T_d} \sigma_j(m) e^{-\beta_j (T_d - s)} dB_s^{(j)} - \frac{1}{2} V(T_f, T_D) \right]} \tag{11.20}$$

Integration yields:

$$\sigma_{T_f, T_d}^2 (T_d - T_f) = \sum_j \sigma_j^2(m) \left(\frac{1 - e^{-2\beta_j (T_d - T_f)}}{2\beta_j} \right) \tag{11.21}$$

We now have all the components for the conditional value:

$$\tilde{E} \left[\max \left(F(T_d, T_d) - F_m(T_f), 0 \right) | \mathcal{F}_{T_f} \right] = e^{-r(T_d - T_f)} F_m(T_f) [\Phi(d_1) - \Phi(d_2)]$$

The only random component of the unconditioned expectation is $F_m(T_f)$, and we know that

$$\tilde{E} [F_m(T_f)] = F_m(0) \tag{11.22}$$

The one remaining challenge is the mechanical aspect of putting this all together on precisely the right calendar days, which is not something to be done by hand. Figure 11.2 shows the pricing results for various β_2 given market data as of February 3, 2010. Over most of the range shown, the value of the forward starter increases with β_2; this is reasonable because, as we saw in Figure 11.1, high β_2 results in higher "spot volatility" σ_2, which is what is driving the difference between the daily spot price and the month fixing. The decrease in value at high values of β_2 is due to weekends: at high mean reversion rates, above roughly $\beta = 90$, the value of the Friday options with the three-day lag to Monday delivery decreases. Our estimates for mean reversions rates in power and weather in Chapter 10 suggest values of β_2 in the region of declining value. It is possible that this is merely an artifact of the model; as "Friday-only" daily options do not trade as a single product, there

---

[2] The prefactor $F_m(T_f)$ could be written as a daily forward for each day. However, becaue we are assuming that the initial forward curve is a step function over each delivery month, the result would be unchanged once we take the expected value in (11.22).

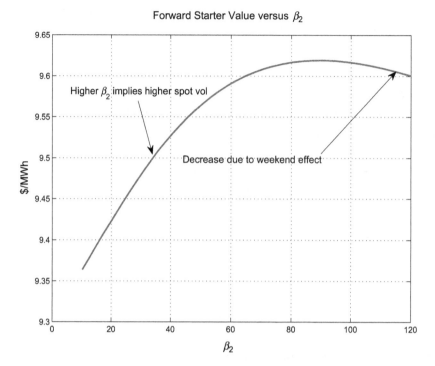

Figure 11.2. Forward starter value as a function of β_2.

is no way to validate market consensus on the point. However, there is good reason to believe that it is not an artifact. The weather analysis in Chapter 10 certainly exhibited decay in autocorrelation functions that would make this phenomenon plausible.

This valuation exercise is our first example of using a multifactor model as an extrapolation device, calibrating to liquid tradables, and using the resulting model to value a nonstandard structure. The question remains – how would we hedge this forward starter in practice?

Once the floating leg fixes at time T_f, our forward starter morphs into a fixed-strike $[K = F_m(T_f)]$ daily option. Standard fixed-strike daily options trade up to a few days before the start of the month, at which point liquidity diminishes rapidly. Near the fixing date T_f we would have a good idea of where $F_m(T_f)$ is likely to settle. At some time $\tau < T_F$, when daily options are still trading, we would take an offsetting position at a strike at or close to $F_m(\tau)$, which can be viewed as the market's estimate of where $F_m(T_f)$ will fix.

Assuming that we had a long position in the forward-starting straddle and, near expiry, sold the daily fixed-strike straddle, by the time the dust settles at T_f, we would have the following spread position for each day d in the month:

$$|F(T_d, T_d) - F_m(T_f)| - |F(T_d, T_d) - F_m(\tau)| \qquad (11.23)$$

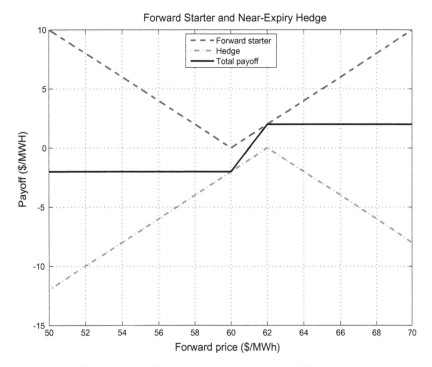

Figure 11.3. Forward starter with straddle hedge.

which is equivalent to a long or short call spread position depending on the sign of $F_m(T_f) - F_m(\tau)$. Assuming, for example, that $F_m(T_f) = 60.00$ and that the short straddle hedge was done at $F_m(\tau) = 62.00$, the resulting terminal payoff is shown in Figure 11.3. We should expect this sort of hedge slippage because of the difference in the strikes $F_m(T_f) - F(\tau)$. Recalling Table 1.1, we know that even a few days can result in meaningful slippage; however, this is a much better proposition than attempting to delta hedge a naked daily option position in the cash month where swaps liquidity is essentially concentrated on two instruments: next-day swaps or balance-of-month swaps (swaps that fix on the remaining days of the month).

This is an important point: limitations in the instruments available for hedging the risk in daily structures result in inherent, and often meaningful, hedge slippage. The next example shows what can happen when we take extrapolation even further.

Working Problem

The current date is April 1, 2011. Value a Henry Hub Gas Daily "peaking" option that pays the best J daily forward-starting call options out of the thirty-one days in January 2012.

This is a *lookback* option. Let $\mathcal{I}_J$ denote the subset of the thirty-one days in January 12 with the largest J values of $\max\left[p_d - F_m(T_f), 0\right]$; t_d, denotes the spot delivery time for day d, and p_d is the Gas Daily spot price for day d. The structure will pay

$$\frac{1}{J} \sum_{d \in \mathcal{I}_J} \max \left[p_d - F_m(T_f), 0 \right] \tag{11.24}$$

We are normalizing the payoff by $1/J$ to afford comparison between structures with different J – normally contracts specify a payoff that is based on the sum only.

Peaking options are more commonly structured as manually exercised so that the holder of the option can exercise a call option J times during month, usually one business day before the delivery date. This is harder to value and manage, and the preceding lookback (or autoexercise) example already illustrates the challenges in managing such structures. See [CS00] or [JRT04] for more detailed discussions.

The relevant market data on April 1, 2011, were

- NYMEX natural gas (NG) for January 12 delivery is trading at \$5.131/MMBtu.
- The standard NYMEX ATM (monthly) call option for January 2012 has a monthly implied volatility $\sigma_M = 0.298$.
- The analogous ATM daily option has an implied volatility of $\sigma_D = 0.324$.[3]

Using these market data and calibrating the Gaussian two-factor model using $\vec{\beta} = [0.30, 40]$ yield $\vec{\sigma} = [0.34, 1.17]$.

The lookback peaking option is amenable to Monte Carlo valuation. The dynamics of $F(t, T)$ are driven entirely by the two OU processes $\vec{Y}_t$ (11.3), which take the forms show in (11.3) with their respective values of β, because we are using big-T calibration. Our goal is to construct the joint distributions of $F_m(T_f)$ and each of the spot prices $F(d, d)$. The mechanics of simulation are discussed in Appendix C.

Given a realization of the OU processes

$$\left[\vec{Y}_{T_F}, \vec{Y}_{t_1}, \ldots, Y_{t_{31}} \right] \tag{11.25}$$

and the initial forward price $F_m(0)$, we compute $F_m(T_f)$ by integrating $F(T_f, T)$ as in (11.2) using $t = T_f$ with $T \in [T_1, T_2]$, where T_1 and T_2 are the start and end times of the delivery month. Recalling that $F_m(T_f)$ is a bid-week construct, we have taken T_f to be four business days before the start of the delivery month.[4]

---

[3] While this option does not commonly trade, the forward starter being the more liquid, we will assume for now that this mark has been made by the trader consistent with observed options trading at or near this date.

[4] It is possible to simulate F_m through bid week (recall the discussion on locational spreads in Appendix D), computing a trade-weighted average using some a priori assumption about the trade weighting, but in practice this is probably "more pain than gain" in accuracy compared with the approach we have taken here.

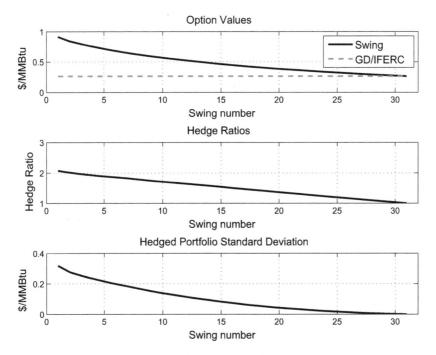

Figure 11.4. Swing option valuation results

The daily spot prices p_d for each delivery day d are given by (11.2), where t is set to be one business day before each delivery time t_d because the fixing for the Gas Daily index occurs for trading on this day. For high-β factors, it is important to keep track of exactly when indices are fixed relative to the delivery time.

Valuation results are shown in Figure 11.4 for a varying J. The number of simulations was 100,000, and the Monte Carlo error was approximately 0.3 percent of the estimated values. The top figure shows the value in \$/MMBtu as a function of swing number. Note that because as we have normalized by J in (11.24), the value decreases with J since lower realized spot prices are included in the average.

The second and third plots show how effectively one can expect to hedge these structures. Using the most relevant liquid option hedge, namely, the standard forward starter call (which corresponds to $J = 31$), a minimum-variance hedge is computed as described in Appendix B. The hedge ratio, shown in the second plot, is the quantity of the forward starter for the optimal hedge; if you are long the swing option, this quantity should be sold to yield the minimum-variance portfolio under the risk-neutral measure. The third plot shows the resulting standard deviation of the hedged portfolio payoff.

When $J = 31$, the swing option is coincident with the forward starter, so the hedge quantity is unity and the hedge variance zero. More important, however, is the large hedge slippage that results at lower values of *J*. The standard deviation of the hedge portfolio is of the order of 20 to 30 percent of the value of the structure as calculated under the risk-neutral two-factor setting – hardly a deterministic outcome. One can consider expanding the set of options to include other strikes, but the gains are minor and the transaction costs nontrivial.

Some traders argue that (somehow) they can delta hedge structures such as these, although such optimism needs to be taken with a healthy degree of skepticism. All that is really available for hedging within the cash month is natural gas for next-day delivery or for the balance of the month. This is a very limited set of instruments with which to extract the extrinsic value of daily structures. For example, if forecasts suggest the likelihood of particularly cold weather five days out, little can be done using these instruments to delta hedge the increased value of the swing call option on that day.

The moral of the story regarding this second working example is that the likelihood of substantial hedge slippage cannot be dismissed as a "higher-order term." The nature of the swing option structure is such that in many cases one can do little more than construct an optimal portfolio prior to the start of the delivery month and then simply watch the cash month realize, summing the settlement results at the end to see what transpired. What this means is that we have pushed the use of the model as a valuation extrapolator beyond reasonable limits and, in the construction of hedge ratios and calculation of residual risks, made the quite arbitrary decision to use the risk-neutral measure as the reference measure for portfolio optimization.

Conclusion

The Gaussian exponential factor framework accommodates two important features of the energy markets commonly encountered:

- Backwardation of volatility
- Separation of time scales – slow mean reversion of price level (at all tenors); fast mean reversion of spot prices

In addition, the flexibility in covariance surfaces that can be obtained through such models makes them useful in a variety of settings, notably in valuation of swaptions and CSOs, as well as other correlation structures. In this modeling paradigm, however, forward returns remain normally distributed, and volatility lookup heuristics are required for skew-dependent structures.

The fact that one can formally evaluate expected payoffs for spot price structures, as in the case of peaking options, does not mean that the underlying tenets of risk-neutral evaluation pertain. Many a trading desk has failed to fully appreciate the deleterious effects that result from a lack of liquid tradables available for hedging. Even with carefully crafted hedges, the substantial residual risks inherent in structures such as the daily swing option example render the realized economics "actuarial"[5] in nature.

Applying models such as (11.1) in such settings is arbitrarily selecting a risk-neutral measure for use as a reference measure in an incomplete market setting in order to facilitate portfolio-optimization calculations. In light of this observation, it is fair to ask why one would not be better off making an effort to craft models of the "physical" measure, performing portfolio-optimization calculations based on such. We will return to this question shortly.

---

[5] By *actuarial*, we mean simply being realized as opposed to dynamically managed.

12

Modeling Paradigms

The original Black-76 framework for risk-neutral forward price dynamics is a model for a single futures contract. While it is easy to generalize Black-76 to the forward-curve setting by considering a set of correlated geometric Brownian motions (GBMs), each driving an individual contract price, this is merely a cosmetic improvement. Modeling the returns correlation structure effectively while maintaining tractability is the hard part. Simply writing martingale diffusions for forward curves in the absence of empirical analysis accomplishes little.

A number of modeling approaches beyond Black-76 have been developed over the past several decades, each intended to capture either observed or postulated attributes of commodities price dynamics. The preponderance of the work has been motivated by a body of thought referred to as the *theory of storage*, discussed earlier in Chapters 2 and 5 in the context of the carry formalism.

The Theory of Storage

The carry formalism decomposes forward yields into three components: the cost of funding, the cost of storage, and the more ethereal convenience yield. All that can be inferred about forward curves for consumption commodities using basic carry arbitrage arguments was given in (2.12):

$$F(t, T) \le F(t,t)e^{[r(t,T)+q(t,T)](T-t)} \tag{12.1}$$

which provides an upper bound on $F(t, T)$ in terms of the spot price $F(t,t)$, the financing rate $r(t, T)$, and the cost of storage represented as a rate $q(t, T)$. The convenience yield $\eta(t, T)$ is the "correction" that renders (12.1) an equality:

$$F(t, T) = F(t,t)e^{[r(t,T)+q(t,T)-\eta(t,T)](T-t)} \tag{12.2}$$

Before proceeding, it is useful to spend a moment discussing the meaning of $q(t, T)$. Does $q(t, T)$ represent the market price for storage or the physical costs associated with storage – for example, losses and fixed costs? As we will see in Chapter 13, the market cost of acquiring storage depends on the forward curve and the volatility structure of the commodity. This is easy to see – if a forward curve is in steep contango, the owner of storage can earn the forward yield net of funding and storage costs and would require a higher price to sell storage capacity than if the forward curve were backwardated. Given that the only quantity observable from the forward curve is $q(t, T) - \eta(t, T)$, it is convenient to treat $q(t, T)$ as purely the cost to the storage owner, expressed as a rate applied to the spot price, to store the commodity over the time interval $[t, T]$. The convenience yield $\eta(t, T)$ is then the aggregate of all other considerations, including the market value for storage capacity.

While we have referred to this as a *carry formalism*, the theoretical underpinnings and empirical analysis of the yield decomposition in (12.2) is referred to as the *theory of storage*. Research under this rubric has spanned the better part of a century at this point. As summarized elegantly by Ng and Pirrong [NP94], the theory of storage refers to two distinct trains of thought. The first essentially posits (12.2), interpreting the convenience yield as a rate of return that owners of storage capacity can achieve by holding the commodity in inventory for sale at a later time. References related to this stream of work include Kaldor [Kal39], Working [Wor49], and Telser [Tel58]. This was followed by work done by Brennan [Bre91] and Williams [Wil86], with related work by Fama and French [FF87].

The second approach to relating forward and spot prices involves explicitly modeling supply and demand balance in the presence of storage optionality – storage operators will buy the commodity in the spot market when it is "cheap" and sell it when it is "expensive." Quantifying what this actually means involves a dynamic control problem, closely related to what we will use in Chapter 13 to value physical storage. This approach was developed by Bresnahan and Spiller [BS86], Williams and Wright [WW91], and Deaton and Laroque [DL91], in addition to more recent work by others, notably Routledge, Seppi, and Spatt [RSS00] and a monograph on the subject by Pirrong [Pir12].

A simple arbitrage argument illustrates the connection between inventory and price dynamics. Denoting current inventory by I_t, in discrete time, the following must hold:

$$
\begin{cases}
F(t, t + \Delta t) = e^{(r+q)\Delta T} F(t, t) & \text{if } I_t > 0 \\
F(t, t + \Delta t) < e^{(r+q)\Delta T} F(t, t) & \text{if } I_t = 0
\end{cases}
\tag{12.3}
$$

where r and q are financing and storage costs over $[t, t + \Delta t]$. This condition can be viewed as an enhancement of (12.2) and illustrates how inventory can affect the joint dynamics of spot and futures prices. Decreasing levels of inventory increase the probability of a stock-out, that is, hitting the zero-inventory boundary, which would decouple spot and forward prices. As a consequence, lower inventory levels should be associated with negative forward yields.

Although the second approach essentially derives the concept of convenience yields from first principles, the consequences of the theory of storage extend far beyond merely the relationship between inventory and forward yields. As summarized in [NP94], the *postulated* consequences for forward dynamics are

1. Low levels of inventory are associated with low (negative) forward yields.
2. Realized returns volatility increases as convenience yields increase and, owing to (1), as inventories decrease.
3. As convenience yields increase, realized volatilities become more backwardated as a result of convexity of the convenience yield as a function of inventory.
4. The correlation between returns at two tenors T and $T+S$, $\rho(T, T+S)$, as defined in (5.11), decays more rapidly in S as convenience yields increase. Equivalently, returns for distinct delivery periods become less correlated as inventories fall.

Just how compelling is the empirical evidence? Ng and Pirrong [NP94], Pirrong [Pir12], and references therein address these matters using sophisticated estimation methods on historical data. We have seen empirical support for the "first law" of the theory of storage, namely, the preceding point (1), in Figures 2.8 and 3.27. A visual survey of the other postulates is useful, if only for comparison with the first.

Figure 12.1 shows realized volatilities of the first nearby and the ratio of the realized volatilities of the second to the first nearby contracts versus forward yields for WTI from 2000 through 2011. Figure 12.2 shows the same results using the first and second calendar strips[1] to mitigate inventory anomalies at the WTI delivery location in the last few years (recall Figure 3.12 and related discussion in Chapter 3). In each case, rolling three-month windows incremented monthly were used; each point represents a three-month statistic. The points corresponding to large positive values of forward yields are at the apex of the credit crisis when massive contango and very high volatilities were observed – both realized and implied. If one excludes volatilities above 0.5, effectively removing this interval, it is possible that structure exists that is consistent with the posited increase in volatility and decreasing volatility ratio as forward yields decrease. This is illustrated by the linear fit, although the regression has $r^2 = 0.084$, suggesting a weak relationship at best. Figure 12.3 shows similar results for Henry Hub natural gas, which are even less compelling. The relationships are weak.

Energy is not necessarily the best place to begin an empirical critique of the theory of storage. Inventory data for crude oil and refined products are incomplete, often not including important global participants. North

---

[1] The daily average of the twelve nearby returns in each strip was used as the strip return series.

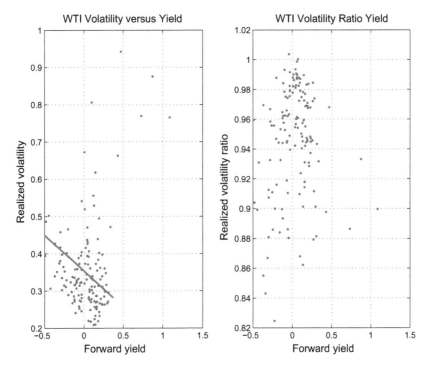

Figure 12.1. WTI volatility statistics versus forward yields: first and second nearby contracts (2000–2011).

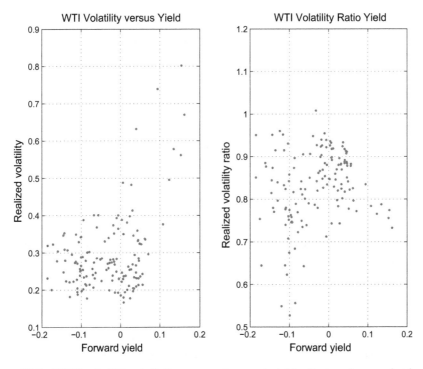

Figure 12.2. WTI volatility statistics versus forward yields: first and second calendar strips (2000–2011).

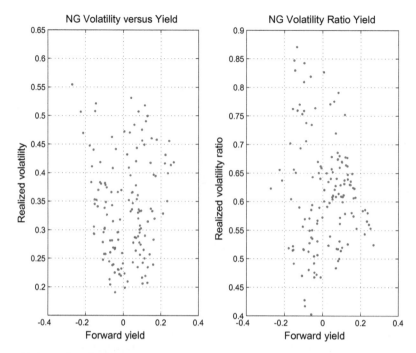

Figure 12.3. NG volatility statistics versus forward yields: first and second calendar strips (2000–2011).

American natural gas has reliable weekly inventory data, but conclusions are much more difficult to draw due to the complexities of seasonality. Some traded metals, on the other hand, have reliable inventory data and relatively stable storage costs. Predictably, much of the research literature has focused on metals, and Figure 12.4 shows results for London Metal Exchange (LME) copper. Here the results are somewhat more compelling, although clearly something unusual was afoot at high forward yields. In summary, the support for the posited consequences of inventory-driven price dynamics provided by a cursory graphic look at the data is underwhelming.

It is important to understand that the stylized facts enumerated earlier are derived consequences from a plausible theory. A good deal of effort has been made by researchers to validate or refute the validity of these predictions empirically. Most analysis has been in nonseasonal commodities, in particular, in metals, where storage costs are explicitly defined by metals exchanges such as the LME. We saw in the case of crude oil that storage costs undoubtedly depend on forward yields in a recursive fashion – recall our discussion is Chapter 2 of the flotillas of tankers, some of which were used for storage in the immediate aftermath of the eruption of the credit crisis. Moreover, in the case of natural gas with its seasonal attributes, an upper bound on storage capacity, and no transparent mechanism for ascertaining the historical physical costs of storage, testing the theory of storage

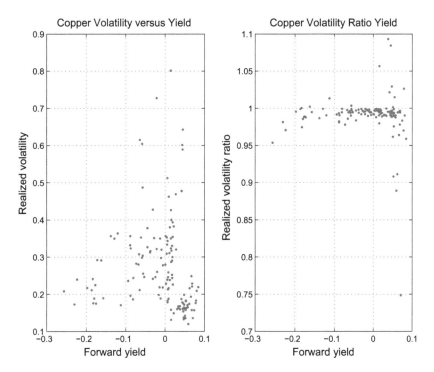

Figure 12.4. LME copper volatility statistics versus forward yields: first and second nearby contracts (2000–2011).

is extremely challenging. Finally, it is clear that volatility can be driven by much more than inventory. Global macroeconomic factors are relevant – the credit crisis resulted in high volatilities even when inventories were high and increasing rapidly. This motivates the use of stochastic volatility in the drivers for inventory models, as suggested by Pirrong [Pir12].[2]

Models for commodity price dynamics can be grouped into three categories: reduced form, econometric, and structure. The postulated behavior enumerated earlier has affected the evolution of the development of each of these.

As in other asset classes, the *reduced-form approach* to valuation refers to modeling frameworks that posit price dynamics in the absence of "fundamental" considerations, specifically without a stylized representation of the actual physical system and market that interact to set spot prices. In the case of some energy commodities, a great deal is known about supply and demand. Examples include generator stacks and load dynamics in power and weather-driven demand dynamics and storage facilities in natural gas. In addition, pricing-setting mechanics can be quite well defined, either

---

[2] The level of complexity of stochastic volatility coupled with the basic stochastic dynamic control problem embodied in inventory optimization is, at this time, numerically intractable for all practical purposes.

through surveys or by means of more rigorous market-clearing algorithms as in power. Models that start with a caricature of the underlying market mechanics, referred to as *structural models*, are in a sense at one end of the modeling spectrum, with reduced-form models at the other.[3] Occupying a space somewhere between reduced-form and structural models are what we will refer to as *econometric models*, which craft regressions tailored to individual markets and are often used in tandem with reduced-form models. In what follows, we will survey these three general modeling paradigms.

Reduced-Form Models

Reduced-form models in commodities start with the thought that the sum of storage costs and convenience yields is a natural stochastic variable because neither component can be ascertained separately from forward prices. Consequently, the convenience yield η net of storage costs q, which we will refer to as the *modified convenience yield*

$$\hat{\eta}(t, T) \equiv \eta(t, T) - q(t, T) \tag{12.4}$$

can take any value. The fact that there are no a priori constraints on $\hat{\eta}$ is at the heart of reduced-form models, which can take the form of models for the joint evolution of spot prices and $\hat{\eta}$, the HJM-style factor models introduced in Chapter 10 and developed in Chapter 11, or hybrids of the two approaches.

We started our treatment of multifactor models in reverse chronological order, beginning with the HJM approach. As in interest-rate modeling, in which short-rate models predated HJM-style forward factor models, the same is true in commodities. The fact that we resorted to empirical analysis of spot price dynamics to guide us in the selection of parameters in (10.4), however, suggests that directly modeling spot price dynamics may have its virtues [Pil98]. Moreover, in many situations, models in the two categories yield identical forward dynamics, much as in the interest-rate setting, as discussed by Baxter and Renie [BR96]. Whereas the direct modeling of spot price and convenience yields introduced in the early 1990s was the dominant paradigm for over a decade, it has been largely supplanted by forward factor models, especially among practitioners.

---

[3] *Fundamental modeling* is another term that is often used and that can be broadly interpreted. These models include large computational efforts to effectively replicate market mechanics and infrastructure in extreme granularity, including, for example, details of transmission constraints, individual generator attributes, or gas pipeline networks, resulting in large-scale optimization problems. One could consider this as defining yet another part of the modeling spectrum, and in fact, Burger, Graeber, and Schindlmayr [BGS07] survey commodities modeling with an emphasis on fundamental models. However, the computational burden and the large number of free parameters limit the utility of such methods in financial mathematics and portfolio management.

The first generation of risk-neutral commodities models, Black-76 aside, started with diffusive models for the spot prices with mean-reverting attributes as introduced by Schwartz [Sch97]:

$$dS_t = \kappa \left(\mu - \log S_t \right) S_t dt + \sigma S_t dB_t \qquad (12.5)$$

In this model, referred to as the *Schwartz one-factor model*, $\log S_t$ mean reverts to a level μ, which can be generalized to a function of time $\mu(t)$ for calibration. This model is related to the earlier work of Brennan and Schwartz [BS85] and is effectively equivalent to a one-factor Gaussian exponential model (GEM) with all the limitations associated with single-factor models of forward dynamics.

A significant step in the evolution of spot models was the coupling of the spot price and the instantaneous convenience yield, as introduced by Gibson and Schwartz [GS90]. This model took the form of coupled diffusions – the spot price being a log-normal diffusion with its drift a function of the convenience yield, and the convenience yield being an Ornstein-Uhlenbeck (OU) process mean reverting to a specified level:

$$\begin{aligned} dS_t &= (r_t - \delta_t) S_t dt + \sigma S_t dB_t^{(1)} \\ d\delta_t &= \kappa \left(\theta - \delta_t \right) dt + \gamma dB_t^{(2)} \end{aligned} \qquad (12.6)$$

with $d\langle B^{(1)}, B^{(2)} \rangle_t = \rho$.

The basic train of thought is simple and compelling. By correlating the two Brownian motions, increases in spot prices can be correlated with increases in convenience yield, which is what is typically observed. Highly backwardated markets, that is, markets exhibiting substantial negative forward yields, are associated with low inventory and commensurately high spot prices.

Figure 12.5 shows this phenomenon for WTI from January 2000 through December 2011 by plotting the forward yield implied by the first two calendar strip prices versus the average of the two strip prices. Calendar strips are used here to look at long-tenor forward yields, avoiding the effects of Cushing surplus as well as financial index rolls[4] that have an effect on forward yields at short tenors. Two regimes are visible, depicted by showing the 2006–2011 interval separately. Aside from the transition period, each shows forward yields decreasing with inventory. The later regime is much more compelling due at least in part to the large range of prices spanned during this interval.[5]

---

[4] Recall that commodity exchange-traded funds (ETFs) move or "roll" their positions from an expiring contract to the next contract on a monthly basis.

[5] A lot was happening in the transition between these two regimes. In addition to OPEC changing reference pricing policy, we will also see in Chapter 17 that open interest in longer-dated contracts increased considerably during this period.

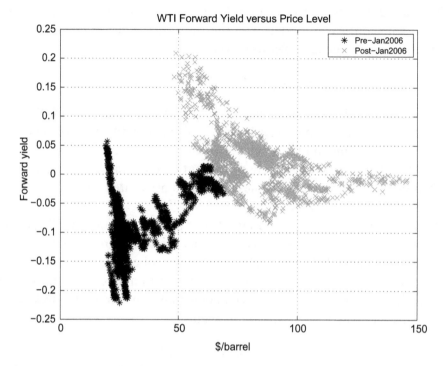

Figure 12.5. WTI calendar strip forward yields versus price level (2000–2011).

Similar phenomena are observed for natural gas, as seen in Figure 12.6. As with oil, there was a similar regime change. Empirical results of this type are observed broadly across energy and commodities more generally and are a feature that can be captured successfully by (12.6).

As with all spot price models, forward prices are obtained via the martingale property:

$$F(t, T) = \tilde{E}(S_T | \mathcal{F}_t) \tag{12.7}$$

When $\delta_t > r_t$, the spot price has a negative drift, and the forward curve is locally backwardated; conversely, if $\delta_t < r_t$, it is in contango.

In the form just specified, it can be shown (see [CL04]) that

$$F(t, T) = S_t e^{\int_t^T r_s \, ds} e^{B(t,T)\delta_t + A(t,T)} \tag{12.8}$$

where

$$B(t, T) = \frac{e^{-\kappa(T-t)} - 1}{\kappa}$$

$$A(t, T) = \frac{\kappa\theta + \rho\sigma\gamma}{\kappa^2} \left[1 - e^{-\kappa(T-t)} - \kappa(T-t) \right]$$

$$+ \frac{\gamma^2}{\kappa^3} \left[2\kappa(T-t) - 3 + 4e^{-\kappa(T-t)} - e^{-2\kappa(T-t)} \right]$$

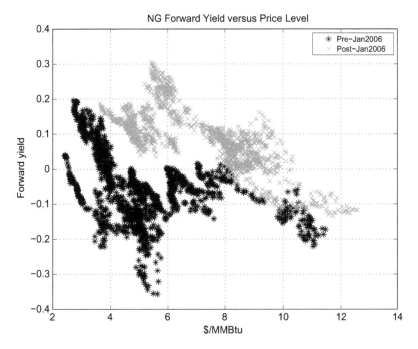

Figure 12.6. Natural gas (NG) calendar strip forward yields versus price level (2000–2011).

An immediate consequence of (12.8) is that differentiation implies

$$\frac{dF(t,T)}{dt} = \sigma \, dB_t^{(1)} + \gamma \frac{e^{-\kappa(T-t)} - 1}{\kappa} dB_t^{(2)} \tag{12.9}$$

which is subsumed by the original GEM formulation (10.4). In short, the Gibson-Schwartz approach is identical to a GEM with the first factor having $\beta_1 = 0$ and the second factor $\beta_2 = \kappa$.

Another way of looking at the relationship is through spot dynamics, which, in the GEM setting, is given by (C.25):

$$\frac{dF}{F}(t,t) = \left. \frac{\partial \log F(t,T)}{\partial T} \right|_{T=t} + \sum_j \sigma_j dB_t^{(j)} \tag{12.10}$$

The spot price drifts at the local slope of the forward yield, a fact that applies to all risk-neutral forward processes

Differentiation of (12.8) yields

$$\left. \frac{\partial \log F(t,T)}{\partial T} \right|_{T=t} = r_t - \delta_t \tag{12.11}$$

as required, and the stochastic drivers are two Brownian motions, establishing equivalence of spot dynamics.

The functional form for $F(t,T)$ implied by (12.8) is very specific, and in order to calibrate (12.6) to a general forward curve, time-varying coefficients are required. This was noted much earlier both in spot rate modeling as discussed by Baxter and Renie [BR96] and surveyed by Hull [Hul12] and as applied specifically to commodities in [Mil03]. This is the awkward aspect of the spot diffusion approach; in forward models, the initial forward curve is the state variable; by construction, it is consistent with observed forwards. Whereas the forward dynamics implied by (12.9) is functionally equivalent to that of (10.4), the initial calibration is more transparent in the latter. In short, these two basic formulations [(10.4) and (12.6)] are equivalent and can generate the observed relationship of forward yields and price levels.

The Gibson-Schwartz model can be represented in an alternative fashion that can be more useful, as shown by Schwartz and Smith [SS07]. The approach decomposes the logarithm of the spot price into short- and long-term components: $\log[S_t] = \chi_t + \zeta_t$, which are driven by correlated diffusions:

$$d\chi_t = -\beta \chi_t dt + \sigma_\chi dB_t^{(1)} \tag{12.12}$$

$$d\zeta_t = \mu_\zeta dt + \sigma_\zeta dB_t^{(2)} \tag{12.13}$$

The short factor is our familiar OU process, whereas the long-term log-price level is a Brownian motion with drift. The equivalence to (12.6) can be established (see [SS07]). The fact that the long-term price level diffuses without any mean reversion, a significant assumption, is equivalent to the fact that the first factor in (12.9) has $\beta = 0$ in the GEM equivalent.

This alternative to the original formulation (12.6) avoids explicitly modeling convenience yields and takes the framework very close to that of the GEMs, in which the two factors with (usually widely) separated decay rates represent spot and long-tenor dynamics. Beyond this esoteric point, empirical estimation of parameters is easier using (12.12). Estimates for the correlation between the Brownian drivers in (12.6) can be relatively high, in some cases above 0.90; the alternative formulation (12.12) yields much lower correlations, allowing more robust estimation.

There are features of price dynamics, empirical or suggested by the theory of storage, that are not captured by the Gibson-Schwartz formulation, or its more general but moral equivalent GEM factor models. Among these are the absence of both skew and a relationship between forward yields and returns volatility. This has spawned an expansive collection of extensions of (12.6) designed to more closely match observed or hypothesized features of forward dynamics. While an exhaustive survey would distract from the main issues, we will briefly mention a few innovations to give a flavor of some of the modeling twists.

Schwartz introduced a three-factor version of the original model in which interest rates are stochastic and correlated with spot and convenience yield drivers [Sch97]

$$dS_t = (r_t - \delta_t) S_t dt + \sigma S_t dB_t^{(1)}$$
$$d\delta_t = \kappa (\theta - \delta_t) dt + \gamma dB_t^{(2)}$$
$$dr_t = \alpha_Z (r_* - r_t) dt + \lambda dB_t^{(3)} \qquad (12.14)$$

This model is functionally equivalent to a three-factor GEM, and closed-form expressions for forward contracts can be computed. Empirical analysis of this model, in comparison with the two-factor model discussed in [Sch97], is ambiguous, with the two models often yielding very similar results. Rather than estimate exponential factors directly, estimates of the interest-rate process were done first using rates data, and then the two-factor $[S_t, \delta_t]$ process was analyzed. The performance of the three-factor model in fitting historical forward prices is not meaningfully better than that achieved by the Schwartz two-factor model. The situation is different when it comes to extrapolation. Estimating parameters empirically and using the current forward curve at short tenors to set S_t and δ_t, the extrapolated values at long tenors can differ significantly between the two formulations. For example, the limiting differential forward yields

$$\lim_{T \to \infty} \frac{1}{F(T)} \frac{\partial F(T)}{\partial T}$$

can vary by several percentage points between the two formulations – a nontrivial difference when valuing assets over long time horizons.

Many additional extensions of the basic Gibson-Schwartz formulation have been made over the years, including the addition of stochastic volatility, stochastic interest rates and jumps, and attempts to couple volatility directly with the state of the forward curve. One example is a two-factor model introduced by Ribeiro and Hodges [RH04] that was designed to allow volatility to vary with forward yield – the second in our list of postulated attributes of forward dynamics. The model takes the form

$$dS_t = (r_t - \delta_t) S_t dt + \sigma S_t \delta^{1/2} dB_t^{(1)}$$
$$d\delta_t = \kappa (\theta - \delta_t) dt + \gamma \delta^{\frac{1}{2}} dB_t^{(2)} \qquad (12.15)$$

The $\delta^{1/2}$ term in the volatility for δ_t is of the Cox-Ingersoll-Ross (CIR) variety [CIR85] used in rates modeling and serves to keep δ_t positive, a necessary feature given the presence of $\delta_t^{1/2}$ in the spot price volatility. Closed-form solutions for the forward curve can be obtained; however, in estimation based on historical realizations of WTI forward prices, the model performs only incrementally better than the Gibson-Schwartz model.

Stochastic volatility extensions are also easily added, although tractability becomes an issue. For example, Hickspoors and Jaimungal [HJ08] consider a class of models of the form $S_t = e^{g_t + X_t}$, where, adopting their notation,

$$dX_t = \beta (Y_t - X_t) \, dt + \sigma_X(Z_t) dB_t^{(1)}$$
$$dY_t = \alpha_Y (\phi - Y_t) \, dt + \sigma_Y dB_t^{(2)}$$
$$dZ_t = \alpha (m - Z_t) \, dt + \sigma_Z dB_t^{(3)} \qquad (12.16)$$

with $\sigma_X(\cdot)$ positive, bounded, and smooth. The stochastic volatility driver Z_t is an OU process, and valuation formulas are obtained using perturbative methods similar to those introduced in [FPS00], with the stationary variance $\sigma_Z^2/2\alpha \ll 1$ the small parameter.

These examples illustrate the importance, certainly in research circles, of the Gibson-Schwartz model as a starting point from which to add extensions. We have also seen that this model is subsumed by the HJM framework, and it is natural to consider working directly with the HJM framework as the starting point. This idea has been championed by Trolle and Schwartz [TS09], who use transform methods to value "vanilla" options under forward dynamics of the form

$$\frac{dF(t, T)}{F(t, T)} = \sum_j e^{-\beta_j(T-t)} v_j^{1/2}(t) dB_t^{(j)} \qquad (12.17)$$

with

$$dv_j(t) = \left[\eta_j - \kappa_j v_j(t) \right] dt + s_j v_j^{1/2}(t) d\tilde{B}_t^{(j)} \qquad (12.18)$$

The intuition here is similar in some respects to (12.15), in that the stochastic volatilities associated with each exponential factor mean revert to stationary expectations with a square-root volatility-of-volatility term. The primary thrust of the work in [TS09] is a detailed analysis of historical options data and statistical evidence of unspanned stochastic volatility – dynamics of the volatility surface that is not a function of the underlying forward dynamics. The presence of unspanned volatility components renders vega exposure unhedgable by purely trading the underlying forwards. While most commodities options traders would consider this self-evident based on their experiences, the class of processes introduced and used in the study is, at the time of this writing, one of the more advanced states of reduced-form modeling.

All of the preceding examples have price dynamics driven by diffusions. Energy commodities, however, frequently exhibit behavior that is far from diffusive in nature. Power markets provide the most striking departures from diffusive behavior, especially at short time scales because of the unstorable nature of the commodity. Figure 12.7 shows a time series of PJM daily average peak spot prices and a QQ plot of spot returns as defined in (10.10) from May through August 2011. The price dynamics near the end of May and in

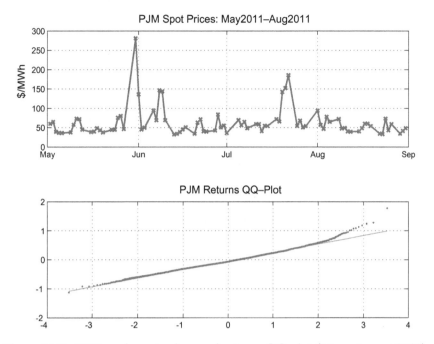

Figure 12.7. PJM peak spot prices and returns QQ plot (May–August 2011).

mid-July certainly could warrant the qualitative description of *spikes*; moreover, basic tests for reject normality resoundingly – not surprising given the appearance of the QQ plot.

Such behavior has spawned additional mutations of reduced-form models in which price spikes are explicitly modeled, as suggested early in the history of power markets by several authors, including Kaminski [Kam97] and Barz and Johnson [BJ98]. Deng [Den00], building on the work of Duffie, Pan, and Singleton [DPS00] on affine models, explicitly incorporated spikes in a sequence of models using Poisson jumps and regime switching. While this was done in a two-commodity setting, with applications to valuation of power generation in mind, the one-factor version of the jump diffusion introduced

$$dS_t = \kappa \left[\mu(t) - \log S_t \right] S_t dt + \sigma S_t dB_t + \Delta J_t \qquad (12.19)$$

is effectively (12.5) supplemented by an additional Poisson jump process ΔJ_t with arrival rate $\lambda(t)$ and jump density $\phi(\cdot)$. This is similar in form to the forward jump-diffusion processes discussed in Chapter 8. The heuristic motivation of this model, as well as more refined versions introduced by Deng and others (see, e.g., [CF05], [GR06], and [Kho05]), is that spikes (ΔJ_t) occur and mean revert to a running level $\mu(t)$, superimposed, of course, on the basic mean-reverting geometric Brownian motion (GBM). In a similar vein, use of the Levy processes in lieu of Brownian drivers has been proposed by several authors (see, for example, [BKMB07] and [BNBV10]).

There is a fundamental incompleteness in such market dynamics. The value function of any derivative is now driven by both the Brownian motion and the jump process. Therefore, delta hedging a derivative on the contract price $F(t, T_m)$ cannot result in a zero-variance outcome because of the jumps – you cannot neutralize both sources of randomness simultaneously. If the jump density $\phi(\cdot)$ is a pointmass, then it is possible (within the framework of such a model) to effect a delta hedging strategy using two forward contracts. The realistic situation, however, is with a continuous jump density that results in an incomplete market given the finite set of forward contracts available for hedging.

The design of reduced-form models is a balance between tractability and retaining empirical features of price dynamics. Proponents of reduced-form models view the number of variations of spot/convenience yield models, and almost equivalently HJM-style factor models, as a sign of a vibrant and evolving paradigm that is yielding increasingly realistic and useful valuation and hedging methods. On the other hand, most of these approaches are used by small subgroups of practitioners, if they are used at all. In fact, production valuation is almost always accomplished using relatively simple models – GEM or near equivalents, if not (in some unadvertised cases) simply Black-76. The lack of instruments available for calibration renders many of these approaches intellectually stimulating but challenging to use in practice. Many of the more sophisticated reduced-form models serve, at best, as "satellite" or off-line desk valuation tools.

Econometric Models

Limitations on the set of liquid tradables to which to calibrate any of the preceding reduced-form models are an exogenous problem arising not from a lack of quantitative methods but from capital limitations, market conventions, and a high level of uncertainty about future developments of rapidly evolving markets. In energy markets generally and power markets in particular, many practitioners have been at the vanguard of developing alternative approaches to valuation that can depart meaningfully from the complete-markets paradigm.

The typical approach to incomplete markets in mathematical finance starts with a parametric specification of price processes on which the ultimate results entirely depend. This renders many of the results of research on incomplete markets less useful in situations where no simple class of processes seems to match observed price behavior and is the primary motivation for econometric and structural models.

The characteristic that distinguishes econometric and structural modeling approaches from reduced-form modeling is that the balance between consistency with empirical behavior and analytical tractability shifts meaningfully toward the former, with much more concern about fitting realized price data. These methods often incorporate known structural attributes of the physical and price-clearing mechanics of the market being analyzed. Econometric methods attempt to construct models for spot price dynamics in the physical measure via regression and simulation, with the structure of the regressions based on known attributes of the market. For example, in power markets we know that temperature affects load and that load and fuel prices affect the ultimate market-clearing spot prices. This hierarchy guides the design of regressions. Structural models can be thought of as turbo-charged econometric models, adding far more detail about mechanical features of the market and effectively creating classes of nonlinearities that would be very challenging to discern using purely econometric methods.

Both the econometric and the structural approaches lead inevitably to a dichotomy in the method of implementation. Once the physical measure is constructed, it can be transformed in some way to be consistent with observed market data, forwards, and options, thereby yielding a risk-neutral measure. Alternatively, the physical measure can be used for construction of optimal hedges using standard portfolio theory. We will illustrate this distinction in the following example of econometric methods for valuation.

Working Problem

Price a TETM3 at-the-money (ATM) January 2013 daily call on December 30, 2011.

While some basis options traders would argue that TETM3 in the Northeast is a reasonably liquid hub and that one could obtain quotes for such an option, such a view on almost any delivery location other than Henry Hub is probably optimistic. Moreover, before hitting or lifting any bid or offer, it would be prudent to independently establish an assessment of fair value.

We encountered TETM3 in Chapter 1, where Figure 1.6 illustrated that rather dramatic locational price dynamics can occur in cold regions where supply depends on long-haul transport for natural gas. We have also seen that basis markets trade between Henry Hub and TETM3, which provide mechanisms for hedging fixed-price risk. In addition, there is a liquid monthly options market at Henry Hub, and there is certainly some measure of activity in daily options markets there. Our approach to this problem will be to apply a model that relates temperature and Henry Hub spot prices to the realized locational spot price at TETM3, thereby allowing us to construct an effective hedge of the TETM3 daily call using both Henry Hub and TETM3 swaps as well as Henry Hub daily options.

A natural variable for regression purposes is

$$\zeta(d) \equiv \log\left[\frac{p_{\text{TETM3}}(d)}{p_{\text{HH}}(d)}\right] \qquad (12.20)$$

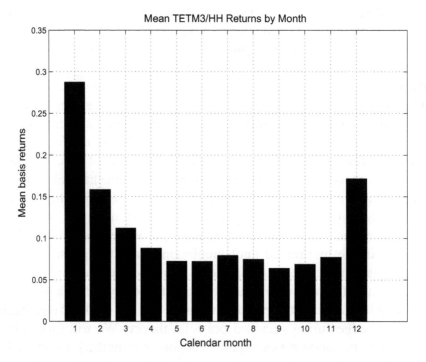

Figure 12.8. Mean TETM3 locational returns by calendar month.

which we will refer to as the locational return. Working with this variable yields a (nearly) price-level-independent problem, allowing us to use data across a much larger time span. In what follows, model calibration uses price and temperature data from January 2002 to December 2011 .

Figure 12.8 shows the average realized values of $\zeta(d)$ by calendar month; the seasonal behavior is manifest. Much of this seasonality is due to temperature effects. The first plot in Figure 12.9 shows realized locational returns $\zeta(d)$ versus temperature $\tau(d)$ at KBOS (Boston), labeled "Actual." Basis dynamics becomes most interesting at low temperatures, as expected.

A plausible representation of this behavior is the following parameterization:

$$\zeta(t) = \alpha + \beta t + \sum_{k=1}^{K} [\gamma_k \sin(2\pi kt) + \delta_k \cos(2\pi kt)] + \sum_{j=1}^{J} \eta_j \theta(t)^j + \epsilon(t) \quad (12.21)$$

where t is measured in units of years, and $\epsilon(t)$ is the residual. The variable $\theta(t)$ is a regularized temperature variable:

$$\theta(t) = \frac{e^{\lambda(t)}}{1 + e^{\lambda(t)}} \quad (12.22)$$

with

$$\lambda(t) \equiv \frac{\tau(t) - \tau_{\text{ref}}}{w} \quad (12.23)$$

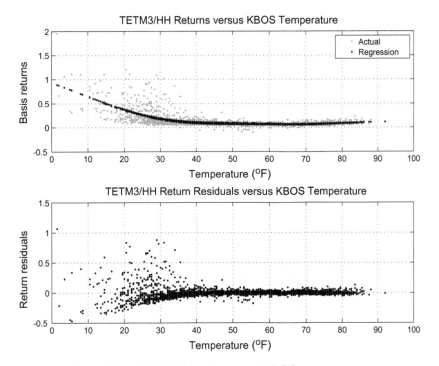

Figure 12.9. TETM3 basis versus KBOS temperature.

with τ_{ref} and w selected to be characteristic mean and width of temperatures realized over the entire data set. The introduction of $\theta(t)$ is purely technical and is required to avoid aberrant behavior of the model (12.21) outside the range of realized temperatures by bounding the independent variable $\theta \in [0,1]$. Although more sophisticated regression models can be envisioned, for example, by including exogenous variables such as pipeline capacity or peak winter demand, this representation does a reasonable job in fitting the data and allows us to illustrate econometric valuation methods.

Out-of-sample model selection keeps one seasonal mode at very low amplitude and a fifth-order polynomial in θ. The resulting historical estimate is shown as the regression points in the top plot in Figure 12.9. The residuals $\epsilon(t)$ are shown as a function of temperature in the lower plot. Higher volatility is observed at extreme temperatures, an effect that also has to be regressed and used to normalize and subsequently fit the residuals with standard time series methods such as ARMA processes.

We are now in a situation where, given a specification of the dynamics for $p_{\text{HH}}(d)$ and $\tau(d)$, we can generate joint realizations of $[\tau(d), p_{\text{HH}}(d),$ $p_{\text{TETM3}}(d)]$ under a physical measure. We have already dealt with temperature in Chapter 10, where the forms of the models were defined in (10.12) and (10.13). A common approach to the modeling of the reference natural gas price $p_{\text{HH}}(d)$ is to use a risk-neutral pricing model, for example,

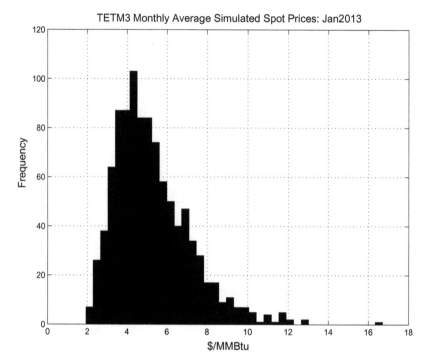

Figure 12.10. Distribution of simulated average monthly TETM3 spot prices (January 2013).

the GEM framework. This is purely a convenient assumption that facilitates construction of a joint physical distribution for the relevant price variables and weather index.[6] In addition, we will assume independence of τ and p_{HH}. While this could easily be generalized to correlated processes, we will see in Chapter 13 that spot dynamics at Henry Hub is positively correlated with Northeast temperature to the tune of an R^2 of roughly 10 percent, making the assumption of independence not unreasonable.

Using these assumptions, (12.20) and (12.21) imply that the temperature and seasonal effects result in an adder to the the Henry Hub implied volatility. This could facilitate closed-form solutions in some situations. However, here we are looking to craft hedges of the monthly strip of daily calls; auto-correlation of weather and prices complicate such calculations considerably. Moreover, more sophisticated approaches could include correlations between temperature and spot returns as well as nonlinearities in p_{HH}, each of which would render any attempt at exact calculation very challenging. Simulation is the preferred approach.

Figure 12.10 shows a histogram for monthly average spot price of the 1,000 simulations generated using the preceding approach. Given the joint distribution of p_{HH} and p_{TETM3} in addition to the market prices of the respective

---

[6] The process for $p_{HH}(d)$ can be replaced by whatever process a user would like to deploy.

swaps and Henry Hub options, we are in a position to perform some rigorous portfolio analysis. As of the pricing date December 30, 2011, the relevant facts are

- The prevailing forward price for January 2013 Henry Hub was $3.882/MMBtu.
- For TETM3, the forward price was $5.341/MMBtu. In contrast, the simulated (physical measure) forward price was $5.162/MMBtu, implying a positive risk premium for winter natural gas at TETM3, a feature generally expected by market participants.
- The value of the ATM Henry Hub daily call option was $0.466/MMBtu. We will use the Henry Hub ATM call as our sole options hedge in the portfolio analysis that follows.

At this stage we face the choice mentioned earlier – use the physical measure directly or "risk-neutralize" it.

If we shift the distribution of spot prices by the risk premium (the difference between the TETM3 forward price 5.341 and the simulated expected spot price 5.162), the result is a distribution that is consistent with the observed forward price. Using this modified distribution to value the daily call option results in a value of $0.855/MMBtu. In more complex situations, where observed market data at the basis location are more extensive, more elaborate mappings from the physical to a risk-neutral distribution are required. The somewhat arbitrary nature of such transformations is a weakness of this approach.

The alternative is to construct hedging portfolios directly from the simulated physical measure. Denoting the payoffs of the three instruments that we have considered as hedges by $\vec{h}$ and the payoff of the basis option by π, the minimum-variance result

$$\vec{\alpha}_* = \underset{\vec{\alpha}}{\arg\min} \operatorname{var}\left(\pi + \vec{\alpha}^\dagger \vec{h}\right) \tag{12.24}$$

yields a portfolio that hedges a long position in the basis option. Note that π and $\vec{h}$ are undiscounted terminal payoffs. For our working problem, the minimum-variance hedge of the long TETM3 option, obtained as discussed in Appendix B, is shown in Table 12.1. As expected, the hedge portfolio involves selling the ATM Henry Hub daily call, which in tandem with the TETM3 option results in a basis position: long TETM3 and short Henry Hub. This is neutralized by the long position in the Henry Hub swap and the short position in TETM3.

In constructing the hedged portfolio

$$\tilde{\pi} \equiv \pi + \vec{\alpha}_*^\dagger \vec{h} \tag{12.25}$$

we receive the premium of $0.466/MMBtu from the Henry Hub daily call option. In addition, the hedged portfolio has a mean $E(\tilde{\pi}) = \$0.469/\text{MMBtu}$,

Table 12.1. *Econometric Analysis: Hedge of TETM3 Basis Option*

HH Swap	TETM3 Swap	HH ATM Daily Option
0.899	−0.786	−0.975

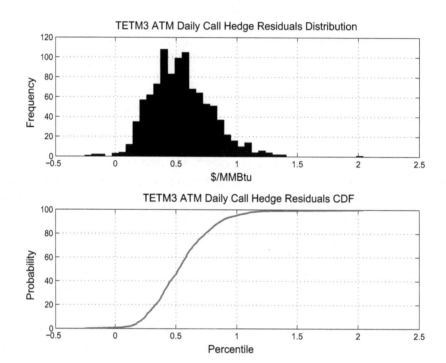

Figure 12.11. TETM3 basis option hedge residuals.

suggesting a midvalue for the TETM3 daily call of the sum of the two values, $0.924/MMBtu. This is approximately 8 percent higher than the value obtained by simply shifting the distribution to match the TETM3 forward price.

Figure 12.11 shows a histogram of $\tilde{\pi}$ as well as the cumulative distribution function. The standard deviation of the hedged portfolio is $0.228/MMBtu, which is a significant fraction of the option premium.

The merit of this approach is that in a situation with illiquid options markets on a commodity that has a relationship with a benchmark commodity that can be parameterized and estimated, the resulting physical measure can be used to construct effective static hedges. This method also yields an estimate of the distribution of realized values of the hedged portfolio – the hedge slippage. This allows one to construct reasonable bid-offer spreads on the structure in question.

Critics of this type of valuation methodology, however, make several valid points. First, the use of a risk-neutral measure for p_{HH} was arbitrary and done for convenience. That said, there is nothing preventing deployment of a preferred rendition of spot price dynamics for the reference hub if one exists. Second, the use of a static hedge and resulting valuation excludes the possibility of rebalancings that would improve hedge effectiveness. In practice, however, the original portfolio typically does not require rebalancing unless regime changes occur that result in basis dynamics that is no longer represented by the original econometric model.

Limitations of Reduced-Form and Econometric Methods

There are merits to each of the previously discussed approaches. The considerable variety of reduced-form models can span a great deal of model "phase space," leaving the ultimate practitioner a menu of models with differing qualitative attributes from which to choose. Econometric approaches are often favored by portfolio managers dealing with less liquid positions because they yield statistical results which bear resemblance to phenomena that have occurred. Even these methods, however, are often layered on top of a generic reduced-form model, as was the case for the basis option example just completed. The reason for this is that locational prices typically reference a benchmark, and developing econometric or structural models for benchmark prices can rapidly expand to include global macroeconomic considerations.

It is useful to revisit reduced-form models regarding consistency with observed forward dynamics. Addressing this issue is not a simple matter because the observed data are in the physical measure. Above and beyond defining the structure of the model to be tested, assumptions must be made about risk premia – assumptions that are usually made with tractability of estimation in mind. For example, it is common to posit constant market prices of risk. In the Gibson-Schwartz setting, this amounts to adjusting the drift terms for the spot and convenience yield processes by constants.

Despite the somewhat ad hoc nature of assumptions on the form of risk premia, there are indeed concerns about the consistency of standard reduced-form models. Carmona and Ludkovski [CL04] analyzed the Gibson-Schwartz (12.6) two-factor model, applying filtering methods to estimate the mean reversion and volatility parameters using WTI spot contracts. With these parameters fixed, they then computed the time series of convenience yields δ_t implied by different forward contracts using (12.8).

The results are disturbing. The convenience yields implied by the rolling three-month contract bear little resemblance to those of the twelve-month contract. Up to the assumptions made about risk premia, it would appear that Gibson-Schwartz, as one example, cannot consistently fit the historical forward prices. This analysis is not conclusive by any means. Gibson-Schwartz is a very specific model, a subset of the GEM framework; allowing the long factor to have mean reversion could improve the results. Other reduced-form models yet to be analyzed in this way may perform better. These results, however, are, cause for concern.

Viewing the issue of consistency from the HJM framework, in which the prevailing forward curve is specified as an initial condition, one might be tempted to argue that the issue is resolved – either by using factor-based models such as GEM or by using the equivalent of adding time dependence to spot-convenience yield models. This notion, however, merely pushes inconsistencies to an intertemporal form; factor dynamics such as those we used in GEM are typically not consistent with realized forward dynamics. In practice, on a daily basis the model is recalibrated to the most recent forward curve; formally

$$F(t+\Delta, T) = F(t, T)e^{\sum_{j=1}^{J}\left[\sigma_j(T)e^{-\beta_j(T-t+\Delta)}Y_j(t+\Delta)\right]-1/2V(\Delta, T)} \tag{12.26}$$

where at each time t the "initial" forward curve is set to $F(t, T)$, and the OU processes are reinitialized to $Y_j(t) = 0$. A consistent model would not require this daily recalibration.

Above and beyond this concern, there are situations that are commonly encountered in energy markets, especially in asset valuation, that exceed the capabilities of reduced-form models at a basic level. For example:

1. *Data limitations.* The maximum tenors at which forwards and options are liquid and therefore useful for price discovery and calibration often fall far short of the tenors required for valuation. Moreover, options liquidity often decays rapidly away from the ATM strikes, rendering skew, as marked by traders, the result of little more than guesswork, perhaps enhanced by parametric extrapolates provided by modeling groups.

2. *Uncommoditized risks.* The payoffs of many structures have components that are not traded but that clearly interact with the price components of the payoff. An example, which we discuss at length in a later chapter, is load swaps in which the payoff is the product of the hourly realized system load and the differential between floating and fixed price: $L_h(p_h - p_{\text{fixed}})$. Load is altogether uncommoditized – vanilla swaps and options on L_h or daily averages thereof do not trade.[7]

3. *Macro changes in price dynamics.* Exogenous forces, for instance, changes in technology, market structure, or regulation, can significantly alter the dynamics of forward prices. A recent example is the introduction of new forms of natural gas exploration, which have resulted in an epochal change in price relationships between natural gas and coal in the United States, fundamentally altering

---

[7] For a brief period of time in the early 2000s, market making for load swaps did occur on Enron's electronic trading platform Enron On Line. This is the only instance that the author is aware of in which such markets existed, and even in this case available tenors were only one or two weeks.

generation stacks around the country. Tax incentives are another case in which regulatory fiat can alter the energy landscape in parts of the world through the subsidized addition of wind, solar, and other renewable generation technologies.

Reduced-form and econometric models have basic limitations in some or all of these situations.

Consider the case where an existing asset with an expected remaining life of ten years[8] requires valuation for the purpose of acquisition. This means that the present value of the asset over its remaining life must be established at tenors beyond the range of market liquidity at the location of the asset. Reduced-form models have only one way of dealing with this – namely, the construction of extrapolations of forward prices and volatilities. Such extrapolation usually involves ad hoc functional forms with no systematic method to accommodate information about future events – think of generation retirements or transmission development, each of which is often announced years in advance. Econometric models, which is based on stationarity of the variables being used to describe the system, fare only slightly better. Regressions can be constructed that include high-level descriptors for system supply and demand growth, but parameterizations of the effects of such fundamental variables are usually the result of educated guesswork.

A greater distinction between the reduced-form and econometric approaches appears in the second situation. Reduced-form models have no concept of uncommoditized variables such as system load. Some practitioners have proceeded by simply decreeing the existence of load forwards and volatilities. However, because such do not trade, these fictional "forwards" and "options" are marked using econometric estimates, with the ultimate result being a peculiar hybrid of physical and risk-neutral measures all being used in a risk-neutral setting. The econometric approach, on the other hand, often explicitly models key drivers such as weather-driven demand, which allows for construction of a physical measure for the joint distribution of both commodities prices and the uncommoditized variables. In this sense, econometric models cover more ground.

High-impact events are another matter altogether. As we will see shortly, changes in the relative value of key fuels such as coal and natural gas have nonlinear effects on the price dynamics of power. Reduced-form models usually depend on specification of constant or deterministic correlations between drivers – a distinctly "linear" approach – and hoping to divine a set of coupled diffusions that would adequately approximate the nonlinearities in the system is not a viable strategy. Econometric models also suffer in this context. Unless there have been historical precedents for fuel switching or changes in the supply stack, little can be done to credibly construct physical distributions in such situations.

---

[8] In many cases, the time horizon is several decades.

These limitations have been appreciated by practitioners for many years. Although reduced-form and econometric methods are quite useful and standard fare on many trading desks, models that utilize known attributes of the mechanics of a market to infer plausible nonlinear relationships, so-called structural models, are the most promising avenue for improvements in valuation methodology.

Structural Models

We will focus our initial discussion of structural models on power markets. Perhaps counterintuitively, the fact that power cannot be stored in any meaningful quantity makes things simpler because there is no actively managed inventory process to cause temporal coupling. The spot prices that balance supply and demand are, to a good approximation, a one-time-period calculation. Temporal coupling at short time scales does in fact occur as a result of the mechanical limitations of generating units – most generation cannot simply switch on and off instantly. For the problem of creating plausible physical distributions, though, this short-time-scale coupling is typically omitted.

In Chapter 3 we introduced the concept of a generation stack, which is the function mapping cumulative capacity to marginal cost of generation. All generation in a region of interest is grouped into a single supply stack without any locational constraints. Given a set of fuel prices, which of course, are essential to the calculation of the cost of both fossil fuel – and nuclear-based generation, the generating capacities of the units $[C_1,\ldots,C_N]$ are sorted in increasing order of cost of generation $[p_1,\ldots,p_N]$. The stack is the step function

$$\Psi\left(C|\vec{F}_t\right) = p_n(\vec{F}_t)\mathbf{1}_{\{C_{n-1}<C\leq C_n\}} \tag{12.27}$$

where $\vec{F}_t$ is the set of relevant fuel prices at the prevailing time t. Typically, the marginal price of a single generator p_n depends on only one component of $\vec{F}$. The reason that this function is of interest is due to the notion that at a given level of system load (demand) L, the clearing price should be (more or less) the marginal cost at level L:

$$p(t) \approx \Psi\left(L|\vec{F}_t\right) \tag{12.28}$$

This is the basic modeling precept underpinning structural models for power.

The concept of a stack, as defined earlier, is replete with ambiguities and flaws of which analysts of power markets are well aware. To begin with, most modern power markets involve nodal pricing – this means that the market-clearing mechanism sets prices at many hundreds of locations as shadow prices from a network optimization, which accounts for system constraints on generation and transmission, enhanced with reliability criteria. Real power markets more closely resemble graphical networks of locational generation and load with constraints than a homogeneous collection of capacity as represented in (12.27). The stack representation assumes that all generation and load sit unconstrained at one location with the price-versus-supply function defined in (12.27). Another issue is that the capacity of a generator C_n is usually taken to be the maximum output of the generator, while in fact the generator can be down owing to forced outages (something breaks, suddenly taking a generator out of the stack) or planned maintenance. Moreover, generators can operate within a range of capacities at different levels of efficiency.

While it is easy to devolve into lengthy discussions about the inadequacies of the stack as an engineering representation of the physical system, this would be a distraction. The point is that a "reasonable" form for the stack Ψ is the basis for a structural model of power prices in a given market, *presumably* capturing key features of the interactions between various types of generation, prevailing fuel prices, and system demand L_t, at a level of detail that facilitates useful computation.

Although the detailed structure of generation stacks varies across control areas, all stacks bear some commonalities. All are nondecreasing functions (by definition), and broadly speaking (i.e., ignoring local roughness), stacks are convex as the maximum system capacity is reached, beyond which a market-specific price cap pertains. The PJM supply stack, shown in Figure 3.38, is a good example. A caricature of this general behavior is shown in Figure 12.12. This is a plot of a functional form for a structural power model introduced by Barlow [Bar02] of the form

$$\Psi(C) = \begin{cases} f_\alpha(C) & \text{if } C < C_{\max} \equiv (1-\epsilon)/\alpha \\ \epsilon^{-1/\alpha} & \text{otherwise} \end{cases} \tag{12.29}$$

where

$$f_\alpha(L) = \begin{cases} \frac{1}{(1-\alpha L)^{1/\alpha}} & \text{if } \alpha \neq 0 \\ e^L & \alpha = 0 \end{cases} \tag{12.30}$$

Barlow derived this form from a simple model for price setting assuming price-inelastic load, and the result is a stack with some of the qualitative features one expects. Prices increase with load as a convex function hitting a maximum (the *bid cap*) of $\epsilon^{-1/\alpha}$ when demand exceeds a threshold level $(1-\epsilon)/\alpha$. The (near) singularity at $C_{\max}$ yields the "price-spike" behavior observed empirically. The case $\alpha = 0$ is a simple exponential stack.

Figure 12.12 shows Ψ using $\alpha = 0.20$ and a bid cap of 1000. The implied value of ϵ yields a threshold on capacity that was scaled by 10,000 in Figure 12.12 to bring units up to levels that are typical of power pools with capacities

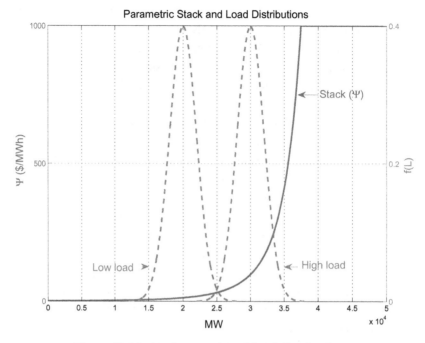

Figure 12.12. Barlow stack and load distributions.

on the order of 10^4 to 10^5 MW in large systems. While Barlow system-
atized the discussions of parametric forms, many researchers have explored
parametric stacks during the same time frame, including [SIC00], [SGI00]
and countless proprietary efforts by industry researchers, some of which are
alluded to in [EW03].

Superimposed on the stack in Figure 12.12 are two normal probability
densities for future loads corresponding to low and high cases. We will
postpone discussion of how distributions of load should be constructed to
Chapter 15 on load hedges. If we assume prices clear at realized loads, this
setup yields a distribution of spot prices. Although Barlow estimated parameters in this framework using realized spot prices and demand, it is useful to
examine the attributes of this model in a risk-neutral setting.

Using the distributions for load to generate a distribution of spot prices
p via the stack Ψ yields a forward price that is $\tilde{E}(p)$. Valuing options
across a grid of deltas produces the implied volatility surfaces as shown in
Figure 12.13. Higher load distributions result in higher implied volatilities
and greater skew. Moreover, these surfaces bear remarkable resemblance
to actual implied volatilities in power markets. This is quite an accomplish-
ment for such a simple model, and clearly, one could go a step further
by implementing calibration methods to observed forwards and options by
allowing some flexibility in the inputs – for example, by adjusting implied
load distributions or using a time-varying maximum capacity.

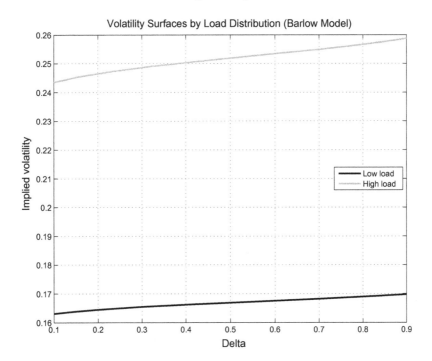

Figure 12.13. Barlow stack implied volatility surfaces.

This type of modeling approach is in stark contrast to the full-blown fundamental engineering models alluded to earlier, which because of their daunting computational requirements, often apply deterministic "expected" loads to dispatch models. It is clear from both the form of (12.29) and the actual physical stacks such as those shown in Figure 3.38 that random load applied to a convex stack yields expected prices that, as a result of Jensen's inequality, can be substantially higher than those obtained using expected load profiles. This is a major weakness in the fundamental approach.

The simplicity of the Barlow stack limits its ability to account for some aspects of spot power prices, including dependence on fuel prices, negative prices, and apparent regime changes. Dependence on fuel prices could be partially remedied simply by rephrasing the stacks Ψ as a heat rate in which the power spot prices become $p_t = G_t \Psi(L_t)$, with G_t the spot natural gas price at time t. This yields a joint distribution of $[L_t, G_t, p_t]$ with nontrivial correlation structure between fuel and power prices as a function of expected load. In addition, this approach allows the use of skew in natural gas markets, which is more observable than in power, to provide extrapolates of power implied volatilities beyond the strike ranges observed.

This simple modification, however, accommodates a stack based on only one fuel. Power markets involve the interaction of generators driven by multiple energy sources, including hydro, nuclear, coal, and refined products, in addition to natural gas. A great deal of work has been done to develop structural models that can account for the interactions between fuel prices and the composition of the stack. The basic challenge in dealing with multiple generation types is that multiple stacks interact in a nonlinear fashion.[9] Grouping each generator by input fuel and representing the "substacks" by $\Psi_j(C|F_j)$, the total stack Ψ is obtained by

$$\Psi^{-1}\left(p|\vec{F}_t\right) = \sum_j \Psi_j^{-1}\left(p|\vec{F}_j\right) \tag{12.31}$$

Because $\Psi^{-1}\left(p|\vec{F}_t\right)$ denotes the total capacity with cost less than p, this result is merely summing the total capacity across all generation types with marginal cost of generation less than p. In certain situations, (12.31) is amenable to direct evaluation. Explict forms for Ψ are constructed by Carmona, Coulon, and Schwarz [CCS13] in the two-fuel setting with exponential stacks.

More general structural models, which remain amenable to closed-form (or nearly closed-form) solutions, have been developed that yield a broader spectrum of price dynamics; see for example, [ACHT09] and [CCS13]. Carmona and Coulon [CC13] have introduced probabilistic stack models in which the spot price takes the value determined by one of a set of substacks $i = 1, \ldots, N$ of the form

$$p_t = (-1)^{\tilde{\delta}_i}(G_t)^{\delta_i} e^{\alpha_i + \beta_i \tilde{L}_t} \tag{12.32}$$

selected with probability π_i of the form

$$\pi_i = \pi_{\text{low}}^{(i)} + \pi_{\text{high}}^{(i)} \Phi\left[\frac{L_t - \mu}{\sigma}(-1)^{\tilde{\delta}_i}\right] \tag{12.33}$$

which is increasing or decreasing with demand depending on the sign of $\tilde{\delta}_i$. Here $\Phi(\cdot)$ is the standard normal distribution function, and $\tilde{L}_t$ is the load bounded by zero and the maximum system capacity $C_{\text{max}}(t)$:

$$\tilde{L}_t = \max\left\{0, \min\left[L_t, C_{\text{max}}(t)\right]\right\} \tag{12.34}$$

The constants $\delta_i, \tilde{\delta}_i \in \{0,1\}$ accommodate the presence or absence of fuel dependence and negative prices. Analytical expressions for forward prices are achievable if L_t and $\log G_t$ are normally distributed.

Extensions of stack models along these lines expand the qualitative dynamics that the models can produce, but at the expense of an increasing set of parameters requiring estimation. The utility of models of this type, in particular, regarding calibration to historical and market data and accurate

---

[9] This also pertains to situations where one considers geographically distinct stacks coupled with a finite transmission capacity between them.

forecasting, has yet to be fully ascertained, although applications are being researched (see [CPS13]).

These models just discussed are parametric structural models with judiciously chosen functional forms and free parameters that have analogues with physical attributes of the market. The maximum capacity $C_{max}(t)$ in (12.29), for example, can be interpreted literally as a maximum available system capacity. This is not how parametric stack models are usually implemented, however. Rather, such parameters are generally used as free variables for calibration. This means that the situation in which significant perturbations to the systems have occurred, or are expected in the future, are difficult to reflect, requiring ad hoc modifications of parameters such as $C_{max}(t)$. This can happen as a result of generation addition and retirement or regulatory-induced regime changes such as the addition of renewable wind generation, as witnessed in the United States in recent years.

Consequently, nonparametric stack models also have been proposed and are used by some practitioners. Here the physical system is described at a granular level, with the engineering attributes of each generator identified and used as the primitive modeling data. The stack at time t is obtained from the $\Psi_i(t)$ associated with each generator:

$$\Psi_i^{-1}(p) = \begin{cases} C_{max}^{(i)} S_i(t) & \text{if } p > p_i(t, \vec{F_t}) \\ 0 & \text{otherwise} \end{cases} \tag{12.35}$$

where $p_i(t, \vec{F_t})$ denotes an engineering estimate of the marginal cost of generation of unit i given fuel prices $\vec{F_t}$ (recall again that typically only one component of $\vec{F}$ matters). We have also introduced a time-varying availability adjustment $S_i(t)$, that is designed to accommodate observed seasonal patterns in generation capacity. Recall Figure 3.45, which showed daily historical available nuclear generation capacity in the United States. The manifest seasonality is due to maintenance schedules, in which operators bring parts of the fleet down for scheduled maintenance and refueling during the less expensive shoulder months in the spring and fall. The same type of behavior is consistently observed for other types of dispatchable generation.

Given the entire set of capacity functions (12.35) for the region in question, one can posit a stochastic model for spot clearing; for example:

$$p_t = \Psi_t \left[L_t(1 + \delta_t) | \vec{F_t} \right] + \epsilon_t \tag{12.36}$$

where Ψ_t is constructed from (12.35) for all i using (12.31). Here δ and ϵ are stochastic processes reflecting uncertain availability of generation randomness in bidding, respectively. Assuming a particular distributional form for each, maximum-likelihood estimation can be affected. Note that normality of the underlying random variables or processes can still yield nontrivial skew and spikes as a result of the nonlinearity of Ψ. For reasons of tractability, significant simplifications have been made – this is after all a structural model not an engineering replica. Use of a single δ_t at each time effectively dilates the entire stack – outages are uniform. Similarly, a single ϵ_t reflects a common aggressive or conservative bidding strategy across generators. In addition, it is usually assumed that the seasonal availability adjustments are common, either across the stack or by generation type, and usually parameterized, for example, as

$$S(t) = \sum_{k=1}^{K} [\gamma_k \sin(2\pi k t) + \delta_k \cos(2\pi k t)] \tag{12.37}$$

This type of approach might be termed *semiparametric structural modeling* because the stochastic drivers are parametric, but the stack itself is (often quite laboriously) constructed from high-level engineering attributes of the system. Such a modeling framework can be used to make predictions about the effects of forced perturbations, such as the addition of large renewable capacity or forced retirements due to emissions, on price distributions. The validity of such predictions has not yet been systematically tested.

Structural models for storable commodities, in contrast to the preceding stack models, have been a topic of research for a very long time. From a perspective of practical implementation as derivatives pricing engines, however, these are actually at an earlier stage of development than the stack models due in large part to daunting numerical challenges. Many versions of structural models for inventory have been proposed, most of which are substantively equivalent. The monograph by Pirrong [Pir12], which motivates much of the following discussion, is an excellent survey of the potential strengths and limitations of such efforts.

The basic assumption of inventory-based structural models is that spot price formation occurs through a market equilibrium based on information about supply and demand drivers and storage capacity. The starting point is the specification of supply and demand functions $p_t = S(q_t^S)$ and $p_t = D(q_t^D)$, respectively, as depicted in Figure 12.14. The equilibrium price is characterized by the intersection of these two functions, where supply and demand balance. An alternative characterization is that the equilibrium price maximizes the sum of the consumer and producer surpluses defined, respectively, as

$$D^*(q) = \int_0^q D(\hat{q}) \, d\hat{q} - qD(q)$$

$$S^*(q) = qD(q) - \int_0^q S(\hat{q}) \, d\hat{q} \tag{12.38}$$

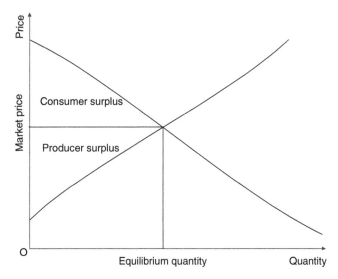

Figure 12.14. Supply and demand equilibrium.

These are also shown in Figure 12.14. The consumer surplus $\mathcal{D}^*(q)$ can be interpreted as the value that would be obtained by all consumers when quantity q is consumed at the demand-curve price $\mathcal{D}(q)$. Consumers who would have purchased at a higher price $\hat{p}$ effectively make the difference $\hat{p} - p$; those who would only consume at lower prices consume nothing. The producer surplus is defined similarly as $\mathcal{S}^*(q)$, but with demand curve also setting price as for $\mathcal{D}^*$. The price at which the sum of the two surpluses

$$\mathcal{D}^*(p) + \mathcal{S}^*(p) = \int_0^q [\mathcal{D}(\hat{q}) - \mathcal{S}(\hat{q})]\, d\hat{q} \tag{12.39}$$

is maximized is the equilibrium price. This is the total shaded area in Figure 12.14. The use of the reference level $q\mathcal{D}(q_t)$ in (12.38) yielded an economic interpretation but was arbitrary in that it nets out in (12.39).

For a system in which agents can make intertemporal decisions involving inventory of a commodity that is produced and consumed, it is the present value of integrated future total surplus that must be maximized. Denoting the level of inventory at time t by I_t, and adding randomness to the demand and supply functions by making them functions of stochastic processes $\vec{X}_t$ and $\vec{Y}_t$, respectively, the optimization problem amounts to computation of the value function:

$$V\left(I_t, \vec{X}_t, \vec{Y}_t\right) \equiv \sup_{[q_D(\cdot), q_S(\cdot)] \in \mathcal{A}}$$
$$\times \tilde{E}\left(\int_t^\infty e^{-r(T-t)} \left\{\mathcal{D}^*[q_D(T), \vec{X}_T] + \mathcal{S}^*[q_S(T), \vec{Y}_T]\right\} \Big| \mathcal{F}_t\right) dT \tag{12.40}$$

Constraints on the allowed actions q_D and q_S are denoted by $\mathcal{A}$ and always include

- Bounds on inventory: $I(t) \in [0, S_{max}]$ for all t.
- Conservation of commodity: $dI/dt = q_S(t) - q_D(t)$. In some cases this constraint is modified to have losses of inventory while in storage.

In addition, there must be consistency of spot price formation

$$p_t = D\left[q_D(t), \vec{Y}_t\right]$$
$$p_t = S\left[q_S(t), \vec{X}_t\right] \tag{12.41}$$

equating the marginal cost of supply and demand. This effectively reduces the decision variables from $[q_D, q_S]$ to q_D.

In the case of valuing a single storage structure, as we will see in Chapter 13, the price process is specified exogenously, and it is assumed that a single storage operator has no impact on price dynamics. Here the key point is that dynamic control of q_D and q_S does not merely effect spot prices – it defines them. Viewed from the perspective of simulation, along any given path at time t, the spot price is obtained from (12.41).

Methods for solution of the dynamic control problem (12.40) are discussed in detail in [Pir12]. In addition to the value function, such solutions also provide the "carry-out" function, which specifies the rate of injection/withdrawal as a function of the current state of the system:

$$\frac{dI}{dT}\left(I_T, \vec{X}_T, \vec{Y}_T\right) \tag{12.42}$$

or in discrete time: $I_{T+\Delta T} = I_T + \Delta I(I_T, \vec{X}_T, \vec{Y}_T)$. With the carry-out function in hand, forward prices can be obtained either via simulation or by solution of a partial differential equation (see [Pir12]). It is important to realize that both steps, the computation of the carry-out function and the computation of forward prices, are numerically challenging, especially if the dimensionality of $[\vec{X}, \vec{Y}]$ is large – and *large* in this case can be viewed as anything more than two factors.

Various authors have studied models of this form or closely related variations, including [DL91] and [RSS00]. Pirrong [Pir12] has the most comprehensive discussion of the behavior of inventory-based structural models, analyzing a two-factor version of (12.40). The results of these studies suggest that models of this form can generate many of the expected results, notably

- The instantaneous variance of returns (spot or forward) decreases with inventory I_t.
- This effect decreases (in general) with tenor, with the ratio of spot to forward returns variances greatest at high demand and low inventory.
- The returns correlation between spot and forward contracts is low at high demand and low inventory and effectively unity at low demand and high inventory.

This class of models also can exhibit plausible volatility surface dynamics and in some cases (see [RSS00]) contango of implied volatilities at short tenors – a phenomenon occasionally observed in market data, as we saw in Figure 5.8.

While the plots shown earlier in this chapter showed little or no relationship between returns volatility and forward yields, there is empirical evidence that structural inventory models are a step in the right direction. Consider the following results from LME copper market data. The ideal markets for empirical studies of the effects of storage are those devoid of seasonality and that have good price and inventory data. Inclusion of seasonality complicates solution of optimization problems such as (12.40) considerably. Although crude oil prices, both spot and forward, can be considered nonseasonal, oil inventories do exhibit some seasonality. Moreover, global inventory data for crude oil are hard to compile, and the data that are available are not considered to be particularly reliable. Crude oil is therefore not a leading candidate. Natural gas has reliable storage data in the United State but is seasonal.

Copper, however, has the merit of being a consumable commodity with reliable inventory data provided by the metals exchanges and is devoid of meaningful seasonality in demand and prices. Copper price dynamics is amenable to direct application of PCA. Figure 12.15 shows historical LME inventory levels, which have clearly spanned a considerable range over the

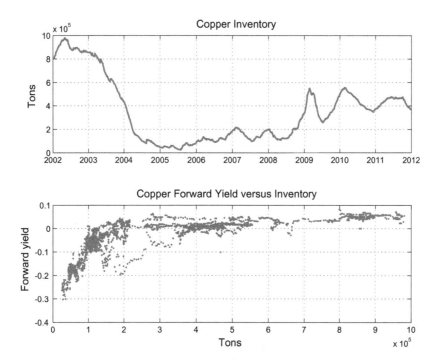

Figure 12.15. Forward yields versus inventory for copper.

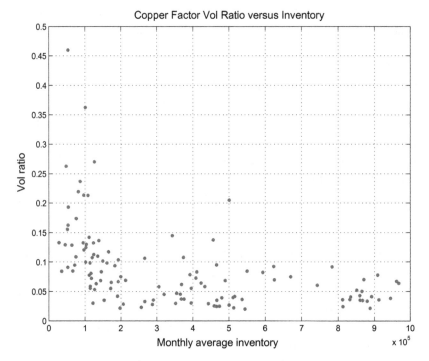

Figure 12.16. PCA for copper.

past decade. The lower plot shows forward yields versus inventory. The monotonicity of forward yields as a function of inventory is similar to what we saw in Figure 3.27, although the convexity in this relationship for copper is much more significant. At high inventory, the change in expected forward yields as a function of inventory is smaller than at low inventory levels, presumably because the marginal cost of increasing storage capacity is relatively low for copper, at least in comparison with the elaborate and costly requirements for natural gas storage.

Returns correlations also show interesting structure as a function of inventory level. Figure 12.16 shows the results of PCA analysis, plotting the volatility of factors $j \geq 2$ over that of the first factor by month versus inventory level over the entire data set. Specifically, the PCA factors $\{\Phi_j\}_{j=1}^J$ are computed over the entire data set in addition to the "factor amplitudes":

$$\alpha_j(d) \equiv \Phi_j^{(m)} \cdot \vec{R}(d) \tag{12.43}$$

The factor amplitude $\alpha_j(d)$ represents the "amount" of Φ_j present in the realized forward returns for day d. The scatter plot shows the ratio

$$\frac{\left[\sum_{d \in m} \sum_{j=2}^J \alpha_j^2(d)\right]^{1/2}}{\left[\sum_{d \in m} \alpha_1^2(d)\right]^{1/2}} \tag{12.44}$$

The noteworthy feature of dependence of this ratio on inventory is that at high inventory levels the forward dynamics are tantamount to one-factor dynamics, with multifactor correlation structure being manifest only at low inventories. Models such as (12.40) exhibit precisely this behavior.

Modeling forward dynamics for, say, copper and, certainly by plausible extension, crude oil or natural gas without inventory effects should be done at one's peril. It is also clear, as emphasized by Pirrong [Pir12], that there are missing ingredients that will be required for consistency with empirical observation, notably stochastic volatility or some moral equivalent in the underlying drivers. Anyone watching oil markets through the credit crisis would have to conclude that volatility, both realized and implied, was anything but stationary during that time. The issue, once again, is tractability of the modeling framework.

Conclusion

Attempts to construct models for commodities forward price dynamics encounter a tradeoff between tractability and consistency with empirical results. We have categorized the large and varied approaches to this task into three categories:

- *Reduced-form models*. These are the workhorse models for the industry, involving posited parametric dynamics, usually consisting of diffusion models of price dynamics.
  - The dominant form in use are the HJM-style models, in which the set of forward prices is the underlying primitive.
  - Spot convenience yield models take the approach of specifying spot price dynamics with drift adjusted by a second process, the local convenience yield. Calibration to forward prices requires time-dependent drifts, which ultimately render these models equivalent (or nearly equivalent) to HJM-style models.
  - The merit of reduced-form models is tractability coupled with some degree of consistency with empirical features of forward curve dynamics.
  - Attempts to capture more subtle behavior, such as price spikes and associated heavy skew, as well as correlation dependence on underlying variables such as inventory, are ad hoc and usually result in complex models with large number of parameters that are challenging to estimate.
  - Application of reduced-form models is predicated on the existence of liquid forward and options markets to facilitate calibration. In the absence of such, extrapolation methods are required.
- *Econometric models*. Econometric models are useful in situations where historical data are abundant and amenable to regression methods, but where market data are scarce and liquidity is limited.
  - The approach is predicated on stationarity of spot price and index data such as weather, to which econometric methods are deployed to construct models that can be used to simulate physical measure realizations of the underlying prices.

- o Incompleteness is explicitly modeled, and optimal hedge construction is an exercise in standard portfolio theory.
- o Econometric modeling relies on stationary time series, rendering estimation challenging when a commodities market is undergoing upheaval through either regulatory changes or shocks to supply and demand profiles.
- *Structural models*. Structural models use known aspects of a particular market to identify plausible nonlinear relationships between fundamental drivers and inputs, such as supply, demand, inventory, and weather, and realized spot prices.
  - o Stack models handle the situation where the commodity cannot be effectively stored, notably in power, which renders the calculation of spot price distributions relatively efficient. Such models are commonly used to generate plausible volatility, skew, and correlation structure in the absence of liquid markets.
  - o As with econometric models, pricing is effected either in the physical measure with portfolio analysis methods used for hedge construction or in a risk-neutral setting with model parameters adjusted to yield price distributions that are consistent with market data.
  - o Inventory-based models attempt to handle the situation in which the commodity is stored, with price distributions resulting from an intertemporal stochastic equilibrium calculation. Research suggests that such models can generate price dynamics and volatility surfaces with features that are more consistent with empirical results than those obtained from reduced-form or purely econometric approaches.
  - o Numerical efficiency is the dominant challenge in the analysis and development of structural models for energy derivatives pricing.

Part V

Advanced Methods and Structures

The structures that we discuss here in Part V combine all the primary valuation issues discussed in Part III and many aspects of the modeling paradigms described in Part IV. We concentrate on three common types of structures that in many respects continue to challenge portfolio managers and valuation specialists.

Natural gas storage facilities are arguably the most challenging and least resolved class of energy structures in the business. We start with storage primarily because it involves a single commodity; complexities arise for several reasons. First, optionality is high dimensional, occurring at the daily level, and more important, each decision point (exercise time) is coupled with optionality in the future. The decision to inject or withdraw from storage affects the state of the system, specifically how much inventory remains, which changes one's degrees of freedom in the future. This coupling means that valuation depends on correlations between returns of different contracts or delivery periods. However, the market implied correlation information is scarce and often of a nature that is not particularly useful for model calibration or hedging. Finally, storage operators, while competitive, are all attempting to achieve much the same thing. Hence the assumption of no feedback of hedging actions into price dynamics is potentially flawed. There is evidence that returns correlations do, in fact, depend on inventory levels, presenting a modeling problem that has yet to be resolved.

Tolling transactions are the second class of structures that we address here. In Chapter 9 we discussed monthly tolling structures; here we focus on the much more pertinent and commonly traded daily structures. The introduction of daily exercise requires estimation or calibration of returns correlations between power and natural gas at the daily level. Here we start by applying the standard two-factor Gaussian exponential models, which turn out to require correlations that are much higher than empirical estimates would suggest in order to be consistent with price levels at which these structures are known to trade. High correlations reduce the value of the structure, which, we argue, is likely a result of market frictions that severely degrade one's ability to extract extrinsic value. Alternative methods to the standard financial engineering models are explored, including econometric and structural models in which we explicitly address market incompleteness via the use of static hedges constructed in the physical measure.

Finally, we conclude Part V with a discussion of variable-quantity swaps. These commonly arise in several contexts. The most common, and the one on which we focus, are load swaps or physical load obligations in which hourly variations of the demand of a tranche of electricity consumers define the notional quantity. The absence of any direct commoditization of load renders the use of quantos irrelevant, and the approach that we follow here is predicated altogether on econometric or structural approaches. Another source of variable-quantity risk is provided by unit-contingent transactions in which the notional is defined by how much a facility is able to produce of the product. The most common examples are unit-contingent off-takes from nuclear generators. In these transactions, the risks associated with variable quantity are largely unhedgeable.

The unifying theme of this section is that the nature of these structures requires extrapolation from traded markets in a manner than renders standard methods challenging to defend and potentially hazardous to use. This has pushed many practicioners into realms of valuation and analysis that revolve around construction of (hopefully) realistic physical measures about which standard portfolio analysis can be applied.

13

Natural Gas Storage

Humanity has continually strived to efficiently store commodities of all types. The purpose of storage is to resolve supply and demand imbalances across time, particularly to accommodate (if not to survive) fluctuations in either supply or demand. All commodities can be stored to a greater or lesser extent. Among energy commodities, coal and oil are the easiest to store, requiring little more than fields and tanks. Electricity, on the other hand, is extremely challenging to store; the amount of storage capacity for power is typically a minute fraction of total generation capacity and insignificant in comparison with the typical hourly variations in demand. This is why electricity production and distribution infrastructure must be extremely reliable; reliability often achieved at the cost of significant redundancies in the physical system.

Natural gas lies somewhere between these two extremes – it can be stored in relatively large quantities, provided that geologic formations exist that can be modified to hold natural gas at required pressures. The development of such facilities is expensive but not prohibitively so. As a consequence, the ratio of working storage capacity to total demand can be substantial. For example, as we saw in Chapter 3, in 2012, the United States had roughly 4.2 tcf of storage capacity with annual consumption of approximately 24 tcf per year. This has historically proven to be adequate to resolve the mismatch between the seasonal variations in demand and the relatively slow changes in production shown in Figure 3.24.

Valuation of a storage facility as a derivative, or *real option*, is astonishingly difficult. There are few practitioners or academics who would contend that the issue is resolved; most view this as one of the major outstanding valuation issues in the business. There are, however, interesting approaches to the problem that are commonly used and that at a minimum provide frameworks about which to construct a toehold on valuation.

In this chapter we will first discuss key attributes of physical storage infrastructure, proceeding subsequently to describe the general valuation problem. We will then turn to virtual storage, which is an idealized facility with no constraints other than maximum inventory. While departing significantly from the realities of actual storage, virtual storage has the merit of being amenable to exact valuation, and analysis of the solution is both informative and intuitive. Moreover, many of the key results pertain, at least qualitatively, to physical storage. This will be followed by a discussion of several commonly used methods for physical storage valuation, accompanied by appropriate words of caution.

Physical Storage

There are several ways to store natural gas. One way is to compress or liquify it, reducing the volumes to levels that engineered structures can handle. The trouble with this is, of course, cost. Such methods are typically used to transport natural gas but are rarely used to store it over the course of a season. As a result, natural gas storage is almost always affected by modifying suitable geologic structures.

Structures engineered to store natural gas are usually grouped into the following three categories:

- *Aquifer storage*. Facilities consisting of large porous rock structures.
- *Reservoir storage*. Depleted natural gas or oil production fields suitably modified for natural gas storage.
- *Salt caverns*. Salt dome formations that can be engineered to store natural gas.

Of the three types of storage, salt caverns most resemble large, uncomplicated tanks with relatively high injection and withdrawal rates that make these facilities particularly useful for meeting rapid changes in demand.

Unlike other physical optionality, such as power generation, where the engineering constraints and capacities, while complex, are extremely well defined, natural gas storage has inherent uncertainties given the dependence on large and only partially observable geology. To clarify this point, total "nameplate" storage capacity in the United States is thought to be around 8,800 bcf as of 2010. Of this, approximately 4,600 bcf holds *base gas* that is injected once at inception to raise the pressure in the storage facilities to required levels. Base gas can be thought of as a minimum inventory level below which withdrawal is not economically viable. The exact level of inventory at which withdrawal would cease to be achievable is only an estimate and could very well change with time, even for a specific facility. The remaining storage capacity, roughly 4,200 bcf, is referred to as *working storage*; this is the useful capacity. Note, however, that given the uncertainty regarding the quantity of working storage, the only way to know the bounds on inventory levels at which withdrawal or injection rates would become effectively zero is to actually hit the engineering limits – this has yet to happen on a macroscopic scale in the United States.

In the presence of engineering uncertainties, storage structures, specifically leases or off-takes (tranches) of a storage facility, are designed within what are thought to be conservative parameters. Physical storage affords the owner the option of injecting and withdrawing natural gas, typically on a daily basis. Each decision affects the future optionality due to constraints on inventory and rates. The owner of a storage facility has the following considerations:

- *Capacity constraints.* Ensure that enough capacity exists to accommodate a storage contract. This involves specifying bounds on contracted capacity: $S(t) \in [0, S_{\max}]$, where $S(t)$ denotes the inventory level at time t.
- *Rate constraints.* Ensure that contracted injection and withdrawal rates can be achieved. This is accomplished by constraints on the rates $s(t) \in [s_*, s^*]$, where $s(t) \equiv dS/dt$ is the injection rate. Here $s_* < 0$ and $s^* > 0$. In practice, as inventory approaches the bounds 0 or $S_{\max}$, these constraints can change – as the tank gets full (empty), putting more in (taking more out) becomes harder. Such constraints take the form $s_* = s_*[S(t)]$ and $s^* = s^*[S(t)]$.
- *Inventory constraints.* All storage contracts specify initial and final conditions, the most common structure being that the facility is to be left with the same inventory at the end of the contract as at the beginning: $S(T) = S(0)$, where T denotes the term of the contract. Often the contract spans the start of the injection season April 1, and terminates at the end of the withdrawal season, March 31 of the following year. It is not uncommon for inventory levels to be constrained to specified inequalities at intermediate times. In general, these limits can take the form of a sequence of constraints through the contract of the form $S_{\vec{\tau}_*} \leq \vec{L}_*$ and $S_{\vec{\tau}^*} \geq \vec{L}^*$ for specific times $\vec{\tau}$ and limits $\vec{L}$. The purpose of constraints of this type is to force cycling of natural gas into and out of the facility, which results in lower migration of natural gas to unrecoverable areas of the geologic structure and prevents the development of pressure gradients that are deleterious to reservoir integrity.

The term *ratchets* is often applied to the rate and inventory constraints, particularly to the latter. From a valuation perspective, these constraints reduce the set of allowable actions of the holder of a storage contract and, therefore, reduce its value.

Storage is often characterized by its *cyclability*, that is, by how many times it can fill and then empty, in the parlance *cycle* or *turn*, in one year. In the case of constant limits, one cycle time is

$$\tau = \frac{S_{\max}}{|s_*|} + \frac{S_{\max}}{s^*} \tag{13.1}$$

and the number of turns is $1/\tau$. Most aquifer and reservoir storage is effectively "one-turn storage," that is, one cycle per year. Salt-cavern storage is much more flexible, with some facilities able to turn several times a year. There is, of course, more option value in facilities with high cyclability.

Finally, to add to what is clearly a set of nontrivial constraints, some aquifer storage can have path-dependent forms for the rate-constraint functions $s_*\left(S_{\leq t}\right)$ and $s^*\left(S_{\leq t}\right)$. Constraints of this form arise as a result of nontrivial times required for equilibration of pressure gradients – if you withdraw quickly now, s_* will increase for some period of time, which is to say that you can withdraw less until the reservoir has returned to equilibrium.

Valuation of natural gas storage involves a confluence of high-dimensional optionality in the daily injection/withdrawal decisions embodied in $s(t)$, accompanied by nontrivial path constraints on actions and inventory trajectories. Coupled with seasonality in volatility and correlation structure, with very limited clarity afforded by traded CSOs, the valuation of natural gas storage is a nontrivial affair. Qualitatively, however, we would expect that "rougher" dynamics of forward curves will result in a higher value of a storage facility, as storage capacity allows one to exploit time spreads in prices. We expect, therefore, that higher volatility and lower returns correlation result in greater value. This actually works both ways – the presence of storage capacity in a market smooths the forward dynamics that would otherwise have transpired in the absence of storage.

Forward Yields, Carry, and Virtual Storage

Valuation of natural gas storage involves the same basic goal associated with any long option position: maximize value. For European options, this is easy – exercise if in the money. For American options, for which the exercise feature is nontrivial, more work is required to ascertain optimal exercise boundaries. For the general storage problem, the situation is much more complex. Before plunging directly into the general formulation, it is quite informative to examine a simple and highly idealized inventory problem.

The simplest storage structure is afforded to us by a slight modification of the CSOs introduced in Chapter 9. Consider options with the following payoff:

$$\max\left[F(\tau, T+U) - e^{rU}F(\tau, T), 0\right] \qquad (13.2)$$

where we are assuming constant interest rate r. This option can be thought of as providing the holder with the ability to purchase natural gas at exercise time τ for delivery at time T at price $F(\tau, T)$, funding the cost to time $T + U$, and simultaneously selling the same quantity forward at time $T + U$. A long position in this option provides the owner with the ability to store the product from time T to $T + U$ or the financial equivalent. Clearly, the holder of such an option will only exercise if the accrued cost of the purchase is less than the forward price at withdrawal; this is equivalent to the forward yield exceeding the financial cost of carry:

$$y(\tau, T, T+U) = \frac{1}{U}\log\left[\frac{F(\tau, T+U)}{F(\tau, T)}\right] > r \qquad (13.3)$$

Although actual storage is much more complex, with constraints resulting in current decisions affecting future value, (13.3) captures one essential aspect of storage – the value is driven by the difference between forward yields and financing costs.

With the CSO example in mind, consider a storage facility where the only constraint is $S(t) \in [0, S_{\max}]$, notably without constraints on injection or withdrawal rates and without inventory ratchets. This type of structure is sometimes referred to as *virtual storage* and is clearly an idealization as the owner can toggle between empty and full instantaneously. One might argue that some commodities infrastructure could be approximated by virtual storage – for example, compressed-air storage for power generation. However, even this is a stretch, and the purpose for considering virtual storage is that it is analytically tractable.[1]

In discrete time, virtual storage can be represented as the sum of nearest-neighbor CSOs:

$$V[T_n, F(T_n, \cdot)] =$$
$$S_{\max} \tilde{E}_{T_n} \left\{ \sum_{m=n}^{N_*} e^{-(T_{m+1} - T_n)r} \max\left[F(T_m, T_{m+1}) - e^{r\Delta T} F(T_m, T_m), 0 \right] \right\}$$
(13.4)

where the problem is defined on the time grid $T \in \{n\Delta T\}_{n=1}^{N_*}$. At each time, the decision is made to hold maximum inventory if the net carry is positive or to hold zero inventory otherwise. Note that the current inventory level S_n is not an argument of V due to the absence of any rate restrictions, which renders S_n irrelevant in the optimization – you can set inventory at any level that you would like to instantly.

Evaluation of virtual storage in discrete time is equivalent to CSO valuation. If we use the Gaussian exponential factor framework in the form

$$dF(t, T) = F(t, T) \sum_{j=1}^{J} \sigma_j(T) e^{-\beta_j(T-t)} dB_t^{(j)}$$
(13.5)

the mth option value is

$$V_{n,m} = e^{-(T_{m+1} - T_n)r} \left[F(T_n, T_{m+1})\Phi(d_1) - e^{r\Delta T} F(T_n, T_m)\Phi(d_2) \right]$$
(13.6)

where

$$d_{1,2} = \frac{\log\left[\frac{F(T_n, T_{m+1})}{e^{r\Delta T} F(T_n, T_m)} \pm \frac{1}{2}\tilde{\sigma}^2 \right]}{\tilde{\sigma}}$$

---

[1] It is also rumored that such structures have occasionally traded purely as derivatives between counterparties, but if so, it has happened very rarely.

with Φ and ϕ the standard normal CDF and PDF, respectively, and

$$\tilde{\sigma}^2 = (T_m - T_n)\left(\bar{\sigma}^2_{m,m+1} - 2\rho_{m,m+1}\bar{\sigma}^2_{m,m}\bar{\sigma}^2_{m,m+1} + \bar{\sigma}^2_{m,m}\right)$$

Here $\bar{\sigma}^2_{m,m}$ and $\bar{\sigma}^2_{m,m+1}$ are the term volatilities of contracts T_m and T_{m+1} over the time interval $[0, T_m]$, respectively, and $\rho_{m,m+1}$ is the term correlation between the two contracts over the same interval. Each term in $\tilde{\sigma}^2$ can be evaluated exactly using (C.19) and (C.21).

A continuous time representation of virtual storage can be obtained from (13.4), which we rewrite as

$$V[T_n, F(T_n, \cdot)] = S_{\max}\tilde{E}_{T_n}\left\{\sum_{m=n}^{N_*} e^{-(T_{m+1}-T_n)r}F(T_m, T_m)\right.$$
$$\left. \cdot \max\left[\frac{F(T_m, T_{m+1})}{F(T_m, T_m)} - e^{r\Delta T}, 0\right]\right\}$$

Taylor expanding $F(T_m, T_{m+1}) = F(T_m, T_m) + \partial F(T_n, T)/\partial T|_{T=T_m}\Delta T$ and taking the limit $\Delta T \to 0$ yield

$$V[t, F(t, \cdot)] = S_{\max}\tilde{E}_t\left\{\int_t^{T_*} e^{-r(T-t)}F(T, T)\left[\frac{\partial \log F(t, U)}{\partial U}\Big|_{U=T} - r\right]^+ dT\right\}$$
(13.7)

where T_* denotes the end of the contract. This result is simply saying that at each time T, if the instantaneous forward yield exceeds the financing cost, it makes sense to have maximum inventory; if the opposite holds, then zero inventory is optimal.

The preceding expression is amenable to exact solution, either by direct evaluation (see [ADS02]) or by series expansion of (13.4). Using the Gaussian exponential model (GEM) framework, direct substitution, and Taylor expansion eventually yields leading-order expressions for $\tilde{\sigma}^2 \sim O(\Delta T^2)$ and $V_{n,m} \sim O(\Delta T)$ with the limiting expression for the value function of the form

$$V(t, \vec{Y}_t) = \int_t^{T_*} e^{-r(T-t)}F(t, T)v(t, T)\left\{h(t, T)\Phi[h(t, T)] + \phi[h(t, T)]\right\} dT$$
(13.8)

where

$$v^2(t, T) = \sum_j \left[\beta_j - \frac{\sigma_j'}{\sigma_j}(T)\right]^2 \frac{\sigma_j^2}{2\beta_j}\left(1 - e^{-2\beta_j(T-t)}\right)$$
(13.9)

and

$$h(t, T) = \frac{1}{v(t, T)}\left[\frac{\partial \log F(t, U)}{\partial U}\Big|_{U=T} - r\right]$$
(13.10)

Here $\vec{Y}_t$ are the GEM state variables – the Ornstein-Uhlenbeck (OU) processes driving the forward curve.

Valuation for virtual storage is therefore reduced either to a discrete sum of CSOs (13.4) or the one-dimensional integral (13.8). In either case, numerical evaluation is significantly less challenging for virtual storage than for physical storage with nontrivial constraints. This is apparent in the calculation of intrinsic value, which is obtained from an inventory trajectory consisting of step jumps from 0 to $S_{\max}$:

$$S_{\text{Intrinsic}}(t,T) = \begin{cases} S_{\max} & \text{if } \frac{\partial \log F(t,U)}{\partial U}\big|_{U=T} - r > 0 \\ 0 & \text{otherwise} \end{cases} \tag{13.11}$$

yielding an intrinsic value of

$$\int_t^{T_*} S_{\max} \left[\frac{\partial \log F(t,U)}{\partial U}\Big|_{U=T} - r \right]^+ dT \tag{13.12}$$

The fact that we have a closed-form solution (13.8) allows us to efficiently explore the behavior of inventory value as a function of $\vec{Y}_t$. Before proceeding to a working problem for natural gas, with seasonality in both forward prices and implied volatilities, it is worth examing an idealized non-seasonal setting. If we consider an infinite horizon setting ($T_* = \infty$), with constant values for the local volatilities ($\sigma_j(T) = \sigma_J$) and with the forward curve asymptotically constant and of the form:

$$F(0,T) = F_\infty e^{\sum_j e^{-\beta_j T} Y_j} \tag{13.13}$$

then the value function depends solely on $\vec{Y}$, with no t dependence.

Figure 13.1 shows the results for a one-factor infinite-horizon valuation using $F(0,T) \equiv 1$, $\beta = 1.00$, $\sigma = 0.50$, and $r = 0.05$. The top figure is the value versus $Y(0)$. Negative values of $Y(0)$ correspond to contango; therefore, the value function must be a decreasing function of $Y(0)$ in order to be an increasing function of the forward yield. The middle figure shows the change in value with respect to $Y(0)$; because this is a single-factor model, the plot shows $\Delta_Y = \partial V / \partial Y$ versus $Y(0)$. Finally, the bottom plot of $\Gamma_Y = \partial^2 V / \partial Y^2$ versus $Y(0)$ illustrates an important point: much as with a simple vanilla option, the convexity of the structure decreases at extreme values of backwardation or contango.[2] Value converges to intrinsic at $|Y(0)| \to \infty$. Just as for standard options, extrinsic value arises near-the-money; in the case of storage, this is when/where the forward curve is relatively flat.

Higher-dimensional analysis exhibits results that are similar to the one-dimensional case shown – in particular, a decay in convexity at extreme

---

[2] The negative values of Γ_Y and the related change in montonoticiy of Δ_Y are due to the fact that Y is a "returns" variable. The structure remains convex in the sense discussed earlier in (9.16).

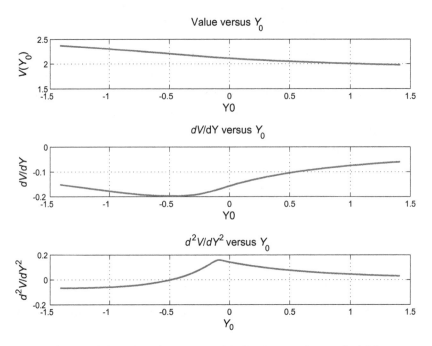

Figure 13.1. Virtual storage valuation versus forward yield.

values, with a greater sensitivity to the value of the high-β factors. Although these results are based on a highly idealized storage structure, the qualitative features pertain to all storage facilities.

Before using virtual storage in the seasonal setting with real market data, there is one remaining issue that we must address. The time scale required for pricing is daily, but market data provide price information at the time scale of monthly delivery. Storage valuation requires that we use forward prices over a given delivery period, notably monthly contract prices, to infer "forward" prices at shorter delivery periods (the quotes are to emphasize the fact that daily forwards do not trade at all but in the cash month).[3] We will digress for a moment on this technical, but important, issue.

Construction of Daily Forward Curves

Storage optimization usually occurs on a daily time scale $\Delta T = 1/365$ as in (13.4), while forward contract price data are at the monthly level. Within the cash month, one can also trade the spot price for next-day delivery as well as the balance-of-the-month price in many locations, but this is not directly relevant to the construction of term daily forward curves. The goal

---

[3] It could be argued that this should have been done earlier for daily fixed strike or forward-starting options. The issue is much less relevant for vanilla daily option setting. Storage optionality depends on differences of daily forward prices, unlike strips of daily optionlets, each of which depends on the spot price on a single day.

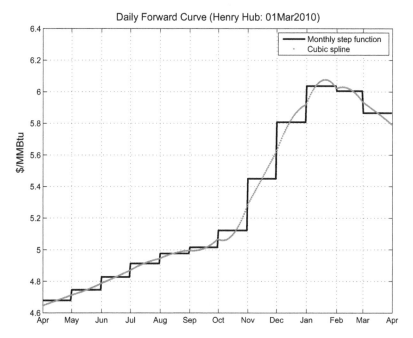

Figure 13.2. NYMEX natural gas (NG) forward curve and cubic spline interpolate.

is to construct daily forward prices from monthly contract prices in a reasonable way. One obvious, though primitive, solution is to use step functions, as shown in Figure 13.2 for Henry Hub on March 1, 2010, which is simply positing that all that the market is telling us is the price for ratable delivery over a month, and one might as well assume that the price is flat. There is, of course, information in neighboring contract prices, which leads us to consider using other methods. The results of one such method are also shown in Figure 13.2; this daily forward curve is consistent with the monthly forwards.

This interpolate was constructed by calculating the cumulative forward value of the commodity:

$$C(\bar{N}_M) = \sum_{m=1}^{M} N_m F_m \qquad (13.14)$$

where N_m is the number of days in month m, F_m is the month forward, and $\bar{N}_M = \sum_{m=1}^{M} N_m$ is the number of delivery days from across all previous delivery months inclusive. The resulting data $\{\bar{N}_m, C(T_m)\}_{m=1}^{M_{\max}}$ were then interpolated using a cubic spline to obtain $C(n)$ for all delivery days $n \in [1, N_{\max}]$. The discrete function $C(\cdot)$ was then differenced to yield a daily forward price $F(0, n)$. Consistency with the monthly forwards is guaranteed because, by construction,

$$N_m F_m = C(N_m) - C(N_{m-1}) = \sum_{d \in m} F(0, d) \qquad (13.15)$$

This clearly yields a more reasonable daily forward curve than the step-function representation, although there are kinks and changes in monotonicity that are not natural.

In continuous time, this approach amounts to constructing an interpolate

$$C(T) = \int_0^{T_*} F(T) \, dT \qquad (13.16)$$

on discrete data $\{T_m, C(T_m)\}_{m=1}^M$ obtained from the monthly prices. The forward price is then $F(T) = \partial C(T)/\partial T$. The presence of the

$$\frac{\partial \log F(t, U)}{\partial U}\Big|_{U=T}$$

in (13.8) would clearly benefit from a high degree of smoothness in $C(T)$, while the cubic spline only guarantees continuity of this term. We will see the effects of this momentarily. More sophisticated interpolation schemes can be used to yield smoother valuation results, but we will use the simple cubic spline as our default method in what follows.

Virtual Storage Results

With daily forward curves at hand, we can now examine the behavior of virtual storage. The purpose in this section is to exhibit qualitative attributes that will also pertain to more realistic storage transactions.

Working Problem:

Our working example will be a contract over one typical season: April 1, 2010 to March 31, 2011. The pricing date will be March 1, 2010.

To start, suppose that we had used the step-function form of daily prices in the discrete CSO evaluation and with our default parameter settings $\vec{\beta} = [0.30, 40]$. The total value of the structure is \$10.71/MMBtu of capacity. However, the intramonth CSOs are effectively at-the-money, and the preponderance of the value is concentrated at the boundaries between contract months where the forward prices jump. Figure 13.3 shows both the total and intrinsic value by delivery date in the top plot. The value spikes at the monthly boundary are almost entirely intrinsic value, with extrinsic value visible only on the intramonth CSOs. The middle plot shows daily deltas, and the bottom plot shows the delta to each monthly contract price. Clearly, the value concentration at the boundaries is counterintuitive, although the monthly contract deltas are reasonable with the dominant long and short positions in the most expensive and cheapest months, respectively.

If we perform the same exercise using daily forwards constructed via the cubic spline method, the result is a total value of \$10.44, which is surprisingly

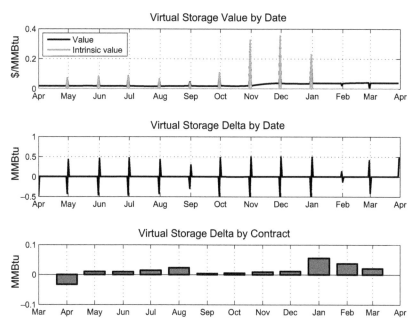

Figure 13.3. Virtual storage value (step-function forward).

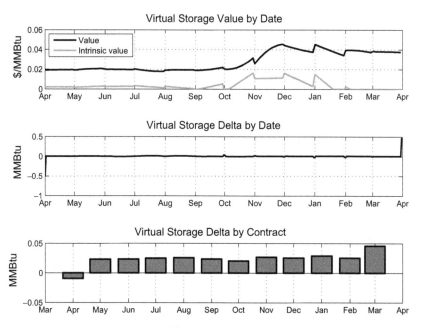

Figure 13.4. Virtual storage value (cubic-spline forward).

close to the preceding result given the difference between the daily forward curves used. The results of the two methods are, as expected, quite different at the daily time scale, as shown in Figure 13.4. The intrinsic-value profile

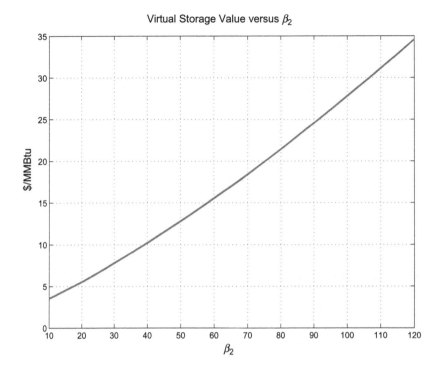

Figure 13.5. Virtual storage value versus β_2.

is more reasonable, concentrated where the forward yields are the highest. The lack of smoothness in the value function and the small outcropping of intrinsic value in February are consequences of the limitations of the cubic-spline interpolate discussed earlier.

The relative computational ease in valuation allows us to easily examine sensitivity to assumptions regarding volatility parameters, much as we did in the case of the forward starters in Chapter 11. Figure 13.5 shows the value of this structure as a funtion of β_2 holding β_1 fixed. The sensitivity of value to the high mean reversion rate is very significant. Replacing $\beta_2 = 40$ with $\beta_2 = 60$, which changes the decay in the returns auto-correlation function from approximately nine days to six days, increases the value by a stunning 50 percent. The value of storage is very sensitive to mean reversion rates. This exposure to estimated parameters is also present in high-turn physical storage.

The General Valuation Problem

The valuation problem for storage structures with constraints on rates and inventory ratchets can be approximated using CSOs, a topic we will return to later in this chapter, but the procedure is more challenging and the results less transparent. The general storage optimization problem must now be phrased in terms of maximizing the expected value of futures cash flows as one injects (spends cash) or withdraws (receives cash). Formally, the valuation problem is

$$V[0, S(0), F(0, \cdot)] = \sup_{s(\cdot) \in \mathcal{A}} \tilde{E} \left\{ \int_0^{T_*} d(0, t)[-s(t)F(t, t) - \kappa\left(s(t), S(t), F(t, t)\right)] \, dt \right\}$$

(13.17)

where

- $d()$ and $F()$ are the discount factor and forward curve, respectively.
- $S(t)$ is the current inventory level, and $s(t) = S'(t)$.
- κ denotes costs associated with injection and withdrawal. For example, a cost that is a fraction of the fuel charge would take the form $\kappa = k|s(t)|F(t, t)$.
- $\mathcal{A}$ denotes allowed controls [e.g., $0 \leq S(t) \leq S_{\max}$].

We will work on the interval $[0, T_*]$ and index time by t. Optimization is over allowed choices of injection/withdrawal $s(\cdot)$. The integrand is the discounted value of the differential inventory change at the prevailing spot price $F(t, t)$: $-s(t)F(t, t)$; it is positive when you withdraw and sell into the market [$s(t) < 0$] and negative when you buy and inject [$s(t) > 0$]. The goal is to maximize the expected present value given the current state of the system: $[0, S(0), F(0, \cdot)]$.

Unless the dynamics are finite-dimensional, such as (13.5), the state space for $F(t, T)$ is infinite-dimensional (or, in discrete time periods such as days, of very high dimension) rendering valuation intractable for practical use. It is common, therefore, to reduce the dimensionality of the problem either by using the GEM framework, in which case the state space becomes $\left[t, S(t), \vec{Y}_t\right]$, or by other approaches, such as Longstaff-Schwartz-type methods.

The constraints $\mathcal{A}$ on $s(t)$ and $S(t)$ are what make the problem challenging. In what follows, we will work with the following constraints:

- $0 \leq S(t) \leq S_{\max}$
- $s_* \leq s(t) \leq s^*$ with constant bounds

Physical storage constraints are often significantly more complex than these, but the essential valuation challenges will become apparent in this relatively simple setting.

Calculating Intrinsic Value

Calculation of intrinsic value is often the first step in any valuation exercise, providing a lower bound on the value of a facility. For most options structures, this is a simple exercise. In the case of storage, however, calculation of intrinsic value already requires a fair amount of work.

Intrinsic value is the zero-volatility solution to (13.17), the value that can be captured by a single static hedge placed at the time of pricing. Because there is no randomness, the value function takes the form $V_I = V_I[S(0)]$

with implicit dependence on the initial forward curve $F(0,T)$. There are two approaches to calculating intrinsic value: the first is computationally faster as a result of reduction of the problem to a linear-programming task; the second uses dynamic control, which is more generally applicable but much slower.

The linear-programming approach can be applied if the cost function is independent of inventory level S and linear in the absolute rate; for example:

$$\kappa = \begin{cases} -k_*s(t)F(t,t) & \text{if } s(t) < 0 \\ k^*s(t)F(t,t) & \text{if } s(t) > 0 \end{cases} \tag{13.18}$$

The intrinsic value $V_I[S(0)]$ is the maximum value over portfolios of forward spreads between all pairs of delivery days (i,j), subject to the constraints of the storage facility:

$$V_I[S(0)] = \sup_{\substack{\vec{v} \in A \\ \vec{v} \geq 0}} \sum_{i,j} v_{i,j} \left(e^{-rT_j}F_j - e^{-rT_i}F_i - K_{i,j} \right) \tag{13.19}$$

Here the portfolio is defined by $\vec{v}$, with $v_{i,j}$ the notional of the (i,j) spread. In addition, $K_{i,j}$ denotes the discounted cost per unit notional of injection at time T_i and withdrawal at time T_j. Although the cost function (13.18) is itself nonlinear in s, this is handled by doubling the size of the state space and using the constraint $\vec{v} \geq 0$. Specifically, by considering positive injection and withdrawal volumes as opposed to signed injection values, the constraints A on inventory level and rates become linear in $\vec{v}$

$$S(T_J) = S(0) + \sum_{\substack{i \leq J \\ j > J}} v_{i,j} - \sum_{\substack{j \leq J \\ i > J}} v_{i,j}$$

$$s(T_J) = \sum_{k \neq J} [v_{J,k} - v_{k,J}] \tag{13.20}$$

and hence amenable to linear-programming methods.

Another approach to calculating V_I is via dynamic programming. Although it is more computationally demanding, the benefit is that general cost functions and inventory constraints can be handled. The idea is based on the notion that to maximize value, one should take the best possible action at each state $[t,S(t)]$. We will work on the discrete time grid

$$t \in \mathcal{T} \equiv [0, \Delta t, 2\Delta t, \ldots, T_*] \tag{13.21}$$

and use the notation

$$t_n = n\Delta t \quad \text{and} \quad p_n = F(0,t_n) \tag{13.22}$$

We will also work with the typical terminal condition for a storage contract

$$V(T_*,S) \equiv 0 \tag{13.23}$$

for all S (you lose whatever inventory you injudiciously left in the facility at the end of the contract), although the method applies to more general boundary conditions. With this as the starting point for a backpropagation solution, the single-step optimization at each state is

$$V(t_n, S) = \max_{x \in \mathcal{A}_{\Delta t}} \left[c(t_n, x, S, p_n) + e^{-r\Delta t} V(t_{n+1}, S + x) \right] \qquad (13.24)$$

where

$$c(t, x, S, p) = -xp - \kappa(x, S, p) \qquad (13.25)$$

Here we have accounted for the fact that the allowed set of transitions depends on Δt using the notation $\mathcal{A}_{\Delta t}$. For example, given Δt, the rate constraint becomes $s_* \Delta t \leq x \leq s^* \Delta t$.

Equation (13.24) is usually solved on a discretized state space for storage:

$$S \in \mathcal{S} \equiv [0, \Delta S, 2\Delta S, \ldots, S_{\max}] \qquad (13.26)$$

in which case (13.24) becomes

$$V(t_n, S_k) = \max_{\hat{k} \in \mathcal{A}_{\Delta t, \Delta S}} \left\{ -(\hat{k} - k)\Delta S p_n - \kappa \left[(\hat{k} - k)\Delta S, S_k, p_n \right] + e^{-r\Delta t} V(t_{n+1}, S_{\hat{k}}) \right\}$$
$$(13.27)$$

Iterating (13.27) yields the value function $V(t_n, S_k)$. In addition, backpropagation yields the optimal control at each state, specifically the $\hat{k}$ obtained from the maximization at each point $[t_n, S_k]$. Denoting this optimum by $k^*(n, k)$ (this is sometimes referred to as the *carry-out function*) and starting at an initial storage level $S_0 = k_0 \Delta S$, the optimal injection and withdrawal path is then obtained by iterating forward in time:

$$k_{n+1} = k^*[n, k_n] \qquad (13.28)$$

Continuing with our working example, we will consider the same storage structure from April 1, 2010 to March 31, 2011, modified by the following constraints and costs.

Working Problem – Modified

- $S_{\max} = 10^6$ MMBtu (1 bcf)
- $[s_*, s^*] = [-\alpha, \alpha] \times S_{\max}$
- $\kappa[s(t), S_u, F(t, t)] = 0.01 F(t, t)$

Figure 13.6 shows the optimal intrinsic inventory profiles for various constraints on injection rates α indexed by turns. Recalling (13.1), turn number N and α are related via $\alpha(N) = 2S_{\max}N$. Note the anticipated change in profile with change in injection rate, ultimately yielding profiles that do not use the full capacity.

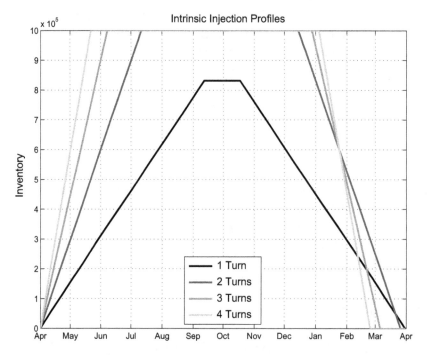

Figure 13.6. Intrinsic inventory profiles.

The intrinsic value of the facility also increases with allowed rates, as shown in Figure 13.7, with incremental increase at high rate limits due to the fact that the derivative of the initial forward curve is bounded in absolute value. In fact, in the limit as $N \to \infty$, the only constraint is the bound on inventory $S_{\max}$, which is exactly the virtual storage case.

Stochastic Dynamic Programming

The dynamic-programming approach that was used earlier to calculate intrinsic value is easily extended to the fully stochastic problem in which forward curves are driven by a discrete set of random factors. In the setting of the Gaussian factor models, this becomes

$$V\left(t_n, S, \vec{Y}\right) = \max_{x \in \mathcal{A}_{\Delta t}} \left\{ c\left[t_n, x, S, p_n(\vec{Y})\right] + e^{-r\Delta t} \tilde{E}\left[V\left(t_{n+1}, S+x, \vec{Y}_{t_{n+1}}\right) \Big| \mathcal{F}_{t_n}\right] \right\}$$

(13.29)

The argument is the same as before: at each possible state, now appended by $\vec{Y}$, which defines the current state of the forward curve, choose the change in inventory that optimizes the sum of the current cost c and the discounted *expected* value at the next time step over the set of allowed changes. There are two key differences between the dynamic programming that was used to compute intrinsic value and the form here. First, the state space must include

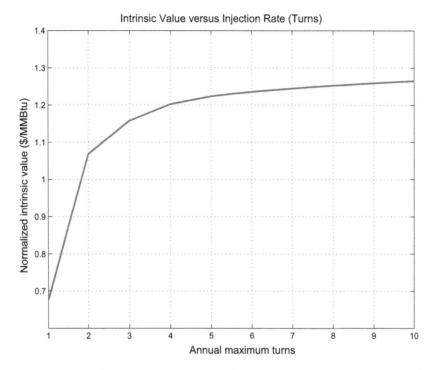

Figure 13.7. Intrinsic value versus rate limit.

the processes that define the forward curve because, unlike in the intrinsic-value (equivalently, the zero-volatility) calculation, the forward curve is changing. Second, the decision involves maximizing expected value, which requires the expectation of the value function in the upcoming time step. Other than these two changes, the concept is identical.

Following the intrinsic-value approach, in which we discretized the relevant state variable S, here one discretizes the $\vec{Y}$ state variables; for example in the one-factor setting,

$$Y \in \mathcal{Y} \equiv [-Y^*, -Y^* + \Delta Y, \ldots, Y^* - \Delta Y, Y^*] \tag{13.30}$$

for a given range $[-Y^*, Y^*]$ over which we choose to compute the value function. The resulting optimization problem becomes

$$V(t_n, S_k, Y_j) = \max_{\hat{k} \in \mathcal{A}_{\Delta t, \Delta S}} \left\{ -(\hat{k} - k)\Delta S p_{n,j} - \kappa \left[(\hat{k} - k)\Delta S, S_k, p_{n,j} \right] \right.$$
$$\left. + e^{-r\Delta t} \sum_j f(Y_j | Y_n) V(t_{n+1}, S_{\hat{k}}, Y_j) \right\} \tag{13.31}$$

where $p_{n,j}$ denotes the spot price at time t_n in state Y_j, and $f(Y_j | Y_n)$ is the transition probability of the OU process Y_t from Y_n to Y_j over a time interval ΔT:

$$f(Y_j|Y_n) = P\left[Y_{\Delta T} \in \left(Y_j - \frac{1}{2}\Delta Y, Y_j + \frac{1}{2}\Delta Y\right) \middle| Y_0 = Y_n\right] \tag{13.32}$$

Note that unlike in the intrinsic case, in which the spot price p was simply $F(0, t_n)$, in the stochastic case it now depends on the state variable Y and is obtained from (C.23).

Recalling that the stationary variance of the OU process Y given in (C.12) is $1/2\beta$, the natural parameterization of boundaries is via $Y^* = z^*/\sqrt{2\beta}$ for a reasonably large value of z^*; for example, $z* = 3$ spans 3σ in the standard normal sense. One can, and should, test for convergence of the solution by examining sensitivity to the value of z^*. Boundary conditions near $\pm Y^*$ require modification of the transition density; here we adjusted $f(Y_j|Y_n)$ so that the expected value of linear functions across the boundary was preserved. This issue, as well as the stability of numerical methods, has been discussed extensively in related contexts; see, for example, [Hul12] and [WHD95].

Before proceeding to numerical results, it is worth mentioning that a continuous-time version of the discrete optimization can be obtained either directly from (13.17) or by taking the limit $\Delta t \to 0$ in (13.24), where Taylor expansion results in the following PDE provided that $c()$ is smooth:

$$0 = \frac{\partial V}{\partial t} - rV + \sup_{s \in \mathcal{A}}\left(\frac{\partial c}{\partial s}s + \frac{\partial V}{\partial S}s\right) \tag{13.33}$$

In this limit, the optimal solution is to inject at the maximum rate s^* if the marginal gain in storage value exceeds the marginal cost of injection, that is, if

$$\frac{\partial V}{\partial S} + \frac{\partial c}{\partial s} > 0 \tag{13.34}$$

and conversely to withdraw at the maximum rate if the opposite inequality holds. Although much research has been done on the existence and general properties of solutions to nonlinear PDEs arising in stochastic control, in practical applications, the nontrivial issues are the design of fast, stable numerical solutions and tests for convergence.

General Valuation Results

Solving (13.31) in practice is tedious, but the concept of maximizing expected value at each point in the state space is simple. The practical problem is the time required for computation. We will show results of this approach applied to both the idealized and working problems that we discussed earlier in the context of virtual storage using the preceding one-factor formulation. Later we will discuss the two-factor setting, which is marginally tractable

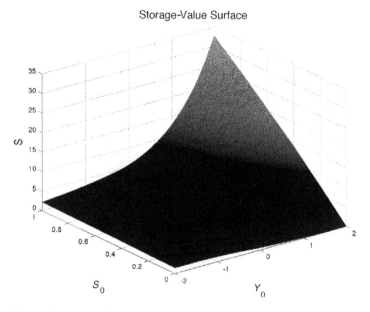

Figure 13.8. Storage-value surface in USD per unit capacity (non-seasonal).

numerically; in higher factor settings the preceding approach is generally viewed as untenable in production.

In what follows we have simplified matters not only by reduction to one factor but also by using constant $\sigma(T) \equiv \sigma$ chosen so that for any value of β we have the same stationary variance of σY; specifically, $\sigma^2/2\beta \equiv C$ for a specified value of C.[4] We will work with the default parameters:

- A stationary variance $C = 0.5$
- A constant short rate $r = 0.05$
- Mean reversion rate of $\beta = 1$
- For the idealized settings, namely, those in which were are not using market forward curves, we take $F(0, T) \equiv 5$.

Starting with the idealized nonseasonal setting with constant initial forward curve, Figure 13.8 shows the value surface as a function of S_0 and Y_0 for a one-year, five-turn storage facility with

$$\kappa\left[s(t), S_u, F(t,t)\right] = 0.01 F(t,t) \tag{13.35}$$

The value is an increasing function of initial inventory as it should be – starting off with more of something worth a positive value is better than starting off with less. At all but the lowest values of S_0, the value function is

---

[4] Modification of (13.31) to accommodate little-t dynamics requires modifying $p(n,j)$. When the local volatility is of the form $v(t)$, the transition density f must be adjusted at each time step, and care must be taken that ΔY is small enough to avoid numerical instabilities over all the range of $v(t)$, which in the explicit scheme we are using would manifest via negative probabilities. Implicit methods are generally preferred.

Storage Extrinsic-Value Surface

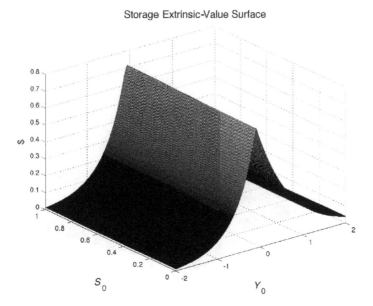

Figure 13.9. Storage extrinsic-value surface in USD per unit capacity (nonseasonal).

increasing in Y_0 – this is due to the fact that the value of initial inventory is $S_0 F_0 e^{\sigma Y_0}$.

The extrinsic-value surface, shown in Figure 13.9, is more interesting, with maximum optionality at $Y_0 = 0$. This is consistent with the results from virtual storage. What is perhaps surprising is that the extrinsic value does not drop appreciably near the boundaries $S_0 = 0$ or $S_0 = S_{\max}$, where one might think that the actions of the operator are constrained to inject and withdraw, respectively. This is due to the fact that the inventory trajectories rapidly pull storage levels away from the boundaries. Figure 13.10 shows the expected inventory as a function of time for three initial values of S_0, all with a flat initial forward curve, that is, $Y_0 = 0$.

Figure 13.11 shows the expected trajectories for various initial Y_0 with $S_0 = 0.5$. At high levels of initial backwardation/contango, the course of action is to withdraw/inject rapidly, as expected.

Inventory optimization is a tradeoff between forward yields and cost of financing inventory. Figure 13.12 shows the expected inventory trajectories for several levels of interest rates using initial conditions $S_0 = 0.5$ and $Y_0 = 0$. The first feature that stands out is the obvious one – namely, that the higher the funding rate, the lower the expected inventory. It is also noteworthy that the expected storage level consistently rises to levels well above 0.5 before converging to zero at expiration. This is due to the fact that forward yields in the risk-neutral measure are biased toward contango. To see this in the case of constant local volatility $\sigma(T) \equiv \sigma$ in the one-factor setting, the expression

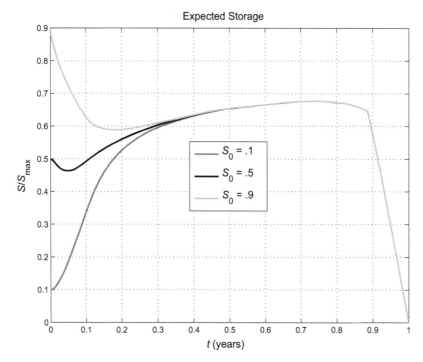

Figure 13.10. Expected inventory trajectories: varying S_0 with $Y_0 = 0$.

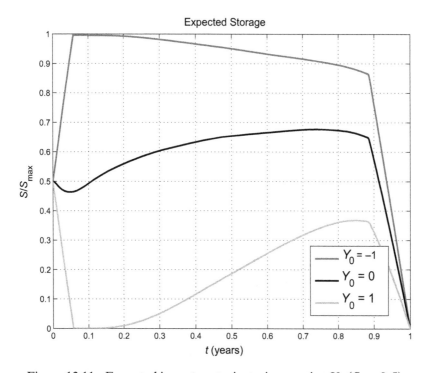

Figure 13.11. Expected inventory trajectories: varying Y_0 ($S_0 = 0.5$).

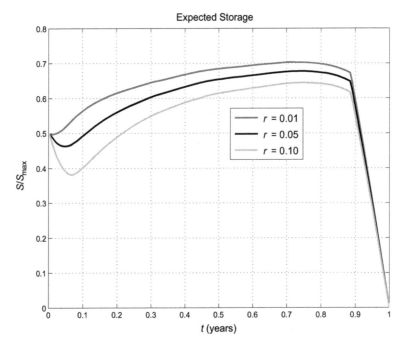

Figure 13.12. Expected inventory trajectories: varying short rate.

for $F(t, T)$ given in (C.9) with the Ito term $V(t, T)$ in (C.19) implies that

$$\log\left[\frac{F(t, T+S)}{F(t, T)}\right] = \log\left[\frac{F(0, T+S)}{F(0, T)}\right] + \sigma\left(e^{-\beta(T+S-t)} - e^{-\beta(T-t)}\right) Y_t$$
$$+ \frac{\sigma^2}{4\beta}\left(e^{-2\beta(T-t)} - e^{-2\beta T} - e^{-2\beta(T+S-t)} + e^{-2\beta(T+S)}\right)$$

although the result that follows applies for any number of factors. Starting at $Y_0 = 0$, the second term is a mean-zero normal random variable. The third term, however, is positive because the function

$$\psi(T) = e^{-2\beta(T-t)} - e^{-2\beta T} = e^{-2\beta T}\left(e^{2\beta t} - 1\right) \tag{13.36}$$

is decreasing in T. This implies a bias toward positive forward yields under the risk-neutral measure and the resulting systematic increase in inventory levels as t increases to intermediate times.

Turning now to our working problem on March 1, 2010, for which we calculated intrinsic-value profiles earlier, for physical storage the behavior of inventory profiles depends on cycling rate. Figure 13.13 shows the value of storage versus turns, which exhibits a similar profile as was seen for intrinsic value. The distributional features of inventory over the season also vary with the flexibility of the facility. Figure 13.14 shows the expected inventory path for one- and five-turn storage. The drop in expected inventory in the

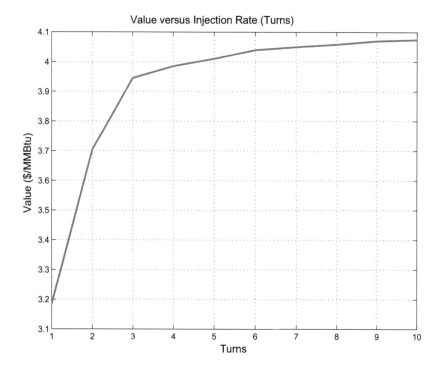

Figure 13.13. Storage value versus turns.

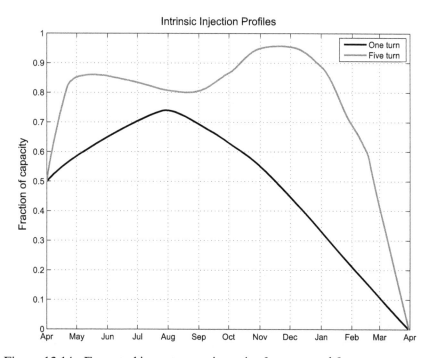

Figure 13.14. Expected inventory trajectories for one- and five-turn storage.

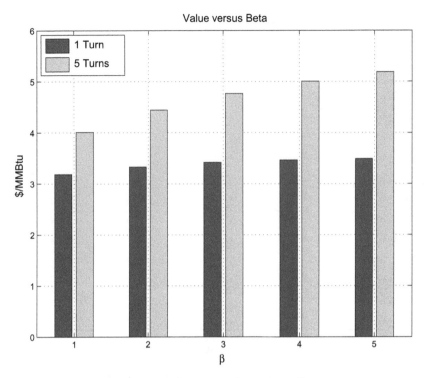

Figure 13.15. Storage values versus beta.

July time frame for the high-turn facility, in contrast to the low-turn facility, shows that it is able to exploit relatively nuanced changes in forward yields.

As a final point, sensitivity to model selection increases as constraints are reduced. Figure 13.15 shows the value of the one- and five-turn facilities as a function of mean reversion rate β. Note that the low-turn, highly constrained structure shows almost no response in value, which is in stark contrast to the high-turn facility. This is both obvious and important – the highly constrained case is much more readily approximated by its intrinsic value, which is model-independent. The situation where you must rely on models, namely, the high-turn situation, is more sensitive to model specification.

Alternative Methods

There is a purity to the dynamic-programming approach – when it can be applied yields, up to the assumptions regarding underlying forward dynamics, the value of the structure. The trouble is that requirements for production application of dynamic programming are severe. First, the methodology is constrained to prescriptions of forward dynamics that can be represented by a finite-dimensional state space. The Gaussian exponential factor class is the canonical example of such. Second, and of even greater concern, computational limitations restrict the modeling universe to one or two factors. All our preceding examples analyzed the one-factor setting for a reason – numerical solution was reasonably fast.[5] Even in the one-factor setting, calculation of the Greeks for all contract months would start to become costly computationally. The size of the grid used in the preceding one-factor analysis, that is, the product of the size of the time grid, S grid, and Y grid, was just under 6×10^6. In two factors this would have been over 500×10^6. In the two-factor setting, which is the least one can imagine being truly useful for high-turn storage, in which response to spot volatility is a significant source of value, the computational requirements are formidable.

Given these challenges associated with direct solution of the dynamic-programming problem, a number of approximate and heuristic approaches continue to be developed, a few of which we will survey briefly.

Longstaff-Schwartz-Type Algorithms

One class of simulation-based approaches to storage valuation is descendant from the Longstaff-Schwartz method for Monte Carlo valuation of American options (see [LS01]). The central idea is that the continuation value of an American option, that is, the value of not immediately exercising but holding the option for another time step versus immediate exercise, can be parameterized by a set of basis functions, with coefficients estimated using least-squares regression applied recursively on a set of simulation paths. Since the value at expiration is well defined, a form of backpropagation results.

In the American option setting, for which the original method was introduced in [LS01], the decision at time t is

$$V(t, X_t) = \max \left\{ (X_t - K)^+, e^{-r\Delta t} E\left[V(t + \Delta t, X_{t+\Delta t}) | \mathcal{F}_t \right] \right\} \quad (13.37)$$

in the case of a call option. Given a set of simulation paths for essentially any stochastic process driving X_t, the functional form of the continuation value

$$C(t, X_t) \equiv E\left[V(t + \Delta t, X_{t+\Delta t}) | \mathcal{F}_t \right] \quad (13.38)$$

is approximated as

$$\hat{C}(t, X_t) \equiv \sum_{j=1}^{J} \alpha_j(t) \phi_j(X_t) \quad (13.39)$$

---

[5] A single solution of the backpropagation using reasonably efficient vectorization in Matlab required approximately two minutes. Simulation required less than a minute for 1000 sample paths. While faster methods exist (see [Pir12] for a discussion in precisely this context), even these are easily overwhelmed by tenor and dimensionality.

for a set of basis functions $\{\phi_j(x)\}_{j=1}^{J}$, and the coefficients $\vec{\alpha}(t)$ are estimated via least squares. The key step is that on each simulation path k at time step t_n the realized continuation value starting from $X_{t_n}^{(k)}$ is (approximately) $\hat{C}\left(t_{n+1}, X_{t_n}^{(k)}\right)$. This provides a data set of size equal to the number of simulation paths on which to estimate the coefficients in (13.39).

Natural gas storage is amenable to an extension of this approach, as described in [BdJ08] and references therein. The idea is similar to the American option approach – namely, approximating the continuation value in (13.29)

$$C\left(t_n, S, \vec{Y}\right) = e^{-r\Delta t} E\left[V\left(t_{n+1}, S + \Delta S, \vec{Y}_{t_{n+1}}\right) | \mathcal{F}_{t_n}\right] \tag{13.40}$$

via a parametric form, with coefficients estimated via regression. In [BdJ08], a one-factor spot price process of the form

$$\frac{dp_t}{p_t} = \kappa\left[\mu(t) - \log p_t\right] dt + \sigma \, dB_t \tag{13.41}$$

is used. In this simplified setting, the continuation function takes the form $C(t,S,p)$.

Rather than proceeding with a general set of multivariate basis-function approximations

$$C(t,S,p) \approx \sum_{j=1}^{J} \alpha_j(t) \phi_j(S,p) \tag{13.42}$$

for which specification of the basis functions is challenging, the approach used is to discretize the storage variable as in (13.26) and run separate regressions for each $k \in \mathcal{S}$ of the form

$$C(t, k\Delta S, p) \approx \sum_{j=1}^{J} \alpha_{j,k}(t) \phi_j(p) \tag{13.43}$$

At each step, the continuation value is approximated over the storage grid $\mathcal{S}$, and optimization takes the form

$$V(t_n, S_k, p_n) = \max_{\hat{k} \in \mathcal{A}_{\Delta t, \Delta S}} \left\{ -(\hat{k} - k)\Delta S p_n - \kappa\left[(\hat{k} - k)\Delta S, S_k, p_n\right] \right.$$
$$\left. + e^{-r\Delta t} \sum_{j=1}^{J} \alpha_{\hat{k}, j}(t) \phi_{\hat{k}}(p_n) \right\} \tag{13.44}$$

Stability of the method depends on the choice of basis functions and the number used.

In the preceding one-factor example, using (13.41), a direct backpropagation would have been the logical choice of method. Furthermore, multifactor extensions are (arguably) computationally as laborious as direct implementation of dynamic programming. The primary value of the least-square-based methods is that more general forward dynamics can be used, in contrast to the dynamic-programming methods, which are confined to low-dimensional factor dynamics.

More sophisticated optimization methods also have been developed that use elements of the Longstaff-Schwartz regression methods with additional innovations. For example, [CL10] introduces an iterative method in which the number of injection/withdrawal actions is akin to the number of exercises in a swing option. As with the preceding methods, the approach is quite general in the type of stochastic process driving spot prices that can be handled.

Rolling Intrinsic

Another simulation-based method that has grown in popularity is based on the observation that a lower bound on the value of storage results from dynamically hedging the intrinsic value of the facility. This idea is compelling due to its simplicity and intuitive appeal. This approach, referred to as the *rolling intrinsic method*, is also motivated by what many portfolio managers tasked with optimizing gas storage facilities do in practice – namely, at inception, they lock in the intrinsic value via a set of forward hedges, rebalancing at later times if the prevailing forward curve implies a higher intrinsic value. This method has been examined and discussed broadly; see, for example, [BCE$^+$08], [EW03], [GK04], and [SLM$^+$10].

Working in continuous time and assuming constant interest rates for simplicity, the approach works as follows. Consider a storage transaction spanning $[T_*, T^*]$. Calculating intrinsic value at time $t = 0$ as in either (13.19) or (13.24) amounts to obtaining the function $w_0^*(T)$ that solves

$$V(0) = \max_{w \in \mathcal{A}} \int_{T_*}^{T^*} e^{-rT} w(T) F(0, T) \, dT \tag{13.45}$$

where we have assumed that the transaction starts in the future ($T_* > 0$) and denoted the constraints on w by $\mathcal{A}$. Note that $w(T) > 0$ corresponds to a forward *sale* of natural gas at time T, so the actual forward hedge required to "lock in" intrinsic value is $-w_0^*(T)$ for delivery time T.

At a later time $t \in (0, T_*)$, the same calculation results, in general, in a different solution $w_t^*(T)$ to the current intrinsic-value calculation:

$$V(t) = \int_{T_*}^{T^*} e^{-r(T-t)} w_t^*(T) F(t, T) \, dT \tag{13.46}$$

In the absence of transaction costs, it makes sense to rebalance the hedge from $-w_0^*(T)$ to $-w_t^*(T)$, if the difference in value:

$$\int_{T_*}^{T^*} e^{-r(T-t)} [w_t^*(T) - w_0^*(T)] F(t, T) \, dT \qquad (13.47)$$

is nonnegative.

This is the idea behind the rolling intrinsic method, and the resulting algorithm is an iterative application of this train of thought. If at any time you can achieve a positive change in the static value implied by the *current* forward curve by rebalancing, then you should do so. In practice, this procedure occurs on a daily basis and must account for transaction costs. Moreover, as the deal starts to amortize (i.e., $t > T_*$), the calculation clearly involves current forward positions.

This procedure can be applied to any realization of the forward curve, and the ultimate value at termination of the transaction is the accrued value of both the initial intrinsic value and the incremental value obtained by the sequential rebalancings. Note, moreover, that no knowledge of future price dynamics is assumed because at each stage decisions are made based solely on the observable forward curve. Many practitioners will in fact run this procedure through historical realizations to benchmark valuation. For forward valuation, however, the procedure is clearly amenable to simulation for any model of forward dynamics and provides useful benchmarks for other valuation methods. While very flexible regarding the type of forward dynamics used, with no constraints on reduced factor dimensions such as in the GEM framework, results are still heavily dependent on the model specification.

CSO Subordinators

We have seen that CSOs are the simplest renditions of commodity storage. It is reasonable to ask whether CSOs can be used in the case of physical storage with nontrivial constraints, if only to establish bounds. Research along these lines appears to have started with the preceding rolling intrinsic valuation method, to which a judicious application of a sequence of inequalities shows that a lower bound on physical storage starting and ending with zero inventory can be obtained by a portfolio of American CSOs; see, for example, [BCE+08] or [Sad11], which are descendant from [EW03] and unpublished references therein.

A more general tack is the brute-force approach of directly constructing subordinating portfolios of CSOs that are consistent with the physical constraints of the storage facility. Recall (13.19), which represented the intrinsic value as the maximum value of all forward spreads that were consistent with the constraints of the storage facility. A similar representation for the value of a facility can be obtained by optimizing over all pairs of CSOs and forward spreads. Denote the present value of the forward spreads and CSOs, respectively, as

$$S_{i,j} = e^{-rT_j}F_j - e^{-rT_i}F_i - K_{i,j}$$

$$C_{i,j} = \tilde{E}\left[\left(e^{-rT_j}F_j - e^{-rT_i}F_i - K_{i,j}\right)^+\right]$$

$$P_{i,j} = \tilde{E}\left[\left(e^{-rT_i}F_i - e^{-rT_j}F_j - K_{j,i}\right)^+\right] \qquad (13.48)$$

We are assuming that $i < j$ and are using the same notation for costs and forwards as before. A lower bound on the value of a storage asset is

$$V[S(0), F(0,\cdot)] = \sup_{\substack{\tilde{v} \in \mathcal{A} \\ \tilde{\alpha}, \tilde{\beta}, \tilde{v} \geq 0}} \left[\sum_{1 \leq i < j \leq J} \left(\alpha_{i,j}C_{i,j} + \beta_{i,j}P_{i,j}\right) + \sum_{1 \leq i < j \leq J} v_{i,j}S_{i,j}\right] \qquad (13.49)$$

The tedious part is specifying $\mathcal{A}$. The point to keep in mind is that, even though each option may or may not be exercised, it must be assumed to be exercised in order to ensure that the constraints are satisfied under all realizations of forward prices and all possible option exercise events. For completeness, the list following describes the set of constraints. To clarify the reasoning, the first constraint listed ensures that under any possible sequence of option exercise, the injection rate at time k does not exceed s^*. Any (k,j) call with the second leg $j > k$, if exercised, results in an injection at time k; the corresponding forward spread always does, and both must be counted. The symmetric argument applies to the puts.

1. $s_k \leq s^*$ $(1 \leq k \leq J)$:

$$\sum_{j>k}\left(\alpha_{k,j} + v_{k,j}\right) + \sum_{i<k}\left(\beta_{i,k} + v_{k,i}\right) \leq s^*$$

2. $s_k \geq s_*$ $(1 \leq k \leq J)$:

$$\sum_{j>k}\left(\beta_{k,j} + v_{j,k}\right) + \sum_{i<k}\left(\alpha_{i,k} + v_{i,k}\right) \leq -s_*$$

3. $S_k \leq S_{\max}$ $(1 \leq k \leq J-1)$:

$$S_0 + \sum_{\substack{1<i\leq k \\ k<j\leq J}}\left(\alpha_{i,j} + v_{i,j} - v_{j,i}\right) \leq S_{\max}$$

4. $S_k \geq 0$ $(1 \leq k \leq J-1)$:

$$S_0 - \sum_{\substack{1<i\leq k \\ k<j\leq J}}\left(\beta_{i,j} + v_{j,i} - v_{i,j}\right) \geq 0$$

Note that the last two sets of constraints apply up to $J - 1$ because the Jth condition would be trivially satisfied as a result of the fact that all involve notional neutral pairs.

This is a linear-programming problem, the solution to which is routine. Given any risk-neutral model for forward dynamics, the relevant CSOs can be valued and (13.49) solved. Typically, this approach is implemented at the level of monthly granularity consistent with the structure of the CSOs that are traded (we will discuss limitations on CSO liquidity shortly).

One often overlooked trouble with this approach is that the solution is not a smooth function of the input market data. Condensing our preceding notation into the values of the tradables involved and the parameters over which optimization occurs, that is,

$$\vec{\pi} \equiv \left[\vec{\alpha}, \vec{\beta}, \vec{v} \right] \qquad \vec{V} \equiv \left[\vec{C}, \vec{P}, \vec{S} \right] \tag{13.50}$$

the optimal holding $\vec{\pi}_* [F(t, \cdot)]$ implies a lower bound on the value

$$V_* [F(t, \cdot)] \equiv \vec{\pi}_*^\dagger [F(t, \cdot)] \, \vec{V} [F(t, \cdot)] \tag{13.51}$$

It is important to note that the solution $\vec{\pi}_*$ depends on the prevailing forward curve (not to mention volatilities and correlations) at the time of the optimization. Because $\vec{\pi}_*$ is the solution of a linear-programming problem, π_* is not a smooth function of the input data $F(t, T)$. Consequently, when the subordinating portfolio is reoptimized over the course of the transaction, a process that is often scripted for daily occurrence, discontinuous changes in the Greeks can occur. Many implementations of this method calculate the Greeks on the static portfolio, for example,

$$\frac{\partial V_*}{\partial F(t, T)} - \vec{\pi}_*^\dagger [F(t, \cdot)] \frac{\partial \vec{V}}{\partial F(t, T)} \tag{13.52}$$

whereas in fact the proper calculation should be

$$\frac{\partial V_*}{\partial F(t, T)} = \vec{\pi}_*^\dagger [F(t, \cdot)] \frac{\partial \vec{V}}{\partial F(t, T)} + \frac{\partial \vec{\pi}_*}{\partial F(t, T)}^\dagger [F(t, \cdot)] \vec{V} \tag{13.53}$$

The second term is not a smooth function in underlying market data, which can result in surprises to the portfolio manager as risk exposures can change discontinuously.

Despite this drawback, the approach is viewed by many practitioners as a reliable method for obtaining conservative estimates of value. As with all the methods described previously, the results are only as good as one's ability to have accurate and hedgable CSO values, which is tantamount to calibrated or estimated volatilities and correlations.

Daily Optionality and Spot Yields

We have discussed the mechanics of valuation using a variety of related methods. In particular, we analyzed storage using dynamic programming at the daily time scale with a one-factor model – a framework generally more suited to longer-time-scale structures. Although we could clearly adjust the single mean reversion rate to higher values and calibrate to daily volatilities, a minimum of two factors is required to represent the value associated with both the intermonth changes in forward yields and the daily optionality embedded in high-turn storage facilities. The CSO subordinator method can be implemented at the daily time scale, much as in the discrete virtual storage setting. However, given what little CSO trading occurs between contract months, this method is almost always deployed in a monthly setting, with the transition to daily exercise during the cash month awkward to effect. Likewise, numerical implementation of the Longstaff-Schwartz approximations are challenging at the daily time scale.

We saw in Chapters 11 and 12 examples of daily structures that could ostensibly be valued using multifactor models. The approach was to calibrate a two-factor model and to compute the expected payoff of the structure either by quadrature or by simulation. The key distinction between various structures is in the ability to hedge the value obtained. In the case of the forward starter, this was not terribly challenging; for the peaking option, limitations on the instruments available rendered hedging very challenging if the number of exercises was small.

High-turn storage facilities fall into the category of "hard to hedge." One can use any of the preceding methods, taking monthly options and forward starters, in addition to the few CSOs that trade, to calibrate a two-factor model. In addition, the monthly forward contract prices coupled with the spot price (for next-day delivery) and the balance-of-month price would be used to construct a daily forward price – perhaps even using weather forecasts to make logical (if unhedgable) views on the likely trajectory of daily spot prices. Dynamic-programming or other methods would yield a value.

The key question remains: Can the extrinsic value be hedged?

The first problem is that whereas valuation used daily forward prices, these don't trade. You can buy or sell natural gas for spot delivery (tomorrow) but not for the next day, at least with any liquidity. The only reliably liquid short-tenor forward is the balance-of-month price. What traders actually do is buy or sell spots and take offsetting positions in the balance of month or first nearby contracts. The trading mechanics implied by the daily CSO presentation, the moral equivalent of which is baked into the daily dynamic programming calculation, cannot be effected.

In addition, the one instrument traders have at their disposal, namely, the forward starters, is, as in the case of the swing option, less than effective at hedging the extrinsic value. This could be demonstrated much as we did for the swing option, but we will adopt a slightly different approach here to illustrate the point.

The extrinsic value of storage depends on changes in the forward yields between relevant spreads, whether these are intermonth (think of monthly CSOs) or intramonth, namely, the cash month, where the storage trader has to decide on a daily basis whether to inject or withdraw. In the later case, the typical consideration of the cash trader is whether the spot price is low (high) enough relative to the first nearby to warrant injection (withdrawal) with offsetting trades in the first nearby. This often causes a segmentation of responsibilities that is less than optimal. Those managing term (longer-tenor) risks will be focusing on positions from the first nearby through the duration of the contract, rebalancing as needed; the cash trader will be focused on the spread between spot prices and the first nearby, often making decisions without accounting for the marginal cost of inventory [the $\partial V/\partial S$ term in (13.33)]. Putting aside the issue of how much value may be lost in this segmentation, this common state of affairs motivates a simple caricature of what can be achieved in high-turn storage.

The top plot in Figure 13.16 shows by month the standard deviation of the daily change of the intramonth forward yield defined as

$$y_{\text{cash}}(d) \equiv 24 \log \left[\frac{p_d}{F_{m+1}(d)} \right] \tag{13.54}$$

The expression for y_d is very similar to the definition of spot returns, with the difference being that the spot price is being compared with the *next* contract, namely, the first nearby. The factor 24 is an approximation for the average yield tenor over the month, namely, 1/24th of a year. This is the yield implied by the spread that the cash trader is watching; the more it changes, the more rebalancings a storage operator can effect versus the first nearby, constrained, of course, by operational limits. The lower plot shows the same statistic by month for the first and second nearby contracts:

$$y_{1,2}(d) \equiv 12 \log \left[\frac{F_{m+2}(d)}{F_{m+1}(d)} \right] \tag{13.55}$$

which is an annualized yield. This is intended to be a metric for rebalancing opportunities in the forward (as opposed to spot) position. The scales on the two plots are not the same, the latter being almost an order of magnitude smaller. The average over all contract months of the cash-yield statistic is 1.28 percent versus 0.10 percent for the nearby yields. It is also clear from the plots that winters are more interesting than summers. Figure 13.17 punctuates this point, showing averages of the preceding results by calendar month. The theme is that the daily option value in the cash month is the dominant contributor to extrinsic value for high-turn storage.

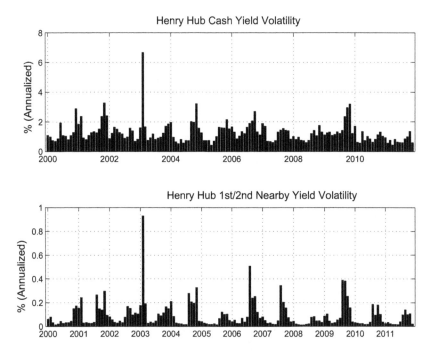

Figure 13.16. Standard deviation of spot and nearby yield changes by month.

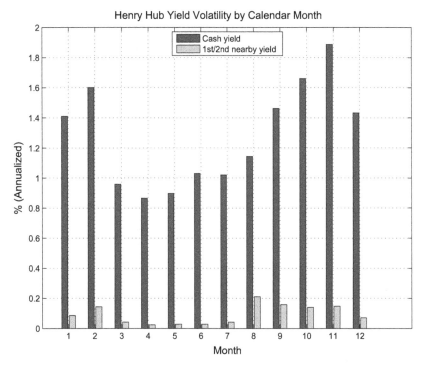

Figure 13.17. Standard deviation of spot and nearby yield changes by calendar month (2000–2011).

Turning to hedging, a simple experiment is to consider the daily straddle payoff for month m:

$$\pi_m(d) \equiv |p_d - F_{m+1}(d)| \tag{13.56}$$

which is the payoff of the spread that the cash trader is watching – devoid of inventory constraints. The hedging instrument is the forward starting straddle

$$h_m(d) \equiv |p_d - F_m(T_e)| \tag{13.57}$$

where, as before, $F_m(T_e)$ denotes the final settlement price of the contact m. Assuming perfect foresight, namely, on a monthly basis, selecting the portfolio $\vec{\alpha}$ of hedges $\vec{h}$ that minimizes the empirical variance of $\vec{\pi} + \vec{\alpha}^\dagger \vec{h}$, the average standard deviation of the unhedged straddles $\vec{\pi}$ of 0.22 was reduced to 0.17. This is hardly an impressive result and exhibits the challenge of capturing the significant extrinsic value of a storage facility with a high turn rate.

As a result, many desks that value and manage physical storage adopt far less rigorous methods than those espoused by unwavering advocates of the complete-markets paradigm. These are typically based on construction of a physical measure of sorts. The problem with using historical data, such as that shown in Figure 13.17, is that it is unclear that you have a enough of it – after all, during this time period there were significant weather fluctuations coupled with large swings in price and inventory levels.

The use of yields, as opposed to price spreads, eliminates a large element of the undesirable price-level effects. Figure 13.18 shows the spot price

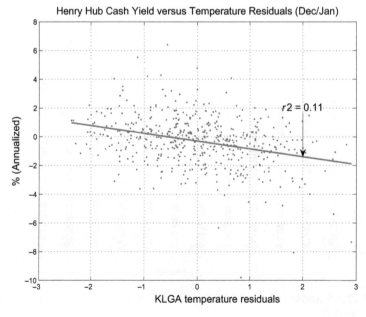

Figure 13.18. Spot yields versus KLGA temperature residuals (2000–2011).

yields, as defined in (13.54), over all December and January months in the data set versus temperature residuals as defined in (10.14) for LaGuardia in New York City. The result shows that high yields are associated with cold temperatures.[6]

The main point is that basic drivers, which are amenable to econometric modeling such as weather and inventory, can be used to construct credible distributions for the daily component of storage extrinsic values. The challenge, which remains unresolved, is how to link the decisions made by the cash desk with the effects on the value of the term position.

Correlation Structure and Inventory Feedback Effects

The methods just surveyed all differ in what are basically mechanical aspects of valuation. Do you decompose monthly forwards into dailies? Do you invoke full dynamic programming using multifactor models or resort to approximations such as the CSO subordinators or Longstaff–Schwartz-type methods for broader classes of forward dynamics? Do you layer an econometric model of cash-month dynamics on top of a monthly risk-neutral method? Various works contrast and compare the results of some of these methods; see, for example, [MLS10], which describes results of extensive comparisons, in addition to introducing some improved methods for constructing valuation bounds.

The real issue, however, is that all these methods depend on the correlation structure of forward returns, which is often barely discernible from market data. The limited nature of correlation products is unnerving. Modelers typically assume a complete set of correlation products, leaving it to traders or portfolio managers to mark CSOs to the best of their ability. This is a seriously flawed approach.

Given our discussions of virtual storage and CSO subordinators, it is fair to say that if we cannot reliably value a family of CSOs spanning all (or nearly all) delivery-month pairs, then deploying any of the methods discussed is questionable at best. Consider Figure 13.19 showing the NG forward curve on November 10, 2010. The obvious seasonality of the curve means that the intrinsic value for all but the most flexible storage facilities is obtained by injecting in the summer and withdrawing in the winter. Extrinsic value, on the other hand, is largely intraseasonal, as labeled in this figure. This is where correlation information is particularly important.

---

[6] The choice of LaGuardia might seem bizarre given that Henry Hub is located 2,000 miles south in Louisiana, but the reason for this selection is that in the winter, cold weather in the Northeast is a dominant driver of spot natural gas prices across a large swath of the country, including Henry Hub. More sophisticated analysis and regressions would include many weather locations across the country.

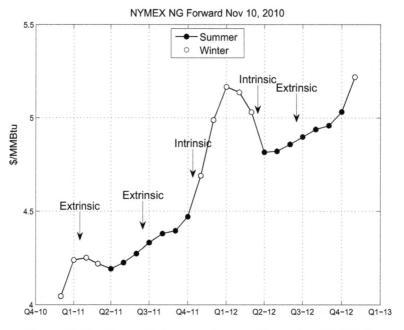

Figure 13.19. Henry Hub forward curve (November 10, 2010).

Now consider the following broker chat on the same date:

```
MARKET LOG FOR MARKET ID:
11/10/10 8:19 AM v11/f12 -.50 call cso .0825-.095
11/10/10 8:34 AM V/F -50call CSO .075 / .10
11/10/10 8:37 AM V/F -50call CSO .075 @ .09
11/10/10 10:57 AM v11/f12 -.50 call cso @ .0875
11/10/10 10:58 AM v11/f12 -.50 call cso .075-.0875
11/10/10 1:43 PM v11/f12 -.50 call cso 6.5/8.25
11/10/10 1:44 PM v11/f12 -.50 call cso 7/8
11/11/10 8:46 AM v1/f2 -.50 call cso: .07 / .085
11/11/10 1:47 PM v11/f12 -.50 call cso .07-.085
11/11/10 1:52 PM v1/f2 -.50 call cso: .07 / .075
11/11/10 1:52 PM v1/f2 -.50 call cso: .07 / .075
11/11/10 1:59 PM v11/f12 -.50 call cso .07-.075
11/11/10 2:11 PM v11/f12 -.50 call cso .0725-.075
11/12/10 10:16 AM
V/F -1.00/-1.25 1x2 put spr CSO .01/.03 to the 2
V/F -.1.25 put CSO .0675/.075
V/F -1.00 put cso .115/.135
V/F -.50 call CSO .065/.075
```

Recall from our earlier discussions of CSOs that the quoting convention is to specify the two contract months, the associated spread between them at the time of the quote (the difference between the first and second forward prices), what type of option is being discussed, and a bid, offer, or both.

What is wrong with this picture? All the quotes shown (and this is a representative state of affairs) are between the October (V) and January (F) contracts, that is, CSOs on the October-January spread between injection and withdrawal seasons. This is exactly where we do *not* need the correlation data – intrinsic value is dominant between the seasons. Correlations matter most when the option is near-the-money and extrinsic value is dominant, in this case, intraseason.

The moral of the story is that market data on correlation are woefully lacking, rendering the discussions about the exact mechanical method for numerical calculation of storage value interesting but one step removed from the real action, which is deciding how to represent and estimate correlation structure.

It is common for practitioners to use a stationary representation of returns correlations. These can, in fact, be reasonably sophisticated. The multifactor exponential class that we have used as a modeling benchmark accommodates many stylized facts, as we saw earlier. Furthermore, allowing for nonstationary correlation structure by permitting the factor correlations to depend on local time, that is, $\rho_{i,j}(t) \equiv \langle dB_t^{(i)}, dB_t^{(j)} \rangle$, creates a great deal of flexibility in the design of covariance structure with very limited implied correlation data from which to calibrate.

Is this good enough?

The answer is almost certainly not, and a set of open problems remains to be addressed and solutions developed. We have seen that inventory levels affect the dynamics of forwards. Both forward yields and volatility structure have discernible relations to relative inventory levels. This is also true for correlation and, as a result, the value of storage. After all, as a storage owner, you are probably optimizing your facility in a manner that is not altogether unlike the way your competitors are optimizing theirs. Consequently, the correlation structure that you should be using to value and hedge your facility almost depends on macro inventory levels and, by proxy, the inventory level of your facility.

Conclusion

Natural gas storage plays an essential role in reconciling the mismatch between highly seasonal demand profiles and relatively predictable supply patterns. At the level of an individual facility, valuation and hedging require the use of optimization methods: either dynamic-programming and related Longstaff-Schwartz methods or linear-programming methods such as the construction of CSO subordinators or rolling intrinsic simulations. Each of these techniques is intended to capture the expected payoff from what at the core is a set of coupled options on forward yields – options to buy, store, and sell over various holding periods.

Although numerical methods and their limitations constitute an important and continuing research effort, the main underlying difficulty is the construction of reliable correlation estimates in the presence of inventory effects on forward dynamics. Inventory level affects correlation structure, meaning that the optimization actions of the totality of portfolio managers changes the inputs to the very valuation that they are using. The absence of a tractable, self-consistent theory of this feedback, coupled with a lack of useful options and correlation hedging instruments, results in a significant and continuing challenge to the acquisition and management of storage.

14

Tolling Deals

Tolling deals are designed to hedge power generators that convert a fuel to electricity. We first encountered tolls in Chapter 9 in the context of monthly exercise spread options between power and natural gas. Analysis was based on the Margrabe valuation framework. Tolls with daily or intraday optionality are by far the more common than those with monthly exercise primarily because the dispatch decisions of physical generation are usually made on the time scale of days and hours.[1] Valuation and hedging daily or intraday tolling structures are considerably more complex than the monthly case.

Although sporadic broker activity may constitute an amusing activity between structured desks to "pick off" their competitors, tolling deals were created and exist to hedge risks inherent in the acquisition or development of generation. Given the billions of dollars invested annually in generation and the associated borrowing requirements, tolls are among the more socially defensible derivatives transactions. Paradoxically, they also have caused some of the greatest damage to commodities desks for reasons that will unfold in what follows.

We will start with standard daily structures in which exercise is into a single standard delivery bucket with a single fuel. These "simple" structures are challenging in their own right while avoiding many of the complexities of physical generation to which we turn to later in this chapter.

Daily Tolls: Mechanics

A toll can involve any structure that replicates the conversion of a fuel, or multiple fuels, into electricity. For nearly two decades, natural gas generation has constituted the dominant addition to generation capacity because of relentless increases in efficiency of combined-cycle generators coupled

---

[1] The term *dispatch*, namely, when and at what output a generator is scheduled to produce electricity, is the power engineering moral equivalent of the term *exercise* for financial engineers.

with (at least sporadically) low natural gas prices. As a result, most tolling structures involve natural gas as the input fuel. Purists insist that the term *tolling deal* refers to physical transactions, with the financially settling equivalents being heat-rate options. The primary difference is in the scheduling and dispatch requirements of the former, with staff required to ensure daily delivery of anticipated natural gas usage and power schedulers required to ensure delivery of the power generated. Moreover, valuation of the physical variety requires analysis of the reliability of the fuel supply, the generation unit itself (they do break down occasionally), and relevant parts of the transmission system. Our focus is on the "derivative" nature of these structures, and we will treat the financial and physical versions of these structures as functionally equivalent from a term-valuation perspective.

The daily payoff of the most basic natural gas toll in a specified delivery bucket is

$$\mathbf{1}_{E_d}[F_B(T_d,T_d) - H_*G(T_d,T_d) - V] \tag{14.1}$$

where we continue to use B to denote one of the standard buckets, for example, "5x16," "2x16," or "7x8." The forward prices for power and natural gas are denoted by $F_B(t,T)$ and $G(t,T)$, respectively, so $F_B(T_d,T_d)$ and $G(T_d,T_d)$ are the respective spot prices on day d. H_* is the unit (transaction) heat rate, and V is the variable operation and maintenance (VOM) costs, usually set to be a proxy for the cost of running and maintaining the unit (typically in the \$3 to \$6/mwH range). E_d is the event that the cash trader calls and exercises the option for day d; the first term is the indicator function of this event $\mathbf{1}_{E_d}$, taking the value one if E_d occurs and zero otherwise.

As with daily power options, while autoexercise (lookback) structures occasionally trade, for most tolls, exercise is manual, requiring a phone call (or in some cases e-mail) prior to say 10 a.m. on the business day preceding the flow date. This means that Sundays and Mondays involve time lags in excess of a day. Moreover, once the option is exercised, the holder is in possession of the one-day swap with terminal payoff

$$F_B(T_d,T_d) - H_*G(T_d,T_d) - V \tag{14.2}$$

At the time of exercise, this underlying swap has value

$$F_B(\tau_d,d) - H_*G(\tau_d,d) - V \tag{14.3}$$

where τ_d denotes the exercise time for the delivery period d. This spread is presumably positive at exercise. In many cases, one-day forward prices are either visible on the screen and easily traded or statistically closely related to those that are. On exercise at τ_d, the resulting long power position is sold at (or near) the price $F_B(\tau_d,d)$, and the short position of H_* units of natural gas is purchased at (or near) $G(\tau_d,d)$, thereby locking in the value (14.3).

The ultimate payoff (14.2) can settle positively or negatively. Given the high volatility of power and natural gas spot prices (recall Figure 1.5), it should come as no surprise that the settlement value (14.2) can be very different from (14.3). The purpose of the hedge at the time of exercise is to eliminate the one-day risk.

Daily Tolls: The Valuation Problem

The valuation problem for the generic structure on a single delivery bucket takes the form

$$V(0) = \tilde{E} \left\{ \sum_m d(0, T_m) \sum_{d \in \mathcal{B}(m)} Q_d \max[F_B(T_d, T_d) - H_* G(T_d, T_d) - V, 0] \right\}$$

(14.4)

where $\mathcal{B}(m)$ denotes the set of delivery days in bucket B in month m, and Q_d is the delivery quantity in MWh. The relevant market data are the two forward curves $F_B(0, \cdot)$ and $G(0, \cdot)$, as well as the monthly and daily volatility surfaces $\sigma_M(T, \rho)$ and $\sigma_D(T, \rho)$, as discussed in Chapter 8.

In the case of monthly tolls discussed in Chapter 9, we used empirical analysis of returns to guide our selection of correlation, especially in the absence of any meaningful trading activity to which we might have calibrated correlations. The rest was routine application of Margrabe. We will proceed similarly here, at least initially. The challenge is not using Margrabe; rather, it is in reaching sensible conclusions about correlation structure at the daily time scale and, of equal importance, the analysis of the viability of the resulting hedging program.

There are several features that distinguish the daily valuation problem from the monthly. In the case of daily structures, we have to address the issue of correlation of spot returns, properly defined, and this necessitates the use of a second factor – ζ in the caricature model (10.18) or the high-β factor in our working problems of Chapter 11. Moreover, unlike for monthly tolls, there is some trading activity in daily heat-rate options in the broker markets – rarely beyond a year or two in tenor and certainly with sporadic activity, but activity nonetheless. Such market data provide information about implied correlations, although the modeling challenge of extrapolation of implied correlations to longer tenors remains.

Much as we knew that monthly and daily implied volatilities had to converge at long tenors, we expect the term correlation – the returns correlation from the present t to delivery T – to approach that of the "long-factor" correlations as T increases. There are two ways of dealing with this problem. One way is to exogenously (somehow) specify a term structure of correlation; the second way is to use a multifactor model, calibrated to implied correlations at shorter tenors, to generate correlation extrapolates. Although the second choice is appealing and is one of the reasons for using a multifactor framework, it is encumbered by questionable hedging requirements, as we will see shortly.

The working problem that we will use in this chapter is a daily toll for 2011.

Working Problem

Price a PJM Western Hub "5x16" versus Henry Hub daily toll with the following terms:

- Pricing date: January 11, 2010
- Heat rate: 8.0
- Delivery period: January 1, 2011 to December 31, 2011
- Standard exercise: "-1b"
- Notional: 400 MW

This is a calendar strip of daily spread options, the hedging of which will illustrate some noteworthy (though often ignored) frictions. Also, most generation hedges do not reference Henry Hub as the natural gas leg, using instead basis locations, which although less liquid than Henry Hub, are more representative of the cost of procuring natural gas for the given generator. This creates additional challenges, not least of which is that implied volatilities at such hubs are often barely observable; there may be liquid swaps markets, but often options markets are at best lightly and sporadically traded.[2] In such situations, one is left with the dual challenge of specification of correlations and implied volatilities. The current structure, as posed, is challenging in its own right and is more than adequate to illustrate the main issues.

Spot Correlation and Moments

We first discussed the ambiguity of spot returns in Chapter 10. For nonstorable commodities, namely, power, as well as commodities such as natural gas, in which constraints on injection and withdrawal frequently bind, returns defined as p_{d+1}/p_d can exhibit extreme statistical attributes that are not particularly relevant to valuation. For this reason, we turned to an alternative definition of spot returns introduced in (10.10) by using a beginning-of-month contract settlement as the reference price

$$\hat{\rho}_d \equiv \log \left[\frac{p_d}{F_m(T_e)} \right] \tag{14.5}$$

---

[2] In some instances, the natural gas basis options markets are less visible than broker-traded tolls referencing the same location.

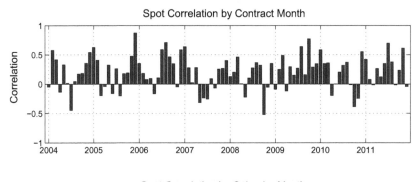

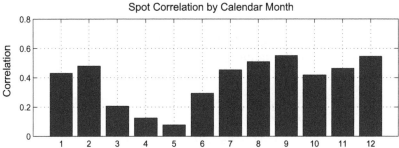

Figure 14.1. Spot returns correlations: PJM versus Henry Hub.

where p_d denotes the daily spot price, and $F_m(T_e)$ is the settlement price for the last trading day of the standard futures or forward contract for delivery in month m. Figure 14.1 shows the realized spot correlation by month between PJM and Henry Hub in the top figure. The lower figure shows the average sample correlation by calendar month. The spot correlation structure between PJM and Henry Hub exhibits pronounced seasonality of a form practitioners would find intuitively reasonable. In summer and winter months, load is firmly on the natural gas part of the stack; in shoulder months, where the distribution of load has more support on baseload generation (historically this has been nuclear and coal), correlations are lower.[3]

Valuation

There is little consensus among practitioners as to the "right way" to value tolls, even simple ones. For now, we will continue to work in the Gaussian exponential model (GEM) framework, which is at its core a log-normal Margrabe setting and which remains one of the more common methods in use. One of the results of this effort will be that the values obtained using empirical returns correlations will be very high in comparison with the prices at

---

[3] In an era of low natural gas prices starting around 2010, natural gas has at times displaced coal, which has the potential of fundamentally altering this correlation structure.

which such tolls typically trade. Rephrased, these structures typically trade at implied correlations that are much higher than one would infer from statistical estimation.

In using the two-factor (per commodity) GEM framework, our notational convention will BE

$$\frac{dF_k(t,T)}{F_k(t,T)} = \sum_{j=1}^{2} \left[\int_0^t \sigma_j^{(k)}(T) e^{-\beta_j^{(k)}(T-t)} dB_j^{(k)}(s) \right]$$ (14.6)

where $k = 1$ will correspond to power and $k = 2$ to natural gas. Calibration is assumed to be effected for each commodity in the manner discussed in Chapter 11.

All that remains is to specify the correlations between the respective Brownian motions. In the same spirit as in our approach for monthly tolls, it is natural to assume

$$\text{corr} \left[dB_1^{(1)}, dB_1^{(2)} \right] = \rho_L$$ (14.7)

$$\text{corr} \left[dB_2^{(1)}, dB_2^{(2)} \right] = \rho_S(t)$$ (14.8)

We will set the long correlation to a constant value $\rho_L = 0.950$.[4]

In addition, we will set all pairwise correlations, other than ρ_L and ρ_S, to zero. Some commodities desks use cross-correlations as a "dial" to increase term correlations. However, empirical results do not show much in the way of cross-correlation between the long and short (spot) factors. Recall that the WTI correlation surface fit yielded a cross-factor correlation of $\rho = 0.119$. Given the high values of β_2 that we will be using for power and natural gas, a reasonable estimate of the factor correlations can be obtained by computing the spot returns with the returns of the first nearby contract. The results for our setting using data from 2007–2011 are shown in Table 14.1. Including these cross-factor correlations would not materially alter the results that follow.

Calculating the term correlation implied by the dynamics (14.6) is, as always, an exercise in evaluating exponential integrals; the result is given in (C.22). Although numerically simple to evaluate, key qualitative features are much more easily gleaned using the spot-model caricature (10.18), which treated spot prices as arising from independent normal returns applied to the first-of-month price. The result related the spot volatility ζ to the monthly and daily implied volatilities via

$$\bar{\sigma}_{D,k}^2 T_D = \bar{\sigma}_{M,k}^2 T_M + \zeta_k^2$$ (14.9)

---

[4] While this is slightly higher than our default assumption of 0.90 in the case of the monthly toll valued in Chapter 9, it is certainly in the range of realized values in Figure 9.5 and is a tacit acknowledgment of the rather low correlations that will result from our first valuation cut.

Table 14.1. *PJM/Henry Hub realized spot
versus first nearby correlations (2007–2011)*

	HH Spot	PJM Spot
HH Fwd	0.029	0.053
PJM Fwd	0.002	−0.113

In a similar vein, the term correlation can be computed as the ratio of the sum of the covariance of the monthly returns and the independent daily returns to the total term variance

$$\rho_{\text{term}}(T_D) = \frac{\bar{\sigma}_{M,1}\bar{\sigma}_{M,2}T_M\rho_L + \zeta_1\zeta_2\rho_S}{\bar{\sigma}_{D,1}\bar{\sigma}_{D,2}T_D} \tag{14.10}$$

Note that ρ_S in general varies by contract month due to seasonality.

This expression, or its more unsightly but moral equivalent (C.22), yields behavior that can certainly be considered reasonable. If the spread between daily and monthly implied volatilities decreases, the traded options markets are implying a reduction in spot volatility ζ during the delivery month via (14.9). The result is an increased contribution of the high value of ρ_L in (14.9). This effect creates a correlation-induced vega because the final spread volatility that is used in Margrabe is of the form

$$\hat{\sigma}^2 = \bar{\sigma}_{D,1}^2 + \bar{\sigma}_{D,2}^2 - 2\rho_{\text{term}}\left(\bar{\sigma}_{M,1},\bar{\sigma}_{M,2},\bar{\sigma}_{D,1},\bar{\sigma}_{D,2}\right)\bar{\sigma}_{D,1}\bar{\sigma}_{D,2} \tag{14.11}$$

Because ρ_{term} depends on all four implied volatilities, the value of the toll using this approach will have exposure, often very large exposure, to both monthly and daily implied volatilities.

Changes in ζ are ostensibly hedgable. In a single-commodity proprietary trading setting, if you believe that the implied value of ζ is too low, you can buy daily straddles and sell monthly straddles to express this view. Similarly, the vega induced by the correlation dependence on volatility can, in theory, be hedged. However, as we will see shortly, the realities of the options markets generally render this prohibitively costly.

Another useful feature of this correlation expression is that the asymptotic behavior of $\rho_{\text{term}}(T)$ is as one would expect. As $T_M \to \infty$, the spot correlation component vanishes in the limit, and $\rho_{\text{term}}(T_D) \to \rho_L$. provided that implied spot volatilities are bounded, simply because in this limit $T_D/T_M \to 1$ and $\zeta_1\zeta_2\rho_S/T_D \to 0$.[5] As a result, these methods could be used

---

[5] The assumption of bounded spot volatility is reasonable. If a power market starts to exhibit high spot price volatility, market participants will quickly install peaking generation to exploit and therefore dampen the effect. In addition, system operators will take what measures they can to encourage availability and demand-side response to "bring things under control," which, in our language here, means "reduce ζ." Moreover, price caps are common in most markets, which also constrain potential growth in spot volatility.

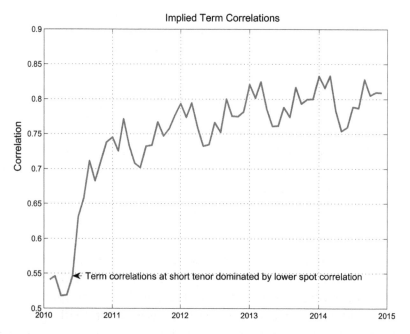

Figure 14.2. Implied PJM/Henry Hub term correlation (January 11, 2010).

as extrapolation devices for implied correlations. Assuming visible implied volatility surfaces for the two underlying commodities, one can use either estimated values of ρ_L and ρ_S or values calibrated to spread option quotes at short tenors to generate extrapolates for the term correlation.

Figure 14.2 shows the term correlation derived from (14.9) using the at-the-money (ATM) implied volatilities as of January 11, 2010. The implied correlation is clearly increasing, with variations at the monthly level. Convergence to the limiting value of $\rho_L = 0.950$ is slow, and even for structures with tenors in the five- to seven-year range, the term correlation remains well below the asymptotic limit.

Given $\rho_{\text{term}}(T)$, we proceed by contract month through the Cal11 strip, with skew treated by the same volatility look-up heuristic used in the one-factor setting in Chapter 9. Denoting the forward prices for month m by $F_j(0, T_m)$ and the respective volatility surfaces parameterized by price ratio π (recall that $\pi = K/F$), the monthly and daily volatilities take the form $\bar{\sigma}_{M,j}(t, T_m, \pi)$ AND $\bar{\sigma}_{D,j}(t, T_m, \pi)$. The volatility look-up procedure is exactly as in Chapter 9, extended to the two-factor setting:

$$\pi_1 \equiv \frac{H_* F_2(0, T_m) + V}{F_1(0, T_m)}$$

$$\pi_2 \equiv \frac{F_1(0, T_M) - V}{H_* F_2(0, T_m)} \tag{14.12}$$

Skew impacts the valuation. The unit heat rate $H_* = 8.0$ is low in comparison with market heat rates, which means that low-strike volatilities are

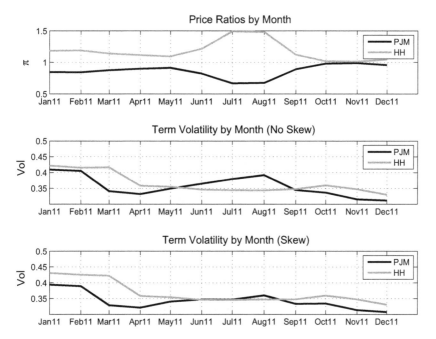

Figure 14.3. Skew effect on implied volatilities for PJM and Henry Hub (January 11, 2010).

used on the power side and high-strike volatilities for the natural gas leg, as shown in Figure 14.3. The top figure shows the price ratios by month. The middle figure shows the ATM implied volatilities for the two commodities. The bottom figure shows the same using the heuristic. The most notable contrast is the spread between power and natural gas volatilities in the summer months. The skew adjustment results in natural gas daily volatilities being either at a discount or near parity to those for power in the summer and at a premium in all other months. As a consequence, the resulting term correlation for July increases from 0.813 to 0.833 because of the effect of skew, approximately 2 percent. This increase in correlation is reasonable. The value of price spikes to a long position in a tolling contract is enhanced for high values of H_*; at low values of H_*, the spread options are in the money to such an extent that the structure is more akin to a swap. Over the entire term, the effect of inclusion of skew effects reduces the extrinsic value by approximately 4 percent.

We have made an implicit assumption that the correlation parameters ρ_L and ρ_S are constant and that any skew in the term correlation is descendant from that of the respective implied volatility surfaces. This is analogous to using a statistically estimated volatility to price options at all strikes in the absence of traded options, an approach that would not result in skew. It is tempting to consider computing implied surfaces for ρ_L and ρ_S from traded heat-rate options. However, liquidity across heat rates H_* is very limited, with the preponderance of trading at combined-cycle heat rates, roughly in the range $7 \leq H_* \leq 7.5$. Coupled with limited reliability of skew marks, especially on the daily volatility surface for natural gas, discerning anything with confidence about implied correlations is, as a practical matter, not achievable. This is one motivation for econometric and structural approaches, to which we turn shortly.

The form of (14.11) appears deceptively simple because it is easy to overlook the nonlinear dependence of ρ_{term} on the four input volatilities $\bar{\sigma}_M$ and $\bar{\sigma}_D$. This functional dependence of term correlation on implied volatilities has a compelling heuristic: the more spot volatility ζ (or σ_2) is implied by the options markets, the lower the term correlation should be. Testing this heuristic, however, would depend on the unrealistic requirement of daily (or at least very frequent) trading activity in all the underlying options markets, both monthly and daily, as well as for tolls. Moreover, even if valid, this heuristic will turn out to result in vega hedging programs that are quite problematic.

For now we will proceed relentlessly to a valuation, returning to this issue momentarily. Given (14.12), the resulting implied volatilities for each commodity leg are used in (C.22) to yield $\hat{\sigma}$ in (14.11), which is used directly in Margrabe. The only innovation is use of the two-factor dynamics and associated monthly and daily volatilities, coupled with correlation estimates, to obtain $\hat{\sigma}$.

We will consider two scenarios:

- Using estimated short correlations $\rho_S(T)$, as shown in Figure 14.1.
- A constant value $\rho_S = 0.900$.

In both scenarios we have taken $\vec{\beta}_P = [0.30, 100]$ and $\vec{\beta}_G = [0.30, 40]$.

The term correlations in these two scenarios are shown in Figure 14.4. The $\rho_S = 0.900$ scenario yields a significantly higher result than that obtained using estimated correlations, as expected given that the average estimated ρ_S over the calendar year is 0.379.

There is a resulting difference in values. Using historical correlations, the value of the toll is \$11.508/MWh with a ratio of intrinsic value to total value of 0.752; in the second scenario, the results are \$10.371/MWh and 0.835, respectively. Stripping out the value of the in-the-money swap, the extrinsic values in the two scenarios are \$2.848/MWh and \$1.712/MWh, with the higher spot correlation reducing extrinsic value by approximately 40 percent. This is significant. During this time period, the broker market trades for tolls at similar heat rates and at these locations yielded implied correlations in the low 90s, roughly corresponding to our second scenario. We will return to the possible explanations for the difference between estimated and implied correlations shortly.

Continuing with the second scenario, Figure 14.5 shows the value of the structure by contract month, as well as the intrinsic-value ratio. Note that

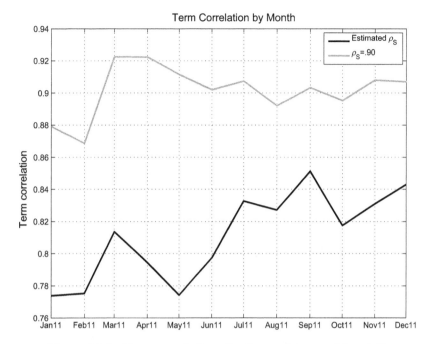

Figure 14.4. Term correlations for the working problem toll.

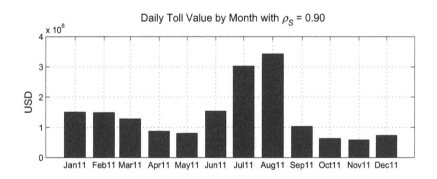

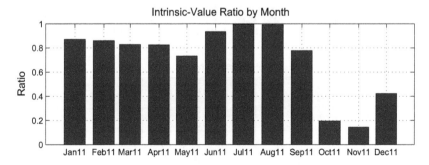

Figure 14.5. Value by month for the working problem toll.

the optionality is primarily in the shoulder months and certainly not in the summer. Although volatilities are typically highest in the summer, the high market heat rates mean that for most generation hedges the call options are far in the money.

The valuation approach illustrated here results in a number of important issues. First, the nonuniform nature of the distribution of extrinsic value over a calendar year is, from a hedging perspective, problematic given the concentration of liquidity in calendar strips. Second, the correlation-induced vega results in a nontrivial and costly hedging program. Because it is the result of a modeling construct, the validity of this vega result requires examination.

Hedging and Spurious Risks

On execution of a tolling transaction, the first order of business at the time of execution is to neutralize the deltas; this is true for all options transactions unless the intention is to create a purely levered speculative position. Figure 14.6 shows the power and natural gas deltas by contract month for our working problem. As expected, the position is long power and short natural gas, with the highest exposures in the summer months where the option is most in the money.

The notional of 400 MW, which is typical of many generation hedges, is large enough to preclude immediate hedging of power exposure due to

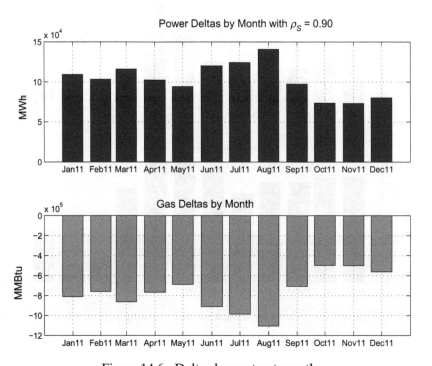

Figure 14.6. Deltas by contract month.

limited liquidity, especially at tenors of more than a few years. Therefore, the first action typically taken at the inception of the transaction is to neutralize net energy delta using a natural gas hedge. For tolls with zero strike, valuation can be rephrased using the natural gas price as the numeraire:

$$V(0,T) = G(0,T)\tilde{E}_G\left[\left(H(T,T) - H_*\right)^+\right] \qquad (14.13)$$

where $H(t,T) \equiv F(t,T)/G(t,T)$ denotes the market heat rate. We saw in Figure 9.10 that forward heat rates do not change particularly rapidly, at least in comparison with underlying commodities prices. At the instant of trade execution, it is changes in $G(t,T)$ that are of immediate concern. A portfolio manager typically will sell natural gas swaps to neutralize either $\partial V(0,T)/\partial G(0,T)\big|_H$ or more sophisticated conversions to gas-equivalent delta's that account for heat-rate dependence on natural gas prices (discussed in Chapter 6). Once this is done, power swaps are sold as liquidity permits, buying back appropriate quantities of natural gas to ultimately neutralize deltas of both legs.

This process is not nearly as clean as it sounds. The preceding valuation, as is almost always the case in commodities, is based on contract-month pricing. Exercise is daily. Swaps liquidity, however, is concentrated in seasonal strips and at longer-tenor calendar strips. As a practical matter, the initial hedge, as well as subsequent rebalancings to capture extrinsic value, must be effected using calendar strips at longer tenors. Figure 14.7 shows deltas by month as well as the total calendar strip delta in both absolute terms and as a percentage difference for the working problem. Note the nontrivial variation from the calendar strip quantity. The problem is exacerbated at higher heat rates, which push the delta into fewer months, making the calendar swap an even clumsier instrument. Figure 14.8 shows the situation for a toll with $H_* = 10$, closer to the heat rate of peaking generation. Limited liquidity in monthly or seasonal swaps can have a deleterious effect on one's ability to extract extrinsic value via delta hedging.

Given the challenges in capturing extrinsic value, there is an inclination by many traders attempting to manage tolls to sell "vanilla" single-commodity fixed-strike options against a long tolling position. These (flawed) arguments proceed along lines similar to that which motivated the volatility look-up heuristic: "After all, can't a toll be thought of as a call option on power struck at the natural gas forward and conversely as a put on natural gas." This would be fine if one of the prices stayed fixed, but that is certainly not what happens. The result is a substantial mismatch in the attributes of the options sold in contrast to the toll.

To illustrate this point, consider a heat-rate option with $H_* = 8$ and with tenor $T = 0.5$ using simple Margrabe valuation, with power and natural gas forward prices of \$50/MWh and \$5/MMBtu, respectively. Using implied

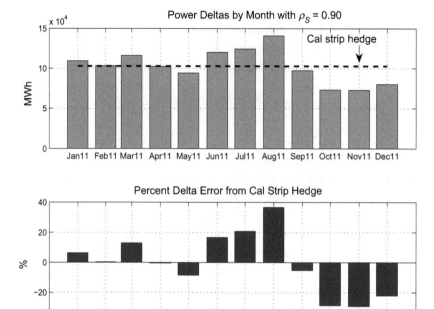

Figure 14.7. Power delta and calendar strip hedge.

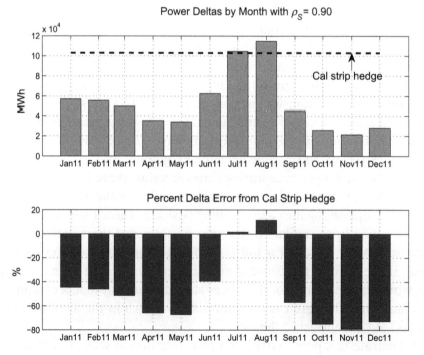

Figure 14.8. Power delta and calendar strip hedge ($H_* = 10$).

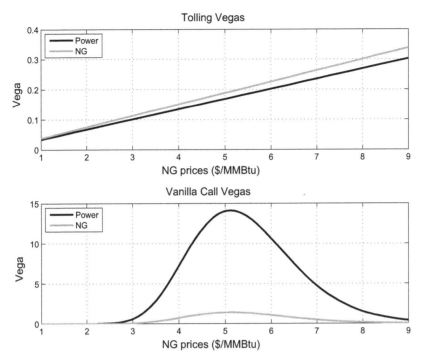

Figure 14.9. Vega behavior: tolls versus vanilla calls.

volatilities of 0.30 on each leg and a correlation $\rho = 0.9$, Figure 14.9 shows the behavior of power and natural gas vegas for the toll across a range of natural gas prices, assuming that the market heat rate remains fixed at 10.[6] The lower figures shows the same behavior for the ATM vanilla calls. The fact that the order of magnitude of the toll vega is much lower is not relevant – hedge ratios would be calculated appropriately. The key point is that the toll vegas do not exhibit the rapid decay as $G(t, T)$ changes. As a result, any attempt to monetize extrinsic value or neutralize vega exposure is destined for many rebalancings of the vanilla options positions because the vega profile of the hedges changes much more rapidly than that for the toll. Given that bid-offer spreads in power options can be several volatility points wide, this is an expensive proposition. The essential problem is that the toll, because it is a spread option between highly correlated commodities, is simply not amenable to replication via single-commodity vanilla options.

If this isn't discouraging enough, the situation gets worse as we delve into the vega implications of the correlation construction in (14.10) or (C.22). Use of this approach implies vega exposures that can be large and unmanageable. The underlying correlation heuristic is reasonable, with the volatility of spot returns in each leg of the spread option driven by the spread

---

[6] Here we again calculate vega as the derivative with respect to volatility in absolute units, not in percentages.

between $\bar{\sigma}_D$ and $\bar{\sigma}_M$. Because spot correlations are usually well below forward correlations, the term correlation can be quite sensitive to the spreads between monthly and daily volatilities via

$$\frac{\partial V}{\partial \bar{\sigma}_D} = \frac{\partial V}{\partial \bar{\sigma}_D}\bigg|_\rho + \frac{\partial V}{\partial \rho}\bigg|_{\bar{\sigma}_D} \frac{\partial \rho}{\partial \bar{\sigma}_D} \qquad (14.14)$$

Vega exposure is not confined to $\bar{\sigma}_D$ for the two commodities, and the vega hedging requirements can be impractical to effect.

Resorting to our simple caricature model, the term volatility $\hat{\sigma}$ that enters the Margrabe formula is

$$\hat{\sigma}^2 = \left(\bar{\sigma}_{M,1}^2 + \bar{\sigma}_{M,2}^2 - 2\rho_L\bar{\sigma}_{M,1}\bar{\sigma}_{M,2}\right)T_M + \left(\zeta_1^2 + \zeta_2^2 - 2\rho_S\zeta_1\zeta_2\right) \qquad (14.15)$$

which is equivalent to (14.10). This allows us to calculate the vegas with respect to each monthly and daily implied volatility holding the other fixed. For example

$$\frac{1}{2}\hat{\sigma}\frac{\partial\hat{\sigma}}{\partial\bar{\sigma}_{M,1}}\bigg|_{\bar{\sigma}_{D,1}} = \left(\bar{\sigma}_{M,1} - \rho_L\bar{\sigma}_{M,2}\right)T_M + \frac{\partial\zeta_1}{\partial\bar{\sigma}_{M,1}}\left(\zeta_1 - \zeta_2\rho_S\right) \qquad (14.16)$$

yields the derivative of the term volatility $\hat{\sigma}$ with respect to the monthly power volatility, holding the daily volatility fixed. The sign of the first term on the right is exactly of the form of the vega in the monthly toll valuation discussed in Chapter 9. The correlation-induced effect on vega results from the presence of $\partial\zeta_1/\partial\bar{\sigma}_{M,1}$ and similarly for the vegas with respect to the other term volatilities.

We know that $\partial\zeta_1/\partial\bar{\sigma}_{M,1} < 0$ and $\partial\zeta_1/\partial\bar{\sigma}_{D,1} > 0$, with similar relationships for all other permutations of volatility type and commodity leg. Figure 14.10 shows the resulting vega exposures for our working toll as of the pricing date. The vegas have been converted to volumes of standard ATM straddles for each commodity – for power in megawatts and natural gas in lots. Long vega in one option type is associated with short vega in the other type. This is the spread effect between monthly and daily volatilities. The natural gas vegas are of the opposite sign of the power vegas due to high correlation.

The options hedges in power are between 100 and 200 MW – while not a small notional, such would usually be achievable at or near inception, although the hedging costs would be nontrivial. More important, these would have to be rebalanced over the life of the transaction, as per our discussion relating to Figure 14.9, which would accrue substantial hedging costs – all of this for one 400-MW toll. A larger portfolio would overwhelm power options markets.

Contrast these results with the "standard" vega calculated without the correlation effect [i.e., using only the first term in (14.14)] shown in Figure 14.11, again in the same straddle-equivalent units. In this case the only volatility

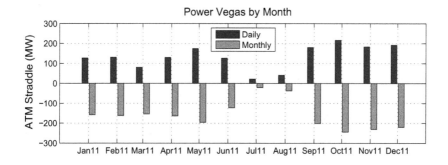

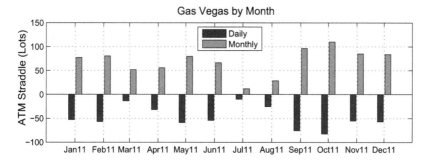

Figure 14.10. Vega by leg and type for daily toll.

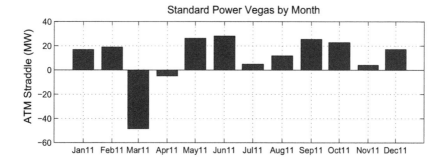

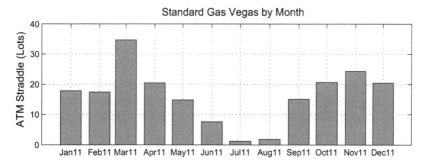

Figure 14.11. Standard vegas for daily toll.

exposure is due to the daily implied volatilities; the monthly vegas arose solely due to the correlation effect. While the sign of the natural gas vegas changes, the magnitude is roughly the same as the sum of the daily and monthly vegas inclusive of the correlation effect. The key point is that much smaller options hedges are required in the simpler approach.

The difference in the preceding two sets of results implies very different vega hedging strategies, with the hedging requirements of the ostensibly more sophisticated approach challenging, if not impossible, to implement. Anyone who has had to trade a power options book would appreciate the difficulties (and costs) of rebalancing several hundred megawatts of options as underlying energy prices fluctuate. This begs the question: Is the correlation-induced vega a real, observable phenomenon or a spurious risk – an artifact of the multifactor model and the long-short correlation heuristic used? Limited market data leave this question unresolved. However, the impracticality of the resulting hedging program in a sense renders the question moot and serves more to motivate alternative approaches that can be implemented given the nature of the mechanics of the markets and limitations in liquidity.

Why Are Implied Correlations So High?

Several themes continue to emerge over the previous chapters. One is the hazards of estimation and extrapolation. Another is the impact of substantial market incompleteness on commonly accepted valuation methods. Tolls provide a vivid example of the issues that can arise on both counts. With the results of our preceding "strawman" valuation in hand, it is a good time to reflect on the issues, in particular, the large gap between prices obtained using empirical correlations versus those at which actual trades occur.

One contributing factor is the one-sided nature of the market. The world is continuously building generation, financing requires hedges, and as a result, dealers are inherently long tolls. This, however, is far from being a complete explanation for the high level of implied correlations. Among those experienced in managing tolls, one fact is almost universally accepted – pricing tolls using empirical correlations results in a very high likelihood of losses over the life of the structure. Hence, if only due to enough desks witnessing (if not becoming) tolling-deal "road kill," tolls trade at high correlation relative to empirical estimates.

Another thought is that using realized spot prices to estimate correlation was not the right thing to do. The typical toll exercises one business prior to the delivery date. A cash trader at 9:30 a.m. who is deciding whether or not to exercise the toll by 10 a.m. is looking at where day-ahead power is trading on the screens; similarly for spot natural gas. Although data are not readily available, it is almost certainly the case that spot correlations estimated one business day before delivery ("-1b") would be substantially higher than the spot correlations that we obtained from real-time spot prices.

Recall, however, that the high decay rate of the second factor is intended to compensate for this. Suppose that we proceeded exactly as we did in the preceding section – calibrating our two-factor model to the standard monthly and daily options but instead valuing a same-day toll, that is, an autoexercise toll that settles on the realized spot prices that we used to estimate correlations. Because the daily options to which we calibrated were "-1b" exercise, when we change expiration to autoexercise the values for σ_D that enter the toll, valuation is higher due to the additional one day of volatility, and when β_2 is large, that extra day of volatility can be large, resulting in a lower term correlation than for the standard "-1b" toll.

A more significant potential flaw in the preceding valuation methodology is the calculation of the term correlation using monthly and spot components. This approach resulted in the spread between daily and monthly implied volatilities appearing as a significant risk factor. Suppose for the moment that our estimates for term and spot correlations ρ_L and $\rho_S(m)$ are in fact stable and stationary, given that tolls trade at much higher implied correlations than those that are implied by the correlation heuristic, could we "arb" the valuation discrepancy? That is, could we buy the toll at the high correlation and engage in offsetting (and dynamic) options hedges to capture the difference? In light of the volatilty-induced correlation effect, these options hedges would involve selling daily options and buying monthly. The bid-offer spreads in power options, the very limited liquidity in daily options in natural gas, and the requirement to rebalance options hedges as energy prices move (recall Figure 14.9) are simply too costly to monetize the posited arbitrage opportunity.

In essence, the vanilla, single-commodity options markets may be effectively decoupled from the tolling markets as a result of the joint effects of relatively high bid-offer spreads and the high volatility of macro energy price levels, which force frequent rebalancings. Add to this delta-hedging frictions induced by calendar strip limitations, and it is not unreasonable to consider abandoning the pursuit of a framework that unifies all vanilla options (monthly, daily, and swaptions) with structures such as tolls.

Some trading shops have followed this train of thought, deploying models for heat-rate dynamics, resulting in a joint distribution of natural gas and power prices that usually has lower variance in heat rates and lower tolling values than using the preceding methods. The heat-rate processes are designed and calibrated to preserve the martingale properties of forward prices, but consistency with single-commodity options prices is often abandoned.

Econometric and structural models, to which we turn shortly, can exhibit spark spread distributions with lower dispersion than implied by the

Margrabe framework. There is some evidence of cointegrating behavior between power and natural gas prices (see, e.g., [JS09]), with such coupling suggesting narrower spark-spread distributions. Results of a comparison of spead options valuation using specific parametric stack models and Margrabe appear in [CCS13] and suggest that structural models can show narrower spark spread distributions and commensurately lower spread-options values owing to the nonlinear coupling of power prices to the underlying fuel prices inherent in the stack construct.

The most common response of portfolio managers to high implied correlations, however, is to simply crank the term correlation up in a standard Margrabe setting. Although compelling in its simplicity, two problems arise. The first is that extrapolation to longer tenors, which is often required, is simply not supported by a plausible underlying heuristic. Fixing term correlations at shorter tenors leaves parametric extrapolation methods, with their inherently arbitrary nature, the alternative. The second weakness, as we will see in the next section, is that the dynamics of heat rates implied by coupled geometric Brownian motions at high correlation are at variance with empirical observations.

Heat-Rate Behavior

We have seen that heat rates typically increase as natural gas prices decrease; recall Figure 6.10. There are several possible explanations for this behavior, the simplest of which is the bidding behavior of generation owners who need to cover costs above and beyond fuel as well as earn a return. This implies spot prices of the form

$$p_{\text{bid}} = H_* G(t,t) + K \tag{14.17}$$

and motivates a forward heat-rate relationship of

$$H(t,T) = H_* + K/G(t,T) + \epsilon(t,T) \tag{14.18}$$

where $\epsilon(t,T)$ can be thought of as a residual to a regression. Fuel switching in the generation stack would enhance the effect. As $G(t,T)$ increases, cheaper alternative sources of generation will appear on the margin, pulling the expected realized heat rates down.

If one scans scatter plots of historical forward heat rates versus natural gas prices across contract months, patterns similar to those shown in Figure 6.10 are the norm. There are exceptions, particularly in shoulder months and in markets dominated by sources of generation other than natural gas. However, it is reasonable to expect a stochastic model of forward prices for power and natural gas to exhibit qualitative behavior similar to Figure 6.10.

The stylized fact that heat rates decrease with natural gas prices has important and tangible consequences. Relationships similar to (6.8) imply that

$$\frac{\Delta F(t,T)}{F(t,T)} = \frac{H_*\Delta G(t,T)}{H_*G(t,T)+K} < \frac{\Delta G(t,T)}{G(t,T)} \tag{14.19}$$

suggesting that monthly power volatilities should be lower than those for natural gas, as is usually the case. This is admittedly a primitive argument – we have assumed that the noise term $\epsilon(t,T) = 0$ when in fact it is a stochastic process that contributes to power volatility. However, the variation in $\epsilon(t,T)$ is small relative to changes in natural gas prices, and (14.19) is the reason that monthly power implied volatilities are systematically below those for natural gas.

What are the implications of the GEM framework or, more broadly, the joint log-normal Margrabe setting on heat-rate behavior when correlations are set to high levels?

Heat rates in the Margrabe setting are given by

$$H(t,T) \equiv \frac{F(t,T)}{G(t,T)} = \frac{F(0,T)}{G(0,T)}e^{t^{1/2}\sigma_F Z_F - 1/2t\sigma_F^2 - t^{1/2}\sigma_G Z_G + 1/2t\sigma_G^2} \tag{14.20}$$

where (Z_F, Z_G) are standard normal random variables with correlation ρ. The implications for the relationship between $H(t,T)$ and $G(t,T)$ are derived in Appendix A, yielding

$$H(t,T) = cXG(t,T)^{\left[\rho\frac{\sigma_F}{\sigma_G}-1\right]} \tag{14.21}$$

where c is independent of $G(t,T)$, and X is a unit-mean log-normal random variable, as shown in (A.40).

For $H(t,T)$ to be a decreasing function of $G(t,T)$, we must have

$$\rho\frac{\tilde{\sigma}_F}{\tilde{\sigma}_G} < 1 \tag{14.22}$$

However, for daily structures, the term volatility for power often exceeds that of natural gas, as can be seen for an $H_* = 10$ toll in Figure 14.12. Simply increasing the term correlation ρ will cause a violation of the expected relationship between natural gas and heat rates. This is yet another reason for exploring modeling alternatives.

Modeling Alternatives: Econometric Models

The preceding discussions should give pause to the rote application of standard risk-neutral methods. High implied correlations are due, at least in large part, to limitations of market liquidity, with dealers requiring a low entry price to compensate for frictions. Increasing the correlation parameters in the coupled diffusions driving the power and natural gas forwards lowers the value of the tolls but can result in price dynamics with features

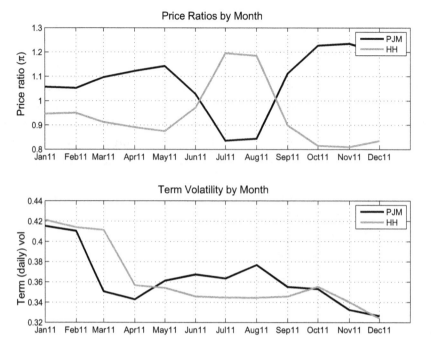

Figure 14.12. Price ratios and term volatilities for an $H_* = 10$ toll (January 11, 2010).

that are at variance with empirical observations. Moreover, in many cases, the implied volatilities required to pursue such an approach are themselves barely visible, and the depth of the options markets is not anywhere near what is required to support the resulting hedging strategies.

Such observations have yielded an ongoing quest for alternative approaches. In this section we will examine econometric models as applied to tolling transactions, followed in the next section by stack models. When we discuss variable-quantity swaps in Chapter 15, these methods will again prove useful.

In Chapter 12 we introduced an econometric approach to valuation of natural gas basis options that was predicated on weather and benchmark natural gas processes as underlying drivers to spot basis prices. Here we will model the behavior of spot heat rates, which we have seen exhibit nonlinear relationships to natural gas prices. Figure 14.13 shows daily spot realizations of PJM/Henry Hub heat rates versus the average daily temperature in Philadelphia (KPHL). Some features are expected; for example, the highest heat rates occur at highest temperatures. Also of note, however, is that at low temperatures spot heat rates can achieve remarkably low values. This happens when high natural gas prices force natural gas generation out of dispatch, effectively capping the power price at the alternative supply.

The results of a regression analysis are superimposed. The regression used data from January 1, 2005 to the trade date of the working problem. These

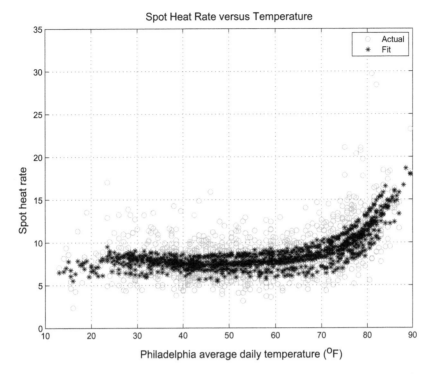

Figure 14.13. PJM peak versus Henry Hub spot heat rates and regression estimates.

estimates do not fall on a one-dimensional curve since temperature is not the only variable. The form of the regression used here is

$$\log\left[\frac{p(d)}{p_{\text{NG}}(d)}\right] = \alpha + \eta p_{\text{NG}}(d) + \sum_{k=1}^{K} \gamma_k \theta(d)^k + \epsilon_d \qquad (14.23)$$

where $p(d)$ denotes the daily spot power price, $p_{\text{NG}}(d)$ is the locational natural gas spot price (in this case TETM3), and ϵ_d are residuals. As in Chapter 12, $\theta(d)$ denotes the nonlinear transformation of daily temperature $\tau(d)$ given in (12.22). The terms to be included in the regression were selected by an out-of-sample criterion.[7] The response to natural gas prices is estimated at $\eta = -0.04$. As in forward markets, spot heat rates can exhibit a statistically significant response to natural gas prices, increasing with decreasing natural gas prices.

Coupled with temperature and natural gas simulations, we are in a position to use (14.23) to generate a joint distribution of $\vec{\pi} \equiv [\tau, p_{\text{HH}}, p_{\text{TETM3}}, p]$. This is enough information to calculate econometric, or "physical" measure,

---

[7] The slight concavity at roughly 25°F is a flaw, not a feature. But the effects on the subsequent analysis are negligible, so we will work with this regression methodology.

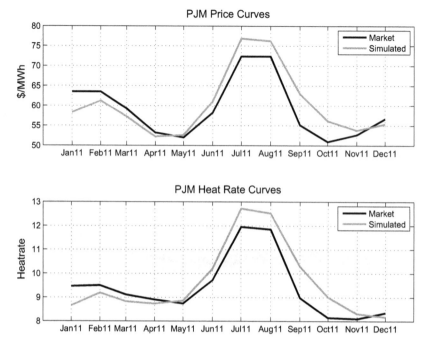

Figure 14.14. PJM and PJM/Henry Hub-heat rate forward and simulated prices as of January 11, 2010.

payoff distributions for power and natural gas forwards, as well as for the tolling payoff.

Figure 14.14 compares the forward power prices and heat rates with those computed under the physical (simulation) measure. The structure is similar between market forwards and simulated future prices, but the differences can be meaningful, with heat-rate differences often above 0.5 and even exceeding unity.

Econometric methods in general yield expected spot prices that differ from those implied by traded markets, resulting in the dichotomy discussed in Chapter 12. Should physical measures be used to value a structure such as a toll? Or should the distributions of the joint price processes $\vec{\pi}$ be transformed in some way to force consistency with forwards and options markets, thereby creating a risk-neutral measure? Such a measure would presumably have distributional features that are more realistic than the log-normal distributions we have used so far while retaining the basic tenets of dynamic hedging and frictionless markets.

Differences between the two approaches are moot if the structure being priced is effectively the same as a common tradable. Suppose that we posit that the only hedging that we will be allowed to perform is at the inception of a transaction and that only swaps can be traded. If the instrument being hedged is identical to a traded swap, then (1) the risk of the structure can be reduced to zero, and (2) the present value of the position will coincide with that of the replicating swaps position, thereby marking the position to market. Whether you effect a risk-neutral transformation before valuing the structure or simply work under the physical measure, the result is the same.

When the structure being priced is not closely related to traded instruments, the two methods can yield very different results, as we will see shortly. Working under the physical measure is an acknowledgment of market incompleteness that has been manifest in so many ways. This is what we will do in what follows, working directly with the physical measure, computing the distribution of the toll payoff by month, and selecting static forward and options hedges using a minimum-variance criterion.

To clarify the term *static*, practitioners acknowledge that some rebalancings can occur over the life of a toll. We have seen, however, that there are serious impediments to dynamically hedging a toll: (1) heat rates must move a great deal to yield a change in delta that exceeds the standard 50-MW contract size, (2) calendar strips are the most liquid products for tenors outside of a year but are less than effective at hedging the inhomogeneous distribution of extrinsic value over individual months, and (3) options rebalancings can be costly. Static hedging in this setting is not far removed from what one can actually achieve in practice and also yields implied correlations that are much closer to those observed.

The tolling payoff for a given contract month m is

$$\Pi_T(m) \equiv \sum_{d \in m} \max[p(d) - H_* p_{HH}, 0] \qquad (14.24)$$

where as before $p(d)$ denotes the daily spot power price for the relevant bucket. We have similar random payoffs corresponding to potential hedges. For example, forward hedges are of the form:

$$\Pi_F(m) \equiv \sum_{d \in m} [p(d) - F_m]$$

$$\Pi_G(m) \equiv \sum_{d \in m} [p_{HH}(d) - G_m]$$

where F and G denote PJM and Henry Hub forward prices. The options hedges that we will consider will be ATM straddles[8]:

$$\Pi_{S_F}(m) \equiv \sum_{d \in m} [p(d) - F_m]$$

$$\Pi_{S_G}(m) \equiv \sum_{d \in m} [p_{HH}(d) - G_m]$$

---

[8] There is a perception among some practitioners that natural options hedges paralleling the volatility look-up heuristic are useful, where the power option strike at $H_* G$ and the gas option strike at F/H_*. The results that we present here are not changed substantially by including these.

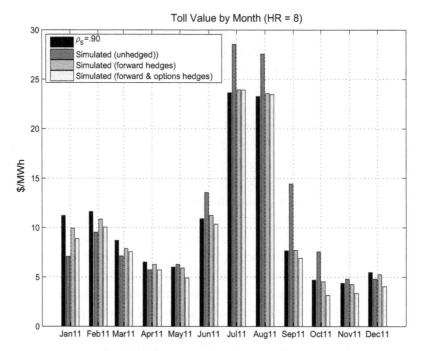

Figure 14.15. Tolling values under various hedging programs.

The expected value of the tolling payoff under the physical measure is $E[\Pi_T(m)]$, but this is not the "market" value of the toll since no hedging has been effected. We next compute the minimum-variance hedges for portfolios of the form $\Pi + \vec{h}^\dagger \vec{X}$, where $\vec{X}$ denotes the set of hedges being considered – for the case where only forwards are used, that is, $\vec{X} = [\Pi_{\mathcal{F}}(m), \Pi_{\mathcal{G}}(m)]$, and where both forwards and options are used, that is, $\vec{X} = [\Pi_{\mathcal{F}}(m), \Pi_{\mathcal{G}}(m), \Pi_{\mathcal{S}_F}(m), \Pi_{\mathcal{S}_G}(m)]$. The optimal hedge ratios are obtained as the solution to

$$\vec{h}_* \equiv \underset{\vec{h}}{\mathrm{argmin}}\,\mathrm{var}\left[\Pi_T(m) + \vec{h}^\dagger \vec{X}\right] \tag{14.25}$$

The resulting expected values of $\Pi_* \equiv \Pi + \vec{h}_*^\dagger \vec{X}$ are shown by contract month in Figure 14.15, as well as the base multifactor valuation using $\rho_S = 0.900$ for comparison. The expected value of each contract month is altered by the hedges since we are working in the physical measure. For example, since the expected spot price exceeds the market forward price in both July and August, the fact that the optimal hedge is to sell power results in an increase in the expected value of the portfolio. Selling power at a higher price than the expected value results in an expected gain. In other months there is a reduction in portfolio value.

The next question is how much was achieved in risk reduction. Figure 14.16 shows the standard deviation of the econometric valuation under the

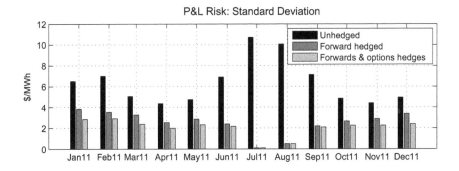

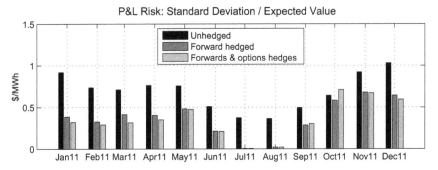

Figure 14.16. Tolling values under various hedging programs.

different programs. The forward hedges reduce risk substantially across all months, largely eliminating the risk in the summer months where an $H_* = 8.0$ option is so far in the money that it is effectively a swap. On the other hand, the addition of the options hedges to the portfolio accomplished relatively little, another manifestation of the fact that single-commodity options have risk characteristics that are very different from spread options and are not particularly useful in "flattening" the portfolio payoff.

Results vary by the unit heat rate H_*. Higher-heat-rate tolls have more extrinsic value and from a risk perspective are more removed from the attributes of a swap than are low-heat-rate tolls. They are therefore harder to hedge. Even the options hedges remain at best marginally useful in risk reduction. Table 14.2 shows the value of the structure obtained by summing the discounted expected values for the various scenarios and normalizing to unit notional.

The econometric approach can yield values that differ considerably from reduced-form methods. This is no surprise – we saw this before in the case of natural gas basis options. The spot prices used are not log-normally distributed. Moreover, the choice of hedging method matters. We did not transform the physical measure to a risk-neutral measure. Instead, we worked directly with the physical measure, which meant that the differences between

Table 14.2. *Valuation Comparison for Call1 Toll as of January 11, 2010 in $/MWh*

Heat Rate	Financial	Simulated Unhedged	Simulated Forwards	Simulated Forwards and Options
$H_* = 8$	10.37	11.28	10.01	9.27
$H_* = 10$	4.06	4.16	3.24	2.43

expected payoffs and market prices, that is, the risk premia, affected the expected value of the hedged portfolio.

This was the case for the July and August months in the tolling example where the heat rates, both market and simulated, were so far above the unit heat rate $H_* = 8.0$ that the payoff was effectively a swap:

$$\max[F(T,T) - H_*G(T,T),0] \approx F(T,T) - H_*G(T,T) \qquad (14.26)$$

Hedging the right-hand side is trivial – sell one power swap and buy H_* natural gas swaps, resulting in a payoff of $F(t,T) - H_*G(t,T)$ under either the risk-neutral measure or the physical measure.

The situation is completely different if the structure departs meaningfully from vanilla tradables. This is the case for the shoulder months in the preceding toll because the standard deviation of the hedged portfolio is only partially reduced. To illustrate this effect more dramatically, consider a higher heat rate $H_* = 12$ that forces even the summer months out of the money. There are two consequences resulting from the fact that simulated (physical) heat rates exceeded market (risk-neutral) heat rates in the summer months that which we saw in Figure 14.14. The first is that the delta resulting from the simulated valuation exceeded that using the risk-neutral measure. The second is that this higher delta requires a larger sale of power at the lower market forward price. Taken together, the hedged value of the summer months is meaningfully higher under the physical measure than under the risk-neutral measure, as shown in Figure 14.17.

We chose to work in the physical measure because transformation to a risk-neutral measure implicitly assumes that dynamic hedging can effectively replicate the payoff of the tolls considered. Econometric or structural models used in the risk-neutral setting are as vulnerable to hedging frictions as were reduced-form models. The actual state of affairs is somewhere between perfectly liquid markets and altogether illiquid. However, when limitations in liquidity are significant, whether originating from calendar strips, block-size limits, or simply high bid-offer spreads, valuation and residual risk

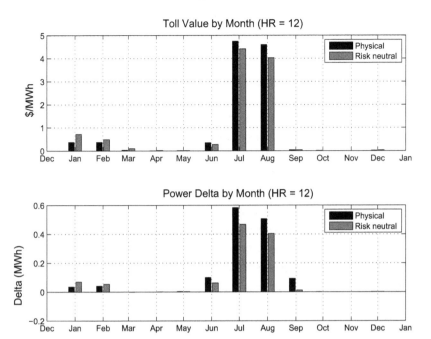

Figure 14.17. Comparison of physical versus risk-neutral valuation ($H_* = 12$).

distributions under the physical measure are (arguably) more reliable than those obtained under risk-neutral valuation.[9]

In practice, dealers who are purchasing tolls do one of three things. Some use financial models with empirical correlations as a basis for establish mid-market values. Those who do this usually end up losing money over the course of the transaction.[10] Others use what little market data are available from sporadic broker trading to set midmarket correlations. However, the depth in these markets is not enough to effectively hedge the correlation risk in a typical long-tenor tolling hedge. Finally, some attempt to explicitly construct a physical measure, as we have just done, with static hedge construction at inception. Those who do this are aware of the fact that rebalancings later in the transaction may occur and that such rebalancings should improve the value of a long options position.

[9] This has been recognized in the academic literature for some time (see, e.g., [AP94], [AMS99], and [FS91]), where the results of minimum-variance and dynamic control approaches to valuation and hedging construction in incomplete markets depend explicitly on the physical measure. In most of work along these lines, the physical measure is assumed to be known and analytically tractable. Realistic dynamics of the interaction between fuels and power prices is considerably more complex and difficult to parameterize, which motivated the econometric methods for generating price distributions.

[10] One would think that natural selection would have eliminated this approach. However, the life cycle of tolling hedges is long (five to seven years), allowing for information loss between generations of portfolio managers. In other words, there seems to be no shortage of future victims of this method.

Modeling Alternatives: Structural Models

Valuation results in incomplete markets depend on the physical measure being used. While relatively straightforward to design and implement, econometric approaches have obvious limitations. Estimation implicitly assumed stationary data, and the use of simulation to value structures is predicated on continuing stationary behavior. Econometric models can be perturbed to test for sensitivities, say, to the response of heat rates to natural gas prices. Such stress testing of models can provide some indication of the magnitude of potential changes in value but are always ad hoc in nature.

The period 2009–2011 provided a very good example of a regime change that would challenge econometric modeling. The drop in natural gas prices in North America arising from the rapid increasing in shale gas production resulted in the changes in the relative cost per MMBtu of NYMEX NG versus Central Appalachian coal shown in Figure 14.18. This figure shows the first nearby contract prices for each commodity in terms of $/MMBtu.[11] The transition from coal being by far the "cheapest MMBtu" among fossil fuels, a world view that was considered unshakable just a few years ago, to effective parity with natural gas in North America is an example of a phenomenon that preexisting econometric models would be challenged to capture given the absence of any historical precedent.

The potential impact of this change in power markets is illustrated in Figure 14.19. Two approximate renditions of the coal and natural gas components of the PJM stack around 2010 are shown corresponding to two natural gas scenarios: $3/MMBtu and $7/MMBtu. The nonlinear nature of (12.31) is apparent because the significant separation between the two stacks at high natural gas prices vanishes in the low-price scenario, with many coal units displaced.

The total separation of the two generation types evident in the high natural gas scenario yields a far simpler dispatch (and modeling) configuration than the lower natural gas scenario, where two types of generation with very different operating characteristics are competing at the same load levels. The implications for the physical system during periods of switching as occurred during 2011 were manifold. Natural gas units are the more flexible in dispatch. When natural gas displaces coal, the coal units are on a part of the stack that would most naturally cycle from low to high output during peak hours – this is not what they were designed to do. Second, historically most coal purchases by generators are long term "take-or-pay," which is jargon for saying that you pay for it whether or not you want delivery. As a result,

---

[11] Coal trades in $/ton. The conversion ratio used was 1 ton of central Appalachian coal is equivalent to 24 MMBtus, which is the minimum acceptable energy content for delivery into the NYMEX futures contract.

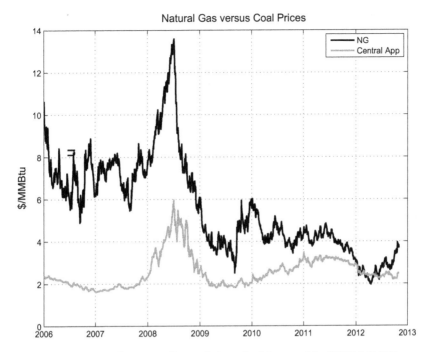

Figure 14.18. NG versus Central Appalachian coal in USD/MMBtu.

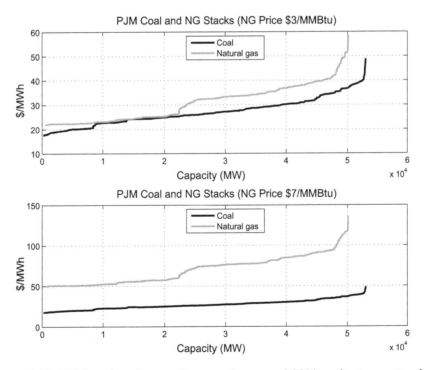

Figure 14.19. PJM coal and natural gas stacks around 2011 under two natural gas price regimes.

coal inventories at generation stations reached capacity, ultimately making estimates of just how much switching would occur quite challenging.

The implications on tolling valuations are similarly complex. In the high natural gas price scenario one would expect correlations between peak power and natural gas spot returns to be higher at typical peak loads than in the low-price scenario, where coal can ultimately set the marginal price. Regime changes such as the shale gas revolution are the dominant motivation for the use of structural models introduced in Chapter 12. The following simple example illustrates the nontrivial effects of fuel switching on price dynamics. In this example, we are purely considering a single-period price clearing with none of the complexities of intertemporal dispatch.

Consider a stack model comprised of two distinct types of generation:

- *Baseload.* The baseload generation is described by the stack with capacity C_B and single marginal price of dispatch p_B:

$$\Psi_B(C) = \begin{cases} p_B & \text{if } C < C_B \\ p_{\max} & \text{otherwise} \end{cases} \tag{14.27}$$

- *Natural gas.* In contrast, the natural gas stack is parameterized by heat rate, which increases exponentially with load:

$$\Psi_{NG}(C) = \alpha G e^{\lambda C} \tag{14.28}$$

where G denotes the spot natural gas price. This form is similar to the exponential case of the Barlow model.

As in the stack models in Chapter 12, spot prices will be set by

$$p_T = \Psi\left(L_T \middle| G_T, p_B\right) \tag{14.29}$$

where L_T is the demand (load) at time T. The stack Ψ is calculated from (14.27) and (14.28) using (12.31).

For the results that follow, we will be assuming that the (nominal) tenor is $T = 1$, that load is normally distributed, and that the log-normal distribution of the natural gas price G_T under the physical measure is the same as under the risk-neutral measure. The parameters used in the results that follow are shown in Table 14.3.

The variable of interest is the baseload price p_B (think of a coal price). When $p_B \ll \alpha G$, the natural gas and baseload stacks are effectively separated, and the distribution of L_T is (with high probability) setting prices solely on Ψ_{NG}. As p_B increases, a switching regime occurs where the two stacks are at near parity. With p_B at higher levels, load once again is set by the natural gas stack. The results shown in Figure 14.20 are consistent with these heuristic arguments. First, the forward heat rate $E[p_t]/G(0,T)$ increases with p_B, as it should. Raising any fuel price results in an increase

Table 14.3. *Structural Stack Model Parameters*

C_B	p_{max}	α	λ	$G(0,T)$	$\bar{\sigma}_G(T)$	μ_L	σ_L
20,000	1000	4.00	2e-05	5.00	0.30	50,000	4000

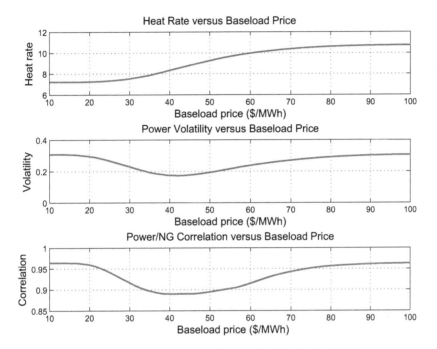

Figure 14.20. Structural model results for fuel switching.

in Ψ. Power volatility shows more structure, decreasing as switching occurs because p_B was assumed to be constant. Similar behavior is shown for correlation between natural gas and power returns.

The preceding experiment suggests that information about the stack, coupled with fuel forward prices, could yield potentially useful estimates for power implied volatilities and cross-commodity correlations and ultimately improved tolling valuation. The relatively short period in which such switching has occurred makes calibration and model testing difficult. However, given the inherently nonlinear nature of the interaction between power spot prices and *multiple* fuel prices, structural models should guide the design and calibration of financial or econometric models, if not replace them outright.

Complex Tolls and Approximation Methods

The analysis of basic tolls is the cornerstone for the valuation of more complex generation structures. These vanilla tolls, which exercise into standard power buckets such as "5x16," "2x16," and "7x8," can only yield approximations to the payoff of real generation assets. Engineers who design or operate physical generation and appreciate the complexities involved or mathematicians who relish challenging problems often deem such approximations inadequate and strive for more realistic representations of physical generation.

In designing hedging structures to support financing of generation construction or acquisition, there is a dialectic between hedge providers and hedgers – the former being more comfortable with structures that are closest to vanilla and the latter preferring the highest degree of replication of the generation unit possible. However, when dealers value complex tolls, constraints are generally rounded to the greatest potential impact and additional flexibility is reduced in value to obtain a lower bound in the form of a vanilla product. This means that the perceived advantage of a more effective hedge is often more costly than the hedger realizes given the lower value the dealer is willing to pay. While vanilla structures are almost always suitable as effective hedges, more complex hedges often transact. In what follows we will take the perspective of the hedge provider, designing approximation methods that result in simple valuation mechanics and *lower* bounds on value.

In Chapter 3 we surveyed common features of physical generation that complicate valuation, usually by coupling the standard buckets and reducing the time scales of exercise (dispatch) to the hourly level. Most generation can operate at output levels within a range $[Q_{min}, Q_{max}]$, referred to as the *lower* and *higher operating limits*, respectively, and heat rates vary with output level, in general being higher (less efficient) at lower operating levels. Moreover, generation cannot instantaneously adjust output; rather, there is a maximum rate (ramp rates) at which output can be changed. In addition, start costs are incurred in transitioning from zero output to positive output. While far from a complete list of the complexities of physical generation, this is certainly enough to allow us to illustrate some of the key issues.

The simplest illustration of subordinating approximation methods is to extend a vanilla toll to include multiple fuels. Some generators are able to burn more than one fuel (usually two), allowing switching between, say, natural gas and fuel oil. In practice, switching requires planning and often is encumbered with regulatory constraints on how much oil can be burned annually due to emissions caps. Assuming that the asset allows a daily choice between fuels, the terminal payoff takes the form

$$\max\left\{F(T,T) - \min\left[H_1 G_1(T,T), H_2 G_2(T,T)\right], 0\right\} \qquad (14.30)$$

where the two fuel prices G_1 and G_2 will, in general, have different heat rates. This structure is ostensibly simple to evaluate by quadrature, given the covariance structure between the three commodities.

Many practitioners, however, have a healthy skepticism about just how readily one can hedge a dual-fuel toll and opt to value and manage such using a "best of" vanilla representation. The payoff (14.30) is equivalently written as

$$\max\left\{\max[F(T,T) - H_1G_1(T,T),0], \max[F(T,T) - H_2G_2(T,T),0]\right\}$$

$$(14.31)$$

Taking the expected value of this expression inside the first maximum yields a lower value in terms of the simpler one-fuel tolls. The result is that a rigorous lower bound on the value of a dual-fuel structure can be obtained simply by valuing the single-fuel toll for both G_1 and G_2 and taking the best value by contract month. The situation is reassessed regularly, and the booking is changed if there has been a reordering of which fuel "wins" in a given contract month. From a portfolio manager's perspective, the advantage of this approach is that the risk of the structure resembles that of more familiar vanilla toll and can be managed as such, aside from the occasional rebalancings required.

The dual-fuel example coupled three commodities at single delivery times. Exercise remained independent from period to period. The situation becomes much more interesting when one includes intertemporal couplings. Consider the following extension of our original working problem, but now include exercise for each of the delivery buckets: "5x16," "2x16," and "7x8." In addition, assume that exercise can be allowed into either lower or higher operating limits Q_L or Q_H and that total (not per-MWh) start charges are K_S. This means that had you elected to not exercise a "7x8" option, for example, and subsequently exercised the following bucket (either "5x16" or "2x16," as the case may be), you incur the additional start charge K_S.[12]

The valuation problem takes the form

$$\tilde{E}\left\{\sup_{\vec{Q}\in\mathcal{A}}\sum_n\left[Q_nN_h(n)(F_n - H_*G_n) - \kappa(n,\vec{Q})\right]\right\} \qquad (14.32)$$

where $N_h(n)$ is the number of hours in bucket n, and Q_n denotes the quantity generated in period n. The set of all allowed dispatch paths is denoted by $\mathcal{A}$, which in this case is simply

$$\mathcal{A} = \{Q: Q_n \in [0, Q_L, Q_H]\ \forall n\} \qquad (14.33)$$

---

[12] Typically, such charges are articulated in cost per start, as done here, or in terms of fuel and power costs. In the latter case, adjustments to equivalent economic output or heat rate are easily made.

Here n indexes buckets chronologically; if n corresponds to a "5x16" delivery bucket, then $n+1$ will be a "7x8" bucket. Coupling between buckets occurs because the start charge takes the form

$$\kappa(n,\vec{Q}) = \begin{cases} 0 & \text{if } Q_{n-1} > 0 \\ K_S & \text{otherwise} \end{cases} \tag{14.34}$$

with a start charge occurring if the quantity generated in the previous bucket is zero. We have set the standard strike K (VOM) to zero for notational ease.

Valuation of this problem is challenging at several levels. First, "7x8" and "2x16" options are hardly ever traded. This means that spread option valuation immediately encounters the obstacle of formulating some plausible estimates for these volatilities. Second, evaluation of (14.32) requires solution of a dynamic-programming problem.

The essential feature of the optionality embodied in (14.32) is that in situations where the spark spread is negative at, say, $n-1$, exercise at Q_L can result in the savings of a start charge in exercise n. Clearly, this would only occur in the situation where the prior spark spread is not too negative:

$$Q_L N_h(n-1)S_{n-1} - \kappa(n-1,\vec{Q}) + K_S > 0 \tag{14.35}$$

where

$$S_n \equiv F_n - H_* G_n \tag{14.36}$$

is the spark spread at time n. Viewed from the perspective of bucket $n-1$, there is often enough transparency in the day-ahead markets to implement the exercise criterion implied by (14.35).

Dynamic-programming methods are one approach to this problem, although the formulation is more challenging than for natural gas storage. If each bucket price is driven by a set of OU processes, the dimensionality of the problem is prohibitive. Alternatively, hourly spot price dynamics can be parameterized in some form, and dynamic control or Longstaff-Schwartz-type methods can be applied (see, for example, [CL08] for a survey and expansion on these issues and methods).

Alternatively, one can construct subordinating portfolios of vanilla tolls. The idea is to consider a variety of permutations of the possible operating configurations, each of which is considered to be a potential representation for the structure to be used *for an entire contract month*. For example, consider the following two structures, each of which is consistent with the operational features of our structure:

- Independent options, one for each of the three delivery buckets ("5x16," "2x16" and "7x8"), each fully loaded with start costs:

$$\tilde{E}\left\{\sum_n \max[Q_H N_h(n)S_n - K_S, 0]\right\} \tag{14.37}$$

- Assume a priori exercise ("must run") on the "7x8" bucket at Q_L, thereby eliminating start costs from the "5x16" and "2x16" blocks:

$$\tilde{E}\left\{\sum_{n \in B_{7x8}} [Q_L N_h(n)S_n - K_S \mathbf{1}_{\{Q_{n-1}=0\}}] + \sum_{n \notin B_{7x8}} \max[Q_H N_h(n)S_n, 0]\right\} \quad (14.38)$$

Because the strike in the "7x8" component depends on the previous exercises, this is not technically a swap, but optionality has been removed via the presumption is that the unit will dispatch in the offpeak bucket at the lower capacity regardless of the value of S_n.

The first configuration is a lower bound on the value (14.32) because start costs are allocated to every option. Dispatch is at Q_H since if the option is in the money, exercising at any level below the maximum capacity would be suboptimal. By replacing the "7x8" option with the form in the second configuration, we are forcing exercise; hence no start cost is applied to peak buckets. However, the "7x8" swap could sustain start costs if the preceding peak bucket was not exercised, resulting in the term $K_S \mathbf{1}_{\{Q_{n-1}=0\}}$. The expected value of this expression is the probability of exercise of the "5x16" or "2x16" option, respectively, calculation of which is straightforward for the log-normal distributions.

The best of the two possible operating states can be selected by month, for the entire month, thereby achieving an optimal (among the two configurations considered) subordinating configuration. The problem is therefore reduced to standard tolling structures and swaps, as well as calculation of exercise probabilities. There are a number of possible configurations for dispatch that would be considered in practice. Each bucket can be in any of the three configurations with time n for each given as

1. Full optionality at Q_H:
   - If the previous bucket is in the option configuration,

$$\max[Q_H N_h(n)S_n - K_S, 0]$$

   - If the previous bucket is in the must-run configuration,

$$\max[Q_H N_h(n)S_n, 0]$$

2. Must run at Q_H:
   - If the previous bucket is in the option configuration,

$$Q_H N_h(n)S_n - K_S \mathbf{1}_{\{Q_{n-1}=0\}}$$

   - If the previous bucket is in the must-run configuration, $Q_H S_n$.

3. Mustrun at Q_L:
   o If the previous bucket is in the option configuration,

$$Q_L N_h(n) S_n - K_S \mathbf{1}_{\{Q_{n-1}=0\}}$$

   o If the previous bucket is in the must-run configuration, $Q_L S_n$.

These permutations differ in their resulting values due to tradeoffs between extrinsic value and reduction in start costs. Valuation of each can be scripted, and the configuration with the highest value can be used as a subordinating representation. As with CSO subordinators in natural gas, the configuration that is optimal can change during the lifetime of the transaction, and rebookings (with associated hedge rebalancings) must occur.

Subordinating methods result in valuation of standard structures that can easily be booked in risk systems. While compelling in simplicity, valuation of the "2x16" and "7x8" options is not straightforward. For one thing, "2x16" and "7x8" swaps are usually not traded individually but rather are quoted together as the union – the *off-peak wrap*. This means that statistical methods for decomposing traded products into these forward buckets are inevitably required.[13] Options on "7x8" and "2x16" power are almost unheard of, rendering the required volatility inputs also subject to estimation and modeling assumptions.

Start costs created a temporal coupling between delivery buckets, resulting in a stochastic control problem, but one that was amenable to subordinating approximations. Physical generation, as well as some structured derivatives hedges, involves dispatch constraints and optionality at the hourly time scale. At short time scales, the problem becomes considerably more challenging. No hourly options trade in the broker markets, and price risk at the hourly time scale must be managed using vanilla swaps and options that involve ratable delivery over the standard buckets. Simulation-based methods are almost always required.

The construction of hourly price simulations can be accomplished in a variety of ways. Hourly loads can be calibrated to temperature and simulated, ultimately driving econometric or structural models. Alternatively, bucket spot prices can be simulated, as discussed in the preceding section, using econometric or structural models. The simulated (daily) bucket spot prices can then be split into hourly price realizations by simulation of "shaping coefficients" $\vec{\alpha}^{(B)}(d)$ for each bucket B on day d. These define the realized hourly spot prices $p_h(d)$ from the bucket $p^{(B)}(d)$ via

$$p_h(d) = \alpha_h^{(B)}(d) p^{(B)}(d) \tag{14.39}$$

---

[13] It is natural to ask why we did not decompose the toll into peak and off-peak buckets. This could have been done, but such a structure bears little resemblance to actual generation dispatch, and tolls of this type are rarely transacted.

Analysis of the dynamics of shaping coefficients is central to the valuation of variable-quantity swaps and is discussed in detail in Chapter 15. For the remainder of this section we will assume the existence of a method to generate simulations of joint realizations of fuel and hourly spot prices.

If the spot price process is driven by diffusions, which have presumably been calibrated in some fashion to historical spot data or existing forward and options data, stochastic impulse-control methods such as those developed in [CL08] are potentially viable. However, the computational requirements for analysis of dispatch at the hourly time scale over tenors spanning many years are daunting.

Most spot price simulation engines are based on nonlinear regressions or structural models and are not amenable to description by a set of coupled Ornstein-Uhlenbeck processes, as often assumed in control theoretic methods. In this case, heuristic methods are frequently used. As a simple example, one can *assume* that the portfolio manager exercising the toll or the operator of the asset has complete knowledge of the (to be realized) hourly spot prices for the upcoming peak and off-peak buckets grouped as pairs. Optimal dispatch for this interval of twenty-four hours, given the end state of the past pair of buckets, is usually directly amenable to linear or quadratic programming methods. This "myopic" optimization can be rapidly solved for each simulation path, yielding random payoffs on time scales that are hedgable. Moreover, the methods of hedge construction and valuation that we used in the preceding section apply. The result is valuation and estimates of hedge slippage with credible assessments of impacts of intraday optionality and constraints.

The weakness in this approach is the assumption of perfect foresight of hourly prices. A more realistic situation is to assume knowledge of the next two bucket prices; these are often visible on the trading screens for the more liquid hubs. In this case, the distributional characteristics of the shaping coefficients used in (14.39) provide the required information for a mean-variance optimization over the next twenty-four hours, which is also usually tractable using quadratic programming methods.

The advantage to such an approach is its flexibility. A broad array of complex constraints can be handled, including pump storage facilities, which involve the additional complication of inventory constraints on the dispatch of the asset.[14]

---

[14] Pump storage facilities are perhaps the only economically viable method for effectively storing power in large quantities. A reservoir of finite capacity can be filled using electric pumps, thereby storing the electricity as potential energy, which can subsequently be converted back into electricity through turbine generators. The loss ratio is usually in the ballpark of 1.4; that is, 1.4 MWh of pumping can yield 1 MWh of generation. As a consequence, pumping usually occurs during the off-peak hours and producing during on-peak hours, subject to limitations on the size of the reservoir.

Conclusion

Valuation and hedging tolling transactions with daily optionality using standard financial models are challenging for a number of reasons.

- The concept of returns correlations at the daily level is ambiguous for nonstorable commodities.
- Estimated returns correlations are chronically below the implied correlations when trading activity in tolls is visible.
- Substantial constraints in liquidity, not only in the sense of low daily trading volume of swaps and options but also due to block size and calendar strip conventions, can result in degradation of the performance of dynamic hedging strategies.
- Hedging volatility and correlation risk using fixed-strike single-commodity options can require large positions and frequent, costly rebalancings.

Alternative approaches based on econometric or structural simulation methods are commonly used. With these, a basic dichotomy exists in implementation.

- *The risk-neutral paradigm.* Modify simulations to yield expected values of traded payoffs that are consistent with market prices, and proceed to calculate the relevant Greeks for dynamic hedging.
- *The physical-measure paradigm.* Construct static hedges at inception based on the physical measure.

The first approach is a less severe departure from the standard liturgy while providing joint distributions of the relevant underlying price process that can be more realistic than GBM or other parametric constructs. The second approach, while failing to account for potential rebalancings, has the merit of avoiding the pitfalls of assuming liquidity that may not exist.

More complex tolling transactions also can be addressed using these various methods. Financial models on subordinating methods have the same potential issues as for vanilla structures. Simulation methods are more robust and easier to implement and provide not only an estimate of expected value and appropriate hedges but also the distribution of residual risks.

15

Variable-Quantity Swaps

The balance between supply and demand of energy commodities can change extremely rapidly. An unusually cold day in a region heated by natural gas results in higher consumption, coupled with statistically higher natural gas spot prices. A hot day in a region in which air conditioning is prevalent results in increased demand for power, again with commensurate price response. The aftermath of 9/11 witnessed a meaningful and nearly instantaneous drop in air travel with an associated drop in jet fuel consumption. The list goes on. A refinery outage can result in a discontinuous drop in supply that can have significant regional pricing (not to mention political) consequences. The same is true for power generators, notably nuclear plants, where unanticipated (forced) outages can last for weeks or even months and result in local and in some instances regional price responses.

The purpose of storage and transportation facilities is to mitigate price dislocations resulting from such events. Large withdrawals from natural gas storage occur when the temperature is low in the Northeast, as we saw in Figure 3.31, and pipeline flows to the region increase. Such responses dampen the price spikes that tend to occur at such times. Nonetheless, despite substantial storage and transportation infrastructure, the price series for TETM3 basis shown in Figure 1.6 is clear evidence that such infrastructure has limitations – otherwise we would not see the regular appearance of basis returns in excess of 100 percent.

Power demand shows even more structure at shorter time scales. Temperature is the dominant driver; recall Figure 3.37, which shows PJM Classic load at 4 p.m. versus daily average temperature in Philadelphia, with the highest levels of demand associated with high temperatures. Load variation at the hourly time scale is significant, as we saw in Figure 3.36. Power, because it is effectively nonstorable, relies on a variety of generation types to accommodate demand fluctuations, with considerable allocation of capacity as backup generation (so-called spinning and nonspinning reserves) in lieu of storage.

Short-time-scale variations in net demand in natural gas and power and, to a somewhat lesser extent, in other energy and consumable commodities are an inherent feature of the markets. This risk must be borne by someone. In regulated markets, the costs associated with dispatching generation to match the varying load or using liquified natural gas (LNG) to react to spikes in natural gas demand are passed through to the end user through rate-setting mechanisms.

In deregulated markets, the suppliers of load must procure power at the market-clearing price. This means that suppliers charging their customers fixed prices will usually choose to hedge their short positions through forward purchases. However, as we have seen, the "vanilla" instruments readily available for such hedging programs are fixed notional contracts with ratable delivery. Such instruments can hedge price risk on long time scales for *expected* supply or demand but are largely ineffective at managing daily or hourly demand/price correlation risk. The result is that a large reservoir of volumetric risk exists across the energy markets without much in the way of risk transfer possible.

In this chapter we discuss some products that have been created that do in fact facilitate hedging volumetric risk. The methods used to value such structures are just as pertinent to the natural holders of volumetric risk, for example, merchant generators that own primarily baseload generation against a short position comprised of a customer load or natural gas distributors with fixed gas-supply contracts against daily variations in customer demand.

Viewing such exposure as a swap with random notional (the realized demand), the fundamental problem arises from the fact that demand is not traded directly – it is an altogether uncommoditized risk. The goal in what follows is to first construct optimal hedging strategies and then to develop methods that characterize the residual risks, which are (arguably) stationary and not dynamically managed – what we will refer to as *actuarial risks*. Pricing is ultimately driven by the value implied by the hedges and a risk adjustment based on the risk preferences of the holder of the risk.

The Basic Problem

A variable-quantity exposure coupled with a fixed notional hedge takes a common form. Consider a short position to an end user, which can consume the commodity as needed, at a fixed contract price of p_f. The terminal payoff for delivery period n is

$$\pi_{\text{short}} \equiv Q_n \left(p_f - p_n \right) \tag{15.1}$$

where Q_n is the (random) demand at time n, and p_n is the associated spot price. Here n could be indexing an arbitrary sequence of delivery periods – monthly, daily, or hourly, as is often the case in power.

The quantity Q_n is a random variable; viewed collectively, $\{Q.\}$ is a stochastic process on which econometric analysis is usually performed to yield estimates for $\bar{Q}_n \equiv E(Q_n)$ in addition to other statistical attributes. The typical hedge invoked by many practitioners is to purchase for forward delivery the expected quantity, which has a terminal payoff of

$$\pi_{\text{hedge}} \equiv \bar{Q}_n (p_n - F_n) \tag{15.2}$$

where F_n is the forward price at which the hedge was transacted. Note that usually this forward price is constant over a set of delivery times n due to the nature of monthly ratable forward contracts. As we will see shortly, hedging using the expected demand as the notional is usually not optimal, but for the moment it serves for expository purposes.

The portfolio payoff is the sum of (15.1) and (15.2), which can be written as

$$\pi_{\text{final}} \equiv (Q_n - \bar{Q}_n)(p_f - p_n) + \bar{Q}_n (p_f - F_n) \tag{15.3}$$

The second term is a constant; the first term is where the action is. Demand is positively correlated with price, rendering the expected value of the first term negative. Correlation risk is against the holder of this position.

If forwards and options markets on Q_n were traded, then π_{final} could be treated as a quanto (see [Hul12]). This observation is often too compelling for people to ignore, and it is not uncommon for trading desks to construct forwards and volatilities for Q_n, estimate some correlations, and treat such structures in precisely this way. The problem with this approach is that derivatives on Q, aside from the rare structured-load swap, are simply not traded; they are never discussed by brokers and are certainly not listed or cleared. Volumetric risk is totally uncommoditized.

Demand for most commodities is effected by macroeconomic considerations. Although we will discuss this in some detail later, most of our attention will be directed to variable-quantity risk categorized according to whether the quantity index Q_n is by weather or by infrastructure failure. The first category includes a variety of natural gas structures, as well as variable-load risk in power. Our focus will be on variable-load risk due to the availability of reliable load data from the ISOs. The methods used, which rely heavily on econometric analysis of weather, demand, and price, pertain to all such structures regardless of commodity. The second category is often referred to as *unit-contigent (UC) risk*. This risk is most commonly traded in the purchase or sale of whatever a physical asset produces. The uncommoditized risk in UC structures is asset performance. The most commonly traded

UC structures are offtakes from a specific generator in which the buyer purchases the actual quantity produced on an hourly basis or tranches thereof. Once again, the methods developed for UC power contracts apply more broadly. Unit-contigent risk is qualitatively very different from the first category of weather-driven demand swaps in that the distribution of Q_n in the UC context is typically very skewed (think of a point mass at zero output) and with large outages rare. The typical duration of such transactions is not long enough to invoke a limit theorem to characterize residual risks.

This topic is a natural successor to the preceding chapter, in which we argued that market incompleteness calls into question the applicability of the usual complete-markets valuation methods. Here such methods are simply not applicable, and econometric or structural methods coupled with portfolio optimization is the only viable approach currently available.

Load Swaps: Origin and Risks

Volumetric risk is most pronounced in electricity markets as a result of the substantial hourly variation in load. The purpose of a competitive power market is to efficiently dispatch generation to meet demand, which is highly variable and largely price-insensitive. The inelastic nature of power demand arises from the lack of direct exposure to and visibility of spot-price risk to end users, although this is slowly changing with new technology and demand-response programs.[1]

Often load is procured in a competitive fashion, either through retail aggregation, in which companies solicit end users, or through large auction processes mandated by regulators. In such auctions, utility customers are tranched according to coarse attributes of consumption patterns – for example, large industrials, small commercials, and residentials. Each tranche consists of a defined set of customers at the time of the auction, and bidders for these tranches typically perform detailed econometric analysis of tranche attributes. The econometric attributes that are pertinent to valuation and hedging span time scales from hours to years:

- *Short-time-scale behavior.* Demand varies daily or hourly for power and for some classes of customers is heavily weather-dependent. The autocorrelation in temperature residuals decays on the order of only a few days, as seen in Figure 10.9. Vanilla bucket hedges are only partially effective as hedging instruments, and entities that serve load can experience meaningful variations in revenue over short time scales.

- *Attrition.* Utility customers in competitive markets have the option to leave utility service for another retail provider. As with prepayment options in mortgages, customers have optionality – if a competitor can provide a lower price, then the

---

[1] *Demand response* is a term that refers to economic incentives for consumers to reduce consumption during periods of particularly high demand. As such, load reduction is akin to another form of power supply and can be viewed as occupying the most expensive part of the stack.

customer can leave the tranche. Details vary by utility and state, but this optionality is a commonly occurring feature. If energy prices systematically decline after an auction-clearing price has been established, customers have economic incentive to leave the tranche. This phenomenon, referred to as either *attrition* or *migration*, has a behavioral component that is challenging to quantify given limited historical data, although some stylized facts are clear. For example, large industrial customers are very price sensitive; residential customers tend to be less price sensitive or *sticky*, in the vernacular.

- *Load growth.* Historically power demand has systematically increased on the order of 1 to 2 percent annually. There are glaring exceptions, notably during the credit crisis, which we will discuss shortly. Hedging strategies depend heavily on estimates of future load growth, and departures of realized growth from estimated are a risk that is inherent in load transactions.

Our primary focus will be on short-time-scale weather-driven risk because of its relative tractability and extensive data. We will also discuss the risks associated with departures of load growth from expected. Attrition is beyond the scope of this treatment in part because, unlike in mortgages, there is limited historical data regarding the behavioral attributes of customers endowed with this regulatory put option.[2]

Load Swaps: Fixed Notional

The form of swap described by (15.1) with Q_n a random variable is the risk inherent in short positions to tranches of customers. The hedge slippage incurred by using vanilla block hedges is illustrated in Figure 15.1, which shows realized PJM Classic load on an hourly basis for July 2010 with plausible "5x16," "2x16," and "7x8" block forward hedges (which happen to be the average realized load by bucket during this month). On a daily basis, the quantity of power required can depart meaningfully from the hedge, resulting in the residual short-time-scale risk. This risk can be decomposed into a deterministic component corresponding to the expected demand and a stochastic component corresponding to the residuals.

Switching notation to the hourly indexing pertinent to power markets, the settlement value for the unhedged structure in contract month m, and bucket $\mathcal{B}$ can be decomposed into the expected volume component and a departure from expected volume:

$$\sum_{h \in \mathcal{B}(m)} \left[\bar{L}_h \left(p_f - p_h \right) + \left(L_h - \bar{L}_h \right) \left(p_f - p_h \right) \right] \tag{15.4}$$

where L_h is the hourly load, and $\bar{L}_h$ is the expected value.

---

[2] In mortgage markets, the data sets span decades, although technological innovations certainly render customer behavior nonstationary and challenging to model in its own right.

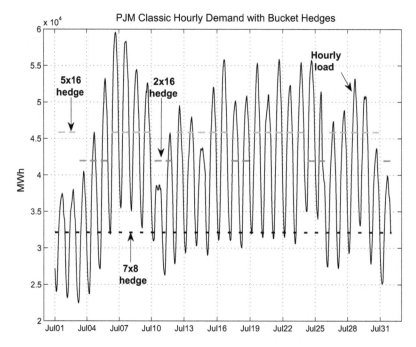

Figure 15.1. Hourly PJM demand with block hedges (July 2010).

We will start by examining the first component in (15.4), which has a deterministic notional that varies by hour; only the price differential is random. Swaps of this form, referred to as *fixed-shape swaps*, transact with some frequency, are traded commonly in part because they are viewed as more benign than swaps that hedge full volumetric risk because of the contractually fixed hourly quantities. Fixed shape swaps live, metaphorically, between vanilla ratable delivery products and structures which hedge total volumetric risk. The reassuring aspect of contractually fixed volumes is actually deceptive, and such structures have more embedded weather risk than most realize.

The standard (and flawed) valuation methodology begins with making the simple observation that as for a constant notional swap, the present value is given by

$$V(t) = \sum_m d(m) \sum_{B \in \mathcal{B}} \sum_{h \in B} \bar{L}_h \left(p_f - F_h \right) \tag{15.5}$$

where m indexes month, $\mathcal{B}$ is the set of delivery buckets over which B is indexed, and h is hour; $d(m)$ is the discount factor, and p_f is the fixed price of the transaction. All that remains is to decide how to compute the hourly "forward" prices F_h that are at best visible for the next day and certainly not discernible from traded markets at longer tenors.

The typical approach is to introduce the concept of *shaping coefficients* or *scalars* $\vec{\alpha}$ that relate the hourly forward to the standard bucket forward multiplicatively $F_h = \alpha_h F_B$. Because F_B refers to ratable delivery, we must have

$$\frac{1}{N(B)} \sum \alpha_h = 1 \tag{15.6}$$

where $N(B)$ is the number of hours in the bucket.

The shaping coefficients are usually obtained via routine regression by bucket and by month. The simplest approach is to define a date range, say, from 2005–2011 in the results that follow, and average the realized daily shaping coefficients by calendar month:

$$\vec{\alpha}_B(j) = \frac{1}{N} \sum_{m=j} \sum_{d \in B(m)} \frac{\vec{p}(d)}{p_B(d)} \tag{15.7}$$

where $\vec{p}(d)$ is the vector of hour spot prices in the bucket, and N is the total sample size. Here $j \in [1, \ldots, 12]$ is indexing calendar month in the sense that $j = 1$ corresponds to all Januarys in the data set. The dimension of $\vec{\alpha}_B$ is equal to the number of hours in bucket B. The required conservation law (15.6) holds as it is satisfied for each sample day.

There are problems with this approach when $p_B(d)$ is small (or negative) owing to negative hourly prices. A day in which $p_B(d) \approx 0$ will dominate the estimate. This is an increasingly common phenomenon with the addition of substantial wind-generation capacity that is subsidized by tax incentives. The structure of the prevailing tax incentives subsidizes generators according to the amount of power generated. This form of subsidy creates a situation in which production at negative spot prices is still economical and has resulted in a frequent occurrence of negative hourly spot prices in some regions of the country, notably in West Texas.

One way to avoid this problem is to change the regression form. The model underlying (15.7) is of the form

$$\frac{\vec{p}(d)}{p_B(d)} = \vec{\alpha} + \vec{\epsilon}(d) \tag{15.8}$$

where $\vec{\epsilon}(d)$ are the daily residuals. This implies that the standard deviation of the realized coefficients versus estimated values $\vec{p}(d)$ scales linearly in $p_B(d)$. Alternatively, a model of the form

$$\vec{p}(d) = \vec{\alpha} p_B(d) + \vec{\epsilon}(d) \tag{15.9}$$

assumes a constant scaling of the standard deviation of the error but avoids the pitfalls of zero denominators. Proceeding once again by contract month, the regression problem amounts to minimizing the L_2 error

$$\min_{\vec{\alpha} \in \mathcal{A}} \sum_d \|\vec{p}(d) - \vec{\alpha} p_B(d)\|_2^2 \tag{15.10}$$

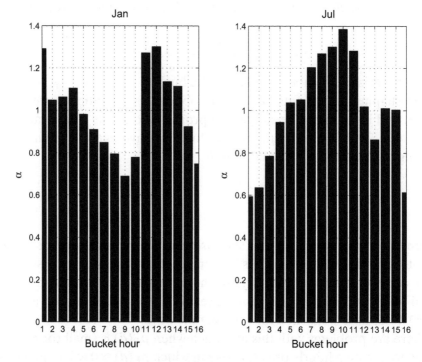

Figure 15.2. Price shaping coefficients for PJM Western Hub "5x16".

subject to the constraints

$$\mathcal{A} = \left\{ \vec{\alpha} \geq 0; \ \frac{1}{N(B)} \sum \alpha_j = 1 \right\} \tag{15.11}$$

This is a quadratic programming problem of the form:

$$\min_{\vec{\alpha} \in \mathcal{A}} \left(\frac{1}{2} \vec{\alpha}^\dagger A \vec{\alpha} + \vec{\alpha}^\dagger \vec{f} \right) \tag{15.12}$$

with $A = \left[\sum_d p_B^2(d) \right] \mathbf{I}$, with $\mathbf{I}$ the identity matrix, and $\vec{f} = \sum_d p_B(d) \vec{p}(d)$. This regression problem is simple to solve numerically and has the merit of avoiding degeneracy in estimation due to near-zero prices.

Figure 15.2 shows the results for PJM Western Hub for January and July. A few qualitative observations add to the credibility of this approach. First, the behavior of summer months, as exhibited by July, is consistent with basic heuristics – maximum load (and hence price) occurs in the hottest hours, with a spike when people return home and crank up their air conditioners. Winter months, January in this case, have the higher ratios early in the morning when heating is usually turned up. Shoulder months such as April and October tend to show relatively flat shaping profiles.

Regardless of method, the standard practice is to estimate shaping coefficients, put them into risk systems (occasionally updating the estimates), and price fixed-shape swaps as any other swap. This approach does yield a useful result – namely, that the delta of such a transaction is not the notional. Rewriting (15.5) as

$$V(t) = \sum_m d(m) \sum_{B \in \mathcal{B}} \sum_{h \in B} \bar{L}_h \left(p_f - \vec{\alpha} F_B\right) \tag{15.13}$$

it is clear that for month m, the delta for bucket B is

$$\Delta_B(m) \equiv \frac{\partial V}{\partial F_B} = -d(m) \sum_{h \in B} \bar{L}_h \alpha_h \tag{15.14}$$

Because most load hedging structures have higher quantities in the hours with the highest shaping coefficient (after all, it is higher expected loads that are responsible for higher shaping coefficients), delta is usually significantly larger than the discounted notional. We will return to this shortly for fully variable-load swaps.

The weakness in the use of shaping coefficients is that, in its simplicity, no connection is made between between spot price and its basic drivers such as temperature, which affect the realized price ratios $p_h(d)/p_B(d)$. Consider Figure 15.3, which shows the daily price ratio for 4 p.m. versus KPHL

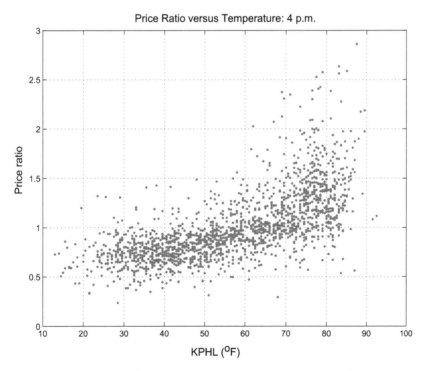

Figure 15.3. 4 p.m. pricing shaping coefficients for PJM Western Hub "5x16" versus KPHL temperature.

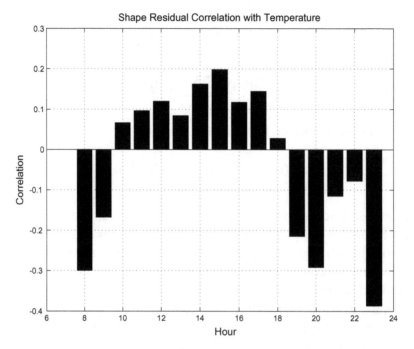

Figure 15.4. July shape residuals for PJM Western Hub "5x16" versus KPHL temperature.

daily average temperature. Shaping coefficients are clearly temperature-dependent. This observation spawns two concerns.

First, the correlation between the realized ratio $p_h(d)/p_B(d)$ and the bucket price $p_B(d)$ results in a lurking convexity. Most structures hedging load have higher values of $\bar{L}_h$ at hours in which $p_h(d)/p_B(d)$ is positively correlated with p_B, which can result in a negative convexity adjustment. Figure 15.4 shows the correlation between the daily shape residuals $\epsilon_h(d) = [p_h(d)/p_B(d)] - \vec{\alpha}$ and temperature in July by hour of the bucket. Given a prescribed load shape, the midmarket value for p_f for a given day d or, by trivial extension, for an entire transaction is obtained by zeroing the expected payoff. Assuming that there is no distinction between risk premia for hourly price risk and those for ratable delivery, this amounts to

$$p_f = \frac{\tilde{E}\left\{\sum_{h \in d} \bar{L}_h [\alpha_h + \epsilon_h(d)] p_B(d)\right\}}{\sum_{h \in d} \bar{L}_h} \tag{15.15}$$

Most pricing systems use only the first term in the numerator and ignore the effects of the correlation $\langle \bar{\epsilon}(d), p_B(d) \rangle$. Under this assumption, the *uplift*, defined as the ratio of the midmarket fixed price p_f to the bucket forward price, takes the form

$$\mathcal{U}_B \equiv \frac{p_f}{F_B} = \frac{\sum_{h \in d} \bar{L}_h \alpha_h}{\sum_{h \in d} \bar{L}_h} \tag{15.16}$$

This uplift is typically greater than unity for the same reason that the delta in (15.14) typically exceeds the notional – the fixed load shapes $\bar{L}$ required for hedging are usually highest when the shaping coefficients are highest. While this expression for uplift omits the convexity adjustment captured by (15.15), in practice, this usually has a relatively minor effect on most load, typically an adjustment in p_f of under a half percent. But why take chances?

The second issue is far more serious. Most shaping-coefficient estimates are made using a few years of historical spot price data. No competent weather derivatives desk would even remotely entertain the notion of trading based on such short data sets. To reinforce this point, the sample standard deviation of the residuals obtained via the simple regression method (15.8) is of the order of 2 to 3 percent depending on hour and month, assuming independence of daily samples. However, with the characteristic time decay in temperature ACFs of three days, give or take, the estimation error is probably closer to an eye-popping 10 percent. This is not acceptable.

The punchline is that even though fixed load shape swaps are somewhat less risky than the fully variable case, a much more effective approach is to calibrate the dynamics of $p_h(d)/p_B(d)$ to temperature. This allows the use of much longer weather data sets to calibrate regressions and subsequently generate simulations of price ratios. Such an approach yields distributions of the realized payoffs of (15.13) directly, facilitating not only better estimation of expected values but also a full characterization of the residual risks.

In the next section we will outline methods for handling the fully variable case, which effectively subsume the required modeling for fixed load swaps.

Load Swaps: Variable Notional

Fully variable load structures of the form (15.1) constitute the energy component associated with serving tranches of actual customer load. In the case of physical load obligations, a number of ancillary services and capacity must be procured in addition to energy.[3] Our focus will be on the short-time-scale implications pertaining to correlation between load and price as a result of temperature as well as the risks arising from estimates of load growth on long time scales. The analysis and pricing of attrition, namely, departures of customers from load tranches to competitive suppliers, are beyond the scope of this book and arguably beyond the scope of current modeling capabilities.

Rewriting (15.1) in an hourly context and assuming that we are working under a risk-neutral measure (we will depart from this assumption shortly),

---

[3] *Ancillary services* in power markets refer to a variety of reliability products that vary in definition between ISO. In one form or another, these compensate the additional generation that must be available to provide capacity in the event of force outages or localized infrastructure failure. Rather than produce power, these generators are on stand-by and earn revenue for being in this state. Suppliers of power must procure such in prescribed quantities in addition to the electricity required.

the mid market fixed price p_f must satisfy

$$p_f = \frac{\tilde{E}[\sum_h L(h)p_h]}{\tilde{E}[\sum_h \bar{L}(h)]} \qquad (15.17)$$

Fair value amounts to estimation of the covariance of load and price at the hourly level.

The problem with (15.17) is the tilde over the expectation – that is, the assumption that we are working under a risk-neutral measure. To make estimates on the joint dynamics of $[L_h, p_h]$, one option is to use econometric or structural models calibrated to historical load and spot data. Alternatively, one can attempt to use reduced-form or structural models calibrated to spot or forward prices to make inferences about load risk premia. Risk premia are notoriously difficult to estimate, even when given a history of both spot and forward prices, and here we are working in the absence of forward load data. Consequently, as we have done previously in the context of basis options and tolls, we will revert to physical-measure hedge construction and valuation based on econometric analysis.

Before proceeding, it is interesting to view this problem from the perspective of the simple Barlow stack model for a single delivery period. Starting with the exponential case in which

$$p_h = p_* e^{\lambda L_h} \qquad (15.18)$$

where p_* is a reference price spot price, and assuming that L_h is normal (μ_L, σ_L), we have

$$\tilde{E}(L_h p_h) = p_* \tilde{E}\left(L_h e^{\lambda L_h}\right) = p_* \frac{d}{d\lambda} \tilde{E}\left(e^{\lambda L_h}\right) \qquad (15.19)$$

which yields

$$\tilde{E}(L_h p_h) = p_* \left(\mu_L + \lambda \sigma_L^2\right) e^{\lambda \mu_L + \frac{1}{2}\lambda^2 \sigma_L^2} \qquad (15.20)$$

In addition, the forward price (being the expected spot price under this risk-neutral setting) is

$$F = \tilde{E}(p_t) = p_* e^{\lambda \mu_L + \frac{1}{2}\lambda^2 \sigma_L^2} \qquad (15.21)$$

This yields the fair-value fixed price, which in the form of a price uplift is

$$\mathcal{U} \equiv \frac{p_{\text{fixed}}}{F} = \frac{\mu_L + \lambda \sigma_L^2}{\mu_L} = 1 + \lambda \frac{\sigma_L^2}{\mu_L} \qquad (15.22)$$

This is a constant-elasticity result, in that uplift depends on convexity of the stack and the ratio of load variance to mean but not on load levels. Had we opted to use a heat-rate stack in which $p_* = H_{\text{ref}} G_h$, provided that natural gas prices are independent of the load process, the same result would pertain.

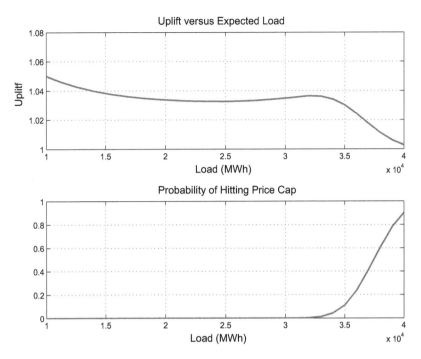

Figure 15.5. Barlow model uplift versus load.

Single exponential stacks are rarely used for a variety of reasons, not the least of which is a lack of skew. The independence of uplift of load in (15.22) shows another limit of such a simple model. We have seen that price-shaping coefficients are correlated with temperature and hence with load, and the same is true of the load/price covariance. The nonexpontential Barlow stack of the form (12.29) exhibits more realistic behavior and demonstrates the nontrivial nature of uplift that can be expected. The top plot in Figure 15.5 shows uplift versus expected load level using parameters discussed in the context of Figure 12.12. The lower plot shows the probability of reaching the price cap versus expected load. The results are interesting in that uplift first decreases and then increases with expected load, ultimately decreasing once load levels are firmly planted in the price-cap region.

The correlation between load and price results in uplift values in excess of unity, and uplift clearly depends on the structure of the stack and the distribution of load. Structural approaches to valuation of load swaps proceeds very much along the preceding lines, either with more complex parametric forms, for example, [ACHT09] or [CCS13], or with actual renditions of the physical stack in a region, as discussed in Chapter 12. Such methods are used by some shops in practice, and the approach remains a subject of active research. Empirical tests of performance remain largely an open issue.

We turn next to the use of econometric methods applied to the following load structure.

Working Problem

Calculate the midmarket fixed price p_f for a variable-load swap of the form

- Pricing date: December 30, 2011
- Delivery: Peak power for Jul12
- Spot price index: PJM Western Hub hourly real-time price
- Load index: PJM Classic preliminary load index[4]

Many load structures reference historical data, such as the load index in this problem, but the methods used in this example pertain to most realistic loads in which good historical data are available.

Figure 3.42 showed a scatter plot of PJM hourly prices versus PJM Classic hourly loads in which the relationship between load and power prices is clearly manifest. Most practitioners begin analysis of a variable load by analyzing historical realizations, and the simplest method for pricing a load transaction is to apply some estimate of historical uplift to forward prices. Although we will develop a more rigorous approach, the historical results provide a reference that, at a minimum, is valuable as a "sanity check."

Given historical data for a month m and bucket B, the implied (in arrears) fair price p_f solves

$$\sum_{h \in B(m)} \left(L_h p_f - L_h p_h \right) = 0 \tag{15.23}$$

The historical uplift is the ratio of p_f to the average realized hourly price, which yields

$$U(m,B) = \frac{\sum_{h \in B(m)} L_h p_h}{\left(\sum_{h \in B(m)} L_h \right) 1/N_{B(m)} \left(\sum_{h \in B(m)} p_h \right)} \tag{15.24}$$

where $N_{B(m)}$ denotes the number of hours in bucket B for month m.

Note that if load L_h were constant, the uplift would be identically one, and any departure from this value would be due to the presence of empirical correlations between load and price.

The results for our working example are shown for the "5x16" and "7x8" buckets in Figures 15.6 and 15.7, respectively. The average uplift by calendar month is shown in the lower plots. Interestingly, the average uplift for the "7x8" bucket is slightly higher (1.033) than for the "5x16" bucket (1.030). Also of note is the high "5x16" uplift in the peak summer months. These facts are qualitatively consistent with the behavior of the Barlow stack.

---

[4] Preliminary load estimates are published by PJM within a few days of the delivery day based on econometric analysis and samples of subsets of consumption. Final load estimates are published a few months later and are typically very close to to the preliminary estimate, which makes the preliminary load index more suited to swaps with monthly settlements.

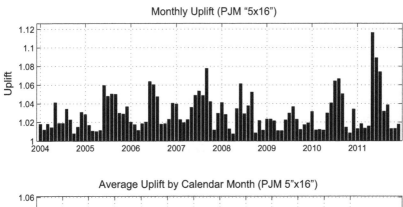

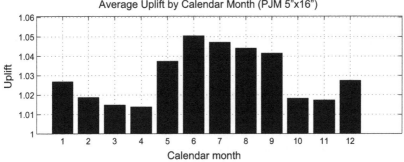

Figure 15.6. Uplift statistics PJM WH versus PJM Classic ("5x16").

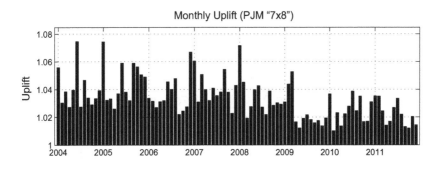

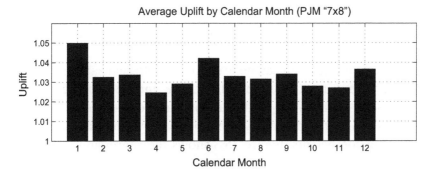

Figure 15.7. Uplift statistics PJM Western Hub versus PJM Classic ("7x8").

A common approach to econometric analysis of load structures proceeds using detailed regressions of hourly loads and covariance estimation with hourly prices or heat rates. However, analyzing load statistics at the hourly level for a long-term transaction is of dubious value given that hedging is always done using vanilla forwards or swaps that deliver (or settle) in the usual buckets. It is sufficient to analyze the joint behavior of the three stochastic processes

$$\bar{X}_d \equiv \left[\bar{L}_B(d), \bar{U}_B(d), p_B(d)\right] \tag{15.25}$$

by bucket, where

$$\bar{L}_B(d) \equiv \sum_{h \in B(d)} L_h \qquad \bar{U}_B(d) \equiv \frac{\sum_{h \in B(d)} L_h p_h}{\left(\sum_{h \in B(d)} L_h\right) 1/N_{B(m)} \left(\sum_{h \in B(d)} p_h\right)} \tag{15.26}$$

A characterization of $\bar{X}_d$ is sufficient to value a load transaction of the form (15.4).

We have previously detailed econometric methods for calibration and simulation of natural gas basis and heat rates, which already provide us with a characterization of the third process $p_B(d)$ earlier. Proceeding similarly, and using the modified temperature $\theta(d)$, as given in (12.22), we will use the following forms in what follows:

$$\bar{L}_B(d) = \alpha + \beta d + \sum_{k=1}^{K_L} \gamma_k \theta^k(d) + \sigma_L(d)\epsilon_L(d) \tag{15.27}$$

and

$$\bar{U}_B(d) = \sum_{k=1}^{K_U} \zeta_k \theta^k(d) + \sigma_U(d)\epsilon_U(d) \tag{15.28}$$

where the drift and polynomial degree are selected according to an out-of-sample criterion.[5] Similar parametric forms for σ_L and σ_U are used. Finally, the covariance structure between the relevant residuals $[\epsilon_L, \epsilon_U, \epsilon_{HR}]$, which is temperature-dependent, needs to be parameterized and esti-mated (the details of which are technical and beyond the scope of this discussion).

The resulting model then can be used to simulate realizations of $\vec{X}$, which is precisely the information required to value and hedge load swaps. The same approach, with minor modifications, can be used for fixed-quantity swaps discussed in the preceding section, thereby avoiding the pitfalls of static shaping coefficients. Figure 15.8 shows the regression results for $\bar{L}_B$

---

[5] The linear form of growth rate used here can be replaced with exponential drift with a minor increase in estimation complexity. Over the time scales typically used for calibration and growth rates of the order of 1 to 2 percent, the differences are typically small.

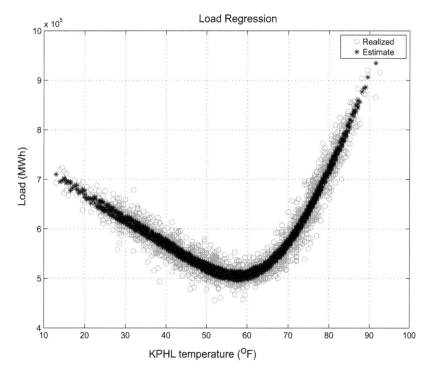

Figure 15.8. Peak load versus temperature: realized and regression.

for the peak bucket using data from 2004 through 2011. The fact that the regression estimates do not fall on a one-dimensional curve is due to drift, which turns out to be negative at roughly -0.440% annually. A negative drift is unusual and is the result of the drop in consumption due to the credit crisis. We will discuss this very important point more shortly.

Armed with the joint distribution of $\vec{X}$, we are now in a position to value and hedge load swaps. Unlike many structures, load swaps are negotiated in terms of the fixed price p_f that an acquirer of a short load position requires for assuming the obligation. This will result in an iterative aspect to valuation. Given a set of potential hedges with terminal payoffs $\vec{\mathcal{H}}$ and current market prices $\vec{p}_{\mathcal{H}}$, for a specified transaction price p_f, the minimum-variance hedge[6] for contract month m is

$$\bar{w}_* \left(p_f \right) = \operatorname{argmin} \operatorname{var} \left\{ \sum_{d \in m} \left[p_f \bar{L}_B(d) - \sum_{h \in B(d)} L_h p_h \right] + \vec{w}^\dagger \left(\vec{\mathcal{H}} - \vec{p}_{\mathcal{H}} \right) \right\}$$

(15.29)

---

[6] It is equally straightforward to use mean-variance criteria or, with a little more numerical work, any of the usual utility-maximizing criteria. In fact, use of minimum or mean variance criteria render the solution for p_f analytically tractable. We will, however, proceed using iteration for generality.

We have explicitly represented the dependence of the optimal hedge $\bar{w}^*$ on the contract price p_f. Given $\bar{w}_*(p_f)$, the midmarket price must solve

$$p_f = \Psi(p_f) \equiv \frac{E\left[\sum_d \sum_{h \in B(d)} L_h p_h - \vec{w}_*^\dagger(p_f)\left(\vec{\mathcal{H}} - \vec{p}_{\mathcal{H}}\right)\right]}{E\left[\sum_{d \in m} \bar{L}_B(d)\right]} \tag{15.30}$$

This equation for p_f can be solved iteratively given an initial estimate $p_f^{(0)}$: $p_f^{(n+1)} = \Psi\left(p_f^{(n)}\right)$.

Returning to our working problem, on the pricing date December 30, 2011, we start by setting $p_f^{(1)}$ as the fair-value peak bucket in Jul12without any hedges:

$$p_f^{(1)} = \frac{E\left(\sum_d \sum_{h \in B(d)} L_h p_h\right)}{E\left[\sum_{d \in m} \bar{L}_B(d)\right]} \tag{15.31}$$

This is our initial estimate for the midmarket fixed price p_f, which in our example is $p_f^{(1)} = \$53.07/\text{MWh}$.

We now have to decide what to include as possible hedges in $\vec{\mathcal{H}}$. Figure 15.9 shows the payoff of the load swap versus the daily bucket spot price $p_{5 \times 16}(d)$. The unhedged load swap is, to leading order, little different from

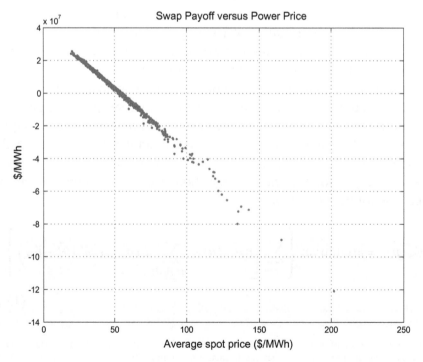

Figure 15.9. Load swap payoffs July 2012 versus power price.

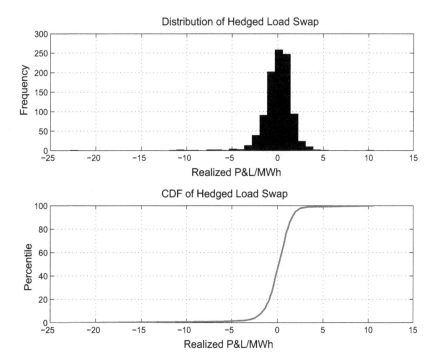

Figure 15.10. Distribution of realized payoff for the hedged load swap payoff.

a vanilla short position. Motivated by this observation, we will use only a single power swap as a hedge. The optimal hedge quantity involves purchasing 1.11 MWh of power per megawatt-hour of expected load, significantly more than the expected notional. This hedge accomplishes a lot. The standard deviation of the load swap payoff is $21.11/MWh; that of the hedged portfolio with this forward purchase was reduced to $1.73/MWh.

Iterating (15.30) with the forward hedge computed earlier yields a fixed point of $p_f = \$57.18/MWh$. This was achieved by the third iteration to within fractions of a cent. Given the forward price of $53.60/MWh, the uplift for the peak bucket in Jul12 was 1.067.

With this fixed price and associated forward hedge, the resulting distribution of monthly profit and loss (P&L) per expected MWh is shown in Figure 15.10. This distributional characterization of the residual risks is very useful in constructing bids or offers on such transactions.

We chose to use a single forward as the sole hedging instrument not only for simplicity but also because arguments for including additional instruments are not terribly compelling. Some practitioners espouse buying out-of-the-money call options in power to hedge against the large downside events that can occur at high power prices. This, of course, requires paying option premium, and in practice, the costs are typically hard to justify given the limited risk reduction achieved.

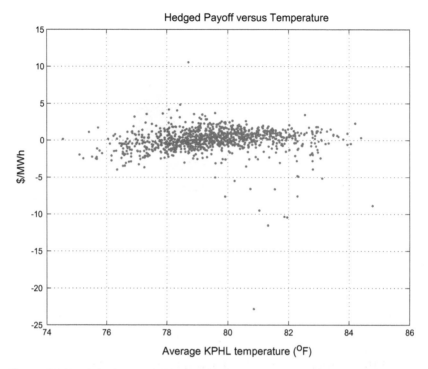

Figure 15.11. Jul 2012 monthly residual payoff versus KPHL Temperature

An alternative that is often contemplated and at times effected is the use of weather derivatives to reduce the tail risk. Figure 15.11 shows the hedged payoff distribution versus the monthly average temperature. Extreme values of the monthly temperature, high or low, are detrimental to the position. However, the impact of weather is far more dramatic at the daily time scale. Figure 15.12 shows the hedged position versus temperature on July 1, 2012. A daily temperature put at low temperatures could be a candidate for a weather derivative hedge.

An issue, however, is that weather derivatives trade in terms of cooling-degree day (CDD) and heating-degree day (HDD) indices averaged over either contract months or seasonal strips (see [Ban02]) and [JB05] for a surveys of weather markets and valuation methods). CDDs and HDDs are defined in reference to $65°F$; the CDD index on day d is defined to be $\max(\tau_d - 65, 0)$, and an HDD is $\max(65 - \tau_d, 0)$. Here τ_d is defined as the arithmetic average of the high and low daily temperatures rounded to the nearest 0.5 degree; this is the index that we have used throughout our econometric analyses. Vanilla swaps and options pay on the sum of these over the defined averaging period. Most load swap risk is in the summer months, during which τ_d is almost always well above the $65°F$ threshold implicit in CDDs. As with temperature swaps, options also pay on the difference between the cumulative CDDs and a strike. The weather structures that are

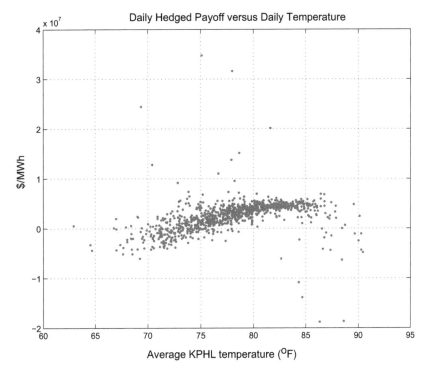

Figure 15.12. July 2012 daily residual payoff versus KPHL temperature.

most effective at hedging this residual risk require off-market strikes and daily optionality. These are not traded as vanilla over-the-counter (OTC) or listed options and require structured weather products that are typically only sold by a few reinsurance companies.

When first launching a load swap or physical load business, it is easy to overlook another aspect of the nature of the risks in these transactions. As in our working example, at inception, the contract price p_f of a load swap is generally close to the vanilla forward price. However, it is likely that sometime in the life of a multiyear transaction the prevailing forward prices will differ substantially from the contract price. This has ramifications for the risks in the transaction.

Figure 15.13 shows the standard deviation of the resulting hedged portfolio, as well as the optimal hedge ratio as a function of the ratio of the fixed contract price to the prevailing market forward price for the month p_f/F_m. The variance of the load swap payoff increases as the fixed contract price departs from the prevailing market price. The reason is simple – referring to (15.3), the economic impact of fluctuations in demand $(Q_n - \bar{Q}_n)$ is proportional to $(p_f - p_n)$. As a consequence, a heuristic estimate of the standard deviation of the hedged portfolio is $\sigma_Q |p_f - F|$, where F is the prevailing forward price. The capital requirements for these transactions demand that one account for the volatility in forward prices over the term of the transaction.

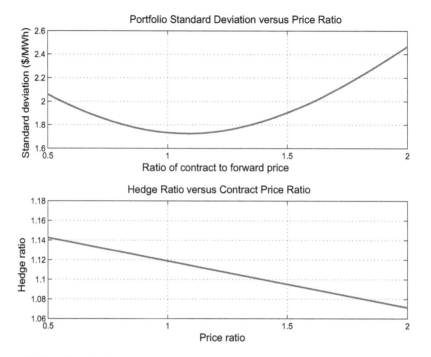

Figure 15.13. Standard deviation of the residual risk of the hedged load swap and optimal hedge ratio.

The preponderance of quantitative effort on loads swaps has been directed at the effects of load/price correlation on the time scale of days or hours. One risk that we have mentioned only fleetingly is that realized load growth can differ meaningfully from the estimates used in pricing and hedging.

Participants in power markets are accustomed to swings in demand of a few percent one way or the other, with the standard folklore being that load tends to grow in most regions at rates between 1 and 2 percent per year. Although occasional outliers have occurred, for example, Atlanta with much higher growth rates in the early 2000s (to the dismay of some suppliers who thought they were hedged), the thought of an outright drop in load growth of any meaningful magnitude was generally viewed as a remote possibility.

Global power demand had increased relentlessly for decades, even during epochs in which high oil prices reduced demand. However, for the first time in decades (recall Figure 3.34), global power demand actually decreased in much the same way that oil demand did. The 2009–2010 period was a rude awakening to the risks implicit in estimates of load growth.

The data set that we chose to use in the working example spanned the credit crisis and resulted in a negative growth rate of −0.440% percent as a result of the drop in load in the 2008–2009 time frame. However, from the perspective of mid-2008, statistics on load growth were very different.

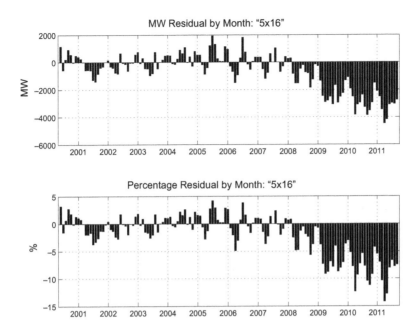

Figure 15.14. Load estimate residuals.

Figure 15.14 shows out-of-sample performance of load estimates made using the preceding regression methods, with data up to July 2008. The plots show the difference between actual load and the expected load given realized temperatures using the load calibration for PJM Classic peak load. Being fully weather-normalized, these residuals are almost solely due to changes in growth rates. The residuals from August 2008 and beyond show remarkable levels of load destruction, often exceeding 10 percent below the a priori estimate. To put this in perspective, the bursting of the tech bubble around 2001 was a drop that was brief and which averaged roughly 2 percent.

In the aftermath of the credit crisis in which this demand destruction occurred, energy prices were also falling, ultimately dropping nearly 60 percent from the highs in 2008. This meant that portfolio managers hedging estimates of expected load found themselves with a long position to the tune of approximately 10 percent, in a dramatically falling price environment. For a sense of the magnitude of the impact, a 1,000-MW load for one calendar year would experience a loss of in excess of $5 million for every 1 percent drop in expected load on the "5x16" component alone. Most load transactions span several years and involve load obligations around the clock, not just during the peak hours. To compound matters, a great deal of migration from utility service to retail aggregators (attrition) exacerbated the imbalance.

The results were felt broadly; writers of load hedges sustained large losses, as did utilities and merchants who were offsetting generation length with load shorts and retail suppliers who had hedged using standard products.

For those left standing, the relevant question is whether the macroeconomic risk inherent in load obligations could be anticipated or hedged. Reflecting on Figure 15.14, the earliest you could have hoped to unambiguously discern the drop in realized load would have been in mid-2009, at which time prices had already collapsed – the damage had been done. How this affects valuation and hedging of load obligations, aside from more cautious bids going forward, remains to be seen. Macro strategies such as buying puts on equity indices or credit protection through CDX[7] indices, which in retrospect would have worked well during this one period, would in general simply increase the risk of a portfolio. It is possible that improved structural models could yield methods by which portfolios of commodity swaps and options are insulated, at least partially, to load growth estimates. For now, the state of affairs can basically be summarized by "price conservatively."

Exotic Swaps

Load swaps are seen almost exclusively in the power markets because ISOs have been publishing reliable demand data for years. Without these historical data, the analysis required to ascribe a value to the transactions would not be possible. Other markets, notably natural gas, do not have such systematic and publicly available daily demand data. End users are at times able to provide historical usage data, and volumetric hedges are transacted based on such. However, in the absence of reliable and large historical data sets, alternatives have been constructed.

As an example, suppliers of natural gas to end users, whether utilities or retail suppliers, sustain risks that are mathematically identical to the load structures just discussed. High natural gas demand and high spot prices tend to occur at low temperatures. This has resulted in the introduction of natural gas swaps that "trigger" on a temperature level. For example, a swap with settlement in month m defined by

$$\sum_{d \in m} \mathbf{1}_{\{\tau_d \leq \tau_*\}} \max(p_d - K, 0) \tag{15.32}$$

provides protection to the supplier for spot prices levels p_d in excess of the strike if the daily temperature τ_d is below the trigger τ_*. The intent is similar to that of load swaps. All that has transpired is that demand has been replaced by temperature and the product of demand and price by the course approximation of a temperature triggered call option.

There are many variations of such structures. In the power markets in the western United States, power forwards have traded that have notional quantities indexed by temperature. The unifying feature, however, is that at

---

[7] CDX refers to indices of groups of credit default swaps compiled by Markit.

a fundamental level these structures are all amenable to analytical methods similar to those we used in the load swap setting.

Unit-Contingent Swaps

Some commonly traded power swaps and forwards have embedded volumetric risk of an altogether different nature. In these so-called unit-contigent (UC) transactions, the purchaser of power receives a prescribed percentage of output from a specific generation unit. If the unit generates, the buyer gets the power. If the unit is experiencing a forced outage, the buyer does not get the power. If the unit is derated and running at less than full output, the buyer gets the prescribed percentage of output. Hence the purchase is referred to as *unit-contigent*.[8] Unit-contigent risk is disarmingly simple to articulate but particularly virulent and difficult to hedge.

Unit-contigent swaps arise because utilities and merchant generation owners, just as producers of crude oil and natural gas, often desire to hedge the output of their generation assets over some horizon. For a baseload generator such as a nuke, the standard hedge is a vanilla swap that takes the usual form (15.3). The generator sells the expected output from the unit in a vanilla transaction and retains the risk of variations between actual output Q_n and $\bar{Q}_n$.[9]

In a unit-contigent sale, the buyer of the commodity assumes the volumetric risk. The payoff is the usual form (15.1) but from the perspective of a purchase: $Q_h (p_h - p_{\text{fixed}})$, where Q_h is the hourly output and p_{fixed} is the contract price. For large facilities such as nuclear generators, which can have capacities in excess of 1,000 MW, hedges are often effected with multiple buyers, each of whom receives a pro-rata tranche of the output.

At the time of the transaction, $p_{\text{fixed}} \lesssim F_n$; the purchase price is at a discount to the price for firm delivery because of the additional risk sustained by the buyer. As with load swaps, the questions are (1) what should the discount to firm delivery be? and (2) can the residual risk be managed?

Figure 15.15 shows the daily available capacity of a generator in upstate New York as reported by the Nuclear Regulatory Commission. This is based on daily availability and is not literally the hourly generation profile of the unit, which is usually proprietary and which exhibits hourly fluctuations

---

[8] Similar transactions occur in other contexts, from refinery output to LNG facilities. Moreover, force majeure clauses present in most physical contracts in a sense constitute a source of ubiquitous volumetric risk.

[9] The discussion that follows assumes that a UC swap is referencing a generator that is unambiguously baseload in the sense of effectively always being economical to run. For natural gas generators, in which economic dispatch is a consideration, the definition of a UC contract requires referencing a declaration of forced outage. Coal units, which were at one time considered baseload, face similar considerations now that natural gas has sporadically displaced coal generation in the stack and is likely to continue to do so.

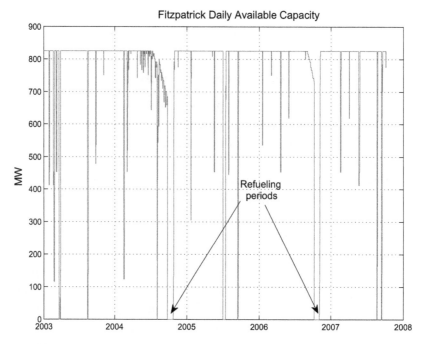

Figure 15.15. Daily available capacity for a nuclear generator (Fitzpatrick).

due to thermal-efficiency effects. Nuclear plants must refuel every eighteen months to two years, and two such refueling periods are shown. These are planned outages and explicitly accounted for in unit-contigent transactions. Most, if not all, other outages or derates were unplanned and would have affected the payoff of any unit-contigent contracts on this unit that may have existed at the time.

The typical approach to quantifying this risk involves several steps that we will only outline here:

1. Using historical data provided by the hedger, characterize the process $[\tau_n, \eta_n, \rho_n]$ econometrically, where τ denotes the arrival (starting) time process of outage events, η is the outage duration process and ρ is the fraction of nameplate capacity available during the outages.[10]
2. Estimate the impact of outages on spot prices. Typically, these contracts settle on nodal or zonal prices that are off-benchmark and closely related to the spot price that the hedger receives. This is effectively an analysis of the effect on the basis between the contract spot location and a liquid benchmark; it is presumed that benchmark prices are unchanged as a result of any individual outage event.
3. Jointly simulate the dynamics of the benchmark forward prices, usually using a risk-neutral process and the processes described in points (1) and (2).
4. Construct minimum-variance hedges using benchmark forward.

---

[10] Such modeling falls under the rubric of renewal theory in stochastic processes.

The results of such an approach are loosely analogous to the analysis used for load swaps. Unlike for load structures, however, there is not an effective law of large numbers at work. For weather-driven risk, the ACF decays on a time scale of approximately three days. Over the course of a three-year transaction, therefore, the effective sample size is of the order of several hundred. Five years of historical load data are more than enough to get reasonable estimates of the relevant statistical attributes.

For UC structures, this is simply not the case – even a decade of performance data is almost certainly inadequate for accurate estimation in point (1) in the preceding list. Changes of ownership, maintenance budgets, and operators usually render historical performance data nonstationary. Moreover, inter-temporal diversification is not particularly strong. Forced nuclear outages tend to be relatively infrequent and long in duration – usually a minimum of several days to fix the problem, and outage durations of weeks or even months are not uncommon. In some cases, a serious problem can result in months of outage.[11] The Fukushima disaster is an extreme example.

The impact of an outage can be severe depending on price level. If prices have risen considerably after the transaction date, an outage adversely affects the hedger who is now short power in a high-price environment. The opposite is also true – higher than expected availability in a lower-price environment can be similarly painful. Consider a UC contract of one-year duration for 500 MW at an initial fixed price of $100/MWh. This contract is of moderate size, consisting of approximately 4.4 million MWh or a total notional value of approximately $440 million. If energy prices dropped by 65 percent to say $35/MWh before the deal starts realizing, the uncertainty associated with actual versus expected generation is significant. Every 1 percent increase in availability results in a loss of roughly $3 million. If you had estimated expected availability at 90 percent and a diligent operator managed to achieve 95 percent for the year, the result is a loss of $15 million that could not have been hedged.

There is certainly less to discuss in the way of hedging methods for UC transactions than for load structures because of the basic attributes of the distribution of the random-quantity process Q. Buying vanilla fixed-strike options to hedge against losses due to variations in expected output is prohibitively costly. One only needs the option as insurance on the rare occasions when an outage occurs. There are only two ways to deal with UC risk. The first is diversification across units – if one UC transaction is too risky,

---

[11] A noteworthy example was provided by the Davis Besse unit in Ohio, in which corrosion in the reactor vessel head, discovered in 2002, resulted in the plant being down for approximately two years by NRC mandate to effect repairs and permit inspections. Whether events such as this impact a given unit-contingent transaction depend on the details of the contract. But the event serves as a striking reminder of the limitations of estimates using historical performance data.

many will be less risky, at least per megawatt-hour of notional. Extraordinary events such the Fukushima disaster and the subsequent shutdown of all nuclear generation in Japan exhibit the limits of diversification, but such events are rare. The biggest impediment to such an approach is simply the capital required to aggregate the risk. The second approach is outage insurance, which is offered by some reinsurers. Such transactions, however, are almost always structured with payout caps, resulting it what is effectively insurance on mezzanine risk, that is, outages of limited duration and during moderate price regimes. The buyer remains exposed to the fearsome events of long outages during unfavorable price regimes.

Conclusion

Variable-quantity risk is inherent in energy commodities markets. End users consume random quantities of refined products, natural gas, or power depending on factors ranging from temperature to macroeconomic events. Producers can experience fluctuations in production owing to weather and mechanical failures. Ultimately, someone bears these risks. Variable-quantity structures transfer this risk from one entity to another, but the methods for pricing and hedging are equally pertinent to the risk management even if the risk is inventoried at its source.

Variable-quantity structures can be grouped into two categories:

- Structures in which the typical fluctuations in the delivery quantity are driven by short-time-scale phenomena, typically weather. Load swaps fall into this category, even though the credit crisis exhibited the potential impact of long-time-scale macroeconomic effects.
  - Correlation risk is against the holder of the risk – high prices are associated with high demand, and conversely, and the impact on hedging is that the delta of the swap exceeds the expected notional.
  - The typically approach to valuation and hedging is based on econometric or structural models calibrated to historical relationships among temperature, load, and commodities prices.
  - The larger the gap between prevailing market prices from the initial transaction price, the greater the risk of the position.
- Unit-contingent transactions in which the dominant risk is mechanical failure of the unit.
  - Statistical methods for modeling outage statistics are impeded by limited historical data and the nature of the outage processes, in which low-probability and long-duration events are both the greatest risk and the hardest to estimate.
  - The structures available for hedging are limited, consisting of outage insurance contracts that provide partial coverage and typically do not protect against the tail risk of long outages in disadvantageous price environments.

Part VI
Additional Topics

Two main themes have arisen consistently in the previous chapters. The first is that energy markets are affected on short time-scales by transient variations in supply and demand and on longer time scales by macroeconomic drivers, technological innovations, and regulatory developments. The second is that many risks that commonly arise in energy markets are only partially hedgable, in some cases being altogether uncommoditized. A variety of methods were introduced in the previous chapters that provided at least partial solutions to valuation and hedging when liquidity is limited or in which the risks of a structure differ substantially from those embodied in common tradables.

In this part we begin with a discussion of risk management and control for enterprises with activities spanning numerous regional energy-trading desks, including institutions with activities across multiple asset classes. The standard risk metrics, such as value-at-risk (VaR), inevitably play a role in risk management and capital requirements. However, a topic of particular relevance to energy trading is the characterization of risks that are outside the "VaR footprint" due to either limited liquidity and price transparency in high-dimensional portfolios or uncommoditized risks such as those arising from variable notional swaps. The methods that we used to analyze risk at the level of individual transactions serve well as starting points for the development of useful metrics at the enterprise level.

We then conclude this book with a discussion of current valuation and risk-management issues in energy markets. The credit crisis of 2008–2009 and its aftermath provided an opportunity to observe the response of markets, and energy markets in particular, to a very large perturbation in the global economy. The implications from a valuation and hedging perspective are on one hand troubling but on the other a motivation for the development of improved methodologies. In addition, while commodities prices in the 2007–2009 time period were a causal result of other global economic factors, the regulatory reverberations have impacted energy markets particularly forcefully. In the last chapter of this book we survey some of the issues and open problems in energy risk management.

16

Control, Risk Metrics, and Credit

The past two decades have witnessed a significant expansion in energy markets. The number of commodities that actively trade has exploded, from a few crude oil contracts to a vibrant global market in refined products, natural gas, electricity, and coal. Daily volume and open interest have increased, and trading activity continues to extend to ever longer tenors, particularly on benchmark contracts. More recently, emissions and weather markets have entered the mix. The variety of instruments traded has also increased, with a broad array of swaps and options arising as more sophisticated hedging programs required new mechanisms to effect risk transfer. This trend could reverse in the prevailing regulatory climate. However, the benefits in this expansion in energy markets have been manifold, enabling entire industries to hedge unwanted energy exposure and facilitating the financing of asset construction and exploration.

One characteristic of the growth of energy markets is that the number of traded delivery locations has grown much more rapidly than the set of instruments that can truly be characterized as liquid; liquid in the sense of unambiguous price transparency and significant daily trading volume. Consequently, the risk profiles of many energy portfolios have become increasingly high dimensional, demanding innovative methods to organize information and requiring the design of effective risk metrics.

Many "blowups" in the history of commodities trading have occurred in the tried and true fashion – excessively large positions in ostensibly liquid markets that went the wrong way. However, it is likely that more (although less publicized) blowups have occurred as a result of large basis positions at less liquid delivery locations and tenors. Some trading desks have run afoul of regulators owing to activities that control groups failed to notice, primarily because the degrees of freedom available to traders are so large that detecting inappropriate (if not illegal) trading activity is not easily accomplished.

Standard risk metrics are useful at the level of the benchmarks or liquid trading hubs but are less effective as liquidity diminishes. Illiquid forward curves are typically marked in reference to benchmarks, with price differentials often held constant for long periods of time simply due to sporadic trading activity. If such price series are used as inputs to the calculation of standard risk metrics, the results can be seriously flawed. It is common, therefore, to map such price points to liquid benchmarks, map in the sense of using benchmark returns in lieu of the historical returns series at illiquid locations. This yields more reliable metrics but also can result in a misguided sense of comfort as the now "invisible" basis risk can fade from the attention of front office and control groups alike. It is important, therefore, to design methods to quantify the risk of these illiquid basis positions – so-called specific risks.

Most risk metrics rely on historical price series. The fulcrum of effective risk-control frameworks is accurate price data, and the logical starting point in a survey of risk measurement and controls is a discussion of how forward curves and volatility surfaces are marked and how they should be validated.

Price Integrity

The dominant consideration in the analysis and control of any portfolio is understanding how the underlying prices are constructed and whether these are consistent with observable market data or industry consensus. All other considerations are of secondary importance. Much of this burden is shouldered jointly by the risk and product control groups in collaboration with the front office.

Ensuring benchmark price integrity on a daily basis through exchange futures contract settlements for locations and tenors at which such are published is straightforward. For less-liquid positions the situation is more challenging. Typically, illiquid curves are marked on a daily basis by traders who are responsible for each particular commodity. The information that they have at their disposal is usually the following:

- Price indications on the exchange screens that, if such exist, are often incomplete in nature, for example, a one-way market for small volume.
- Daily pricing sheets in which indicative bid-offer prices are disseminated by brokers, ostensibly in an unbiased fashion. Brokers base their daily market summaries on information such as recent trades, indications, or even informal discussion. It is important to bear in mind, however, that brokers earn their living via commissions from trading activity. In the absence of genuine market activity, brokers tend to be more amenable to arguments made by their best customers.
- Historical forward and spot prices.
- Recent actual transactions at the same or closely related locations and tenors.

From this information, traders usually have their own customized spreadsheets designed to construct nonbenchmark prices, often requiring decomposition of strip pricing into monthly contract prices.

The upshot is that construction of prices from limited data is often happening on the trading desk in a manner that is commonly outside the typical modeling control framework.[1] How should an organization attempt to validate marks in, for example, a regional power swaps book that could have positions in several dozen delivery locations and buckets for tenors of up to a decade or more? The prices to which such portfolios have exposure number in the many thousands, with only a few percent on which there is consistently observable trading activity.

One method for price verification of illiquid positions is the regular auction of subsets of portfolios. If performed regularly, with no perception of a distressed sale, the resulting firm bids from counterparties is perhaps the most reliable validation of marks and models that one can obtain. However, this is rarely used in practice – a substantial amount of work is required to design portfolios which will shed light on pricing while not disrupting the management of the existing portfolio and ongoing commercial activity.

Exchange settlements are an important source of information, providing a daily value for an ever-increasing array of nonbenchmark products. This value, however, is often simply the view of the exchange because daily volume may very well have been zero for some contracts. Exchanges may clear trades, but they cannot create trading activity. Even so, exchange settlements are important – because trades clear on the exchange, settlements too far afield from "market consensus" would rapidly result in an avalanche of complaints. This form of feedback, from the market to the exchanges, serves to enhance the relevance of such settlement prices.

Another useful source of external information is provided by consensus service providers, at least for products and tenors in which an adequate number of market participants have commercial interest. The typical procedure is for participants to submit either midmarket or bid-offer pricing by contract month on a set of forward curves. Outliers are excluded, and the statistics on the remainder are calculated by the service provider. These statistics are then provided to each participant over the range of prices in which their submissions were accepted, thereby preventing a form of gaming in which clearly bogus prices are thrown into the survey simply to learn how other shops are setting prices.

---

[1] It is not uncommon for those involved in valuing a complex transaction to focus more on the mathematical aspects of the effort than on the validation of pricing inputs. The first order of business for any valuation effort is to perform due diligence on the integrity of the marks, regardless of how mundane a task this may seem to be.

The labor involved in constructing submissions to consensus providers on a large set of forward curves is substantial and is usually performed periodically, often on only a monthly basis. Consensus surveys are a useful source of information, but it is important to note that these are based on indications. In the course of daily commercial activity, if a trader consistently makes indications to counterparties or brokers but fails to transact anywhere near the quotes, word spreads, and credibility diminishes. Anonymity in consensus surveys has no such implicit reputational imperative. This allows a form of consensus to emerge, if only by iteration. If you are rejected, you can usually obtain qualitative indications as to why you were rejected, allowing you to adjust your marks to avoid rejection on the next submission. Eventually, much like the economics metaphor of "hot dog stands on a beach," everyone converges (more or less) to a stable consensus price. How much consensus prices tell you about where you could actually transact is unclear.

Despite these concerns, availability of consensus information is a dramatically better situation than when it is absent. Even in the absence of consensus marks, however, reasonable control frameworks can be constructed.

Take, for example, the situation of any product – crude oil, gasoline, natural gas – at rarely traded delivery locations and tenors. Trader marking methods are usually straightforward regressions based on either historical spreads or ratios that relate the illiquid location to a closely related liquid delivery point. A control framework should be able to detect an erroneous mark of significant magnitude. Given the high dimensionality of the risks, control groups should deploy automated comparisons of marks with historical price relationships. These can take the form of more complex calibration and simulation methods or much simpler approaches akin to those typically used by traders.

Consider, for example, two pricing hubs for power in PJM: PECO and PJM Western Hub (the benchmark). A simple method for establishing an estimate of the PECO/PJM Western Hub basis would be a regression of the form

$$\frac{p_{\text{PECO}}(d)}{P_{\text{PJM}}(d)} = \sum_{k=1}^{K} [\gamma_k \sin(2\pi kt) + \delta_k \cos(2\pi kt)] \tag{16.1}$$

where K is obtained through an out-of-sample selection method, as discussed earlier in the context of temperature. This form accommodates the likely seasonal effects of load variation. Applying such an approach using data from 2006 through 2011 yields the result shown in Figure 16.1. This ratio applied on a monthly-average basis to PJM forwards is a credible sanity check.

While purely illustrative, because PECO does in fact trade and usually appears in consensus surveys, at less liquid hubs or nodes an approach such as this might even exceed the quality of whatever analysis was behind the

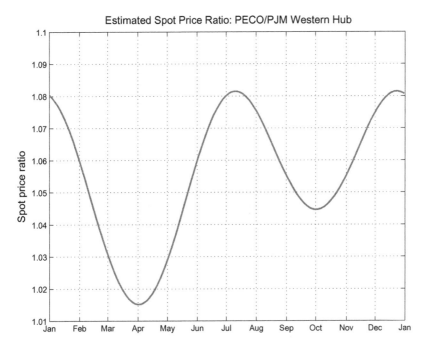

Figure 16.1. Fourier estimate of spot price ratio by time of year: PECO versus PJM Western Hub.

trader mark.[2] No claim is being made that such results would in fact be the prices at which transactions would occur. However, meaningful departures from plausible estimates can flag price anomalies and result in useful discussions.

Similar control issues pertain to volatility and correlation marks. For volatility surfaces, the situation is less onerous with respect to the number of surfaces that need to be examined – it is rare to encounter options books with exposure other than at benchmark locations or the most liquid hubs. Validation of volatility surfaces, however, has historically proven surprisingly problematic.

One of the fundamental reasons that volatility-surface anomalies are not detected is that in focusing on implied volatilities, one is examining what is effectively an integral of the underlying local volatility – the relevant underlying variable. Figure 16.2 shows a hypothetical implied volatility surface for a seasonal commodity. It is hard to see anything unusual in this surface. However, Figure 16.3 shows the local volatility surface, which essentially differentiates the term implied volatility. Anomalous behavior is visible in this surface at high strikes with the 2014–2015 winter months. Actual local

---

[2] The language used is not to imply a lack of cooperation or intelligence of the traders marking the curves. In fact, most would welcome such methods to assist in what is a very challenging task of marking a high-dimensional book. All too frequently, however, this is low on the list of front-office technological and modeling priorities.

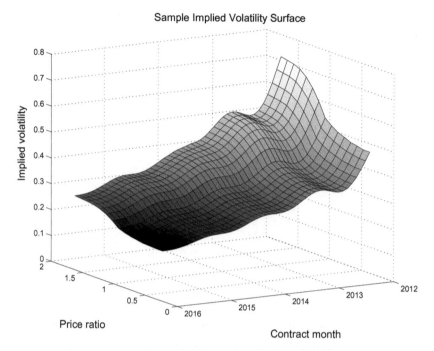

Figure 16.2. Hypothetical seasonal implied volatility surface.

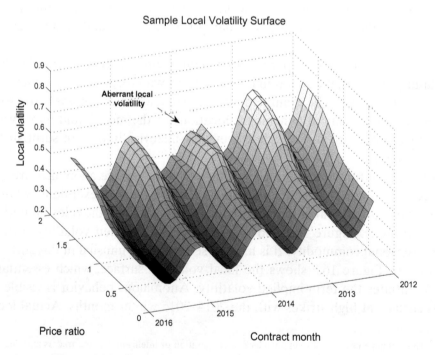

Figure 16.3. Hypothetical seasonal local volatility surface.

volatility surfaces are rarely this smooth, as we saw originally for WTI in Figure 7.10. The point, however, is that variations in "sensible" patterns are more easily discerned in local volatility space; a fact that has been alluded to more broadly in other asset classes (see, e.g., [Dup94] and [DK94]).

Risk Metrics: Context

Trading operations with any semblance of a control framework rely, to a greater or less extent, on a set of standard risk metrics designed to provide quantitative measurements of risk and capital usage.[3] Such metrics are used at all levels of the business and must be applicable broadly across all asset classes. This requires a level of generalization that can obscure large risk concentrations at low levels of a trading operation.

The most commonly used metric is value-at-risk (VaR). Given a random variable X, interpreted as the profit and loss (P&L) of a *static* portfolio over the next N trading days and a probability α, the VaR of the portfolio is the threshold θ such that the probability of a loss exceeding θ is no larger than $1 - \alpha$. Formally, this amounts to

$$\mathcal{V}_{N,\alpha}(X) \equiv \inf_{\theta} P(X < -\theta) \le 1 - \alpha \qquad (16.2)$$

where $\mathcal{V}_{N,\alpha}(X)$ is the VaR corresponding to the parameters (N, α). For example, a VaR of $10 million on a 10-day/95th percentile basis means that the P&L distribution over a ten-trading-day horizon is estimated to have no greater than a 5 percent probability of losses in excess of $10 million.

By convention, the percentile thresholds are usually 95 or 99 percent. VaR is almost always calculated and reported on short time scales, with one- and ten-day VaR being the most common. Consequently, it is often interpreted as an estimate for the losses one might sustain while attempting to unwind a portfolio of liquid positions under "normal" market conditions. This interpretation must be taken as heuristic, in that neither market depth nor transaction costs are considerations in the computation of $\mathcal{V}_{N,\alpha}$; the portfolio was assumed static.

The literature on VaR methodologies and limitations is exhaustive; see, for example, basic discussions in [Hul12] or more expansive references such as [Jor06]. VaR has known technical flaws related to its behavior under decomposition of portfolios and alternatives, and so-called coherent risk metrics have been promulgated since the 1990s and may in fact find their way into future Basel frameworks; for one of the original treatments, see [ADEH99]. At a broader level, the literature and public debate

---

[3] Even hedge funds, which often rely on customized characterizations of performance relative to capital usage, are almost always required to report standard metrics such as VaR to investors.

are replete with criticism of the usage of VaR as a primary metric for portfolio risk, largely centered on two issues: the ability to accurately estimate low-frequency, high-impact events and the inability to obtain credible price series for the large number of instruments comprising a typical portfolio.

Limitations on the viability of estimating the probability of "tail" events is seen by many as warranting the dismissal of VaR as a relevant risk metric (see [Tal07] for an example of such a critique). Estimation of, say, the first percentile of a distribution requires *large* and *stationary* data sets. In the context of rapidly evolving and sporadically turbulent markets, *large* and *stationary* are, for all practical purposes, mutually exclusive criteria. Moreover, knowing a loss percentile tells you little about the magnitude of the values that exceed the threshold. Finally, as has been known since the inception of modern financial markets, events can occur that have not occurred in the past. Usually (if not always), subsets of market participants are anticipating and trading on forecasts of an imminent, unprecedented event (hedge funds who made fortunes on the credit crisis are an example), and their views, while not actively advertised, are often known and visible to the market broadly. These contrarian views, when discerned, should spawn stress tests that complement statistical metrics and partially remedy their shortcomings.

The second issue is that the breadth of instruments over which one requires returns series to calculate VaR is often extremely large. As a result, many asset prices are "mapped" to liquid benchmarks, reducing the dimensionality of the calculations and avoiding questionable price series. Such mappings, by construction, eliminate a set of basis risks, making it very easy to lose sight of them. Unusual circumstances can cause these seemingly benign (and certainly optically risk-free) basis positions to turn ugly, as various periods of market turbulence have demonstrated.[4] Some purists might argue that the precise recorded history of all marks should be used in the calculation of generic risk metrics, especially in an era where an increasing number of traded instruments are cleared. This notion is flawed and can result in random distortions in the results. Consider the implications of Figure 16.4, which shows the price series for the July 2011 PJM Western Hub contract and a synthetic illiquid zonal price in the top plot. The lower plot shows the change in the basis between the zonal and hub prices.

Although only a caricature, basis marks for illiquid delivery locations are qualitatively of this form – infrequent intervals of clustered trading or price-framing activity. Rather than improving matters, throwing such series into algorithms predicated on daily liquid marks distorts the results. Portfolio VaR can change owing to minor perturbations of when the basis-price

---

[4] The shareholder report on UBS's write-downs [AG08] is a very interesting document on the failings of basic risk management and which comments on the mapping of illiquid credit spreads to liquid proxies at UBS without additional processes in place to monitor such risks.

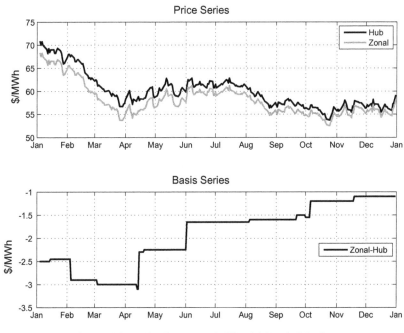

Figure 16.4. Caricature of Illiquid Basis Marks.

changes "occurred" – on what exact day the trader talked to the right broker and concluded that there was enough information to warrant a change in the mark. Collapsing illiquid exposures onto liquid benchmarks results in more useful characterizations of short-time-scale risks but also necessitates separate and rigorous treatment of the residual basis risks. Mapping illiquid risks to benchmarks does not eliminate basis risk; it just makes it easy to ignore.

The concept of VaR in energy is similar to that in any asset class. However, for portfolios with a preponderance of highly illiquid positions, VaR requires a different interpretation: it is an estimate of the potential change in the present value of the portfolio over a time horizon in which *benchmark* exposures could be liquidated. A full unwind of a complex energy portfolio can take months, if not years, and risk metrics for such portfolios require a distinctly different approach than rote application of VaR.

There are several aspects of the typical energy portfolio that particularly limit the value of standard risk metrics and motivate supplementary approaches to characterizing risk:

- High-dimensional risk profiles are common in energy trading, and the illiquid nature of many (often the substantial majority) of forward curves can severely limit VaR as a mechanism for detecting risk concentrations or estimating capital usage.
- The seasonality inherent in the price dynamics of many energy markets complicates matters. This is especially true for enterprises such as banks, with activities that span multiple asset classes, most of which are devoid of seasonal structure.

- Energy portfolios often have exposure to uncommoditized risks that, even when optimally hedged, involve realizing residual payoffs that are quasi-stationary as opposed to diffusive in nature. The residual risks in load structures and unit-contingent transactions are good examples. Additional risk metrics are required which are more suited to such "actuarial" risks.

The characteristic time scales for fundamental drivers such as temperature and infrastructure failure are short, and as a result, years of spot price data constitute a large sample from which to make estimates of the distribution of future P&L resulting from holding an illiquid position to maturity. This is not to say that outliers, dislocations at variance with such estimates, cannot occur. However, used properly, spot data can vastly improve the quality of the metrics being applied to illiquid positions.

We will proceed in two stages, starting with a review of standard methods for calculating VaR, with a focus on issues unique to energy portfolios. Our discussions here would pertain equally to alternatives, such as coherent risk measures. We will then discuss approaches to developing metrics that are pertinent to nonbenchmark price exposures that cannot be readily captured using standard methods.

Risk metrics at the enterprise level are typically discussed in the context of large portfolios and trading operations – it is, after all, a broad issue. Breadth, however, often results in an element (if not an excess) of abstraction, and there is an imperative that arises when one works through how specific trades should be handled. This is the tack that we will follow using a single specific trade to illustrate the key points.

Working Example

Quantify the risks of an Algonquin City Gate (ALCG) natural gas daily swap as of valuation date December 30, 2011:

- Contract term: November 2012 through March 2013.
- Notional: $N = 4$ lots per day.
- Natural gas reference price: Algonquin City Gate (ALCG) Gas Daily spot price.
- Strike: $K = \$6.00/\text{MMBtu}$.

The swap has a daily payoff of

$$\pi(d) \equiv N[p(d) - K] \tag{16.3}$$

where $p(d)$ is the ALGC spot price. Both ALGC and TETM3 , to which it is highly correlated, manifest high spot volatility in the winter months.

The reason that a discussion of such a specific trade warrants a place in a chapter on enterprise risk is that it spans the central issues. ALCG falls (arguably) into the set of delivery locations that are illiquid and without the daily forward marks that would render it amenable to standard VaR treatment.[5] Analysis of this trade requires that we extract benchmark price risk from the position in order to calculate a meaningful VaR and subsequently characterize the nonbenchmark residual risks of the position.

Risk Metrics: Liquid Price Risk

Value-at-risk (VaR) is the workhorse metric for liquid risks. While the metric is unambiguously defined in (16.2), in practice, a number of estimation methods are used. These are usually classified according to (1) the method of generating the price change distributions and (2) the method of computing the change in the portfolio value given a change in prices.

Most methods for generating the distributions of returns fall into one of two categories:

- *Parametric.* This approach is predicated on a parametric form for returns processes of the assets in question. Often returns are assumed to be multivariate normal random variables, an assumption made solely for convenience since all subsequent calculations are based on a returns covariance matrix.[6] Nonnormal parametric forms also have been espoused (see, e.g., discussion of MVAR in [Zan96] and [BPC09]), although the increased implementation challenges make such methods less commonly used.
- *Historical.* In this method, historical returns over a prescribed range, for example, the past five years, define the distribution of returns. Although this approach is minimalist in mathematical sophistication, it does have the merit of being easily validated and is more likely to generate the extreme returns observed empirically than would the normal parametric approach.

The second classification relates to the method of computing the response of portfolio value to a given set of price changes, with the typical dichotomy being

- *Taylor series.* Given the current value of the portfolio $V(t)$, as well as a set of Greeks, the change in value over a time increment Δt is approximated by

$$V(t+\Delta t) = V(t) + \frac{\partial V}{\partial t}\Delta t + \nabla_{\vec{X}}V\Delta\vec{X} + \frac{1}{2}\Delta\vec{X}^{\dagger}\mathcal{H}_{\vec{X}}(V)\Delta\vec{X} \qquad (16.4)$$

where X are the dynamic risk variables, $\nabla_{\vec{X}}V$ is the gradient (linear) response of V to the risk variables, and $\mathcal{H}_{\vec{X}}(V)$ is the Hessian (second-order derivatives). This last term is required to handle the convexity in options positions.
- *Exact.* For the new set of risk variables, the exact change in value $V(t+\Delta, \vec{X}_{t+\Delta}) - V(t, \vec{X}_t)$ is computed.

---

[5] There is an element of judgment here because ALCG has witnessed increasing trading activity in recent years. If only for the purpose of exposition, we will assume that ALCG is not amenable to direct VaR analysis.

[6] This method is often referred to as the *variance-covariance method* for this reason.

All four combinations of these approaches are used in practice. In the case of parametric dynamics and Taylor-series valuation, the results can often be computed in closed form.[7] This tractability is accompanied by a significant loss of relevance because the probability of large returns is usually underestimated, and Taylor series can yield poor approximations for the large returns that substantively affect the value of $\mathcal{V}_{N,\alpha}(X)$. See [Jor06] for a more extensive comparison of methodologies and backtesting methods.

Application of these methods to energy portfolios is functionally similar to that of other asset classes with two substantial differences: (1) seasonality in price dynamics, and (2) the preponderance of high-dimensional illiquid positions.

While seasonality in price dynamics is particularly challenging for entities such as banks, which trade in multiple asset classes, it cannot be ignored. Recall the seasonality in returns volatility, both by delivery month and for a rolling calendar strip, shown in Figures 5.19 and 5.20. Natural gas returns distributions at similar tenors are statistically of higher variance when viewed from the winter in comparison with the shoulder months of April and October. To produce reliable results, VaR calculations must include such effects.

An organization that trades purely energy can handle seasonality in a straightforward fashion simply by using historical data or covariances estimated from such centered at the time of calculation. On a given date t, the returns used for estimation can be restricted to intervals $[t - W, t]$, $[t - 1 - W, t - 1 + W]$ through $[t - N - W, t - N + W]$, where N is the historical date range, and W is an estimation window, usually of order one month in duration. Any estimation or historical simulation is using returns history from the appropriate time of the year – in December historical returns "near" December are used to obtain a returns distribution.

Financial institutions need to calculate risk metrics across a broad array of asset classes, most of which are nonseasonal in nature. Such institutions have historically used contiguous data sets given the lack of seasonal structure in most asset classes. This clearly disqualifies the simple method of using subsets of historical data.

A common solution to this problem is equivalent to that used to modify standard PCA for seasonal time series in (5.13). This procedure involves estimating a local volatility $s[\theta(t)]$ using rolling nearby contracts or strips, where $\theta(t)$ denotes the fraction of year corresponding to date t. We saw in Chapter 5 that the impact on the spectrum and factors can be small; however, the seasonality in volatility is nontrivial. The estimated seasonal local volatility is then used to rescale historical returns for the purpose of calculating VaR

---

[7] Many use the term *parametric VaR* to mean exactly this situation. In addition, using only the linear terms in tandem with normal returns, the so-called delta-normal method, is analytically tractable.

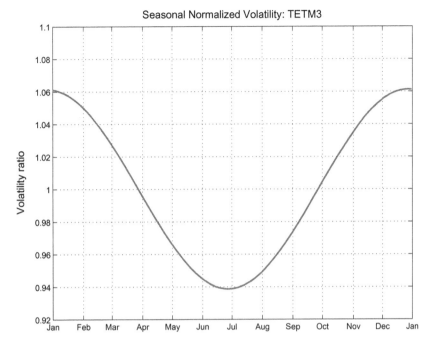

Figure 16.5. Seasonality in TETM3 returns volatility.

on the current date t. For example, the historical return $r(t_n, T)$ on day t_n is scaled by the ratio of the "current" local volatility $s(t)$ to the local volatility $s(t_n)$ on t_n:

$$\tilde{r}(t_n, T) = \frac{s[\theta(t)]}{s[\theta(t_n)]} r(t_n, T) \tag{16.5}$$

which is then used in VaR calculations.

Figure 16.5 shows a Fourier estimate for the realized volatility of the first thirty-six nearby contracts of TETM3 displayed over a single calendar year. We will use this profile later in our working problem.

Illiquid curves have embedded benchmark price risk, which is usually the dominant driver of daily P&L. To quantify this risk, the exposure, namely, the change in value of an illiquid position resulting from changes in the related benchmark price, must be estimated. Recall the concept of the risk hierarchy described in Chapter 6, represented pictorially in Figure 6.11. Such hierarchies are designed, in large part, based on the mechanics of how spreads trade.[8]

Figure 16.6 is a graphic representation of a sample risk hierarchy in the Northeast natural gas and power metamarket, with NYMEX natural gas (NG) futures at the apex as the most liquid benchmark. Liquidity is coarsely

---

[8] One can certainly envision statistical algorithms to automatically construct such hierarchies, but market mechanics is an important element of a useful design. Correlation analysis comes into play to "break the tie" if there are ambiguities in the assignment of a location to a parent in the tree.

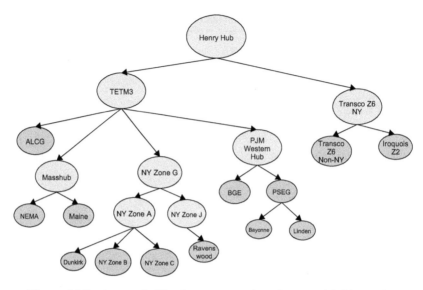

Figure 16.6. A sample Northeast natural gas/power risk hierarchy.

represented by the size of the node – those in light shading have adequate
liquidity to qualify as curves to which standard VaR metrics apply. The
nature of the hierarchy can change with tenor – at long tenors the set of
liquid benchmarks is smaller.

To compute VaR for a portfolio with exposures on such a hierarchy, one
needs to infer the value change of the positions at each illiquid node, given
a set of returns at the benchmark nodes. The typical approach is the simple
one: the forward curve at the illiquid node (ALGC in our working problem) will sustain the same returns as the location to which it is mapped
(TETM3) in VaR calculations. Although easy to implement, simply mapping
locational returns ignores the effects of important nonlinearities. Recall the
relationships shown in Figures 6.5 and 6.10. If these nonlinearities can result
in noticeable effects on hedge ratios, as we saw in Chapter 6, they should
certainly be included in VaR calculations, given that it is the large returns
that affect VaR results.

There are two situations that can arise – the first being when there is adequate historical forward data to facilitate regressions and the second being
when there is not, and spot data constitute the only information available?

In the first situation, regression results can be used to calculate VaR by
propagating the price change at the benchmark nodes to illiquid nodes.
Using the notation of Chapter 6, and denoting the illiquid node by $\mathcal{I}$ and
its parent in the hierarchy by $\pi(\mathcal{I})$, regressions relate the forward price $F_{\mathcal{I}}$
to that of its parent $F_{\pi(\mathcal{I})}$. For example, if $\mathcal{I}$ corresponds to PSEG, the parent $\pi(\mathcal{I})$ is PJM Western Hub. Regressions relate PSEG forward prices
by contract month to those of the regional benchmark for power. These

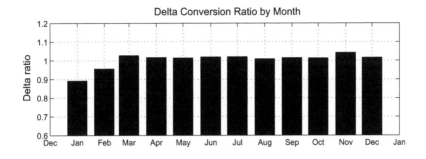

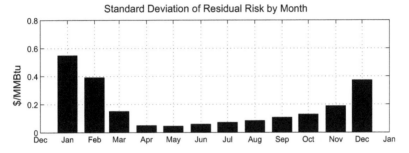

Figure 16.7. Basis swap equivalent TETM3 delta.

relationships take forms similar to those shown in (6.9):

$$F_{\mathcal{I}} = \Phi_{\mathcal{I}}\left(F_{\pi(\mathcal{I})}\right) + \epsilon_{\mathcal{I}} \qquad (16.6)$$

VaR is then calculated using any of the methods discussed in the preceding section.

In the absence of forward price regressions, the situation is more challenging. Here the methods developed earlier in the context of basis options in Chapter 12 and for tolls in Chapter 14 are useful. Designing variance-minimizing hedges for the positions at an illiquid node using swaps and options at the nearest liquid node yields the equivalent benchmark exposure. This is the approach we will work through now for the ALCG swap in our working problem.

The closest liquid node to ALCG in the risk hierarchy is TETM3, which will be the basis for a VaR calculation. Regressing each spot price process, as in (12.20) and (12.21), yields residuals that can be jointly simulated. The result is the distribution of $\vec{\zeta}(d) \equiv [\tau(d), p_{\mathrm{HH}}(d), p_{\mathrm{TETM3}}(d), p_{\mathrm{ALGC}}(d)]$, where τ denotes the temperature at KBOS in Boston. From this we can obtain the optimal TETM3 hedges for the ALCG swap payoff (16.3).

Figure 16.7 shows the TETM3 delta of the basis swap by contract month in the top plot. These are the (unsigned) volumes of TETM3 swaps that minimize the variance of ALCG swaps per MMBtu and by contract month. The lower plot shows the standard deviation of the residual portfolio payoff with such hedges in place.

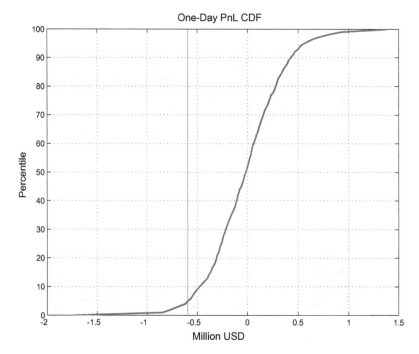

Figure 16.8. Basis swap one-day P&L distribution function and 5th percentile.

The delta-equivalent exposures at TETM3 of the ALCG swap is what we need to calculate VaR. The procedure is as follows:

- Calculate TETM3 nearby returns for the five-year period 2007 through 2011.[9]
- Use the profile in Figure 16.5 to normalize the returns relative to the pricing date as per (16.5).
- Apply these nearby returns to the individual contract months in the structure, using the deltas in Figure 16.7 to compute the change in value.

When applied to the basis swap, the result is a distribution of one-day P&L shown in Figure 16.8. The one-day 95 percent VaR of −600,000 is also shown.

What this procedure accomplished was a projection of the ALCG basis swap risk onto the liquid TETM3 node of the hierarchy, allowing the embedded benchmark risk to be handled as any other. Moreover, this approach applies to a broader set of structures than merely swaps. Although we will not address vega risk here, the principle is identical. The method of hedge construction used to obtain the results in Table 12.1 for basis options applies generally, and vega exposures are aggregated in the same way as forward price exposures. More general structures such as tolls and load swaps are

---

[9] Here we are rolling each contract fifteen business days before the contract month, which allows diversified VaR results to be calculated for a variety of energy commodities all of which expire after this roll date.

also amenable to the simulation-based methods for computing equivalent benchmark exposures.

Hierarchical representations and regression relationships are pertinent to other commodity groups. Bunker fuel delivered in New Orleans might be mapped to fuel oil (3 percent sulfur), which would then link to fuel oil at New York Harbor, which itself would then be mapped to the Brent futures contract. Similar constructs exist naturally in international crude products markets and coal markets. The concept is broadly applicable.

Whether forward or spot price regressions are used, the idea is the same: use historical relationships, which are often nonlinear, to reduce portfolio risks to equivalent exposures at the liquid price points. This avoids the distortions due to the sporadic nature of price changes that haunt the less liquid nodes and is an improvement on the direct linear mapping of returns, yielding more realistic estimates of the potential losses due to *benchmark* price moves.

Risk Metrics: Illiquid Positions

Illiquid exposures, whether originating from simple basis trades or exotic structures with uncommoditized risks, have embedded benchmark price risk. Once these are neutralized, the residual risks to the portfolio are outside the VaR paradigm. The remaining task is to say something useful about these residual risks, often referred to as *specific risks*.

The preceding methodology yielded (ostensibly) stationary residuals that can be modeled through any of a variety of time-series methods. The statistical attributes of these residuals characterize the P&L distribution of holding the illiquid position to termination. Figure 16.9 shows the distribution of the hedge slippage of the entire ALCG swap obtained by applying the benchmark hedges and calculating the distribution of the cumulative cash flows of the hedged position.[10]

This approach of constructing optimal hedges and then computing the statistical attributes of the residual risk applies just as easily to uncommoditized risks. For example, the PJM Western versus PJM Classic load swap analyzed in Chapter 15 yielded a PJM "5x16" Jul12 exposure of 1.11 for each MWh of expected load. This effectively projected the load swap risk profile onto the vanilla product on which VaR analysis is legitimately performed. The residual risks, shown in Figure 15.10, are analogous to those in Figure 16.9; there is no difference in interpretation or utility of the results.

---

[10] These approaches do not attempt to account for the possibility of an unwind sometime during the life of the position. While there may arise opportunities to hedge at favorable levels, attempting to include such dynamic management in risk metrics is laden with modeling assumptions and computational difficulties.

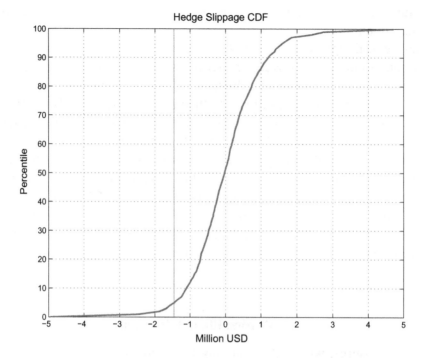

Figure 16.9. Residual basis swap risk and 5th percentile.

To fully implement the preceding methods, all nodes of the risk hierarchy must be linked via forward price regressions or joint distributions of spot prices and some objective method for hedge construction (e.g., minimum variance). This may seem like a daunting task. On the other hand, it would not be unreasonable to view such analysis as a prerequisite for even entering into an illiquid exposure.

Credit Risk

The risk associated with credit exposure is ubiquitous. Managing credit risk in energy portfolios is in some ways more challenging than for other asset classes for many of the same reasons that pertained to valuation and hedging of price risk. High volatility of the underlying price processes requires more frequent rebalancing of credit hedges in a market in which liquidity is limited. Moreover, the nature of commonly occurring credit support structures can complicate the assessment of credit exposure.

Credit risk affects all the transactions that we have discussed in the previous chapters without exception. It is tempting to think of spot purchases or cleared transactions as free of credit risk, but this is not so. Spot purchases of a commodity involve a time differential between the delivery of the commodity and ultimate payment. Typically, the physical commodity is delivered first, with cash payment from the buyer transpiring a few days or weeks later. The amount of this cash obligation is a receivable risk, often referred to as *delivered-not-paid* (DNP). DNP is a short-term credit risk but often of high notional exposure. For example, a physical contract for 100 MW (a mere two contracts) of on-peak power over a single contract month involves delivery of roughly 35,000 MWh of power. At a spot price of say $50/MWh, this relatively small position results in almost $2 million of DNP credit exposure, payment for which usually occurs roughly two weeks into the following month. The seller is taking this credit risk.

Clearing trades on exchanges definitely mitigates credit risk to a considerable degree. However, the centralized clearing of trades results in exposures, presumed to be quite small, to the solvency of the exchanges and their clearing members. Although not seriously contemplated as a risk on most (if any) credit desks, in a world of multiple exchanges with an increasing percentage of total transaction volume being cleared, credit risk to exchanges will likely be of greater concern in the future.

The real action on the credit front is the risk managed by the credit desks, so-called credit-valuation-adjustment (CVA) groups. The purpose of the CVA desks is to value and manage the credit risk inherent in term bilateral transactions. Bilateral trading is governed by ISDA[11] master agreements and credit-support annexes (CSAs), including specific forms for power and natural gas trading.[12] These contracts define the general terms applicable to all OTC transactions between two counterparties, addressing in particular

- *Margining thresholds.* The present-value thresholds beyond which a counterparty must post margin. If the value of the portfolio with the given counterparty exceeds the threshold, the differential must be posted as collateral of a specified form, which can include cash, securities, or letters of credit. Credit downgrades can result in changes in thresholds and increased collateral posting requirements.[13]
- *Netting.* The terms that define whether or not exposures between different legal entities under the same corporate umbrella are netted – that is, portfolio present values are summed. Netting is a critical factor in determining credit exposure because it reduces credit risk; in the absence of netting provisions, potentially offsetting exposures remain between the two counterparties.[14]

---

[11] International Swaps and Derivatives Association

[12] These include Edison Electric Institute (EEI) master netting agreements, referred to as EEIs, for power and North American Energy Standards Board contracts for natural gas.

[13] A notorious example of failure to properly compute the exposure to potential collateral requirements due to downgrades was provided by Constellation Energy Group, which in 2008 was obliged to announce that exposure to collateral calls in the event of downgrade was roughly double what had previously been communicated to investors. This announcement had meaningful impacts on ratings, stock price, and managerial structure.

[14] The Lehman default illustrates the relevance of netting. Lehman Brothers Holdings, Inc., filed for bankruptcy protection on September 15, 2008. Lehman's energy trading subsidiary Eagle Energy Partners filed a few days later. Both the time lag and a lack of netting between entities made the energy aspect of the Lehman event particularly complex. Offsetting exposures constituted separate claims, and offsetting positions were terminated on different days, complicating risk management and doubling the task of assessing unwind and replacement-cost damages.

- *Events of default or termination.* The definition of what occurrences constitute failure to adhere to the terms of a trade or set of trades. These can include events spanning outright bankruptcy filing, failure to make contractual payments or delivery as per terms of an individual contract, credit downgrades, or specific criteria related to tax or regulatory events. Often included are cross-default and cross-acceleration provisions, which allow the holder of one side of a trade to declare a counterparty in default as a result of the counterparty's failure to adhere to terms of a trade with another (third) counterparty.
- *Close-out provisions.* In the event of default or termination, the protocol by which trades with the defaulting counterparty are terminated and replaced in the market and the manner in which economic costs of such termination and replacement are calculated.
- *Hierarchy.* The position (seniority) of claims in the capital structure of the defaulting counterparty.

Managing credit portfolios involves valuation and hedging of both credit risk and commodity price risk. Moreover, this has to be done individually for each counterparty. Across asset classes, the basic information required to characterize the credit risk of a counterparty are

- *Portfolio value.* The value of the current portfolio $V(t,\vec{X}_t)$ for any given time t and underlying risk factors $\vec{X}_t$. For example, the value of a single swap on a given contract month depends on the forward price for that month and the associated discount factor; these two factors comprise $\vec{X}_t$ in this case. The credit exposure to a swap depends on the implied volatilities of the underlying in order to model the future potential exposure.
- *Margining provisions.* The terms defining the collateral posting requirements of the counterparty, often defined by two thresholds, $L < C_{\max}$, with the collateral requirement at time t being

$$\min\left\{\max\left[V(t,\vec{X}_t)-L,0\right],C_{\max}\right\} \tag{16.7}$$

This means that the counterparty does not have to post collateral until an exposure exceeds the lower threshold L, with the total posting capped at $C_{\max}$. Credit exposure, as a function of V_t, increases to L, remains flat up to $L+C_{\max}$, and then increases linearly beyond this cap. These levels can be dependent on credit rating, becoming more onerous as downgrades occur. Margining substantially reduces credit exposure. In the absence of thresholds, counterparties post collateral on the entire exposure (*dollar-for-dollar*), and credit risk is reduced to replacement costs of a transaction if a counterparty defaults, which is usually comprised of a one-day price move and bid-offer spread.

The exposure implied by (16.7) is the uncollateralized residual:

$$\tilde{V}_t \equiv \begin{cases} 0 & \text{if } V_t \leq 0 \\ V_t & \text{if } 0 < V_t \leq L \\ L & \text{if } L < V_t \leq L+C_{\max} \\ V-C_{\max} & \text{if } L+C\text{max} < V_t \end{cases} \tag{16.8}$$

which is always nonnegative. The cost of the associated credit exposure is

$$C_t \equiv \tilde{E}\left[d(t,\tau)\left(\tilde{V}_\tau - R_\tau\right)\mathbf{1}_{t \le \tau \le T_*}\,\middle|\,\mathcal{F}_t\right] \tag{16.9}$$

where τ is the default time, $d()$ is the discount factor, and T_* is the maximum tenor on which exposure to the counterparty exists. R_τ is the recovery on default, which is bounded by V_τ (you cannot recover more than your exposure) and in most cases is simply a percentage of the exposure V_τ. However, in general, R_τ can depend on not just $V(\tau, \vec{X}_\tau)$ but also on the underlying market prices, which are functions of $\vec{X}_\tau$. This situation arises when credit support is provided by liens on assets owned by the counterparty. For example, a producer may provide a lien on a set of oil and natural gas fields to a consortium of dealers. This adds a degree of complexity to valuation and management of the position given the dependence of the value of the collateral on the underlying risk factors.

Evaluating (16.9) requires a model for the joint distribution of $\left[\tau, \vec{X}_\tau\right]$. Methods for construction of such models vary in sophistication; for surveys, see, for example, Cossin and Pirotte [CP01] or Schönbucher [Sch03]. In practice, the assumption that τ is uncorrelated with $\vec{X}$ is extremely common because of the resulting decrease in complexity of the calculation. Under this assumption, (16.9) becomes

$$C_t = \tilde{E}\left[\int_t^{T_*} \lambda(\tau)d(t,\tau)(V_\tau - R_\tau)\,d\tau\right] \tag{16.10}$$

where $\lambda(\tau)$ is the hazard rate.[15] The hazard rate $\lambda()$ is generally obtained from the market price of traded credit instruments, particularly credit-default swaps (CDS), by bootstrapping or similar yield-curve construction algorithms.

Credit-default swaps are the primary mechanisms for hedging credit risk. While CDS mechanics are laden with details, the basic structure is as follows[16]:

• The buyer of credit protection pays quarterly coupons to the seller of credit protection until the time of default τ, at which point the coupon accrued from the last payment to τ is paid to the seller and coupon payments cease. Since 2009, standard CDS contracts have coupon payments on a fixed grid (e.g., 100 or 500 basis points), with the difference from market value paid in the form of an up-front payment between buyer and seller.

---

[15] Formally, the probability that the default time τ has not occurred by time $t+s$, viewed from the current time t, is $P(\tau > t+s|\mathcal{F}_t) = e^{-\int_t^{t+s} \lambda(u)\,du}$.

[16] Details can be found in a variety of industry surveys. See, for example, [SGHSA10], as well as the standard references such as [Hul12, CP01, Sch03].

- If a credit event, as defined in the CDS contract, occurs during the term of the CDS ($0 < \tau < T$, where T is the tenor of the CDS), the seller pays the par value of a reference asset (usually a bond), and the buyer delivers the bond to the seller. This is referred to as *physical settlement*. In the case of *financial settlement*, the seller of protection pays the buyer the difference between the par value and the recovery amount R for the reference asset, where R is determined by procedures articulated in the terms of the contract.

Credit-default swaps trade at quarterly tenors, with liquidity typically concentrated on the five-year instrument. Given the hazard rate $\lambda()$, evaluation of (16.10) is usually accomplished by simulation of the risk factors $\vec{X}$ relevant to the exposure, often using the same models employed for basic derivatives valuation. The resulting value function C_t has the usual commodity Greeks as well as exposures to the hazard rate $\lambda(\cdot)$ or, equivalently, the strip of CDS contracts.

Although the essential aspects of valuing and hedging are common across asset classes, managing credit risk in energy portfolios faces certain unique challenges. These include the difficulties in assessing the impact of the assumption of no correlation between the default time τ and the underlying commodity price processes, the impact of high price volatility on hedging structures of the form (16.10), and limited or nonexistent liquidity in CDS for many counterparties.

The assumption of uncorrelated default times τ and price processes causes a good deal of debate on energy desks, typically framed in terms of right-way or wrong-way risk. *Right-way risk* refers to a negative correlation between hazard rates $\lambda()$ and the portfolio exposure $\tilde{V}_t$ in (16.8); *wrong-way risk* refers to a positive correlation. If a credit risk is right-way, default is more likely to occur when exposures are small, and the value of the credit exposure will be lower than the value obtained from (16.10) under the zero-correlation assumption.

The train of thought on this issue is often simplistic – if a producer is hedging, the dealer is buying the commodity from the producer at a fixed price. The dealer is long. Exposure to the producer increases if prices increase, but because the producer is inherently long the commodity, the credit risk of the producer "must surely decrease if prices increase." This would suggest that changes in hazard rate λ are negatively correlated with the price returns of the relevant commodity. For consumers, the opposite should be the case. If a dealer is selling energy to a producer of steel, aluminum, or petrochemicals, which require large quantities of energy, credit exposure arises in a falling price environment, which, at least at a simplistic level, should benefit such consumers of energy.

Historical CDS spreads shed little light on this matter. Table 16.1 shows the correlation between changes in five-year CDS spreads versus returns of rolling calendar strips for Henry Hub natural gas and WTI futures over

Table 16.1. *Correlation between CDS Spread Changes and*
1st Cal Strip Fuel Returns

Name	Apache	Chesapeake	Alcoa	Delta Airlines
NG	−0.10	−0.19	−0.23	—
WTI	−0.25	−0.32	−0.40	−0.08

ten-trading-day intervals from January 2007 to December 2012.[17] Natural
gas was excluded from the Delta Airlines analysis because airlines do not
burn natural gas. The first two series, which correspond to producers, look
promising because credit spreads appear to decrease with increasing fuel
prices. However, the energy consumers Alcoa and Delta Airlines do not
show the expected response. This is far from an exhaustive study of the matter, but the point is that simple arguments such as these are compromised by
macroeconomic risks. Rapid and substantial decreases in fuel prices, such
as witnessed in late 2008, usually coincide with weak global macroeconomic
outlooks, which tend to hit producers of metals and transportation sectors
particularly hard.

Direct analysis of CDS spreads is compromised by the fact that default is
a low-probability event for all but the weakest credits, rendering the impact
of fuel prices difficult to detect. Equity prices can exhibit more discernible
responses to energy prices. Figure 16.10 shows the residuals resulting from
regressions of the form

$$p_{\text{Name}}(d) = \alpha + \beta p_{\text{SPY}}(d) + \epsilon(d) \tag{16.11}$$

over the same date range, with p_{Name} corresponding to three individual
equity or index prices, as labeled, and with p_{SPY} corresponding to the S&P
500 ETF. This standard regression is intended to remove the market risk factor represented by SPY, and the residuals are scattered against the twelfth
WTI nearby; the twelfth nearby was used solely as a representation of
North American oil prices, avoiding idiosyncracies of near-dated contracts,
especially in light of the inventory effects discussed in Chapter 3.

The first equity price, XLE, is an ETF comprised of a collection of energy-
related equities, spanning majors, such as Exxon Mobil and Chevron, to
energy logistics and services companies such as Schlumberger. Note that
XLE outperforms the broader index as oil prices increase. The same occurs
for Apache (APA), a North American oil and natural gas producer. Representing the short side, Delta Airlines (DAL) shows an obvious short
exposure to energy prices relative to SPY.

---

[17] Delta airlines statistics ran from Q4 2007 to December 2012.

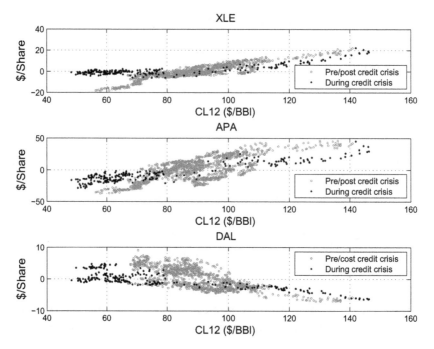

Figure 16.10. Equity price residuals versus WTI (2007–2012), with points in the interval July 2008 to June 2009 highlighted.

The structure of the results in Figure 16.10 suggests an element of right-way risk – energy producers tend not to go bankrupt in an increasing energy price environment. The impact of macroeconomic effects is visible in the During Credit Crisis series. The broader energy index and APA, to a somewhat lesser extent, presumably benefit from a "flight to quality," given the unambiguous nature of hydrocarbon reserves in contrast to fiat currency. For the airline, the situation was the opposite – falling energy prices of the magnitude witnessed in the 2008–2009 period were a direct consequence of the global credit crisis, which never bodes well for the travel business. In this case, DAL underperformed both SPY and CL12 values.

Credit spread or equity price response to relevant factors, in particular, to energy prices, is one component of right-way or wrong-way risk. The form of credit support also affects matters. Recalling the discussion following (16.9), for lien-based credit-support, the value of the collateral can depend on underlying prices. Formally, this means that recovery takes the form $R\left[V(\tau,\vec{X}_\tau),\vec{X}_\tau\right]$. If, in fact, a producer is more likely to default in a low-price environment, the value of the asset pledged is also low at the time of default. This is a source of wrong-way risk, with the value obtained by assumption of no correlation underestimating the actual exposure. This complexity is compounded by the fact that most lien-based credit support structures involve a group of dealers, each of whom may be providing hedges to the counterparty. With the ultimate claim on the assets being pari passu,[18] the actual recovery depends not only on the value of the current portfolio and the assets under lien but also on the size of the exposure of the other dealers in the consortium.

The moral of the story is that arguments for right-way risk in valuation need to be taken with a considerable degree of skepticism. Causal factors for energy price movements can have effects beyond the obvious direct impact of energy prices.

Our second key issue is that consistently higher volatility in energy makes structures of the form (16.9) or (16.10) more difficult and costly to manage. The credit exposures of the form (16.10) are correlation structures involving two underlying risks. The greater the volatility in each underlying, the more delta hedging is required, and single-name CDSs are not known for liquidity and narrow bid-offer spreads.

To illustrate the point, consider a single-time-period credit exposure of the form

$$C_t = \tilde{E}\left(\tilde{V}_T \mathbf{1}_D | \mathcal{F}_t\right) \tag{16.12}$$

where D is the event of default; both payoff and default occur only at time T. Under the assumption that the event D and the distribution of $\tilde{V}_T$ are uncorrelated, this takes the simple form $\tilde{V}_t P_t(D)$, where $P_t(D)$ is the probability of default conditioned on information available at time t. The risk associated with changes in $P_t(D)$ is identical to the risk of changes in the hazard rate $\lambda(t)$ or, equivalently, changes in the term structure of CDS spreads. The amount of CDS protection one needs to acquire to hedge this risk depends on $\tilde{V}_t$, which is a function of the underlying forward curves, as well as implied volatilities.

The volatility of $\tilde{V}_t$ is directly related to the volatility of the underlying commodity prices, which is easily a factor of two greater than other asset classes. This means that more rebalancing in the CDS markets is required. The bad news is that the bid-offer spreads on single-name CDSs such as APA and DAL are of the order 20 basis points at the five-year maturity; for the three-year CDS it is closer to 30 basis points; a one-year CDS is roughly 120 basis points. In contrast, the bid-offer spreads on the credit benchmarks, namely, CDX investment-grade or high-yield indices, which are essentially baskets of single-name CDSs, is only a few basis points. Using these indices to hedge is more efficient from a transaction-cost perspective. However, the correlations between the changes of energy CDS spreads and those of the

---

[18] When a set of separate credit claims is pari passu, it means that all are on equal footing pro rata in the division of recoverable assets.

indices are not high enough for the indices to be effective hedges. For example, from January 2010 to December 2012 the correlation between ten-day spread changes between APA 5Y CDSs and the 5Y CDSs IG (investment grade) and 5Y CDS HY (high yield) indices was 0.47 and 0.45, respectively. The airline DAL had similar levels of correlation. The indices have low effectiveness due to the limited presence of energy names in their composition. Frequent rebalancing requirements due to high energy volatility collide with limited benchmark effectiveness.

Conclusion

In this chapter we have covered four cornerstones of risk management of energy portfolios[19]: price integrity, benchmark risk metrics, nonbenchmark (specific) risks, and credit risk. The common features of high volatility and high-dimensional risk profiles affect each of these significantly.

Maintaining proper controls on price integrity in a high-dimensional energy portfolios requires

- Standard verification of price formation on benchmark and hub forward curves and volatility surfaces
- Regular and quasi-automated comparison with consensus surveys and exchange settlements when such exist
- Rigorous statistical benchmarking of illiquid positions
- Comparison of marks to recent transactions

Calculating useful metrics for benchmark price risks requires

- Hierarchical organization of risks based in part on market structure, with statistical analysis used when nodal relationships are ambiguous
- Properly parameterized and calibrated relationships between risks at each level of the hierarchy, which facilitates aggregation of benchmark exposures
- Application of standard risk metrics to aggregate benchmark risks, modified for seasonality in returns

The residual nonbenchmark or so-called specific risks are the most challenging. In energy, these exposures constitute a substantial component of many portfolios. Statistical analysis of spot data can provide credible distributional estimates of nonbenchmark basis risks.

Management of credit risk depends on reliable approaches to the preceding three topics. In addition,

- The assumption of uncorrelated default and price processes and corrections to this assumption (so-called right-way or wrong-way risk) are particularly pertinent to energy desks. The risk profiles of many counterparties are heavily concentrated in

---

[19] This is not to say that the list was complete – operation risk, for example, is significant in commodities businesses but is outside of the scope of this work.

one or two commodities, and heuristic arguments for right-way exposure are partially supported by equity price behavior. However, the complexities of global macroeconomic factors and the dependence of credit support on commodities prices complicate even the qualitative assessment of right-way or wrong-way risk.

- High volatility coupled with limited effectiveness of benchmark hedging instruments adds to the complexity and cost of managing an energy CVA book.

These four facets of energy risk management have common features. An effective risk platform involves unifying the manner in which these risks are handled, with particular attention focused on the linkages between benchmark information and pricing and the residual risks inherent in both the price and credit aspects of the business.

17

Conclusions

Energy markets exist to provide efficient mechanisms for balancing supply and demand intertemporally and geographically. This is accomplished through price signals, with transparency and effectiveness depending on the nature of the market. Regardless of market construct, the resulting price risk is always present. Someone must shoulder the burden of price and volumetric risk or else make investments in infrastructure to mitigate it.

In fully regulated markets, rates of return for investments and operations are set by regulatory bodies, and it is usually consumers who are, often unknowingly, on the receiving end of the gamut of risks and the costs to mitigate them.[1] Some would argue that in regulated markets, risk management and commercial strategy tend to be of dubious value because decision makers are typically not directly bearing the financial consequences of their actions. Contrast, for example, the nuclear build in the 1970s with recent strategic assessments of the viability of new nuclear generators. In the case of the former, promises of electricity that would be "too cheap to meter" were followed by billions of dollars of cost overruns, shouldered in large part by rate increases to the consumer. In the latter case, potential investors in new nuclear generation have consistently exhibited remarkable trepidation regarding such investments; the prospect of being responsible for a bad $10 billion investment has a way of directing objective analysis to the economic prospects and risks associated with such projects.

In deregulated markets, risks are dispersed across the spectrum of market participants. Naturals, namely, producers and large-scale consumers and suppliers, can transfer risks to intermediaries such as banks and commodities trading shops. Alternatively, they can choose not to hedge, opting to inventory risks, in which case their shareholders sustain the exposure. Some

---

[1] In the extreme case where energy prices for end users are fixed through government subsidies, it is the taxpayers who ultimately bear price risk.

oil majors minimize hedging activity, acting under the reasonable assumption that energy price risk is desired by their investors. Merchant generators, as another example, often opt to manage their assets directly, hedging only portions of the commodity risk and keeping embedded optionality in-house.

A significant and growing amount of hedging activity occurs on futures exchanges. However, despite best efforts to standardize hedges to facilitate clearing, much of the risk transfer that we have discussed in the previous chapters is likely to remain over the counter (OTC). Hedges for refiners, gas storage, and tolls are often highly customized to match the idiosyncratic risks of each physical asset, requiring deal-specific complexities that are anathema to the standardization on which exchange clearing is predicated. Moreover, credit support for such hedging activities has often been in the form of liens on physical assets – whether oil and natural gas fields or a fleet of wind-generation turbines. Nonstandard credit support, as useful and valid as such is at facilitating bona fide hedging activity, is not part of the futures exchange lexicon.

In the preceding decade, banks assumed an increasingly prominent role as commodities intermediaries, holding long-tenor, illiquid positions. This has been the focus of considerable attention, usually negative, and a reduction in activity in recent years. It is hard, however, to see why this activity is any different from others in which banks are expected to engage – namely, taking short-term deposits and making long-term loans to borrowers of all sorts with idiosyncratic business and funding requirements. In facilitating the dissemination of credit, banks are using liquidity where it is abundant to create liquidity where it is required. This is exactly the role of intermediaries in energy markets.

Regardless of the mechanisms by which risks are transferred and capital is allocated, given that the fundamental risks are not going to vanish into thin air, the need for valuation and risk management persists under all market structures. Even in a regulated framework, regulators should be (and often are) acutely interested in the economic consequences of their decisions. If banks and insurance companies are removed from the pool of intermediaries as a result of regulatory developments, others will step in or risks will be inventoried by naturals. Whoever ends up holding the risks needs to be at the forefront of better ways to value and to manage their positions.

Mathematical models in finance are, first and foremost, a framework in which to organize one's thoughts about value and risk. There are no Holy Grail models that capture all features of a market – very few experienced portfolio managers or financial engineers take models literally. In contrast, quantitative modeling serves two primary purposes. First, done properly, it yields plausible valuation, practical hedging strategies, and in some cases predictions of market evolution. Second, it exposes key parameters or risks about which little can be said with certainty. This second purpose is important and often overlooked.

Take, for example, unit-contingent transactions discussed in Chapter 15, in which the quantity of energy purchased depends on the actual realized production of a generator. Regardless of the level of complexity of modeling such a structure, all approaches have as a key input an estimate of the availability of the unit – equivalently, the likelihood that at any given time the unit will fail to produce energy. The moment that such transactions are contemplated, the relevance of this availability estimate is immediately discerned by traders and senior management alike – and thoughts abound. What could cause a systemic shutdown of an entire fleet of nuclear generators?

Nobody around the table believes that such an event could be modeled statistically. However, the possibility of such an event is acknowledged, and conjectures are made about how it could occur – a terrorist strike or a severe mechanical failure or meltdown requiring the immediate and long-term shut down of a broad swath of generation. It is unlikely that anyone would have said, "What about an earthquake in Japan causing a tsunami that floods emergency generators, resulting in the failure of the cooling systems and eventually a government-mandated shutdown of all nuclear generation in Japan?" The point is that while it would take remarkable powers of divination to predict the details, the concept and potential impact of such a systemic event are forced into the discussion by the modeling.[2] In the absence of reliable statistical estimates, position limits for such transactions are usually put in place based on management tolerance (a judgment call) of the potential economic impact of such an event.

The past decade has witnessed significant evolution in modeling methods in energy markets. There remain, however, many open problems and issues that limit the effectiveness of current approaches. A few warrant special mention.

At a basic level, limitations on computational speed continues to substantially constrain modeling efforts. Despite the remarkable improvements in computing power over the past decades, there are many important circumstances where limits in computing speed preclude proper analysis of the response of energy markets to foreseeable developments. Moreover, many promising avenues for modeling that could render seemingly nonstationary behavior in forward price dynamics stationary are of little value in the absence of faster computers or better algorithms.

---

[2] Contrary to popular press accounts, very few events in financial markets, if any, have occurred that were not contemplated in advance by a meaningful percentage of market participants, even if a minority.

The second issue is that correlation structure in commodities has exhibited striking changes over the past decade. Nonstationarity haunts all markets, but energy markets have exhibited some remarkable changes in the past decade. The dynamics of crude oil forward curves has become increasingly one-dimensional, one-factor in the parlance of our earlier models. Moreover, the correlation of commodities returns with other asset classes has also increased meaningfully since the first signs of the credit crisis manifest themselves. The origin of these changes, which affect many aspects of commodities trading and investment, are not well understood. This issue constitutes a major modeling challenge.

Finally, the regulatory landscape has always kept market participants on their toes due to rapid evolution and relative youth of the markets. However, in the aftermath of the credit crisis, the regulatory dynamic has taken on a new imperative, especially in the United States, reaching a pitch that would almost lead one to believe that commodities trading caused the credit crisis. Justified or not, and opinions vary greatly on the matter, the Dodd-Frank Act and the Volker Rule are substantially altering the way in which energy markets function.

There are many other topics that could legitimately warrant discussion. The demand destruction witnessed in 2009 suggests a possible need to couple valuation with macroeconomic drivers or other markets. The relationship between equities and commodities, touched on briefly in Chapter 16 in the context of credit risk management, is an arena where a good deal of innovation has yet to occur. However, these three topics illustrate the breadth of issues that confront efforts to value and manage energy structures and assets.

Computational Limitations

Production risks systems are typically predicated on relatively "vanilla" representations of even complex structures. Ensuring that the official P&L and risk positions of a trading desk are completed before whatever deadline management has imposed is usually accomplished in the brute-force manner – more machines. In a world of decreasing hardware costs, this is a perfectly acceptable solution.

The real impact of computational limits occurs in "satellite" analytics – models outside the production valuation environment, which serve a variety of purposes. These include, for example, the analysis of market dynamics and the impacts of potential changes in market structure or fundamental drivers, estimation or calibration of slow-moving parameters for use in production risk systems, and the construction of vanilla approximations of complex transactions for the purposes of booking in production risk systems. We have touched on two examples in previous chapters: stack models and inventory-based models for forward curve dynamics.

The stack models described in Chapter 12 were high-level, stylized representations of power markets. Even for these, calibration of parameters to
historical price data is computationally intensive; calibrations often require
days to converge. The inherently high-dimensional risks resulting from
nodal pricing in power markets renders more sophisticated modeling simply
"out of scope" for anything other than basic scenario analysis. Numerous
vendors sell software that purports to estimate market-clearing prices at
a very granular level. However, the nonlinear equations governing power
flow and the large number of loads, assets, and transmission lines comprising a power market render calculation of clearing prices for a single scenario
(specified loads, fuel prices, transmission, and generation outages) extremely
time-consuming. Using such software to produce useful probabilistic results
is simply not viable at this point in time.

A consequence of this limitation is that it is difficult to make accurate
predictions of the impact of changes to the system. Public information
on project development, permitting, or regulatory perturbations such as
emissions regulations is commonly available years in advance of implementation or completion. Transforming such information into quantitative
actionable predictions remains problematic. Moreover, even when the qualitative features of technological advances become clear, making quantitative
predictions of market response all too often is not possible.

One example is afforded by the shale gas revolution, which is having a
fundamental effect on the dynamics of natural gas prices in North America. Changing volatility and correlation structure affects everything from
vanilla option pricing to the valuation of physical storage. The near parity in the cost of natural gas versus coal in power generation is affecting
the dispatch of entire fleets of generation (recall Figure 14.19). Translat-
ing this macro phenomenon into useful parameterizations of volatility and
correlation structure remains an open problem.

Renewable energy sources provide another example of note, in particular,
with the introduction of wind generation in several parts of the world. West
Texas provides a good example. Starting in roughly 2006, substantial wind
turbine capacity was built in the ERCOT, primarily in West Texas, reaching nearly 10,000 MW of installed wind capacity, a meaningful quantity in
a system with total capacity of roughly 75,000 MW. Limited transmission
from West Texas to the demand centers, namely, the large cities, resulted
in a dramatic change in price behavior. Figure 17.1 shows historical West
Texas "7×8" power prices in the top plot and a ninety day moving average
of spot heat rates (versus Henry Hub) in the bottom plot. Note the fundamental change in price dynamics that ensued, specifically the frequent and
significant negative spot prices,[3] as well as a visible drop in spot heat rates to

---

[3] Tax incentives make wind generation at negative prices economical.

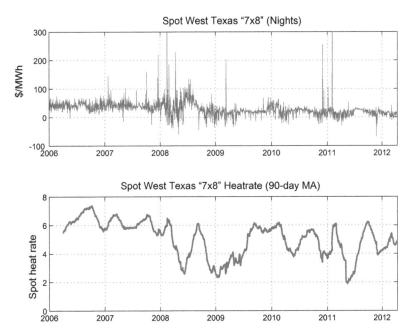

Figure 17.1. ERCOT West Texas "7x8" spot prices and heat rates.

remarkably low levels. Forecasting the response of clearing prices as a result of this largely foreseeable development was, and remains, in the domain of rough "order of magnitude" estimation.

In short, current modeling capabilities are a (large) step behind the complexity of power and natural gas markets, as well as, arguably, oil, refined products, and coal, which face different but conceptually similar issues.

Inventory-based models, also introduced in Chapter 12, address price dynamics at a more fundamental level. We have seen evidence that returns covariance structure is affected by inventory levels, at least in the case of copper (recall Figure 12.16). For seasonal commodities such as natural gas or refined products, one can only begin to make qualitative statements.

Currently, most valuation methods used in practice assume that the covariance structure is constant or deterministically varying with time. Absent a unifying framework in which the actions of market participants managing inventory affect forward price dynamics, realistic models based on stationary underlying processes will continue to prove elusive.

Such a framework could potentially be built around inventory-based models such as those discussed by Pirrong [Pir12], but computational methods are not up to the task of solving the required stochastic control problems on time scales short enough to be truly useful. As a consequence, this promising avenue remains a provocative source of little more than "numerical heuristics," pending some combination of faster computers and cleverer models.

Evolving Correlations

Correlation structure is affected by market participants as well as by fundamental drivers, and the covariance structure of returns is unquestionably evolving. Recall Figure 5.11, which showed a marked decrease in the backwardation of volatility over time. Such changes in volatility structure are a substantial source of risk to structured portfolios.

A more refined look at this phenomenon is shown in Figure 17.2. The top plot displays the ratio of the rolling one-year realized volatility for the twelfth nearby contract returns to that of the second nearby. The results are plotted versus the midpoint of the calendar averaging window. The lower plot shows the ratio of higher-order total volatility to the that of the first factor $\left(\sum_{j=2}^{24} \lambda_j\right)^{1/2} / \lambda_1^{1/2}$ from principal-components analysis (PCA) of the first twenty-four nearby contracts applied over the same rolling one-year windows.

These two plots are different representations of the same phenomenon. The first plot shows the flattening of the term structure of volatility to be expected with an increasingly dominant first factor. The second plot shows that the variance of the higher factors is contributing less to the overall volatility of the forward curve. Although there were significant fluctuations in each series in the 2001–2002 time frame, the dynamics of the West Texas Intermediate (WTI) forward curve has become increasingly one-dimensional in nature.

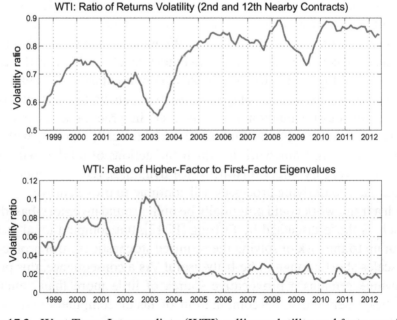

Figure 17.2. West Texas Intermediate (WTI) rolling volatility and factor analysis.

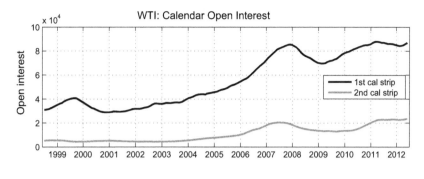

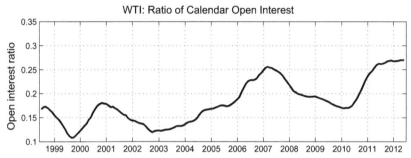

Figure 17.3. WTI rolling open interest analysis.

This phenomenon occurred over the interval 2003–2005, remaining largely unchanged since – aside from surprisingly small variations at the apex of the credit crisis – and could be evidence of what is commonly referred to as the *financialization* of commodities markets, with increasing investment in commodities index funds from a broader spectrum of investors. In fact, open interest in futures contracts has increased significantly, and the ratio of open interest in longer-tenor contracts relative to shorter-tenor contracts has also increased. The top plot in Figure 17.3 shows the the open interest in the first two calendar strips, once again displayed in the same rolling one-year fashion. The lower plot shows the ratio.

There has been a fundamental change in the trading activity of market participants, with greater liquidity at longer tenors a potential factor in the decrease in volatility backwardation. Flatter volatility results in less special-ness; less decoupling of short-tenor contracts from longer-tenor contracts. More regular price dynamics makes hedging more efficient, which is a good thing. It should be noted, however, that the period that witnessed the great-est change in correlation structure was in fact exhibiting nothing particularly unusual in the gradual increase in volume and tenor. The origin of this change in correlation structure remains unclear.

A closely related topic of interest to investors is whether the correla-tion between commodities (energy in particular) and other asset classes

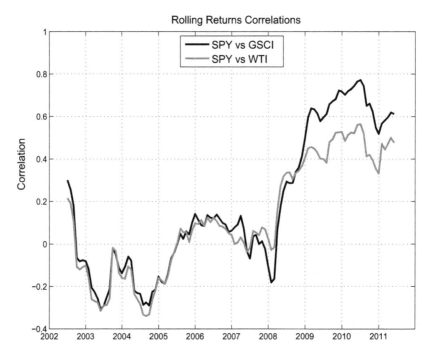

Figure 17.4. Rolling returns correlation: SPY versus GSCI and WTI.

has changed. This topic has received much attention, including claims that such correlation has increased meaningfully, affecting investment strategies and altering the behavior of commodity price dynamics. See, for example, analysis by Tang and Xiong [TX12], which suggests that the presence of a commodity in an index such as the Standard & Poor's (S&P) GSCI[4] alters its correlation behavior with other asset classes, or alternatively Hamilton and Wu [HW12], who find no meaningful relationship between notional index positions and risk premia.

To illustrate the issue, consider Figure 17.4, which shows rolling correlations of five-day returns between SPY (the S&P 500 ETF) and two commodity series (again, using a one-year window), the first being the S&P GSCI and the second being the first WTI nearby contract. The two correlations track closely because of the substantial crude oil component in the GSCI. It is clear that something interesting has been occurring, with correlations transitioning from a range of $[-0.2, 0.2]$ to roughly 0.5. What is also noteworthy is that this "phase transition" occurred several years after the change in correlation structure shown in Figure 17.2, beginning at the inception of the credit crisis and occurring during a period of decreasing open interest.

The overarching theme in these two examples is that fundamental aspects of price behavior can exhibit nontrivial changes over the period of a few

---

[4] This was formerly the Goldman Sachs Commodity Index.

years and that explaining, let alone predicting, such changes remains a substantial modeling and econometric challenge.

The Regulatory Landscape

Participants in any traded market have to grapple with the impact of regulatory developments. These include not only regulations such as Basel capital requirements for banks and high-profile regulatory endeavors such as Dodd-Frank Act,[5] but also much more frequent events such as changes in market design and structure, tariffs, emissions, and even tax incentives for the development of renewable energy sources.

Deregulated natural gas and power markets are a relatively recent phenomenon, taking firm root in parts of the North America in the last fifteen years, more recently in Europe, and hardly at all in Asia. New markets experience gyrations as flaws are discerned and remedied or as fundamental changes are made, such as a power market shifting from zonal to fully nodal pricing, instantaneously expanding the set of locations at which the commodity is priced from a few zonal prices to many hundreds of delivery locations. Even relatively minor changes to the mechanics of price formation can result in measurable changes in price dynamics.

More mature markets are not immune from sudden structural changes. In 2005, OPEC altered the composition of its reference basket price, the so-called OPEC Reference Basket (ORB) to which OPEC references target price ranges, ranges that are also adjusted on occasion. Such events can result in discernible changes in price dynamics. The moratorium on drilling and permitting in the Gulf of Mexico occurred almost overnight as a result of regulatory response to the *Macondo* oil spill. The regulatory response to the Fukushima disaster in Japan was global in nature, with many countries, particularly in Europe, slowing development or accelerating the decommissioning of nuclear generation. These events affected supply and demand and ultimately energy prices globally.

There are two complementary actions that a trading operation can take in dealing with a changing regulatory environment. The first is to try to anticipate changes and quantify potential effects. The second is to identify and maintain a record of the timing of relevant regulatory changes. Doing so prevents flawed results arising from analysis that spans differing regulatory regimes and in some cases allows for estimation of biases induced by changes, allowing for more robust data sets once such biases are removed.

Most regulatory developments are limited in nature, having the potential to affect a particular transaction or even regional activity but not fundamentally alter the commercial viability of a large enterprise. In stark contrast,

---

[5] The Dodd-Frank Wall Street Reform and Consumer Protection Act.

the post – credit crisis Dodd-Frank legislation and the associated Volker Rule[6] are potential game changers. The Dodd-Frank body of legislation is expansive, and a detailed discussion is well beyond the scope of this section. Moreover, the form of the ultimate implementation continues to evolve, due both to litigation and technical difficulties in implementation.

The aspects of Dodd-Frank most pertinent to energy trading are

- Previously unregulated swaps markets would be brought under the purview of the CFTC.
- Swaps dealers and major swap participants (once defined) would be subject to stringent capital requirements and reporting obligations.
- Standardized swaps (once defined) would be required to be exchange-traded or cleared.
- Position limits on exposure to a core set of commodities would be implemented.

In addition, dealers must provide detailed information regarding the mid-market value of trades, as well as the impacts of price-change scenarios, on customer request.

One effect of this legislation so far has been to dampen hedging activity pending clarification of exactly what form it will ultimately take. One can only conjecture about what the long-term consequences might be.

Centralizing credit risk at exchanges certainly simplifies trading and reduces the large amount of labor involved in supporting bilateral trading activity. Constraining commercial activity to standardized trades will simplify portfolios. Instead of having a limitless variety of almost identical trades, netting and novation of positions between counterparties will be much easier to effect.

The effort to push more trading onto exchanges, however, is also likely to have some detrimental effects. First, more onerous capital requirements for uncleared transactions could discourage the use of customized structures most effective at hedging the idiosyncratic features of energy infrastructure, potentially increasing the costs to finance development. Lenders like effective hedges. In addition, the use of lien-based credit support could become problematic, also potentially increasing costs to hedgers who will have to post collateral in the traditional sense.

Finally, the effort to force clarity on the markets in the form of reporting midmarket value of transactions with clients is, on the face of it, a good thing – arguably long overdue in other asset classes such as municipal bonds. However, for long-tenor transactions in less-liquid markets, there is likely to be significant ambiguity regarding what would constitute erroneous data. Paradoxically, this could result in a trend toward structuring trades in illiquid locations, diffusing liquidity from benchmarks.

---

[6] The Volker Rule refers to a part of Dodd-Frank that would limit proprietary trading by U.S. banks.

From the perspective of valuation and risk management, Dodd-Frank introduces a variety of technical issues surrounding reliable, near-real-time reporting of trades and dissemination of accurate information to clients regarding valuation. Far more interesting, however, is the potential impact of position limits.

Even relatively modest energy trading operations have several traders all trading the usual benchmarks. Developing methods to dynamically allocate the use of "position limit capacity" within an organization, particularly large financial institutions, is far more than a mere technical problem. While bearing similarities to issues such as allocation of risk capital (VaR in many shops), the time scale required for allocation of notional capacity is much shorter. The position of a single book can change substantially intraday in the regular course of a client-oriented business. Most institutions appear to be opting for fixed allocations, with ad hoc adjustments as needed. Internal clearing markets for such notional capacity would yield more efficient allocation of what could become a scarce resource in this new regulatory regime. Design and implementation of better methods to allocate position limits remain an open problem.

Conclusion

Managing an energy portfolio is difficult even under "normal" circumstances. Routine weather-driven spikes in basis prices, infrastructure failure, and perturbations to supply or demand due to hurricanes or oil spills all result in a trading environment that requires the ability to process large amounts of information, both internal risk positions and external risk drivers, quickly and accurately.

The incomplete nature of energy markets, with many risks being managed using a limited number of benchmark instruments, is not merely a "rounding error" to the results of standard financial models. Even under the best of conditions, limited liquidity results in an inventory of risk positions for extended periods of time. New methods have been, and continue to be, developed that depart dramatically from the complete-markets framework. Most of these methods are heavily dependent on statistical estimation and modeling of complex, high-dimensional systems.

Paradoxically, a market that is confronted with such circumstances is also having to grapple with a high degree of nonstationary behavior. A changing investment landscape with greater interest in energy and commodities broadly as an asset class, while potentially enhancing liquidity, has contributed to changes in price dynamics. The rapidly evolving and unpredictable regulatory environment ultimately may yield significant benefits. It will, however, also add constraints to the activities of hedgers and portfolio managers, who are already working with a very limited set of hedging instruments in the first place.

Even after several decades of research and development of analytical frameworks for energy, in many respects the progress made has just scratched the surface. The problems are challenging – risk management in energy involves fully uncommoditized risks and a level of complexity that exceeds that of other asset classes. Given the outstanding issues, progress will continue to be made, and there is a strong likelihood that some of the most meaningful innovations in mathematical finance in the upcoming years will occur in this arena.

Appendixes

Appendix A

Black-76 and Margrabe

In this appendix we survey the standard valuation approaches to "vanilla" single-commodity options and spread options.

Black-76

Black-76 refers to a modification of the standard Black-Scholes option pricing framework to the situation in which the underlying price process is that of a generic forward or future contracts. As with Black-Scholes, returns are normally distributed, and the underlying price process is a geometric Brownian motion (GBM) with constant volatility:

$$\frac{dF(t,T)}{F(t,T)} = \sigma \, dB_t \qquad \qquad (A.1)$$

Letting $Y_t = \log[F(t,T)]$, Ito's formula yields

$$dY_t = -\frac{1}{2}\sigma^2 dt + \sigma \, dB_t \qquad \qquad (A.2)$$

which integrates to

$$Y_t = Y_0 - \frac{1}{2}\sigma^2 t + \sigma B_t \qquad \qquad (A.3)$$

Exponentiating yields

$$F(t,T) = F(0,T)e^{-1/2\sigma^2 t + \sigma B_t} \qquad \qquad (A.4)$$

Turning to derivative pricing, by Ito's formula, the value of a European option $V_t = V(t, F_t)$ will evolve according to

$$dV_t = \frac{\partial V}{\partial t} dt + \frac{\partial V}{\partial F_t} dF_t + \frac{1}{2}(\sigma F_t)^2 \frac{\partial^2 V}{\partial F_t^2} dt \qquad \qquad (A.5)$$

447

Assuming that the holder of a long option position shorts a number Δ of futures contracts, the portfolio evolves according to

$$dV_t - \Delta dF_t = \left(\frac{\partial V}{\partial t} + \frac{1}{2}\sigma^2 F_t^2 \frac{\partial^2 V}{\partial F_t^2}\right)dt + \left(\frac{\partial V}{\partial F_t} - \Delta\right)dF_t \qquad (A.6)$$

Delta hedging, that is, choosing $\Delta = \partial V/\partial F_t$, yields an instantaneously risk-free portfolio. Therefore, the drift in the portfolio value should equal the carry of the value of the portfolio under the risk-free rate, which implies

$$\frac{\partial V}{\partial t} + \frac{1}{2}\sigma^2 F_t^2 \frac{\partial^2 V}{\partial F_t^2} = rV \qquad (A.7)$$

with boundary data specified by $V[T_e, F(T_e, T)]$ for a European option payoff, where T_e denotes the expiry of the option. The absence of a term involving $\partial V/\partial F$ is due to the absence of a drift in the underlying dynamics (A.1).

Comment on Discounting

In what follows we will discount to the delivery time T. This is tantamount to rendering the terminal payoff of a call, for example, as

$$V[T_e, F(T_e, T)] = e^{-r(T-T_e)}\max[F(T_e, T) - K, 0] \qquad (A.8)$$

continuing the assumption of constant interest rates. In practice, T is set to be consistent with the exact mechanics of settlement for each particular transaction.

The familiar formulas for call and put valuation have a slightly simpler appearance than for cash assets (those that at purchase require up-front expenditure and hence a cost of carry) because of the absence of the drift term:

$$C(t, F) = e^{-r(T-t)}[F\Phi(d_1) - K\Phi(d_2)] \qquad (A.9)$$

$$P(t, F) = e^{-r(T-t)}[K\Phi(-d_2) - F\Phi(-d_1)] \qquad (A.10)$$

where C and P are values for the European call and put, respectively, and with

$$d_{1,2} = \frac{\ln(F/K) \pm \frac{1}{2}\sigma^2(T_e - t)}{\sigma\sqrt{T_e - t}}. \qquad (A.11)$$

Here Φ denotes the cumulative distribution function of a standard normal random variable.

These results can easily be extended to the case of deterministic time-varying volatility of the form

$$\frac{dF(t, T)}{F(t, T)} = \sigma(T-t)dB_t \qquad (A.12)$$

which is commonly used to accommodate volatility backwardation. The preceding arguments are unchanged in this setting and result in the following extension of (A.7):

$$\frac{\partial V}{\partial t} + \frac{1}{2}\sigma(T-t)^2 F^2 \frac{\partial^2 V}{\partial F^2} = rV \tag{A.13}$$

with the same boundary conditions.

Valuation of any payoff expiring at $\tau \in [0, T]$ using (A.13) proceeds by using a standard time-change $s(t)$ that, when applied to (A.13), yields

$$\frac{\partial V}{\partial s} + \frac{1}{2}\bar{\sigma}_\tau^2 F^2 \frac{\partial^2 V}{\partial F^2} = rV \tag{A.14}$$

with $s(0) = 0$ and $s(\tau) = \tau$. The time change that accomplishes this is

$$s(t) = \tau - \frac{\int_t^\tau \sigma^2(T-u)\, du}{\bar{\sigma}_\tau^2} \tag{A.15}$$

where

$$\bar{\sigma}_\tau^2 = \frac{1}{\tau} \int_0^\tau \sigma^2(T-u)\, du \tag{A.16}$$

Note the fact that $ds/dt = \sigma^2(T-t)/\bar{\sigma}_\tau^2$, when applied to (A.13), yields (A.14). The result implies that the average variance over the term of the option is all that matters when local volatility is deterministic.

Margrabe: Valuation

The Margrabe approach to spread option valuation was originally developed for cash assets, amounting to evaluation of

$$e^{-rT}\tilde{E}[\max(X_T - Y_T, 0)]$$

In the Margrabe setting, the spot prices of two assets X and Y under the money-market measure (see Chapter 4) are modeled as two GBMs:

$$dX_t = rX_t dt + \sigma_X X_t dB_t^{(X)}$$
$$dY_t = rY_t dt + \sigma_Y Y_t dB_t^{(Y)}$$

The correlation between the Brownian motions is assumed to be a constant ζ.

Change of numeraire ([Hul12],[CD03]) is the most efficient approach to this problem. In the Y measure, $\tilde{E}_Y$ in which Y_t is the numeraire, all assets discounted by Y must be martingales. Denoting the value of the option at time t by $V(t, X_t, Y_t)$ since V must be an $\tilde{E}_Y$ martingale, we have

$$\frac{V(0, X_0, Y_0)}{Y_0} = \tilde{E}_Y\left[\frac{V(T, X_T, Y_T)}{Y_T}\right]$$

which implies that

$$V(0, X_0, Y_0) = Y_0 \tilde{E}_Y \left[\left(\frac{X_T}{Y_T} - 1 \right)^+ \right]$$

The ratio

$$R_T \equiv \frac{X_T}{Y_T} = \frac{X_0}{Y_0} e^{\sigma_X B_X(T) - \sigma_Y B_Y(T) + \mathcal{I}(T)} \tag{A.17}$$

is a log-normal random variable, where $\mathcal{I}(T)$ denotes drift terms arising from Ito's formula. In addition, the exponent in (A.17) has variance

$$\hat{\sigma}^2 \equiv \mathrm{var}[\sigma_X B_X(T) - \sigma_Y B_Y(T)] = T_e \left(\sigma_X^2 + \sigma_Y^2 - 2\zeta \sigma_X \sigma_Y \right)$$

Finally, as R is log normal with variance, $\hat{\sigma}^2$ satisfies

$$E[\max(R - K, 0)] = E(R)N(d_1) - KN(d_2) \tag{A.18}$$

where

$$d_{1,2} = \frac{\log \left[\frac{E(R)}{K} \pm \frac{1}{2}\hat{\sigma}^2 \right]}{\hat{\sigma}} \tag{A.19}$$

Assembling these facts, we have

$$V(0, X_0, Y_0) = Y_0 \left[\tilde{E}_Y \left(\frac{X_T}{Y_T} \right) N(d_1) - N(d_2) \right]$$
$$= X_0 N(d_1) - Y_0 N(d_2)$$

where

$$d_{1,2} = \frac{\log(X_0/Y_0) \pm \frac{1}{2}\hat{\sigma}^2}{\hat{\sigma}} \tag{A.20}$$

This is (perhaps) intuitively reasonable: the value of the option is as if we used Black-Scholes with X as the underlying and the strike set to Y_0, with the implied volatility $\hat{\sigma}$ the variance of $\log[X_T/Y_T]$. There is no discounting because funding is embedded in the Y asset.

Margrabe: Hedging

Turning to the Greeks, we will work through the example of a call, the put case following by analogy. For ease of calculation, note that the value in (A.20) is equivalent to a Y_0 notional quantity of calls on underlying $U_t \equiv X_t/Y_t$ with strike 1:

$$V(0, X_0, Y_0) = Y_0 [U_0 N(d_1) - N(d_2)] \tag{A.21}$$

Working in (Y, U) variables renders $d_{1,2}$ functions of U only. We also know from standard Black-Scholes that

$$\frac{\partial V}{\partial U} \bigg|_Y = Y_0 N(d_1) \qquad \frac{\partial^2 V}{\partial U^2} \bigg|_Y = \frac{Y_0}{U\hat{\sigma}} N'(d_1) \tag{A.22}$$

Note that $\hat{\sigma}$ has an embedded $T_e^{1/2}$. From (A.22) we have

$$\frac{\partial V}{\partial X} = \frac{\partial V}{\partial U}\bigg|_Y \frac{\partial U}{\partial X} = N(d_1) \tag{A.23}$$

$$\frac{\partial V}{\partial Y} = \frac{\partial V}{\partial Y}\bigg|_U + \frac{\partial V}{\partial U}\bigg|_Y \frac{\partial U}{\partial Y} \tag{A.24}$$

$$= UN(d_1) - N(d_2) + YN(d_1)\left(-\frac{X}{Y^2}\right)$$

$$= -N(d_2)$$

providing us with the two deltas for the spread option. Note that $\partial V/\partial X$ increases and $\partial V/\partial Y$ decreases as $U \equiv X/Y$ increases.

The calculation for the Hessian Γ proceeds in a similar fashion. Beginning with the first term:

$$\frac{\partial^2 V}{\partial X^2} = \frac{\partial}{\partial U}\left(\frac{\partial V}{\partial U}\bigg|_Y \frac{\partial U}{\partial X}\right)\frac{\partial U}{\partial X} \tag{A.25}$$

$$= \left(\frac{\partial^2 V}{\partial U^2}\bigg|_Y \frac{\partial U}{\partial X} + \frac{\partial V}{\partial U}\bigg|_Y \frac{\partial^2 U}{\partial X^2}\right)\frac{\partial U}{\partial X}$$

$$= \left[\frac{Y}{U\hat{\sigma}}N'(d_1)\frac{1}{Y}\right] = \frac{1}{X\hat{\sigma}}N'(d_1)$$

This is identical in form to the result for a fixed-strike call option with the modified volatility $\hat{\sigma}$. As in the simpler setting, $\partial^2 V/\partial X^2$ decreases with increasing T as $\hat{\sigma}$ increases with tenor (recall that T is implicit in $\hat{\sigma}$).

Similarly,

$$\frac{\partial^2 V}{\partial Y^2} = \frac{\partial - N(d_2)}{\partial U}\left(\frac{-X}{Y^2}\right) \tag{A.26}$$

$$= \frac{-N'(d_2)}{U\hat{\sigma}}\left(\frac{-X}{Y^2}\right) = \frac{N'(d_2)}{Y\hat{\sigma}} = \frac{XN'(d_1)}{Y^2\hat{\sigma}}$$

where we have used the fact that $N'(d_2) = (X/Y)N'(d_1)$.

Finally,

$$\frac{\partial^2 V}{\partial X \partial Y} = \frac{\partial[-N(d_2)]}{\partial U}\left(\frac{1}{Y}\right) \tag{A.27}$$

$$= \frac{-N'(d_2)}{UY\hat{\sigma}} = -\frac{N'(d_2)}{X\hat{\sigma}} = -\frac{N'(d_1)}{Y\hat{\sigma}}$$

Both $\partial^2 V/\partial X^2$ and $\partial^2 V/\partial Y^2$ are positive, as is expected by analogy with vanilla calls and puts. The cross-gamma term $\partial^2 V/\partial X \partial Y$ is negative: Increasing Y lowers the moneyness of the option, thereby reducing $\partial V/\partial X$. Viewed collectively as a Hessian, the Γ matrix

$$\Gamma = \frac{N'(d_1)}{\hat{\sigma}} \begin{pmatrix} \frac{1}{X} & -\frac{1}{Y} \\ -\frac{1}{Y} & \frac{X}{Y^2} \end{pmatrix} \tag{A.28}$$

is positive definite because

$$\vec{\alpha}^t \Gamma \vec{\alpha} = \frac{1}{X} \left(\alpha_1 - \frac{X}{Y} \alpha_2 \right)^2$$

The spread option payoff is an option: when delta hedged, all directions point up.

Turning to vega, as with a single asset call option, $\partial V / \partial \hat{\sigma}$ is positive:

$$\frac{\partial V}{\partial \hat{\sigma}} = XN'(d_1)\frac{\partial d_1}{\partial \hat{\sigma}} - YN'(d_2)\frac{\partial d_2}{\partial \hat{\sigma}} = XN'(d_1) \tag{A.29}$$

By the chain rule, we have

$$\frac{\partial V}{\partial \sigma_X} = \frac{\partial V}{\partial \hat{\sigma}}\frac{\partial \hat{\sigma}}{\partial \sigma_X}$$

Implicit differentiation yields

$$\frac{\partial \hat{\sigma}}{\partial \sigma_X} = \frac{T^{\frac{1}{2}}(\sigma_X - \zeta \sigma_Y)}{\left(\sigma_X^2 + \sigma_Y^2 - 2\zeta \sigma_X \sigma_Y\right)^{1/2}}$$

with a symmetric result for $\partial \hat{\sigma} / \partial \sigma_Y$. Therefore,

$$\frac{\partial V}{\partial \sigma_X} = XN'(d_1)\frac{T^{1/2}(\sigma_X - \zeta \sigma_Y)}{\left(\sigma_X^2 + \sigma_Y^2 - 2\zeta \sigma_X \sigma_Y\right)^{1/2}} \tag{A.30}$$

and

$$\frac{\partial V}{\partial \sigma_Y} = XN'(d_1)\frac{T^{1/2}(\sigma_Y - \zeta \sigma_X)}{\left(\sigma_X^2 + \sigma_Y^2 - 2\zeta \sigma_X \sigma_Y\right)^{1/2}} \tag{A.31}$$

each of which scales as $T^{1/2}$.

One final comment is in order, given that all applications of Margrabe in the commodities setting involve forwards, not cash assets. All the preceding results must be discounted. Letting $X_t = F(t, T_1)$ and $Y_t = G(t, T_2)$, the forward prices for two (possibly the same) commodities, the terminal value of a call option with expiry T_e is

$$e^{-r(T-T_e)}\max[F(T_e, T_1) - H_*G(T_e, T_2), 0] \tag{A.32}$$

where we are assuming settlement at a defined time T for both legs. The $t = 0$ value of this option is

$$V[0, F(0, T_1), G(0, T_2)] = e^{-rT}[F(0, T_1)N(d_1) - H_*G(0, T_2)N(d_2)] \tag{A.33}$$

with

$$d_{1,2} = \frac{\log\left[\frac{F(0,T_1)}{H_* G(0,T_2)}\right] \pm \frac{1}{2}\hat{\sigma}^2}{\hat{\sigma}} \tag{A.34}$$

and

$$\hat{\sigma}^2 = T_e \left(\sigma_F^2 + \sigma_G^2 - 2\zeta\sigma_F\sigma_G\right)$$

Note that if all volatilities are set to zero, the value of the option is the intrinsic value $e^{-rT}\max[F(0,T_1) - H_*G(0,T_2),0]$. Similarly, all the preceding Greeks require discounting.

Margrabe: Distributional Calculations

In the Margrabe setting, each underlying has a log-normal marginal distribution. The relationship between one leg, say, $G(t,T)$, and the ratio $F(t,T)/G(t,T)$ is often of empirical interest. In the context of power and natural gas, the ratio is referred to as the *market heat rate*.

For ease of notation, let

$$\tilde{\sigma}_F = \sigma_F t^{1/2}$$
$$\tilde{\sigma}_G = \sigma_G t^{1/2}$$

where σ_F and σ_G are volatilities of the two underlying forward prices (in the case of time-varying local volatility, these are the implied volatilities for $[0,t]$). We will also denote the normal deviates corresponding to the two underlyings at time t by Z_F and Z_G, respectively, and the correlation between these by ζ.

The forward price ratio is therefore

$$H(t,T) \equiv \frac{F(t,T)}{G(t,T)} = \frac{F(0,T)}{G(0,T)} e^{\tilde{\sigma}_F Z_F - \frac{1}{2}\tilde{\sigma}_F^2 - \tilde{\sigma}_G Z_G + \frac{1}{2}\tilde{\sigma}_G^2} \tag{A.35}$$

Writing $Z_F = \zeta Z_G + \sqrt{1-\zeta^2}W$, where W is independent of Z_G, yields the appropriate correlation ζ and allows us to rewrite (A.35) as

$$H(t,T) = \frac{F(0,T)}{G(0,T)} \left(e^{\tilde{\sigma}_F\sqrt{1-\zeta^2}W - \frac{1}{2}(1-\zeta^2)\tilde{\sigma}_F^2}\right)\left(e^{(\zeta\tilde{\sigma}_F - \tilde{\sigma}_G)Z_G - \frac{1}{2}(\zeta^2\tilde{\sigma}_F^2 - \tilde{\sigma}_G^2)}\right) \tag{A.36}$$

We have arranged the W component to have the martingale property. From this we can see that the heat rate $H(t,T)$ is not a martingale, in general, because the third term has a nontrivial expected value:

$$\tilde{E}\left[e^{(\zeta\tilde{\sigma}_F - \tilde{\sigma}_G)Z_G - \frac{1}{2}(\zeta^2\tilde{\sigma}_F^2 - \tilde{\sigma}_G^2)}\right] = e^{\frac{1}{2}[(\zeta\tilde{\sigma}_F - \tilde{\sigma}_G)^2 - (\zeta^2\tilde{\sigma}_F^2 - \tilde{\sigma}_G^2)]}$$

$$= e^{\tilde{\sigma}_G(\tilde{\sigma}_G - \zeta\tilde{\sigma}_F)}$$

A relationship between $H(t,T)$ and $G(t,T)$ implied by the Margrabe approach can now be established. Using the fact that

$$G(t,T) = G(0,T)e^{\tilde{\sigma}_G Z_G - \frac{1}{2}\tilde{\sigma}_G^2} \tag{A.37}$$

we have

$$Z_G = \frac{1}{\tilde{\sigma}_G} \log \left[\frac{G(t,T)}{G(0,T)} \right] + \frac{1}{2}\tilde{\sigma}_G \tag{A.38}$$

Inserting this into (A.36) yields

$$
\begin{aligned}
H(t,T) &= \frac{F(0,T)}{G(0,T)} \left(e^{\tilde{\sigma}_F \sqrt{1-\zeta^2}W - \frac{1}{2}(1-\zeta^2)\tilde{\sigma}_F^2} \right) \\
&\quad \cdot \left(e^{(\zeta\tilde{\sigma}_F - \tilde{\sigma}_G)\left\{ \frac{1}{\tilde{\sigma}_G} \log[G(t,T)/G(0,T)] + \frac{1}{2}\tilde{\sigma}_G \right\} - \frac{1}{2}(\zeta^2\tilde{\sigma}_F^2 - \tilde{\sigma}_G^2)} \right) \\
&= \frac{F(0,T)}{G(0,T)} \left(e^{\tilde{\sigma}_F \sqrt{1-\zeta^2}W - \frac{1}{2}(1-\zeta^2)\tilde{\sigma}_F^2} \right) \\
&\quad \cdot e^{\frac{1}{2}\zeta\tilde{\sigma}_F(\tilde{\sigma}_G - \zeta\tilde{\sigma}_F)} \left[\frac{G(t,T)}{G(0,T)} \right]^{(\zeta\tilde{\sigma}_F/\tilde{\sigma}_G - 1)}
\end{aligned}
\tag{A.39}
$$

This establishes that in the Margrabe log-normal setting, $H(t,T)$ is related to $G(t,T)$ via

$$H(t,T) = cXG(t,T)^{(\zeta\tilde{\sigma}_F/\tilde{\sigma}_G - 1)} \tag{A.40}$$

where c depends on t, and X is a unit-mean log-normal random variable with returns variance $\tilde{\sigma}_F \sqrt{1-\zeta^2}$.

Appendix B
Portfolio Mathematics

In this appendix we will survey basic mean-variance optimization methods used in portfolio management across all asset classes (see [JI87], [Lue98], or [Shr04] for general treatments).

Covariance calculations in finance typically address questions of the following mean-variance form: given a set of terminal prices $\bar{X}_T$, find a set of weights $\bar{w}$ that maximizes the expected value of the portfolio $\bar{w}^\dagger \bar{X}_T$[1] subject to a variance penalty. Written as a minimization problem, the formulation becomes

$$\min_w \left[\text{var}\left(\bar{w}^\dagger \bar{X}_T \right) - \lambda E\left(\bar{w}^\dagger \bar{X}_T \right) \right] \tag{B.1}$$

where λ is the reward of gains in expected value relative to variance.[2]

The solution to this problem is well known and proceeds by expanding the preceding term as

$$\min_w \left(\vec{w}^\dagger A \vec{w} - \lambda \vec{w}^\dagger \vec{\mu} \right) \tag{B.2}$$

where $\vec{\mu}$ and A denote the mean and covariance matrix of $\vec{X}$, respectively. Minimizing over each component of $\vec{w}$ yields the equation

$$A\vec{w} - \frac{\lambda}{2}\vec{\mu} = 0$$

from which we obtain

$$\vec{w} = \frac{\lambda}{2} A^{-1} \vec{\mu} \tag{B.3}$$

For the one-dimensional case in which the covariance matrix A is simply the variance σ_X^2, the optimal holding is $w = \lambda\mu/2\sigma^2$. The investment weight is increasing with mean and decreasing with variance as expected.

---

[1] Here $\bar{w}^\dagger$ denotes the transpose of $\bar{w}$.

[2] Far more general utility optimization is routine in finance, including path-dependent problems in which the optimization is over a continuous time interval. See, for example, [KS91], [Oks10], or [Set00].

A common variation of the mean-variance paradigm is the minimum-variance criterion used frequently in hedge construction.[3] The setup for minimum-variance hedge construction is that the investor is endowed with an existing portfolio consisting of $\Pi = \vec{\pi}^{\dagger}\vec{X}$ and seeks to construct a variance-minimizing hedge using another set of tradables with payoffs $\vec{Y}$.

The minimum-variance criterion is

$$\min_{w} \text{var}\left(\vec{w}^{\dagger}\vec{Y} + \vec{\pi}^{\dagger}\vec{X}\right) \tag{B.4}$$

Proceeding similiarly, the quadratic form requiring minimization is

$$\min_{w}\left(\vec{w}^{\dagger}A_{YY}\vec{w} + 2\vec{w}^{\dagger}A_{YX}\vec{\pi} + \vec{\pi}^{\dagger}A_{XX}\vec{\pi}\right) \tag{B.5}$$

where the As are the respective covariance matrices between the subscripted random vectors. Minimization yields

$$A_{YY}\vec{w} + A_{YX}\vec{\pi} = 0$$

with the resulting optimal hedge given by

$$\vec{w} = -A_{YY}^{-1}A_{YX}\vec{\pi} \tag{B.6}$$

For the situation in which both X and Y are one-dimensional, the preceding result reduces to the well-known solution

$$w = -\frac{\rho_{XY}\sigma_X}{\sigma_Y} \tag{B.7}$$

with the intuition being that at unit correlation, the appropriate hedge ratio is given by the ratio of the two volatilities [Hul12].

The application of minimum-variance hedging that we will use most is over short time scales when $\vec{\pi}^{\dagger}\vec{X}$ is a weighted sum of price changes across an entire forward curve, and $\vec{Y}$ is the set of price changes of a subset of forward price changes, usually at short tenor, for which hedging is efficient and transaction costs minimal. The simplest case occurs when the existing portfolio consists of a position on a single contract with forward price $F(t,T)$, and the hedge instrument is a single forward $F(t,S)$. The optimal hedge obtained from (B.6) is given by

$$w(t,S,T) = -\frac{d(t,T)}{d(t,S)}\frac{\text{cov}\left[dF(t,S),dF(t,T)\right]}{\text{var}\left[dF(t,S)\right]} \tag{B.8}$$

The discount factors $d(t,\cdot)$ are required because the change in present value of a forward contract is discounted.

---

[3] In the presence of transaction costs, optimal hedge construction is nontrivial because a pure minimum-variance calculation will pay anything to minimize risk. For now, however, we will do the simple calculations in the absence of frictions.

Letting $r(t,T)$ denote the (random) return at time t and tenor T,

$$w(t,S,T) = -\frac{d(t,T)}{d(t,S)}\frac{F(t,T)}{F(t,S)}\frac{\text{cov}\left[r(t,S),r(t,T)\right]}{\text{var}\left[r(t,S)\right]}$$

$$= -\frac{d(t,T)}{d(t,S)}\frac{F(t,T)}{F(t,S)}\frac{\sigma(t,T)}{\sigma(t,S)}\rho(t,S,T) \tag{B.9}$$

where $\sigma(t,T)$ is the returns volatility for contract T, and $\rho(t,S,T)$ is the returns correlation between the S and T contracts each at prevailing local time t.

Appendix C
Gaussian Exponential Factor Models

In this appendix we develop the key results related to the multifactor forward dynamics described by

$$\frac{dF(t,T)}{F(t,T)} = \sum_{j=1}^{J} \left[\sigma_j(t,T)e^{-\beta_j(T-t)} \, dB_t^{(j)} \right] \tag{C.1}$$

where the volatilities σ_j are deterministic functions of t and T, and the Brownian motions have a constant correlation structure $\rho_{j,k} \equiv \text{corr}\left[dB^{(j)}, dB^{(k)} \right]$.

$F(t,T)$ Is Log-Normally Distributed

The integral of the returns for factor j over the time interval $[0,t]$, for delivery T, is

$$\int_0^t \sigma_j(s,T)e^{-\beta_j(T-s)} \, dB_s^{(j)} \tag{C.2}$$

Because any stochastic integral of the form $\int_0^t \phi(s) \, dB_s$ is normally distributed with mean zero, $F(t,T)$ has a log-normal distribution.

We also know that[1]

$$E\left\{ \left[\int_0^t \phi(s) \, dB_s \right]^2 \right\} = \int_0^t \phi^2(s) \, ds \tag{C.3}$$

for deterministic ϕ. Therefore, in the case where the Browian motions are uncorrelated, the returns variance $V(t,T)$ for $F(t,T)$ is

$$V(t,T) = \sum_{j=1}^{J} \int_0^t \sigma_j^2(s,T)e^{-2\beta_j(T-s)} \, ds \tag{C.4}$$

---

[1] This is known as the *Ito isometry* and is the basic mechanism by which stochastic integrals are constructed [KS91].

The general result with correlated factor returns is

$$V(t,T) = \sum_{j=1}^{J}\sum_{k=1}^{J} \int_0^t \sigma_j(s,T)\sigma_k(s,T)\rho_{j,k}e^{-\beta_j(T-s)}e^{-\beta_k(T-s)}\,ds \qquad (C.5)$$

These results ultimately provide us with the implied volatilities for options on $F(t,T)$, as well as the following expression for $F(t,T)$ obtained via Ito's formula:

$$F(t,T) = F(0,T)e^{\sum_{j=1}^{J}\int_0^t \sigma_j(s,T)e^{-\beta_j(T-s)}dB_s^{(j)} - \frac{1}{2}V(t,T)} \qquad (C.6)$$

The separation of the volatility terms $\sigma_j(t,T)$ from the exponential terms is purely optical, and for models of this form to be of use, judicious assumptions regarding the form of the volatility terms are required.

Separable Volatility Structure and Ornstein-Uhlenbeck Processes

If we assume that each volatility function factors into functions of spot and delivery time, respectively, $\sigma(t,T) = v(t)\sigma(T)$ (omitting the factor subscripts for the moment), then the integral of (C.2) can be written as

$$\sigma(T)e^{-\beta(T-t)}\int_0^t v(s)e^{-\beta(t-s)}\,dB_s = \sigma(T)e^{-\beta(T-t)}Y(t) \qquad (C.7)$$

where

$$Y(t) \equiv \int_0^t v(s)e^{-\beta(t-s)}\,dB_s \qquad (C.8)$$

Of note is that $Y(t)$ is independent of T.

In this case, considering all factors, (C.6) becomes

$$F(t,T) = F(0,T)e^{\sum_{j=1}^{J}\sigma_j(T)e^{-\beta_j(T-t)}Y_j(t) - \frac{1}{2}V(t,T)} \qquad (C.9)$$

which, in spite of appearances, constitutes a meaningful improvement because the entire forward curve is now a function of a finite number of state variables: $\{Y_j\}_{j=1}^{J}$.

To characterize the dynamics of these state variables, differentiation of (C.8) with respect to t yields

$$dY = -\beta\left[\int_0^t v(s)e^{-\beta(t-s)}\,dB_s\right]dt + v(t)dB_t \qquad (C.10)$$

or, more succinctly,

$$dY = -\beta Y dt + v(t)dB_t \qquad (C.11)$$

The Y processes mean revert to zero, with mean reversion rates specified by the βs and driven by an additive Brownian motion with volatility $v(t)$.

When $v(t)$ is a constant, diffusions of the form (C.11) are referred to as *Ornstein-Uhlenbeck (OU) processes*. This is the "big-T" framework discussed in Chapter 7, in which $\sigma_j(t, T) = \sigma_j(T)$.

The generic OU process

$$dY = -\beta Y dt + dB_t \tag{C.12}$$

is amenable to exact integration

$$Y_t = Y_0 e^{-\beta t} + \int_0^t e^{-\beta(t-s)} dB_s \tag{C.13}$$

This can be verified by differentiation but is best viewed as a direct analogue from linear ordinary differential equations, where the initial value decays exponentially to zero at rate β, as do all perturbations dB_s from the time such occur.

Equation (C.13) allows us to establish a few facts that will be useful.

First, the mean decays at rate β is

$$E(Y_t|Y_0) = Y_0 e^{-\beta t} \tag{C.14}$$

which follows by taking the expected value of (C.13).

Second, the conditional variance is

$$\mathrm{var}(Y_t|Y_0) = \frac{1 - e^{-2\beta t}}{2\beta} \tag{C.15}$$

which follows from (C.13) and (C.3).

By taking the limit $t \to \infty$ in (C.15), we see that the stationary variance of the OU process is:

$$\mathrm{var}(Y_\infty) = \frac{1}{2\beta} \tag{C.16}$$

The relevance of this fact is that when mean reversion rates are positive, the limiting distribution of the forward prices is stationary.

Finally, the autocorrelation structure can be obtained from (C.13), which implies that

$$Y_{t+s} = e^{-\beta s} Y_t + \int_t^{t+s} e^{-\beta(u-t)} dB_u \tag{C.17}$$

As the second term is mean zero and independent of Y_t, the auto correlation function is

$$\langle Y_{t+s}, Y_t \rangle = e^{-\beta s} \tag{C.18}$$

Variances and Correlations

The variance $V(t,T)$ that makes $F(t,T)$ a martingale can be calculated exactly when the local volatilities take the form $\sigma_j(T)$ (the big-T setting):

$$V(t,T) = \sum_{j=1}^{J}\sum_{k=1}^{J}\sigma_j(T)\sigma_k(T)\rho_{j,k}\left[\frac{e^{-(\beta_j+\beta_k)(T-t)} - e^{-(\beta_j+\beta_k)T}}{\beta_j+\beta_k}\right] \quad (C.19)$$

In the case where the Brownian motions are uncorrelated, this reduces to

$$V(t,T) = \sum_{j=1}^{J}\sigma_j^2(T)\left(\frac{e^{-2\beta_j(T-t)} - e^{-2\beta_j T}}{2\beta_j}\right) \quad (C.20)$$

Similarly, the returns covariance of contracts S and T over $[0,t]$ is

$$V(t,S,T) = \sum_{j}\sigma_j(S)\sigma_j(T)\int_0^t e^{-\beta_j(S-u)}e^{-\beta_j(T-u)}\,du$$

$$= \sum_{j}\sigma_j(S)\sigma_j(T)\left(\frac{e^{-\beta_j(S+T-2t)} - e^{-2\beta_j(S+T)}}{2\beta_j}\right) \quad (C.21)$$

The term returns correlation between the two contracts is obtained by normalizing (C.21) by the two returns volatilities obtained from (C.4).

A similar calculation yields the term covariance and correlation between two different commodities. In the case of spread options, the typical situation is for common delivery times for both legs, as for calendar spread options (CSOs) and tolling transactions. Denoting the two commodities by superscripts, the same calculation that yielded (C.4) results in a covariance of the form

$$V_{1,2}(t,T) = \sum_{j=1}^{J}\sum_{k=1}^{J}\sigma_j^{(1)}(T)\sigma_k^{(2)}(T)\tilde{\rho}_{j,k}\left[\frac{e^{-\left(\beta_j^{(1)}+\beta_k^{(2)}\right)(T-t)} - e^{-\left(\beta_j^{(1)}+\beta_k^{(2)}\right)T}}{\beta_j^{(1)}+\beta_k^{(2)}}\right] \quad (C.22)$$

where $\tilde{\rho}_{j,k}$ denotes the correlation between factor j of the first commodity and factor k of the second. Term correlations used in valuation are, as before, obtained by normalizing $V_{1,2}(t,T)$ by the respective volatilites obtained from (C.4) for each commodity leg.

Spot Price Dynamics

Spot price dynamics can be inferred from (C.9) (C.11). Continuing in the big-T setting, with volatilities of the form $\sigma_j(T)$ and assuming that the factors are uncorrelated, the spot price is given by

$$F(t,t) = F(0,t)e^{\sum_{j=1}^{J}[\sigma_j(t)Y_j(t)]-\frac{1}{2}V(t,t)} \quad (C.23)$$

with

$$V(t,t) = \sum_{j=1}^{J} \sigma_j^2(t) \left(\frac{1 - e^{-2\beta_j t}}{2\beta_j} \right) \tag{C.24}$$

Ito's formula implies

$$\frac{dF}{F}(t,t) = d\log[F(t,t)] + \frac{1}{2} \frac{< dF(t,t) >}{F^2(t,t)}$$

$$= \left[\frac{\partial \log F(0,T)}{\partial T} \bigg|_{T=t} - \sum_j \sigma_j \beta_j Y_t^{(j)} + \frac{1}{2} \sum_j \sigma_j^2 - \frac{1}{2} \frac{\partial V(t,T)}{\partial T} \bigg|_{T=t} \right] dt + \sum_j \sigma_j dB_t^{(j)}$$

which reduces to

$$\frac{dF}{F}(t,t) = \left[\frac{\partial \log F(0,T)}{\partial T} \bigg|_{T=t} - \sum_j \sigma_j \beta_j Y_t^{(j)} + \frac{1}{2} \sum_j \sigma_j^2 \left(1 - e^{-2\beta_j t} \right) \right] dt + \sum_j \sigma_j dB_t^{(j)}$$

Because

$$\log F(t,T) = \log F(0,T) + \sum_j e^{-\beta_j(T-t)} \sigma_j Y_t^{(j)} - \frac{1}{2} V(t,T)$$

we have

$$\frac{\partial \log F(t,T)}{\partial T} \bigg|_{T=t} = \frac{\partial \log F(0,T)}{\partial T} \bigg|_{T=t} - \sum_j \sigma_j \beta_j Y_t^{(j)} + \frac{1}{2} \sum_j \sigma_j^2 \left(1 - e^{-2\beta_j t} \right)$$

This means that

$$\frac{dF}{F}(t,t) = \frac{\partial \log F(t,T)}{\partial T} \bigg|_{T=t} + \sum_j \sigma_j dB_t^{(j)} \tag{C.25}$$

The implication is that the spot price return has a drift equal to the local slope of $\log F(t,T)$.

The mean reversion rates $\bar{\beta}$ also relate to distributional attributes of spot dynamics including the autocorrelation function (ACF). Letting

$$\rho_t \equiv \log \left[\frac{F(t,t)}{F(0,t)} \right] \tag{C.26}$$

(C.23) yields

$$\rho_t = \sum_{j=1}^{J} \sigma_j(t) Y_j(t) - \frac{1}{2} V(t,t) \tag{C.27}$$

The correlation between $\rho(t)$ and $\rho(t+s)$ is therefore

$$\langle \rho_t, \rho_{t+s} \rangle = \left\langle \sum_j \sigma_j Y_j(t), \sum_j \sigma_j Y_j(t+s) \right\rangle \tag{C.28}$$

Assuming that the underlying OU processes are uncorrelated, (C.15) and (C.18) imply

$$\langle \rho_t, \rho_{t+s} \rangle = \frac{\sum_j \sigma_j^2 \left(\frac{1-e^{-2\beta_j t}}{2\beta_j} \right) e^{-\beta_j s}}{\sum_j \sigma_j^2 \left(\frac{1-e^{-2\beta_j t}}{2\beta_j} \right)} \tag{C.29}$$

The preceding expression reduces to a form useful for statistical estimation over short time scales when one factor has a high volatility and mean-reversion rate relative to the others. Working in the two-factor setting for simplicity, in the limit $t \to 0$, with $\beta_1 t \to 0$ while $\beta_2 t$ is held constant, the auctocorrelation is asymptotically

$$\langle \rho_t, \rho_{t+s} \rangle \sim e^{-\beta_2 s} \tag{C.30}$$

This facilitates econometric estimation of β_2 using the ACF of β_2 when returns dynamics exhibits a large separation of time scales ($\beta_1 << \beta_2$), as for power. This is also useful in estimation of spot volatilities and correlations by setting the reference price $F(0,t)$ equal the settlement price $F_m(T_e)$, where m indexes month, and using $F(t,t)$ as the daily spot prices during the month.

Simulation

Simulating the dynamics of (C.1) in the case of separable local volatilities is equivalent to simulating the processes $\bar{Y}_t$ given in (C.11). Once realizations of these underlying factors are obtained, computation of $F(t,T)$ on any sample path is straightforward.

In the case where $v_j(t) \equiv 1$, (the big-T setting), the diffusions $\bar{Y}_t$ are OU processes (C.12). Simulating a transition from Y_t to Y_s is achieved by generating normal random deviates, because (C.13) implies that the distribution of Y_s given Y_t is normal with

$$E(Y_s|Y_t) = e^{-\beta(s-t)} Y_t \qquad \text{var}(Y_s|Y_t) = \frac{1-e^{-2\beta(s-t)}}{2\beta} \tag{C.31}$$

If simulation is on a uniform time grid $[0, \delta, 2\delta, \ldots]$, the dynamics is identical to an $AR(1)$ (see [BD02]) process:

$$Y_{(n+1)\delta} = e^{-\beta\delta} Y_{n\delta} + \sigma_\delta Z_{n+1} \tag{C.32}$$

where $\sigma_\delta^2 = (1 - e^{-2\beta\delta})/2\beta$, and $\bar{Z}$ are independent standard normal deviates. Commercial time-series or signal-processing software can be used for efficient simulation.

In the case of nontrivial $v(t)$ structure, it is common for $v(t)$ to take the form of a step function, in which the preceding approach can be performed piecewise.

Appendix D
Common Tradables

In this appendix we describe some of the commonly traded instruments in the primary markets discussed in this book: crude oil and refined products, natural gas, and power. Rather than organizing this appendix by market, given the common nature of many of the instruments, the discussion that follows is organized by class of trade, namely, linear instruments (futures, forwards, and swaps), single-commodity options, and cross-commodity options.

Those experienced in the markets will recognize that many trades that do occur with some frequency are not included in this summary. The purpose here is to clarify the topics in the body of the text, as well as to create a quick reference. The variety of swaps and options that trade in each market is substantial, and details can be obtained through the various exchange websites or directly from trade confirms. In addition, Geman [Gem05] provides a very useful survey of markets and instruments.

Linear Instruments

Benchmark Futures Contracts

Futures contracts are traded by delivery month. The dominant benchmark contracts in energy are West Texas Intermediate (WTI) and Brent for crude oil and Henry Hub, NBP, and TTF for natural gas futures. For example,

- *NYMEX WTI futures contract.* Sometimes referred to as the *light sweet crude oil futures*, owing to the high quality of WTI, delivery is at pipeline or storage facilities in Cushing, Oklahoma, and must occur sometime during the delivery month. The standard contract size is 1,000 barrels. The last trading day of the contract is specified by the exchange via a date rule (three business days before the first business day at or before the twenty-four day of the previous month), which corresponds to roughly two-thirds of the way through the preceding calendar month.
- *ICE brent futures contract.* The Brent contract is described by the exchange as physically settling with an option to settle financially. The contract expires on the last business day on or before the fifteenth day of the preceding month.

Financial settlement is based on the ICE Brent Index as published on the day after settlement. This index is computed using the arithmetic average of physical forward trades for the next two delivery months, with the second month price linearly adjusted by the average price at which spreads traded during the day. The set of crude oil streams on which the index is calculated has been expanded to the broader Brent, Forties, Oseberg, and Ekofisk (BFOE) basket due to the deleterious impact on liquidity resulting from diminishing production of Brent fields.

- *NYMEX Henry Hub futures contract.* Referred to as the *NG futures*, the contract size is 10,000 MMBtus. Delivery occurs ratably (uniformly) over the delivery month at Henry Hub, Lousiana. Futures expiration is three business days prior to the delivery month.

Fixed-Price Swaps

Fixed-price swaps settle on the product of the contracted notional N and the difference between a floating price p_{float} and the contractual fixed price K. The payoff, from the perspective of the holder of the long position, is

$$N(p_{\text{float}} - K) \tag{D.1}$$

The distinctions in swaps arises in the mechanics of computing p_{float} and in conventions regarding calculation of the notional N.

- *WTI Asian swaps.* These are monthly swaps that reference the WTI futures contract, settling on the average of the first nearby contract price over the contract month:

$$p_{\text{float}}(m) = \frac{1}{K_m} \sum_{d \in m} F_1(d) \tag{D.2}$$

where K_m is the number of trading days in month m, and $F_1(d)$ denotes the settlement price of the first traded contract on day d. The floating price is therefore roughly a two-third to one-third the average of two distinct contract prices.
- *NG penultimate swaps.* These are monthly swaps in which p_{float} is the settlement price of the the natural gas futures one day before contract expiry; equivalently four business days before the delivery month.
- *NG L3D swaps.* A generalization of the penultimate swap, these swaps settle on p_{float} computed as the average of the last three trading days (hence the name L3D) of the NG futures contract. The purpose of the averaging is to mitigate the effects of any unusual price dynamics associated with options or futures expirations.
- *Monthly power swaps.* Financially settling power contracts in which p_{float} for month m is the average hourly spot price over the delivery period:

$$p_{\text{float}}(m) = \frac{1}{K_h} \sum_{h \in B(m)} p_h \tag{D.3}$$

where K_h is the number of hours h in the delivery bucket $B(m)$. This delivery bucket is defined by contract month and hour bucket, with peak and off-peak buckets the most liquid. The definitions vary by location. In the United States, the two buckets are defined as

o Peak ("5x16")
  * *Eastern markets*: 7 a.m. to 11 p.m. EST Monday through Friday excluding holidays
  * *Western markets*: 7 a.m. to 11 p.m. PST Monday through Saturday excluding holidays
  * *Texas (ERCOT)*: 6 a.m. to 10 p.m. CST Monday through Friday excluding holidays
o *Off-peak*: The complement of peak

where holidays are in reference to the NERC[1] holiday calendar. The total notional is the product of the quoted notional rate (e.g. 50 MW) and the number of hours K_h.

Locational Spreads

Commonly referred to as *basis trades*, these take a variety of forms in each of the primary markets. The simplest situation is where pairs of futures at different delivery locations effectively trade as a package, as in the ICE Brent-WTI futures spread. Such transactions are nothing more than coupled futures contracts.

The more interesting situation occurs when benchmark futures contracts are linked to different locational risks with different settlement mechanisms. Of note are natural gas basis swaps, which link the Henry Hub futures contract with the near-equivalent at particular delivery locations. Both legs are floating, and settlement is on the difference. In the United States, basis swaps settle on the product of the notional and the spread differential:

$$N[F_D(T_{\text{BW}}) - F_{\text{Hub}}(T_e)] \tag{D.4}$$

where $F_{\text{Hub}}(T_e)$ is the settlement price on the expiration date T_e of the Henry Hub futures contract for the given month. $F_D(T_{\text{BW}})$ is the bid-week price for the specified delivery location. The bid-week price is a volumetrically weighted average of transaction prices during the five trading days prior to the delivery month, as established by index vendors.

Swaps of this form transfer risk from the benchmark, namely, Henry Hub in this example, to the desired delivery location. Similar locational swaps exist across the energy commodities spectrum, from refined products to power, with the basic feature that settlement is defined by two floating legs corresponding to two delivery locations of the same commodity.

---

[1] NERC is the North American Electric Reliability Corportation.

Time Spreads

Commonly referred to as *calendar spreads* or *rolls*, this category of trade is used to change the tenor (*roll*) risk positions more efficiently than doing two individual trades. Such trades are the equivalent of a long position in a futures or swap contract (or strip of contracts) and an offsetting short position of equivalent (or nearly equivalent) notional.

Calendar spreads are quoted with the convention that backwardation is premium. For example, in natural gas, a "Cal13/Cal14 roll" quoted at $-\$0.30$ means that the Cal13 strip is trading at a discount of 30 cents to the Cal14 strip. In crude oil, these usually take the form of a swap or futures contract on the spread between two contract months; at long tenors, the December-December spreads are the points of liquidity. For natural gas, monthly spreads are quoted at short tenors; at longer tenors, liquidity is concentrated in calendar strip spreads.

Another important example are the Gas Daily/IFERC[2] swaps, often referred to as *index swaps*, which convert the monthly price risk associated with the bid-week price $F_D(T_{BW})$ in (D.4) to the Gas Daily spot price as published by Platts. The payoff is therefore the product of the notional and difference between the average spot price $p_{GD}(d)$ over the month and the bid-week price $F_D(T_{BW})$:

$$N \sum_{d \in M} [p_{GD}(d) - F_D(T_{BW})] \tag{D.5}$$

where N is the daily notional. We categorize these swaps as time spreads as these effect a risk transfer from a monthly settlement price to future spot prices. These are, however, usually viewed as swaps that effect the mechanical step of converting benchmark price risk to daily spot price risk in the natural gas markets.

Cross-Commodity Spreads

Two commonly encountered cross-commodity swaps in energy are between refined products and crude oil and between electricity and input fuels, usually natural gas. Crack spreads are futures or swaps on the spread between a refined product (or a basket of several products) and a crude oil. The term *crack spread* often refers to the simple concept of paired trading between some quantity of refined product futures contracts and a crude oil contract. Although refined products are usually quoted in cents per gallon, the lot size of 42,000 gallons is equivalent to the 1,000-barrel lot size of a crude contract. In addition to the basic heating oil and gasoline crack spreads, which are usually a one-to-one ratio of the single product to a crude oil, standard

---

[2] IFERC is an abbreviation for "Inside FERC", a set of indices published by Platts.

basket crack spreads are commonly traded, for example, the 3-2-1 spread that comprises three oil contracts against two gasoline and one heating oil contract.

The different settlement conventions on each leg of the basic futures crack spreads can result in risks appearing as legs expire on different dates. The RBOB[3] gasoline NYMEX futures contract, for example, expires on the last business day preceding the delivery month, whereas the WTI contract expires roughly ten days earlier. As a consequence, exchange-traded crack spread futures are usually financially settled on the average of the first nearby contracts, just as for WTI Asian swaps. For example, the NYMEX RBOB gasoline crack spread future settles on the realized average first-nearby spread:

$$s_{\text{float}}(m) = \frac{1}{K_m} \sum_{d \in m} \left[F_1^{\text{RBOB}}(d) - F_1^{\text{WTI}}(d) \right] \tag{D.6}$$

In a similar fashion, cross-commodity swaps arise in the power and natural gas markets, caused by the coupling between the two commodities resulting from the prevalence of combined-cycle generation. In North America, some power markets commonly trade as spreads to natural gas. The usual reference is the Henry Hub futures contract, and the forward or swap is priced as a heat rate to natural gas. A heat-rate swap struck at H_* involves two floating legs until the natural gas leg expires, at which time the swap converts to a fixed-strike power swap, where the floating leg is exactly as defined in (D.3), and the fixed price is $H_* F_{\text{Hub}}(T_e)$. For example, if the swap was traded at $H_* = 9.0$ and the natural gas futures contract settled at \$4.00/MMBtu, the power swap has a fixed price of \$36/MWh.

Single-Commodity Options

The primary single-commodity options are monthly, daily, and calendar swaptions. Calendar spread options also fall into this category.

Swaptions

These are options that, on exercise, result in a swap position in a strip of contracts at a fixed strike K. Often the strip is one calendar year. The swap at expiry has a value per unit notional of

$$V_\tau = \frac{1}{12} \sum_m d(\tau, T_m) \left[F(\tau, T_m) - K \right] \tag{D.7}$$

where τ is is the expiry of the swaption. A call swaption, for example, has a terminal value of the form $\max(V_\tau, 0)$.

---

[3] RBOB refers to "Reformulated gasoline Blend stock for Oxygen Blending."

Monthly Options

Monthly options are the most commonly traded energy options, involving settlement on either a futures or swap price for a given contract month or on the average of an index over the month.

Exchange-traded monthly options, or *look-alikes*, settle on the value $F(\tau, T_m) - K$, where $F(\tau, T_m)$ is the value of the futures contract at expiration/exercise τ, and K is the strike. Call or put option payoffs are applied to this spread. The exercise date τ is usually within a few business days of the expiration of the futures contract. Exchange-traded options of this type often have American exercise features. If the mechanics of the exchange involves an up-front premium payment, the American feature is nontrivial; the value will exceed that of its European counterpart (see Chapter 4).

Monthly options can be either cash-settled or can result in a position in the underlying futures or swaps. For example, NYMEX natural gas options expire one business before the futures contract expiry and exercise into a futures contract. Likewise, monthly options in power typically exercise two business days before the delivery month into a financial swap on the underlying power index.

Another common variation of monthly options is Asian options, closely related to the Asian swaps discussed in the preceding section. The call or put feature is applied to the Asian average of the first nearby defined in (D.2).

Daily Options

Daily options trade most commonly in power and to a lesser extent in natural gas. Daily options trade by contract month; for example, a daily option for a particular month for peak power consists of a set of distinct options, one for each delivery day in the month.

In power, options liquidity is concentrated in the peak buckets and at the most liquid hubs. A daily option on a contract month, therefore, typically has twenty to twenty-two discrete "optionlets" corresponding to the number of business days in the month. The typical form of exercise is manual (phone) exercise by 10 a.m. on the business day before delivery. Settlement is financial. For example, the settlement amount for a call option is

$$\sum_{d \in m} \mathbf{1}_{E_d} [F(\tau_d, T_d) - K] \qquad \text{(D.8)}$$

where $d \in m$ denotes the set of delivery days in the option during month m, and E_d denotes the event that the option was exercised one business day (τ_d) before delivery day d; $\mathbf{1}_{E_d}$ is one if exercise occurred and zero otherwise. Less commonly traded are autoexercise (lookback) daily options, which settle on $\sum_{d \in m} \max[F(T_d, T_d) - K, 0]$.

Another type of daily option trades primarily in the natural gas markets. These are forward-starter options, which are options on the index spread defined in (D.5). The term *forward starter* (sometimes referred to as a *Cliquet feature*) is due to the fact that the first-of-month price $F_D(T_{BW})$ acts as a floating strike until it fixes during bid week. Once fixed, this structure constitutes a set of fixed-strike daily options with strike $K = F_D(T_{BW})$.

Calendar Spread Options (CSOs)

Options on calendar spreads trade in oil and natural gas markets. The underlying spread is of the form

$$F(\tau, T_2) - F(\tau, T_1) - K \tag{D.9}$$

on which call or put payoffs are applied. An at-the-money CSO corresponds to a strike $K = F(0, T_2) - F(0, T_1)$, effectively serving to reference the expiration spread to the current spread. These options, when traded, provide information about the returns correlation structure between different contract months of the same commodity.

Cross-Commodity Options

Cross-commodity options are essential to hedging basic conversion infrastructure – particularly refining and generation. Although substantially less liquid than the single-commodity options on future exchanges or over the counter (OTC), these are often transacted in sizable notionals in structured hedges.

Crack Spread Options

Options on crack spreads are based on the structure of crack spreads futures and swaps discussed in the first section. For example, a NYMEX NY Harbor heating oil crack spread option versus WTI expires on the business day preceding the expiration of the WTI futures contract, at which time the holder of a call option on exercise assumes a long heating oil contract and a short WTI futures contract. The two futures contract prices are set according to a detailed price-rounding protocol, which effectively amounts to setting the WTI price at the WTI futures settlement price and the heating oil contract at the sum of the price of the WTI settlement and the strike price. This price is divided by 42 to convert the result to units of gallons in which the heating oil futures contract trades.

The other flavor of crack spread option is the Asian variety, which settles financially on the call or put option payoff applied to (D.6).

Tolling (Spark-Spread) Options

Technically, the term *tolling option* or *contract* refers to physical control of a generator. In this text we use the term interchangeably with *spark-spread options*, which are also referred to as *heat-rate options*.

These options trade OTC with sporadic liquidity and are usually a component of structured hedges for builders or buyers of generation seeking financing. Tolls almost always involve daily exercise, with exercise one day prior to the delivery day. The payoff, therefore, is a modification of (D.8), with the fixed strike modified by a cost of natural gas:

$$\sum_{d \in m} \mathbf{1}_{E_d}[F(\tau_d, T_d) - H_* G(\tau_d, T_d) - K] \tag{D.10}$$

As before, E_d denotes the event of exercise at expiry τ_d. The natural gas price at time τ_d for delivery at T_d is denoted by $G(\tau_d, T_d)$, and H_* is a deal-specific heat rate.

Bibliography

[ADEH99] P. Artzner, F. Delbaen, J. M. Eber, and D. Heath. Coherent measures of risk. *Mathematical Finance* 9(3):203–228, 1999.

[ADS02] H. Ahn, A. Danilova, and G. Swindle. Storing arb. *Wilmott* 1:78–83, 2002.

[AG08] UBS AG. Shareholder Report on UBS's Write-Downs, UBS, 2008. url=http://books.google.com/books?id=_t0OSQAACAAJ

[AMS99] H. Ahn, A. Muni, and G. Swindle. Optimal hedging strategies for mis-specified asset price models. *Applied Mathematical Finance* 6(3):197–208, 1999.

[ACHT09] R. Aid, L. Campi, A. N. Huu, and N. Touzi. A structural risk-neutral model of electricity prices. *International Journal of Theoretical and Applied Finance*, 12(07):925–947, 2009.

[AP94] M. Avellaneda and A. Paras. Dynamic hedging portfolios for derivative securities in the presence of large transaction costs. *Applied Mathematical Finance* 1(2):165–194, 1994.

[AV11] C. Alexander and A. Venkatramanan. Closed form approximations for spread options. *Applied Mathematical Finance* 1:1–26, 2011.

[Ban02] E. Banks. *Weather Risk Management: Markets, Products and Applications*. Palgrave, Basingstoke, UK, 2002.

[Bar02] M. Barlow. A diffusion model for electricity prices. *Mathematical Finance* 12(4):287–298, 2002.

[BBLP05] G. Burghardt, T. Belton, M. Lane, and J. Papa. *The Treasury Bond Basis: An in-Depth Analysis for Hedgers, Speculators, and Arbitrageurs*. McGraw-Hill Library of Investment and Finance. McGraw-Hill, New York, 2005.

[BCE+08] J. Breslin, L. Clewlow, T. Elbert, C. Kwok, and C. Strickland. Gas storage: Overview and static valuation. *Energy Risk* Nov:62–68, 2008.

[BD02] P. Brockwell and R. Davis. *Time Series and Forecasting*. Springer, New York, 2002.

[BdJ08] A. Boogert and C. de Jong. Gas storage valuation using a monte carlo method. *Journal of Derivatives* 15(3):81–98, 2008.

[BGS07] M. Burger, B. Graeber, and G. Schindlmayr. *Managing Energy Risk: An Integrated View on Power and Other Energy Markets*. Wiley, Hoboken, NJ, 2007.

[BJ98]   G. Barz and B. Johnson. Modeling the prices of commodities that are costly to store: The case of electricity. *Proceedings of the Chicago Risk Management Conference.* Chicago, IL, Volume 5, 1998.

[BKMB07]   F. E. Benth, J. Kallsen, and T. Meyer-Brandis. A non-Gaussian Ornstein-Uhlenbeck process for electricity spot price modeling and derivatives pricing. *Applied Mathematical Finance* 14:153–169, 2007.

[Bla76]   F. Black. The pricing of commodity contracts. *Journal of Financial Economics*, 3(1):167–179, 1976.

[BNBV10]   O. E. Barndorff-Nielsen, F. E. Benth, and A. E. D. Veraart. Modeling energy spot prices by levy semistationary processes. Technical report, Volume 18, 2010.

[Bou11]   I. Bouchouev. The inconvenience yield or the theory of normal contango. *Energy Risk Magazine*, September 2011.

[BP12]   British Petroleum. *Statistical Review of World Energy*, London, June 2012.

[BPC09]   K. Boudt, B. Peterson, and C. Croux. Estimation and decomposition of downside risk for portfolios with non-normal returns. *Journal of Risk* 11(2):79–103, 2008–2009.

[BR96]   M. Baxter and A. Rennie. *Financial Calculus: An Introduction to Derivatives Pricing.* Cambridge University Press, Cambridge, UK, 1996.

[Bre91]   M. Brennan. The price of convenience and the pricing of commodity contingent claims. In D. Lund and B Oksendal (eds.), *Stochastic Models and Options Values.* Elsevier, New York, 1991.

[BS85]   M. Brennan and E. Schwartz. Evaluating natural resource investments. *Journal of Business* 58(2):135–157, 1985.

[BS86]   T. Bresnahan and P. Spiller. Futures market backwardation under risk neutrality. *Economic Inquiry* 24:429–441, 1986.

[Car12]   S. Carollo. *Understanding Oil Prices.* Wiley, Hoboken, NJ, 2012.

[CC13]   R. Carmona and M. Coulon. A survey of commodity markets and structural approaches to modeling electricity. In Fred Benth, Valery Kholodnyi, and Peter Laurence (eds), *Quantitative Energy Finance.* Springer-Verlag, New York, 2013.

[CCS13]   R. Carmona, M. Coulon, and D. Schwarz. Electricity price modeling and asset valuation: A multi-fuel structural approach. *Mathematics and Financial Economics* 7(2):167–202, 2013.

[CD03]   R. Carmona and V. Durrleman. Pricing and hedging spread options. *SIAM Review* 45(4):627–685, 2003.

[CF05]   A. Cartea and M. Figueroa. Pricing in electricity markets: A mean reverting jump diffusion model with seasonality. *Applied Mathematical Finance* 12(4):313–335, 2005.

[CIR85]   J. C. Cox, J. E. Ingersoll, and S. A. Ross. A theory of the term structure of interest rates. *Econometrica* 53:385–408, 1985.

[CL04]   R. Carmona and M. Ludkovski. Spot convenience yield models for the energy markets. *Mathematics of Finance* 351:65–79, 2004.

[CL08]   R. Carmona and M. Ludkovski. Pricing asset scheduling flexibility using optimal switching. *Applied Mathematical Finance* 15(6):405–447, 2008.

[CL10]   R. Carmona and M. Ludkovski. Valuation of energy storage: An optimal switching approach. *Quantitative Finance* 10(4):359–374, 2010.

[Cou]   ISO/RTO   Council.   http://www.isorto.org/site/c.jhKQIZPBImE/b
          .2604471/

[CP01]   D. Cossin and H. Pirotte. *Financial Approahces and Mathematical
          Models to Assess, Price, and Manage Credit Risk*. Wiley, New York,
          2001.

[CPS13]   Michael Coulon, Warren B. Powell, and Ronnie Sircar. A model for
          hedging load and price risk in the Texas electricity market. *Energy
          Economics*, 2013.

[CS99]   L. Clewlow and C. Strickland. A multi-factor model for energy deriva-
          tives. Working paper, University of Technology, Sydney, Australia,
          1999.

[CS00]   Les Clewlow and Chris Strickland. *Energy Derivatives: Pricing and
          Risk Management*, Volume 124. London, Lacima Publications, 2000.

[Cul04]   C. Culp. *Risk Transfer: Derivatives Trading in Theory and Practice*.
          Wiley Finance, Hoboken, NJ, 2004.

[Den00]   S. Deng. Stochastic models of energy commodity prices and their
          applications: Mean-reversion with jumps and spikes. *Technical report,
          University of California Energy Institute*, 2000.

[DK94]   E. Derman and I. Kani. Riding on a smile. *Risk* 7:32–39, 1994.

[DL91]   A. Deaton and G. Laroque. On the behavior of commodity prices.
          Review of Economic Studies 59:1–23, 1991.

[Dow09]   M. Downey. *Oil 101*. Wooden Table Press, 2009.

[DPS00]   D. Duffie, J. Pan, and K. Singleton. Transform analysis and option
          pricing for affine jump-diffusion. *Econometrica* 68:1343–1376, 2000.

[Dup94]   B. Dupire. Pricing with a smile. *Risk* 7:18–20, 1994.

[EIA]   U.S. Energy Information Administration. *Annual Energy Outlook
          2013*. http://www.eia.gov/forecasts/aeo/pdf/0383(2013).pdf

[EW03]   A. Eydeland and K. Wolyniec. *Energy and Power Risk Manage-
          ment: New Developments in Modeling, Pricing and Hedging*. Wiley,
          Hoboken, NJ, 2003.

[Fat11]   Bassam Fattouh. *An anatomy of the crude oil pricing system*. Oxford
          Institute for Energy Studies, 2011.

[FF87]   E. Fama and K. French. Commodity futures prices: Some evidence
          on forecast power, premiums and the theory of storage. *Journal of
          Finance* 43:1075–1093, 1987.

[FPS00]   J. Fouque, G. Papanicolaou, and R. Sircar. Derivatives in financial
          markets with stochastic volatility. *International Journal of Theoretical
          and Applied Finance* 3:101–142, 2000.

[FS91]   H. Föllmer and M. Schweizer. Hedging of contingent claims. *Applied
          Stochastic Analysis*. 5:389–414, 1991.

[Gab91]   J. Gabillon. The term structure of oil futures prices. Working paper,
          Oxford Institute for Energy Studies 17, 1–43, 1991.

[Gat06]   J. Gatheral. *The Volatility Surface: A Practicioner's Guide*. Wiley,
          Hoboken, NJ, 2006.

[Gem05]   H. Geman. *Commodities and Commodity Derivatives: Modeling and
          Pricing for Agricultural, Metals and Energy*. Wiley, Hoboken, NJ,
          2005.

[GHR07]   G. Gorton, F. Hayashi, and K. G. Rouwenhorst. The fundamentals
          of commodity futures returns. *NBER Working Paper 13249*. National
          Bureau of Economic Research, Cambridge, MA, 2007.

[GK04]   J. Gray and P. Khandelwal. Towards a realistic gas storage model. *Commodities Now*, 1–4, June:75–79, 2004.

[Gla04]   P. Glasserman. *Monte Carlo Methods in Financial Engineering*. Springer-Verlag, New York, 2004.

[GO09]   H. Geman and S. Ohana. Forward curves, scarcity and price volatility in oil and natural gas markets. *Energy Economics* 31:576–585, 2009.

[GR06]   H. Geman and A. Roncoroni. Understanding the fine structure of electricity prices. *Journal of Business* 79(3):1225–1261, 2006.

[GS90]   R. Gibson and E. S. Schwartz. Stochastic convenience yield and the pricing of oil contingent claims. *Journal of Finance* 45(3):959–976, 1990.

[Har06]   C. Harris. *Electricity Markets: Pricing, Structures and Economics*. Wiley, Hoboken, NJ, 2006.

[Hic46]   John R. Hicks. *Value and Capital*, Volume 2. Clarendon Press, Oxford, 1946.

[HJ08]   S. Hikspoors and S. Jaimungal. Asymptotic pricing of commodity derivatives using stochastic volatility spot models. *Applied Mathematical Finance* 15(5–6):449–477, 2008.

[HJM92]   D. Heath, R. Jarrow, and A. Morton. Bond pricing and the term structure of interest rates: A new methodology for contingent claims valuation. *Econometrica* 60:77–105, 1992.

[HKLW91]   P. Hagan, D. Kumar, A. Lesniewski, and D. Woodward. Managing smile risk. Oxford Institute for Energy Studies, Oxford, UK, 1991.

[Hul12]   J. Hull. *Options, Futures, and Other Derivatives*, 8th ed. Prentice-Hall, Englewood Cliffs, NJ, 2012.

[HW12]   James D. Hamilton and Jing Cynthia Wu. Effects of index-fund investing on commodity futures prices. Technical report, Working paper, University of California, San Diego, 2012.

[IEA10]   International Energy Agency (IEA). Key World Energy Statistics. Technical report, 2010.

[JB05]   S. Jewson and A. Brix. Cambridge University Press, Cambridge, UK, 2005.

[JI87]   J. Ingersoll, Jr. *Theory of Financial Decision Making*. Rowman & Littlefield Publishers, Maryland, USA 1987.

[Jor06]   P. Jorion. *Value at Risk: The New Benchmark for Managing Financial Risk*, 3rd ed. McGraw-Hill, New York, 2006.

[JRT04]   P. Jaillet, E. Ronn, and S. Tompaidis. Valuation of commodity-based swing options. *Management Science* 50(7):909–921s, 2004.

[JS09]   C. De Jong and S. Schneider. Cointegration between gas and power spot prices. *Journal of Energy Markets* 2(3):27–46, 2009.

[Kal39]   N. Kaldor. Speculation and economic stability. *Review of Economic Studies* 7:1–27, 1939.

[Kam97]   V. Kaminski. The challenge of pricing and risk managing electricity derivatives. *The US Power Market*, 3:149–71, 1997.

[Kam12]   V. Kaminski. *Energy Markets*. Incisive Media, London, 2012.

[Key50]   J. M. Keynes. *A Treatise on Money*, Vol. 2. Macmillan, London, 1950.

[Kho05]   V. Kholodnyi. Modeling power forward prices for power with spikes: a non-markovian approach. *Nonlinear Analysis: Theory, Methods and Applications* 63(5–7):958–965, 2005.

[Kir95] E. Kirk. Correlation in the energy markets. *Managing Energy Price Risk*, 71–78, 1995.

[KS04] D. Kirschen and G. Strbac. *Fundamentals of Power System Economics*. Wiley Online Library, 2004.

[KS91] I. Karatzas and S. Shreve. *Brownian Motion and Stochastic Calculus*. Springer-Verlag, New York, 1991.

[LS01] F. A. Longstaff and E. S. Schwartz. Valuing American options by simulation: A simple least-squares approach. *Review of Financial Studies* 14(1):113–147, 2001.

[Ltd11] Argus Media, Ltd. VLCC booked for more crude storage in the U.S. Gulf, June 2011; available at: www.argusmedia.com.

[Lue98] D. Luenberger. *Investment Science*. Oxford University Press, Oxford, UK, 1998.

[Mar78] W. Margrabe. The value to exchange one asset for another. *Journal of Finance* 33:177–186, 1978.

[Mil03] K. Miltersen. Commodity price modelling that matches current observables: A new approach. *Quantitative Finance* 3(1):51–58, 2003.

[MLS10] F. Margot, G. Lai, and N. Secomandi. An approximate dynamic programming approach to benchmark practice-based heuristics for natural gas storage valuation. *Operations Research* 58:564–582, 2010.

[NP94] V. Ng and C. Pirrong. Fundamentals of volatility: Storage, spreads, and the dynamics of metals prices. *Journal of Business* 67(2):203–230, 1994.

[OECD10] Organization for Economic Cooperation and Development Factbook 2010: Economic, environmental and social statistics. Technical report, 2010.

[Oks10] B. Oksendal. *Stochastic Differential Equations: An Introduction with Applications*. Springer-Verlag, New York, 2010.

[Ovi06] R. Oviedo. The suboptimality of early exercise of futures-style options: A model-free result, robust to market imperfections and performance bond requirements. Working paper, McGill University, Montreal, Canada, 2006.

[Pil98] D. Pilipovic. *Energy Risk: Valuing and Managing Energy Derivatives*. McGraw-Hill, New York, 1998.

[Pir12] C. Pirrong. *Commodity Price Dynamics*. Cambridge University Press, Cambridge, UK, 2012.

[RH04] Diana R. Ribeiro and Stewart D. Hodges. A two-factor model for commodity prices and futures valuation. *EFMA 2004 Basel Meetings Paper*, 2004.

[RSS00] B. Routledge, D. Seppi, and C. Spatt. Equilibrium forward curves for commodities. *Journal of Finance* 55:1297–1338, 2000.

[Sad11] A. Sadeghi. Hedging the extrinsic value of a natural gas storage. *Energy Risk* 64–68, November, 2011.

[Sch97] E. S. Schwartz. The stochastic behavior of commodity prices: Implications for pricing and hedging. *Journal of Finance* 52(3):923–973, 1997.

[Sch03] P. Schönbucher. *Credit Derivatives Pricing Models: Model, Pricing and Implementation*. Wiley, Hoboken, NJ, 2003.

[Set00] S. Sethi. *Optimal Control Theory: Applications to Management Science and Economics*. Kluwer Academic Publishers, Boston, 2000.

[SGHSA10] C. Schwarz, T. Gibney, H. Haworth, C. Somaia, and A. Ali. Fixed Income Research Credit Suisse. Technical report, June, 2010. www.credit-suisse.com/researchandanalytics

[SGI00] P. Skantze, A. Gubina, and M. Ilic. Bid-based stochastic model for electricity pricing. MIT E-Lab report MIT-EL 00-004, Massachusetts Institute of Technology, Cambridge, MA, 2000.

[Shr04] S. Shreve. *Stochastic Calculus for Finance II: Continuous Time Models*. Springer, New York, 2004.

[SIC00] P. Skantze, M. Ilic, and J. Chapman. Stochastic modeling of electric power prices in a multi-market environment. *IEEE Power Engineering Society Winter Meeting, 2000*, 2(23–27):1109–1114, 2000.

[SLM$^+$10] N. Secomandi, G. Lai, F. Margot, A Scheller-Wolf, and Duane Seppi. The effect of model error on the valuation and hedging of natural gas storage. Tepper working paper (E71), Carnegie Mellon University, Pittsburgh, PA, 2010.

[SS07] E. S. Schwartz and J. E. Smith. Short-term variations and long-term dynamics in commodity prices. *Management Science* 46(7):893–911, 2007.

[Stu97] F. Sturm. *Trading Natural Gas: Cash, Futures, Options and Swaps*. Penwell Publishing, Tulsa, OK 1997.

[Tal07] N. Taleb. *The Black Swan: The Impact of the Highly Improbable*. Random House, New York, 2007.

[Tel58] L. Telser. Futures trading and the storage of cotton and wheat. *Journal of Politcal Economy* 66:233–255, 1958.

[Tre08] L. Trevino. Liberalization of the electricity market in europe: An overview of the electricity technology and the market place. *College of Management of Technology. Federal Polytechnic School of Lausanne*, 2008.

[TS09] A. B. Trolle and E. S. Schwartz. Unspanned stochastic volatility and the pricing of commodity derivatives. *Review of Financial Studies*, 22(11):4423–4461, 2009.

[TX12] K. Tang and W. Xiong. Index investment and financialization of commodities. *Financial Analysts Journal* 68(6):54–74, 2012.

[Wha86] R. E. Whaley. On valuing American futures options. *Financial Analysts Journal* 42(3):49–59, 1986.

[WHD95] P. Wilmott, S. Howison, and J. Dewynne. *The Mathematics of Financial Derivatives*. Cambridge University Press, Cambridge, UK, 1995.

[Wil86] J. Williams. *The Economic Function of Futures Markets*. Cambridge University Press, Cambridge, UK, 1986.

[Wil07] P. Wilmott. *Paul Wilmott Introduces Quantitative Finance*. Wiley, Hoboken, NJ, 2007.

[Wor49] H. Working. The theory of the price of storage. *American Economic Review* 39:1254–1269, 1949.

[WW91] J. Williams and B. Wright. *Storage and Commodity Markets*. Cambridge University Press, Cambridge, UK, 1991.

[Zan96] Peter Zangari. A VaR methodology for portfolios that include options. *Risk Metrics Monitor*, 1:4–12, 1996.

Index

Lightning Source UK Ltd.
Milton Keynes UK
UKHW031528021218
333292UK00015B/714/P